A MODERN HISTORY OF TANGANYIKA

BOOKS IN THIS SERIES

A MODERN HISTORY OF TANGANYIKA

JOHN ILIFFE

Fellow of St John's College, Cambridge
Assistant Director of Research in History

CAMBRIDGE UNIVERSITY PRESS

CAMBRIDGE

LONDON · NEW YORK · MELBOURNE

Published by the Syndics of the Cambridge University Press
The Pitt Building, Trumpington Street, Cambridge CB2 1RP
Bentley House, 200 Euston Road, London NW1 2DB
32 East 57th Street, New York, NY 10022, USA
296 Beaconsfield Parade, Middle Park, Melbourne 3206, Australia

First published 1979

Printed in Great Britain at the
University Press, Cambridge

Library of Congress Cataloguing in Publication Data
Iliffe, John.
A modern history of Tanganyika.
(African studies series ; no. 25)
Bibliography: p.
Includes index.
1. Tanganyika – History. I. Title. II. Series.
DT447.I39   967.8'2   77-95445
ISBN 0 521 22024 6 hard covers
ISBN 0 521 29611 0 paperback
ISBN 0 521 29612 9 special paperback
edition for sale in East,
West and Central Africa only

In memory of my father
Arthur Ross Iliffe

Contents

Contents

Contents

Maps and Tables

Preface

I did most of the research for this book while teaching at the University of Dar es Salaam, where I was fortunate to have colleagues and students who helped me to enjoy and understand Tanganyika in its first exciting years of independence. I have written the book at Cambridge while working so closely with John Lonsdale that I do not know which of my ideas are really his. Many scholars have generously allowed me to use their unpublished work. Andrew Roberts made valuable comments on a draft of this book. I am grateful to all those who have helped me.

Cambridge   JOHN ILIFFE
June 1977

Acknowledgments

The following individuals have kindly allowed me to use unpublished material: Dr A. V. Akeroyd, Professor M. L. Bates, Dr C. Brantley, Dr M. von Clemm, Professor S. Feierman, Dr J. T. Gallagher, Mr H. Gillman, Professor P. H. Gulliver, Dr G. C. K. Gwassa, Lt-Col. F. C. Hallier, Dr C. R. Hatfield Jr, Mrs P. Huxham, Dr J. A. P. Kieran, Dr L. E. Larson, Mr A. C. Ledger, Dr A. A. Lema, Professor M. Lowenkopf, Dr P. S. Maro, Dr A. H. Nimtz Jr, Dr C. K. Omari, Mr N. Pearson, Dr P. M. Redmond, Dr S. G. Rogers, Dr A. M. H. Sheriff, Dr L. W. Swantz, Dr G. E. T. Wijeyewardene.

I am also grateful to the authorities of the following institutions for permitting me to consult records in their keeping: Bundesarchiv-Militärarchiv, Freiburg i.B.; Deutsches Zentralarchiv, Potsdam; Kipalapala Pastoral Centre; Kwiro Mission; Makerere University Library; Ministry of Labour, Dar es Salaam; J. B. Morrell Library, University of York; Peramiho Abbey; Public Record Office, London; Rhodes House, Oxford; School of Oriental and African Studies, London; Tanganyika African National Union; Tanzania National Archives, Dar es Salaam; United Society for the Propagation of the Gospel, London; University Library, Dar es Salaam.

Terminology

Since Tanzania now uses the metric system, I have converted all weights and measures to their metric equivalents. In order to simplify the variety of currencies used in Tanganyika during the last 200 years, I have taken as the standard unit the East African shilling, which was equal in value to the British shilling until Tanganyika became independent. One shilling contained 100 cents. Twenty shillings made up one pound. All other currencies have been converted to pounds, shillings and cents at their contemporary values. The Maria Theresa dollar current in the nineteenth century has been valued at Shs. 4.17. Until 1914 one German Mark was equal in value to one shilling. The German East African rupee fluctuated in value until 1905, when fifteen rupees became equivalent to twenty Marks. (The fluctuations can be found in German annual reports on the protectorate.) The German East African rupee contained 64 pesa (pice) or 100 Heller.

Abbreviations

AA	African Association
AAKA	Auswärtiges Amt, Kolonial-Abteilung
ADMB	Admiralstab der Marine, Abteilung B
APO	Assistant Political Officer
BA	Bezirksamt
BA-M	Bundesarchiv-Militärarchiv, Freiburg i.B. [below, p. 579]
BNS	Bezirksnebenstelle
BSOAS	*Bulletin of the School of Oriental and African Studies*
CIGS	Chief of the Imperial General Staff
CO	Colonial Office [records in Public Record Office, London: below, p. 579]
CP	Commissioner of Police
CPO	Chief Political Officer
CS	Chief Secretary
DA	Director of Agriculture
DAO	District Agricultural Officer
DAR	District Annual Report
DC	District Commissioner
DCS	Deputy Chief Secretary
DE	Director of Education
DOAG	Deutsch-Ostafrikanische Gesellschaft
DPO	District Political Officer
EAISR	East African Institute of Social Research
FCB	Fabian Colonial Bureau
FO	Foreign Office [records in Public Record Office, London: below, p. 579]
FS	Financial Secretary
IJAHS	*International Journal of African Historical Studies*
JAA	*Journal of African Administration*
JAH	*Journal of African History*
KCCU	Kilimanjaro Chagga Citizens Union
KNCU	Kilimanjaro Native Cooperative Union
KNPA	Kilimanjaro Native Planters Association
KUAS	*Kyoto University African Studies*
LC	Labour Commissioner

LD	Labour Department
LKV	Landkommissionsverhandlung
LO	Labour Officer
LR	Landregister
MDS	*Mitteilungen aus den deutschen Schutzgebieten*
MLC	Member of Legislative Council
MMRP	Maji Maji Research Project [records in University Library, Dar es Salaam: below, p. 578]
MOH	Medical Officer of Health
MPG	Minute Paper German
MS	Municipal Secretary
MSOS	*Mitteilungen des Seminars für orientalische Sprachen zu Berlin*
MUL	Makerere University Library [below, p. 578]
PAR	Provincial Annual Report
PC	Provincial Commissioner
RG	Registrar-General
RH	Rhodes House, Oxford [below, p. 579]
RKA	Reichskolonialamt [records in Deutsches Zentralarchiv, Potsdam: below, p. 578]
RS	Registrar of Societies
RT	*Stenographische Berichte über die Verhandlungen des Reichstages*
RTA	*Stenographische Berichte über die Verhandlungen des Reichstages: Anlagenbände*
RTU	Registry of Trade Unions
SA	Secretary to the Administration
SAO	Senior Agricultural Officer
SC	Senior Commissioner
SG	Secretary-General, Tanganyika African National Union
SP	Superintendent of Police
TAA	Tanganyika African Association
TAGSA	Tanganyika African Government Servants Association
TANU	Tanganyika African National Union [below, p. 578]
TJH	*Transafrican Journal of History*
TNA	Tanzania National Archives [below, p. 577]
TNR	*Tanganyika [Tanzania] Notes and Records*
TSGA	Tanganyika Sisal Growers Association
TTACSA	Tanganyika Territory African Civil Services Association
UEASSC	University of East Africa Social Science Conference
ULD	University Library, Dar es Salaam [below, p. 578]
UMCA	Universities Mission to Central Africa [records at the United Society for the Propagation of the Gospel, London: below, p. 579]
UNTC	United Nations Trusteeship Council
WO	War Office
YUL	York University Library [below, p. 579]
ZES	*Zeitschrift für Eingeborenensprachen*

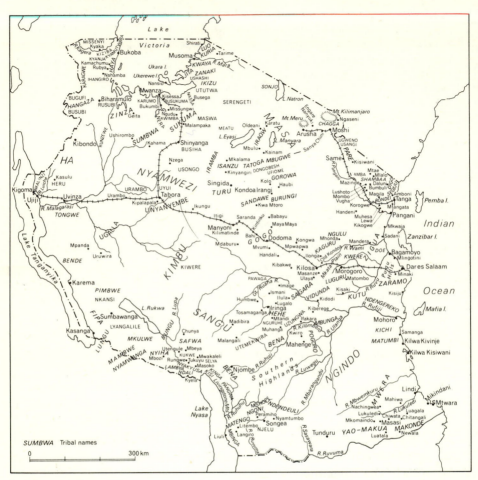

I Tanganyika

CHAPTER 1

Intentions

This is a modern history of Tanganyika based on written sources and concentrating on the colonial period. Tanganyika as defined by its colonial borders is the appropriate unit of study in this period, although the name will also be used in a purely geographical sense to describe the same area before colonial rule. The book seeks to synthesise research by many scholars working in Tanganyika since it became independent in 1961, in the hope that despite the difficulty of the task and the vast areas of ignorance remaining, a synthesis by one author may help to focus thought and stimulate research.

The book is a general history which deals with many aspects of Tanganyika's past and with numerous small societies. It is written in the belief that the essence of history is complexity. To comprehend such diversity and write a connected history of such a land requires organising themes. Those chosen are the five most important aspects of Tanganyika's modern experience. Most have attracted the attention of particular scholars, so that to outline themes is also to identify recent approaches to Tanganyikan history. The approaches are not mutually exclusive: each is merely a narrow beam of light penetrating the obscurity of the past. Sometimes the beams merge and a larger area becomes visible. Sometimes the themes connect and true historical understanding becomes possible.

The first theme is enlargement of scale. The world in which Tanganyikans lived has become immensely larger in modern times. Through alien rule and their own political creativity they have come to live in larger polities. Through economic change and improved communications they have extended their relations with men beyond their political borders. Through literacy they have extended their relations with the dead. This is a process best analysed by social anthropologists, whose work has provided much of the intellectual basis for the modern study of African history. In particular, it was two anthropologists working in Tanganyika, Godfrey and Monica Wilson, who systematised the idea of enlargement of scale.[1] They argued that although the scale of a society varied according to the number of men with whom its members had relations, the total quantity of relations between any individual and other men was a constant, so that the larger a society became, the less intense, on average, were the relations among its members. The implication was that as Tanganyikans came to live in a larger world so their small communities lost coherence. The Wilsons also argued that the individual members of a society experienced enlargement of scale to varying degrees: some lived more in the larger world, some more in the smaller. The argument implied differentiation between the more modern and the more deprived. Modernisation and deprivation were two sides of the same process. These ideas underlie much of this book, especially its sections on culture, religion, and social change. Moreover, although the Wilsons concentrated on differentiation among the members of a small society, the same process differentiated between one society and another, and even between one region or country and another. The resulting tensions provided much of the dynamic of Tanganyika's modern history, especially in the political sphere.

Yet Tanganyikans were not drawn into just any larger world. They were drawn into a capitalist world. The impact of capitalism and the growth of capitalist relations among Tanganyikans is the book's second theme, and it is the most contentious subject in modern African history. While some have seen European capitalism as providing Africa with the incentive and the means to escape historic underpopulation, isolation, and poverty, others have argued that capitalism bred underdevelopment: unequal exchange, immiseration, the transfer of economic surplus from Africa to Europe or Asia, and the impover-ishment of African economies and societies as they were specialised in the production of certain primary goods demanded by external metropoles.[2] This book argues that capitalism's impact on Tanganyika did not fit either of these models, but combined elements from each. Capitalism did not impoverish Tanganyika as a whole, but impover-ished some of it all of the time and all of it some of the time. Capitalism did transfer surplus to Europe, but also generated surplus which remained in Tanganyika. Capitalism did specialise some

[1] Godfrey and Monica Wilson, *The analysis of social change* (reprinted, Cambridge, 1968), esp. ch. 2.
[2] For the contrasting views, see A. G. Hopkins, *An economic history of West Africa* (London, 1973) and Walter Rodney, *How Europe underdeveloped Africa* (London, 1972).

Tanganyikans in producing primary exports, but specialised others in supplying the needs of the export-producers. It did provide the means to escape historic poverty, but obstructed that escape within the colonial period. This, supremely, is a subject whose essence is complexity. That is true also of the second issue surrounding capitalism: the extent to which, and the means by which, Tanganyikans accepted capitalist values and entered capitalist relationships before Independence. Although this question has bred less academic dispute, it has been a crucial ambiguity in Tanzanian political debate. In 1967, for example, President Nyerere wrote that 'there has been a general acceptance of the social attitudes and ideas of our colonial masters', but a year later he declared that 'the masses of the people did not become capitalist, and are not filled with capitalist ideas'.[1] Like most important issues in modern Tanganyikan history this needs further research, but the argument here is broadly that although relatively few Tanganyikans became capitalists during the colonial period, capitalist values and aspirations spread very widely indeed.

Both capitalism and enlargement of scale were imposed on Tanganyika from outside. By contrast, the liveliest history written by Africans and the most important historical research in Tanganyika during the last two decades has stressed African initiative. This work has taken two forms. One has sought to understand the inner working of pre-colonial societies: 'to understand Shambaa in Shambaa terms', as Professor Feierman has put it.[2] Based largely on oral research, this work has transformed understanding of the experience which Tanganyikans carried with them into the colonial period. In particular, the depth of pre-colonial history now revealed – and still being revealed – has led some to stress the capacity for survival of African traditions and institutions. In discussing the Maji Maji rebellion of 1905, for example, Dr Gwassa has stressed 'its demonstration that traditional ideas can be a progressive force'.[3] Here the approach merges with a second which has been concerned with the history of popular action, following a trend recently current in the writing of European and Asian history.[4] Such work appears in this

[1] Julius K. Nyerere, *Freedom and socialism* (Dar es Salaam, 1968), pp. 340, 17.
[2] Steven Feierman, *The Shambaa kingdom: a history* (Madison, Wisconsin, 1974), p. 5.
[3] G. C. K. Gwassa, 'The outbreak and development of the Maji Maji war 1905–7', Ph.D. thesis, University of Dar es Salaam, 1973, p. 505. See also Isaria N. Kimambo, 'Mbiru: popular protest in colonial Tanzania 1944–1947', in Bethwell A. Ogot (ed.), *War and society in Africa* (London, 1972), pp. 237–58.
[4] See Terence O. Ranger, *The recovery of African initiative in Tanzanian history* (Dar es Salaam, 1969).

3

book in accounts of resistance and rebellion, in studies of labour organisation and popular culture, and in the analysis of nationalism. It makes possible an escape from a history of kings and colonialists to an understanding of Africa's modern history both as an ordeal to which men responded with extraordinary resilience and as a process by which men long isolated from the mainstream of world history learned to survive in and profit from the larger world.

The fourth issue is periodisation. A distinctive feature of Tanganyika's history was a double restructuring of its economies and societies, first in the nineteenth century when long-distance trade drew them into relations with the outside world, and then again in the early colonial period when Europeans sought to remould economies and societies according to their own ideas and interests. In each period change occurred in a dialectical manner, with old and new long co-existing in contradiction and ambiguity. This was true also of the third major phase of change, which took place during the middle of the colonial period. Here the analysis follows Professor Berque's work on North Africa, where he has argued that the colonial period divided into two phases which merged dialectically between the two world wars at the moment when colonial society both took its most complete form and 'bore within itself...its own negation'.[1] A similar transition in Tanganyika between 1929 and 1945 is the pivot of this book. Both the creation and the dissolution of colonial society were dialectical processes. Colonial society incorporated much of Tanganyika's pre-colonial experience, while nationalism was, in one aspect, a means by which Tanganyikans internalised many of colonial society's values and incorporated many of its institutions, notably its administrative state, into their independent country.

The creation and dissolution of colonial society occupy the front of the stage. Behind them stands a longer process. A central theme of Tanganyika's history has been its people's colonisation of the land and their struggle with their enemies in nature. The theme is especially important in Tanganyika because it was one of the last areas of Africa to be at all densely colonised by men and its history is quite literally written on the face of the land. Yet the subject is of more than local significance, for the colonisation of their immensely difficult continent has been the African people's chief contribution to human history and one of the great adventures of man's past. Only recently have

---

[1] Jacques Berque, *French North Africa: the Maghrib between two world wars* (trans. J. Stewart, London, 1967), p. 19.

4

historians of Africa begun to understand this, and as yet they have scarcely begun to relate the story of colonisation to other aspects of Africa's past.[1] To do so in one country is the central purpose of this book. It is an attempt to show how relationships between men and nature in modern Tanganyika have intertwined with relationships between men and men.

[1] The seminal work is John Ford, *The role of the trypanosomiases in African ecology: a study of the tsetse fly problem* (Oxford, 1971). For Tanganyika, see Helge Kjekshus, *Ecology control and economic development in East African history* (London, 1977). For an attempt to integrate ecological and general history, see Leroy Vail, 'Ecology and history: the example of eastern Zambia', *Journal of southern African studies*, III (1977), 129–55.

CHAPTER 2

Tanganyika in 1800

Nature and men

The eastern arm of the great rift valley cuts southward through Tanganyika and divides it into natural regions. To the west a plateau stretches away for 600 kilometres towards Lake Tanganyika. Woodland savannah 1,000 to 1,500 metres above sea level and seldom receiving more than 1,000 millimetres of rain in a year, this western plateau presents few obstacles to the movement and mingling of peoples. On its north-western rim it merges into the region of higher land, heavier rainfall, and more luxuriant vegetation which borders the western shore of Lake Victoria. At its southern edge the plateau gives way to the Southern Highlands, mountains and high plateaux running south-westwards to encircle the northern shore of Lake Nyasa. East of the rift, by contrast, the land slopes gently down towards the Indian Ocean. To the south of the River Rufiji this eastern region is predominantly rolling woodland savannah, but in the north high mountain outcrops – Kilimanjaro, Meru, Upare, Usambara, Uluguru – thrust abruptly from the plain as islands of high rainfall and forest vegetation. These five regions – the western plateau, the north-west, the Southern Highlands, the south-east, and the north-east – are Tanganyika's natural divisions. Ecological diversity has been the first determinant of its history.

The men followed the dictates of the land. Africa's peoples speak languages belonging to four families, and variants of each were spoken in Tanganyika in 1800.[1] The earliest recognisable inhabitants were hunters and gatherers who spoke Khoisan ('click') languages. At least one large Khoisan-speaking group survived in Tanganyika: the Sandawe, who lived close to the country's geographical centre on the

---

[1] The classification follows Joseph H. Greenberg, *The languages of Africa* (The Hague, 1963). For the history of settlement, see Roland Oliver, 'The East African interior', in Roland Oliver (ed.), *The Cambridge history of Africa*, III (Cambridge, 1977), pp. 621–69 and the references therein.

rim of the plateau overlooking the rift valley. Other Khoisan-speakers had doubtless been assimilated by peoples of different origin who had entered Tanganyika later. One group of these spoke Cushitic languages akin to those of Ethiopia. They herded and cultivated but did not initially use iron. They probably arrived from the north many centuries before the birth of Christ and occupied the rift valley and its environs as far south as the Southern Highlands, for Cushitic words remained in many languages spoken in the region and surviving Cushitic-speakers included the Burungi, Gorowa, and Iraqw, all close neighbours of the Sandawe on the rift valley's rim whose history still remains to be written. The third language family, Chari-Nile, was also represented by men who had come from the north, probably in a series of migrations of which the more recent brought Nilotic ancestors of the largely pastoral Tatoga, who ranged between the northern rift valley and Lake Victoria, and, much later, the almost wholly pastoral Masai, who had seized the rift valley by the eighteenth century.[1] Meanwhile a fourth group of immigrants had arrived: Bantu-speaking, iron-using cultivators who came from the west during the centuries immediately before and after the birth of Christ. Archaeology suggests that they were settled in the modern Bukoba district west of Lake Victoria by about 500 B.C.[2] Over the centuries they colonised most of Tanganyika, presumably absorbing earlier peoples until more than ninety per cent of the population spoke Bantu languages. These Bantu languages formed large groups which broadly followed the country's natural divisions: one probably in the south-east and another in the Southern Highlands, a third around Lake Victoria, and a fourth covering the western plateau and stretching across to embrace the north-east, where, however, a distinct Bantu language group survived in the mountain blocks of Kilimanjaro, Meru, and North Pare.[3] Pottery techniques show a similar development of regional styles during the more than a thousand years which still remain unknown to the historian between Bantu settlement and the earliest oral traditions.

Khoisan hunters, Cushitic herdsmen and cultivators, Nilotic pastoralists, and Bantu agriculturalists composed Tanganyika's popula-

[1] Alan H. Jacobs, 'Maasai pastoralism in historical perspective', in Theodore Monod (ed.), *Pastoralism in tropical Africa* (London, 1975), p. 411.
[2] Peter R. Schmidt, 'A new look at interpretations of the Early Iron Age in East Africa', *History in Africa*, II (1975), 128.
[3] This is my interpretation of research in progress by D. Nurse and G. Philippson. I am grateful to Dr Nurse for discussing their findings with me.

tion. That it was the only country in Africa where all four major
languages were spoken indicated how incomplete the process of
assimilation and colonisation remained. In 1800 Tanganyika was still
frontier territory which was being penetrated by colonists from all
directions, with most of its population concentrated in the more
fertile regions around the edges, and with its arid core – modern
Ugogo and its environs – either occupied by hunters or scarcely
inhabited, for until the mid nineteenth century a man could walk for
a fortnight across western Ugogo and see scarcely a dozen hamlets.[1]
Tanganyika's earliest traditions are dominated by stories of migration,
but there are scarcely any traditions of migration out of Tanganyika.[2]
Probably the areas of most vigorous immigration in 1800 were the
south-east and the west. In 1616 a Portuguese traveller had found the
south-east virtually uninhabited, but by 1800 its basic population,
ancestral to modern Ngindo and Ndendeuli, was being swollen by
immigrant Makonde and other groups from Mozambique, just as
ancestors of the Bende and their neighbours continued to arrive from
modern Zaire and Zambia to the west.[3] Tradition often pictures great
tribal or clan migrations from distant places to new homelands. Such
migrations were possible, especially for pastoralists like the Masai, but
they were rare. Careful use of tradition suggests, rather, that
migration was usually more complex, with families of hunters or
shifting cultivators gradually spreading over the land, adapting to new
environments, mingling with existing occupants, and then perhaps
sending out new migrants to repeat the sequence.[4] So slow, complex,
and unmemorable was this process that historians will never reconstruct it.

Early nineteenth-century Tanganyika was not inhabited by discrete,
compact, and identifiable tribes, each with a distinct territory,
language, culture, and political system. The need to describe makes
the use of collective names inescapable, but they distort and oversimplify a vastly more complex reality. Normally one group merged

[1] Richard F. Burton, 'The lake regions of central equatorial Africa', *Journal of the Royal Geographical Society*, xxix (1859), 155–9.
[2] For rare exceptions, see J. Forbes Munro, 'Migration of the Bantu-speaking peoples of the eastern Kenya highlands: a reappraisal', *JAH*, viii (1967), 26; Oliver in Oliver, *Cambridge history*, iii, 645–6.
[3] Sir John Gray, 'A journey by land from Tete to Kilwa in 1616', *TNR*, xxv (1948), 43–4; Edward A. Alpers, *Ivory and slaves in East Central Africa* (London, 1975), p. 5; A. Lechaptois, *Aux rives du Tanganika* (Alger, 1913), ch. 2.
[4] T. O. Beidelman, 'Myth, legend and oral history: a Kaguru traditional text', *Anthropos*, lxv (1970), 74–97; Isaria N. Kimambo, *A political history of the Pare of Tanzania c. 1500–1900* (Nairobi, 1969), ch. 3.

imperceptibly into another. Sandawe, for example, spoke a Khoisan language. Their culture was built upon a hunting and gathering past. Their poetry and praise songs celebrated the chase. Even their word for 'homeward' meant 'to the water'. Yet for centuries they had mingled with Cushitic, Bantu, and Nilotic neighbours. Pottery associated with Bantu-speakers of the first millennium A.D. has been found in Usandawe. Sandawe shared a tradition of rock-painting with Cushitic-speaking Burungi and Bantu-speaking Turu. Some Sandawe had begun to herd and cultivate, taking the necessary vocabulary from the Turu. Today several 'Sandawe' clans claim Turu origin, while the chief rain-making clan claims to be Tatoga. Yet these peoples were culturally and linguistically the most diverse in Africa.[1]

Tanganyika was not composed of tribes. Its groups and identities were formed in other ways. In the north-east the Shambaa occupied one of the several isolated mountain blocks, 'a green island in a brown sea'. 'The Shambaa', their historian has written, 'are people who live in a particular botanical environment' which existed only in that area.[2] Its local name, Shambaai, meant literally 'where bananas thrive', and the people contrasted it with the surrounding *nyika*, the arid lowlands. Such categorisation by adaptation to a specific environment was normal throughout eastern Tanganyika where mountains and plains were sharply juxtaposed. The Shambaa's lowland neighbours included the Bondei, literally 'people of the valley'. To the south lived Ngulu, Kaguru, Luguru, Vidunda, Sagara, Matumbi, Ndengereko – all literally 'highlanders', just as Khutu and Zaramo were 'lowlanders', Kichi were men of 'the waterless country', and Makonde inhabited a 'thicket-covered plateau'. West of the rift valley, however, these sharp physical contrasts gave way to the monotony of the open plateau. Here most of the names which evolved to classify people were either political – the inhabitants of a particular chiefdom – or simply indicated direction. Those who were to be called Sukuma were 'northerners' to their southern neighbours. The central Gogo (whose name was not yet invented) described northern Gogo as Sandawe. Identifi-

---

[1] James L. Newman, *The ecological basis for subsistence change among the Sandawe* (Washington, D.C., 1970), pp. 26, 42–3, 48–50; Eric ten Raa, 'Sandawe prehistory and the vernacular tradition', *Azania*, IV (1969), 93, 94 n. 1, 101; *idem*, 'Dead art and living society: a study of rockpaintings in a social context', *Mankind*, VIII (1971), 56; J. E. G. Sutton, 'Archaeological sites in Usandawe', *Azania*, III (1968), 167–74. For group identity in this region generally, see Patrick Pender-Cudlip, 'The Iramba and their neighbours', in K. Ingham (ed.), *Foreign relations of African states* (London, 1974), pp. 55–66.
[2] Feierman, *Shambaa kingdom*, p. 20.

cation was 'totally relative to the spatial position of the speaker'.[1] By moving his home and adapting to a new environment a man changed his identity. Turu became Sandawe. Shambaa who left the mountains commonly ceased to be Shambaa.

A people's adaptation to its environment was its civilisation. Shambaa had a great legend about Mbegha, the hero believed to have founded their kingdom.[2] The story told that he was a hunter of wild pigs in Ungulu to the south. His kinsmen withheld his inheritance because he was mystically dangerous, having as an infant cut his upper teeth first. He therefore fled, living as a hunter, until he reached Usambara. There he met Shambaa. Mbegha gave them meat and they gave him vegetable food. When he killed the wild pigs which ravaged their crops, they gave him a wife. When he killed a lion which attacked their cattle, they made him their king. Among its many levels of meaning, the story contrasted the life of the hunter with that of the agriculturalist, and meat with vegetable food. As a hunter Mbegha was dangerous, beyond civilised society, until the Shambaa civilised him by giving him vegetable food and bringing him into their culture. Shambaa conceptions of civilisation centred on this dichotomy between field and forest, between cultivated land and the wildness of the *nyika* and the mountain rain-forest which they had been clearing for generations. All Tanganyika's peoples, except perhaps pastoralists, seem to have recognised this dichotomy, but the perceived relationship between field and forest varied. The idea that they were antagonistic was strongest among those who lived in high-rainfall areas. 'The bush is full of dangers', said a Chagga proverb from Kilimanjaro. Similar ideas were held by those who inhabited permanent villages in more arid country, notably the Fipa of the highlands above Lake Tanganyika, where many villages have existed for so long that their founders are unknown. Fipa stress 'the village's properly dominant role in relation to the surrounding bush'. However, most inhabitants of the woodland savannah lived in scattered homesteads, ate much forest produce, and found the bush more hospitable. Sandawe held that every home should be surrounded by ample trees for firewood and building, fruit-gathering and honey-collecting, so that the bush was 'virtually synonymous with the best place to live', but this was an extreme view derived from a hunting past. More commonly the

---

[1] Peter Rigby, *Cattle and kinship among the Gogo* (Ithaca, New York, 1969), pp. 15–18.

[2] See Feierman, *Shambaa kingdom*, chs. 2–3. Whether the legend was fully formed by 1800 is unknown.

rituals of savannah peoples expressed ambivalence, an 'all-pervasive contrast and harmony of field and forest', or, like the myths of the Kimbu of the western plateau, stressed that it was the function of political and ritual leaders to mediate the dichotomy between nature and culture.[1]

Men faced four obstacles in colonising the land. One was the poverty of the soils, which, except in rare volcanic areas, were shallow, leached by the heavy rains of the wet season, and deficient in humus and phosphates. In Buhaya, on the western shore of Lake Victoria, the fertility of the cultivated areas – perhaps a fifth of the whole – had been deliberately built up by transferring grass and animal manure from surrounding pastures.[2] The second obstacle, except in mountain and lakeshore regions, was scarcity of water, due less to low rainfall than to its irregularity, which meant that only 20 per cent of the country could reliably expect more than 800 millimetres of rain each year and that large areas remained unoccupied on account of annual flooding while neighbouring regions might be uninhabitable because domestic water was lacking for several months of the year.[3] Wild animals were a third enemy. Their profusion may explain why hunting and gathering peoples survived so long in eastern Africa. Tanganyika's folktales and legends, like the story of Mbegha, laid emphasis on animals and hunting. So did artistic decoration. It was widely believed that the border between human and animal could be crossed, and that to do so spelled evil and danger. Pare prayed:

> Our God protect us
> Our country and families
> All our enemies, which are epidemics, wild animals and the witches
> Let them be blind and
> Let them come not to us.[4]

Disease was the most serious obstacle to colonisation. A visitor to the coast in 1776 was told that smallpox existed throughout the south.

[1] Michael von Clemm, 'People of the white mountain: the interdependence of political and economic activity amongst the Chagga', D.Phil. thesis, Oxford University, 1962, p. 300; Roy G. Willis, *Man and beast* (reprinted, St Albans, 1975), p. 8; Newman, *Sandawe*, p. 35; A. R. W. Crosse-Upcott, 'The social structure of the KiNgindo-speaking peoples', Ph.D. thesis, University of Cape Town, 1956, p. 275; A. E. M. Shorter, 'Religious values in Kimbu historical charters', *Africa*, XXXIX (1969), 227–37.

[2] G. Milne, 'Essays in applied pedology: III – Bukoba', *East African agricultural journal*, IV (1938), 15.

[3] C. Gillman, 'A population map of Tanganyika Territory', *Geographical review*, XXVI (1936), 354, 370.

[4] Quoted in C. K. Omari, 'God and worship in traditional Asu society', Ph.D. thesis, University of East Africa, 1970, p. 195.

Malaria was endemic below 1,000 metres and seasonal in many higher areas. Often fatal to the young and debilitating to their elders, it was presumably an important constraint on population growth and a further reason for preferring the highlands. Shambaa highlanders understood the connection between mosquitoes and malaria and feared to spend a single night in the *nyika*.[1] In the woodland savannah the most dangerous vector of disease was the tsetse fly, which survived in tropical Africa but not in other continents. Tsetse flourish in wooded country and feed on blood, chiefly taken from game. They carry parasites called trypanosomes. Several of these are fatal to animals lacking acquired immunity, while two infect men with sleeping sickness. Since tsetse can live only in the bush they must withdraw where men cultivate the land intensively or browsing cattle destroy the scrub. The incidence of tsetse in pre-colonial Tanganyika is an important subject for research, but it was certainly uneven. In the south-east, where scattered homesteads were the rule, cattle were very rare and tsetse carrying fatal trypanosomes were probably wide-spread. Further west a broad swathe of tsetse-free land stretched from north-east to south-west across the country, including the rift valley and the Southern Highlands. Sandawe had no word for tsetse. The western plateau formed a third region. Here, over the centuries, men had cleared stretches of bush, but these cultivated regions were separated by wider belts of tsetse-infested woodland – *Grenzwildnisse*, border wildernesses, as Dr Ford has called them. Whether these harboured sleeping sickness is an unanswered question.[2] Seen from the air, early nineteenth-century Tanganyika would have appeared as a carpet of woodland broken by settled clearings: large clearings on the mountains and lakeshores, smaller and less compact clearings on the plateaux, and thousands of tiny glades occupied by individual homesteads. Men would have seemed very small and unevenly dis-tributed in the vast and empty land.

Mbegha crossed a *Grenzwildnis* as he travelled from Ungulu to rule the cultivated land of Usambara. He braved the perils of malaria and hunted wild pigs, the scourge of cultivators and the preferred hosts of tsetse. In the *Grenzwildnis* he was 'half man, half animal: a

[1] G. S. P. Freeman-Grenville, *The French at Kilwa Island* (Oxford, 1965), p. 121; David F. Clyde, *Malaria in Tanzania* (London, 1967), ch. 1; Robert Koch, 'Report on West Usambara from the point of view of health' (trans. V. Blessly), *TNR*, xxxv (1953), 10–11.

[2] Eugène de Froberville, 'Notes sur les Va-Ngindo', *Bulletin de la Société de Géographie*, 4th ser., III (1852), 426–30; Kjekshus, *Ecology control*, pp. 61–2; Newman, *Sandawe*, p. 136; Ford, *Trypanosomiases*, p. 123; below, p. 164.

dangerous creature who existed between categories'.[1] Not until he regained the safety of cultivated land was he civilised. The myth caught the danger and the excitement of colonisation:

> In all their examination they did not see any human foot-prints – not even the foot-prints of one man. Moreover they did not find any other sign, such as a single tree having been cut by man. So they realised that this country was uninhabited, and that it was a country that belonged to God only. Oh, how happy they were! 'Now we have acquired a country', they said, 'and we shall rule it ourselves.'[2]

Production, exchange, and social organisation

Men measured out their lives in famines. Chiefly due to unreliable rainfall, they and disease were the main reasons for underpopulation. Not even the most favoured regions were spared. Bananas might thrive in Usambara, but its traditions record a famine at least once every fifteen years. Chagga believed that a red glow on Kilimanjaro's summit at night presaged dearth. 'Deliver us from death by starvation', men prayed in fertile Unyakyusa on the shore of Lake Nyasa. Many Haya legends told of dearth, and famine is the chief explanation of migration and social change in most Tanganyikan traditions. Men came to distinguish two kinds: ordinary food shortages, and 'famines that kill', the ultimate horrors of mass starvation which destroyed kinship obligations, broke down the distinctions between forest and field, and turned men into animals.[3]

When the rains failed men had two alternatives. Some sought food in the bush. Here hunting and gathering skills were crucial and such experts as the Sandawe were less often decimated than their neighbours. Others fell back on the reserves embodied in their cattle, not eating them but exchanging them for grain with more fortunate groups, or exploiting the social ties created by prior exchanges of cattle. 'Many corpses are the result of not having livestock', said a Shambaa proverb.[4]

[1] Feierman, *Shambaa kingdom*, p. 61.
[2] This Bungu tradition is quoted in Aylward Shorter, *Chiefship in western Tanzania: a political history of the Kimbu* (Oxford, 1972), p. 40.
[3] Feierman, *Shambaa kingdom*, p. 23; Bruno Gutmann, *Dichten und Denken der Dschagganeger* (Leipzig, 1909), p. 6; John S. Mbiti, *The prayers of African religion* (London, 1975), p. 85; Abel G. M. Ishumi, 'The kingdom of Kiziba', *Cahiers d'histoire mondiale*, XIII (1971), 726; Frederick J. Kaijage, 'Kyamutwara', *ibid.*, 553; A. R. W. Crosse-Upcott, 'Ngindo famine subsistence', *TNR*, L (1958), 1–2.
[4] Eric ten Raa, 'Bush foraging and agricultural development: a history of Sandawe famines', *TNR*, LXIX (1968), 33–40; Rigby, *Cattle*, p. 47; Feierman, *Shambaa kingdom*, p. 34.

Yet the first line of defence against famine was the cultivator's skill. It was the opposite of a modern, large-scale farmer's skill. He seeks to control the environment and produce a few specialised crops. The Tanganyikan cultivator sought to adapt to the environment and produce as many crops as possible. 'Since communications and markets were relatively poorly developed', Professor Feierman has written, 'the farmer had to sow a great variety of crops with a great variety of characteristics, in order to survive no matter what the climatic variations: so that he would not be, in effect, wiped out. By taking a single ecological zone, understanding its complexity with a thoroughness incomprehensible to even a rural westerner, developing a rich and subtle language with a profusion of terms for the understanding of local ecology, planting dozens of crops to which the environment was peculiarly suited, the farmer sought to defeat famine, to cheat death.'[1] Only long experience could give such skill, on which rested the authority of age. 'The men who are skilled in choosing ground for hoeing', a twentieth-century Nyakyusa explained, 'are those who have been long familiar with the soil. They know how soils differ and that one soil is best for maize...one for peas, another for beans...Whenever a man is hoeing a field for millet or ground-nuts or sweet-potatoes, he can tell just from the soil whether his crop will do well or not.'[2]

By the early nineteenth century Tanganyika's varied environments supported many different agricultural systems.[3] One practice in the woodland savannah was to cut and burn the bush, sow grain for a few seasons, and then plant crops requiring less fertility – possibly root crops – before the exhausted soil was abandoned for perhaps a generation. Repeated burning had entirely destroyed the forest in some areas and converted them into 'cultivation steppe' where a grass fallow was practised. Such systems of extensive, long-fallow cultivation conserved labour and the soil's fertility but supported only sparse populations, perhaps a dozen people to the square kilometre. Their staple crops were millet and sorghum, which resisted drought but matured slowly, gave low yields, and required much communal labour. They were the daily bread of most Tanganyikans, enshrined in myth and sanctified in ritual. Twentieth-century Turu diviners invoked the Pleiades: 'Send flowers to all sorts of millet – bulrush millet, long-

---

[1] Feierman, *Shambaa kingdom*, p. 19.
[2] Godfrey Wilson, *The land rights of individuals among the Nyakyusa*, Rhodes-Livingstone papers no. 1 (Livingstone, 1938), pp. 8–9.
[3] Generally, see William Allan, *The African husbandman* (Edinburgh, 1967).

headed sorghum, short-headed sorghum, red sorghum, white sorghum, pumpkins, cowpeas, sunflower, castor; crown with your flowers, Kiimia.'[1] By contrast, the staple of the high-rainfall areas was the banana, a permanent crop. In Usambara every village was enclosed in banana groves. They supported far denser populations than long-fallow agriculture and required less labour, leaving men free for war, politics, or reflection.

Much of Tanganyika's history might be written around the contrast between millet and bananas, but it was not a total contrast. Many peoples grew both staples. All agricultural systems rested on the labour of homesteads with the same simple technology – axes, hoes, digging-sticks – for apart from occasional use of donkeys or canoes, transport and agriculture depended entirely on human labour because cattle were not used either as pack or draught animals – a circumstance which has never been adequately explained. Despite this similarity, however, each agricultural system was specialised to minimise the risk of famine. Nyamwezi and Sukuma ridged their fields. Fipa planted in earth-covered mounds of vegetation, having deforested their plateau. The mountain peoples of the north-east – Chagga, Meru, Pare, Shambaa – had complicated systems of irrigation furrows. The poor soils of Ukara Island in Lake Victoria were so laboriously enriched with animal and vegetable manure as to support over 300 people on each square kilometre in the early twentieth century. Equally specialised was the wholly pastoral economy which the Masai chose to practise.[2]

The little evidence available suggests that everywhere (except perhaps Ukara) the colonist who undertook the immense drudgery of clearing new land controlled it and could welcome or refuse later settlers. Among the Iraqw the colonist's descendants became 'county heads' and preserved the right to allocate land. Where there were political authorities, village headmen might allocate cleared land abandoned by its original owner, but virgin land was so ample in the savannah that the colonist did not even need to consult a chief before clearing it.[3] The colonist's rights remained even in areas of permanent

[1] Marguerite Jellicoe, 'Praising the sun', *Transition*, XXXI (1967), 31.
[2] N. V. Rounce and others, *A record of investigations and observations on the agriculture of the cultivation steppe* (Dar es Salaam, 1942), pp. 12–13; Allan, *Husbandman*, pp. 139–40, 199–206; Kjekshus, *Ecology control*, pp. 33–6; Alan H. Jacobs, 'African pastoralists: some general remarks', *Anthropological quarterly*, XXXVIII (1965), 151.
[3] E. H. Winter, 'Some aspects of political organization and land tenure among the Iraqw', *KUAS*, II (1968), 6; R. G. Abrahams, *The peoples of Greater Unyamwezi* (London, 1967), pp. 61–2.

cultivation, but here considerations of inheritance intervened. Most of Tanganyika's peoples were patrilineal, but there are indications that many had once been matrilineal, and certain matrilineal peoples – the Zaramo, Luguru, Mwera, Makonde, and their neighbours – survived in the south-east, where tsetse may have prevented men from acquiring cattle to bequeath to their sons.[1] Patrilineal inheritance of banana plots was the norm in the high-rainfall areas, where clans or corporate villages generally occupied and controlled specific areas of land. Partial exceptions were Buhaya and Bugufi, to the west of Lake Victoria, where unusually powerful chiefs gave their officers estates, known as *nyarubanja* or *ntore*, which were the only approximations to landlordism existing in Tanganyika.[2] This outline oversimplifies the real position, however, for although land was freely available, the best land was not, so that men often had different rights in different types of land. Shambaa, for example, appear to have bought and sold the favoured land whose location enabled men to exploit both highland and *nyika* environments, while exceptionally fertile plots in Unya-kyusa's extinct volcanic craters have long belonged to particular families.[3]

The division of labour between the sexes varied. In human societies generally, hoe-agriculture has tended to coincide with low levels of economic differentiation, the extensive use of female labour in agriculture, polygyny, the payment of bridewealth as recompense to the family losing a woman's labour and fertility, and the importance of extended families where survival remained tenuous and men owned little property which they wished to keep within a nuclear family.[4] This was broadly Tanganyika's social pattern. In most areas women did much of the repetitive agricultural work while men herded, hunted, cleared the forest, and managed the homestead, but there were also areas where men were energetic farmers. Nyakyusa and Nyamwezi were keen cultivators, 'boasting about their strength in

[1] T. O. Beidelman, *The matrilineal peoples of eastern Tanzania* (London, 1967), *passim*; de Froberville, 'Va-Ngindo', p. 433; Crosse-Upcott, 'Social structure', p. 20; Robert F. Gray, 'The Mbugwe tribe', *TNR*, xxxviii (1955), 40, 47–8; David F. Aberle, 'Matrilineal descent in cross-cultural perspective', in David M. Schneider and K. Gough (ed.), *Matrilineal kinship* (Berkeley, 1961), p. 680.

[2] P. C. Reining, 'The Haya: the agrarian system of a sedentary people', Ph.D. thesis, University of Chicago, 1967, pp. 250–61; J. C. Clarke, 'A note on the *ntore* system in Bugufi', *TNR*, v (1938), 76–8.

[3] Steven Feierman, 'Concepts of sovereignty among the Shambaa and their relation to political action', D.Phil. thesis, Oxford University, 1972, p. 30; Monica Wilson, *Good company: a study of Nyakyusa age-villages* (reprinted, Boston, 1963), p. 46.

[4] Jack Goody, *Production and reproduction* (Cambridge, 1976), *passim*.

hoeing, and praising those who are diligent'.[1] Polygyny existed in most
areas when accounts first become available, although presumably only
a minority of men were polygynists. Sandawe apparently did not
practise polygyny until they adopted agriculture from their Bantu
neighbours.[2] Bridewealth was also common but not universal. The.
Ndendeuli of the south did not know of it.[3] Where cattle existed they
were the normal gifts in bridewealth. 'Kinship is cattle', said the
Nyakyusa.[4] Those who lacked cattle might obtain brides by labour.
Nyakyusa recognised two forms of marriage: marriage by cattle,
practised by the rich, where children belonged to the father; and
marriage by service to the bride's parents, who then owned the
children. Kimbu men worked for three to five years for their
fathers-in-law, treating them with extreme deference, while Nyamwezi
suitors had to pay bridewealth *and* perform service.[5] Control of women
enabled older men to control and exploit their juniors. In Unyakyusa
'the opposition of generations is taken for granted' and was institu-
tionalised, as among some other East African peoples, into a regular
and ceremonial transfer of authority to a new generation.[6] Although
exploitation was masked by every man's expectation of becoming an
elder, generational tension may have been the most important form
of social conflict in all but the politically most sophisticated of
Tanganyikan societies. Yet these were not immobile gerontocracies,
for they were colonising societies where not only success but survival
depended on individual effort.

Exploitation of women and young men was the corollary of men's
inability to exploit each other by economic means. Slavery illustrates
the point. Except on the coast, the institution appears to have been
confined to the courts of powerful chiefs, where it was a relationship
of dependence rather than chattel slavery. Shambaa or Kerewe slaves
were people without descent groups who had become attached to a
chief's court: prisoners of war, men unable to pay legal indemnities,
or men so uncontrollable that their kinsmen disowned them and gave
them to the chief. The relationship was protective as well as servile,

[1] Wilson, *Good company*, p. 55.
[2] Otto Dempwolff, *Die Sandawe* (Hamburg, 1916), p. 137.
[3] P. H. Gulliver, *Neighbours and networks: the idiom of kinship in social action among the Ndendeuli* (Berkeley, 1971), pp. 311–12.
[4] Monica Wilson, *Rituals of kinship among the Nyakyusa* (London, 1957), p. 201.
[5] *Idem*, 'Zig-zag change', *Africa*, XLVI (1976), 400; Shorter, *Chiefship*, p. 74; Wilhelm Blohm, *Die Nyamwezi* (2 vols, Hamburg, 1931–3), II, 94–5.
[6] Monica Wilson, *Communal rituals of the Nyakyusa* (London, 1959), p. 160. See also O. F. Raum, *Chaga childhood* (London 1940), p. 289.

'a combined penal and welfare system with the majority of slaves coming from within the kingdom'.[1] Slaves could usually marry, acquire wealth, cultivate their own land, and redeem themselves. There is no evidence that they were bought or sold. Slavery was an outgrowth of political rather than economic power and appears to have existed only where political institutions were strong. It was unknown in the small chiefdoms of Unyakyusa.[2]

Skilled crafts were the basis of economic specialisation and exchange. Most women made pottery, but volcanic areas lacked suitable clay and so depended on specialists like the Kisi women of the Nyasa lakeshore who bartered their pots from house to house in Nyakyusa villages or the people of Ngaseni who traded their huge beer pots along the road which ran around the upper slopes of Kilimanjaro.[3] Cloth was widely made, either from bark, as in Buhaya and Unyakyusa, or from locally-grown cotton. In the latter case the spindle – a hollow reed in Ufipa – was rolled on the spinner's thigh and then passed backwards and forwards between threads strung lengthwise on a wooden loom, the weft being beaten home with a lathe, but the technology seems to have varied widely in different areas. Such looms were found in most western villages in the mid nineteenth century and also in the south-east. It is not clear whether weaving had ever been practised in the north-west or the north-east. It may have spread from the southern coast, where there is archaeological evidence of weaving from before the thirteenth century.[4]

Iron-smelting was more specialised. Worthwhile outcrops of ironstone were rare, although widely dispersed, and the craft required technical knowledge which was jealously guarded. The technology of smelting was already highly developed in Buhaya by 500 B.C. Smelters and smiths were often caste-like endogamous groups (as among Tatoga and Masai), distinct clans (as in Meru and Ukerewe), or men of chiefly families (as in Upare and Unyakyusa), although probably the most important industry, in Buzinza, was apparently open to anyone who paid to learn the skill. Smelting was often associated with

---

[1] Gerald W. Hartwig, 'The Bakerebe', *Cahiers d'histoire mondiale*, XIV (1972), 366–7. See also Feierman, *Shambaa kingdom*, pp. 174–5.

[2] Meyer to Soden, 12 February 1892, TNA G9/26/79.

[3] Monica Wilson, 'Traditional art among the Nyakyusa', *South African archaeological bulletin*, XIX (1964), 58; Georg Volkens, *Der Kilimandscharo* (Berlin, 1897), pp. 177, 232.

[4] Kjekshus, *Ecology control*, pp. 105–9; Petronella Lyimo, 'The role of crafts in the economy of Sumbawanga district: the case of cotton weaving in the Rukwa valley 1870–1975', M.A. thesis, University of Dar es Salaam, 1975, *passim*; de Froberville, 'Va-Ngindo', pp. 428, 432; Neville Chittick, *Kilwa* (2 vols, Nairobi, 1974), I, 376.

the forest. A Nyamwezi myth told that the lord of the animals had taught the first blacksmith his craft. Given such specialisation, iron was an important item in regional trading networks. In the north-east the Chagga and Masai obtained it from Pare smelters, while early in the nineteenth century the Mamba chiefdom became the iron-working centre for much of Kilimanjaro. In the south-west, Fipa smiths exchanged their produce for cloth woven in the Rukwa valley, while Nyakyusa climbed the Livingstone mountains to barter food for the products of Kinga furnaces. Iron was a scarce and precious commodity. Only the wealthiest Nyakyusa possessed iron hoes. Those used on Kilimanjaro at this time were only a few centimetres broad. The Sandawe used them until they were worn down to the tang.[1]

The other staple of regional exchange was salt, a necessity of life to men who lived chiefly on vegetable foods. Most peoples produced small quantities by burning grass or collecting surface deposits, but high-quality sources were rare. The most famous were the brine springs of Uvinza, on a tributary of the Malagarasi which flowed into Lake Tanganyika. These had probably been exploited since the first millennium after Christ. The brine was evaporated by boiling after a priest had invoked the tutelary spirits. Anyone could boil salt at Uvinza, provided that he paid a tithe to the local chief. The product was traded throughout the western plateau.[2]

Pots, cloth, iron, and salt were the staples of regional trade, but each area contributed the speciality which helped to define its identity. Nyakyusa produced none of the staples but were expert mat-makers. Kisi fishermen exchanged their catch for cattle from the plains of Usangu. Tobacco was probably the most widely traded agricultural product; standardised packages from Usambara were reaching the coast by the early nineteenth century.[3]

The peoples of Tanganyika were neither isolated nor in a state of permanent 'tribal war'. Where contrasting environments and cultures

---

[1] Kjekshus, *Ecology control*, pp. 81–92; Peter R. Schmidt, 'An investigation of Early and Late Iron Age cultures through oral tradition and archaeology: an interdisciplinary case study in Buhaya', Ph.D. thesis, Northwestern University, 1974, pp. 56–65, 339–48; Elias Nchoti, 'Some aspects of the iron industry of Geita c. 1850–1950 A.D.', M.A. thesis, University of Dar es Salaam, 1975, p. 17; R. Stern, 'Die Gewinnung des Eisens: Ueberlieferungen bei den -Nyamwezi', in Franz Stuhlmann, *Handwerk und Industrie in Ostafrika* (Hamburg, 1910), pp. 152–63; Kathleen M. Stahl, *History of the Chagga people of Kilimanjaro* (The Hague, 1964), p. 294; H. A. Fosbrooke, 'The defensive measures of certain tribes in north eastern Tanganyika', *TNR*, XXXVII (1954), 124.

[2] J. E. G. Sutton and A. D. Roberts, 'Uvinza and its salt industry', *Azania*, III (1968), 45–86; Kjekshus, *Ecology control*, pp. 92–105.

[3] Feierman, *Shambaa kingdom*, p. 132.

were juxtaposed, antagonism often co-existed with a lively exchange of goods. Fipa highlanders distrusted the Nyika of the Rukwa valley but valued their cloth. Nyakyusa despised their Kinga neighbours in the Livingstone mountains as 'dirty in habit and obsequious in manner' but eagerly sought Kinga iron, believed that their chiefs were immigrants from Bukinga, and watched with trepidation as Kinga priests descended the mountain paths each year to venerate their common ancestors.[1] Early traditions rarely mention warfare among agricultural peoples. Hunters, not warriors, are their heroes. Weapons – bows, arrows and spears – were simple and freely available. Cattle-raiding was common, but warfare often had a ritual quality and caused few casualties. Despite a long history of victimisation by their neighbours the Iraqw had no military organisation or admiration of violence.[2] By contrast, cultivator and pastoralist were hereditary enemies. Tanganyika lay on the frontier of Bantu Africa. Nilotic pastoralists had played a large part in its history. Not only their economies but their organisation differed. The cultivators were relatively numerous but tied to the land and their social organisation was fluid and small in scale. The pastoralists were less numerous but vastly more mobile and possessed wider-ranging social institutions. Their young men often formed a single age-set, and they alone in Tanganyika genuinely constituted tribes. Antagonism was very deep. 'A hero', in Sandawe definition, 'is a man who must previously have killed Tatoga', and the Tatoga bulk large as enemies in the traditions of all the peoples between the rift valley and Lake Victoria.[3] Masai aggression threw the whole of northern Tanganyika into disorder during the eighteenth and nineteenth centuries. In the Chagga languages of Kilimanjaro even the word for war is of Nilotic origin.[4] Yet relations were not solely antagonistic. Tatoga rain-making clans were scattered among cultivating societies – even the Sandawe – like the communities of a religious order. Masai married Chagga women and traded with Pare for iron. Cultivator could become pastoralist, and pastoralist cultivator.[5] Most important of all, interaction between the two had often created political organisation.

[1] Wilson, *Communal rituals*, pp. 2, 27.
[2] de Froberville, 'Va-Ngindo', p. 433; Feierman, 'Concepts', pp. 342–3; Winter, 'Aspects', p. 14.
[3] Dempwolff, *Sandawe*, p. 141.
[4] Christopher Ehret, *Ethiopians and East Africans* (Nairobi, 1974), p. 91; below, p. 23.
[5] John L. Berntsen, 'The Maasai and their neighbours: variables of interaction', *African economic history*, II (1976), 1–11.

Political organisation

The political systems existing in Tanganyika in 1800 ranged from complete statelessness to chiefdoms administered by appointed officers. Interaction between the two, with their very different ideologies and political cultures, was a central theme of the country's history. States were not necessarily more 'advanced' than stateless societies. Many of Africa's most cultured peoples were stateless. Rather, these were adaptations to different circumstances, for it was in the political sphere that relations between men and nature were most closely interwoven with those between men and men. Generally, high rainfall, permanent agriculture, and dense population made an articulated political system likely. This was not always so. Despite dense settlement, intensive agriculture, and long conflict with ethnically diverse neighbours, the Iraqw, very remarkably, had created no centralised political institutions whatever, whereas one of the most elaborate chiefdoms, Nkansi in Ufipa, occupied rolling, treeless hills overlooking Lake Tanganyika. Yet there was a significant correlation between population density and political organisation. The reason lay in the dynamics of colonisation, for although pioneering enabled men to move away from political control, it also stimulated political organisation by mingling peoples with different customs and mutually advantageous specialities who needed superior authority to facilitate their interaction and arbitrate their disputes.[1]

Statelessness was most common in the sparsely-populated, tsetse-infested south-east. Makonde, for example, possessed two main units of organisation: a matrilineal kinship grouping (of which several hundreds existed) and the *chirambo*, a territorial group led by an *mkulungwa*, normally descended from a pioneer colonist. The *mkulungwa* possessed only a limited ritual and judicial leadership over anyone who chose to remain his neighbour. As settlement extended, the *chirambo* divided and new ones formed. No wider organisation existed – each *chirambo* had its own initiation rites – and the Makonde appear never to have united for any purpose. Such structures were common throughout the region between Lake Nyasa and the sea.[2] 'If a case arose', Ndendeuli recalled, 'a father of the village concerned

[1] My argument generally follows B. A. Ogot, 'Kingship and statelessness among the Nilotes', in J. Vansina and others (ed.), *The historian in tropical Africa* (London, 1964), pp. 284–302.
[2] J. Gus Liebenow, *Colonial rule and political development in Tanzania: the case of the Makonde* (Nairobi, 1971), ch. 3. See also de Froberville, 'Va-Ngindo', pp. 425–43.

would invite the father of another village, saying, "Please, there is a case in my village. Two of my sons have quarrelled. Come and help me decide the case." So they came together and decided the case."[1] More surprisingly, statelessness also characterised the better-watered Southern Highlands, occupied by the ancestors of the modern Bena, Hehe, Sangu, and Pogoro. It was not simply an absence of organisation but a form of organisation with its own rationale and ideology.

Political consolidation through the mingling of cultures was especially clear in the ecologically diverse north-east. One ancient political system was the Gweno state in the North Pare mountains, said to have been formed by the Shana clan of ironsmiths and then taken over by another clan, the Suya, who united the scattered colonising groups through a common initiation system, a hierarchy of councils, and centrally-appointed administrative officers.[2] Similarly, the neighbouring Shambaa initially formed several small clan-chiefdoms, but these were threatened by immigrant Cushitic pastoralists, the Mbugu, whose tribal institutions were incompatible with the neighbourhood organisation of the cultivators. According to tradition, the old culture found its saviour in Mbegha, the wandering hunter from Ungulu. By violence, cunning, diplomacy, and marriage into leading families he united the Shambaa under his rule. His kingdom was an embodiment of the old culture. The royal capital, Vugha – estimated in 1857 to house 3,000 people – was built as a huge Shambaa village. Kinship was the basis of the state. The monarchy sought to break the power and integrity of the clans, but lineages resolved their internal disputes and were corporately responsible for their members. The political structure was identified with the royal descent group, the Kilindi, who were Mbegha's descendants by Shambaa wives. Kilindi sub-chiefs were restrained by their maternal uncles, who were commoners. The king had a council of commoners. He alone had power of life and death. He could seize property without compensation and women without bridewealth. He levied tribute and redistributed it to his agents. He alone controlled rain medicine. At his ceremonial recognition the people shouted, 'You are our King, but if you don't treat us properly, we will get rid of you.' Yet without him there was no civil society, no distinction between Shambaa and stranger, hill and plain, field and forest. Born of cultural mingling, the Shambaa

---

[1] Daudi Lukeyile, quoted in Joseph T. Gallagher, 'Islam and the emergence of the Ndendeuli', Ph.D. thesis, Boston University, 1971, p. 408.
[2] Kimambo, *Political history*, ch. 4.

kingdom was the highest embodiment of the civilisation of Tanganyika's Bantu-speaking peoples.[1]

Political consolidation on Kilimanjaro seems also to have resulted from interaction between Bantu and Nilotic immigrants, most recently the Masai who were at their apogee at the beginning of the nineteenth century under a great ritual leader named Subet. By the early nineteenth century certain clan leaders on Kilimanjaro had emerged as territorial chiefs: the Orio clan of Kibosho on the western slopes, Rongoma of Kilema in the south, and Horombo of Keni in the east. They had probably taken from the pastoralists the initiation rites which seem to have been the core of chiefdom identities. Rongoma, the first great chief, imitated Masai spears, while Horombo armed his age-group with Masai spears and died fighting the Masai.[2]

Western Tanganyika's political history reveals two important differences from the north-east. One was environmental. Whereas the relatively dense agricultural populations of the north-eastern highlands were organised to resist incursions from the plains, the open western plateau had few human concentrations. Although its peoples were equally mixed, therefore, its political units were small. The Kimbu, for example, were divided into more than thirty chiefdoms created by three groups of immigrants: the Nyisamba, who claimed to originate from Usumbwa to the north-west; the Nyitumba, from Usagara in the east; and the Igulwibi chiefdoms created by Kimbu returning from Iramba to the north-east. Kimbu chiefs ruled huge areas of woodland containing at most a few thousand men. Lacking cattle or other scarce goods to bind men to them, their strictly political power was small. 'The Kimbu chief', Dr Shorter has written, '. . .did not really rule his chiefdom himself. His power had a markedly ritual emphasis, and much of the real executive and judicial power was in the hands of his council, which had power both to appoint and depose him.'[3] Similar ritual chiefdoms, each occupying a woodland clearing and separated from its neighbours by *Grenzwildnisse*, existed among the Nyamwezi.[4]

[1] Feierman, *Shambaa kingdom*, chs. 1–4. The quotation is from Feierman, 'Concepts', p. 244.
[2] Edward A. Alpers and Christopher Ehret, 'Eastern Africa', in Richard Gray (ed.), *The Cambridge history of Africa*, IV (Cambridge, 1975), pp. 491–5; Alan H. Jacobs, 'The traditional political organization of the pastoral Masai', D.Phil. thesis, Oxford University, 1965, pp. 54–6; Stahl, *History*, pp. 154–7, 297–302, 347–50.
[3] Shorter, *Chiefship*, p. 148.
[4] Andrew Roberts, 'The Nyamwezi', in Andrew Roberts (ed.), *Tanzania before 1900* (Nairobi, 1968), pp. 118–22.

The Fipa lived on the south-western rim of the plateau. During the previous centuries the established population had been augmented by immigrants from the west, from Luba country in modern Zaire, who created several ritual chieftainships. The central one – Milansi, 'the eternal village' – was headed by a dynasty of ironsmiths. Somewhat later these dynasties were superseded by new immigrants, of unknown origin, named Twa. Organised as a single clan, in contrast to Fipa neighbourhoods, the Twa usurped power by force and cunning and established themselves as an aristocracy. The Milansi dynasty retained ritual power and the right to install the Twa chief, but the Twa exercised a territorial, administrative authority through appointed officials who transmitted orders to elected village headmen. While originating from the mingling of peoples, the Fipa state – for here the word is legitimate – was more stratified, had more precise borders, and was governed in a more strictly administrative manner than the other polities of the plateau.[1]

The Fipa state highlights the second difference between western and eastern Tanganyika. The west bordered major centres of African political development. Luba country was one. The other was the region west and north of Lake Victoria whose permanent agriculture had long supported kingdoms where pastoralists and agriculturalists coexisted. By 1800 several small kingdoms of this kind fell within Tanganyika's modern borders.[2] One group contained the Haya states on the western shore of the lake, Karagwe in the high grasslands to the west, the Zinza state on the south-western lakeshore, and Ukerewe Island. Their traditions claimed that a hero named Ruhinda had created a single kingdom in the region and that his descendants, the Hinda clan, ruled the successor chiefdoms, although the ruler of the most northerly Haya chiefdom, Kiziba, belonged to a rival clan, the Bito, who also ruled Buganda to the north. In these chiefdoms, and especially in Karagwe, the pastoralists, known as Hima, held a distinct social predominance which may have resulted from their ability to make cultivators their clients by loaning cattle. Yet the kings attempted to exert an independent authority over both classes of men, prohibiting blood feuds between clans, appointing royal relatives as

[1] Roy G. Willis, 'The Fipa', in *ibid.*, pp. 82–7.
[2] Interlacustrine history is too contentious to be discussed fully here. The best introduction is Oliver, *Cambridge history*, III, 630–46. But see also David P. Henige, *The chronology of oral tradition* (Oxford, 1974), pp. 105–18; Luc de Heusch, *Le Rwanda et la civilisation interlacustre* (Bruxelles, 1966), *passim*; Schmidt, 'New look', pp. 127–36. For Karagwe, see Israel K. Katoke, *The Karagwe kingdom: a history of the Abanyambo of north western Tanzania c. 1400–1915* (Nairobi, 1975).

sub-chiefs and village headmen occupying *nyarubanja* estates, waging a long and largely successful struggle to control the mediums of the *kubandwa* cult which dominated local religion, and organising elaborate courts at which each clan performed a specialised function. In Karagwe, unlike Ufipa, villagers did not even elect their headmen or allocate land. It was Tanganyika's most stratified and authoritarian society, and its cultivators' misery struck several early visitors.[1]

Until the eighteenth century the interlacustrine region had been dominated by Bunyoro, but at the end of the century Karagwe expelled a Nyoro force, its king becoming known as Ntare the Nyoro-slayer. Deprived of Nyoro protection, the Bito kingdom of Kiziba sought aid from Buganda against its Hinda neighbours. By 1800 Ganda had killed the Hinda chief of Kyamutwara at his court and the chiefdom had split into four, two sections (Kianja and Bukara) being ruled by Hinda and two (Bugabo and Lesser Kyamutwara) by Nkango, a Hima clan. Shortly afterwards the Ganda intervened in another Hinda chiefdom, Ihangiro, and in Karagwe itself. Meanwhile, further south, another group of kingdoms was threatened, for the Tusi rulers of Buha – possibly the same people as the Hima – had flourished in the eighteenth century but were now threatened by the emergence of Burundi, which was to annex large parts of Buha in the early nineteenth century.[2]

Even in the most highly organised regions the extent of specifically political authority must not be exaggerated. African states were webs of relationships which grew steadily weaker with distance from the capital until they merged into the statelessness of peripheral peoples. A ruler's authority grew with age and declined with senility. Haya states were composed of clans, not individuals. Mbegha's descendants judged cases between descent groups but did not intervene in one group's affairs unless life was to be taken. Even in the most sophisticated polities descent remained the core of a man's identity, many loyalties were still personal to a leader, and much violence and naked power survived. Men still had many loyalties: to nuclear family, extended family, descent group, clan, village, patron, chiefdom, perhaps even tribe. One was relevant in one situation, another in another. Yet – and this is the key point – the societies of 1800 were in the midst of the dynamic, autochthonous change which came from the mingling of diverse colonists.

[1] E.g. J. A. Grant, *A walk across Africa* (London, 1864), p. 177.
[2] Alpers and Ehret in Gray, *Cambridge history*, IV, 500; J. Vansina, 'Les peuples de l'Afrique orientale: aperçu historique', *Cahiers d'histoire mondiale*, XIII (1971), 35.

The problem of evil

We do not know what inland Tanganyikans believed in the early
nineteenth century. They were pre-literate, and the religions of
pre-literate peoples not only leave little historical evidence but are
characteristically eclectic, mutable, and unsystematic. Yet religious
change has been so important in Tanganyika's modern history that
some foundation for discussing it is essential. If we cannot know what
Tanganyikans believed, we may discover a little about what they did.
Some specifically historical data on religious practices survive. In
addition, it is possible, although risky, to argue backwards from the
religious practices existing in the twentieth century, much as linguistic
history can be reconstructed from existing languages. When combined,
these two approaches suggest that most peoples shared a common
corpus of religious practices to which many groups added practices
peculiar to themselves (and possibly their neighbours). The common
practices will be discussed first.

In the twentieth century most Tanganyikan peoples shared four
main religious practices. First, they recognised a single deity.[1] God
had many names to describe his various attributes. Several were widely
used. Those derived from the root *-uba* or *-uva*, together with the use
of the sun as a divine symbol, were common throughout the broad
linguistic area of the western plateau and the north-east. The sun
symbolised both God's remoteness and his enveloping warmth:

O Sun, Creator, you have opened. You are praised by the cock and by the
morning warbler, by the male donkey and the male goat; by the eland of the
forest... At midday pause over a homestead with ten houses, spread out your
blessing there; to a homestead with only one house also send goodness. Do not
burn us; do not be too hot. In the evening return safely those who have gone
herding and those travelling in the forests. Take with you to the west the
poisonous snakes, rhinoceroses, lions. Take with you all fevers of our people
and our herds... See that no sleeping child is caused to fall into the fire.[2]

Legends told how after creating the world God withdrew from its
affairs. He might maintain the laws of the universe or cause great
communal misfortunes. Sacrifices for rain might be directed to him,

---

[1] Only for Nyakyusa and Pangwa is this sometimes denied. See Wilson, *Communal rituals*,
pp. 18, 156; Hans Stirnimann, 'Zur Gesellschaftsordnung und Religion der Pangwa',
Anthropos, LXII (1967), 409–10.
[2] This twentieth-century text is quoted in Jellicoe, 'Praising the sun', pp. 30–1. For the
sun as a divine symbol, see Winter, 'Aspects', p. 7; Berta Millroth, *Lyuba: traditional
religion of the Sukuma* (Uppsala, 1965), ch. 1; Raimo Harjula, *God and the sun in Meru
thought* (Helsinki, 1969), *passim:* Shorter, *Chiefship*, pp. 99–100, 189.

or his name might be mentioned when invoking lesser spirits. Diviners might praise him. Men might appeal to him when all else failed. But he was rarely concerned with human morality and seldom the object of a cult or priesthood. These conceptions were so widespread in the twentieth century that they probably existed earlier.

In misfortune – if they or their animals sickened, if their crops failed or their relatives died – men consulted diviners, the intellectuals of these pre-literate societies.[1] In the twentieth century diviners often ascribed misfortune either to ancestral spirits or to witchcraft. Where kinship and age were the basis of social organisation, men often believed that ancestors survived death as spirits who intervened in their descendants' affairs by ensuring prosperity or causing misfortune. 'Do not come to us in dreams', Nyakyusa sang at funerals.[2] Propitiatory offerings were made at ancestral graves, at shrines in descendants' houses, or at special huts.

An alternative explanation of misfortune was witchcraft. Lacking scientific knowledge and rarely satisfied by the notion of chance, men could take action in misfortune by identifying and countering witches. Witchcraft accusations were made in most twentieth-century Tanganyikan societies and were especially common where men lived in villages, stressed neighbourly and egalitarian virtues, and favoured explanations in personal terms. Images of witches varied, for they were the reverse of all that was good. Fipa witches were supposed to be carried upside down at night by their wives while working evil. Kaguru witches were white and naked, walked on their hands, worked at night, and treated human beings as animals and animals as humans. Shambaa associated witchcraft with the forest; dangerous medicines had to be kept in the horns of wild animals and hidden in the bush. By contrast, the Kimbu – a forest people – saw witchcraft as a village activity. In stratified societies witchcraft was usually attributed to commoners. It was, in Professor Wilson's phrase, 'the standardized nightmare of a group'.[3] Witch beliefs were probably very old in many

[1] I owe this phrase to Professor J. R. Goody. See especially Colby R. Hatfield Jr, 'The *nfumu* in tradition and change: a study of the position of religious practitioners among the Sukuma', Ph.D. thesis, Catholic University of America, 1968; Blohm, *Nyamwezi*, II, 39.
[2] Godfrey Wilson, 'An African morality', *Africa*, IX (1936), 81.
[3] Willis, *Man and beast*, p. 94; T. O. Beidelman, 'Witchcraft in Ukaguru', in John Middleton and E. H. Winter (ed.), *Witchcraft and sorcery in East Africa* (London, 1963), p. 67; Feierman, *Shambaa kingdom*, p. 47; Shorter, *Chiefship*, p. 59; Wilson, *Communal rituals*, p. 68; Monica Wilson, 'Witch beliefs and social structure', *American journal of sociology*, LVI (1951), 313.

areas. Mbegha was clearly a witch before the Shambaa domesticated him. Makua traditions tell that they burned witches as soon as they crossed the Ruvuma into Tanganyika, and the right to murder a habitual witch was a Shambaa community's only right to kill.[1] It was in their treatment of supposed witches that the insularity and cruelty of the old Tanganyikan societies was most vividly revealed.

The fourth common practice was the use of medicines to harm or protect, to ensure health and fertility in peace, safety and victory in war. Some medicines were herbal remedies, others purely magical. Some were common knowledge, others the property of guilds or individual specialists. Medicines were a 'free-floating' device and probably an area of frequent change.[2]

Much of this is speculation. Historical reconstruction becomes possible – although still difficult – for those religious practices peculiar to certain peoples and more specifically related to their general history. Five kinds can be identified. The first were the religious actions of political leaders. Most commonly ancestor propitiation was extended to make a chief's ancestors influential over the welfare of the territory they had ruled. Regular sacrifices might be made at their graves, or they might be propitiated in communal misfortune. This was the basis of ritual chieftainship on the western plateau. A Nyamwezi chief poured beer on his predecessor's grave:

Here is your water!
Give me rain! Let it rain!
Why have you abandoned me? [Are you not still] my master?
I inherited the office from you. It was not stolen.
[Yet] you have abandoned me.
If you [continue to] abandon me, so that there is not rain in the land, the people will depart.
See, here is your goat, and this is your sheep![3]

Rainmaking was often a specialised activity separate from political office. Practitioners were usually those thought to have first colonised the land. Over large areas of the western plateau a single rainmaking tradition appears to have existed. It needs further study, but it probably originated with the Ghawog Mang clan of the Tatoga, who provided Tanganyika's most famous rainmakers. The Alagwa rain-

---

[1] J. A. R. Wembah-Rashid, *The ethno-history of the matrilineal peoples of southeast Tanzania* (Wien, 1975), p. 27; Feierman, 'Concepts', p. 319. For different viewpoints, see Crosse-Upcott, 'Social structure', p. 297; below, p. 81.
[2] See especially Hatfield, 'The *nfumu*', ch. 3; Wilson, *Communal rituals*, ch. 10.
[3] Blohm, *Nyamwezi*, II, 66.

makers of the Sandawe were of Tatoga origin. So, probably, were Isanzu, Iraqw, Turu, and Mbugwe ritual experts, and also the Masai *laibon*, for most Masai ritual terms were of Tatoga origin. Several Sukuma chiefs consulted Tatoga experts, while the Nyitumba who created several chiefdoms in Ukimbu introduced rainmaking techniques probably derived ultimately from the Tatoga. They attracted clients from far beyond Ukimbu.[1]

The third category of special practices were cults of nature spirits, which flourished chiefly in societies stressing territoriality rather than kinship. They often embodied notions of relationships between field and forest. In the Fipa cult, for example, spirits associated with rocks, mountains, groves, and lakes had each a shrine where a priest tended a sacred python whose domestication symbolised man's control of nature.[2]

Four areas possessed territorial shrines, normally in caves associated with water, where hereditary priests sacrificed for rain and fertility to a god (often symbolised by a python) whose authority extended over all who lived in the region, whatever their ethnic identity. They are much in need of research, but all four groups of shrines existed in the nineteenth century and may be very old indeed. The most northerly was the Tiita rain shrine of Unyaturu, which was part of the widespread religious system combining rainmaking with a god symbolised by the sun.[3] The other three were in the east and south. One consisted of at least three shrines, at Kibesa on the Rufiji, on the eastern face of the Uluguru mountains, and in the Ngulu hills. The god venerated was named Bokero at Kibesa and Kolelo at the other shrines. Heads of descent groups made annual pilgrimages for rain and fertility medicines, bringing black beasts, the colour of rain clouds. The god communicated by possessing a resident medium.[4] Further

---

[1] Morimichi Tomikawa, 'The distribution and the migrations of the Datoga tribe', *KUAS*, v (1970), 1–46; George J. Klima, *The Barabaig* (New York, 1970), p. 81; C. W. Werther, *Die mittleren Hochländer des nördlichen Deutsch-Ost-Afrika* (Berlin, 1898), pp. 31–2; above, p. 9; Winter, 'Aspects', pp. 10–15; Marguerite Jellicoe, 'The shrine in the desert', *Transition*, xxxiv (1967–8), 43–9; Gray, 'Mbugwe', pp. 39–44; information from Dr D. Nurse; Shorter, *Chiefship*, p. 191.

[2] Willis, *Man and beast*, p. 113; Winter, 'Aspects', pp. 8–9.

[3] Jellicoe, 'Shrine', pp. 43–9.

[4] G. C. K. Gwassa, 'Kinjikitile and the ideology of Maji Maji', in T. O. Ranger and I. N. Kimambo (ed.), *The historical study of African religion* (London, 1972), pp. 202–17; Lloyd W. Swantz, 'The role of the medicine man among the Zaramo of Dar es Salaam', Ph.D. thesis, University of Dar es Salaam, 1974, pp. 75–83; Richard F. Burton, *The lake regions of central Africa* (reprinted, 2 vols, New York, 1961), I, 88–9; Mtoro bin Mwenyi Bakari, 'Safari yangu ya Udoe hatta Uzigua', in C. Velten, *Safari za Wasuaheli* (Göttingen, 1901), p. 180.

west, on the face of the escarpment above the Kilombero, was the shrine of Chanzi, 'the beginner', again apparently associated with some subterranean water movement interpreted by priests.[1] The fourth group of shrines surrounded the northern and eastern shores of Lake Nyasa. Here several peoples appear to have possessed oracular shrines, some of those on the lakeshore being similar in operation to Chanzi's or Kolelo's. Subsequently, however, several seem to have become associated with a hero-cult of the ancestors of Nyakyusa chiefs.[2] Such shrines had specialised priesthoods with wider authority than many political leaders. The Kinga priests who sacrificed annually at the shrine of Lwembe in Unyakyusa belonged to a lineage claiming to antedate the Kinga chiefs. They monopolised ritual functions and exercised authority in selecting chiefs and collecting tribute.[3]

The last special religious practice was spirit possession. Men believed that spirits – ancestors, heroes, nature spirits, or divine manifestations – communicated by possessing them. Those possessed might be specialised mediums, like those of Kolelo, or ordinary men to whom the spirits announced themselves by misfortune, in which case ritual was performed to enable the spirit to communicate and so release his host from the misfortune. It is difficult to know how widespread possession was in 1800. Probably it was less common than in the twentieth century but existed in some regions. The *simbo* possession dance of the Sandawe, in which the dancers imitated lions as a means of combating witchcraft, is depicted in rock-paintings and is probably ancient. Zaramo and Ngindo traditions of spirit possession appear to antedate the nineteenth century.[4] Moreover, one form of possession undoubtedly existed at this time. It was found in the north-west, chiefly in Buhaya where it was called *kubandwa* ('to be possessed') but extending also into surrounding areas. Although never adequately studied in Buhaya, it is the most illuminating of all Tanganyika's religious practices.[5]

[1] *Missions-Blätter...der St Benediktus-Genossenschaft*, June 1908.

[2] I am here extending the argument in Marcia Wright, 'Nyakyusa cults and politics in the later nineteenth century', in Ranger and Kimambo, *Historical study*, pp. 158–9.

[3] George K. Park, 'Kinga priests', in Marc J. Swartz and others (ed.), *Political anthropology* (Chicago, 1966), pp. 229–37.

[4] Eric ten Raa, 'A record of some pre-historic and some recent Sandawe rockpaintings', *TNR*, LXXV (1974), 11, 13; Marja-Liisa Swantz, *Ritual and symbol in transitional Zaramo society* (Lund, 1970), pp. 187–200; Crosse-Upcott, 'Social structure', pp. 299–301.

[5] The following account is based chiefly on de Heusch, *Rwanda, passim*; E. Césard, 'Le Muhaya', *Anthropos*, XXXII (1937), 16–18; Iris Berger, 'The *kubandwa* religious complex of interlacustrine East Africa', Ph.D. thesis, University of Wisconsin, 1973, *passim*; Schmidt, 'Investigation', chs. 4–6, 15–16.

The possessing spirits of the *kubandwa* cult were chiefly the Chwezi, who were said to be related to a dynasty which supposedly ruled the interlacustrine region before the Hinda and Bito gained power, although this legend may have disguised an ancient, pre-Hinda religious system. The most important spirit in Buhaya was Wamara, lord of the underworld and supposedly the last Chwezi king. Other spirits included heroes (notably Lyangombe, Wamara's herdsman), nature spirits (Mukasa, the spirit of Lake Victoria, and Irungu, lord of the bush), and dead Hinda kings. Possession was restricted to priest-mediums who served each spirit at sanctuaries scattered through the country, but each clan had a patron spirit and its ancestors were believed to live in Wamara's underworld kingdom and to return to communicate with their descendants. Thus the cult had incorporated most other religious practices, especially the ancestral cult, while at the same time being brought under political control, perhaps after long conflict.

The cult also spread to Unyamwezi, where it was known as *buswezi* and differed greatly in structure. Outside Hinda control it was a peripheral cult of heroes who had resisted Hinda dominance. Its central figure was Lyangombe, who at his death had established the mysteries and promised initiates that 'whoever will adore and pray to me, I shall come to his aid in all his needs'.[1] The cult was open to ordinary men. Diviners might advise clients experiencing misfortune to seek Lyangombe's aid through initiation by a possession ritual. Initiates formed a semi-secret society independent of political chiefs, who might join but not hold office. Tusi pastoralists brought the cult to Unyamwezi and it is not clear whether it existed by 1800, although it was present by the mid nineteenth century.

Kubandwa illustrates many aspects of Tanganyikan religious practice. It shows the immediacy of religious life. Africans were not necessarily particularly religious, but their ritual and symbolism were often remarkably powerful. Neglect of ritual might drive a man mad, kill his children, or prolong his death agonies. Ritual was not merely symbolic: to many it was real. Lyangombe *possessed* his initiates. Nothing can be more real to a man than possession by the spirit of another. The cult also shows that religions were not static and unchanging. The product of a historical process, it changed with time and place until its meaning in Unyamwezi differed from that in Buhaya. Religion too was shaped by the movement and mingling of

[1] Text in Fridolin Bösch, *Les Banyamwezi* (Münster, 1930), p. 206.

31

peoples. Throughout the western plateau men sacrificed to the four points of the compass. The west often belonged to Ruhinda; the east to Ngalangai, a Tatoga or Masai diviner; the south to Sungwa Nyanyika, a Nyamwezi diviner and warrior; and the north to Mukasa, whose cult, it has been remarked, must be almost as old as Lake Victoria itself.[1]

In Buhaya the Chwezi cult had become a state religion, in Unyamwezi a potentially oppositional mystery cult. This dialectic between religion and the social order was to continue throughout Tanganyika's modern history. Further, the cult permits a rare, if limited, insight into the spiritual life of the early nineteenth century. An important part of the rites in Unyamwezi was prayer to Lyangombe to raise up those imitating death. When the rites ended initiates were told to be joyful. Elsewhere in the interlacustrine region initiates believed that after death they would live with Lyangombe in paradise while other men would be cast into the depths of volcanic craters. Such beliefs were very rare, for most African religions were concerned with prosperity in this world, rarely connected divinity with morality, and had only faint notions of an after-life. Twentieth-century Nyakyusa religion, for example, saw the spirit world as merely a shadowy reflection of the human world and had only the vaguest idea that a man's conduct might affect his eternal fate. Nyakyusa religion sought fertility and prosperity in this world; the sanction of morality was fear of supernatural punishment on earth. But as a corollary, Nyakyusa blamed their misfortunes on their faults. They were 'dogged by a sense of guilt' and terrified of death.[2] Most African religions were this-worldly, and this-worldly religions must be pessimistic. It is difficult to conceive the level of anguish in a society whose beliefs attributed a woman's barrenness to her personal failings. Unlike followers of world religions, few Africans had transformed suffering and fear of death into hope of life. They were naked before evil.

---

[1] The many accounts of this ceremony give different names and explanations. See Millroth, *Lyuba*, pp. 165–9, 184–6; Bösch, *Banyamwezi*, pp. 157–8; Harjula, *God and the sun*, p. 27; M. Maurice, 'Les sorciers *abalodi* chez les Bapimbwe', *Bibliotheca Africana*, III (1929), 15. The comment on Mukasa is from J. E. G. Sutton, 'The aquatic civilization of middle Africa', *JAH*, XV (1974), 544.

[2] Monica Wilson, 'Nyakyusa ritual and symbolism', *American anthropologist*, LVI (1954), 228–41.

Music and dance

Compared with west or central Africa, Tanganyika's peoples produced little plastic art.[1] Their main cultural forms were oral literature, ritual, music, and dance. This section is about dance and music. In addition to their cultural significance, these became valuable indicators of social change in later years, and they were probably the most sophisticated of the arts.[2] Almost all that may be inferred about this subject in 1800 comes from Dr Hartwig's research in Ukerewe.[3]

Ukerewe Island in Lake Victoria was an area of high fertility, supporting dense forest, banana groves, millet and other grains. Its initial inhabitants were sections of Bantu-speaking clans who lived also on the mainland. Subsequently the area was drawn into the inter-lacustrine civilisation by immigrants from the western lakeshore who described themselves as Sese and were led by a ruling clan, the Silanga, who claimed kinship with Ruhinda. The Silanga intro-duced the Haya political system, with an elaborate court and a territorial administration of appointed headmen belonging to the Silanga clan or those married into it. The indigenous people learned to speak the 'Sese' language, but were socially inferior to the immigrants. Ukerewe was a cultural colony of the interlacustine civilisation. Its chiefs eagerly welcomed new arrivals from the western lakeshore.

The historical evidence for the dance and music practised in Ukerewe comes from traditions attached to the musical instruments which survived into the twentieth century. (Other instruments may have disappeared.) The earliest surviving instruments were used by hunters and antedated the Silanga. The *enzomba*, for example, was the animal horn blown by a messenger as he ran through the villages calling the men to hunt small game and vermin which threatened the crops. If it returned successful, the party announced itself with horns, while the feast which followed was accompanied by singing, always in an antiphonal pattern of leader and chorus. Another very old instrument, also used only by hunters, was the *omwomba*, a tree branch,

---

[1] See G. W. Hartwig, 'East African plastic art tradition', *Genève-Afrique*, VII (1968), 48–52; Ladislav Holý, *Masks and figures from eastern and southern Africa* (London, 1967), pp. 16–27.

[2] Rose Brandel, *The music of central Africa* (The Hague, 1961), p. 101.

[3] This section is based on Gerald W. Hartwig, 'The historical and social role of Kerebe music', *TNR*, LXX (1969), 41–56; *idem*, *The art of survival in East Africa: the Kerebe and long-distance trade, 1800–1895* (New York, 1976), *passim*; Charlotte M. Hartwig, 'Music in Kerebe culture', *Anthropos*, LXVII (1972), 449–64.

four to six inches in diameter, hollowed out with one end closed and blown like a transverse flute.

By the eighteenth century two more specialised forms of hunting had their own instruments. The Nyaga society contained men from any clan who hunted hippopotamus. They had their own horn and songs. So too did buffalo hunters, a specialised skill introduced from neighbouring Usukuma. Fishermen were also organised as a craft with their own horn and songs, some of which they sang as they paddled. They venerated the spirit of the lake, Mukasa, while hunters invoked Lyangombe. Dancing had no part in hunting practices. Each group's music and instruments were its sole property. 'Parties of fishermen from widely separated villages could use one another's songs', Dr Hartwig writes, 'but they would never consider using songs from, for example, the hippopotamus hunters.'

The *enanga* was a seven-stringed trough zither which the Silanga were said to have brought in their canoes from Buhaya, where every chief had a court orchestra. Individuals played the *enanga* to accompany their songs. Staid, plaintive, reflective, its music was the exclusive property of the elders, who enjoyed it as they exercised their privilege of drinking millet beer. Women had their own styles of singing. The older form used at weddings was supplemented in the late eighteenth century by a new style from Buzinza. The leader accentuated the rhythm by shaking a calabash containing dried seeds.

Dance is more difficult to document. Dr Hartwig is unsure whether the Kerewe yet performed in 1800 the dance which became a feature of all major festivities. Men and women formed two lines facing each other. The women kept their feet firmly planted on the ground while gently rolling their shoulders. The men danced more vigorously, stamping the rhythm with their right feet while moving their shoulders energetically. A transverse flute accompanied the dance.

The last surviving instruments were drums, but music was scarcely their function. Throughout the interlacustrine region they were royal regalia. In Haya tradition, to seize the royal drum is to usurp the throne. Although less dominant in Kerewe symbolism, drums were still ritual objects rather than instruments for entertainment. Katobaha, founder of the Silanga dynasty, had first brought drums on his journey from Buhaya. They were played at the selection, installation, and wedding of a chief, and at his funeral, to warn his ancestors of his approach. A special drum, *matwigacharo*, 'the ears of the country', warned of imminent danger. Important headmen also had drums.

Clan heads owned small replicas and beat them at the clan's ancestral site when the new moon appeared. Diviners used them to accompany their rites.

The Kerewe evidence is unique. Similar instruments – horns, flutes, zithers, rattles and drums – were common elsewhere, with bells and musical bows in addition.[1] Isolated instruments and dances were clearly ancient.[2] But no other cultural history exists to compare with Ukerewe's. It illustrates once more the mingling of peoples, but it also shows that to mingle was not necessarily to mix, for Kerewe society was highly differentiated, although by origin, status, and function rather than by class or wealth. On the other hand, tradition may exaggerate, and Ukerewe was by no means typical. Quite different cultural forms probably existed among such egalitarian, colonising peoples as the Sukuma. One process of modern Tanganyikan history was to be the interaction of these cultures and the breakdown of categories, until young Kerewe played the *enanga* and danced to the beat of drums.

The larger world

The existence of a literate, Muslim, commercial society along the coast was to give a particular character to modern Tanganyika. This society had long been isolated from inland peoples. Although it was an area of high rainfall, the soils of the coast were infertile, malaria was endemic, and it was separated from population concentrations in the interior by arid plains and low hills bisected by unnavigable rivers. When Bantu-speaking peoples occupied the region in the first millennium A.D. it was already known to the mercantile peoples of the Indian Ocean as a source of ivory, rhino-horn, tortoise-shell, and coconut-oil.[3] From that time, at least, the rhythm of coastal history followed the changing commercial patterns of the Indian Ocean, whose seamen came and went with the monsoon.

In the early centuries the coast's centre of gravity was in modern Zanzibar, Somalia, and Kenya. The Tanganyikan coast first became commercially important around 1200 through its position on the route

---

[1] Eric ten Raa, 'Sandawe musical and other sound producing instruments', *TNR*, LX (1963), 23–48, and LXII (1964), 91–5; Wilson, 'Traditional art', p. 60; Elise Kootz-Kretschmer, *Die Safwa* (3 vols, Berlin, 1926–9), I, 124–8.

[2] For example, the Kimbu ghost horn (Shorter, *Chiefship*, pp. 99–101) and the Sandawe *phek'umo* dance, on which see Eric ten Raa, 'The moon as a symbol of life and fertility in Sandawe thought', *Africa*, XXXIX (1969), 38.

[3] J. E. G. Sutton, *The East African coast: an historical and archaeological review* (Nairobi, 1966), pp. 7–9.

between the Middle East and the ports of modern Mozambique which exported the gold of Rhodesia. Along the coastline grew up small, independent trading towns and villages which Dr Sheriff has likened to the beads of a rosary, 'clustering in places and widely spaced elsewhere, threaded through by coastal shipping'.[1] The most important was Kilwa Kisiwani, on a small island just off the southern coast which was the most southerly point Arabian ships could easily reach. Its first known ruler, Ali bin al-Hasan, gained power around 1200.[2] He claimed to be a 'Shirazi', by implication a Persian, but his Persian ancestors had probably long been settled on the coast of modern Somalia. He and his town were Muslim, of the Shafii school of orthodox Sunni Islam. In 1410/11 Kilwa's ruler made a recorded pilgrimage to Mecca.[3] His subjects included Arabs from the Hadhramaut and individual settlers from other Indian Ocean shores as well as Africans from the mainland. 'The last outpost of the civilization of medieval Islam',[4] Kilwa was already experiencing commercial decline and political instability when Portuguese ships arrived via the Cape of Good Hope to storm and loot the town in 1505. The next 250 years were a time of impoverishment and decay. The coast's centre of gravity again moved northwards. The Portuguese sought to redirect Indian Ocean trade towards their bases at Mozambique and Goa. In 1698 they were expelled from the coast north of the Ruvuma through a combination of local insurrection and intervention by Arab seamen from Oman, but although Omanis thereafter claimed authority over the region their control was sporadic, weakened by Persian invasions of Oman and continuous civil wars among themselves.[5]

Yet the seventeenth and eighteenth centuries were a formative period for coastal society. In the absence of effective outside control, colonists from the Somali coast, claiming to be Shirazi and often known locally as Barawi, consolidated themselves as *diwani* or rulers of many settlements on the Mrima coast between the Rufiji delta and the Pangani estuary, often becoming Africanised in the process.[6] The

[1] Abdul M. H. Sheriff, 'The rise of a commercial empire: an aspect of the economic history of Zanzibar, 1770–1875', Ph.D. thesis, University of London, 1971, p. 10.

[2] For Kilwa, see Chittick, *Kilwa*, I, ch. 18.

[3] B. G. Martin, 'Arab migrations to East Africa in medieval times', *IJAHS*, VII (1975), 374.

[4] G. S. P. Freeman-Grenville, *The medieval history of the coast of Tanganyika* (London, 1962), p. 205.

[5] Alpers and Ehret in Gray, *Cambridge history*, IV, 527–36; Chittick, *Kilwa*, I, 242; J. B. Kelly, *Britain and the Persian Gulf 1795–1880* (Oxford, 1968), pp. 2–16.

[6] H. Neville Chittick, 'The peopling of the East African coast', in Chittick and Robert I. Rotberg (ed.), *East Africa and the Orient* (New York, 1975), p. 41; Walter T. Brown, 'A pre-colonial history of Bagamoyo', Ph.D. thesis, Boston University, 1971, ch. 3.

Sultan of Kilwa, who drove out the Omani governor and garrison in 1771, called himself a Shirazi, but in 1776 a French visitor named Morice described him as an African, clearly distinct from the 'Arabs', by which Morice meant the Omani and other visiting traders from the Middle East, and the 'Moors', by which he meant long-settled, Swahili-speaking Arabs and 'Shirazi'. Morice reckoned that the Moors formed between a tenth and a twelfth of Kilwa's 2,000–3,000 people, while free Africans were about a third and the remainder were African slaves. He reported that Africans and Moors shared a common antipathy to Arabs.[1] That a distinct coastal identity was forming at this time is also suggested by the fact that the earliest known written document in the Swahili language – which is basically Bantu with much Arabic vocabulary – dates from 1711 and that the earliest known Swahili poem may have been composed in the seventeenth century. The word Swahili, to describe the coast, its language and inhabitants, became current early in the nineteenth century. In 1800, when this study begins, coastal society may have been more homogeneous than at any other time.[2]

The coast's economy rested on agriculture and fishing, on its position as commercial intermediary between the mainland and the Indian Ocean, and on the water-borne transport which distinguished it from inland economies. Many of the African inhabitants were doubtless cultivators. Men of property, such as the Moors of Kilwa, owned agricultural slaves, for even if Morice's figures were exaggerated this was nevertheless a society more dependent on slavery than any in the interior. Outlying villages also produced food for the towns and for export along the coast. Kilwa stood at the head of a trade route leading south-westwards across the Ruvuma to Lake Nyasa and beyond, but only in the eighteenth century did the hinterland peoples permit the Swahili to venture far inland, just as Kilwa's inhabitants banned mainlanders from visiting the island. Until then exchange took place at the coastal ports. No other town stood on a long-distance trade route, but all exchanged goods with the hinterland and thus, indirectly, with inland peoples.[3] The coasting trade was largely carried in Swahili-owned boats called *mitepe*, locally built with matting sails and ranging from twelve to twenty tonnes. Overseas trade depended entirely on Arab and Indian vessels. 'The Moors who live

[1] Freeman-Grenville, *French at Kilwa*, pp. 78–82, 92, 170.
[2] Wilfred Whiteley, *Swahili* (London, 1969), pp. 18, 38; C. S. Nicholls, *The Swahili coast, 1798–1856* (London, 1971), p. 19 n. 1.
[3] See below, pp. 40–2.

on the coast are not rich enough to have their own ships', Morice reported.[1] In the 1770s Kilwa exported ivory, slaves, hippo-teeth, tortoise-shell, cowries, wax, gum, and indigo. It imported cloth (largely made in western India), hardware, dates, beef (from nearby Mafia Island), salt, arms, ammunition, and money.[2]

The coastal towns had a long history of particularism. Each had its sultan, *diwani*, or *jumbe*, often claiming Shirazi origin and advised by the leading merchants. As in the interior, the ruler possessed elaborate regalia including a horn, umbrella, and drums. Nineteenth-century sources describe a hierarchy of social behaviour as elaborate as Ukerewe's.[3] *Diwani* wore special turbans and sandals. Freemen took off their hats and shoes when greeting them. Slaves doffed their hats to freemen. Propertied men flaunted their pedigrees with almost Arabian insistence. The African villages surrounding each town were politically independent but recognised its commercial and cultural leadership. Their headmen were Africans, Morice reported, but 'wish to pass as Moors'.[4]

The coast was distinguished from inland societies by its religion and culture. The religion contained two elements. One was the rigorous monotheism of orthodox Islam, which taught that the proper response to misfortune was patient expectation of recompense in an after-life on which great emphasis was laid. Alongside this, however, existed a popular cult centring on subordinate spirits, good or evil, Islamic or purely African, who intervened in men's earthly lives, often causing misfortune, and populated a highly-coloured universe of miracles, angels, and devils.[5] Orthodoxy struggled continuously against the popular cult and may have gained. One striking example of Islam's cultural influence was the position of women. Although regarded as inferior in status, intellect, and moral strength, they could wield considerable political influence and were spared the agricultural drudgery which was their lot in most inland societies. Morice noted that in contrast to mainlanders the men of Kilwa were 'slow, very gentle and very fond of women'.[6]

The coastal culture was eclectic, but its ideal was *ustaarabu*, 'Arabness', a notion of civilisation strongly marked by Arab racialism

---

[1] Freeman-Grenville, *French at Kilwa*, p. 163.
[2] Nicholls, *Swahili coast*, chs. 1 and 3.
[3] See Lyndon Harries (ed.), *Swahili prose texts* (London, 1965), pp. 192–213.
[4] Freeman-Grenville, *French at Kilwa*, p. 151.
[5] See Jan Knappert, *Traditional Swahili poetry* (Leiden, 1967) and *Swahili Islamic poetry* (Leiden, 1971).
[6] Freeman-Grenville, *French at Kilwa*, p. 171.

and cultural arrogance. The model of *ustaarabu* was Muhammad's life of service and humility as described in the most popular of all poems, al-Barzanji's eighteenth-century *Maulidi* or Life of the Prophet, which came to be read or recited at most communal ceremonies.[1] This ideal conflicted with the lively competition of small trading towns, the ceremony surrounding their rulers, and the distinctions of a slave society, but it enabled the Swahili to feel culturally superior to the inland peoples. They contrasted their own literary language with the *vilugha*, 'little languages', of the interior. Swahili poetry encapsulated their culture, just as the Mbegha legend embodied that of the Shambaa, although the Tanganyikan coast was a cultural backwater which did not produce poetry of its own. Towards the inland peoples the Swahili had long been indifferent. Morice reported that although Kilwa claimed authority as far as Lake Nyasa, in practice 'the interior is not known at all' and the Swahili encountered the inland peoples chiefly when they visited the coast to trade.[2]

By the late eighteenth century, however, this indifference was at last breaking down. The merchants of Kilwa anxiously awaited the increasingly frequent caravans from the unknown interior. Morice himself was a portent, for he was a slave trader from the Mascarene Islands, the outpost of French power in the Indian Ocean. In 1784 or 1785 Kilwa was reoccupied by an Arab force from Oman, which was soon to become a satellite of British power in India. The European conquest of Asia was beginning and Tanganyika's long isolation was ending.

[1] Knappert, *Islamic poetry*, pp. 48–60.
[2] Freeman-Grenville, *French at Kilwa*, pp. 76, 106.

CHAPTER 3

The nineteenth century

During the nineteenth century Tanganyika's inland peoples made contact with the outside world through a long-distance trading system based on Zanzibar, which became a satellite of Europe's growing power in the Indian Ocean. Tanganyika experienced a transformation more intense than any other region of tropical Africa at that time. It is the essential background to the colonial period. Yet the transformation was not a straightforward replacement of old by new. Men and societies experienced enlargement of scale most unevenly. Some participated enthusiastically in the new trading system while others resisted it. Some created new political systems while others defended their old polities or saw them shattered by change. Some adopted elements of the coastal culture while others reformulated inherited ideas and customs. These reactions formed a spectrum comparable to the later spectrum of responses to colonial rule. And they affected relationships between men and nature. More detailed and reliable traditions and the first European travellers' accounts make the period less obscure than earlier centuries. This chapter describes the long-distance trading system and examines its political, economic, cultural, and religious impact.

The growth of long-distance trade

In 1776 the trade route leading south-westwards from Kilwa to the dense populations around Lake Nyasa was the only route inland from the Tanganyikan coast. It was pioneered in the sixteenth century when the Portuguese seized the gold trade and forced Kilwa's merchants to trade with their own hinterland. Imported cloth from India penetrated the regional trading network of the Yao people of Mozambique and attracted them to carry ivory to the coast. Oman's conquest of Kilwa in 1698 led the Yao to travel instead to Mozambique Island, but by 1776 Kilwa was reviving. One reason was the growth of slave exports, first to the Persian Gulf and then to the Mascarene Islands, French plantation colonies developed after 1735. During the eighteenth century Kilwa became East Africa's chief slaving port, drawing first on the sparse and stateless peoples of south-eastern Tanganyika and then on the Lake Nyasa area. The Yao returned to Kilwa, now as slave traders. Kilwa's revival further profited from the resurgence of Oman, where the Busaidi dynasty seized control in the 1740s, built up their mercantile strength, and became satellites of British power in India. Oman's base on the coast was Zanzibar. When the French slave trade threatened to bypass Zanzibar the Omanis reoccupied Kilwa in 1784 or 1785 and obliged Europeans to trade through Zanzibar. Zanzibar's resulting prosperity attracted Asian[1] merchants from Mozambique, where high customs duties were crippling the ivory trade.[2]

Zanzibar's prosperity and rising ivory prices around 1800 probably explain the development of a new long-distance trade route through central Tanganyika at that time. Some foreign goods reached inland societies via this region during the eighteenth century, probably through exchange between one regional trade network and another. This apparently stimulated certain inland peoples to hunt elephants for ivory. Then the most active traders of the western plateau, the Sumbwa and western Nyamwezi, penetrated to the coast around 1800, travelling through Ugogo. 'They came back again', it is said, 'and began looking for ivory...When the Arabs saw this, they wanted to go to the countries where the ivory was obtained.'[3] By 1811 coastal traders had opened a more southerly route along the Ruaha valley, reaching Ukimbu on the plateau by about 1825. There they met Nyamwezi ivory caravans and persuaded some Nyamwezi to become porters. With their aid coastal traders entered Unyamwezi. By 1831 they reached Ujiji on Lake Tanganyika. From Unyamwezi routes were opened to Katanga and Buganda (probably reached by 1852). Centrally placed and rich in ivory, Unyamwezi became the traders' inland base. From 1852 their headquarters was at Tabora in the Unyanyembe chiefdom.

---

[1] Throughout the book this term refers to Indians and Pakistanis.

[2] Alpers, *Ivory, passim*; Edward A. Alpers, 'The French slave trade in East Africa (1721–1810)', *Cahiers d'études africaines*, x (1970), 80–124; Sheriff, 'Commercial empire', chs. 1–2.

[3] Text quoted in Andrew Roberts, 'Nyamwezi trade', in Richard Gray and David Birmingham (ed.), *Pre-colonial African trade* (London, 1970), p. 48. See also Apolo Kaggwa, *The kings of Buganda* (trans. M. S. M. Kiwanuka, Nairobi, 1971), pp. 99, 195; Shorter, *Chiefship*, pp. 233–42; Sheriff, 'Commercial empire', ch. 3.

A third long-distance route was opened from Tanga and Pangani on the northern coast, following the Pangani to Kilimanjaro and Masailand. Although regional trade existed here previously, long-distance trade was always controlled by coastal merchants, who probably pioneered the route some time after 1800.[1]

Rising ivory prices drove the traders forward. At Surat in western India ivory prices doubled between 1803/4 and 1808/9. At Zanzibar they increased roughly sixfold between the 1820s and the 1890s.[2] Western India was the chief market and also supplied the cloth exchanged for ivory. Tanganyika's second most important export was slaves. There is little evidence that they were shipped from the mainland until Oman's conquest of Kilwa in 1698. In the 1770s the French took some 1,500 each year, and another 1,500–2,000 went to Zanzibar and the Middle East. Subsequent figures are contradictory, but by 1834 mainland exports may have grown to some 6,500 a year, and by the 1840s to 13,000–15,000. Part of the increase may have gone to the Middle East, but the French trade was banned in 1822 and the increased exports went chiefly to Zanzibar, where Arab planters began to grow cloves soon after 1810, employing very large numbers of slaves for an unusually seasonal crop.[3] In the 1850s Zanzibar's 150,000 people may have included 60,000 slaves, but estimates varied widely.[4] The island's prosperity attracted foreign merchants. Asians had a monopoly until the 1830s, but then American merchants began to import their own cloth into Zanzibar. Thanks to slave-grown cotton and steam-driven mills it competed successfully with Indian domestic products. British and German traders followed, but Americans predominated until their civil war in 1861. Their factory-made goods, including firearms, further stimulated long-distance trade.[5]

As Zanzibar grew prosperous, Sayyid Said ibn Sultan, Oman's ruler since 1804, spent much time in the island and finally moved his capital there in 1840. When he died in 1856 Zanzibar became independent of Oman. Sayyid Said sought to extend and control East Africa's trade while minimising expenditure on political administration. The core of

---

[1] Sheriff, 'Commercial empire', pp. 141–4; Feierman, *Shambaa kingdom*, pp. 123–30; Kimambo, *Political history*, pp. 124–7.
[2] Sheriff, 'Commercial empire', p. 100; Norman R. Bennett, *Studies in East African history* (Boston, 1963), p. 89.
[3] H. Neville Chittick, 'The East Coast, Madagascar and the Indian Ocean', in Oliver, *Cambridge history*, III, 185; Alpers, 'French slave trade', pp. 80–124; Alpers, *Ivory*, pp. 234–8; Sheriff, 'Commercial empire', ch. 4.
[4] Nicholls, *Swahili coast*, pp. 266, 288.
[5] Sheriff, 'Commercial empire', ch. 5.

his dominions was Zanzibar Island, a complex slave society whose underlying violence – 'none but women and slaves leave the house unarmed', it was observed in 1857, and one major slave revolt is recorded[1] – was masked by Islamic law, paternalism and subtle gradations of unfreedom. Asians dominated commerce but had little political power. Sayyid Said greatly extended Zanzibar's authority over the mainland coast. Whereas in 1800 only Kilwa had an Omani governor, in 1856 only Sadani lacked one. The last Sultan of Kilwa was deported to Oman around 1843; legend says his horn of office was thrown into the sea.[2] Despite much resentment at Zanzibar's control, the towns were too disunited to resist. Zanzibar enforced a tariff policy to attract trade. Export duties were highest on the Mrima, where Omani control was strong and the people had no alternative to trading with Zanzibar. North and south along the coast the duties fell away in order to attract trade into Zanzibari territory. Tariffs discriminated in favour of Zanzibaris, who paid approximately Shs. 2.50 per kilogram on ivory from Unyamwezi while the Nyamwezi themselves paid Shs. 4.00.[3] Most inland peoples could trade with Zanzibar only through coastal middlemen who demanded substantial fees. Europeans were prohibited from trading on the coast, but Asians were allowed to settle there. In 1871 there were 230 in Kilwa and its vicinity, 191 in Bagamoyo, 105 in Dar es Salaam, and 80 in Tanga, as well as 2,550 in Zanzibar and smaller numbers elsewhere.[4]

Zanzibari control changed the position of the *diwanis* who had previously ruled the coastal towns. They continued to lead their wards, receive tribute – over a shilling on each slave exported from Kilwa – and enjoy much ceremonial respect. In Bagamoyo, at least, they also prospered as private traders. But they normally required Zanzibar's recognition, they had to visit the island each year, they formed only one of several propertied groups, and their external affairs were in Arab hands. Moreover, commercial expansion transformed coastal society. Boom towns emerged, notably Bagamoyo, whose agricultural hinterland, open beaches suited to dhows, and proximity to Zanzibar made it the leading town of the Mrima after 1850. Relationships with hinterland peoples deteriorated. The Zigua burned Sadani in the

[1] Richard F. Burton, *Zanzibar: city, island, and coast* (2 vols, London, 1872), I, 384; Frederick Cooper, *Plantation slavery on the East Coast of Africa* (New Haven, 1977), pp. 202–3; G. A. Akinola, 'Slavery and slave revolts in the Sultanate of Zanzibar in the nineteenth century', *Journal of the Historical Society of Nigeria*, VI (1972), 220–3.
[2] Nicholls, *Swahili coast*, pp. 313–14; Freeman-Grenville, *French at Kilwa*, p. 37.
[3] Sheriff, 'Commercial empire', p. 380.
[4] Kirk, 'Annex no. 1' [early 1871] FO 84/1344/129.

early 1850s. Bagamoyo paid tribute to the Zaramo well into the nineteenth century, and when the Sayyid sent troops to protect it against a threatened Zaramo attack in 1875 the *diwani* apparently sympathised with the Zaramo in common hostility to Arab control. Moreover, the influx of slaves and up-country Africans changed the towns' social composition. The old rivalry between wards apparently gave place to antagonism between established residents and new-comers. In late nineteenth-century Tanga and Pangani, for example, inter-ward dancing competitions appear to have taken second place to rivalry between Darisudi and Darigubi societies, representing established townsmen and up-country immigrants. Nevertheless, the coastal peoples increasingly shared a common relationship to the inland peoples and communicated more frequently among themselves. Growing solidarity later facilitated resistance to European invasion.[1]

In the 1850s inland peoples still conducted most of the long-distance trade. Richard Burton met their caravans on the central route in 1857:

The Wanyamwezi make up large parties of men, some carrying their own goods, others hired by petty proprietors, who for union and strength elect a...leader...The porters trudge from sunrise to 10 or 11 a.m., and sometimes, though rarely, they travel twice a day, resting only during the hours of heat. They work with a will, carrying uncomplainingly huge tusks, some so heavy that they must be lashed to a pole between two men...Their shoulders are often raw with the weight, their feet are sore, and they walk half or wholly naked to save their cloth for displays at home. They ignore tent or covering, and sleep on the ground; their only supplies are their country's produce, a few worn-down hoes, intended at times to purchase a little grain or to be given as blackmail for sultans, and small herds of bullocks and heifers that serve for similar purposes.[2]

By contrast, caravans financed by coastal traders were more hierarchical. At first they had employed slaves, but by the late 1850s they relied chiefly on up-country porters. On the central route most were 'Nyamwezi' from the central plateau. Later, in the 1880s, slaves again became important and other inland peoples joined the occupation, but most porters were always Nyamwezi. Their numbers are difficult to gauge. A missionary reckoned that 15,000–20,000 Nyamwezi visited the coast each year in the 1880s. Other observers guessed that more than

[1] Kirk to Granville, 25 January 1872, FO 84/1357/88; Walter T. Brown, 'Bagamoyo: an historical introduction', *TNR*, LXXI (1970), 69–83; Kitchener to Salisbury, 10 February and 15 March 1886 (and enclosures) FO 84/1797/158 and 84/1798/33; T. O. Ranger, *Dance and society in eastern Africa 1890–1970* (London, 1975), pp. 35–40.
[2] Burton, 'Lake regions', pp. 408–9.

100,000 Africans travelled the central caravan route each year around 1890. At peak seasons, it was said, Bagamoyo contained 30,000–40,000 porters. If correct, these figures suggest labour migration almost as widespread as in the colonial period.[1] Wages were also comparable. In 1871 H. M. Stanley paid his porters about twelve shillings a month and in 1874 twice as much, which became the standard rate among European employers thereafter, although other employers may well have paid less. Unskilled labourers in Tanga in the late 1880s normally earned about thirteen shillings a month. They earned the same thirty years later and only a shilling or two more in 1935.[2] It was through porterage that capitalist relations, appropriating labour by economic means, first entered Tanganyika. Europeans constructing a road inland from Dar es Salaam in 1877 found an ample supply of daily wage-labour. Those first drawn into the cash nexus were the young. Burton was struck by the youth of the porters. Doubtless exaggerating, a missionary observed that 'not one of them was allowed to marry before he had carried a load of ivory to the coast'.[3]

A coastal caravan's personnel were highly specialised. Guards, personal servants, cooks, and guides were distinguished from porters. Status was expressed in the order of march. First came the guide, with a light load, a special dress, and a drummer behind him. Next marched the aristocrats of the caravan, the ivory porters, with cattle bells tied to the tusks they carried. They were followed, in descending order of prestige, by carriers of cloth, beads, wire, and the caravan's domestic requirements. Slaves came next, then women and children – for by the middle of the century many Nyamwezi wives accompanied their husbands. Armed guards were stationed along the line and a strong party, often including the proprietor, brought up the rear and herded stragglers. Endless walking bred a kind of mesmerism with symptoms akin to drunkenness. 'Head somewhat sunken, eyes on the ground, they pay attention to nothing but the legs of the man in front and the narrow path reflecting the glaring sun', a traveller wrote, 'and they set one foot before the other so mechanically that eventually the

[1] Norman R. Bennett, *Mirambo of Tanzania, 1840?–1884* (New York, 1971), p. 12; Paul Reichard, *Deutsch-Ostafrika* (Leipzig, 1892), p. 199; H. F. von Behr, *Kriegsbilder aus dem Araberaufstand in Deutsch-Ostafrika* (Leipzig, 1891), p. 138; below, p. 157.
[2] Norman R. Bennett (ed.), *Stanley's despatches to the 'New York Herald'* (Boston, 1970), p. 160; Oscar Baumann, *Usambara und seine Nachbargebiete* (Berlin, 1891), p. 304; *RTA*, 1910/11, no. 179, p. 6,533; Longland, 'Report on labour matters in sisal areas: no. 1: Tanga', 29 March 1936, TNA 23544.
[3] Kirk to Derby, 22 August 1877, FO 84/1486/36; Burton, *Lake regions*, I, 337–8; A. J. Swann, *Fighting the slave-hunters in central Africa* (London, 1910), p. 58.

45

path seems to slide backwards faster than they themselves move forwards.'[1]

To minimise the hazards of caravan life, joking relationships – previously employed to restore peace – were used to ensure hospitality and mutual aid between the inland peoples and those through whose territory they passed.[2] Custom and practice ruled the caravans, determining the length of marches, the weight of loads, and the bonus for extra duty. Carriers of especially heavy tusks received double rations but no extra pay. Nyamwezi were jealous of their reputation as porters. Desertion was common but deserters often left their loads and could justly be flogged if recaptured. A distinct pattern of labour relations grew up. The employer appointed the headmen and settled routine problems with them, but strikes were frequent and were conducted as collective actions to prevent the employer identifying ringleaders, a distinction between appointed spokesmen and anonymous action common in the early stages of labour organisation and carried forward to colonial plantations.[3]

Most coastal caravans were financed by Asians. They gave trade goods on credit to Arabs or Swahili who undertook to repay two or three times the original sum in ivory on their return. The most powerful capitalist was Taria Topan of Zanzibar, who financed Tippu Tip, Rumaliza, and other entrepreneurs who penetrated west of Lake Tanganyika in the 1860s.[4] Leading a caravan was a distasteful, dangerous, but potentially profitable business. 'But few leave with the caravans for the interior', wrote a visitor to Zanzibar, 'other than the fairly poor Arabs who do not have a small piece of land and three or four hundred pounds of cloves.'[5] A few successful journeys could make a penniless man into a planter. Yet many failed. Tabora was full of traders unable to visit Zanzibar for fear of creditors or the Sayyid's displeasure. The only surviving account of a journey by an ordinary trader is a catalogue of violence and extortion which earned those who returned from Lake Tanganyika a total profit of a hundred pounds.[6]

---

[1] Richard Kandt, *Caput Nili* (2nd edn, Berlin, 1905), p. 108.

[2] J. A. K. Leslie, *A survey of Dar es Salaam* (London, 1963), pp. 33–7.

[3] For labour relations, see Burton, 'Lake regions', pp. 408–16; Robert Cummings, 'A note on the history of caravan porters in East Africa', *Kenya historical review*, I (1973), 109–38; below, p. 310.

[4] W. H. Whiteley (ed.), 'Maisha ya Hamed bin Muhammed el Murjebi yaani Tippu Tip', *Swahili*, XXVIII–XXIX (1958–9), supplement, p. 31.

[5] Loarer, quoted in Sheriff, 'Commercial empire', p. 342.

[6] Selemani bin Mwenye Chande, 'My journey up-country in Africa', in Harries, *Prose texts*, pp. 234–60. See also Sir John Gray, 'Trading expeditions from the coast to Lakes Tanganyika and Victoria before 1857', *TNR*, XLIX (1957), 226–46.

When a caravan leader regained the coast 'his friends will go to wait for him in the open country...And each person has rice in a cup. When they see him they scatter the rice over his head. His elders say to him, "Is it peace, father? Have you had a peaceful journey?" This is greatness.'[1]

The coastal traders claimed to carry their civilisation, *ustaarabu*, to the benighted interior. 'There is no lack of dignity in passing from the abominable yoke of a negro tyrant to the protective tutelage of an Arab', Tippu Tip was quoted as saying. '...The [slave] trade has always existed in the interior, and it is the African who does not want it suppressed. He would sell himself if you emancipated him!'[2] The traders seldom raided for slaves in Tanganyika. They were chiefly ivory merchants, who entered what to Muslims was the vile trade of slave-dealing only when ivory was scarce.[3] Nor were they usually powerful enough to raid. Only a few hundred Arabs and one or two thousand Swahili were in the interior at any time, and they were much divided. With their armed slaves they might intervene in conflicts between Africans, but their independent power was less than that of many African leaders and they depended on free African porters. Only Tippu Tip ever fought a successful war against important African rulers, in the far western chiefdoms of Uvinza and Ugalla, and most traders deplored his aggressive methods.[4] As Burton observed, the traders' problem was that they were too strong to yield without fighting but too weak to fight with success.[5] They therefore relied on their relations with African rulers. These varied greatly. The traders were strongest where, as at Kondoa-Irangi, they formed separate colonies among weak and mutually hostile peoples.[6] Sometimes they could attach themselves to African leaders and influence them. A former slave and Swahili trader, Songoro, established himself in the Busukuma chiefdom near Lake Victoria, married into the neighbouring Kerewe royal family, and reorganised Busukuma into a 'second Zanzibar'.[7] Normally the trader was the junior partner. An example was Mwinyi Kheri, a Swahili who married a daughter of the Tusi Chief

[1] Harries, *Prose texts*, p. 185.
[2] Jérôme Becker, *La vie en Afrique* (2nd edn, 2 vols, Paris, 1887), II, 45–6.
[3] Reichard, *Deutsch-Ostafrika*, p. 485. Generally, see Norman R. Bennett, 'The Arab power of Tanganyika in the nineteenth century', Ph.D. thesis, Boston University, 1961.
[4] See Whiteley, 'Maisha', pp. 43, 99–101.
[5] Burton, *Lake regions*, I, 327.
[6] See Franz Stuhlmann, *Mit Emin Pascha ins Herz von Afrika* (Berlin, 1894), pp. 803–8; G. A. von Götzen, *Durch Afrika von Ost nach West* (Berlin, 1895), pp. 23–5.
[7] Quoted in Gerald W. Hartwig, 'The Victoria Nyanza as a trade route in the nineteenth century', *JAH*, XI (1970), 549.

Rusimbi of Nkalinzi and governed Ujiji on his behalf.[1] In the early
1880s Chief Kapufi of Nkansi in Ufipa had an Arab 'prime minister'.[2]
But normally the merchant's role was commercial. The Arabs of
Tabora governed their settlement, were exempt from tax, and
frequently intervened in local politics, but they never gained enduring
control of the Unyanyembe chiefdom. Traders often occupied a
special quarter of a chief's capital, as in Usambara.[3]

By the 1880s, however, the coastal traders were more willing to fight
and dominate Africans. The model was Tippu Tip's strategy in the
Manyema, the eastern region of Zaire inhabited by stateless peoples
unwilling to act as porters or even, in some cases, to hunt elephants,
so that the merchants created gangs of armed slaves which gained them
political control. Rumaliza copied this strategy around Lake
Tanganyika after 1881, constructing a personal dominion by attacking
and deposing African leaders, installing compliant successors or slaves,
levying tribute, and establishing outposts of armed retainers. Lake
Nyasa witnessed a similar process, while a Swahili merchant, Mwinyi
Mtwana, set himself up as Chief of Mdaburu in the middle of the
central caravan route.[4] Some historians detect a concerted Arab
campaign, encouraged by the Sayyid, to establish Zanzibar's political
control before Europeans occupied the mainland,[5] but there is little
evidence for this and the explanation probably lies rather in rising
prices, falling profits, and growing competition for trade. Zanzibar had
preferred the cheapness of informal empire but now found that it no
longer worked.

The change was due to the dynamics of the ivory trade.[6] Until the
late 1850s most ivory came from inside Tanganyika. Both coastal
traders and inland peoples profited. Nyamwezi ivory caravans predominated on the central route. But Tanganyika's elephants were
rapidly being destroyed. Ivory prices at Tabora were said to have

[1] Bennett, 'Arab power', pp. 43–55.
[2] Joseph Thomson, *To the central African lakes and back* (2nd edn, 2 vols, London, 1968), II, 217.
[3] Alfred C. Unomah, 'Economic expansion and political change in Unyanyembe (ca. 1840 to 1900)', Ph.D. thesis, University of Ibadan, 1972, pp. 180–93; Feierman, 'Concepts', p. 284.
[4] Melvin E. Page, 'The Manyema hordes of Tippu Tip', *IJAHS*, VII (1974), 69–84; Beverly Brown, 'Muslim influence on trade and politics in the Lake Tanganyika region', *IJAHS*, IV (1971), 629; Bennett, *Studies*, pp. 76–80.
[5] Roland Oliver, *The missionary factor in East Africa* (2nd edn, London, 1965), pp. 101–3; B. G. Martin, 'Muslim politics and resistance to colonial rule', *JAH*, x (1969), 474–6; *idem, Muslim brotherhoods in nineteenth-century Africa* (Cambridge, 1976), pp. 166–8.
[6] This argument is based on Sheriff, 'Commercial empire', ch. 7.

increased tenfold between 1846 and 1858. Yet demand was insistent; ivory prices at Zanzibar rose between 1850 and 1890 from £600 to £2,100 per tonne.[1] The hunters therefore penetrated ever wider, until eventually most left Tanganyika entirely. In the 1860s they entered the Manyema and penetrated the great Congo forest whose wealth in ivory and slaves brought a fortune to Tippu Tip and 'a sort of California gold-fever' to Ujiji. Twenty years later coastal traders reached Bunyoro, which soon became the 'paradise for ivory'.[2]

The advance of the ivory frontier dislocated the whole trading system. African chiefs had come to depend heavily on ivory for their revenues. The most powerful rulers of the 1870s and 1880s, such as Nyungu ya Mawe of Ukimbu and Mkwawa of Uhehe, monopolised ivory collected in their territories. Lesser chiefs claimed one tusk of every elephant killed, often 'buying' the other from the hunter. Many rulers employed professional hunters. Elsewhere villagers hunted in the dry season, forming special guilds with their own initiation rites, dances, magic, and leaders who cast the first spear or fired the first shot.[3] The advance of the ivory frontier deprived chiefs of revenue, weakening their capacity to control men or even to defend their territories. Their subjects ceased to be ivory exporters – Nyamwezi ivory caravans became increasingly rare as the century progressed – and were reduced to porterage or supplying food to passing caravans. The community of interest between inland peoples and coastal traders broke down. One response was to seek greater political control over trade, which explains much of the political conflict of the later nineteenth century. Another was to seek a new export product.

For some peoples the new product was slaves. Estimates of the trade remain speculative. If exports from the mainland averaged around 15,000 a year in the 1840s, they probably rose to something over 20,000 a year by 1873. Most still came from the south, where Kilwa's exports increased between 1862/3 and 1866/7 from 18,500 to 22,038.[4] The prohibition decree which the British imposed on the Sayyid in 1873 was only slowly implemented. Kilwa was forced into line in 1876, but both smuggling and an overland trade to northern coastal ports

[1] Burton, *Lake regions*, II, 370; Bennett, *Studies*, p. 89.
[2] Livingstone, 1870, quoted in Bennett, 'Arab power', p. 41; Herrmann to Government, 3 September 1892, RKA 639/123.
[3] Reichard, *Deutsch-Ostafrika*, pp. 422–48; Victor Giraud, *Les lacs de l'Afrique équatoriale* (Paris, 1890), p. 186.
[4] Sheriff, 'Commercial empire', table 2; Churchill to Gonne, 4 March 1868, FO 84/1292/101.

flourished for several years. By the mid 1880s relatively few slaves were leaving the mainland, but instead they were employed there, so that internal demand became more important than the export market.[1] Certainly the trade expanded geographically during the second half of the century. The ivory-rush into the Manyema was followed by slave-raiding of an extent and brutality which sickened even the experienced Livingstone. In the 1870s the interlacustrine region became an important supplier, the southern shores of Lake Tanganyika were invaded, and civil war in Usambara made Pangani a slave port to rival Kilwa and Bagamoyo.[2]

Although Arabs rarely raided for slaves in Tanganyika, their willingness to buy them was obviously the main stimulus to the trade. Some militarised African peoples raided their stateless neighbours systematically, especially in the south. More slaves were probably ordinary war-captives. Some were victims of localised brutality or social oppression. Most of those whose personal stories survive were kidnapped as children, for adult males were too prone to escape.[3] Men also continued to sell their relatives or even themselves during famine. As the trade became increasingly pervasive, attitudes to life and freedom were brutalised. There are stories of men selling their wives for guns in Upare. By the 1890s the Doe were paying bridewealth in slaves and a traveller found the Chief of Ubungu playing the African board game, *bao*, with bullets for counters. Convicted criminals were often sold into slavery, which apparently replaced the death penalty for some offences, especially witchcraft, in several areas. The penalty was sometimes extended to the offender's family. A missionary watched the King of Usambara order the sale of a murderer's children. Nyamwezi chiefs seized the families of convicted witches.[4]

Intensified slaving accompanied a change in import patterns. Cloth remained the most important import. Like the ivory frontier, the cloth

---

[1] Carla Glassman, 'A quantitative social history of the illegal, seagoing, East African slave trade, 1873–1900', typescript, 1977, in Miss Glassman's possession; François Renault, *Lavigerie, l'esclavage Africain, et l'Europe, 1868–1892* (2 vols, Paris, 1971), I, 82–96, 284–5, 349.

[2] Horace Waller (ed.), *The last journals of David Livingstone* (2 vols, London, 1874), II, 133–6; Herrmann, 'Bericht über den Sklavenhandel östlich und südlich des Victoria Nyanza' [July 1892], RKA 1029/34; V. L. Cameron, *Across Africa* (4th edn, 2 vols, London, 1877), I, 272; Kirk to Granville, 25 January 1872, FO 84/1357/88.

[3] See the recollections in A. C. Madan (ed.), *Kiungani* (London, 1887), *passim*.

[4] Hartwig, *Art of survival*, p. 53; Kimambo, *Political history*, p. 129; Stuhlmann, *Mit Emin Pascha*, p. 37; H. H. Johnston, 'British Central Africa', *Proceedings of the Royal Geographical Society*, NS, XII (1890), 732; de Froberville, 'Va-Ngindo', p. 439; J. L. Krapf, *Travels, researches, and missionary labours* (2nd edn, London, 1968), pp. 396–7; Bösch, *Banyamwezi*, p. 443.

frontier gradually advanced. Unyamwezi's domestic textile industry was ailing in 1857 and almost disappeared during the next sixty years, first along the trade routes and then in more remote villages. The same happened in the south-east. Further west, similar industries largely collapsed in the early colonial period. Imported cotton began to replace barkcloth in remote Buhaya in the early 1890s. Missionaries arriving in highland Unyakyusa at that time were besieged by demands for cloth.[1] Yet the important shift in the import trade was the increased supply of firearms. In the 1840s Zanzibar probably shipped some 5,000 guns to the mainland each year. Forty years later the figure was nearly 100,000 a year. Besides the smooth-bore muzzle-loaders first supplied, later imports included rifled muzzle-loaders discarded by European armies in favour of breech-loading rifles. Few breech-loaders, and still fewer magazine rifles, reached Tanganyika.[2] Perhaps half of Tanganyika's peoples used guns as their chief weapons in 1890. In 1857 a musket was a valued gift for a Nyamwezi chief, but in 1873 it was reckoned that half the men in some Nyamwezi chiefdoms owned firearms. In 1871 Livingstone noticed Nyamwezi children making toy guns and using ashes for powder.[3]

Firearms had varied and complicated effects. The Masai and other peoples who used spears at close quarters in disciplined formations did not adopt firearms until German machine-guns made the older tactics redundant, but they were exceptions. Many peoples accustomed to small-scale warfare with few casualties found it transformed by firearms. Guns had great drawbacks. They were generally poor in quality and difficult to maintain, although the Nyamwezi became skilled in repairing them. Their use depended on powder supplies, although some peoples manufactured their own, the Kimbu using local potassium nitrate and castor oil plant. Muskets were usually fired either at arm's length or from the hip. Using low-quality powder, their range was little more than fifty or a hundred metres. They were slow to load and wildly inaccurate – German officers were to be astonished at their few casualties – but it was often enough to wound, for

[1] Burton, *Lake regions*, II, 311; Reichard, *Deutsch-Ostafrika*, p. 354; Oscar Baumann, *Durch Masailand zur Nilquelle* (Berlin, 1894), p. 232; Blohm, *Nyamwezi*, I, 152; Karl Weule, *Native life in East Africa* (trans. A. Werner, London, 1909), pp. 225–9; Kjekshus, *Ecology control*, p. 109; Stuhlmann, *Mit Emin Pascha*, p. 717; A. Merensky, *Deutsche Arbeit am Njassa* (Berlin, 1894), p. 200.

[2] Nicholls, *Swahili coast*, pp. 330–1, 336–7, 359; Euan Smith to Salisbury, 28 June 1888, FO 84/1907/342. Generally, see Gavin White, 'Firearms in Africa: an introduction', *JAH*, XII (1971), 173–84.

[3] Burton, *Lake regions*, II, 308; Cameron, *Across Africa*, I, 201; Waller, *Last journals of Livingstone*, II, 227.

gangrene did the rest. The value attached to guns is clear from the energy devoted to obtaining them. Many porters worked specifically to earn a gun. Success in preventing Africans around Lake Tanganyika from obtaining firearms was one reason why the coastal peoples could raid and dominate that region.[1] Firearms gave a temporary advantage to those who first obtained them. In the lower Pangani valley they were the Zigua, whose guns made them predominant in the region by 1850, while in the upper valley the Arusha first obtained firearms and drove off the Masai.[2] But muskets were chiefly defensive weapons, as the First World War was to prove. They encouraged the construction of elaborate stockades which could be taken only by lengthy siege or a bloody assault demanding the discipline of professional soldiers. In this way – and not because they were scarce – firearms professionalised warfare and strengthened the political power of the military. By the 1890s Safwa children were playing at assaulting fortresses. Yet muskets were poor weapons for aggression. Nyamwezi musketeers were repelled by Nyaturu bowmen.[3] The musket dominated stockade and bush, but the spear still controlled the open plain.

By the late 1860s long-distance trade was bringing Tanganyika to a crisis. Dwindling ivory supplies bred political conflict. Slaving increased, mercenary armies proliferated, and warfare became common even among agricultural peoples. The two phases of trade, dividing during the 1860s, underlay nineteenth-century political change.

The politics of survival

It is a commonplace of African history that long-distance trade often encouraged large-scale political organisation. Trade developed communications and created wealth to support central governments. Rulers used scarce goods to secure loyalty. Traders needed protection and backed stability. They often lived in towns, which were relatively easy to govern, and possessed skills, especially literacy, which facilitated administration. Where trade brought firearms, rulers might monopolise them. Nineteenth-century Tanganyika is often thought to

[1] Becker, *La vie*, II, 38, 507; Shorter, *Chiefship*, pp. 56–7; Merker to Kommando, 2 October 1905, Kriegstagebuch Thetis, Anlageband I, BA-M; Feierman, *Shambaa kingdom*, pp. 172–3; Bennett, *Stanley's despatches*, pp. 116–17.

[2] Feierman, *Shambaa kingdom*, pp. 136–8; G. A. Fischer, *Das Massai-Land* (Hamburg, 1885), pp. 57–8.

[3] Kootz-Kretschmer, *Safwa*, I, 37; Singida district book, TNA.

exemplify these processes, and in some areas that was so, but other regions had exactly the opposite experience and suffered political disintegration. One way of explaining the different experiences is to look for variable factors, but they were very numerous. Some peoples were active traders; others waited for trade to reach them. Some lived on trade routes, others distant from them. Trade goods varied. Peoples became involved in long-distance trade at different times. Above all, each people's prior historical experience and political organisation was unique. Generalisation on these lines is impossible. An alternative approach is to seek processes underlying both consolidation and disintegration. Dr Roberts has suggested two. He has argued, first, that whereas in 1800 leadership in Tanganyika commonly rested on ritual power, the nineteenth-century tendency was towards 'the development of military and economic power rather than ritual power as a basis for leadership'. Second, whereas in 1800 men generally obtained political office by birth, the nineteenth-century tendency was towards 'emphasis on personal achievement and loyalty rather than kinship as a qualification for political office'.[1] Recruitment to office by achievement is commonly regarded as a symptom of bureaucracy and modernity. Some historians have regarded such polities as more stable and durable than their predecessors.[2]

The changes identified by Dr Roberts did take place widely in nineteenth-century Tanganyika, but their nature and limitations need careful definition. Military and economic power did not *supersede* ritual power as bases of leadership but became alternatives to it, sometimes complementary but more frequently contradictory. The outcome was often ambiguity, conflict, and disorder. Similarly, men were not recruited by achievement and loyalty instead of kinship, but different men were recruited by different qualifications and then came into conflict, while some men – often successful men – combined both qualifications. In concrete terms, successful nineteenth-century chiefs controlled guns *and* rain, while able but low-born subordinates commonly married royal women. 'Bureaucratisation' in nineteenth-century Tanganyika was superficial and produced polities which were less stable and durable than either those existing in 1800 or those created in the nineteenth century on different principles. To illustrate these points it is best to begin with the last and to examine two stimulants of political change other than trade: the Ngoni invasion of the south and the continuing pastoral impact in the north.

[1] Roberts, *Tanzania*, p. xv.   [2] Shorter, *Chiefship*, pp. 313–16.

The Ngoni were originally refugees from the Mfecane which convulsed southern Africa early in the nineteenth century and produced the Zulu and other military states. Two Ngoni groups reached Tanganyika after incorporating conquered peoples on the way. One, led by Mputa ('The Smiter') Maseko, reached the modern Songea district early in the 1840s, while the other, led by Zwangendaba, reached Ufipa. There Zwangendaba died in the later 1840s and his followers divided, one section moving northwards to settle at Runzewe, north-west of Tabora, while two other sections led by military commanders, Zulu Gama and Mbonani Tawete, turned southwards and joined Mputa Maseko's followers in Songea about 1858.[1]

Like other Tanganyikan peoples the Ngoni were colonists, but their experience during the Mfecane and the long trek north had given them an unprecedented organisation. Their young men formed regiments extending across the whole society and were armed with the *assegai*, the short stabbing spear whose use by disciplined formations made war 'no longer a game', as their victims bewailed, but bloody and ruthless.[2] The Ngoni were thus an agricultural people who had evolved the military organisation and tactics previously confined to pastoralists. Recruits were taught to despise non-military peoples as slaves. Any man carrying a long throwing-spear had it broken before his eyes. 'You must have a spear with which you can cut, as you draw a knife across a chicken's throat', they were told.[3] Their law inflicted only mild punishment on a murderer who killed in fair fight. They were governed by rank and deference. At their head stood chiefs and aristocrats who originated from South Africa. The military commanders (*manduna*) usually came from the ranks of assimilated captives. The most famous *nduna* in Tanganyika, Songea Mbano, was a Shona captive from Rhodesia, as also was the main ritual leader, Chikusi Mkaranga. When the Ngoni finally settled, the *manduna* became territorial sub-chiefs.

On reaching Songea, Mputa Maseko's followers asserted control

[1] See J. D. Omer-Cooper, *The Zulu aftermath* (London, 1966), pp. 64–79; Elzear Ebner, *History of the Wangoni* (Peramiho, 1959), *passim*; Patrick M. Redmond, 'A political history of the Songea Ngoni from the mid-nineteenth century', Ph.D. thesis, University of London, 1972, chs. 1–3.

[2] Edward A. Mwenda, 'Historia na maendeleo ya Ubena', *Swahili*, XXXIII (1963), 106.

[3] W. P. Johnson, *Nyasa, the great water* (reprinted, New York, 1969), p. 106.

over the stateless Ndendeuli and related peoples. 'Before the Ngoni
wars the Ndendeuli did not know how to fight', they recalled. 'The
Ndendeuli did not know what tribe they were.'[1] Many were incorporated into the regiments and forbidden to marry until demobilised.
When Zulu Gama, Mbonani Tawete, and their followers arrived they
initially recognised Mputa's authority, but in 1862 or 1863 they
rebelled and killed him with the support of dissident Ndendeuli. In
the subsequent disorder many Ndendeuli fled north-eastwards to the
Kilombero valley, where they recreated the Ngoni military system and
became known as Mbunga.[2] Other Ndendeuli were incorporated into
the two states formed by the new conquerors: Mshope in the north,
ruled by Mbonani's descendants, and Njelu in the south, ruled by
Zulu's. Mshope was the smaller and more tightly organised, with
regiments embracing men from the whole chiefdom. It experienced
only one secession, in 1881, when Chabruma, a formidable traditionalist, acceded to the throne and his uncle, Mpepo, took his following
away to the north-east and settled at Kilosa kwa Mpepo. In Njelu, by
contrast, effective power soon passed to the ten *manduna*, each of whom
organised his own regiments.[3] Tributary areas surrounded each state.
The Matengo and Pangwa to the west supplied grain and slaves, while
Masasi to the east paid an annual tribute in salt. In more distant areas
Ngoni raiding-parties made regular forays. Historians may have
exaggerated Ngoni militarism – it is a question which needs research
– but the terror which Ngoni warriors inspired is beyond dispute. 'It
is difficult for those who have not seen it to realize what this perpetual
fear and periodical destruction meant', wrote a missionary. '. . . The
weird cry of *Koto! Koto!* (Danger! Danger!) alone is bad to hear at any
time; it is the native tocsin. And if, as often, with the dreadful sound
comes the sight of huts burning in the distance, how much it means!
Not only burning homes and death and separation, but hunger; all
food destroyed or plundered.'[4] In the 1870s most raids were to the
north and west. After 1882 they concentrated on the east. This was
Songea Mbano's raiding area, while Mshope's forces also terrorised

---

[1] Faraji Makuti, quoted in Gallagher, 'Islam', p. 418. Generally, see P. M. Redmond,
'Some results of military contacts between the Ngoni and their neighbours', *TJH*,
v (1976), 75–97.
[2] Lorne E. Larson, 'A history of the Mahenge (Ulanga) district, c. 1860–1957', Ph.D. thesis,
University of Dar es Salaam, 1976, pp. 13–17.
[3] P. H. Gulliver, 'Political evolution in the Songea Ngoni chiefdoms, 1850–1905', *BSOAS*,
XXXVIII (1974), 85–95.
[4] Johnson, *Nyasa*, p. 109.

the region every year into the 1890s. By then the Ngindo, Mwera, Makonde, and other stateless peoples of south-eastern Tanganyika had retreated to defensive positions on the plateaux, leaving vast stretches of empty land.[1]

The Ngoni impact transformed the Southern Highlands, where in 1800 there were no political units larger then clan-chiefdoms. The first to experience the impact were clans who became known as the Sangu. Their history is little known but they were apparently organised into a military force in the 1830s by a petty chief, Merere I Mwahavanga, probably in response to coastal ivory-traders. The Sangu were then attacked by the Ngoni and adopted their weapons and tactics, which enabled them to dominate the Southern Highlands until about 1860, when Merere I's death led to civil war.[2] Meanwhile other groups imitated the Sangu example. One, the Kinamanga family, ruled Utemekwira, on the south-eastern edge of the Iringa plateau. During the 1860s – possibly in reaction to the flight northwards of the Ndendeuli – they took control of the upper Kilombero valley, forcing the Pogoro to take refuge on the Mahenge plateau.[3] Another figure was meanwhile emerging on the central Iringa plateau. This was Munyigumba of the Muyinga family, one of some fifteen ruling families among the peoples who were to become the Hehe. The Muyinga were hereditary rulers of the Nguruhe chiefdom. Munyigumba and his father extended their territory by marriage into neighbouring clans. From this base, Munyigumba, who probably acceded between 1855 and 1860, gradually conquered and incorporated the remainder of northern and central Uhehe and created the nucleus of a unified state. In the process – or possibly slightly later – his followers, hitherto tributary to the Sangu, adopted Ngoni military tactics from them, even borrowing Sangu regimental names and the praise-names of the Sangu chief.[4]

By the late 1860s the politics of the Southern Highlands were widening into a regional contest between Mshope, Usangu (now emerged strengthened from civil war), Utemekwira, and Uhehe. The Sangu were eliminated first. Attacked by Munyigumba, Merere II abandoned his capital in 1874 and retreated westwards to Usafwa,

[1] Alfons M. Adams, *Lindi und sein Hinterland* (Berlin, [1902?]), pp. 28–36.
[2] Marcia Wright, 'Chief Merere and the Germans', *TNR*, LXIX (1968), 41–3.
[3] Larson, 'History', pp. 20–3.
[4] Alison H. Redmayne, 'The Wahehe people of Tanganyika', D.Phil. thesis, Oxford University, 1964, chs. 4–5; *idem*, 'The Hehe', in Roberts, *Tanzania*, pp. 37–58. My account of the Hehe state is based on Dr Redmayne's work, save where otherwise stated.

where he forced the loosely-organised peoples to build him a massive stone fortress near modern Mbeya. Munyigumba next turned on the Kinamanga, overwhelming them in 1875 at the battle of Mgodamtitu and driving them from the plateau into their newly-acquired territory in the Kilombero valley. Hehe and Ngoni then faced each other. War began in 1878 when the Hehe invaded Mshope and ended in 1882 in a peace of exhaustion which partitioned Ubena between them. For the next ten years they avoided conflict. Chabruma of Mshope raided eastwards outside the southern borders of Uhehe. Munyigumba's son Mkwawa expanded his power northwards towards the central caravan route. When the Germans arrived there in 1890, the Hehe were the dominant power in southern Tanganyika.

Mkwawa's state typified the military chiefdoms which Ngoni tactics brought to Tanganyika, just as the Shambaa kingdom embodied older political principles. In contrast to chiefdoms which grew up around the arms trade and employed professional musketeers, Hehe power rested on spears, on the disciplined force of armed citizens. Hehe despised Arabs and had little to exchange for guns. Their open plains favoured spears. After 1878 – when they still had no guns – firearms became steadily more important, but the spear remained their chief weapon and Munyigumba's military organisation remained the dominant element in Hehe life. Every adult man was a warrior. The youngest lived at the capital, Iringa, where they were stiffened by semi-professional warriors. Mkwawa had an immediate following of some 2,000–3,000 men in the early 1890s. The remainder of the 20,000 or so men of fighting age were mobilised as required by sub-chiefdom units from their scattered homesteads, as their military reputation made fortified villages unnecessary.[1]

Munyigumba's state had few civil institutions, myths, or rituals, although Mkwawa introduced more ceremonial and sacrificed regularly at his father's grave.[2] There was no bureaucracy. Sub-chiefs were drawn from three groups: the Muyinga family; descendants of earlier independent rulers who had submitted; and parvenus who had distinguished themselves in royal service and married royal women. All authority derived from the chief's will. All his agents, from the most powerful sub-chief to the humblest messenger, bore the title *mzagila*, perhaps best translated as representative. All important *wazagila* were bound to the Muyinga family by blood or marriage. The system had

[1] Freiherr von Schele, 'Uhehe', *MDS*, ix (1896), 71.
[2] See Alfons M. Adams, *Im Dienste des Kreuzes* (St Ottilien, 1899), pp. 24–6.

many weaknesses. The conquered provinces, especially Usagara and Ubena, were not assimilated but held by force. As in Njelu, the importance of military command gave great power to outstanding generals. Reliance on kinship threatened civil war at each succession. Munyigumba apparently intended that at his death the state should be divided between two of his sons, Mkwawa taking the north and Muhenga the south. In fact a succession dispute was triggered by Mwambambe, a Nyamwezi slave whose military prowess had made him Munyigumba's son-in-law and the popular commander of the vital south-western frontier with Mshope and Usangu. Mwambambe seized Muhenga, refused the ritual spear-washing of allegiance to Mkwawa, murdered other members of the royal family, and gained control of the state. Only his brutality, the loyalty of the northern provinces to Mkwawa, and the latter's success in gaining external support enabled him to defeat and kill Mwambambe at Ilunda Matwe, 'the place where heads are piled'.

The Hehe state was thus an unsophisticated political system, entirely lacking bureaucratic principles. Yet it proved successful and durable. A visitor sensed an arrogant confidence which he had not found elsewhere,[1] and Hehe identity was to survive all colonial pressures. The state's strength lay in its spears, which made it not only disciplined and victorious but participatory. This was the great contrast between the states created in response to the Ngoni invasion and those based on control of mercenary musketeers.

Between those extremes lay an experience which occurred in the north-east, where the initial stimulus to change came from the Masai. Their power was waning by the late nineteenth century. Early in the century they apparently adopted a more formidable type of stabbing-spear[2] and began a series of civil wars which lasted until colonial invasion. Their root cause was perhaps the fact that unsuccessful pastoralists could more easily survive in the rift valley than in the arid northern regions of Kenya where Masai pastoralism had probably evolved. Some wars were apparently contests between sub-tribes over cattle, grazing, and water. Others may have been disputes between adherents of different ritual leaders. Many were remembered as wars between 'Masai proper' and 'Iloikop' who either were or subsequently became less exclusively pastoral – possibly a conflict between an inner circle of Masai who scarcely interacted with agriculturalists and an outer circle whose external contacts were greater. Like the Mfecane,

[1] Giraud, *Les lacs*, pp. 102–56.   [2] I owe this information to Dr R. D. Waller.

these wars flung out of Masailand many refugee groups who tried to recoup by raiding east to the coast, west as far as Buha, and south to the borders of Uhehe. But the wars drained Masai strength, which was also diminished when agriculturalists, especially the Arusha, acquired firearms. By the 1880s the Masai were still the terror of their neighbours, but they were no longer unchallenged masters of the north-east.[1]

Masai pressure had affected the Chagga by 1800 when chiefs like Rongoma and Horombo were apparently using initiation and age-grades to integrate clan groups into political chiefdoms. Although long-distance trade certainly reached Kilimanjaro early in the nine-teenth century, it had little immediate effect on political organisation. Chagga chiefdoms remained small and depended on citizen armies of spearmen who preserved the egalitarian ideology associated with age-grade organisation. 'If you go as an age-class', young men were instructed, '...you must all be equals...Even if you take with you the son of the chief, he is still only your comrade.'[2] A visitor observed in 1861 that a Chagga chief

cannot be considered as a despot; rather, if one goes to the root of the matter, his power is almost non-existent, at least in peacetime, since the warriors as a group share a sizeable part of it. Without their goodwill he can achieve nothing. He must abstain from much that he would like to do, in order to keep his 'praetorians' in good humour, and must even share with them the dues which the caravans pay him. And at times he is even more dependent on his relatives. A strange contradiction – to be the absolute master of all living things and at the same time a shadow king![3]

Firearms first became common in the next decade. Their extensive use was pioneered by the ambitious and far-sighted Rindi of Moshi. Threatened by a longer-established and more populous chiefdom, Kibosho, Rindi welcomed coastal traders, stockpiled firearms, and entered into regional diplomacy, employing Taita and Arusha mercenaries. These tactics made war more ruthless than before. They were imitated with even greater success by Sina of Kibosho, who maintained a monopoly of guns in his chiefdom and fed a thousand warriors a day. The struggle between Moshi and Kibosho dominated Chagga politics until the 1890s and led to a wider adoption of guns,

---

[1] Jacobs, 'Pastoral Masai', ch. 2; John L. Berntsen, 'Maasai and Iloikop: ritual experts and their followers', M.A. thesis, University of Wisconsin, 1973, *passim*.

[2] Bruno Gutmann, *Die Stammeslehren der Dschagga* (3 vols, München, 1932–8), I, 111.

[3] Otto Kersten (ed.), *Baron Carl Claus von der Decken's Reisen in Ost-Afrika* (4 vols, Leipzig, 1869–79), I, 271.

which were more effective in Kilimanjaro's dense vegetation than on the open grasslands of Uhehe; however, firearms still remained secondary to spears, which were estimated by a German officer to outnumber guns by ten to one in the 1890s.[1] Sina himself gained the throne as the warriors' candidate, while a visitor wrote of Rindi that 'one side of his character he is totally Masai'.[2] These chiefdoms were to retain political vitality throughout the colonial period.

The political effects of trade and firearms must be set against this background. Their varied impact is illustrated by the fate of those few states which already in 1800 possessed administrative institutions. The rulers of Ufipa, especially Mwene Kapufi (c. 1860–90), made alliances with coastal traders and the state experienced stability and outward prosperity. On entering Ufipa, a visitor paid a small tribute and then became the chief's guest. Each village provided him with accommodation and carried his loads to the next. Not itself aggressive, Ufipa obtained enough firearms to deter most potential aggressors. Beneath the surface, however, there were more destructive consequences. The local weaving industry decayed, while firearms 'enabled and encouraged the Twa chiefs to exact much heavier contributions in goods, livestock, and labour from their subjects'.[3] The Kerewe state experienced greater difficulty. Early in the century new diseases, irregular rainfall, and competition to control the resources resulting from the ivory trade led to social tension and rivalry for the chieftainship. Five chiefs held office between about 1820 and 1840. In the second half of the century local ivory supplies dwindled and Ukerewe became a strategic point on a larger trade route contested between coastal traders and the Ganda. Nevertheless, the state's political institutions survived this experience, perhaps largely because trade was not controlled by territorial sub-chiefs but by officials, *abasiba* or 'watchmen', who has no political followings and were ineligible for the chieftainship.[4] By contrast, the most stratified administrative state of the eighteenth century, Karagwe, was in full decay by the 1880s. Although it lay across the route to Buganda, its rulers failed to adopt

---

[1] Stahl, *History*, chs. 9 and 11; Julius Augustiny, 'Geschichte der Häuptlinge von Madschame', *ZES*, XVII (1926–7), 174; Volkens, *Kilimandscharo*, pp. 136–7; A. Widenmann, *Die Kilimandscharo-Bevölkerung* (Gotha, 1899), pp. 55–9.

[2] Moritz Merker, 'Rechtsverhältnisse und Sitten der Wadschagga', *Petermanns geographische Mitteilungen*, Ergänzungsband XXX (1903), 36; Charles New, *Life, wanderings, and labours in eastern Africa* (2nd edn, London, 1874), p. 454.

[3] R. G. Willis, 'Kaswa: oral tradition of a Fipa prophet', *Africa*, XL (1970), 248. See also Reichard, *Deutsch-Ostafrika*, p. 400; Willis, *Man and beast*, pp. 102–6, 127.

[4] Hartwig, *Art of survival*, passim.

firearms or create a standing army, while Ganda and coastal traders had a common interest in a compliant ruler. In the 1850s they imposed such a chief, Rumanyika, whose inability to levy tolls earned him the traders' favour. When he died in 1878 or 1879, succession disputes, brief reigns, and child rulers brought chaos, until even the traders abandoned Karagwe for the water route across Lake Victoria.[1] Even worse disaster occurred in Ugweno, the oldest known political unit in the north-east. In the eighteenth century its southern district, Usangi, acquired some autonomy at the cost of allowing Mbaga allies from South Pare to establish a separate chiefdom in part of Usangi. Trade widened these divisions. Being close to the coast, Pare rulers could not monopolise commerce. Individual traders attached themselves to powerful men, supplying firearms in return for ivory and slaves. Both chiefdoms in Usangi had important slave markets, while the Gweno royal clan was split by competition for trading profits. Stronger powers – Usambara and the Chagga chiefdoms – sought to control the trade route below the Pare mountains. Eventually Ghendewa of Ugweno sought the aid of Rindi of Moshi, only for Rindi's forces to invade Ugweno and kill Ghendewa. By 1890 Ugweno was divided into a dozen units and racked by famine which tradition blames on political disorder.[2]

Thus trade and firearms had varied effects on established administrative states. A further problem is whether trade made possible enduring political units larger in scale and more sophisticated in structure than their predecessors. This is best answered by examining Unyamwezi, the region most deeply involved in trade. For centuries most Nyamwezi had lived in the best-watered northern and western regions of their country, where chiefdoms had the longest royal genealogies and pioneered trade with the coast.[3] By contrast, southern and eastern Unyamwezi were sparsely settled and took little part in early trade. This and their proximity to the coast led them to welcome the arrival of coastal traders.[4] The most hospitable chiefdom was Unyanyembe, where the coastal traders established their headquarters at Tabora.[5] Trade made its earliest and deepest impact in Unyanyembe, where a ritual chiefdom characteristic of the western plateau became possessed of a valuable product, ivory, before obtaining guns in any quantity. The result was conflict between the chief and wealthy

[1] Katoke, *Karagwe*, chs. 7–9.   [2] Kimambo, *Political history*, pp. 122–97.
[3] I owe this information to Fr F. Nolan, W.F.
[4] Sheriff, 'Commercial empire', p. 381.
[5] This account is based on Unomah, 'Economic expansion', *passim*.

private traders, *wandewa*, many of whom were originally headmen. When Chief Swetu died in the early 1840s the electors to the chieftainship ignored the previous rule of matrilineal succession and chose Fundikira, Swetu's son, who had managed his father's commercial activities and was actually travelling with a caravan when elected. Fundikira reorganised the chiefdom, appointing *wandewa* to many offices. Chieftainship in Unyanyembe was no longer purely ritual but also patrimonial, in that the ruler used scarce goods to bind men to him – the classic means of evolution from kinship to state organisation. At the same time, however, the chief was the candidate, the ally, and in part the prisoner of the *wandewa*. These free-trading merchants, with their Arab allies and counterparts, sought to prevent the chief taxing trade or monopolising its profits. The contest dominated Unyanyembe's politics for the rest of the century. In 1860 the traders deposed a chief, Mnywa Sele, who sought to control trade, but during the 1870s attacks by other Nyamwezi leaders and the arrival of firearms enabled Chief Isike to create a standing army and a more centralised polity.

As the stronghold of free trade and coastal influence in Unyamwezi, Unyanyembe was the enemy of Mirambo, the most famous of Tanganyika's nineteenth-century rulers.[1] Mirambo's homeland was north-west of Tabora, in the old centre of Nyamwezi settlement and commerce where coastal intrusion was most resented, but he rose to prominence in the late 1860s, when firearms gave new strength to chiefs, local ivory supplies were exhausted, and power rested on the control of trade routes, especially those leading north and west from Tabora to Lake Victoria and the Manyema. In one aspect, then, Mirambo was a conservative; like Mbegha, he was the champion of the old culture. His 'empire' was not based on new political principles. A minor hereditary ruler, he conquered neighbouring chiefdoms and replaced rulers by their more compliant relatives. He exercised a hereditary chief's ritual functions and was a noted rainmaker. Yet in another aspect Mirambo was simply the greatest of nineteenth-century warlords. His name meant 'corpses' and was given him by his *rugaruga*, his small standing army of brutalised young gunmen of the kind whom firearms bred throughout eastern Africa. 'We never take middle aged men or old men to our wars', Mirambo was quoted as saying, 'always youths not yet troubled with wives or

[1] The following account is based chiefly on Bennett, *Mirambo*; John B. Kabeya, *Mtemi Mirambo* (Nairobi, 1966); Roger Fouquer, *Mirambo* (Paris, 1966).

children. They have keener eyes and lither limbs. . . Fifteen of our boys died at one spot for the sake of one piece of red cloth.'[1] Unlike other Nyamwezi chiefs, Mirambo personally led his men to war and was idolised by them. His visitors recognised, as in Uhehe, that 'we were amongst men who felt they belonged to a great kingdom'.[2]

Alongside the conservative and the warlord, there was a third element in Mirambo's character. He is almost the only leader of his time whose mind is accessible to historians, and his conversations with European visitors reveal a man with larger conceptions than his contemporaries. His campaigns were in effect a bid for control of the whole western plateau. He sought alliance, unsuccessfully, with Kabaka Mutesa of Buganda and the British Consul in Zanzibar. He welcomed a European missionary 'to teach the people how to make guns and powder and cloth'.[3] 'Here there are too many chiefs', he told a traveller in 1882:

Only two or three are needed, allied with one another. . .If the Arabs had thought of coming to terms with me, Mutesa, and Isike, the country would be at peace. . .But the Arabs are proud and jealous. . .They regard me as a savage *mshenzi*. . .I hate them, but I am not so devoid of sense as to prefer continual warfare to a clearly defined common interest.

Although seeing the problem so clearly, however, Mirambo knew he could not solve it. 'My headmen', he confessed, 'obey me only out of fear. . .As for my captains, they are good for nothing but war.'[4] When he died on 2 December 1884 his 'empire' collapsed.

This mingling of conservatism and innovation also marked the career of Mirambo's contemporary and ally, Nyungu ya Mawe.[5] Nyungu (the name meant 'pot of stone') was a member of the Nyanyembe royal family who created a private army of *rugaruga* with firearms and conquered southwards into Ukimbu, which was an important source of ivory but divided into many small chiefdoms. A man of appalling cruelty, Nyungu took to its logical extreme the brutalisation common throughout Tanganyika. His power rested on mercenary troops who included contingents of youths less than sixteen years old – known as *mwitikila*, 'wasps' – comparable to the adolescent armies, born of social collapse, which terrorised Zaire in the 1960s:

---

[1] Richard Stanley and Alan Neame (ed.), *The exploration diaries of H. M. Stanley* (London, 1961), pp. 117–18.
[2] Swann, *Fighting the slave-hunters*, p. 58.   [3] Bennett, *Mirambo*, p. 102.
[4] Becker, *La vie*, II, 167–8.
[5] See Shorter, *Chiefship*, ch. 8. Dr Shorter's assessment of Nyungu is more positive than mine.

The *ruga-ruga* were wild young men without roots or family ties. Many of them were deserters from caravans or runaway slaves. For this reason they owed loyalty only to Nyungu and went anywhere to fight under his command. Like the Ngoni they wore a costume designed to inspire terror. For example, they often wore mutilated parts of the bodies of their enemies as ornaments... The *ruga-ruga* were encouraged to smoke Indian hemp to make them fearless and excitable... All booty had to be brought to Nyungu who distributed it according to the bravery of individual *vatwale* [captains] and *ruga-ruga*. If they were brave, *ruga-ruga* could be promoted to the rank of *mutwale*. In Nyungu's manner of speaking, only the brave were real men. Others he referred to as 'logs'. When ordering reinforcements he would shout: 'More logs! More logs!'[1]

Under Nyungu's rule Kimbu chiefs retained a shadowy existence but their power passed to six or seven provincial governors chosen from the military *vatwale*. The governors' main task was to forward ivory to the capital. Lacking ritual authority or independent resources, the *vatwale* could not acquire political independence. The system survived Nyungu's death in 1884 until the Germans destroyed it in 1895. Yet it would be absurd to describe it as based on bureaucratic principles. Like Mirambo, Nyungu possessed royal blood and made full use of ritual power appropriated from Kimbu chiefs, but his rule was essentially a crude military despotism. Later generations remembered him, but as Ili-Nyungu, 'Nyungu the Terrible'. No enduring human society could be built of logs.

Thus wealth and military strength provided new sources of power. Some men gained office through achievement. But these developments either complemented ritual and heredity or conflicted with them. Both Mirambo and Nyungu possessed royal blood and exercised ritual authority. Many *wandewa* were former headmen. Mkasiwa of Unyanyembe adopted one of his military commanders and married his daughter to another. Mwambambe married Munyigumba's daughter. Songea married his chief's sister. Whatever their military talent, *vatwale* could not be chiefs. Mkwawa's descendants were men of power while Mirambo's and Nyungu's were insignificant. The limits on change are clear, and one further point reinforces them. All the instances of popular action in nineteenth-century Tanganyika were backward-looking. Four types can be identified. One was revolt against a new overlord led by previous rulers. When Mkwawa gained the throne he successfully exhorted his father's Bena subjects to revolt against the Sangu chiefs imposed over them during the Hehe

[1] Aylward Shorter, *Nyungu-ya-Mawe* (Nairobi, 1969), pp. 13–14.

interregnum.[1] A second type of action was resistance by stateless peoples, often led, in the absence of effective political leaders, by religious figures. Nyiha prophets inspired opposition to Sangu invasion, while Ndendeuli resistance to Ngoni conquest was led by prophets who took as their names the attributes of God: Chapanga (the Creator), Ngalwala (the Immortal), Mwenekazi (the Almighty).[2] Thirdly, there were small-scale popular attacks on slave traders or exploitative chiefs. These occurred in the north-east during the 1870s and 1880s, when the Mbugu of Gare in Usambara murdered a Kilindi chief and the Pare of Mbaga besieged a slave traders' settlement at Kisiwani.[3]

The fourth and most important popular movement was the Kiva rebellion of 1869, which originated in the dissolution of the Shambaa state brought about by long-distance trade.[4] The rebels were the Bondei people who lived in the plains to the east of Usambara and had been conquered and incorporated into the Shambaa kingdom early in the nineteenth century. As previously stateless people, the Bondei benefited from personal allegiance to a king who could reconcile otherwise irresolvable internal conflicts, but they gained little from the state. Bonde was a punishment station for Kilindi too dangerous to rule in Usambara. The Bondei were far from the capital and received few redistributed goods in return for the tribute exacted from them. When visiting Vugha they were treated as strangers and forbidden to enter the town.

Although the Shambaa kingdom reached its apogee under Kimweri ya Nyumbai, who ruled from about 1815 to 1862, it was already threatened. The Zigua, a lowland people, acquired firearms in the 1830s, gained control of the Pangani valley, and threatened the mountain kingdom. 'The war-horn is now silent', Burton wrote in 1857, 'and the watch-fire never leaves the mountain.'[5] Ruling a conservative state from a mountain capital remote from the trade routes, Kimweri was slow to see the importance of guns, but his border chiefs welcomed them and acquired external allies. One of Kimweri's junior sons, Semboja, ruled Mazinde, just above the caravan route,

---

[1] Zacharia Chaula in MMRP 4/68/4/3.
[2] Kootz-Kretschmer, *Safwa*, II, 261–2; James J. Komba, 'God and man: religious elements of the Ngoni', D.Th. thesis, Pontifical Urbanian University, Rome, 1958–9, p. 105.
[3] Feierman, *Shambaa kingdom*, pp. 179–81; Kimambo, *Political history*, pp. 175–6.
[4] This account is based on Feierman, *Shambaa kingdom*, chs. 5–8; Feierman, 'Concepts', *passim*; Abdallah bin Hemedi 'lAjjemy, *The Kilindi* (trans. J. W. T. Allen, Nairobi, 1963), pp. 88–238.
[5] Richard F. Burton and J. H. Speke, 'A coasting voyage from Mombasa to the Pangani river', *Journal of the Royal Geographical Society*, XXVIII (1858), 215.

and accumulated guns and followers. Kimweri's death in 1862 split the kingdom. His grandson and successor, Shekulwavu, had little control over the sub-chiefs, who were his uncles. In 1868 he quarrelled with his senior uncle, who then backed Semboja as pretender to the throne. Shekulwavu replied by seeking Bondei support. 'My uncles the Kilindi of Shambalai and here in Bonde dislike me', he is said to have told them. 'If you subjects find them attacking you, you can drive the Kilindi from these districts.'[1] Shortly afterwards Semboja's mercenaries attacked Vugha and expelled Shekulwavu. The Bondei begged him to let them oust the Kilindi, for 'we are not their subjects but Kimweri's'.[2] He agreed, and the Bondei expelled all Kilindi from Bonde. Shekulwavu then died, but his brothers took up the legitimist cause and hatched a new plot with the Bondei, who feared Kilindi reprisals. The Kilindi were invited back to Bonde and assured of their safety, only to be massacred. Then the Bondei swept into Usambara, freeing slaves, killing Kilindi, and calling on Shambaa commoners to rise, but as they neared Vugha resistance hardened, until finally Semboja's forces drove them back.

Within Usambara Semboja did not win the throne, for his brothers wanted a weak king and shrewdly chose his young son. Royal power decayed. Vugha was reduced to a small village. After a period of chaos known locally as *pato*, 'rapacity', each chiefdom became almost independent. As in the Southern Highlands and the western plateau, the conflict extended into a regional struggle involving coastal traders and Taita, Masai, and Zigua mercenaries. Trade and guns had destroyed the interdependence of rulers and subjects. Chiefs no longer relied on tribute and spearmen but on gunmen who collected slaves to pay for firearms. Semboja employed Masai to raid Vugha, while Bumbuli, traditionally the heir apparent's chiefdom, was raided by its own ruler, a Yao slave. The war between Semboja and Shekulwavu's relatives continued indecisively for two decades. Each side had guns and each had certain of the king's ritual powers. Victory was impossible. The Bondei retained their independence but returned to statelessness, refusing allegiance to Shekulwavu's party once the king himself was dead. Far from containing any revolutionary element, Kiva had been traditionalist in inspiration and destructive in effect.[3] It epitomised the limitations of the political change associated with long-distance trade.

[1] Abdallah bin Hemedi, *Kilindi*, p. 118.
[2] *Ibid.*, p. 176. Kimweri here means Shekulwavu.
[3] Here I disagree with Feierman, *Shambaa kingdom*, pp. 162–7, and 'Concepts', pp. 380–1.

The restructuring of indigenous economies

At the root of the nineteenth-century economy was a paradox. Trade rested on the hunting and gathering of natural products – ivory, copal, rubber and men – and stimulated the older and more primitive hunting sector of indigenous economies. Yet trade needed not only ivory, but porters to carry the ivory, food to feed the porters, tools to grow the food and iron to make the tools. Since almost all transport was by human labour, far more men were involved in the system than if trade had been carried by animals. The international economy had established an outpost in Zanzibar and its impact spread through the mainland like ripples on a pool. Regions and individuals made specialised contributions to the new structure. New patterns of exchange developed. New social groups emerged. Tanganyikan economies were gradually restructured around the export trade. But some resisted the process, which remained incomplete when the German occupation initiated a different pattern of reconstruction. This dual transformation is the core of Tanganyika's modern economic history.

The long-distance trading system generally stimulated the regional trade networks which it embraced. Nyamwezi caravans carried not only ivory but salt and iron hoes with which to buy food along the route. Fipa exchanged grain with Lungu slave raiders in return for slaves, with whom they bought guns from coastal traders.[1] Indigenous textile industries could not compete with imported cloth, but long-distance trade stimulated less skilled crafts. In 1891 Tabora re-exported some 150,000 iron hoes, chiefly from Usumbwa and Usukuma. Iron tools replaced wooden ones in several areas. In Uluguru, for example, the ebony hoe survived only as ritual implement with which to open the cultivating season. Buzinza's iron industry was the most successful in nineteenth-century Tanganyika, perhaps because it was free of restrictions which elsewhere impeded the expansion of output.[2]

In 1872 Stanley described the vigorous mingling of regional and long-distance trade at Ujiji market:

There were the agricultural and pastoral Wajiji, with their flocks and herds; there were the fishermen from Ukaranga and Kaole, from beyond Bangwe, and even from Urundi, with their whitebait, which they call *dogara*...there

---

[1] Roberts in Gray and Birmingham, *Pre-colonial trade*, pp. 52–4; Swann, *Fighting the slave-hunters*, p. 98.

[2] Sigl to Government, 1 January 1892, RKA 639/114; Kjekshus, *Ecology control*, p. 82; above, p. 18.

were the palm-oil merchants, principally from Ujiji and Urundi, with great five-gallon pots full of reddish oil, of the consistency of butter; there were the salt merchants from the salt-plains of Uvinza and Uhha; there were the ivory merchants from Uvira and Usowa; there were the canoe-makers from Ugoma and Urundi; there were the cheap-Jack pedlers from Zanzibar, selling flimsy prints, and brokers exchanging blue mutunda beads for sami-sami, and sungomazzi, and sofi.[1]

Such permanent markets were common on the coast and in its immediate hinterland. Amboni market, just inland of Tanga, often contained a thousand people exchanging food, mats, wooden articles, tobacco, and other goods. Further inland, Umba's market met each Thursday and supplied much grain to the coast, Magila's met every nine days, and Hababara's, although not frequented by coastal traders, saw a lively exchange of food and tobacco for cloth, beads, and dried shark. The Shambaa, Pare, Chagga, Meru, Sumbwa, and Ha had regular markets, which existed also at the inland Arab settlements and the capitals of powerful chiefs like Mirambo. But these were exceptions. More commonly exchange took place irregularly at caravan halts or centres of craft production.[2]

No single currency was in general use. Buhaya used cowrie shells, Ujiji employed special beads, and Pare utilised maize cobs, but none had a fixed value elsewhere. Tabora relied on barter, although lengths of calico served as units of value and account. A bewildering variety of coins circulated at the coast. The most common – Austrian dollars and Indian pice – gained currency in coastal villages in the 1850s and in the immediate hinterland in following decades. Pice were current along the northern caravan route as far as Gonja in the 1880s and were accepted for seven days journey inland along the central route in 1883. Coastal traders obtained credit through notes on Zanzibar, and Tippu Tip secured about £1,000 in this way in Ubena in the early 1860s. The only African ruler known to accept such notes was the compliant Rumanyika of Karagwe.[3] Few non-economic barriers impeded free exchange of goods; the pedestrian caravan trade was too pervasive for such conservatism to survive.

Commercial centres drew outlying areas into relationships of

[1] H. M. Stanley, *How I found Livingstone* (new edn, London, 1895), pp. 387–8. Thomson (*Lakes*, II, 90) thought this over-written.
[2] Reichard, *Deutsch-Ostafrika*, p. 190; J. P. Farler, 'The Usambara country in East Africa', *Proceedings of the Royal Geographical Society*, I (1879), 87, 89; Roberts in Gray and Birmingham, *Pre-colonial trade*, pp. 63–4; Kjekshus, *Ecology control*, pp. 112–16.
[3] Roberts in Gray and Birmingham, *Pre-colonial trade*, pp. 64–5; Burton, *Lake regions*, II, 388–9; Baumann, *Usambara*, p. 284; Giraud, *Les lacs*, p. 58; Whiteley, 'Maisha', p. 13.

economic dependence. Unyanyembe obtained its meat supplies from Usukuma. New specialists – hunters, traders, soldiers, porters, and craftsmen with novel skills like repairing firearms – emerged chiefly in the commercial centres. These were mostly in the plains, so that wealth and power tended to shift from the skilled agriculturalists to the savannah peoples whose economies rested more on cattle, game, trade, or warfare. The Zigua challenge to Usambara exemplified this. Yet there is little evidence that agriculture was generally neglected, for two reasons. One was that it profited enormously from the spread of two new food crops of American origin, maize and manioc, together with an Asian crop, rice – all of them being carried along the caravan routes to supplement the millet, sorghum, and banana staples. Since the sixteenth century American crops have spread almost everywhere in the world and their high yields for relatively low labour inputs have everywhere permitted larger populations. This may have been the case in Tanganyika.

Originally brought by the Portuguese, maize was grown at the coast in 1800 and perhaps also in the extreme west, where it arrived from Zaire. Morice observed that maize was common on Kilwa Island in 1776 but was not grown on the mainland. Its expansion into the interior of the country is difficult to trace. Mid nineteenth-century Ngindo appear to have seen maize as a recent and foreign crop. By 1857 it was widely grown in the Pangani valley. Twenty years later it was the staple food of the Bondei and was also common in Usambara, where one tradition associated its spread with the expansion of Kilindi rule. Nyamwezi obtained maize seed from Zaire or from the Bende who had colonised the eastern shore of Lake Tanganyika in the eighteenth century. Nyamwezi cultivated maize in the early nineteenth century and carried it to Usandawe. Kerewe porters brought maize seed from the south early in the century. By the 1880s it was also widespread in the Southern Highlands, where every homestead in Uhehe was surrounded by a large maize field. Yet there were still areas remote from the trade routes, such as northern Usukuma and Unyaturu, where the crop was unknown.[1]

Manioc was probably confined to the vicinity of such Arab centres

[1] Freeman-Grenville, *French at Kilwa*, pp. 77, 92; de Froberville, 'Va-Ngindo', pp. 426, 429; Burton, *Zanzibar*, II, 173, 220; Farler, 'Usambara', p. 92; Clegg, 'Addendum to Mlalo Rehabilitation Scheme monthly report for the month of July 1947', TNA 4/269/6/45; Reichard, *Deutsch-Ostafrika*, pp. 376, 384; ten Raa, 'Sandawe prehistory', p. 93; Hartwig, *Art of survival*, p. 73; Giraud, *Les lacs*, p. 125; Stuhlmann, *Mit Emin Pascha*, pp. 750, 754, 851; *RTA*, 1898/1900, no. 50, p. 235.

as Tabora and Ujiji in the mid nineteenth century, but thereafter it spread rapidly along the caravan routes. It resisted drought but was widely despised as 'a valueless food, reserved for times of scarcity'. Morice observed a little at Kilwa in 1776, but never saw it eaten.[1] Rice was a much older crop, possibly domesticated in Africa, but in Tanganyika white rice was essentially a coastal grain carried by Arabs, and consequently spread alongside the others. It was common in the extreme south-east, but along the central caravan route in the 1850s it was grown only as far inland as Ukhutu and then again in Unyamwezi, where it had recently been introduced by coastal traders and was not widely accepted by the Nyamwezi for another decade or two. Elsewhere its introduction was generally attributed to Arabs.[2]

Maize and rice were more productive but less reliable than millet and sorghum. If agriculture had been neglected, their introduction would probably have caused more frequent famine, especially when added to more extensive warfare and a growing reliance on agriculture rather than hunting. Until the last decades of the century the evidence on famine is sparse. Sukuma traditions suggest that it became more common, but this may result from clearer memories of more recent events.[3] Great famines were certainly remembered, especially from the 1830s when Masai turned on their Iloikop rivals and Kimbu experienced 'the famine which comes even when there is food' because a fungus rotted the harvested grain. Kilimanjaro experienced an exceptionally prolonged famine during the 1850s.[4] Yet two especially susceptible peoples of the 'arid core', the Gogo and Sandawe, remembered only one serious famine in each decade in the 1860s and 1870s, not an unusual number for them. The next decade was, however, a disaster. Ugogo experienced famine in 1881, 1885, and 1888–9. The *mnyime* famine throughout the north-east in the late 1880s was a true 'famine that kills', when social ties, already weakened by slaving and warfare, collapsed and men abandoned their families or

[1] Burton, *Lake regions*, I, 332, and II, 70; Reichard, *Deutsch-Ostafrika*, p. 314; Giraud, *Les lacs*, p. 83; Freeman-Grenville, *French at Kilwa*, p. 169.
[2] M. D. Gwynne, 'The origin and spread of some domestic food plants of eastern Africa', in Chittick and Rotberg, *East Africa*, p. 250; George Shepperson (ed.), *David Livingstone and the Rovuma* (Edinburgh, 1965), pp. 99, 189; Burton, *Lake regions*, I, 97, 331; Newman, *Sandawe*, p. 53.
[3] Charles F. Holmes, 'A history of the Bakwimba of Usukuma', Ph.D. thesis, Boston University, 1969, p. 146.
[4] Jacobs, 'Pastoral Masai', pp. 62–5; Shorter, *Chiefship*, pp. 249–55; Johannes Schanz, 'Mitteilungen über die Besiedlung des Kilimandscharo durch die Dschagga und deren Geschichte', *Baessler-Archiv*, Beiheft IV (Leipzig, 1913), p. 33.

sold them into slavery.[1] But the problem of the earlier decades remains. Ukerewe, for example, suffered severe famines in the 1820s and 1830s but thereafter expanded food production and became a granary for surrounding regions. In twentieth-century Tanganyika improved communications and greater inter-regional trade made famine less destructive. These improvements may have begun to operate in the nineteenth century.[2]

The second reason for thinking that agriculture was not generally neglected was increased agricultural specialisation and exchange. Zanzibar's demand for food penetrated steadily further into the mainland, converting the hinterland peoples into peasants. In 1811 the island was already drawing rice from the Mrima. Sixty years later the Kisiju area specialised in growing manioc to feed slaves awaiting shipment from Kilwa, Mwera grew millet and manioc for export, and the Rufiji valley – which Stanley declared the most populous area he had seen in Africa – was so famed for its rice that the delta was known as Little Calcutta.[3] But Zanzibar's main source of food was the northern hinterland. 'Almost daily', a traveller wrote in the 1880s, 'one sees the Digo carrying their long, pointed, fibre sacks of millet and maize for sale at the Tanga market.' Their neighbours, the Bondei, grew rice chiefly for export to Zanzibar. 'From almost all parts', a visitor to Usambara observed, 'small caravans take honey, butter, tobacco, molasses, beans or some rubber to the coastal towns...in order to exchange these for European goods.' The Zigua, whose rainfall was exceptionally unpredictable, sold large quantities of grain to Pangani and Sadani in good years.[4] Further inland, Nyamwezi bought cattle in Usukuma and drove them to the coast, while the Shambaa of Misozwe purchased cattle from the Kamba to the north and fattened them for the Zanzibar market.[5] Agricultural products also reached more distant consumers. Tanga exported millet to Arabia. Sesame seed from Uzaramo and the southern hinterland was

[1] Clarke Brooke, 'The heritage of famine in central Tanzania', *TNR*, LXVII (1967), 20; ten Raa, 'Bush foraging', p. 37; Kirk to Granville, 10 March 1881, FO 84/1599/196; Kirk to Granville, 30 January 1885, FO 84/1724/122; Rigby, *Cattle*, p. 21; Kimambo, *Political history*, pp. 192–4.
[2] Hartwig, *Art of survival*, pp. 107, 163; below, pp. 315, 576.
[3] Brown, 'Pre-colonial history', p. 110; J. F. Elton, *Travels and researches among the lakes and mountains of eastern and central Africa* (London, 1879), p. 85; Edward Steere, *A walk to the Nyassa country* (Zanzibar, 1876); Bennett, *Stanley's despatches*, pp. 139–47; Kjekshus, *Ecology control*, p. 32.
[4] Reichard, *Deutsch-Ostafrika*, p. 190; Baumann, *Usambara*, pp. 126, 182, 273.
[5] Roberts in Gray and Birmingham, *Pre-colonial trade*, p. 58; Woodward to Steere, 16 March 1881, UMCA A/1/IV/647.

shipped to Marseilles for conversion into 'olive oil'. Copra production extended on the coast from the 1860s. Sugar was exported from Pangani and the swamps below the Pare mountains. Rubber – collected wild rather than grown in plantations – became Kilwa's chief export after 1876 as increased world demand coincided with the end of the slave trade, making Zanzibar second only to Brazil as the world's chief rubber supplier. By 1880 rubber traders had penetrated to the Southern Highlands.[1] Little is known about the supply of food to caravans, standing armies, and other unproductive specialists. The *wandewa* of Unyanyembe employed slaves to grow food for sale, as did several other slave-importing peoples. One Arab at Tabora abandoned trade and became a professional manioc planter.[2] Yet these were exceptions. The extreme unreliability of caravan food supplies suggests that they commonly depended on cultivators who sold surplus crops in good seasons.

East Africa was probably the only part of the world where slavery became markedly more common throughout the nineteenth century, and it is a subject still needing much research. Given Tanganyika's extreme underpopulation, slavery was a means both of exploiting labour where purely economic methods were ineffective and of relocating manpower to accord with economic restructuring. As the century progressed slavery both increased and changed character. The initial change took place at the coast as a result of plantation agriculture, first in Zanzibar and then on the mainland.[3] The old pattern of coastal slavery as a system of personal dependency was varied to distinguish newly-arrived plantation slaves who knew no Swahili (*watumwa wajinga*, 'ignorant slaves') from those born on the coast and brought up in its culture – a distinction probably shaped by the deep-rooted distinction in coastal thought between Islamic 'civilisation' and the 'savagery' of the inland peoples. Plantation slaves generally worked five days a week for their masters, leaving the remaining time for their own plots. Their social life was little supervised, but they could be bought and sold. Their 'home-born' children possessed higher status. They were rarely sold, they could marry freeborn women, and they almost belonged to their owners'

---

[1] Kirk to Derby, 9 November 1875, FO 84/1417/354; Thomson, *Lakes*, I, 143; below, p. 73; Kirk, 'Report on the India rubber plants of the coast near Dar-es-Salaam' [1879] FO 84/1547/122; Holmwood to Kirk, 30 January 1880, FO 84/1574/190.

[2] Unomah, 'Economic expansion', p. 105; Becker, *La vie*, II, 30.

[3] The basic study (which deals only with Zanzibar and Kenya) is Cooper, *Plantation slavery*.

families, but their own children – if both parents were slaves – remained in slavery.[1] 'If my master comes [to show] I am a slave, the woman will be divorced', states a surviving marriage contract from Bagamoyo.[2] A freeman's children by a slave concubine were theoretically equal to those by a freeborn wife, and all the nineteenth-century Sayyids of Zanzibar after Sayyid Said were his children by slave girls, but the fact that some observers believed that this reduced the rulers' status illustrates the contradiction between Islamic law and Arab prejudice.[3] Slave revolts were mounted only by plantation slaves, who became numerous on the mainland after 1873 when their export was prohibited. Along the Pangani estuary Arab landowners built 'great houses' and established sugar plantations – the classic slave crop – whose labour regime was far more rigorous than that of the clove plantations. Here fugitive slaves established an independent 'republic' at Kikogwe, probably shortly before 1873 when they repelled an expedition from Zanzibar. Similar 'maroon communities' existed inland of Tanga, in the Rufiji delta, and at Luagala on the Makonde plateau, where a Yao adventurer named Machemba, himself a slave trader, attracted followers from among the slaves of Lindi.[4]

Coastal conceptions of slavery gradually penetrated inland societies along the lines of trade, for large-scale slavery is impossible without large-scale trade. Little touched by commerce, the Nyakyusa were entirely ignorant of slavery,[5] but elsewhere slaves came to be bought and sold over long distances, so that the typical slave was no longer a kinless personal dependent from within the society but a stranger acquired by economic means and utilised for economic purposes. Such slaves became especially common after exports were banned. Zaramo headmen had gangs working their fields. Gogo exchanged ivory for slaves to cultivate their land, as did the Nyamwezi of Unyanyembe. In the 1880s the Makonde collected wild rubber and exchanged it for cloth with which they bought slaves to cultivate land in their absence. Arusha employed slaves to cultivate while young warriors raided. Ngindo bought slaves from Ulanga, Haya from Buganda, and Kerewe

[1] Harries, *Prose texts*, pp. 184, 210.
[2] C. G. Büttner, *Suaheli-Schriftstücke in arabischer Schrift* (Stuttgart, 1892), p. 88.
[3] Euan Smith to Salisbury, 24 February 1890, FO 84/2059/351; Portal to Rosebery, 12 October 1892, FO 84/2233/513; Cooper, *Plantation slavery*, pp. 195–9.
[4] Behr, *Kriegsbilder*, pp. 216–17, 224; Kirk to Granville, 29 August 1873, FO 84/1375/245; Kirk to Granville, 8 December 1873, FO 84/1376/167; Reichard, *Deutsch-Ostafrika*, pp. 120–1; Akinola, 'Slavery', pp. 223–6; Holmwood to Kirk, 30 January 1880, FO 84/1574/190.
[5] Meyer to Soden, 12 February 1892, TNA G9/26/79.

from Lake Victoria's eastern shore. Manyema slaves rarely reached Zanzibar, being absorbed en route.[1] Many old notions survived alongside the new. Digo slaves could marry free women, own farms, and even own other slaves. In Unyamwezi a slave's children had a higher status than their father and maltreated slaves could find sanctuary with chiefs, who alone could kill them. 'If a man buys a slave', it was reported of Bonde, 'he calls his own children and says, "Behold your brother".'[2] Most notably, few masters feared to arm their slaves, perhaps because discontented slaves could escape so easily that they had little need to rebel. Yet as slaves became more numerous and the nature of their work changed, so their status declined and their assimilation became more difficult. Those who owned many slaves often treated only the most trusted as personal followers. With no tradition of slavery and little regard for the cultivation of land, Gogo were said to treat agricultural slaves severely. Nineteenth-century agricultural slaves in Ukerewe were less often redeemed that the domestic slaves of the past. Several inland societies took over the coast's cultural ideal of the *mwungwana*, the free gentleman.[3]

To understand its full implications, long-distance trade must be set within the context of colonisation. There are indications that population and settlement grew markedly in nineteenth-century Sukuma-land, 'a country thickly populated and rich in cattle'. Rindi and other Chagga chiefs organised the colonisation of new land.[4] Immigration from all directions continued, possibly outweighing slave exports. Rundi entered Busubi, Luo moved south along Lake Victoria's eastern shore, and groups from Zaire crossed Lake Tanganyika. Makonde continued to cross the Ruvuma, followed by Makua and Yao hunters and traders, well-armed bands whose leaders – Matola of Newala, Nakaam of Chiwata, Machemba of Luagala – established small chiefdoms between the Sasawara and the coast. The Yao settled

[1] Burton, *Lake regions*, I, 113, 304; Unomah, 'Economic expansion', p. 105; Holmwood to Kirk, 30 January 1880, FO 84/1574/190; Fischer, *Massai-Land*, p. 57; Crosse-Upcott, 'Social structure', p. 369; Stuhlmann, *Mit Emin Pascha*, p. 726; Hartwig, *Art of survival*, p. 127; Kirk to Salisbury, 7 November 1879, FO 84/1548/244.
[2] H. M. T. Kayamba, 'Notes on the Wadigo', *TNR*, XXIII (1947), 96; Bösch, *Banyamwezi*, pp. 440–5; Reichard, *Deutsch-Ostafrika*, p. 466; August Schynse, *Mit Stanley und Emin Pascha durch Deutsch Ost-Afrika* (Köln, 1890), p. 17; Godfrey Dale, 'An account of the principal customs and habits of the natives inhabiting the Bondei country', *Journal of the Anthropological Institute*, XXV (1895), 230.
[3] Reichard, *Deutsch-Ostafrika*, p. 464; Becker, *La vie*, I, 151; Hartwig, *Art of survival*, pp. 128–9; Crosse-Upcott, 'Social structure', p. 69.
[4] C. F. Holmes and R. A. Austen, 'The pre-colonial Sukuma', *Cahiers d'histoire mondiale*, XIV (1972), 386–7; Bennett, *Stanley's despatches*, p. 206; Bruno Gutmann, *Das Recht der Dschagga* (München, 1926), p. 303.

along the caravan routes, and the same tendency is observable further north. The arid plains west and east of Ugogo which travellers on the central route most feared were gradually settled by Kimbu and Nyamwezi colonists. Nyamwezi settlements grew up throughout central Tanganyika and several Gogo chiefs had Nyamwezi advisers. Shambaa colonists settled the trade route below the Pare mountains.[1] From the 1860s, however, the coming of firearms caused ribbon-like settlements along the trade routes to give way to fortified villages. Many Nyamwezi chiefs insisted that round huts should be replaced by more defensible square *tembes*. A Lambya chief later asserted that during the 1880s all his people lived in a single enormous stockade. Fortifications became increasingly elaborate. Mirambo's capital was a walled enclosure 200 metres square containing a circular, palisaded citadel where the chief lived, while his headmen and *rugaruga* occupied the remainder of the enclosure. The most elaborate defences of all – including a high, encircling stone wall – surrounded Utengule Usafwa, the refuge which Merere's Safwa subjects built for him in the 1880s.[2] Many peoples had never previously lived in concentrated settlements and hated them. Ngindo regarded them as incompatible with a freeman's dignity and despised those who thus compromised their independence. Missionaries said that concentrated villages caused neglect of cultivation and herding.[3] Famine became more likely where plots were vulnerable to localised drought or depredations by game. Stockaded settlements probably strengthened the authority of political leaders.[4] They may have brought more witchcraft accusations, more exploitation of peripheral areas, more competition for accessible land,[5] and more control of the young by their elders. But this is partly speculation.

Changing patterns of settlement and colonisation affected the balance between cultivated land and the natural ecosystem of bush, game, and tsetse flies. In Unyamwezi, for example, villages became even more markedly islands in a sea of bush. 'Were one to ascend by a balloon and scan the whole of Unyamwezi', Stanley wrote in 1871,

---

[1] Burton, *Lake regions*, I, 281–2; Cameron, *Across Africa*, I, 127; Reichard, *Deutsch-Ostafrika*, p. 332; Roberts in Gray and Birmingham, *Pre-colonial trade*, p. 68; Kimambo, *Political history*, ch. 10.

[2] Reichard, *Deutsch-Ostafrika*, p. 358; Monica Wilson, *The peoples of the Nyasa-Tanganyika corridor* (Cape Town, 1958), p. 30; Becker, *La vie*, I, 418–19; Alison Redmayne, 'Mkwawa and the Hehe wars', *JAH*, IX (1968), 414 n. 21.

[3] Crosse-Upcott, 'Social structure', p. 375; C. F. Holmes, 'Zanzibari influence at the southern end of Lake Victoria', *IJAHS*, IV (1971), 493.

[4] Swantz, *Ritual*, p. 99.   [5] D. W. Malcolm, *Sukumaland* (London, 1953), p. 12.

'he would have a view of one great forest, broken here and there by the little clearings around the villages, especially in and around Unyanyembe', where much tsetse bush had been cleared and cattle introduced.[1] The balance of Nyamwezi population had shifted from north and west to south and east,[2] while porterage had withdrawn male labour from the economy on a massive scale and warfare had depopulated certain regions of men and cattle, especially during Mirambo's campaigns.[3] There are indications that tsetse flies reconquered areas of the western plateau in the second half of the century. A traveller noted the death of the buffalo herds – and apparently many human beings – in Ukabende near Lake Tanganyika.[4] 'We had lots of *tsetse* fly every day from Ugogo till we came here', a missionary wrote in 1878 from Urambo, 'and Mirambo says his country is full of it and one has only to look at his cattle to see the truth of this statement...Long ago there was no fly in Mirambo's country. There were a thick population and lots of cattle, but there has been so much fighting among them that the people are all scattered and destroyed and since then the fly has come and there is now very few cattle.'[5] In the colonial period a southern Sukuma chief declared that his people had moved north-westwards to escape Mirambo's raids, with the result that game and tsetse re-occupied the deserted area. Similar explanations were given in northern Unyamwezi. Zinza villagers withdrew north towards the lake to escape Ngoni raids.[6] The evidence is frail and the subject needs much further study, but man's defences may have been weakened at a key point, on the western fringe of the plateau. Through this region tsetse were to spread eastwards across the country during the early colonial period.[7]

Tanganyika's nineteenth-century economic history might appear as 'progress towards an inevitable dead end'.[8] Ivory and slaves, so it might be argued, were wasting assets on which no lasting economic progress

---

[1] Bennett, *Stanley's despatches*, p. 38; Unomah, 'Economic expansion', p. 7.

[2] I owe this point to Fr Nolan.   [3] See Schynse, *Mit Stanley*, p. 16.

[4] Becker, *La vie*, I, 259. See also James B. Wolf (ed.), *Missionary to Tanganyika: the writings of Edward Coode Hore* (London, 1971), pp. 93, 140, 148.

[5] Thomson to Mullins, 4 August 1878, London Missionary Society archives (School of Oriental and African Studies, London), Central Africa correspondence 1/3/D. I owe this reference to Fr Nolan.

[6] D. W. I. Piggott, 'Shinyanga (Mwankini) – Nindo boundary', in Shinyanga district book, TNA; Swynnerton, 'Tsetse fly in the Nzega sub-district. First report', 31 August 1924, CO 691/73/415; Paul Kollmann, *The Victoria Nyanza* (trans. H. A. Nesbitt, London, 1899), p. 106.

[7] Below, pp. 163, 270.

[8] Dr Roberts uses this phrase (with qualifications) to describe Nyamwezi trade in Gray and Birmingham, *Pre-colonial trade*, p. 73.

could rest. They created little fixed capital to be carried forward into a new phase of economic activity and few skills useful outside the ivory trade. As African entrepreneurs, the *wandewa* of Unyanyembe were exceptional; normally their place was taken by the coastal peoples and Asians. No Tanganyikan ruler developed agriculture even to the extent of Sayyid Said. Many domestic textile industries collapsed. Much-needed manpower was exported. Tsetse may have re-occupied cultivated land. Tanganyika, so it might appear, experienced a particularly vicious form of underdevelopment, becoming specialised in the production of ivory and slaves at the cost of other economic activities, only for the supply of ivory and the demand for slaves to collapse at the time of colonial invasion, leaving the country peculiarly ill-equipped to respond to the colonial period. Much of this is true, but it needs qualification. New products, notably rubber, did begin to supplement ivory during the 1870s. Much domestic textile production collapsed, but certain other trades prospered, notably iron-working. The caravan system was in itself an economic asset carried forward into the twentieth century. Many Tanganyikans became accustomed to wage-labour, commercial exchange, and the export of agricultural produce, which prepared them for economic activity in the colonial period. Trade and wider communications spread new crops, the most important economic gain of the century. Whether these outweighed the destructive effects of trade is an unanswerable question. Historically, the important process was structural change.

Innovation and resistance in culture and religion

Improved communications accelerated the mingling of cultures and ideas. Many people were for the first time exposed to the coastal culture, where they encountered literacy, a more sophisticated technology, and a world religion. Their reactions varied in a spectrum of responses from wholehearted acceptance through eclecticism to outright rejection, a spectrum comparable to later reactions to European culture. Yet Africans were also exposed to other African cultures. For many the agents of change were Nyamwezi and Yao rather than Swahili. For most, it was a time of uncertainty and danger which required adaptation, explanation, and prophylaxis.

Those most involved in long-distance trade naturally responded most positively to the material culture of the coast. The Yao were especially receptive. 'Now I have changed Yao so that it resembles the coast', said Chief Mataka after rebuilding his capital in coastal style and embellishing it with mango trees.[1] On the northern trade route Semboja built his capital at Mazinde in coastal manner, wore Arab dress, and had his wives taught to cook *à la Mrima*. Rumanyika's palace in Karagwe was full of stuffed birds, mirrors, clocks, and musical boxes. Isike of Unyanyembe – who may have visited Zanzibar in his youth – had 'the finest Arab clothes and a nice house equipped with pillows and a thick soft carpet'. Kiwanga of lowland Ubena visited the coast for medical treatment. Even Mkwawa's fortress was divided into quarters known as Zanzibar and Bagamoyo.[2]

The acquisition of coastal culture was mostly superficial, but occasionally the impact was deeper. Islam spread among the peoples of the coastal hinterland. Numbers of Segeju and Digo became Muslims. Missionaries found a substantial Islamic presence in Bonde in the 1870s. 'In nearly all the towns there is a little mosque', one wrote, 'and in the larger ones an Arab School.' The Zigua are said to have proselytised in Bonde, and certainly Islam penetrated Uzigua at this time. In Usambara it was little more than a veneer for a few Kilindi, although one who lived in Bonde was remembered as 'a devout Muslim, who fasted and prayed, and paid his dues and gave alms and built mosques in every one of his places'. A similar penetration took place further south, notably among Machemba's heterogeneous followers on the Makonde plateau.[3] One of the rainmaking chiefs of Uluguru, Kingalu mwana Shaha, became a Muslim. Further inland only one African leader is known to have been a serious Muslim: Kilanga bin Ilonga, ruler of Ubungu on the Lake Rukwa shore in the 1850s and 1860s. A slave-raider closely allied to the Arabs who had a quarter and mosque at his capital, he wore Arab dress and sent three of his children to school in Zanzibar. Isike of Unyanyembe was probably less committed to Islam, but in the early 1880s he appears to have observed Ramadhan. The Nyamwezi Chief Mayembe of Uyui

[1] Yohanna B. Abdallah, *The Yaos* (trans. M. Sanderson, Zomba, 1919), p. 51.
[2] Feierman, *Shambaa kingdom*, pp. 197–200; Arye Oded, *Islam in Uganda* (New York, 1974), p. 32; Norman R. Bennett, 'Isike, *Ntemi* of Unyanyembe', in Mark Karp (ed.), *African dimensions* (Boston, 1975), pp. 55–61; Per Hassing and Norman R. Bennett, 'A journey across Tanganyika in 1886', *TNR*, LVIII (1962), 138; A. T. and G. M. Culwick, *Ubena of the rivers* (London, 1935), p. 49; Mbaraka bin Shomari, 'Shairi la bwana mkubwa', in C. Velten, 'Suaheli Gedichte', *MSOS*, xx (1917), 156.
[3] E. C. Baker, 'Wanyika and Wadigo', manuscript notebook, Baker papers, RH; Farler to Steere, 30 September 1876, UMCA A/1/vi/398; Feierman, *Shambaa kingdom*, p. 200; Baumann, *Usambara*, pp. 141, 153, 273–4; Abdallah bin Hemedi, *Kilindi*, p. 109; *Central Africa*, March 1885.

may also have become a Muslim.[1] Otherwise Islam made little impact on inland peoples, but some incorporated coastal practices into their eclectic religions. Makonde began to sacrifice cloth before journeys or during crises. Perhaps most striking was the incorporation of the Sayyid into the sacrificial ceremonies which peoples of the western plateau made to the four points of the compass. After honouring Ruhinda and his peers, a Sukuma officiant turned to the east: 'You, Saidi Bargashi, from your realm derive many objects used in our *tambiko* [sacrifice], strings of beads, cloth.'[2]

Swahili spread more widely than Islam. Burton found it spoken widely by Sagara and Gogo in the 1850s and added, 'almost every inland tribe has some vagrant man who can speak it'. Thirty years later Swahili was very widely known in the coastal hinterland, while almost every inland village was said to contain someone who understood it.[3] Important chiefs found it indispensable. Rindi, Semboja, and Ruma-nyika spoke it fluently. Semboja's son, Kimweri Maguvu, was literate in Swahili in Arabic script. Merere of Usangu employed a Swahili secretary, as did Mirambo's successor, while Shambaa rulers had conducted their diplomacy in Swahili since at least the 1840s.[4]

Yet language indicates that the coastal culture was not always pre-ponderant. Swahili was not the *lingua franca* of the trade routes but only the language for dealing with coastal traders. The commercial language of the southern route was Yao. Semboja's trading centre at Mazinde spoke Zigua. On the western plateau the main language of trade was Nyamwezi, especially a standardised dialect known as *kiru-garuga* which was understood, according to a missionary, 'everywhere between the Victoria Nyanza and Kiwere [in Ukimbu]'. While many peoples borrowed Swahili words, others – such as the Nyamwanga – took them from Nyamwezi.[5] While Ngindo and Luguru admired the

[1] E. A. Alpers, 'Eastern Tanzania in the nineteenth century', *Tanzania zamani*, XII (1973), 8–9; Aylward Shorter, 'The rise and decline of Bungu power', *TNR*, LXXIII (1973), 1–18; A. C. Unomah and J. B. Webster, 'East Africa: the expansion of commerce', in John E. Flint (ed.), *The Cambridge history of Africa*, V (Cambridge, 1976), p. 304; Oded, *Islam*, pp. 236–8.
[2] Terence O. Ranger, 'The movement of ideas, 1850–1939', in I. N. Kimambo and A. J. Temu (ed.), *A history of Tanzania* (Nairobi, 1969), pp. 164–5.
[3] Burton, *Lake regions*, I, 234, 307; Burton, *Zanzibar*, I, 438; Becker, *La vie*, II, 50.
[4] New, *Life*, p. 377; Feierman, *Shambaa kingdom*, pp. 198–9; J. H. Speke, *Journal of the discovery of the source of the Nile* (London, 1863), p. 203; Selim bin Abakari, 'Safari yangu ya Nyassa', in Velten, *Safari*, p. 63; Roberts in Roberts, *Tanzania*, p. 136; Krapf, *Travels*, p. 279.
[5] Adams, *Lindi*, p. 31; Feierman, *Shambaa kingdom*, p. 199; 'Moravian Church, Central Tanzania: extracts from *Periodical accounts*', September 1909 (typescript, MUL); Christopher St John, 'Kazembe and the Tanganyika-Nyasa corridor', in Gray and Birmingham, *Pre-colonial trade*, p. 222.

waungwana for their sophistication, Chagga and Pare found their models in the Masai, and Hehe and Mbunga imitated Ngoni.

The history of dance remains to be written, but it was probably subject to extensive innovation. A Nyakyusa leader told a European traveller that his porters' dances would be current in the area within a month. In Ukerewe the modes of specialised status groups were supplemented by dances borrowed from Sukuma elephant-hunters, Jita lion- and leopard-hunters, and Ganda traders, warriors, and canoeists. Chagga adopted Masai dances. Safwa borrowed almost all their songs. Nyamwezi travellers introduced drums to Usandawe, where the most famous composer of songs in the late nineteenth century was Mugonza, a blind Kimbu minstrel. Slaves and colonists from Zaire introduced their styles of dance and carving. In return the Nyamwezi traders who conquered the Luba state took with them the *buswezi* cult, while other Nyamwezi spread their societies of diviners, snake-experts, and the like throughout the western plateau.[1]

As cultures mingled, so, paradoxically, 'tribes' became more distinct. Like the Hehe, the Nyamwezi, as an entity, were a nineteenth-century creation, their name – perhaps implying 'people of the new moon' – being given them by peoples further east, just as passing Nyamwezi caravans first gave the Gogo their name, and coastal traders invented the word Chagga.[2] As in the twentieth century, the mingling of peoples stimulated many to stress their identity and oppose foreign innovations. Despite – or perhaps because of – their trading experience, the Nyamwezi, a long-settled agricultural people, were remarkably resistant to foreign culture. Only a few notables took any interest in Islam. When visiting the coast Nyamwezi stressed their rusticity in contrast to the urbanity of the Swahili. Nyamwezi colonies elsewhere long remained culturally distinct. In Unyamwezi itself innovation was either absorbed into the indigenous order – as the Ngoni invaders became simply one more chiefdom – or encapsulated like the Arabs of Tabora. Similarly, Islam has no impact whatever in Karagwe.[3]

[1] Giraud, *Les lacs*, p. 194; Hartwig, 'Historical and social role', pp. 43–9; Widenmann, *Kilimandscharo-Bevölkerung*, p. 86; Kootz-Kretschmer, *Safwa*, I, 128–9; ten Raa, 'Musical instruments', p. 28; Dempwolff, *Sandawe*, p. 172; G. W. Hartwig, 'The role of plastic art traditions in Tanzania', *Baessler-Archiv*, NF, XVII (1969), 29; de Heusch, *Rwanda*, p. 362; Shorter, *Chiefship*, p. 28.

[2] Roberts in Roberts, *Tanzania*, p. 117; Rigby, *Cattle*, p. 20; Smith to Rosebery, 30 December 1892, FO 84/2238/102.

[3] Oded, *Islam*, pp. 32, 236–7; E. Quass, 'Die Szuri's, die Kuli's und die Sclaven in Zanzibar', *Zeitschrift für allgemeine Erdkunde*, NF, IX (1860), 448; Stuhlmann, *Handwerk*, p. 88; Fonck, 'Bericht über meinem Marsch', 10 August 1894, RKA 285/30; information from Fr Nolan.

The main areas of resistance to coastal culture, however, were those remote from the caravan routes, whose inhabitants were often the deprived of the nineteenth century. Nyakyusa loathed the Swahili as corrupt and diseased. The Ha of Heru apparently banned coastal traders for several years. Bondei initially killed Muslims in effigy during initiation ceremonies. It was forbidden to wear imported cloth during these rites or to wrap a corpse in imported cloth in Unyiha or Unyamwanga, two centres of domestic textile production. Even Yao and Makua initiation rites required the wearing of barkcloth. 'Coastal people ravage the country', sang the Sandawe, 'their language I do not understand.'[1]

Evidence for nineteenth-century religious history is slender, but perhaps three patterns of change can be identified. One concerned methods of combating witchcraft. Enslavement became a common penalty for this crime, presumably often replacing death. Two rulers – Mashombo of Mbaga in Upare and Shatu of Mshihwi in Usambara – had military units of enslaved witches. Often a witch's relatives were also sold. 'If a man is accused of witchcraft', Bondei rebels complained, 'no evidence is called but he is killed and his children are taken and sold.' Burton believed that witchcraft accusations multipled when their victims became marketable, and this may have happened.[2] Alternatively, accusations may have increased in response to the insecurity of the period. Trade spread old maladies like smallpox and brought the new diseases, notably syphilis and cholera, which invariably attend the integration of any previously isolated region with the outside world. Trade also stimulated political and economic competition. Some historians believe that these changes led men to hold witches responsible for otherwise inexplicable misfortunes, and Dr Hartwig holds that Kerewe sorcery beliefs actually originated at this time, but apart from certain Kerewe traditions there is no evidence that witchcraft accusations increased. External contacts may even have discouraged witchcraft beliefs in some areas – Rindi, for example, was remembered for his scepticism towards them.[3] What does appear is

---

[1] Wells, Neu Langenburg DAR 1918–19, TNA library; A. Leue, *Dar-es-Salaam* (Berlin, 1903), pp. 276–82; Dale, 'Account', p. 192; Baumann, *Usambara*, p. 132; O. F. Raum, 'German East Africa: changes in African tribal life', in V. Harlow and E. M. Chilver (ed.), *History of East Africa*, II (Oxford, 1965), p. 192; T. Bachmann, 'Ambilishiye', *Missions-Blatt der Brüdergemeine*, LXXXI (1917), 65; Weule, *Native life*, p. 277; Dempwolff, *Sandawe*, p. 166.

[2] Kimambo, *Political history*, p. 151; Feierman, *Shambaa kingdom*, p. 175; Abdallah bin Hemedi, *Kilindi*, p. 220; Burton, *Lake regions*, II, 369.

[3] Beverly and Walter T. Brown, 'East African trade towns', in W. Arens (ed.), *A century of change in eastern Africa* (The Hague, 1976), pp. 190–1; Fischer, *Massai-Land*, p. 54;

that methods of handling supposed witchcraft may have changed. Experts in Islamic magic were probably in great demand: by 1848 they were resident on Kilimanjaro and in Usambara.[1] But the chief innovation was probably the use of the *mwavi* poison ordeal to convict or clear those accused of witchcraft. Poison ordeals were probably already widespread in Tanganyika, but *mwavi* probably supplanted them throughout the southern two-thirds of the country. It probably came from central Africa. Nyakyusa attributed it to 'Nyasaland'. Some said the Ngoni had brought it. Zaramo considered it an alien importation. On the coast its introduction was attributed to up-country immigrants. Its expansion in the nineteenth century illustrates the wider communications of the period. Moreover, *mwavi* was commonly controlled by political leaders: in Unyakyusa it was one of their few powers, while the Nyamwanga paramount kept the poison and distributed it to village headmen on request.[2] It may have enabled chiefs to assert control over witchcraft when their authority was often questioned, and since they alone usually had the power to kill or sell supposed witches, it may have encouraged slave exports. But this does not prove that witchcraft accusations increased or that those convicted of witchcraft were treated more cruelly than before.

The second religious change concerned the territorial shrines especially common in the south. Their extensive influence made their priests and mediums vulnerable to political change. Mkwawa destroyed the whole priestly clan of the Chanzi oracle, but no details survive. At the shrine of Kyala on the Lake Nyasa shore the hero's living embodiment was replaced by a new priestly lineage in the mid nineteenth century, perhaps following occupation by Nyakyusa colonists – again the evidence is slender.[3] The nature spirits of Ufipa, previously venerated at specific shrines, developed after Ngoni invasion into spirits capable of possessing female diviners. The Kolelo cult may have experienced a similar but more extensive transformation

Bösch, *Banyamwezi*, p. 296; Becker, *La vie*, II, 318; James Christie, *Cholera epidemics in East Africa* (London, 1876), *passim*; Hartwig, *Art of survival*, ch. 5; Petro I. Marealle, 'Notes on Chagga customs', *TNR*, LX (1963), 74.
[1] J. Rebmann, 'Narrative of a journey to Jagga', *Church Missionary intelligencer*, I (1849), 19; Krapf, *Travels*, pp. 390–1.
[2] Anne Retel-Laurentin, *Sorcellerie et ordalies: l'épreuve du poison en Afrique Noire* (Paris, 1974), *passim*; Wilson, *Communal rituals*, p. 152; J. M. Makwetta, 'Maji Maji in Ubena', MMRP 4/68/1/1; Lloyd W. Swantz, 'The Zaramo of Tanzania', M.A. thesis, Syracuse University, 1956, p. 62; Harries, *Prose texts*, p. 217; Wilson, *Good company*, p. 137; Roy G. Willis, *The Fipa and related peoples* (London, 1966), p. 38 n. 173.
[3] *Missions-Blätter der St Benediktus-Genossenschaft*, June 1908; Wright in Ranger and Kimambo, *Historical study*, p. 159.

by which Kolelo's spirit possessed first diviners and then ordinary people, who exorcised it by ritual.[1]

The 'vulgarisation' of the Kolelo cult is inexplicable at present. It is tempting to see it as a consequence of change which weakened those who had previously controlled the spirit (as the Ngoni temporarily broke the power of the Fipa aristocrats) and created new anxieties interpreted as the work of possessing spirits. Here 'vulgarisation' links with the explanation commonly offered for a third identifiable religious change, the expansion of spirit possession cults. Professor Feierman has explained, for example, that in the past some Shambaa had ascribed tensions or misfortunes to possession by local nature spirits. In the nineteenth century other spirits were believed to become active: first a Zigua spirit, then those of other African peoples – Pare, Masai, Bondei – and finally the *pepo* and *shetani* spirits long recognised by the coastal peoples. Bondei, similarly, introduced a spirit named Jinni Bakari who 'is a swell, likes a white cloth, rice and fowls'. The Swahili, for their part, adopted both Arabian spirits and those of up-country peoples into their galaxy, and similar innovations happened elsewhere. By the end of the century the *kizungu* spirit of Europeans was already present at coastal possession rites.[2] The mingling of cults clearly followed commercial expansion. Perhaps they also gave an illusion of control over change by absorbing its manifestations into an existing framework. Most observers have seen the cults as responses to increased anxiety and social disorder. Dr Willis has described the Fipa cult as 'a "populist" response to what was experienced by ordinary people as social deprivation'.[3] As with witchcraft accusations, however, certainty is impossible, for possession may have been only a new way of dealing with long-standing maladies.

Nevertheless, social tension probably did increase, especially towards the end of the century. The expansion of slavery, the greater cruelty of warfare, the brutality of Nyungu and the ruthlessness of Mkwawa, the Kiva rebellion and the time of 'rapacity' – all these suggest growing oppression and misery for the weak. The often horrifying autobiographies of women caught up in nineteenth-century disorder show an intense desire for security and protection and a

[1] Roy G. Willis, 'Changes in mystical concepts and practices among the Fipa', *Ethnology*, VII (1968), 140; Swantz, *Ritual*, pp. 188–205.
[2] Feierman, *Shambaa kingdom*, pp. 200–2; Dale, 'Account', p. 221; Ann P. Caplan, *Choice and constraint in a Swahili community* (London, 1975), ch. 6; C. Velten, *Desturi za Wasuaheli* (Göttingen, 1903), p. 167.
[3] Willis, 'Kaswa', p. 249.

preoccupation with the nuclear family which might provide it. Bridewealth increased in certain areas, while rich men accumulated wives in others. Ndendeuli claim that their Ngoni conquerors first introduced bridewealth.[1] Young men gained mobility and the opportunity to make careers as porters or *rugaruga*, but the increase in movable property, agricultural slavery, and concentrated settlements may have worked the other way. Returning Nyamwezi porters often gave their wages to their fathers, who distributed the cloth among the family.[2]

These indications of social change find support in another area of religious history: African response to the earliest work of Christian missionaries. By 1885 five missionary societies were working in Tanganyika.[3] The first to arrive were French Holy Ghost Fathers. They settled in Zanzibar in 1863, moved their headquarters to Bagamoyo in 1868, and in 1877 built their first inland station at Mhonda in Ungulu, later establishing themselves also in Uluguru. The next group were Anglicans of the Universities Mission to Central Africa, who also settled first in Zanzibar, in 1864, and shortly afterwards began work on the mainland at Magila, on the border between Bonde and Usambara, and at Masasi, in the extreme south. Another Anglican body, the Church Missionary Society, established a station at Mpwapwa on the road to Uganda in 1876. The London Missionary Society – a British Non-Conformist organisation – began work at Mirambo's capital in 1878 and was also active along Lake Tanganyika. Finally, the White Fathers, members of a largely French society formed explicitly for work in Africa, reached Ujiji in 1879, and later established bases at Unyanyembe in 1881 and at Karema, on the south-eastern shore of Lake Tanganyika, in 1885.

Until the late 1870s the Holy Ghost Fathers and the UMCA concentrated on settlements of freed slaves. These were closed, stockaded colonies under the missionaries' paternalistic control. At Bagamoyo in the late 1870s, for example, each villager worked some twelve hours a day, five days a week, for the mission, in return for food, clothing, and a plot of land to cultivate in any spare time. Church attendance was compulsory, there was a curfew at 10.00 p.m., and no resident might leave the village without the priest's permission. Minor

---

[1] Marcia Wright, 'Women in peril', *African social research*, XX (1975), 800–19; Hartwig, *Art of survival*, p. 105; Gulliver, *Neighbours*, p. 311.

[2] I owe this information to Fr Nolan. On generational tension, see also Raum, *Childhood*, p. 289.

[3] For the origins of mission work, see Oliver, *Missionary factor*, chs. 1–2.

offences were punished by 'penances' and more serious ones by imprisonment. The freedmen often considered themselves still in servitude. Several strikes and protests are recorded. The missionaries designed these closed settlements to protect the freedmen from re-enslavement and provide a milieu in which clergy and evangelists could be trained to convert the free inland societies. All instruction at the seminary in Bagamoyo was in French, Latin was studied in preparation for the priesthood, and Swahili was forbidden. By 1895 at least six pupils had received further training in Europe.[1] The UMCA had sent fifteen young men and two young women to Britain by 1895.[2] This intensive European education naturally led the young freedmen to adopt the missionaries' culture. 'It is a very curious trait in the character of the boys', a teacher wrote from the UMCA school at Kiungani,

> that they always try to evade any questioning about their life before they came to the Mission House. If one only asks them what they called such and such a thing in their own native dialect...they will turn away...they seem to want to forget utterly everything connected with their past life, even so far as to disown their own relations...Another peculiarity of the boys is their amazing fondness for everything English...They one and all want very much to come to England.[3]

By the early 1880s the missionaries were dissatisfied with this strategy. Some feared that 'conversion' in the artificial atmosphere of closed villages was superficial and even fraudulent. The Holy Ghost Fathers did not find a single serious vocation for the priesthood and despaired of ever finding one among freed slaves. Associated with slavery, the villages were despised by neighbouring peoples. 'Only slaves pray', Bende leaders told the White Fathers.[4] Often the missionaries found themselves becoming political rulers, for villages like Mhonda, stockaded and defended by armed freedmen, were powerful military centres. The villages absorbed time and funds, obstructing the evangelisation of free peoples. The new mission societies entering Tanganyika in the late 1870s were pushing straight for the great lakes, threatening to cut their predecessors off from the interior, and seeking coherent African societies to convert as units.

---

[1] John A. P. Kieran, 'The Holy Ghost Fathers in East Africa, 1863 to 1914', Ph.D. thesis, University of London, 1966, chs. 2, 5, 6; Frits Versteijnen, *The Catholic mission of Bagamoyo* (Bagamoyo, 1968), *passim*.

[2] Zanzibar mission diary, 1863–94, UMCA A/1/VI.

[3] Goodwin to ? [1886?] in Gertrude Ward (ed.), *Letters of Bishop Tozer and his sister* (London, 1902), p. 136.

[4] Renault, *Lavigerie*, I, 418.

Finally, their contacts with the inland societies showed the missionaries that the response to their evangelisation came from unexpected directions.[1]

The different responses of inland societies resulted from the restructuring which they had experienced during the nineteenth century. Many powerful societies involved in regional commerce and diplomacy welcomed the missionaries chiefly as experts with valuable skills. Kimweri invited the first missionary he met to settle in Usambara as a teacher, preferably bringing a doctor with him. 'I want you very much to return to Moche', Rindi told a missionary, 'particularly if you can bring some artizans with you. I shall be glad to have my young people taught to read and write...I want paints and dyes of all colours; I want tools – saws, planes, a brace and bits, a screw-making machine, etc., etc.'[2] Yet a powerful ruler's interest did not ensure the missionary a serious response to specifically Christian teaching. The LMS discovered that despite Mirambo's interest in western technology the only way to attract his young subjects to school was to pay them. It was 28 years before this mission baptised its first convert. When Rindi obtained his mission, he was so disappointed at its failure to supply firearms that he kept it in a state of constant insecurity.[3]

The missionaries' problem was not that Urambo and Moshi were immobile 'traditional' societies. Quite the reverse: the problem was that they were in the midst of rapid transformation. Moshi and Urambo had not only been destructured by nineteenth-century change; they had been restructured around it. By contrast, the societies which responded positively to Christian teaching were those whose old order had collapsed and not been replaced by a new one, while the individuals who rallied to the missionaries were those whose old ways of life had been undermined but who had found no adequate substitute.

Thus it was no accident that the most positive response came in Bonde, where the UMCA missionaries, who arrived shortly after Kiva, found the country still in disorder. The Bondei had destroyed Kilindi control but relapsed into statelessness. Semboja was trying to reconquer the area. Slave hunters were active. So too was Islam. Many Bondei therefore saw the missionaries as valuable allies, willing to seek

---

[1] The missionaries' thinking is analysed in Kieran, 'Holy Ghost Fathers', chs. 5–6.
[2] Krapf, *Travels*, p. 280; New, *Life*, p. 433.
[3] Bennett, *Mirambo*, p. 109; 'Moravian church: extracts', September 1908; Johannes Schanz, *Am Fusse der Bergriesen Ostafrikas* (Leipzig, 1912), pp. 25–6.

guns for them and exert diplomatic influence on their behalf. Social instability favoured mission work. Of the first people baptised at Magila, some were surviving but déclassé Kilindi, others were Bondei leaders, others again slaves or their children. Several were Muslims, for Islam 'has broken the ground of indifference for us' by accustoming people to religious choice and the combination of doctrine and observance which the missionaries taught. Bondei society could not restrain those attracted by mission teaching. 'Let every man do what seemeth right in his own eyes' was one headman's attitude.[1]

Individual response followed similar patterns. No known early convert had been a *rugaruga* or a caravan porter, for porters and *rugaruga* were no longer marginal men, and it was from among the marginal men that most early converts came: slaves, refugees, dispossessed aristocrats, ritual experts, and the like. Above all, the first converts were *young*. The reasons for this are considered in detail later.[2] Here it is enough to say that Christianity fed on generational conflict, one of the most dynamic forces for change that Tanganyikan societies possessed. The early converts – so accurately described as 'mission boys' – were the counterparts of Mirambo's *rugaruga* or the caravan porters whose youth so impressed Burton. They were *vanyamati vangu*, 'my young warriors', as one missionary described them.[3]

Response to Christianity suggests how deeply nineteenth-century change shaped the manner in which Tanganyikans would react to colonial invasion. It set society against society and man against man, thus ensuring that the Europeans would enter a situation of intense rivalry and competition. It broke such cultural isolation as these societies had possessed, making some responsive to innovation and providing others with the resources for resistance. It wrought much economic devastation while drawing many into a participation in the international economy which made them responsive to the economic changes of the early colonial period. It divided rulers from subjects and from each other, while providing them with military resources to resist the coming aggression.

---

[1] Farler to Steere, Low Sunday 1877, in *UMCA occasional paper*, VIII, USPG library; list prefaced to Mkuzi mission diary, TNA; Farler to Steere, 30 September 1876, UMCA A/1/VI/398; Yorke to Steere, 15 July 1878, in *UMCA occasional paper*, IX, USPG library.
[2] Below, pp. 223–8.
[3] S. N. M. Kilimhana, 'The Maji Maji rising in Ilembula', MMRP 4/68/3/1.

CHAPTER 4

The German conquest

German invasion and coastal resistance

The decision to create a German colony in East Africa was taken on 23 February 1885 by the Imperial Chancellor, Otto von Bismarck.[1] To this day his reasons remain obscure. The underlying reasons for German colonial expansion lay in the country's industrialisation and its unification in 1871. These gave it the material power for overseas expansion. Industrialisation also divided Germans and produced an economy with a growing need for governmental management. Together with universal suffrage, this made the government increasingly concerned to take advantage of any opportunity to advance economic stability and growth. Overseas markets were one such opportunity. As Germany and other European powers mounted export offensives, they threatened Britain's previous commercial domination of the non-European world. Some Britons feared that their new rivals might establish colonies with protective tariffs. Some Germans feared that the British might exclude their rivals by converting commercial predominance into formal empire. Fears escalated until a region's existing commercial value became less important than its possible future value.

Bismarck was little impressed by this 'closed door' panic. His eyes were fixed on Europe. He was an elderly aristocrat anxious to preserve Germany's social order amidst industrial change. But he was also a great opportunist who knew that stability depended on manipulating rather than resisting change. Despite long-held beliefs in free trade, therefore, he bowed to political pressure in 1879 and

[1] Hans-Ulrich Wehler, *Bismarck und der Imperialismus* (Köln, 1969), p. 342. My account of the origins of German imperialism is based on this work and on Helmut Washausen, *Hamburg und die Kolonialpolitik des Deutschen Reiches 1880 bis 1890* (Hamburg, 1968) and Henry A. Turner, 'Bismarck's imperialist venture', in Prosser Gifford and W. Roger Louis (ed.), *Britain and Germany in Africa* (New Haven, 1967), pp. 47–82.

introduced protective tariffs. He also supported Germany's export offensive, increasing the number of German consulates from 488 to nearly 700 between 1879 and 1881. Until 1883 he went no further. Enthusiasts were urging that Germany should create an overseas empire like Britain's. In 1882 they formed the German Colonial Association. But they were opposed by most of the merchants of Hamburg and Bremen, who feared British reprisals against existing German trade, and by the agrarian conservatives, small-town radicals, workers' representatives, and Roman Catholics who formed a majority of Germany's parliament, the Reichstag. As late as 1884 the Reichstag refused to subsidise German shipping lines. Bismarck himself feared that colonies would be expensive to govern and defend, would bring international complications threatening Germany's security, and would 'widen the parliamentary parade ground'. Yet these were calculations. He had no ideological objection to colonies if the interests of conservatism should demand them.

During 1883 and 1884 events swayed Bismarck towards limited colonial acquisitions. In April 1883 he began to suspect that Britain and France were conspiring to discriminate against German trade in West Africa. Many German merchants now favoured a 'trading colony' there. Then the British informed him that they would resist German claims in hitherto independent South-West Africa. Early in 1884 Britain and Portugal seemed ready to close the Congo to German merchants. Bismarck decided to take a stronger line. On 8 April an official suggested that he could avoid trouble with the Reichstag by merely protecting merchants who formed chartered companies to govern colonies. Bismarck seized on this idea and during the next four months established German protectorates in South-West Africa, Togo, and the Cameroons. His chief motive may well have been a sense of obligation to protect German commercial interests. In addition, colonies might please sections of a new Reichstag which was to be elected in 1884. They also gave Bismarck a voice in African issues and encouraged tension between France and Britain.

Why Bismarck then added an East African protectorate during 1885 is doubly obscure. German merchants had traded with East Africa since 1847, but their interest lay in good relations with Zanzibar.[1] Both the election and any diplomatic flirtation with France were already over. Instead, Bismarck's decision was provoked by an adventurer named Carl Peters. Twenty-eight years old, Peters longed to 'engrave

[1] See Washausen, *Hamburg*, pp. 83–102.

my name once for all in German history'.[1] Reading and family contacts with Britain directed his ambition towards colonies. In March 1884 he and some friends formed a Society for German Colonisation. When Bismarck warned them off Latin America, Rhodesia, or Angola, they decided to undertake an expedition to Usagara, attracted by Stanley's highly-coloured descriptions.[2]

The government knew this, disavowed Peters in private, but did not obstruct him in public.[3] His party marched inland from Sadani. Reaching an Ngulu village on 23 November 1884, they made blood-brotherhood with the headman, read aloud a German treaty, explained it through an interpreter, obtained some scribbled crosses, fired three salvoes, and 'Mafungu Biniani, Lord of Kwatunge Kwaniani etc., Sultan of Unguu...herewith cedes the territory of Kwaniani Kwatunge in Unguu...for all time and at full discretion, to Dr Peters as representative of the Society for German Colonisation'.[4] Three weeks later a delirious Peters was carried into Bagamoyo clutching twelve treaties covering a notional 140,000 square kilometres.

'To acquire territory is very simple in East Africa', Bismarck later observed. 'For a few muskets one can obtain a paper with some native crosses.'[5] Yet he advised Peters to extend his territorial claims and create a chartered company. Peters obliged. The Congo Conference was then meeting in Berlin. Bismarck waited until it ended on 26 February 1885. Next day the Kaiser granted imperial protection to the German East African Company's possessions.[6]

Bismarck despised Peters. The Chancellor may have believed that German merchants in East Africa would ultimately need protection. He may have wished to preserve German access to the disputed Congo region. He may have thought that Germany would have little opportunity to acquire territory if the Congo Act precipitated a real scramble. He may have used Peters as a model for the West African merchants whom he was urging to form chartered companies. Whatever the reasons, Peters won his protectorate just before

[1] Peters to his mother, 2 September 1884, quoted in Wehler, *Bismarck*, p. 337.
[2] Carl Peters, *Wie Deutsch-Ostafrika entstand* (3rd edn, Leipzig, 1940), chs. 2–3.
[3] Wehler, *Bismarck*, pp. 162–8, 335–41; Fritz Ferdinand Müller, *Deutschland-Zanzibar-Ostafrika: Geschichte einer deutschen Kolonialeroberung 1884–1890* (Berlin, 1959), pp. 118–20, 523–5.
[4] Text in Kurt Büttner, *Die Anfänge der deutschen Kolonialpolitik in Ostafrika* (Berlin, 1959), p. 120.
[5] Verbal comment recorded 18 July 1886, quoted in Müller, *Deutschland*, p. 538.
[6] Text in Büttner, *Die Anfänge*, p. 123.

parliamentary difficulties and international tension again tilted Bismarck's calculations against colonial acquisitions. He made no more after May 1885[1] and his successors were equally uninterested.

The moment had been well chosen. Bismarck insisted that colonies should not seriously harm relations with Britain, whose policy was to support the Sayyid of Zanzibar and his claims on the mainland. But Britain was at odds with France and needed German friendship. Assured that Bismarck has no designs on the island of Zanzibar, the British gave him a free hand on the mainland and disowned the Sayyid's protests.[2]

Between 1884 and 1886 the German East African Company (DOAG) despatched eighteen expeditions to make treaties extending its territory. It also established eighteen small trading and experimental stations on the mainland by April 1888.[3] These stirred much hostility. The headman of Dunda, inland of Bagamoyo, asked the Company to remove its station lest 'eventually white people will be masters of the land'. The Zigua boycotted a station at Korogwe. Early in 1887 two stations in Uzaramo were attacked. The possibility of fighting the Germans was widely discussed during 1886 and 1887, notably by Bwana Heri, the ruler of Sadani.[4]

Meanwhile events in Europe hastened conflict. At Bismarck's prompting a group of bankers transformed the Company into a serious commercial undertaking in February 1887. An Anglo-German agreement of November 1886 fixed the protectorate's northern border inland to Lake Victoria. A month later the southern border with Mozambique was settled. The western border was already defined by Germany's recognition of the Congo Free State. In December 1886 the Sayyid acquiesced in an Anglo-German agreement limiting his mainland possessions to a ten-mile strip along the coast and permitting the Company to control and collect customs at Pangani and Dar es Salaam. The Germans occupied Dar es Salaam on 25 May 1887. They next demanded control of the customs throughout the coast. This was granted on 28 April 1888 by a newly-installed Sayyid, an ignorant and unstable British puppet.[5]

---

[1] Apart from a limited authority in Samoa in 1889. See Wehler, *Bismarck*, pp. 398–400.
[2] Ronald Robinson and John Gallagher, *Africa and the Victorians* (reprinted, London, 1972), pp. 192–4.
[3] Müller, *Deutschland*, pp. 228–9; Rochus Schmidt, *Geschichte des Araberaufstandes in Ost-Afrika* (Frankfurt a.O., 1892), p. 20.
[4] Eugen Krenzler, *Ein Jahr in Ostafrika* (Ulm, 1888), p. 89; Bennett, 'Arab power', p. 157; J. A. Kieran, 'Abushiri and the Germans', in Bethwell A. Ogot (ed.), *Hadith 2* (Nairobi, 1970), pp. 161–2.   [5] Müller, *Deutschland*, pp. 142–76, 252–62, 271–86.

When the Company's agents landed to take over seven coastal towns in August 1888 tension finally escalated into violence.[1] Sayyid Khalifa had unwillingly told his *liwalis* to hand over their houses and the Zanzibar flag. He appears also to have instructed them secretly to ensure that his treaty with the Germans was observed strictly. The *liwalis* of Kilwa, Lindi, and Mikindani left for Zanzibar. In Bagamoyo the Germans obtained the Sayyid's flag only by felling the flagpole. The main crisis occurred in Pangani. There a German officer, Emil von Zelewski, secured the *liwali's* acquiescence only by calling in 110 marines from a German warship. The townsmen later accused them of searching the *liwali's* house and harem, breaking up a service in the mosque, freeing convicts from the prison, and felling the flagstaff. 'With the ship at Maziwe', an eye-witness wrote, 'the whole town was humbled and the Europeans strode about the streets...not a free man said a word'.[2] Zelewski issued decrees creating a German-style administration, imposing taxes, prohibiting imports of guns and ammunition, and ordering property owners to prove their titles. As tension mounted, the more cautious notables locked the Germans in their house until the Sayyid's troops evacuated them on 8 September. Twelve days later a decision to resist the Germans was taken at a meeting held at a plantation outside Pangani owned by an Arab named Abushiri bin Salim.

Resistance had already begun elsewhere.[3] Early in September a warship was fired on at Tanga and replied by shelling the town. Warriors from the hinterland flocked into southern coastal towns, where on 21 September the Germans were given two days to leave. Those in Lindi and Mikindani escaped, but the two officials in Kilwa barricaded themselves on the roof of their house for two days until they were killed. Dar es Salaam and Bagamoyo remained in German hands. 'Apart from fear and terror, only the deepest peace reigns here', the German commander reported from deserted Dar es Salaam.[4] His colleague in Bagamoyo was attacked by 8,000 men on 22

---

[1] My account of the coastal resistance is based chiefly on Schmidt, *Geschichte*, *passim*; Müller, *Deutschland*, pp. 357–452; Robert D. Jackson, 'Resistance to the German invasion of the Tanganyikan coast, 1888–1891', in Robert I. Rotberg and Ali A. Mazrui (ed.), *Protest and power in black Africa* (New York, 1970), pp. 37–79; Kieran in Ogot, *Hadith* 2, pp. 157–201.

[2] Hemedi bin Abdallah el Buhriy, *Utenzi wa vita vya Wadachi kutamalaki Mrima* (trans. J. W. T. Allen, Dar es Salaam, 1960), p. 41.

[3] There is no evidence of co-ordination, although coincidence would be remarkable.

[4] Leue to Generalvertretung, 12 October 1888, quoted in Müller, *Deutschland*, p. 390.

September, but was relieved by 260 marines who cleared the town, 'killing every one they saw'.[1]

The Germans called the movement 'the Arab revolt', implying that it was the work of slave traders. In fact it involved many sectors of the heterogeneous coastal society, permeated by slavery and divided by racial and cultural distinctions. Omani administrators and Asian merchants generally withdrew to Zanzibar wherever possible. 'The wealthy, propertied families...saw their livelihood injured by the rising and therefore supported the Germans', an officer remarked of Pangani.[2] Leadership therefore passed to those 'Old Arabs' – descendants of families settled in Zanzibar before Sayyid Said's arrival – who lived on the coast. Their leader was Abushiri, some forty years old, son of an Arab father and Galla mother, who had traded around Lake Tanganyika and fought against Mirambo before settling as one of the slave-owning sugar planters of the Pangani estuary. Of the Harith clan – hereditary enemies of the Busaidi – Abushiri was wanted for debt in Zanzibar, had beaten off a Zanzibari force seeking to arrest him, and no longer recognised the Sayyid. 'What do I care about the Sultan?' he asked a German captive. 'I hate him and have not set foot inside his town of Zanzibar for twenty years, since I should be beheaded there immediately. Now I respect him even less for not being ashamed to sell our land to foreigners.'[3]

His immediate followers came from the armed slaves and hetero-geneous personnel of the caravan trade, men like his brother-in-law and fortifications engineer, Jahazi, a Comorian who spoke English and had served Stanley as an artilleryman in the Congo. Support also came from the *diwani* who had lost power during the nineteenth century but now, more committed to the coast's independence, took the lead in attacking the Company's agents in Bagamoyo, Kilwa, and perhaps elsewhere. As *waungwana*, all these groups distrusted the hinterland villagers who flocked into the towns during September and at this stage provided most of the resistance forces. Zaramo helped to attack Bagamoyo. The escaped slaves of Kikogwe rallied to Abushiri at Pangani. The most radical elements at Kilwa and Mikindani were Yao from the interior. The coastal people's nineteenth-century experience gave them sufficient unity to mount the common resist-ance to the Germans which they had not presented to Portuguese or

---

[1] Euan Smith to Salisbury, 25 September 1888, FO 84/1905/123.
[2] Behr, *Kriegsbilder*, p. 8.
[3] Oscar Baumann, *In Deutsch-Ostafrika während des Aufstandes* (Wien, 1890), pp. 138–9.

Omani. But slavery and racial tension ensured that the unity was fragile.

The coast's natural leader was the Sayyid, to whom the stateless coastal peoples stood in much the same relationship as the Bondei to Kimweri. Omani regarded the Sayyid as a personal lord. 'Old Arabs' saw him as a powerful usurper. *Diwani* resented his control but acknowledged his primacy. Hinterland peoples rejected his rule but sought his mediation and recognition. Bwana Heri resisted Zanzibari attempts to occupy Sadani but sought the Sayyid's recognition of his own position as its chief. 'I am neither a subject of Sultan Said Barghash nor of anyone else', a Bondei headman declared in 1885; '... but since we all know that the Sultan is a powerful man who knows what is right, we have therefore presented ourselves voluntarily before his governor in Pangani when disputes have taken place amongst us'.[1] In 1888, however, Sayyid Khalifa abdicated his role. Abushiri later accused him of encouraging the resistance. Probably he did encourage it initially, he refused at first to aid the Germans with troops, his efforts to check resistance were futile, he was in contact with the leaders throughout, and many coastal men believed they had his blessing. Abushiri secured a European safe passage by describing him as the Sayyid's guest. Others saw it differently. Late in 1889 there were rumours of mutiny in Khalifa's army, although none took place. 'You children of Seyyid Said are changed and have given your territory to the Germans', the *diwani* of Mikindani complained.[2] Abushiri believed that the Sayyid had been forced to betray the coast. So did Bwana Heri, whose son 'complained bitterly of the Seyid for selling their country'.[3] Some saw the dilemma fully:

We are loyal to the Sultan of Zanzibar, but we know that he lives on an island and can easily be overawed by big ships and big guns; we cannot believe that it is his real wish that strangers should come into his dominions and cut down his flag or hoist another beside it.[4]

During September 1888 the coastal peoples made it clear to the Sayyid that they were willing to return to his allegiance but not to accept German control.[5] But by then the Sayyid knew that continued resistance threatened his throne. He tried first to end the

[1] 'Notiz betr. die Häuptlinge und Bewohner von Usambara', 22 April 1888, RKA 404/7.
[2] Abdareheman bin Nangoma and others to Sayyid Ali, 22 March 1890, FO 84/2061/172.
[3] Pruen to Euan Smith, 24 November 1888, FO 84/1911/3.
[4] Bishop Smythies's summary of views in Pangani, in *Central Africa: a monthly record of the work of the Universities Mission*, February 1889.
[5] Euan Smith to Salisbury, 4 October 1888, FO 84/1909/347.

war before German intervention escalated, then to create a peace party.

The leadership vacuum was not filled by Islam, for coastal Islam was pacific and lacked institutions linking the towns together. Instead, the resistance relied on the loyalties of the past, on personal ties between notables and followers, on long-standing symbiosis between towns and coastal villages, and on the authority of the *diwani* in each town. The only exception was Abushiri's personal position. Early in the war he exercised a certain authority throughout the Mrima, but his ambition to dominate an entirely independent coast was unacceptable to particularistic notables, who also distrusted his reliance on Arabs, from whom he created a force of mercenary riflemen to stiffen the volunteers who were beginning to fade away back to their homes by November 1888.

Meanwhile the Germans prepared their response. When the Company first asked Bismarck's aid in September, he refused. 'I would rather abandon the whole colonial experiment in East Africa than authorise military operations by the Empire in the interior', he wrote, and he ordered that the Sayyid be given a month to restore order.[1] In October Bismarck was still talking of abandoning East Africa for twenty years, but he was coming to recognise that Germany must restore control or see the colonial experiment collapse. He arranged a blockade of the coast and decided to ask the Reichstag to finance an expedition. The Reichstag's balance was held by the *Zentrum*, a Roman Catholic party hitherto averse to colonial expansion. To win its support, Bismarck exploited anti-slavery sentiment and persuaded the Reichstag to vote £100,000 for measures 'to suppress the slave trade and to protect German interests in East Africa'.[2] To command the expedition he chose Hermann von Wissmann, a 34-year-old soldier and African traveller who 'regarded the Arab as the enemy of the human race'.[3] 'You are thousands of miles away', the Chancellor told him, 'Stand on your own feet. I am giving you a single mission: Win!'[4] Wissmann recruited 21 officers, 40 N.C.O.s, 18 medical staff, 600 unemployed Sudanese mercenaries from the slums of Cairo, and 400 Shangaan warriors from Mozambique. He calculated that African troops would best survive the climate and parliamentary criticism.

When Wissmann reached Zanzibar in April 1889 the resistance had

[1] Note of Bismarck's reaction, 18 September 1888, in Müller, *Deutschland*, pp. 547–8.
[2] *RT*, 1888/9, 26 January 1889, p. 603.
[3] Euan Smith to Salisbury, 29 September 1890, FO 84/2064/336.
[4] A. Becker and others, *Hermann von Wissmann* (5th edn, Berlin, 1914), p. 179.

reached stalemate. Abushiri had failed to take Bagamoyo and had withdrawn to a nearby fortress. Bwana Heri held Sadani. Local forces controlled the other towns except Dar es Salaam and Bagamoyo, still in German hands. Disillusioned, Abushiri had tried unsuccessfully to surrender to the British[1] and had then accepted a truce with the Germans. Wissmann broke it, citing Abushiri's cruelty, and marched his almost untrained troops against Abushiri's fortress on 8 May. The battle determined the character of the second stage of the war. Abushiri relied on his mercenaries, his modern rifles, and the 2½-metre-high palisade of Jahazi's fortress. Field guns destroyed the defences. Accurate rifle fire drove the defenders from the walls. 'Wherever I put my hand there was a bullet', one recalled.[2] Then the Germans stormed the stockade and the defenders fled, leaving 106 dead, mostly Arabs. Abushiri hid in the grass nearby while the victors celebrated.

Next month Wissmann took Sadani after fierce fighting. Bwana Heri retreated inland. Pangani was shelled from the sea and captured on 8 July. Tanga – divided between Arabs urging war and Africans desiring peace[3] – capitulated two days later. The Germans were masters of the northern coast. Meanwhile Abushiri's following was disintegrating. The peace party at Pangani told the German consul that 'almost all Arabs, especially all the landowners, want peace'.[4] Jahazi joined Bwana Heri. Others melted away. 'I can find no rest anywhere', Abushiri declared at this time.[5] Rejecting flight, he retreated to Mpwapwa, destroyed the Company's only surviving inland station, and then recruited the Mbunga of Kisaki,[6] whose raids had terrorised the coast for two decades. Abushiri's hopes revived. 'I have seen my star', he wrote, 'It has told me that...I shall conquer the Germans, kill them.'[7] Instead the Germans attacked the Mbunga camp just outside Bagamoyo in their first battle against the massed shields and stabbing-spears of an Ngoni-style army, killing 400 and dispersing the survivors. Abushiri again escaped, moving northwards through Uzigua with £750 on his head, perhaps seeking a route overseas through Kenya. But by mobilising the Mbunga he had finally lost coastal support. He was betrayed to the Germans by a Zigua

[1] Euan Smith to Salisbury, 9 and 20 March 1889, FO 84/1977/235 and 407.
[2] Hemedi bin Abdallah, *Utenzi*, p. 69.
[3] Kurt Blümcke, *Der Aufstand in Deutsch-Ostafrika* (Berlin, n.d.), p. 29.
[4] Michahelles to Bismarck, 2 June 1889, RKA 698/6.
[5] Quoted by Kieran in Ogot, *Hadith 2*, p. 180.   [6] Larson, 'History', p. 41.
[7] Quoted by Jackson in Rotberg and Mazrui, *Protest*, p. 71.

headman, Magaya of Kwa Mkoro. 'In the dark room', an officer wrote, 'lay a half-naked figure, clothed only in a native cloth, his hands and feet shackled with heavy iron chains, his head and neck jammed into one of those notorious forked sticks in which slaves were harnessed.'[1] He was led in chains to Pangani and hanged on 15 December 1889, implicating the Sayyid, blaming Jahazi, offering to serve the Germans, but also defying his captors.

Only Bwana Heri still held out in the north, a more formidable enemy with followers from many sources who refused to let him negotiate peace.[2] After losing Sadani he built a fortress with a four-metre-high palisade at Mlembule, seven kilometres inland. Early in January, in what Wissmann described as the hardest fighting of the war, this fortress withstood artillery fire for four hours, the 1,500 defenders interspersing accurate rifle fire with prayer. Bwana Heri retreated deeper into Uzigua, but now he had neither food nor hope. The Sayyid's mediation enabled him to surrender at Sadani on 5 April 1890:

Even at a distance an endless column could be seen approaching across the plain. At its head a magician leaped to the beat of a native drum, his body decorated with a lion's skin and his head with a large eagle's feather at either side. The drummer followed him, a few servants and women, and then Bwana Heri himself with his commanders and a great number of white flags.[3]

Since Bwana Heri was not an Arab, Wissmann regarded him as an honourable enemy and told him to rebuild Sadani. Now only the southern coast remained. Lindi and Mikindani negotiated peace. Kilwa had shed German blood and was bombarded for three days before the Germans took it against feeble resistance on 3 May 1890.

The coastal resistance was over. Weakened by the divisions of a slave society, by lack of leadership, and by vulnerability to seapower and artillery, the townsmen had nevertheless extended Wissmann's scanty forces. One consequence of resistance was indeed the small but formidable army with which the Germans conquered Tanganyika, for the Sudanese were fine though brutal soldiers and their German officers came from the best army in the world. Another consequence was to give the new regime its first collaborators, the peace party among the Omani Arabs. The third and most important was to commit Germany to full-scale colonial rule. On 1 January 1891 the Company's

[1] Behr, *Kriegsbilder*, p. 331.
[2] Bwana Heri to Wissmann, 2 July 1889, FO 84/1979/193.
[3] Behr, *Kriegsbilder*, p. 327.

administrative functions passed to the imperial government, whose vanguard was already marching inland.

The struggle for the caravan routes

Of Tanganika's five natural regions, the first to attract Wissmann's attention was the south-east. Once the coast was occupied in May 1890, most hinterland leaders hastened to submit. The chief exception was Machemba, the Yao adventurer, part Spartacus and part slave raider, who dominated the Makonde Plateau from Luagala and typified the innumerable quasi-brigands, born of the trading system, who seemed predestined to fight the Germans. Although friendly to missionaries – men with an Anglican education wrote his letters – Machemba refused German orders to visit the coast:

> I have heard your words, but I do not seen any reason why I should obey you. I would rather die...If it is a matter of friendship, I shall not refuse, today and always, but I shall not be your subject...I shall not come. If you are strong enough, come and get me.[1]

Wissmann replied with three expeditions. Struggling hopelessly lost through the dense bush, they were harried by Machemba's men, but their destruction of crops and villages persuaded him to seek a truce. In March 1891 Machemba visited Lindi and made peace. He did not observe the conditions, but when a missionary warned him not to underestimate the Germans, Machemba replied that he was in his followers' hands. He enjoyed eight years of substantial freedom until systematic administration caught up with him. Early in 1899 he maltreated a messenger sent to discover why he had not collected tax. Another massive expedition plunged into the bush. Machemba offered peace but refused to surrender his guns until it withdrew. The Germans replied by sweeping the thickets with machine-guns before clearing a path by hand. They found Luagala empty except for quantities of poisoned food. Machemba was already in Mozambique, where he later conducted another long resistance against the Portuguese.[2]

The conquest of the north-east was also a lengthy process. Early in

[1] Machemba to Wissmann, n.d., in Müller, *Deutschland*, pp. 455–6. See also Schmidt, *Geschichte*, p. 225.
[2] Schmidt, *Geschichte*, pp. 230–7, 240–3; Tom von Prince, *Gegen Araber und Wahehe* (Berlin, 1914), pp. 31–9; Smythies to Travers, 30 December 1893, Smythies letters x, UMCA; Natzmer, 'Bericht über die Matschemba-Expedition', 5 August 1899, RKA 289/186; Heinrich Fonck, *Deutsch-Ost-Afrika* (Berlin, 1907–10), pp. 142–50.

1891 Wissmann set out from Pangani to assert German control of the
northern trade route. In Bonde he met no opposition, for, paralysed
by their disunity, the Bondei had already fallen under German
control, taking their cases to the district officer at Tanga for
arbitration.[1] In Usambara Wissmann found a more complicated
situation. In the fragmentation following Kimweri's death, such
central power as survived lay with Semboja at Mazinde. His son,
Kimweri Maguvu, was a puppet king in Vugha. Their rivals were the
relatives of the dead Shekulwavu – his brother, Kibanga, and son,
Kinyashi – who had taken refuge in eastern Usambara. Kimweri
signed a treaty with a German agent in 1885, but Semboja refused.
He initially sympathised with the coastal resistance, but Wissmann's
campaigns changed his mind. He tried to patch up an understanding
with Kibanga in order to face the Germans more effectively, but
Kibanga refused, hoping to regain Vugha. Semboja therefore urged
the other Kilindi to submit. When German forces reached Mazinde
in February 1890, Semboja agreed to raise their flag. Anxious to keep
the trade route open, the Germans then recognised Semboja's
authority over West Usambara and the caravan route. When Wissmann reached Mazinde he confirmed the agreement.[2] But when he
moved on, Usambara's power struggle continued. Kibanga ingra-
tiated himself, selling tracts of eastern Usambara to German planters.
Influential Germans wanted Semboja humbled, but the government
preferred to wait. When Kimweri died in 1893 local officers tried to
install Kinyashi, but Semboja objected and instead another of his sons,
Mputa, was recognised. In March 1895 Semboja at last died. The man
on the spot seized his opportunity and hanged Mputa. After long
hesitation – fearing his father's fate – Kinyashi accepted the throne in
September 1895. The verdict of the Shambaa civil war was reversed
and the Germans – because they had been willing to wait – conquered
Usambara without firing a shot.[3]

As Wissmann marched onwards from Mazinde early in 1891 he
recognised Semboja's candidates as chiefs of the Shambaa villages
below the Pare mountains, but most of his time was absorbed by Pare

[1] Magila mission diary, 14 October 1889 and subsequent entries, TNA.
[2] Above, pp. 65–6; 'Notiz betr. die Häuptlinge und Bewohner von Usambara', 22 April
1888, RKA 404/7; Farler, 'Memorandum on Dr Juhlke's "treaties"', 6 November 1885,
FO 84/1729/148; Müller, *Deutschland*, pp. 447–8; *Central Africa*, November 1889; Clegg
to SAO Lushoto, 7 November 1947, TNA 4/269/6/74; Behr, *Kriegsbilder*, p. 219;
Schmidt, *Geschichte*, p. 175; Feierman, *Shambaa kingdom*, pp. 203–4.
[3] Storch to Government, 30 April 1895, RKA 404/49; Richard C. Thurnwald, *Black and
white in East Africa* (London, 1935), pp. 37–40.

chiefs who climbed down the hillsides to secure recognition in the shape of certificates, flags, and fezzes. Several of those recognised had little serious claim.[1] When Wissmann's column reached Kilimanjaro it entered an even more complicated web of intrigue. Rindi of Moshi had welcomed his first German visitors and even sent emissaries to Berlin in 1889 to present a huge elephant tusk to the Kaiser. Appropriate presents were returned:

While the soldiers presented arms, I...encircled his shoulders with the coronation cloak...from the Berlin Opera House and placed on his head the helmet under which Niemann once sang Lohengrin...[Rindi declared:] 'You have brought me many wonders, but none of the cannon which my people saw in Berlin.'[2]

Rindi needed the cannon. Sina of Kibosho had defeated him a few months earlier. Both were fighting to install their candidates in the Machame chiefdom. The first German embassy reached Sina in August 1890:

'I hear that Sina is troubling Ngameni [in Machame] and sending his warriors against him...What business have Kibosho's warriors in Machame?'
    'Ngameni has attacked me. I am defending myself.'
    'But Ngameni is now my friend.'
    'If Ngameni is your friend', Sina replied, 'Shangali is mine.'[3]

A month later Sina attacked Ngameni again. Inflamed by Rindi, German relations with Sina deteriorated until his destruction was the main object of Wissmann's expedition.

With some 300 soldiers and 400 auxiliaries provided by Rindi, Wissmann entered Kibosho on 12 February 1891. Within minutes he was lost in thick banana groves and under heavy fire. Only by chance did he stumble on the stone fort which Sina had been building for ten years. He shelled and stormed it, losing control of his troops, who slaughtered every living thing inside. Sina escaped and harried the German withdrawal. But Kibosho had lost 200 dead and 60 wounded. Threatened with deposition, Sina submitted. He saved his throne, other Chagga chiefs hurriedly declared loyalty, Rindi gained several thousand cattle, and Sina killed every man in Kibosho who had hesitated to support him. 'In my twelve years' experience in Africa', Wissmann concluded, 'never have I met negroes so brave as Sina's men.'[4]

[1] Kimambo, *Political history*, ch. 11.   [2] Ehlers to Kaiser, 17 April 1890, RKA 385/64.
[3] A. Le Roy, *Au Kilima-Ndjaro* (Paris [1914]), p. 289.
[4] Wissmann to Caprivi, 11 February and 8 and 28 March 1891, RKA 748/9, 19, 39; Prince, *Araber und Wahehe*, pp. 52–8; Bruno Gutmann, *Das Dschaggaland und seine Christen* (Leipzig, 1925), p. 47.

Rindi's death in November 1891 opened the way for a new German ally, Marealle ('the Indefatigable') of Marangu, the most brilliant of all the chiefs who manipulated the Germans, Marealle was Sina's nominee for the Marangu chieftainship and a pawn in the struggle between Kibosho and Moshi until, appreciating European power, he befriended European travellers and joined Wissmann's expedition against Sina. When Rindi died, Marealle induced the local German commander to move his headquarters to Marangu. (The commander was Peters and the inducements included Marealle's wives.) This achieved, Marealle embarked on a series of intrigues. Early in 1892 an askari was killed in a private quarrel in a chiefdom subordinate to Meli of Moshi, Rindi's young son. Probably incited by Marealle, the German commander panicked and marched into Moshi, brushing aside Meli's peace overtures. Equipped with newly-acquired breech-loaders, Meli surrounded the column in the banana groves, shot down its officers, and forced it into a nightmare flight to the coast.[1] While Marealle tried to deceive the other chiefs that German troops still held Marangu, Meli demanded their submission. But the chiefs had no love for Rindi's son and welcomed the Germans who re-occupied Marangu three months later. Sina offered to 'lead Meli to [the Germans] by the hand like a child' if supplied with ammunition.[2] Meli negotiated half-heartedly, fearing German revenge and knowing that his people opposed capitulation. In August 1893 the governor led 566 askari into Moshi and captured Meli's fortress. He kept his throne but lost the overlordship of Uru to Sina and of Kirua and Kilema to Marealle. His people were compelled to build a military station on the site of the chief's house.[3]

Marealle now became effective paramount of eastern Kilimanjaro, controlling 27 of the 44 Chagga chiefdoms. Sina died in 1897, allegedly poisoned on Marealle's orders.[4] Two years later Marealle's career reached its climax. On 21 December 1899 German outposts fired on what they took to be the combined forces of Moshi, Kibosho, and various smaller chiefdoms, together with Masai, Arusha, and Meru contingents. Whether there was any such combination, or whether Marealle invented it, is still unclear. Captain Johannes, Marealle's

[1] Stahl, *History*, pp. 259–64, 320–3; correspondence in RKA 280–1 and FO 84/2229–34; Volkens, *Kilimandscharo*, pp. 35–7, 114–15.
[2] Johannes to Soden, 16 November 1892, TNA G1/18/79.
[3] Johannes to Soden, 31 January 1893, RKA 1033/15; Schele, 'Gefechtsbericht', 13 August 1893, RKA 283/79; 'Bedingungen, unter welchen am 15. August 1893 der Friede mit dem Häuptling Meli geschlossen worden ist', RKA 283/142.
[4] *RTA*, 1894/5, no. 89, pp. 381–2; Stahl, *History*, p. 192.

friend, took Chagga warriors to devastate Meru and Arusha; then, on regaining Moshi, he arrested Meli, Molelia of Kibosho, and seventeen other notables and hanged them from a tree outside the military station. Marealle became the most powerful ruler Kilimanjaro had ever known.[1]

As Wissmann rested at Moshi in February 1891 he knew only that his victory over Sina had transformed the situation in the north-east. The Arusha people of Mount Meru – the leading military power in that area and one of the expedition's original targets – sued for peace, which Wissmann granted. The peace lasted five years, until in 1896 two Lutheran missionaries sought to settle among the Meru, who were the Arusha's semi-dependent neighbours. With Johannes looking on, the Meru chief gave the missionaries land but warned them that his warriors opposed their presence. That night Meru and Arusha warriors killed them. With 6,000 Chagga auxiliaries, Johannes forced his way along the narrow mountain paths, killing more than 500 Arusha spearmen. He let the Chagga loot and kill until the missionaries' goods were surrendered, after older Arusha warriors had killed a number of young extremists. Johannes then raided Meru until 'there was nothing more to fight or plunder'. He returned again in 1900, hanging the Meru chief and Arusha spokesmen. This time he left a garrison to build a permanent military station.[2]

In asserting predominance in the north-east, Wissmann superseded the region's earlier masters, the Masai. Since the Germans were based on the coast, they did not need Masai allies, while the Masai knew that their spears were useless against rifles. On his way inland Wissmann pushed aside a party demanding tribute. On his return he found their herds devastated by rinderpest. Shortly afterwards, the death of their *laibon*, Mbatyan, left the Masai divided behind rival candidates, Senteu and Olonana. Those who survived the rinderpest either retreated with Senteu into the Serengeti plains, where they were long outside German control, or were concentrated into a reserve in

---

[1] Stahl (*History*, pp. 194–8, 272–4, 331–2) ascribes this incident to Marealle's intrigue. Contrary views include Johannes to Government, 30 December 1899 and 3 March 1900, RKA 290/31 and 35; Augustiny, 'Geschichte', pp. 185–6.

[2] Wissmann to Caprivi, 11 February and 28 March 1891, RKA 748/9 and 39; 'Bericht des Kompagnieführers Johannes über seine Expedition vom 12. bis 22. Oktober [1896]', RKA 287/154; Johannes, 'Bericht über die Expedition nach dem Meru-Berg vom 31. Oktober bis 20. November 1896', RKA 287/161; Johannes to Kommando, 21 November 1896, RKA 287/172; Johannes to Government, 3 March 1900, RKA 290/35.

1905 to separate them from European ranchers settling around Kilimanjaro and Meru.[1]

While Wissmann operated in the north-east, a second column advanced up the central caravan route towards the western plateau. Its leader was Emin Pasha, an eccentric Austrian doctor with orders 'to break or undermine Arab influence', to establish a German base on Lake Victoria, and to be ready to act in Buganda if circumstances were propitious.[2] In fact the Germans conceded Uganda to Britain before he arrived there, while Emin ignored his instructions and instead left 'everything in chaos from Mpwapwa to Karagwe'.[3] Leaving Bagamoyo in April 1890 he traversed Ugogo, destroying nineteen villages and looting some 2,000 cattle when a chief's demand for tolls led to an askari's death.[4] Late in July Emin met an Arab deputation from Tabora which offered friendship and invited him into the town. Disregarding his orders, he accepted. The Arabs then told him of the implacable hostility of Isike of Unyanyembe, who had used his standing army during the 1880s to tax trade and assert control over the *wandewa* and their Arab allies. A delegation from Isike's enemies in Urambo confirmed the allegations. Emin therefore made a treaty with the Arabs, promising them religious freedom and an elected *liwali* to lead them in return for renunciation of slave-trading and acceptance of German overrule. Isike maintained a cool reserve. 'It is really astonishing', Emin reflected, 'how shameless one can be.'[5]

Emin then departed northwards, leaving only 24 soldiers in Tabora. Eighteen months of uneasy peace masked a polarising situation. Isike had Nyanyembe rivals led by Bibi Nyaso, a cousin of the Mnywa Sele who had been deposed in favour of Isike's father in 1860. The German officer in Tabora allied with Unyanyembe's enemies, Mtinginya of Usongo and Katukamoto of Urambo (Mirambo's son), while Isike unsuccessfully sought a British protectorate. In June 1892 a private expedition reached Tabora and the foolish local commander led three unsuccessful assaults on Isike's boma, Isiunula, 'the Impreg-

[1] Wissmann to Caprivi, 11 February and 28 March 1891, RKA 748/9 and 39; Jacobs, 'Pastoral Masai', pp 95–103; Johannes to Government, 28 February 1896, RKA 287/37; John Iliffe, *Tanganyika under German rule 1905–1912* (Cambridge, 1969), pp. 59–60.
[2] Georg Schweitzer, *Emin Pasha, his life and work* (trans. R. W. Felkin, 2 vols, Westminster, 1898), ii, 41–2.
[3] Stokes to Wissmann, 29 October 1890, RKA 271/106.
[4] Stuhlmann, *Mit Emin Pascha*, pp. 46–7.
[5] Schweitzer, *Emin Pasha*, ii, 55–7, 68, 77–9; Unomah, 'Economic expansion', ch. 6; Bennett in Karp, *Dimensions*, pp. 62–7; Wilhelm Langheld, *Zwangzig Jahre in deutschen Kolonien* (Berlin, 1909), pp. 46–8; Franz Stuhlmann (ed.), *Die Tagebücher von Dr Emin Pascha*, VI (Braunschweig, 1927), p. 293.

nable'. Yet Isike's victories were hollow. His councillors urged an enduring peace and three important military commanders deserted to Nyaso's side when he refused. The German governor sent his best fighting soldier, Lieutenant Tom von Prince, to resolve the situation. 'Diplomacy was useless here', Prince concluded. 'The people wanted war, were indeed at war.' With 46 askari, 93 nervous recruits, and Nyaso's following he attacked Isiunula in December 1892 while many of Isike's *rugaruga* were campaigning in Unyamwezi. Isike watched the Germans approach the fortress under artillery cover. His attempt to surround them failed. At dawn on the third morning Prince's men stormed the boma. As they reached Isike's house he exploded his magazine. His barely conscious body was strung up on the nearest tree. His young son was shot on the spot. Nyaso was enthroned a fortnight later as Chief of Unyanyembe.[1] Thereafter only mopping-up operations were needed in Unyamwezi. Isike's chief minister, Swetu, fought a guerrilla war for two years before retreating to Uhehe. Katukamoto of Urambo, held responsible for murdering an askari, was imprisoned in 1898 and what remained of Mirambo's empire was dismantled. Tabora and Unyamwezi, the heart of the western plateau, were in German hands. So was Lake Tanganyika, where the Arabs of Ujiji had hastened to make peace.

Emin's march took him northwards through Usukuma, where he founded a station at Mwanza whose garrison fought innumerable minor engagements against the Sukuma until an effective German administration was established early in the twentieth century.[2] In November 1890 Emin at last reached the western shore of Lake Victoria and chose Bukoba for his military station. Two considerations dominated the reactions of the surrounding Haya chiefdoms.[3] One was the continuing struggle to reunify and control Kyamutwara, which had fragmented in the late eighteenth century into four chiefdoms. In 1890 the most powerful contestant was Kayoza of Bugabo. His main enemies, Mukotani of Lesser Kyamutwara and Kahigi of Kianja, had both sought Ganda support against him. This Ganda intervention was the second vital element in Haya politics. 'I can readily understand that the people everywhere receive us with open arms as their

---

[1] Unomah, 'Economic expansion', ch. 6; treaties in TNA G50/1; Isike to British Consul, 19 March 1891, FO 84/2147/401; correspondence in RKA 1030; Prince, *Araber und Wahehe*, pp. 187–213.

[2] Ralph A. Austen, *Northwest Tanzania under German and British rule, 1889–1939* (New Haven, 1968), pp. 30, 41–2, 49–52.

[3] The following account is based on *ibid.*, chs. 2–6.

deliverers from the Waganda', Emin reported.[1] But the Ganda had allies, notably Mutatembwa of Kiziba.

Bukoba was in Lesser Kyamutwara. Its chief, Mukotani, welcomed the Germans, provided labour and building materials, and incited the Europeans against the two major powers, Kayoza of Bugabo and Mutatembwa of Kiziba. Emin raided Bugabo; Kayoza hastened to help build the station. Mutatembwa relied on the Ganda, continued to pay them tribute, and was brought into line by military defeat. Mukotani's diplomacy was bearing fruit. But in the meantime his rival, Kahigi of Kianja, was establishing an even more fertile relationship with the Europeans. Kahigi was the weakest of the chiefs and had hitherto kept his throne only by paying tribute to all his neighbours. But he was also the most intelligent, for like Marealle he saw that a lasting alliance with the Germans depended on accepting their new order rather than simply using them as weapons in old quarrels. Kahigi not only made a treaty with Emin and helped to build Bukoba; he also sent men there to learn Swahili. The next ten years witnessed Kahigi's rise to dominance. His first victim was Mukotani, deposed in 1895 when Kahigi persuaded the Germans that Mukotani had stolen rifles from them. Kahigi took four Kyamutwara parishes. Six years later Kahigi worked the same trick against Bukara and obtained part of its territory. He now dominated Greater Kyamutwara. Meanwhile the rest of Buhaya decayed. Bugabo suffered several weak rulers. Kiziba was racked by a succession dispute until 1903, when Mutahangarwa gained the throne. Ihangiro, in the extreme south, was accommodating but remote, and was made subordinate to Kahigi. Karagwe was in chaos from civil war, child rulers, brutal regents, smallpox, and rinderpest until the Germans installed an alien regent early in the twentieth century. He was Kahigi's brother-in-law.

Emin left Buhaya in February 1891, having, like Wissmann in the north-east, established initial relations with the African peoples. It is well to reflect on the pattern of African reactions.[2] Students of this subject often identify three African responses to invasion – armed resistance, negotiation, and collaboration – and argue that certain kinds of African societies were especially likely to fight, negotiate, or collaborate. This did not happen in Tanganyika. Many peoples reacted in different ways at different times. Machemba, most persistent

---

[1] Schweitzer, *Emin Pasha*, II, 121.
[2] This account draws on T. O. Ranger, 'African reactions to the imposition of colonial rule in East and Central Africa', in L. H. Gann and Peter Duignan (ed.), *Colonialism in Africa 1870–1960* (5 vols, Cambridge, 1969–75), I, 293–324.

of opponents, negotiated at intervals. Sina began by fighting and ended as a reliable ally. Armed resistance was not especially common among the most militarised societies. The Masai were in no position to fight. Unyanyembe had a less warlike past then Urambo. Nor was it less enlightened peoples who fought. A traveller described Isike as 'the most civilized native I have yet seen'.[1] Nor did every people fight when its 'national cause' was threatened,[2] for many, like the Shambaa, could not resist when that moment arrived. Rather, armed resistance, negotiation, and collaboration were tactical choices, alternative means of achieving the same end: the greatest possible independence and power. Tactics were chosen by decision-makers, so that to understand African reactions it is necessary to concentrate on decision-making processes. This is difficult, for little evidence survives. What is clear, however, is that almost all Tanganyikan peoples were divided about how to deal with the Germans. Each had its war and peace parties, its hawks and doves.[3] The coastal resistance was divided in this way. Machemba claimed to be in the hands of his followers. Isike's advisers counselled peace. To understand the decisions reached, therefore, it is necessary to discover why some men were hawks and others doves at particular moments, and to ask why either hawks or doves triumphed. This will not fully explain different responses, for the variables were too numerous. But it suggests certain generalisations.

Hawks were most common among locally dominant peoples, except where internal social conflict threatened their leaders' authority. Isike had more to lose than Nyaso from German overrule. The Germans allied with Kibanga rather than Semboja, Rindi and Marealle rather than Sina. On the coast, however, where differentiation was greater, the previously dominant groups were most anxious to negotiate, while where leadership was very weak – as among the Arusha – leaders often sought to restrain the bellicose young. Favourable prior experience of foreigners also encouraged negotiation. 'The first to come was a man called Emin Pasha and we...thought that he came to trade', Ihangiro tradition records.[4] Moshi had been especially receptive to long-distance trade. This pattern was not universal. Urambo's long antipathy to

[1] Thomson, *Lakes*, II, 257.
[2] John D. Hargreaves, 'West African states and the European conquest', in Gann and Duignan, *Colonialism*, I, 206.
[3] This approach is taken from Ivor Wilks, *Asante in the nineteenth century* (Cambridge, 1975), ch. 12.
[4] H. H. Allsopp, 'Ihangiro', in Bukoba district book, TNA.

Arabs did not prevent negotiation with Germans. But the correlation was significant. The balance between hawks and doves also tilted towards negotiation where there was time for a people to observe its neighbours' fate before reaching a decision. Abushiri's experience led Semboja to negotiate. The Arabs of Ujiji learned from those of Tabora, who learned from those of the coast.

As a broad generalisation, therefore, the peoples most likely to fight were locally dominant, relatively homogeneous, little experienced in profiting from alien intervention, and obliged to face the Europeans at an early stage in their conquest. If one asks in what circumstances was resistance most successful, two points emerge. Prolonged and effective resistance required skilful use of the country. Bwana Heri's campaign, Machemba's long resistance, the bitter fighting on Kilimanjaro and Meru – all were cases where the land favoured mobile tactics of ambush and withdrawal. Such warfare required exceptional unity of purpose so that scattered groups could pursue common action where normal communication and command were lacking. Yet this conflicted with the further point that effective resistance demanded maximum use of firearms, inter-tribal alliances, and other nineteenth-century innovations. Defensive alliances between independent groups were achieved only on the coast and in Unyamwezi, where nineteenth-century change had been greatest, but that change itself had tended to weaken unity of purpose, as the divisions within the coastal resistance and Unyanyembe suggest. The two desiderata, unity and modernity, proved incompatible.

There was another vital element in all these situations: European intentions. The Germans forced Sina and Isike and Mutatembwa into war by allying with their enemies. The Germans left Semboja to die in peace. The Germans ultimately held the initiative. And they too had their hawks and doves. Two divided groups faced each other at each confrontation. Their interplay is best examined in the Southern Highlands, where the German conquest culminated in an epic confrontation with the Hehe.

Mkwawa and Hehe resistance

In 1885 Mkwawa, like Bismarck, invaded Usagara. Hehe expansion southwards was blocked by Ngoni, Sangu, and Kinamanga resistance. Mkwawa therefore looked northwards, occupying territory in Usagara and threatening the caravan route east of Mpwapwa from a base at

Ulaya.[1] There he learned of the German invasion. He apparently sought alliance with Chabruma of Mshope, unsuccessfully.[2] The news may also have led him to construct a stone-walled fortress at Iringa on the Little Ruaha:

When the Hehe had finished building the fort they trusted in it greatly...the women were singing, saying – there is nothing which can come in here, unless perhaps there is something which drops from the heavens. And the old people were also in the fort and they were not afraid of anything.[3]

Mkwawa did not halt his northward expansion, but he sent emissaries to the Germans at Mpwapwa. A Hehe delegation was well received by the German governor, although Mkwawa himself refused to visit the coast. In February 1891 his forces raided almost to the walls of Kilosa boma.[4]

The Germans were divided in dealing with the Hehe. On returning from Kilimanjaro in March 1891 Wissmann was superseded. Reichstag moderates criticised his inland expeditions and his extravagance – he had spent £450,000 instead of £100,000. He was replaced by a civilian, Julius von Soden, a diplomat who had governed the Cameroons and was known to Africans as 'Mr Paper'. Soden was told to practise strict economy and intended to confine his administration to the coast, encouraging trade and maintaining only diplomatic relations with inland peoples. But he had little control over the military, who were furious at Wissmann's dismissal.[5] These hawks were led by the commander of the Defence Force (as it was now called), the same Zelewski who had precipitated resistance at Pangani. Hearing of Hehe raids in Usagara, Zelewski won Berlin's approval for an expedition to 'chastise the thieving and disobedient Hehe'. Soden doubted its necessity but acquiesced, for the troops were not needed on the coast and could come to no harm.[6] Zelewski reached Usagara on 30 July 1891. He had 13 Europeans, some 320 askari, 170 porters, machine guns, and field artillery. He took few precautions. 'The fellows haven't even got guns, just shields and spears', he sneered.[7] He intended to fight.

---

[1] Redmayne, 'Mkwawa', pp. 415–16; Kirk to Granville, 30 June 1885, FO 84/1726/261; Kieran in Ogot, *Hadith 2*, p. 164.
[2] Ernst Nigmann, *Die Wahehe* (Berlin, 1908), p. 15.
[3] Text in Redmayne, 'Mkwawa', p. 429. The date of the building is uncertain.
[4] *Ibid.*, pp. 417–18; Schweitzer, *Emin Pasha*, II, 58; Kieran in Ogot, *Hadith 2*, p. 192.
[5] Alfred Zimmermann, *Geschichte der deutschen Kolonialpolitik* (Berlin, 1914), pp. 175–9; Velten, 'Gedichte', p. 72 n. 15; Marcia Wright, 'Local roots of policy in German East Africa', *JAH*, IX (1968), 624; Schmidt, *Geschichte*, ch. 16.
[6] Zelewski to Caprivi, 8 June 1891, RKA 279/9; Soden to Caprivi, 15 June 1891, RKA 279/7.
[7] Prince, *Araber und Wahehe*, p. 88.

As the inhabitants of Usagara retreated, he burned villages and shot three men who came within range. On 14 August he scaled the escarpment and entered Uhehe.[1]

Mkwawa had tried to avoid war. Zelewski did not know it, but the three men he had shot were Hehe envoys. Now, urged on by his chiefs, Mkwawa mobilised his standing regiments and provincial levies. A few received muskets, but most carried only shields and stabbing-spears. On 16 August 1891 Zelewski camped at Ilula. Next day, when he reached Lugalo, he would have to pass between low, rock-strewn hills bordering the track to Iringa. Here the Hehe laid ambush. Early on the morning of 17 August their men – perhaps some 3,000, led by Mkwawa's brother, Mpangile – took position behind the rocks, some only thirty metres from the track. A single gunshot would signal the attack.

Zelewski broke camp at 6.30, riding a donkey at the head of the column. As its centre reached the waiting Hehe, an officer shot at a bird. The Hehe grasped their spears and charged. The askari fired only one or two rounds before they were overwhelmed. A sixteen-year-old boy speared Zelewski on his donkey. Within ten minutes most of the column was dead. The rearguard escaped, occupied a hill, raised its flag, and sounded bugle calls to rally survivors. The Hehe fired the grass, burning the wounded and hoping to encircle the rearguard. Three Europeans, 64 askari, and 74 porters regained the coast. Some 300–400 Hehe followed but did not attack. They had already lost 60 dead. Another 200 later died of wounds.

Mkwawa gave three cattle to the youth who killed Zelewski, but he forbade mourning, to conceal his losses. He began to strengthen Iringa and is said to have sworn never again to fight Europeans in open battle.[2] Within a few months his envoys were explaining that the attack had been a misunderstanding and Mkwawa wanted peace.[3] The doves were again in control. Soden vetoed revenge. Until he left, eighteen months later, all expeditions were banned. Semboja and Isike were left alone. Meli's victory on Kilimanjaro went unavenged. 'We should at least have digested the coast before we devoured the interior',[4] Soden wrote, and he opened negotiations with the Hehe through Holy Ghost missionaries at Kilosa, demanding that Mkwawa send envoys

---

[1] This account is based on Tettenborn to Soden, 30 August 1891, RKA 279/91; Eschke, report, 19 September 1891, RKA 279/154; Nigmann, *Wahehe*, pp. 15–17; Redmayne, 'Mkwawa', pp. 418–20.
[2] Adams, *Im Dienste*, p. 47.   [3] Soden to Caprivi, 10 January 1892, RKA 280/51.
[4] Soden to Caprivi, 17 November 1892, RKA 282/15.

to the coast, pay a fine, abandon raiding, give hostages, surrender captured guns, and open Uhehe to traders and missionaries.[1] The Hehe replied:

The Great Chief's desire has always been to live at peace with the Germans...Several times he has sent peace envoys to the Germans...With regard to Zelewski's expedition in particular, he was bound to defend himself (not wishing to die like a woman) when, at two separate attempts, his delegates were fired on, and when several tombs were...desecrated.[2]

The missionaries were not convinced, but they believed Mkwawa feared reprisals and wanted peace. They advised his envoys to visit Soden.

Mkwawa's real views are unknown. Slender, quick-moving, sharply intelligent, he was autocratic, unpredictable, suspicious, and cruel: one of his praise-names was 'the Madness of the Year'.[3] He believed fervently in charms and medicines. Such a man – so totally different from Rindi's supple rationality – could scarcely adapt to European control. Yet the Germans believed that Mkwawa personally desired a settlement before Zelewski's invasion and for about a year afterwards. They thought that Hehe hawks subverted the negotiations. In any event, Mkwawa could scarcely have accepted any terms which the Germans could have offered, for Soden's minimum demands were free access to a 'protected' Uhehe and an end to raiding. Moreover, Soden was not in full control. He had entrusted a chain of forts on the northern border of Uhehe – Kisaki, Kilosa and Kilimatinde – to Tom von Prince. And Prince was determined on revenge. In June 1892 he raided into Uhehe and built a new station within its borders. Mkwawa retaliated by annihilating a German garrison at Old Kondoa and rejecting further peace overtures.[4]

Soden left Tanganyika early in 1893, his policy in ruins. His successor, Colonel Freiherr von Schele – 'a handsome man whose talents were generally considered very mediocre'[5] – was the ultimate hawk, convinced that the interior must be conquered. 'Success is everything', he told Prince.[6] In March 1893 Schele welcomed Isike's

[1] Soden to Caprivi, 12 March 1892, RKA 280/78.
[2] Courmont to Soden, 27 February 1892, RKA 280/80.
[3] Redmayne, 'Mkwawa', p. 433.
[4] Roitière to Courmont, 15 May 1892, RKA 280/116; Prince to Soden, 15 August 1892, RKA 281/105; Köhler, 'Bericht über den Einfall der Wahehe in Kondoa', 16 October 1892, RKA 281/142; Prince to Soden, 29 October 1892, RKA 282/19; Prince, *Araber und Wahehe*, pp. 131–83; Velten, 'Gedichte', pp. 92–127.
[5] N. Rich and M. H. Fisher (ed.), *The Holstein papers* (4 vols, Cambridge, 1955–63), I, 163.
[6] Prince, *Araber und Wahehe*, p. 283.

destruction. In August he defeated Meli, seeing it as a training exercise for war against the Hehe. And meanwhile his officers constructed alliances to encircle Mkwawa with African enemies.

The first and firmest ally was Kiwanga, the lowland Bena chief of the Kilombero valley whose father had been driven from the Iringa plateau by the Hehe. Kiwanga met the Germans in Kilwa in 1890 and realised he could use them to destroy Mkwawa. By May 1893 German troops were stationed at his capital for the assault on Iringa. In December Schele arrived to finalise plans.[1]

The next ally was Merere of Usangu. He too had lost his homeland to the Hehe. The German arrival gave him new hope. In July 1891 his envoys were in Bagamoyo seeking a German flag. Mkwawa's victory at Lugalo terrified him. 'If you have a mind to defeat the Hehe', he wrote to Soden in January 1892,

I ask you to come quickly. I and my men will show you the way...and we will also stand by you in the war...The Hehe are gathering their men to defeat me, so I beg you not to leave me alone this year.[2]

Early in 1893 Prince reached Usangu. He aided Merere against his enemies and promised to restore him to his homeland if he guarded Uhehe's western border against Mkwawa.

Other links were fitting into the chain. In December 1893 Schele invaded Umbunga, defeated its forces, and hanged a leading chief. Then he moved southwards, skirting Uhehe, and turned westwards into Ungoni. Here his success was more limited. Njelu was divided and ill-placed to resist. Its leaders greeted Schele warmly, but he left no garrison and raiding continued. Further north, in Mshope, Chabruma refused to meet the governor but did not resist; he was watching events. Nevertheless, Schele's preparations were complete. In May 1894 he received final approval for war.[3]

Mkwawa seems to have sensed this. In January 1894 his envoys again reached Kilosa. The Germans thought they were serious, but themselves no longer wanted peace. They imposed a new condition: a military station at Mkwawa's capital. This was surrender. Mkwawa did not reply.[4]

[1] Culwick, *Ubena*, pp. 28–52; Schele, 'Bericht über die expedition des Gouverneurs von Deutsch-Ostafrika in das Gebiet des Rufidji und Ulanga, am Nyassa-See und in das Hinterland von Kilwa', 27 March 1894, RKA 284/56.
[2] Merere to Soden [January 1892] TNA G9/26/53. See also Wright, 'Merere', pp. 41–9.
[3] Schele, 'Bericht', 27 March 1894, RKA 284/56; Richthofen to Schele, 31 May 1894, RKA 284/112.
[4] Wrochem to Caprivi, 30 January 1894, RKA 284/10.

On 26 October 1894 Schele's expedition debouched on to the Iringa plateau. He had 609 askari and three machine-guns, and this time the Germans were prepared. The Hehe found no opportunity for ambush and feared an open battle. Instead they fell back into Iringa. On 28 October Schele camped outside the fortress:

The town lay picturesquely in a broad, basin-shaped valley. Through it flowed the Ruaha...The town was surrounded by a wall some five kilometres in circumference...mostly built of stone and about four metres high. Inside, on both banks of the Ruaha, was situated a relatively open space on which numerous herds of cattle were visible. The remaining area of both halves of the town was covered with rows of houses and a few prominent buildings...Only in the two easily distinguishable inner fortifications, one in each half of the town, did the tops of a few thatched roofs stand up above the rest. These and their surroundings were pointed out by the guides as Mkwawa's own bomas. In the streets and open places of the town thousands of people were to be seen. As the Company approached, the warriors in their finery streamed with cries to the outer circumference wall. This wall itself was provided at every 100 metres with a square bastion. The houses and house-complexes inside were all similarly equipped for independent defence with strong walls and bastions.[1]

The Germans were delighted to attack a fixed position. Schele poured shrapnel into the fortress while his machine-guns, mounted in trees, commanded the open spaces inside the boma.

'There is nothing which can come in here', the Hehe had sung, 'unless perhaps there is something which drops from the heavens.' They had no experience of defensive war or European artillery. Their spears were useless, they had few guns, and Mkwawa distributed only 100 of the 300 rifles he had seized from Zelewski. Nobody knew how to operate the two captured machine-guns. Only Swetu's Nyamwezi were experienced marksmen. The Hehe did not sally from the fortress. They knew the power of German firearms and probably expected a long siege like their own investments of Merere's boma, but during the night Prince found a weak spot in the southern wall. At dawn next day, 30 October 1894, he led the assault. The defenders saw two columns make for the southern wall amidst rapid fire from Swetu's men. After ten minutes the Germans broke in, captured the wall, mounted their machine-guns on it, and began to take the town. The Hehe abandoned the western half but defended the eastern section house by house. Mkwawa wanted to die in the inner fortress,

---

[1] Schele, 'Bericht über den bisherigen Verlauf des Feldzuges gegen die Wahehe', 1 December 1894, RKA 285/108. See also Prince, *Araber und Wahehe*, pp. 288–309; Redmayne, 'Mkwawa', pp. 421, 430–1.

but his warriors insisted that he should flee. They followed hastily: of the 250 Hehe killed, most were shot in flight. When he reached a safe distance, it is said, Mkwawa sat and wept. Then he watched the Germans from a nearby hill until they withdrew on 3 November, beating off an ambush by the Chief of Image.

Schele's victory won him the *Pour le Mérite*, Germany's highest military decoration. It also destroyed him. The Reichstag doves attacked his forward policy and the government subordinated the military to the civilian colonial authorities in Berlin. Schele resigned in protest and was followed by two years of weak and pacific government until General Eduard von Liebert inaugurated a new military regime in 1896.[1] In the interim the Germans again sought terms with Mkwawa, and the Hehe, too, proved conciliatory. In October 1895 envoys led by Mkwawa's uncle, Mpoma, signed a treaty which freed captives and ended raiding by both sides, the Hehe agreeing to surrender guns, fly the German flag, and allow free access to Uhehe. When this was presented to Mkwawa he accepted the terms but refused to sign, saying 'it would kill him'. He returned his captives, sent six chiefs to Dar es Salaam, and in April 1896 even sought German aid in disciplining Mbeyela, a Bena chief whose allegiance he claimed.[2]

Then the men on the spot intervened again. German officers still wanted conquest. Mkwawa's request for aid against Mbeyela offered the opportunity. From their posts on the borders the officers converged on Iringa. One was refused access to Mkwawa's palace – 'Here live Mkwawa who tolerates no European' – and was told to pay five guns for entering the country.[3] This violated the treaty and gave Prince his chance. Mkwawa refused to see him or let him build a station anywhere in Uhehe except just within the borders. Meanwhile the chief sought allies, but the long Hehe supremacy stood against him. Mbeyela turned back Mkwawa's emissaries and welcomed a German garrison. Mlamiro of Njelu promised the Germans his neutrality. Chabruma ostentatiously flew a German flag. Finally Prince wearied of negotiations, announced that he was fighting Mkwawa alone, and started to build his station only eleven kilometres from Iringa. Hehe chiefs began to submit. Mkwawa executed

[1] Zimmermann, *Geschichte*, pp. 199–200.
[2] Elpons to Wissmann, 14 October and 18 November 1895, RKA 286/101 and 163; Wissmann to Hohenlohe, 23 December 1895, RKA 287/14; Natzmer to Hohenlohe, 24 August 1896, RKA 287/62.
[3] Natzmer to Hohenlohe, 24 August 1896, RKA 287/62.

two, then withdrew westwards and let his brother Mpangile surrender.[1]

By September 1896 the Hehe were divided. Prince had constructed a peace party of chiefs and installed them in the main chiefdoms. On 10 December, before a thousand unarmed Hehe warriors, Merere of Usangu was re-installed in the capital he had lost 22 years earlier and made ruler of the western half of the former Hehe state. The east was given to Mpangile, who raised the German flag over the ruins of Iringa.[2]

Mkwawa was now an outlaw. Fleeing Iringa in August 1896, he moved westwards towards the Ruaha, evading patrols, still sure of the protection of subjects who 'threw themselves on the advancing soldiers, literally sacrificing themselves to give Mkwawa time to escape'.[3] In December, finding the country too open, he turned south-eastwards into Uzungwa, the high mountain range cloaked with dense rain forest which formed Uhehe's southern and eastern border. From Uzungwa he raided the lowlands for food, ambushed patrols, and attacked German outposts. Aided by Merere's warriors and 'loyal' Hehe, a German force swept Uzungwa in July 1897 and stumbled on Mkwawa's camp. The chief fired once and escaped.[4] Any Hehe aiding him was now subject to the death penalty. The people of Uzungwa were concentrated into strategic hamlets whose fields could be guarded day and night. In November another massive force swept Uzungwa, seizing over a thousand captives and burning Mkwawa's camp. But Mkwawa evaded it and moved into Viransi, the inaccessible heart of the mountains. There, in January 1898, a patrol discovered his whereabouts. Prince hastened to the scene:

The thickness of the forest obliged us to use a path whose last kilometre formed literally a tunnel of foliage. The camp consisted of some 250 huts of the crudest kind, the best of them not even Mkwawa's...We saw it first when we emerged from the tunnel in front of the huts, where we were immediately met by rifle-fire. We charged through the village towards Mkwawa's hut... But at the same moment the village was abandoned... The pursuit brought in a hundred women and children...In many cases the people were mere

[1] Wissmann to Hohenlohe, 16 December 1895, Natzmer to Hohenlohe, 24 August 1896, Prince to Government, 20 September 1896, and Bornhardt to Government, 9 September 1896, RKA 287/9, 62, 115, 136; Adams, *Im Dienste*, p. 48; Magdalene von Prince, *Eine deutsche Frau im Innern Deutsch-Ostafrikas* (3rd edn, Berlin, 1908), chs. 1–2.

[2] 'Auszugsbericht über den Kriegszug des Kompagnieführers bezw. Hauptmann Prince in Uhehe von 12. Juli bis 25. Dezember 1896', RKA 288/25; Prince to Government, 26 January 1897, RKA 288/52.

[3] Prince to Government, 26 January 1897, RKA 288/52.

[4] Liebert to Hohenlohe, 7 September 1897, RKA 288/189.

skeletons. In the whole camp of a thousand souls there was not a single load of grain. Even in Mkwawa's hut were only sweet potatoes.[1]

Mkwawa was now on the move again, living mainly by hunting elephant. Ten days after fleeing his camp he attacked a German outpost at Mtandi, killing its garrison of thirteen before moving on.[2] His route took him through the heart of Uhehe towards the northern border. On 10 July 1898 he crossed the Ruaha into northern Pawaga, the low, torrid, desolate plain which formed the north-western border of Uhehe. He had with him only four young boys and a man from Uzungwa and his wife. Carrying his rifle, Mkwawa reached the house of a man named Kanalire, introduced himself as Fundi Maludi, made blood-brotherhood, and stayed there. Learning of this, the Germans patrolled Pawaga and on 16 July found the Zungwa woman searching for food. She said that Mkwawa was again moving southwards. The Germans hunted unavailingly for his trail. In fact he had recrossed the Ruaha and was trying to make his way back to Uzungwa. On the evening of 18 July, it is said, he shot his Zungwa companion, apparently fearing betrayal. He was now alone except for two young boys, Musigombo and Lifumika Mwamsombwa.

The boys were terrified that Mkwawa might kill them. On the morning of 19 July 1898 Lifumika fled. As he climbed down a hill near Humbwe, half-way between Iringa and the Great Ruaha to the north, he was spotted by a German patrol returning to Iringa to report failure. Lifumika ran but was caught. Forced to talk, he told Sergeant-Major Merkl that Mkwawa lay sick in the bush three hours away. Merkl ordered Lifumika to lead them:

After half an hour we heard a shot in a south-westerly direction. The boy suggested Mkwawa was shooting game. At 2.30 the boy said we were near the camp. We took off our boots and packs and crawled forward on our stomachs to a baobab tree. I climbed this in order to observe, but could see nothing. We crawled further over very stony ground as far as a dry watercourse, in which we saw the camp a hundred metres away. We crawled within thirty metres of it. We now saw two figures lying before it, apparently asleep. The boy pointed out one of them as Mkwawa. Since the stones prevented us getting closer unnoticed, we took aim, fired, and ran forward.

Both figures were dead – the one identified by the boy as Mkwawa, for about one-and-a-half hours: cold but not stiff. *Mzagila* Mnia Urambo identified this body immediately as Mkwawa's. Apparently he had shot himself when we heard the shot previously mentioned. Around his body he wore, besides various medicines, a half-filled cartridge belt. His carbine was considerably

[1] Prince to Kommando, 17 January 1898, RKA 289/19.
[2] Prince to Kommando, 29 January 1898, RKA 289/31.

cracked at the muzzle and in places much charred in the fire beside him. Musigombo's body was already completely stiff. Beside him lay a sporting rifle. Between them the two bodies carried 117 cartridges. My caravan soon arrived. The Hehe recognised Mkwawa immediately and remained for a long time in dejected silence.[1]

The consolidation of German rule

When Mkwawa died in 1898 the Germans controlled all Tanganyika's main population centres and lines of communication. Their next task was to extend their authority over the many small-scale societies remote from the caravan routes. This required a welter of local violence which defies detailed description, but certain general points can be isolated.

First, the extension of German control was essentially a local process. Military commanders and African leaders made bargains or fought wars in which ignorance, ambition, and sheer accident were far more important than large policy considerations. The establishment of German control on the eastern shore of Lake Victoria is an example. The main cause of disturbance in this region was the southward migration of the Luo. It led a threatened Kuria headman, Kibore Machera, and a Jita leader, Nyakulinga of Munguru, to seek the aid of German troops from Mwanza. During 1898 Captain Schlobach toured the region and established almost arbitrary relations with its peoples. In Buzanaki he was welcomed by Sange of Bumangi, known to the Germans as Kirangozi because he agreed to guide Schlobach's expedition. Other Zanaki resisted until their main leader, Monge, sent an embassy to offer submission, only for the ambassador, Fundi Kanyeka, to secure recognition as an independent ruler. In Majita Schlobach recognised Nyakulinga as chief. In Bukuria he was welcomed by Kibore Machera, but the Sweta group resisted strongly from a stone-walled hilltop fortress until overcome. 'Continuing our march', one of Schlobach's auxiliaries recalled, 'we met large hordes of raiding Kavirondo [Luo] natives, but these having heard of Suruba's [Schlobach's] victory over the Basweta did not assume the offensive.'[2] The expedition's original purpose – to chastise the Luo –

---

[1] Merkl to Iringa, 22 July 1898, RKA 289/64. There are further details in Gordon to CS, 31 August 1920, CO 691/36/35. For a remarkable but untrustworthy reconstruction, see Mwenyi Shomari bin Mwenyi Kambi, 'Kufa kwa Mkwawa', in Velten, 'Gedichte', pp. 152–74.

[2] D. C. MacGillivray, 'History of European settlement and government...through the eyes of Kiyumbi, native of Mwagalla' (1931), in Maswa district book, TNA.

had disappeared. But careers had been made and broken, political systems distorted and recast, and men killed and maimed throughout the region.[1]

The early German regime much resembled a new 'empire of the *rugaruga*'. It used its bands of gunmen to maintain authority over compliant local leaders much as Mirambo had done, and its 'conquest' was often an extension of tribal war in which the Germans shared the plunder. Captain Johannes' 'expeditions' around Kilimanjaro always showed a financial profit, carefully accounted.[2] In such situations conquest was not an event but a process. The Matengo who inhabited the mountains between Songea and Lake Nyasa provide a good example. When the Germans founded their military station at Songea in 1897 the two main Matengo leaders were Howahowa of Langiro and Mandawa of Litembo. Mandawa was summoned to Songea in 1897 and given a flag. Next year a German officer found the Matengo friendly. Then European pressure increased. In 1899 missionaries settled in the mountains. Two years later askari began to press people to carry lime to Songea to help build the boma. A few houses were burned and anger rose. When the next askari entered Litembo, in March 1902, the people tore the badges off his uniform and sent him hurrying back to Songea. Sergeant Müller arrived with fourteen askari, found 800 armed men, and withdrew hastily to a nearby hill. Three days later the full German force appeared. Now the Matengo retreated to a hilltop fortress which they defended with arrows, spears, and stones until they had lost forty men. Mandawa fled, was captured, escaped, was captured again, taken to Songea, fined, reinstated, and finally deposed in 1904 in favour of a more compliant brother. From 1904, perhaps, one may say that the Matengo were conquered.[3]

Stateless societies were easy to defeat but difficult to rule. The Sandawe were such a people. The first German visitors to Usandawe reported that such authority as existed there was wielded by Mtoro, leader of a recently-established Nyamwezi colony. The officer in far-off Kilimatinde therefore made Mtoro headman of Usandawe. His settlement, Kwa Mtoro, became the headquarters of the region. The Sandawe loathed the Nyamwezi settlers, however, and expelled them in 1902, seizing their cattle. Lieutenant Kohlermann entered Usan-

[1] Schlobach, 'Bericht über die Expedition Magalla, Ntussu, Nassa, Uschaschi u.s.w.', 20 September 1898, RKA 289/128.
[2] Johannes, 'Bericht über die Expedition nach dem Meru-Berg vom 31. Oktober bis 20. November 1896', RKA 287/161.
[3] Kigonsera mission diary, 1901–4, Peramiho archives.

117

dawe and killed 800 men in three days without suffering a casualty.[1]
A second expedition captured 1,100 cattle and gave most of them
to the Nyamwezi. The district commander reported progress:

The rock-strewn land of Usandawe, 3–6 days march N.E. of the station, is
inhabited by a still thoroughly uncivilised, warlike, predatory, and unexplored
mountain people whose members do not recognise German rule, live far apart,
tolerate no headmen or superiors, and have hitherto rid themselves in drastic
fashion of those experimentally installed by the station. In the valleys live loyal,
agriculturally most productive, taxable Nyamwezi, who are incessantly
harrassed by the wholly unproductive Sandawe.

Among the Sandawe revolts which the history of the colony shows to be
annual occurrences, last year's was energetically subdued, so that after its
repression a few Sandawe appeared at the station – for the first time since its
establishment – to demonstrate their submission.[2]

Encouraged, he withdrew his military contingent from Kwa Mtoro.
The Sandawe attacked it as it retreated, harried the Nyamwezi again,
and announced their willingness to take on a new expedition. Further
massive bloodshed followed until the post at Kwa Mtoro was made
permanent and Sergeant Linke 'pacified' the region. 'A single man,
Herr Linke, brings us famine', sang the Sandawe; '. . . Our country
is dying out. . . We are losing all our dances.' Linke chose 22 headmen,
mainly from the rainmaking clan. The Sandawe now had chiefs. 'If
anyone defies my orders', one said, 'I will appeal to the European.
He is a man who punishes with fetters and the whip. . . Therefore, my
people, see that you live in peace.'[3]

To the end of their occupation, German rule was spread most
unevenly over Tanganyika. Many *Grenzwildnisse* remained almost
entirely ungoverned. As late as 1911 the government killed 548 Ha
before deciding that Buha was not worth taxing.[4] In the more settled
regions, however, the Germans had created an administration.[5] Soden
converted the main coastal towns into headquarters of administrative
districts and appointed civilian district officers. Further inland administration also grew outwards from strategic garrisons but was
transferred to civilian hands more slowly. In 1914 Tanganyika was
divided into 22 administrative districts of which two – Iringa and
Mahenge – were still ruled by soldiers. The chief characteristic of
German rule was the power and autonomy of the district officer. Sheer

[1] Baumann, *Masailand*, p. 193; Stuhlmann to AAKA, 12 December 1902, RKA 699/105b.
[2] Nigmann to Government, 30 May 1903, TNA G55/8.
[3] Dempwolff, *Sandawe*, pp. 168–9, 111.
[4] Methner to RKA, 2 December 1911, RKA 702/165.
[5] This account is based on Iliffe, *German rule*, ch. 7.

lack of communications dictated this. Orders from the capital might take months to reach remote districts. Telegraph wires reached Mikindani in 1897, Mwanza in 1905, Iringa in 1910. In August 1914 the district officer in Tukuyu had to ask his British counterpart in Nyasaland whether they were at war.[1] No provincial commissioners supervised district officers. A remote station could expect a visit from a senior official only once a decade. The district officer exercised full jurisdiction over 'natives', for although legislation specified the punishments he might impose, nothing defined the offences for which he might impose them. Officers were encouraged to remain in one post. Major Willibald von Stuemer administered Bukoba from 1904 to 1916. In 1914 seven of the twenty district officers had held their posts for seven years or more. Their rule was openly based on force and few travelled without armed escorts. Their offices were massive bomas sited to command the best fields of fire. That the district officer *was* the government was to be vividly displayed during the Maji Maji rebellion of 1905, when many district offices were attacked but no serious threat was made to the capital. With their brutal soldiers and police, German officials inspired great terror. In 1903 the Chief of Mkulwe hid for three weeks in the bush when told that a single askari was approaching. Six years later Chagga children were reported to be making toy machine-guns. Violence bred fear, and so did the sheer incomprehensible arbitrariness of European behaviour. 'Why were they imprisoned?' an old woman was asked. 'For nothing', she replied, '...It was the European who imprisoned them.'[2]

Two broad phases of district administration can be identified in German times. In the 1890s its aims were military security and political control and its methods were violence and alliance with accommodating African leaders. The search for collaborators led to a new balance of forces in each region, a rearrangement of power and privilege within and between societies. These 'local compromises', as they may be called, had common characteristics. The administration's demands were small: recognition of German paramountcy, provision of labour and building materials, use of diplomacy rather than force in settling disputes. In return the Germans offered equally limited advantages: normally only political and military support for their allies. The relationship demanded little change in the societies

[1] Charles Hordern, *Military operations, East Africa*, 1 (London, 1941), p. 170 n. 1.
[2] *Chronique trimestrielle de la Société des Missionnaires d'Afrique*, October 1903; Raum, *Childhood*, p. 284 n. 1; Mlachuma binti Simbo in MMRP 1/68/2/4/5/2.

concerned. Stateless peoples had to accept headmen. Many chiefdoms had to accept changes in leadership. But even those who allied with the Germans generally saw them as a new factor in existing conflicts, not yet as making those conflicts redundant. Tanganyika in 1898 was still in the diplomatic phase of colonial rule. The core of each local compromise was the emergence of collaborators who often exercised a form of sub-imperialism over former rivals. In return the sub-imperialists provided the support and services which made European rule possible. Marealle dominated eastern Kilimanjaro and supplied Johannes with auxiliaries. Kiwanga and Merere encroached on Mkwawa's kingdom while helping to hunt him down.

The imposition of tax in 1898,[1] together with Mkwawa's death, initiated a transition to a second phase of administration whose chief characteristic was the collapse of the local compromises established in the 1890s. The old collaborators did not necessarily lose power, but to survive they had to adapt themselves and often to reorganise their societies. Local compromises collapsed for three main reasons.[2] One was the Germans' growing military security, which made them less dependent on powerful allies. Where earlier officers often welcomed their collaborators' power, later ones suspected it. This happened to Mtinginya of Usongo, a powerful Nyamwezi chief who had aided the Germans against Isike. By 1901 he headed the district commander's list of potential adversaries, and when Mtinginya died a year or two later, his chiefdom was deliberately dismantled.[3]

Another solvent of local compromises was the fact that sub-imperialism could itself become a source of danger once its victims recovered from defeat and substituted intrigue for spears. Marealle suffered such a fate. The most powerful ruler Kilimanjaro had known, he was too successful. By destroying his rivals he made his military support less necessary. His very skill in intrigue aroused German suspicions. His exploitation of Rombo clashed with the needs of the European farmers who settled on Kilimanjaro after 1900 and also wanted Rombo's labour. These tensions culminated in 1904 in a crisis whose details are still obscure. Either Chief Sengua of Mashati in Rombo or ex-Chief Mbararia of Mwika – both Marealle's enemies – persuaded the district commander that Marealle was planning a revolt with Masai backing. The officer panicked, arrested several of Mare-

[1] Below, pp. 133–4.
[2] In the south the Maji Maji rebellion was a fourth. See below, p. 200.
[3] Gausser to Government, 30 March 1901, RKA 1030/96; F. W. Bampfylde, 'Tribal government' (1934), in Nzega district book, TNA.

alle's councillors, and warned local Europeans that a rising was imminent. Friendly missionaries passed this on to Marealle. Knowing how dangerous the Germans were when frightened, Marealle fled to Kenya. He later returned to rule Marangu, but his paramountcy over other chiefdoms was abolished.[1]

Marealle's experience also illustrates the third reason for the collapse of the local compromise: the tension between the needs of political control and the needs of efficient administration.[2] Control required powerful allies with obedient followings. Administration required efficient agents who could impose uncongenial innovations. Only rarely could one man fulfil both functions successfully as the Germans began to make more extensive demands on their subjects. Tax-collecting was the most important innovation. 'The old rainmaker is not to be converted into an autocrat by artificial means', a district officer wrote when explaining why Sukuma chiefs could not collect tax.[3] The dilemma was most acute in previously stateless societies. Government-appointed headmen in Unyaturu often found they could remit tax only by paying much of it themselves and recouping in other ways.[4] But the same pressures also affected major chiefs. In 1902 Kinyashi of Usambara abdicated rather than face the unpopularity and possible witchcraft which he incurred by implementing German demands for tax and labour.[5]

Not all the early collaborators lost power. There were two ways of surviving. In remote areas where administrative demands were minimal, unswerving political loyalty could still win freedom to resist such uncongenial innovations as mission schools. Kasusura of Rusubi in Buzinza survived the whole German period in this way, but at the cost of seeing his country degenerate into a tsetse-infested and famine-stricken backwater. For those closer to German control, however, survival required positive acceptance of innovation. Some Haya chiefs were especially successful at this, for they controlled elaborate administrative systems which the Germans were anxious to preserve. Kahigi of Kianja survived by loyal and efficient rule and active support for economic development, although he opposed

---

[1] Correspondence in RKA 1033; Haber to Government, 5 March 1905, RKA 700/93; Willmann, 'Bericht über den Missionar Schanz', 25 December 1904, TNA G9/31/105; *Evangelisch-Lutherisches Missionsblatt*, March 1905; Stahl, *History*, pp. 333–4.
[2] I have taken this formulation from G. M. A. Bakheit, 'British administration and Sudanese nationalism 1919–1939', Ph.D. thesis, Cambridge University, 1965, p. 183.
[3] Gunzert, 'Jahresbericht Muanza mit Schirati 1908/09', TNA G1/5.
[4] Eberhard von Sick, 'Die Waniaturu', *Baessler-Archiv*, v (1915), 59–60.
[5] Feierman, 'Concepts', p. 397.

education and mission work. His rival, Mutahangarwa of Kiziba, took adaptation further and actively welcomed education, thus giving Kiziba a lead over the rest of Buhaya, although he refused to become a Christian himself and disinherited his eldest son for doing so.[1]

Conquest and response dominated Tanganyika's political history during the 1890s. The transition to adaptation initiated a more constructive phase of colonialism, but the experience of defeat and alien rule remained traumatic. Generations earlier the hunter of wild pig, Mbegha, had killed a lion and become king in Vugha. In 1896 the women of Vugha exclaimed, 'Where once a lion sat, there is now a pig.'[2]

[1] Iliffe, *German rule*, pp. 171–4.
[2] Steven Feierman, 'The Shambaa', in Roberts, *Tanzania*, p. 13.

CHAPTER 5

Colonial economy and ecological crisis, 1890–1914

Two processes dominated Tanganyika's economic history under German rule. One was the re-ordering of economies into a colonial pattern, just as they had previously been re-ordered around trade with Zanzibar. The colonial economy took over certain nineteenth-century structures – notably the lines of communication – but was otherwise sharply discontinuous with pre-colonial economic patterns. Nineteenth-century structures were not easily broken, however. It was not until railway-building accelerated in the early 1900s that a recognisably colonial economy emerged.

Alongside this process went a more dramatic experience. European invasion accelerated Tanganyika's incorporation into the world's disease environment as well as its economy. The last decade of the nineteenth century was a time of appalling natural disaster. To European occupation and intensified warfare were added human and animal diseases, locust invasions, drought, and famine, on a scale unparalleled in traditions of earlier periods. Immediate suffering and probable demographic decline were followed by an expansion of the natural ecosystem of bush, game, and parasites at the expense of men, livestock, and cultivation.

The central problem of Tanganyika's economic history in this period is to identify the relationship between the impact of capitalism and ecological change. Hypotheses must be tentative, for research has only recently begun and the available evidence is inadequate. There are no reliable population figures, for example, while the German government's statistics, although copious and superficially exact, are probably trustworthy only where they concern foreign trade. Nevertheless, the colonial government's records in Tanzanian and German archives provide a wealth of information not available for earlier periods.

Disaster and survival in the 1890s

A decade of natural catastrophes opened when rinderpest (cattle plague) entered northern Tanganyika early in 1891, having apparently been introduced into Ethiopia in diseased cattle bought from India by the Italian army. Fatal to livestock and many game species, rinderpest often killed 90–95 per cent of the cattle: all but 35 of the 600 at the Bukoba military station, all but a hundred of the several thousand beasts in Unyanyembe, and, according to legend, every bull in Bukuria save one delighted animal.[1] Pastoralists such as the Masai suffered most: .

There were women wasted to skeletons from whose eyes the madness of starvation glared...'warriors' scarcely able to crawl on all fours, and apathetic, languishing elders. These people ate anything. Dead donkeys were a feast for them, but they did not disdain bones, hides, and even the horns of the cattle...Parents offered us children to buy for a scrap of meat, and when we refused the exchange they cunningly hid the children near the camp and made off.[2]

Estimates of Masai deaths ranged from two-fifths to three-quarters of the entire people, the warriors surviving best. Ancient enemies – Mbugwe, Iraqw, and the like – slaughtered and dispersed the survivors. Some 'went Dorobo' and hunted the diminished game. Others sought refuge with Arusha, Chagga, or Sukuma and turned to agriculture.[3]

The consequences of rinderpest extended far beyond immediate hunger and death. In the north-west it broke the power of Karagwe's pastoral aristocrats. 'Sad as a Mtusi woman' became a common proverb. Competition for the few surviving cattle intensified local warfare. Merere raided Unyakyusa in 1892 to replenish his herds and many of Mkwawa's campaigns probably had the same motive. Cattle were both capital and the cement of social relations, especially marriage. There are indications of subsequent malnutrition, especially among children.[4]

With rinderpest came smallpox. It killed 600 people – a tenth of the population – in Dar es Salaam during 1893. Then a new plague

---

[1] Ford, *Trypanosomiases*, pp. 138–40; Langheld, *Zwanzig Jahre*, p. 93; Sigl to Government, 1 January 1892, RKA 639/114; information from Dr M. Ruel.

[2] Baumann, *Masailand*, pp. 31–2.

[3] *Ibid.*, pp. 165–6; Jacobs, 'Pastoral Masai', pp. 95–9; Widenmann, *Kilimandscharo-Bevölkerung*, p. 90.

[4] Katoke, *Karagwe*, ch. 11; information from Fr Nolan; Marcia Wright, *German missions in Tanganyika 1891–1941* (Oxford, 1971), p. 49; Kjekshus, *Ecology control*, p. 138.

arrived: sand fleas or jiggers, originally from Latin America, which ate into hands and feet, causing appalling injuries. Finally came the locusts. Many regions had experienced them before, but the plague of the 1890s seems to have been exceptionally widespread. They appeared three times: first in 1893–5, when almost every part of the country suffered; then in 1897–9, when most areas were affected but especially Usukuma and the north-east; and finally a smaller visitation in 1903–4, largely confined to the north-east.[1] In Bonde the locusts arrived in April 1894 and ate the first crops sown.[2] In June they destroyed the second sowing and famine became serious. Many Bondei sought work in Tanga, leaving only the old in the villages. By October many depended on food distributed by the Anglican mission. In December 1894 and again in April 1895 locusts returned and destroyed the growing crops. 'The old folk are dying off', a missionary reported. Then in July 1895 the plague retreated, a good harvest was reaped, and grain prices fell. The respite was brief. The locusts returned in January 1898, followed by a drought which killed even the manioc. Bonde experienced a 'famine that kills':

Many people died anyhow in their wanderings in search of food. Strong folk did porter's work and so secured money with which to buy food, but many separated from their wives because they were no longer able to support them. When they went away as porters they did not return home, in order to escape the cries of their children. Mothers lost their love and pity for the children they were suckling and left their children to their husbands and ran away, never to return. These were days when everyone was concerned only with his own welfare.[3]

A Bondei woman put it more simply: 'People are dying everywhere like animals, two and two.'[4] Elsewhere the famine's severity was captured in its remembered names: 'the wide and extended one', 'famine of the bush', 'famine of the legs', 'scraping coconuts', and, simply, 'locusts'.[5]

Disease and famine, together with widespread armed resistance, helped to delay the restructuring of Tanganyika's economies into a colonial mould. The impetus to do so was in any case weak during

[1] Kjekshus, *Ecology control*, pp. 132–6, 138–40.
[2] The following account is based on *Central Africa*, 1894–9.
[3] Samuel Sehoza in *ibid.*, March 1933.   [4] Blandina Limo in *ibid.*, June 1899.
[5] S. von Sicard, *The Lutheran Church on the coast of Tanzania 1887–1914* (Lund, 1970), pp. 124–5, 132 n. 1; John Salaita, 'Colonialism and underdevelopment in Unyanyembe ca. 1900–1960', M.A. thesis, University of Dar es Salaam, 1975, p. 30; A. O. Anacleti, 'Pastoralism and development: economic changes in pastoral industry in Serengeti 1750–1961', M.A. thesis, University of Dar es Salaam, 1975, p. 32; Rigby, *Cattle*, p. 21.

the 1890s. Bismarck had not acquired the territory because Germany had any immediate economic need for it. Germany had little surplus capital for overseas investment and there were many more enticing outlets for it than Tanganyika, which consequently suffered an acute shortage of investment, especially in this early period. The financiers who controlled the DOAG undertook in 1891 to build a railway inland from Tanga to Korogwe, but they laid only forty kilometres of unsatisfactory track before its cost obliged them to abandon the project to the government in 1899.[1] By 1901 the DOAG had invested £169,000 in plantations and received only £13,650 in return. Not until 1904 did it begin to make substantial profits. No plantation company showed a profit before 1902, when European enterprises produced only an estimated 13 per cent of the colony's exports.[2] Their main product was coffee, and indeed for Europeans the 1890s were dominated by disillusionment with the coffee crop.

The DOAG and its associates concentrated their plantation experiments in the north-east, the only region where a substantial highland area, Usambara, was close to the coast. The Shambaa civil war had depopulated large areas of Usambara which seemed suitable for settlement,[3] while the existence of rival parties led by Semboja and Kibanga facilitated European intervention. Usambara therefore became the goal of the railway from Tanga. In August 1891 the DOAG established the colony's first coffee plantation at Derema in the foothills of East Usambara. By 1895 there were fifteen plantations in the region. Seven were on the coast and produced copra. The remainder grew coffee in Bonde or East Usambara.[4]

Land alienation in the Usambara region escaped the government's control because the DOAG had concessionary rights there and African leaders claimed vast unoccupied areas. Kibanga leased the Rheinische-Handei Plantagengesellschaft some four thousand hectares for a hundred years at less than two cents per hectare per year. His nephew, Kinyashi, sold even larger areas to the DOAG. One Kurt Hoffmann bought 20,000 hectares from the DOAG in 1896 with the object of 'creating myself a small principality'.[5] The scandal continued until Wissmann returned as governor in 1895 and ordained that

[1] M. F. Hill, *Permanent way* (2 vols, Nairobi, 1950–7), II, 62–6.
[2] Rainer Tetzlaff, *Koloniale Entwicklung und Ausbeutung: Wirtschafts- und Sozialgeschichte Deutsch-Ostafrikas 1885–1914* (Berlin, 1970), pp. 59–60; *Koloniale Rundschau*, IV (1912), 506; Wilhelm Arning, *Deutsch Ostafrika, gestern und heute* (Berlin, 1936), p. 339.
[3] Baumann, *Usambara*, p. 292.   [4] *RTA*, 1895/7, no. 88, pp. 880–2.
[5] Correspondence in TNA MPG 2233 and LR Dar es Salaam 12; Hoffmann to RKA, 3 December 1909, RKA 366/117.

Africans owned only the land they cultivated, that they could not alienate land without the governor's approval, and that all other land was 'ownerless Crown Land' which only the government could distribute. He then called a meeting in January 1896 to investigate existing claims. The most extravagant were rejected or curtailed; the remainder were confirmed as 100-year leaseholds, with the option of purchase once cultivated.[1] Wissmann thus corrected the worst abuses and established a procedure to prevent further speculation. But he was too late to prevent the alienation of enormous areas of virgin land in East Usambara and Bonde, which became the centre of Tanganyika's plantation agriculture. By 1911 the DOAG's 'Union' plantation complex encompassed 110 square kilometres of East Usambara and more than a dozen other holdings of over twenty square kilometres existed in Tanga district alone.[2]

In 1896 slightly less than a thousand Europeans lived in Tanganyika. Only 55 were agriculturalists.[3] Perhaps the only true settler – a permanent farmer on his own land rather than a plantation manager on contract – was Ludwig Illich, who farmed in the mountains of West Usambara. There the best land lay in relatively small patches in valleys overlooked by Shambaa hilltop villages. This and its cool climate made West Usambara more suitable for private farming than large plantations. In the late 1890s further settlers arrived and the governor ordered that all vacant land in Usambara west of Vugha should be reserved for farms not larger than two hundred hectares. By January 1904 there were 186 Europeans in Lushoto district, mostly in the mountains.[4]

The pioneer faced grave obstacles. From railhead at Korogwe (opened in March 1902) he organised a caravan to carry his goods further along the Pangani and then up the escarpment into the mountains. Having located his farm, his first task was to build a mud hut for protection from the approaching rains. This done, he laid out a small vegetable garden and purchased a few local cattle. Only then could he turn to his main business, which was to supervise Shambaa workers whose hoes prepared the shallow, stony soil of the plantation for the coffee bushes on which the pioneer's future depended. The

[1] *Die Landesgesetzgebung des Deutsch-Ostafrikanischen Schutzgebiets* (2 vols, Dar es Salaam, 1911), I, 212–8; Protokoll, Tanga, 18–21 January 1896, TNA MPG 3498.
[2] List of plantations in Tanga district, 17 June 1912, TNA MPG 6316.
[3] *RTA*, 1895/7, no. 624, p. 2,969.
[4] Liebert to Wilhelmstal, 3 July 1899, TNA BA Wilhelmstal xxv/A/I; *RTA*, 1903/5, no. 540, p. 3,011.

government warned him to bring a minimum of £450 capital and not to expect a profit for at least three years. '*Impecunious Europeans*', it warned, '*have not the slightest chance of success.*'[1]

These warnings rested on unhappy experience. In 1903 Lushoto district office reported that not a single settler had yet made a profit. The main problem was the cash crop, coffee. In the eight years after 1890 its world price halved, declining further to an absolute minimum in 1910. While Brazilian producers were throwing sacks of coffee into the Atlantic there was little chance of establishing a profitable industry in remote Usambara. Moreover, Usambara was a poor environment for coffee. The lower land was too hot and dry, while West Usambara was too cool and damp. Both had shallow, acidic soils which produced only low yields, a quarter of those later obtained on Kilimanjaro. In 1903 German East Africa exported only 337,344 kg of coffee worth £36,546. And this was the supposed vanguard of colonial enterprise.[2]

In reality much of Tanganyika's nineteenth-century economic structure survived into the twentieth century. Attempts to detach the mainland from dependence on Zanzibar failed. In 1902 Zanzibar still took 67 per cent of German East Africa's exports and supplied 57 per cent of its imports. Not until 1899 did the German East African Line – a subsidised shipping firm partly owned by the DOAG – begin to ship goods directly from Europe to Tanganyika. Wm. O'Swald and Company, the longest-established German firm in East Africa, did not move its headquarters from Zanzibar to the mainland until 1902.[3] It is true that Bagamoyo's share of total foreign trade fell between 1890 and 1903 from over 40 to 24 per cent while Dar es Salaam's rose from 9 to 25 per cent,[4] but the figures concealed an important difference. The capital's trade was almost entirely in goods imported for European consumption. Only government caravans used the port. By contrast, Bagamoyo remained the colony's main export harbour at the terminus of the central caravan route. The towns themselves illustrated the contrast. Popularly known as Little Potsdam, the capital contained some 20,000 people at the turn of the century.[5] Its European, Asian,

[1] *Auskunft für Ansiedler in Usambara und anderen Gebieten von Deutsch-Ostafrika* (1902): copy in TNA BA Wilhelmstal xxv/A/1.
[2] *RTA*, 1903/5, no. 540, pp. 3,080–5; Iliffe, *German rule*, p. 68.
[3] Heinrich Brode, *British and German East Africa* (London, 1911), appx. A; Liebert to AAKA, 6 October 1899, TNA G1/28/107; O'Swald to Dernburg, 20 March 1907, RKA 641/50.
[4] Tetzlaff, *Entwicklung*, p. 185; *RTA*, 1903/5, no. 540, pp. 2,964–5.
[5] *RTA*, 1900/2, no. 437, p. 2,966.

and 'Native' quarters were already largely distinct. A curfew prohibited non-Europeans from entering the European quarter after 10.00 p.m. The town's whole life revolved around the government offices. By contrast, Bagamoyo's population remained static at 10,000–15,000 throughout the 1890s. Four hundred Arabs, nearly a thousand Asians, and more than a thousand domestic slaves diversified a population whose social hierarchy still rested on commerce, slave-owning, and Islam.[1] When O'Swalds moved their headquarters from Zanzibar in 1902 they settled in Bagamoyo.

Statistics of the caravan trade for the early 1890s are scarce and unreliable, while for the late 1890s they are copious and contradictory. In the 1880s some 100,000 people a year may have travelled the caravan route running through Mpwapwa between Tabora and Bagamoyo.[2] At the turn of the century the number was probably much the same. Between 1901 and 1904 an average of 21,131 porters arrived at Bagamoyo each year and 32,647 departed – according to official figures.[3] Sadani's caravan trade may have declined by half between 1896 and 1902.[4] On the other hand, Dar es Salaam became an important depot when the government transferred its traffic there from Bagamoyo in 1894. Between 1901 and 1903 it despatched an average of 17,971 loads inland each year, roughly balancing the decline in Bagamoyo and Sadani.[5] Thus the caravan trade of the Mrima appears to have remained broadly stable from 1890 to the early 1900s. Figures for inland centres support this impression. In 1903 some 29,395 porters passed through Mpwapwa from the coast and 24,382 in the opposite direction.[6] The figures for Tabora are more fragmentary, but the 19,955 people who left the town in caravans for the coast in 1904 may be compared with the 15,000–20,000 Nyamwezi said to visit the coast each year as porters in the 1880s.[7] For the northern caravan route there is little useful evidence. Figures are also scarce in the south, but there the evidence suggests that after the slave raids and Ngoni expeditions of the nineteenth century, German rule brought a brief prosperity until the Maji Maji rebellion of 1905. This region was the centre of the rubber trade which flourished in the 1890s and a traveller noted that the Ngindo, who collected much of the rubber,

---

[1] *RTA*, 1898/1900, no. 50, p. 226.   [2] Above, p. 45.
[3] *RTA*, 1903/5, no. 540, p. 2,961; *RTA*, 1905/6, no. 175, p. 2,722; *RTA*, 1907/9, no. 41, p. 39.
[4] *RTA*, 1897/8, no. 94, p. 958; *RTA*, 1907/9, no. 41, p. 39; *RTA*, 1903/5, no. 540, p. 2,961.
[5] *RTA*, 1903/5, no. 540, p. 2,961.
[6] *Ibid.*, p. 2,962.
[7] *RTA*, 1905/6, no. 175, p. 2,723; above, p. 44.

were very much better clothed than other inland peoples.[1] The south-east also continued to supply Zanzibar and other coastal ports with grain. 'At the time of the millet harvest', it was reported in 1898, 'innumerable tiny stores are set up in the millet districts by coastal people who take a small parcel of goods on credit from Indians.'[2] In that year Kilwa exported nearly 1,500,000 kg of millet. Prosperity swelled the caravan statistics. Kilwa despatched 5,050 loads into the interior in 1897, rising in 1903 to 11,334, of which 2,832 went to Ungindo, 1,952 to Mahenge, and 2,515 to Songea.[3] The Maji Maji rebellion was to take place in the one area of the colony which was clearly prospering.

Like the caravan trade, the overall level of German East Africa's foreign trade remained fairly constant during the 1890s. Exports fell from an annual average of £334,878 in 1890–3 (a figure swollen by ivory reserves accumulated during the coastal resistance) to £214,878 in 1894–7 and £209,415 in 1898–1900. Average imports for the same periods were £412,783, £403,020, and £578,461.[4] Imports of cotton cloth, the best indicator of African purchasing power, rose from an annual average of £169,765 in 1892–5 to £242,104 in 1897–1900.[5] Products of hunting and gathering rather than agriculture remained the export staples. Yet beneath these overall figures economic patterns were changing. Throughout the period the colony's most valuable products were ivory and wild rubber, but whereas in 1892–4 ivory provided 43 per cent of exports and rubber 12 per cent, the equivalent figures in 1900–2 were 18 and 23 per cent.[6] Most of Tanganyika's elephants had been exterminated in the nineteenth century. After 1890 the closing of political borders strangled the remaining trade. By 1891 little ivory was reaching Tabora from Zaire. Ujiji was soon deep in depression. Western Uganda was shut off by the British. German game laws put hunting beyond the reach of a poor and law-abiding man. The staple product of the nineteenth-century economy became a trophy for wealthy tourists. By contrast, rubber boomed. The 1890s – the 'red rubber' decade in King Leopold's

[1]   Adams, *Im Dienste*, p. 132.   [2]   *RTA*, 1898/1900, no. 518, p. 2,892.
[3]   *RTA*, 1898/1900, no. 50, p. 228; *RTA*, 1903/5, no. 540, p. 2,962; Rode to Government, 19 May 1903, TNA G1/29/52.
[4]   Liebert to AAKA, 6 October 1899, TNA G1/28/107; *RTA*, 1900/2, no. 437, p. 2,922; *RTA*, 1903/5, no. 54, p. 98.
[5]   *RTA*, 1895/7, no. 88, p. 885; *RTA*, 1895/7, no. 624, p. 2,977; *RTA*, 1900/2, no. 152, p. 952; *RTA*, 1900/2, no. 437, pp. 2,980–1.
[6]   *RTA*, 1895/7, no. 88, pp. 884–5; *RTA*, 1900/2, no. 437, pp. 2,982–3; *RTA*, 1900/2, no. 814, pp. 5,360–1; *RTA*, 1903/5, no. 54, pp. 202–5.

Congo – saw a great hunt for wild rubber throughout the world. German East Africa's rubber exports grew from an average annual value of £34,482 in 1892–4 to £90,682 in 1902–4.[1] Roughly a third was smuggled from Zaire, but the main sources were in the southern hinterland: the densely-wooded highlands on either side of the Lukuledi and Kilombero rivers. 'Where much rubber is collected', it was reported, 'cultivation generally leaves a good deal to be desired.'[2] Another forest product whose collection had ill effects on agriculture was beeswax, whose annual exports averaged £13,457 between 1902 and 1904. In the past, it was observed, Mwera had collected honey and thrown away the wax; now they collected wax and discarded honey.[3]

The replacement of ivory by rubber may have benefited commoners at the expense of rulers, as has been suggested for the Ngoni.[4] It is more certain that the first decade of German rule destroyed the wealth and influence of slave-owners. By the end of the century slave-trading survived only in the most remote regions. Two slave markets existed in the Heru chiefdom of Buha as late as 1903, but whereas the courts imposed an average of 43 sentences a year for slaving between 1894 and 1900, the equivalent figure for 1905–12 was only four a year.[5] The government's approach to slavery as a social institution was more cautious. Officials were empowered to free slaves who complained of maltreatment. Slaves could also buy their freedom, the normal price for an uneducated adult being Shs. 40–67 on the coast and Shs. 33 in the interior. Between 1891 and 1912, 52,313 certificates of freedom were issued, the annual number increasing from an average of 880 in 1891–6 to 3,890 in 1907–12. Purchase by slaves accounted for 40 per cent of the certificates, while 24 per cent were freed by the government and 36 per cent by their owners.[6] Many doubtless gained freedom without the government's knowledge. In addition, government decreed that all children born after 31 December 1905 were automatically free. But district officers hunted down slaves who simply fled their masters.[7] In 1912 government estimated that 165,000 slaves

---

[1] *RTA*, 1895/7, no. 88, p. 885; *RTA*, 1903/5, no. 54, pp. 202–5; *RTA*, 1903/5, no. 540, pp. 3,080–5; *RTA*, 1905/6, no. 175, pp. 2,816–9, 2,828–9.
[2] Quoted in Tetzlaff, *Entwicklung*, p. 73.
[3] *RTA*, 1903–5, no. 54, pp. 202–5; *RTA*, 1903/5, no. 540, pp. 3,080–5; *RTA*, 1905/6, no. 175, pp. 2,816–9; *RTA*, 1898/1900, no. 518, p. 2,892.
[4] Redmond, 'Political history', pp. 202–3.
[5] Kummer to Ujiji, 16 January 1903, RKA 290/235; Fritz Weidner, *Die Haussklaverei in Ostafrika* (Jena, 1915), p. 101.
[6] Weidner, *Haussklaverei*, pp. 138–40.
[7] *Landesgesetzgebung*, I, 332; information from Fr Nolan.

still existed, but this was merely a guess. British officials later declared the figure a gross exaggeration, but after the First World War they estimated that 1,000 slaves survived in Pangani district, 1,500 in Tanga, and 4,000 in Kilwa and Mafia.[1]

The Arab planters of the coastal hinterland suffered most from the decline of slavery. The sugar planters of the lower Pangani were slowly ruined. In 1894 the 105 Arab planters there, with 1,000–1,200 slaves, exported 1,250,000 kg of crude sugar. Locusts devastated the crop in the late 1890s. Much land passed through mortgage to Asian financiers. The DOAG's attempt to establish a processing factory failed in 1903. As their slave holdings fell, the Arabs lacked the resources and attitudes to become capitalists. In 1908 the area's sugar exports were only 10,381 kg and the industry had almost disappeared.[2]

Two further symptoms of the advancing colonial economy were visible during the 1890s: monetisation and taxation. Considering the extent of commercial activity, the use of money was surprisingly rare before 1890, but the Germans gave monetisation high priority, paying their employees in cash and gradually demanding that tax should be paid in specie and not in kind. Broadly speaking, by the early 1900s cash was current in the more accessible half of each region. In the north-east, coins were the normal currency in Shambaa markets by 1900 and were current at the Machame market – a centre of exchange between Chagga and Masai – as early as 1894. On the other hand, tax could not be collected in cash in most parts of Kilimanjaro in 1898, while in the remote Mbulu area, as late as 1906, 'a rupee was placed on a stone in the house for fear that it might sink into the ground'.[3] The picture was similar elsewhere. In 1903 coins were current everywhere in Kilimatinde district except remote Usandawe. In Tabora, four years earlier, cash was acceptable only within a fairly narrow radius of the town, but by 1906 it was current throughout the district except the most remote parts of Buha and Buzinza – the latter area still having little use for cash as late as 1913. Further south, most of Tukuyu district's tax was paid in kind in 1906, but it was the only district where this was common.[4]

[1] Weidner, *Haussklaverei*, p. 41; Reid, Pangani DAR 1920–1, TNA 1733/1921/13; Byatt to Churchill, 19 July 1921, CO 691/45/414.
[2] *RTA*, 1895/7, no. 88, pp. 877, 882; *RTA*, 1909/11, no. 179, p. 412.
[3] *RTA*, 1900/2, no. 437, p. 2,975; Johannes to Government, 1 July 1894, RKA 385/107; *RTA*, 1898/1900, no. 518, p. 2,896; A. L. Malley, 'Dagharo Gharghara', seminar paper, University College, Dar es Salaam, n.d.
[4] Nigmann to Government, 27 February 1903, TNA G55/8; Bezirkschef Tabora to Government, 1 April 1899, TNA G1/35/157; *Deutsches Kolonialblatt*, 15 May 1907; diary

The consequences of monetisation need research, but they may have been limited because of Tanganyika's long experience of commerce. One revealing indication is that tax proved remarkably easy to collect, resistance being confined almost entirely to areas isolated from long-distance trade. There were exceptions: Machemba refused to collect tax and an Mbunga chief, Simbamkuti, was deposed for lacking the power to do so.[1] But resistance came chiefly from those for whom tax implied a quite new level of alien interference. In Usambara the Mbugu pastoralists – but not the Shambaa cultivators – resisted collection. There was unrest in Ukabende, Utongwe, Uvinza, and Buha when huts were counted in 1911.[2] The most serious resistance came from the Matumbi, who lived in the hills behind Kilwa and had resisted both Ngoni raiders and coastal slave-traders. Tax-collectors met the same hostility:

When that European arrived he asked, 'Why did you not answer the call by drum to pay tax?' And they said, 'We do not owe you anything. We have no debt to you. If you as a stranger want to stay in this country, then you will have to ask us.'[3]

The 'war of the pumpkins' which followed taught Matumbi the reality of European power. By 1903 their seclusion was broken:

While the Matumbi people previously isolated themselves and sold their products to traders on the fringes of the hills – allowing no trader to enter their mountains – small traders are today established throughout the area and the Matumbi bring their products to Kilwa, Samanga, and Mohoro. Even in 1897–8, during several marches through the country, I saw the people almost solely clothed in skins. Today they dress...like the coastal people.[4]

Introduced in 1898 as an annual levy of one to four shillings on each hut, tax was designed to have precisely the 'educational' effect which the Matumbi case suggests: to make people use money, sell surplus crops, work for Europeans, and obey a distant government.[5] In this it succeeded: tax became the symbol of subjection and the chief stimulus to participation in the money economy:

of Clement Gillman, 4 August 1913, RH; 'Gouvernementsrat beim Gouvernement von Deutsch-Ostafrika. Fünfte Sitzung', 26 March 1906, RKA 1055/168.
[1] Above, p. 98; Fiedler to Government, 21 November 1902, TNA G1/91/164.
[2] Stuhlmann to AAKA, 13 November 1900, RKA 290/98; Paschen to Government, 27 October and 10 December 1911, RKA 702/174 and 184.
[3] Quoted in G. C. K. Gwassa and John Iliffe (ed.), *Records of the Maji Maji rising: part one* (Nairobi, 1968), p. 3.
[4] Rode to Government, 19 May 1903, TNA G1/29/52.
[5] See Alexander Bursian, *Die Häuser- und Hüttensteuer in Deutsch-Ostafrika* (Jena, 1910), p. 10.

On 1 August [1900] news arrived that all adult males were to go to the district office in Iringa to work in lieu of tax. That stirred the Muhanga mountains to life. The last reserves of maize were pounded and ground into meal for the journey. Sweet potatoes were uprooted and bound in bundles. Young and old were busy with preparations for travel...On the morning of 3 August everyone who could walk assembled before dawn in front of our chapel in Muhanga. A colourful scene: women with their husbands' provisions on their heads and children with their fathers' walking-sticks or their indispensable rolls of tobacco in their hands...On 31 August the people returned home gaily from Iringa. I have been told that they behaved themselves well.[1]

Elsewhere the consequences might be grimmer. The askari who often collected tax in remote areas frequently confiscated the local cattle and ate them until the tax was brought forward. In southern Ubena the procedure was to hold the chief hostage until his people paid. As late as 1906 the station commander in Mwanza needed half a company of troops and a machine-gun to collect the public revenue.[2]

At the turn of the century tax and the growing use of cash were drawing Africans increasingly into a territorial economy. Yet the process was essentially a slow expansion of nineteenth-century economic patterns to encompass those who had previously resisted their embrace. The caravan trade, exchanging cloth for forest products, remained the basis of the exchange economy, just as the cultivation of millet and bananas remained the basis of the subsistence sector. Europeans had not yet reshaped the economy to their own purposes. On their Kaiser's birthday in 1902 the Germans of Dar es Salaam made carnival:

> However fine our German colony,
> The businessman its future cannot see,
> For, so he says, in fifty years, he's sure,
> There'll be no Europeans any more.
>
> The governor will be a nigger then,
> And so will all the other leading men.
> Indians will have a trade monopoly –
> God help us, what a splendid place to be!

Outstanding was the mask of the gentleman who represented the black governor...Not lacking, even, was 'the last European'.[3]

[1] Report by Neuberg, late 1900, TNA G9/11/73.
[2] Hans Stirnimann, *Existenzgrundlagen und traditionelles Handwerk der Pangwa* (Freiburg, Schweiz, 1976), pp. 17–19; report by Gröschel, 1901, TNA G9/11/73; Gunzert, 'Jahresbericht Muanza mit Schirati 1908/09', TNA G1/5.
[3] *Deutsch-Ostafrikanische Zeitung*, 15 February 1902.

Railways and the colonial economy

Alongside literacy and institutions of territorial government, new means of transport were the crucial innovations of the colonial period. Railways in the German period and motor vehicles in British times opened the possibility of escaping ancient constraints of distance, disease, and underpopulation. But they also opened the country to more intensive European domination, enabling the international economy to absorb indigenous economies and restructure them to meet its needs. The locomotives which steamed inland drew the colonial economy behind them.

German colonial enthusiasts quickly realised that railways were the key to development and profit in East Africa. In 1891 the DOAG undertook to build a line inland from Tanga through the projected plantation area around Usambara to Kilimanjaro and possibly Lake Victoria. An alternative line along the central caravan route was temporarily rejected as more expensive and less likely to advance plantation development.[1] The Tanga line was built slowly, inefficiently, and with much forced labour. 'The railway company has made a loss', an African teacher complained in 1897. '...They are forcing everyone to work without pay, neither wages nor food...Poor us! The people have no way of escape, they fear to be beaten...Truly this is not justice.'[2] By 1899 only forty kilometres were completed. They carried two trains each week and lost over £1,500 each month. The government then took over, but the Reichstag's parsimony dictated that not until 1905 did this northern railway reach Mombo, 129 kilometres inland and railhead for West Usambara.

The northern railway initially made little economic impact and only discouraged further construction. The stimulus to railway-building came rather from the British-built Uganda railway, which reached Lake Victoria in 1901 and quickly transformed a hinterland which included the German lake ports. Between 1903 and 1906 Mwanza's exports rose from £3,559 to £97,898. In 1903 Mwanza district collected £1,341 in tax; in 1908, £27,000. Mwanza also attracted long-distance trade away from the central caravan route. In 1904–5 Tabora despatched 7,242 loads of wax, hides, skins, and rubber to Bagamoyo and 3,259 to Mwanza; two years later 2,375 went to

[1] 'Protokoll über die am 5. März 1891...veranstaltete Beratung in Sachen des Eisenbahnbaues in Deutsch-Ostafrika', TNA G12/1/17. My account of railway policy is based on Tetzlaff, *Entwicklung*, pp. 63–70, 81–100; Hill, *Permanent way*, II, part 2.
[2] Mdoe to Travers, 20 November 1897, Travers letters box 2, UMCA.

Bagamoyo and 11,275 to Mwanza. The Germans were losing their hinterland.[1]

The Uganda railway transformed German transport policy. Its existence argued against extending the northern railway to Lake Victoria, yet the trade of the Tanganyikan interior had somehow to be recaptured. The Uganda line also showed that a long, expensive railway into the interior could be indirectly profitable by stimulating commerce and could meet its interest charges by increasing African taxability. This last point offered the Germans a means of financing railway construction without continuing to rely on cautious financiers or fickle politicians. Then the Maji Maji rebellion of 1905–7 so devastated southern Tanganyika as to rule out a railway there. It also demonstrated the military need for a railway through the heart of the colony and convinced Governor Freiherr von Rechenberg (1906–11) that railways must be built to make African cultivators sufficiently prosperous to acquiesce in colonial rule without repeated uprisings.[2]

The debate on railway policy in the last decade of German rule produced five decisions. One was to build a central railway along the caravan route from Dar es Salaam to Kigoma on Lake Tanganyika (reached in 1914), in order to stimulate the economy of the western plateau, improve military security, and recapture the trade of the interior. A second, implicit decision was not to build a southern railway. The third was to aid European settlers by extending the northern line from Mombo to Moshi (reached in 1912) and Arusha (completed by the British in 1930). Fourth, it was decided in 1914 to build a new railway north-westwards from Tabora to densely-populated Rwanda, although only forty kilometres of track were laid before the war intervened. The final decision underlay the others: these railways were financed by public loans raised from private investors, the Government of German East Africa owning the railways and paying (essentially from African taxes) a fixed interest rate guaranteed by the Imperial Government. By 1913 the colony's public debt of £8,677,550 included £6,400,000 for the central line and £2,150,000 for other railway purposes. Interest charges absorbed over a quarter of public revenue.[3]

[1] *RTA*, 1903/5, no. 540, p. 3,109; *RTA*, 1907/9, no. 622, p. 3,714; *RTA*, 1907/9, no. 1,106, p. 6,552; *RTA*, 1909/11, no. 179, p. 554; R. Hermann, 'Die Ugandabahn und ihr Einfluss auf Deutsch-Ostafrika', *Zeitschrift für Kolonialpolitik, Kolonialrecht und Kolonialwirtschaft*, VIII (1906), 580–93.

[2] Iliffe, *German rule*, pp. 71–81, 92, 102–3, 126–7, 203.

[3] Max Fleischmann, 'Die Verwaltung der Kolonien im Jahre 1913', *Jahrbuch über die deutschen Kolonien*, VII (1914), 112; 'Protokoll über die Sitzung des Gouvernementsrats am 20. Juni 1912', RKA 813/130.

The northern railway was easy to build, but the central line was a major technical undertaking, although less difficult than the railway built to Zambia in the 1970s. The main obstacles were to tunnel through the Pugu Hills, climb the western wall of the rift valley at Saranda – where the gradient reached the maximum then possible – and cross the marshes of the Mkata Plain and the Ruvu and Malagarasi valleys. Unlike the Uganda railway the Tanganyikan lines were built by African labourers, working in huge gangs with only the simplest tools. At its peak the central railway employed some 20,000 men. Conditions depended on the country. About 100 men died each month while working in the marshes east of Kilosa. Yet men generally preferred railway to plantation work. Wages were higher – averaging fifteen shillings for thirty days worked in 1909–12 – and the additional food and medical care were probably better.[1]

The railways struck at the heart of the nineteenth-century economy, the caravan trade. Whereas in 1900 some 35,000 porters arrived at Bagamoyo and 43,880 departed for the interior, in 1912 only 851 arrived and 193 departed.[2] In 1903 Bagamoyo's total foreign trade was worth £211,763, as against Dar es Salaam's £217,301; by 1912 the equivalent figures were £58,550 and £1,616,050.[3] Caravan trade survived in the south, where there was no railway, and local porterage may well have increased until motor vehicles became common in the 1920s. The First World War was to demonstrate Tanganyika's dependence on human carriers. Yet by concentrating trade at the deep-water ports at Tanga and Dar es Salaam the railways – together with direct shipping from Europe – substituted a colonial dependence on Europe for the mainland's previous dependence on Zanzibar. In the decade after 1902 the proportion of the colony's exports shipped to Zanzibar fell from 57 to 8 per cent, while Germany's share of its colony's exports increased from 29 to 57 per cent and its share of imports from 23 to 51 per cent.[4]

The railways affected many spheres of life. They ruined the Zinza iron-smelters who had produced the iron for hoes which caravans used as currency. Lower transport costs enabled European manufactures to penetrate new areas. By 1914 domestic weaving and iron-smelting

---

[1] *Die deutschen Schutzgebiete in Afrika und der Südsee 1912/13* (2 parts, Berlin, 1914), II, 79; *Deutsches Kolonialblatt*, 15 November 1909; Kuhlwein to Eisenbahn-Kommissar, 3 June 1909, TNA G17/66.
[2] *Die deutschen Schutzgebiete 1912/13*, I, 48.
[3] *RTA*, 1903/5, no. 540, pp. 2,964–5; *Die deutschen Schutzgebiete 1912/13*, II, 204–5, 220–1.
[4] Brode, *East Africa*, appx. A; *RTA*, 1903/5, no. 54, p. 100; *Die deutschen Schutzgebiete 1912/13*, II, 154–7, 170–3, 200–3, 218–21.

were increasingly rare, their technological skills reduced to uncomprehended magic, although the wider availability of iron (as scrap) may well have benefited blacksmiths. Better transport extended markets and enabled large producers to oust small: the early twentieth century was a prosperous time for Kisi potters. In 1904 a joint stock company took over the ancient brine springs at Uvinza and converted the salt dealers into porters. To dance 'like steam engines' became a synonym for a successful party.[1]

During the last decade of German rule, Asian shopkeepers, the crucial intermediaries of Tanganyika's colonial economy, secured control of retail trade in the interior. They had long settled on the coast, where over 600 lived in 1871. They came from western India. The first were Hindus, members of the Bhattia and Lohana castes from Cutch, followed by Banias from Kathiaward and Patidars from Gujarat. By 1871, however, Hindus were outnumbered by Muslims belonging to Shia sects: Ithnasharis, Ismaili Bohras, and Ismaili Khojas, with the last forming the majority. Immigration accelerated under German rule until in 1912 there were 8,698 Asians in German East Africa. Most immigrants were impoverished countrymen, often driven into the towns by famine and then lured to East Africa by hopes of wealth.[2] By 1895 the Aga Khan, the Living Imam of the Ismaili Khojas, was encouraging and occasionally commanding migration. His followers were Hindu converts whose Islamisation continued during the colonial period, but they had abandoned caste divisions for a tight community organisation which balanced councils of local notables against their Imam's growing authority, held to equal that of the Koran and strongly backed by the British regime in India for whom he was a crucial ally. These characteristics made Ismaili Khojas the most adaptable and progressive Asian community, much as African states commonly operated more successfully than stateless peoples under colonialism. Unlike Hindus, Ismaili Khojas brought their womenfolk to East Africa and settled permanently, which gave them an important commercial advantage.[3] Unrestrained by caste rules, they

---

[1] Nchoti, 'Iron industry', p. 42; Kjekshus, *Ecology control*, pp. 91–2; M. S. Mbwillo, 'Pottery industry in Ukinga', B.A. thesis, University of Dar es Salaam, 1974, pp. 4, 20; Tetzlaff, *Entwicklung*, p. 172; *Rafiki yangu*, May 1912.

[2] Kirk, 'Annex no. 1' [1871] FO 84/1344/129; David F. Pocock, '"Difference" in East Africa: a study of caste and religion in modern Indian society', *Southwestern journal of anthropology* XIII (1957), 290–2; Shirin R. Walji, 'Ismailis on mainland Tanzania, 1850–1948', M.A. thesis, University of Wisconsin, 1969, chs. 1–2; *Die deutschen Schutzgebiete 1912/13*, II, 38–9.

[3] For Ismaili Khojas, see Walji, 'Ismailis'; *idem*, 'A history of the Ismaili community in Tanzania', Ph.D. thesis, University of Wisconsin, 1974; J. N. D. Anderson, 'The

concentrated entirely on trade: 172 of the 180 Ismailis in Dar es Salaam in 1893 were traders but only 35 of the 124 Hindus, most of whom practised hereditary crafts.[1] Religious constraints on commensality and intermarriage tended to divide Hindus, whereas by the 1880s Ismaili Khojas had a single Jamatkhana (meeting house) at Bagamoyo and community officers in other towns. Indeed the very strength of their organisation and its leader's growing pretensions were the chief dangers to the Ismaili Khojas in German times, for during the 1890s roughly a third of those in East Africa seceded to the less centralised Ithnashari community. That the seceders included many wealthy merchants suggests resentment of the *dasond*, the annual community levy of one-eighth of income. Having failed to reconcile the seceders while visiting East Africa in 1899 and 1905, the Aga Khan excommunicated them and strengthened his remaining followers by establishing a provincial council on the mainland. Other communities tended to concentrate in particular towns. Tanga was a Bohra stronghold, for example, while Ithnasharis long dominated Bukoba's trade.[2]

Most Asian immigrants arrived penniless – there is no example of a wealthy man transferring his business from India – and looked to relatives to find them jobs with established merchants. This apprenticeship – 'service' in the derogatory Gujarati term[3] – was endured until a man could break away, first as itinerant trader and then as resident shopkeeper, taking his stock on credit from a wholesaler. One whose store in Uzaramo was destroyed in 1905 valued his stock at £20 – balls of rubber, sacks and baskets of maize and rice, and 'money kept in the maize in the bark drum'. He set no value on most of his clothes or possessions.[4] Poverty, isolation, and grinding effort left Asians intensely proud of their pioneering self-reliance and intensely ambitious for wealth and security. Struggling storekeepers dreamed of becoming great wholesalers like Alidina Visram, the Ismaili Khoja who started by buying 'country produce' and expanded until he sent more caravans along the central route than the DOAG in 1898 and

Ismaili Khojas of East Africa', *Middle Eastern studies*, I (1964), 21–39; H. S. Morris, 'The divine kingship of the Aga Khan', *Southwestern journal of anthropology*, XIV (1958), 454–72; Hatim M. Amiji, 'Some notes on religious dissent in nineteenth-century East Africa', *IJAHS*, IV (1971), 603–16.

[1] *RTA*, 1894/5, no. 89, p. 391.

[2] Hatim Amiji, 'The Bohras of East Africa', *Journal of religion in Africa*, VII (1975), 38–9; Seyyid Saeed Akhtar Rizvi and Noel Q. King, 'Some East African Ithna-Asheri *jamaats* (1840–1967)', *ibid.*, V (1973), 21.

[3] Pocock, '"Difference"', p. 292.   [4] List in TNA G35/8.

employed over 500 Asians ten years later. Yet no merchant of the next generation equalled his success, for European control, improved transport, and greater competition made fortunes more difficult to amass. Nor were they easy to bequeath where so much depended on individual entrepreneurship. Visram's heirs eventually paid their creditors two per cent.[1]

However rich an Asian merchant, to the Germans he was a native because he could not observe German civil law.[2] This greatly offended Asians among whom colour racialism was deeply engrained. Their chief political aim throughout German times was to secure a higher legal status than Arabs and Africans. Their complaints culminated in 1914 when the Asians of Tanga explicitly, but unsuccessfully, demanded a separate legal status and formed a professedly non-political body called the Tanga Indian Association. Yet protests were cautious, for Asians were vulnerable and politically impotent. Their status as British subjects, which strengthened their position in British colonies, was doubly suspect to Germans. Three Asians were expelled from Kilwa in 1895 for selling gunpowder to 'rebels' and the whole Kilwa community was fined £1,333. Others were convicted of gun-running during the Maji Maji rebellion. Their business methods were blamed for African discontent. Although German merchants regarded Asians as indispensable local agents, settlers were openly hostile. In 1911 the chief European political organisation resolved that Asians should be excluded 'for ever from any political influence', prevented from owning land, required to keep their accounts in Swahili or a European language, and subjected to controls on health or immigration. Government bowed to this pressure in 1912, prohibited the further sale of land to Asians in Dar es Salaam, began to divide the capital formally into racial quarters, and restricted the immigration of destitute Asians.[3] Yet most Asians were concerned less with a struggle for communal status than with the great push inland. Whereas in 1901 only 58 of 3,420 Asians are known to have lived in interior districts, by 1912 the figure was 2,591 out of 8,698. German administrative centres attracted storekeepers. When Captain Prince settled at Iringa in 1896, for example, he was followed by nearly a thousand traders and their dependents. But railways were the most

[1] Kannenberg to Government, 27 December 1898, TNA G1/35/120; J. S. Mangat, *A history of the Asians in East Africa, c. 1886 to 1945* (Oxford, 1969), pp. 51–3, 77–82.
[2] See 'Rechtsverhältnisse der Inder in Deutsch-Ostafrika' [c. 1901] TNA Handakten Referat VIII P.
[3] Iliffe, *German rule*, pp. 94–6, 203.

potent stimulus. In 1895 there were three Asians in Tabora district; in 1910, 51; in 1912 (when the railhead reached Tabora) 496.[1]

With better access to imported goods, export markets, credit, and commercial skills and information, Asian shopkeepers commonly drove out Arab and African competitors. Between 1908 and 1909 the number of Asian shopkeepers in Morogoro district increased from 79 to 116, while the number of Arab and African shopkeepers fell from thirteen to six. Yet at the same time itinerant traders and cattle-dealers – normally Africans or Arabs – increased from 116 to 222 and sellers of local beer from 91 to 249.[2] As is normal, capitalism ousted small men from the economic centres but multiplied opportunities for them at the peripheries. Bukoba supported a thousand Haya traders in 1913, alongside some 600 other Africans, 100 Asians, and 30 Arabs. During 1912 the north-eastern plantations imported some 12,000 slaughter cattle.[3] There were small areas – Nzega in Unyamwezi, Ufipa, Ujiji, Daluni to the north of Usambara – where Arab shopkeepers successfully resisted Asian competition, but generally Arabs, like Africans, had to move to the peripheries. Arab residents of Tabora declared that once the railway reached their town they would have to move to Ujiji. There was comment in Tanga as Asian settlement encroached on the African residential area.[4] But opposition to Asian expansion normally failed. The *wandewa* of Unyanyembe disappeared from the records. In the crucial and little-known area of inland trade, discontinuity between nineteenth and twentieth centuries seems to have been almost complete.

The clearest indication of the colonial economy's advance was increasing white settlement. Between 1904 and 1913 Tanganyika's European population grew from 1,390 to 4,998; of the latter figure, 882 were male adults engaged in agriculture. The numbers were small, but similar to Kenya's at the same date.[5] The increase owed little to

[1] *RTA*, 1900/2, no. 437, p. 2,965; *Die deutschen Schutzgebiete 1912/13*, II, 38–9; Prince to Government, 4 November 1896, RKA 1039/9; Leue to Government, 30 October 1895, RKA 1030/88; *Die deutschen Schutzgebiete 1909/10*, II, 20.

[2] Lambrecht, 'Jahresbericht des Bezirks Morogoro für 1908/9', TNA G1/5.

[3] BA Bukoba to Government, 7 February 1913, TNA G9/48/146; G. Lichtenheld, 'Ueber Rinderrassen Rinderzucht und ihre wirtschaftliche Bedeutung in Deutsch-Ostafrika', *Der Pflanzer*, IX (1913), 273.

[4] Fergus C. Wright, *African consumers in Nyasaland and Tanganyika* (London, 1955), pp. 108–9; Willis, *Fipa*, p. 72; Shunya Hino, 'The occupational differentiation of an African town', *KUAS*, II (1968), 101–5; Gillman diary, 10 February 1939, RH; *Deutsche Kolonialzeitung*, 15 July 1911; *Kiongozi*, August 1911.

[5] *RTA*, 1903/5, no. 540, p. 3,011; *Die deutschen Schutzgebiete 1912/13*, II, 10–13; M. P. K. Sorrenson, *Origins of European settlement in Kenya* (Nairobi, 1968), p. 145.

government policy. Governor Graf von Götzen (1901–6) favoured settlement and supported schemes to establish Afrikaner refugees from the Boer War and impoverished Germans from Russia on the foothills of Meru, but he regarded settlement as experimental and enforced the rule that settlers might not buy their farms until they were cultivated.[1] His successor, Rechenberg, also regarded settlement as experimental but privately hoped that it would fail. 'Any settlement of Europeans on a large scale', he warned, 'must lead to a conflict with the natives, which could be settled only in bloody fashion.'[2] In practice he obstructed settlement in many minor ways, raising land prices, insisting on strict observance of leasehold provisions, and regulating the settlers' treatment of African labourers. The last two years of German peacetime rule, under Governor Schnee, saw a more accommodating attitude, but he too refused to dispossess Africans of their land.[3]

Lacking direct official support, European settlement was piecemeal. The colonists were extraordinarily diverse. Many influential settlers were retired officers from the colonial defence force or the metropolitan army whose pensions gave them a security which others lacked. There were also several former N.C.O.s. Some Germans had first arrived as employees of trading or plantation companies. In 1907 some 70 per cent of the settlers were Germans. Many of the others were Afrikaner refugees from British rule in the Transvaal, and there were also communities of Greeks and Italians, often impoverished peasants who began as railway contractors and ended as sisal growers in Kilosa or coffee planters in Moshi.[4]

Early in the new century most settlers aimed for West Usambara, hoping to combine mixed farming with small coffee plantations. By 1911 there were 41 farms in the mountains.[5] The settler normally selected partly-cultivated land in a valley between Shambaa villages. The district officer held a land commission consisting of himself, the local *akida* or government agent, and the headmen concerned. They decided to concentrate the Africans on part of the land and alienate the rest. The common pratice was to leave Africans four times the area they cultivated or four hectares per family. Those moved received a

[1] Iliffe, *German rule*, pp. 59–63, 128–9.
[2] Rechenberg to RKA, 21 December 1910, RKA 15/211; Iliffe, *German rule*, chs. 4–6.
[3] Iliffe, *German rule*, pp. 203–4.
[4] *RTA*, 1907/9, no. 622, p. 6,563; Nikos Georgulas, *Minority assimilation in Africa: the Greeks in Moshi*, Maxwell Graduate School, Eastern African Program, occasional paper 22 (New York [1965]).
[5] Methner to RKA, 28 March 1911, RKA 80/80.

few shillings compensation. The land vacated was declared Crown Land and leased for 25 years. The settler had to cultivate one-tenth each year and could buy twice as much as he cultivated. These regulations were frequently but not invariably observed.[1] 'Such hatred circulates among the people', a West Usambara settler noted in 1908,

and it will not be much longer before we once again have the finest of rebellions!...I believe that Captain Prince, who is taking possession of everything still available, bears a large part of the blame for it. He already has fifteen plantations. No wonder that this hits the people hard, for he mostly buys out the natives with a few rupees.[2]

Prince often allowed Shambaa to remain on his land in return for labour service. In 1912, however, shortage of land and labour persuaded the government to close West Usambara to settlement. More than half the cultivable land then remaining to Africans was said to be cultivated at any time, fallow periods were falling to destructive levels, and food production was declining.[3] Yet European farming did not prosper in West Usambara. Coffee failed as a cash crop. Dairying and European vegetables were tried, but the market was small and communications appalling. Most settlers grew African cereals to feed plantations in the valley below the mountains. As generally in Tanganyika, European mixed farming proved less viable than plantations or ranching.[4]

From West Usambara intending settlers gazed westwards to the wider spaces around Kilimanjaro and Meru. Here the situation was quite different. Instead of living in scattered hilltop villages, the Chagga, Meru, and Arusha peoples were settled relatively densely on the middle slopes of the mountains where bananas flourished. Below their *vihamba* – banana groves and home farms – was *shamba* land where Chagga (who stall-fed their cattle) grew maize and Meru and Arusha cultivated grain and grazed cattle. The lower plains had once been occupied by the Masai, but civil war and rinderpest had left them apparently empty.[5]

The Germans initially believed that there was ample land for

[1] Iliffe, *German rule*, pp. 128–9.
[2] M.-L. von Horn, diary, 15 April 1908, quoted in Detlef Bald, *Deutsch-Ostafrika 1900–1914* (München, 1970), pp. 185 n. 30, 187 n. 44.
[3] Report by Schmidt, August–September 1913, TNA blue 33. A translation is in CO 691/29/375.
[4] *Die deutschen Schutzgebiete 1910/11*, I, 17.
[5] P. H. Johnston, 'Some notes on land tenure on Kilimanjaro', *TNR*, XXI (1946), 1–20; Clemm, 'White mountain', chs. 13–14; P. H. Gulliver, 'Interim report on land and population in the Arusha chiefdom', duplicated, 1957, ch. 3 (TNA library).

European settlement in Kilimanjaro's *vihamba* belt. A few settlers, mostly Greeks, bought *vihamba* land from amenable chiefs, notably Marealle. Once inter-chiefdom warfare ended, however, Chagga occupied the border regions between chiefdoms and government began to doubt whether *vihamba* land was really available. In 1907 it decided to alienate only apparently unused land in the *shamba* belt and the foothills, leaving gaps between farms to allow access to the lowlands. The idea was to limit Chagga expansion so that population growth would provide settlers with a labour force growing parallel with their needs. From 1910 world coffee prices rose rapidly and it became clear that coffee flourished on Kilimanjaro. Government now resisted demands for further alienation, and Rechenberg banned all further settlement on Kilimanjaro in 1911 until a native reserve could be created 'to protect the Chagga tribe...against uprooting and proletarianisation'. Nevertheless some 200 square kilometres of arable land and 567 of pasture had been alienated by 1913. Only 60 square kilometres of the arable were cultivated.[1]

Perhaps the worst effects of land alienation were avoided on Kilimanjaro. Certainly the Chagga were not proletarianised by land shortage. Nevertheless, alienation produced localised land hunger. In 1913 the Chagga – estimated at 110,000 – had some 468 square kilometres of land in the *vihamba* belt, or 4,200 square metres per head. A settler had acquired all the pasture in Mrau chiefdom. Kirua had lost a third of its *vihamba* land. Pasture was short in Marangu and people were reduced to using that of other chiefdoms. Scores of landless people squatted on Roman Catholic mission land at Kilema. In Kibosho, where Sina's successor had alienated recklessly, the people had to grow their maize on European land.[2]

A similar, perhaps more serious, problem emerged on Mount Meru. European colonists reached this area later than Kilimanjaro and only two settled in the banana belt around the mountain, but the situation in the foothills and the plain was especially difficult, for two reasons. One was that Arusha was the focus of Götzen's planned settlement schemes, so that very large areas around the base of Meru, bordering

---

[1] Johannes to Government, 16 November 1892 and 1 June 1893, TNA G1/18/79 and 123; Iliffe, *German rule*, p. 63; Rechenberg to Moshi, 10 October 1911, TNA LKV Moshi 157; Erdmann to Moshi, 30 July 1913, CO 691/29/373.

[2] Erdmann to Moshi, 30 July 1913, CO 691/29/373; Knaak to Government, 23 May 1912, TNA LKV Moshi 81; Bald, *Deutsch-Ostafrika*, p. 189; Wahl to Government, 20 February 1914, TNA LKV Moshi 97; G. O. Ekemode, 'German rule in north-east Tanzania, 1885–1914', Ph.D. thesis, University of London, 1973, p. 324; Lueg to Government, 8 November 1915, TNA LKV Moshi 180.

immediately on African holdings, became almost a European reserve. By 1910, 37,720 hectares had been distributed in this way. The second problem was that Meru's foothills were less well watered than Kilimanjaro's. The European settlers appropriated almost all the lower land with access to streams, making expansion from the banana belt exceptionally difficult.[1]

In 1914 slightly less than one per cent of Tanganyika's land was occupied by Europeans. As so often in colonial history, the chief losers had been the pastoralists, especially the Masai confined to their 'ludicrously inadequate' reserve.[2] Usambara, Kilimanjaro, and Meru were the centres of European agriculture, as they remained until Independence. Early plans to settle Uhehe, highland Unyakyusa, and other parts of the Southern Highlands foundered on lack of transport. A few coffee planters obtained land in Buhaya. The only other settlement area was Morogoro district, where the central railway enabled 82 plantations to be opened by 1911.[3]

The failure of coffee before 1910 led Europeans to experiment with cotton, rubber, and sisal. Cotton generally failed as a plantation crop, despite rising prices after 1905 as German cloth manufacturers sought to free themselves from American monopoly suppliers. Two massive plantations were established. The Leipzig Cotton Spinners took up 330 square kilometres in the Ruvu flood plain near Sadani in 1907 and a Stuttgart millionaire named Otto opened a plantation on a similar scale near Kilosa. By 1912 they had failed. Both had employed too many expensive Europeans – Otto's plantation was known locally as 'the convict settlement'. Both had spent vast sums on expensive steam ploughs which cut so deep that they turned up infertile subsoil. In 1910 the Leipzig Spinners cultivated 2,500 hectares at a cost of £75,000, while Otto's 240 hectares of growing cotton had cost him £80,000. That year the plantations were hit by curly-leaf disease, which forced the Leipzig Spinners to withdraw completely. Otto struggled on until the war, producing little cotton but endless expansion projects. Like the later Groundnut Scheme, plantation cotton showed that capital and technology alone made little impression on Tanganyika's environment.[4]

The fate of rubber was even more spectacular. Until 1912 world

---

[1] *Die deutschen Schutzgebiete 1909/10*, I, 27; Kitching, 'Native land in the Arusha district', 3 December 1930, TNA 25369/I/A/13.
[2] Kitching, 'Native land', 3 December 1930, TNA 25369/I/A/13.
[3] *Die deutschen Schutzgebiete 1910/11*, II, 8–9.
[4] Iliffe, *German rule*, pp. 77–8, 99–100; Tetzlaff, *Entwicklung*, pp. 136–54; R. Kaundinya, *Erinnerungen aus meinen Pflanzerjahren in Deutsch-Ostafrika* (Leipzig, 1918), *passim*.

demand was almost insatiable. At first almost all was wild rubber, but experiments with plantation rubber began in German East Africa as early as 1892. The variety was manihot (*Ceara glaziovii*), a quick-growing, low-quality product which required less moisture than the more common *Hevea brasiliensis*. By 1902 the DOAG was developing a large plantation at Lewa, a tapping method had been devised, and other planters were experimenting. Towards the end of 1908 world rubber prices began to rise in an astonishing boom. Best quality Brazilian rubber on the Hamburg market rose by 132 per cent between the first half of 1908 and the early months of 1910. Thereafter it fell gradually, but high prices continued until the end of 1912. Between 1909 and 1912 German East Africa's exports of plantation rubber rose from 218,468 to 1,018,807 kg and their value from £20,798 to £362,012. European enterprise in the north-east became genuinely profitable for the first time. Money could be made from producing rubber, but still more could be obtained by establishing a plantation and selling it as a going concern. By October 1910 British companies had paid some £350,000 for 16,000 hectares of rubber plantations in German East Africa and a few poor men had made fortunes. The boom collapsed early in 1913. By the year's end the price of East African manihot had fallen to a quarter of its 1910 peak, rendering the whole crop uneconomic. Three factors destroyed it: the enormous investment in *hevea* plantations elsewhere, especially South-East Asia; manihot's inability to compete with high-quality *hevea*, for German East Africa's rubber was reckoned the worst in the world; and the fact that plantation growth outran labour supply and pushed up production costs, which rose from Shs. 1.70 per kg at Lewa in 1907 to an average of Shs. 3.20–5.00 in 1913. By 1914 many rubber plantations were abandoned. Others were being uprooted to make way for sisal.[1]

As a plantation crop, sisal had the qualities which coffee, cotton, and rubber conspicuously lacked. It flourished in the shallow, laterite soils of the north-east, the central railway area, and the southern coast, where it was grown by what was essentially shifting cultivation. It withstood unpredictable rainfall. Plantation production was essential to provide bulk transport and a regular supply of leaves to the expensive processing machines. Sisal was a high-quality product with a premium over its nearest competitor, Mexican henequen. Demand for sisal and henequen fluctuated little because they formed only a tiny proportion of the costs of the consuming industries, notably as binder

[1] Iliffe, *German rule*, pp. 100–1, 140, 203; Tetzlaff, *Entwicklung*, pp. 123–30.

twine in agriculture. Finally, sisal had the enormous advantage for a new colony that its supply was inelastic. Since it took seven years to reach maturity, it rode out price fluctuations which might have destroyed an annual crop like cotton. On several occasions the Tanganyikan sisal industry survived depressions chiefly because it was so unadaptable. Sisal plants possessed an equanimity which their growers often lacked.

The introduction and development of sisal was the work of the DOAG, one of whose plantation managers imported the first plants from Florida in 1893 and planted them at the Kikogwe plantation near Pangani. World prices then fell, but rose again by 1898–9, when Kikogwe installed processing machinery and produced its first fibre. Substantial planting followed in the lower-lying estates of the north-east. Then the cyclical pattern of the hard fibre market once more asserted itself as excessive planting came into bearing. Between 1906 and 1911 the price of German East African sisal at Hamburg fell from £38–45 to £23–27 per ton, only slightly above the estimated production and transport cost. As usual, sisal survived this recession until demand once more outstripped supply. From 1911 the price rose sharply, reaching £38 per ton on the Hamburg market in 1912. The Sisal-Agaven-Gesellschaft paid 25 per cent dividends in 1912 and 1913. With the collapse of rubber, sisal exports, worth £376,961, formed 23 per cent of the colony's exports in 1912.[1]

Investment in Tanganyika rose substantially in the last decade of German rule. In 1905 the fourteen largest companies investing in the colony had paid-up capital of £1,892,970, while in 1913 company and private capital together was estimated at £4,800,000, made up of £1,050,000 in railways, £2,400,000 in agriculture, £1,100,000 in trade, industry, and mining, and £250,000 in banking.[2] Individual business histories are lacking, but all the main banks and trading companies and about half the agricultural undertakings seem to have been profitable.[3] The highest profits were made in trade, banking, and shipping, chiefly by the financiers who had invested in the DOAG after

[1] Iliffe, *German rule*, pp. 69, 100, 139–40, 203; Tetzlaff, *Entwicklung*, pp. 118–23; Richard Hindorf, *Der Sisalbau in Deutsch-Ostafrika* (Berlin, 1925), *passim*; Stuhlmann, 'Aufzeichnung über Deutsch-Ostafrikanischen Sisal-Hanf', 2 December 1912, RKA 8201/92; *Die deutschen Schutzgebiete 1912/13*, II, 158–73, 206–21.

[2] *RTA*, 1905/6, no. 175, pp. 3,018–9; Heinrich Schnee (ed.), *Deutsches Kolonial-Lexicon* (3 vols, Leipzig, 1920), s.v. Kapitalanlagen. Both figures exclude shipping companies and public railway investment.

[3] Max Fleischmann, 'Die Verwaltung der Kolonien im Jahre 1912', *Jahrbuch über die deutschen Kolonien*, IV (1913), 164.

1887 and were thereby strategically placed to benefit from further investment opportunities. Following the principle of 'never standing aside', the DOAG came to control the German East African Bank; the Commercial Bank for East Africa (based in Tanga); the German East African Railway Company (which operated both railways); the German Tanganyika Company; the Central African Mining Company (exploiting Uvinza's salt); the Lindi Trading and Plantation Company and the East Africa Company (sisal estates in the south); the German East African Plantation Company, Rhenish-Handei Plantation Company, and Ngomeni Plantation Company (plantations in the northeast); and the Usambara-Magazin (trade). The DOAG directly employed 120 Europeans and some 4,400 Africans and Asians. In 1910 and 1911 it paid 8 per cent dividends. It also held mortgages on much private land, often demanding 5–7 per cent interest per annum and a selling monopoly of the settler's crops at a commission ranging up to 2½ per cent.[1] 'The majority of settlers in German East Africa have been reduced to a class of vassals of the DOAG', a colonist complained in 1907.[2] A latent conflict of interest between metropolitan financiers and 'red-eyed settlers' existed throughout German East Africa's history, but it was restrained by European solidarity against the other races.

As European residents became increasingly numerous and prosperous – in 1912 their undertakings produced 57 per cent of export value – they sought political power. Early German colonial administration was almost entirely bureaucratic. Europeans were entitled to the privileges of German law and all money collected or spent in the colony had to pass through the Reichstag's budgetary procedures, but otherwise legislative and executive power devolved from the Kaiser through the Imperial Chancellor and a colonial department of the Foreign Office – which in 1907 became an independent Colonial Office – to the governor and his civilian district officers or military district commanders. After 1898 certain Europeans in settled districts were nominated to advisory councils administering 'communal' funds for local development, spending these chiefly on European interests. Another all-European body, the Governor's Council, first met on 27 April 1904. It had an official majority until 1909 and was purely an advisory body, unlike the Legislative Council of British times. The settlers' 'drive for mastery' during the last decade of German rule

---

[1] Schnee, *Lexicon*, s.v. DOAG; Tetzlaff, *Entwicklung*, pp. 164–9; Iliffe, *German rule*, p. 97.
[2] Karl Perrot, quoted in Tetzlaff, *Entwicklung*, p. 114.

centred on an attempt to control these advisory bodies, make them elective, and give them decision-making powers. The campaign was provoked by Governor Rechenberg, who opposed European settlement and wished to see Tanganyika developed through African cash-crop production and trade with Germany. His actions politicised the settlers. Small associations of planters had existed in the Tanga area since 1898 and in West Usambara since 1903. In June 1908 they came together with other local bodies to form the Territorial Business League of German East Africa, skilfully led by a plantation manager and former officer named Carl Feilke.[1]

A tiny minority, often isolated and vulnerable, the settlers believed that Africans were permanently on the verge of revolt which only vigilance could prevent. They saw Rechenberg as a 'nigger-lover' whose 'lax handling of the negroes...contains within it the awful danger of a sudden rising'.[2] His programme threatened the settlers' livelihood, which depended heavily on the use of political power to distort economic forces to their advantage. He also represented the old German authoritarian state against which the Europeans set the claims of local self-government. Another important element in settler thinking was racialism. This was universal among early twentieth-century Germans and embodied some of the best scientific opinion of the time. All men, it was believed, could be classified into races as animals could be classified into species. Each race had a distinct skin colour, physique, mentality, character, history, and cultural attributes. Like animal species, human races represented different stages in the scale of evolution, with the white races at the top and the black at the bottom. Each race contained sub-groups which could also be classified on an evolutionary scale, so that Bushmen were a lower form than Bantu, who were themselves lower than 'Hamites' like the taller, lighter-skinned, pastoral Masai. Even the most humane Germans thought in these terms. Rechenberg, an exceptionally cool-minded man, doubted if Africans were capable of being Christian priests. Governor Schnee, a man of liberal sympathies and academic temperament, compared the distinction between aristocratic, pastoral Hamites and plebeian, earthy Bantu to that between antelope and cattle.[3] Less sophisticated minds held that since Africans stood so low on the evolutionary ladder they belonged as much to the animal as

[1] Iliffe, *German rule*, pp. 30–8, 84–9, 108–15; Bald, *Deutsch-Ostafrika, passim.*
[2] Gillman diary, 11 November 1906, RH; *Usambara-Post*, 30 January 1909.
[3] Rechenberg to RKA, 23 September 1910, TNA G9/21/5; Bald, *Deutsch-Ostafrika*, p. 127 n. 7.

to the human world, their characteristics being exactly the reverse of those which the settlers ascribed to themselves. Africans were marked by 'savagery [*Roheit*], laziness, cunning, and repulsive ugliness',[1] but also by loyalty and obedience to a master who was 'just but firm', for the African 'is a born slave, who needs his despot like an opium addict needs his pipe'.[2] Only compulsion made such creatures work, and 'education for work' recurred endlessly in German writings. It was used to justify recourse to flogging both by employers and by the authorities. Between 1901 and 1913 the government sentenced 64,652 Africans to corporal punishment, or an average of five a week at every district office in the country.[3] A newly-arrived engineer recorded the lore of the cafés:

In the evening I had an interesting talk with old experienced Africans [i.e. settlers] about the natives: 'They must feel, that the white man is the mbana', the master. The white must act with the necessary tact and justice, but must always be strict and have all their orders obeyed to at once. If necessary the wip must come in helping.

Kindness is absolutely no good with the niggers, who are used to have someone above them, and it is to a great deal due to the fact, that missionarys are too kind and familiar with them, that the present [Maji Maji] rebellion broke out...

Whether they are the born slaves, as was said by a man, who ought to know them well enough, I can't make out yet, and therefore can't quite agree with the idea, that the putting an end to slavery was a great pity to the country – as the above mentioned gentleman thinks.[4]

The settler newspapers became noticeably more preoccupied with race as time passed and the European population grew.[5]

Although racialism was universal, German attitudes towards Africans were extremely varied. Germany itself was a deeply divided country amidst dislocating socio-economic change. Rechenberg's contest with the settlers embodied these divisions. Both sides drew their strength chiefly from political support in Germany: Rechenberg from humanitarians, Roman Catholics, and socialists, the settlers from militant right-wing nationalists. The settlers won. By 1914 they possessed a degree of political power which European unofficials were never again to exercise in Tanganyika. European unofficial

---

[1] Kaundinya, *Erinnerungen*, p. 31.
[2] Carl Peters, 'Gefechtsweise und Expeditionsführung in Africa' (1892), in his *Gesammelte Schriften* (3 vols, München, 1943), II, 520.
[3] Fritz Ferdinand Müller, *Kolonien unter der Peitsche* (Berlin, 1962), p. 114.
[4] Gillman diary, 29 October 1905, RH. Gillman did not accept these views.
[5] Ida Pipping-Van Hulten, *An episode of colonial history: the German press in Tanzania 1901–1914* (Uppsala, 1974), p. 11.

representatives, chosen by presentative election,[1] held twelve of the sixteen seats on the Governor's Council, which, with Schnee's support, was pressing vigorously for decision-making powers. There were as many Europeans in Tanganyika as in Kenya. They were better organised, better represented in public bodies, more influential in metropolitan politics, far more important economically, and able to ignore the Asian political demands which the British in Kenya had to heed. It is more likely than not that if Tanganyika had remained under German rule it would have become a white man's country like Kenya or even Southern Rhodesia.[2]

The struggle for labour

Plantation development in the north-east introduced a capitalist sector into Tanganyika, with smaller sectors in other areas of white settlement, in the towns, and along the railways. Just as Zanzibar's impact had radiated through the country during the nineteenth century, so the plantations' impact radiated outwards in German times. Like Zanzibar, they appropriated vast quantities of African labour by a mixture of political and economic means, with the former somewhat less overt than in the nineteenth century but still extremely important. Most workers were migrants from distant regions, since the economic and environmental conditions which made plantations possible in the north-east also enabled the Africans of that region to commercialise their own agriculture. The result was differentiation between labour-importing and -exporting regions. In the importing regions African societies tended to develop towards peasant organisation, a trend accentuated by subordination to a distant government and growing adherence to world religions. By contrast, the labour-exporting regions tended to stagnate or even retrogress. Many labour-importing regions were high-rainfall areas, which thus began to regain the cultural lead they had lost during the nineteenth century. One of the most important aspects of the German impact on Tanganyika was its unevenness.

The peoples of the north-east generally escaped conversion into plantation labourers. Their settlements became native reserves interspersed with European plantations, 'little attols in a big Pacific Ocean of sisal' as they were later described.[3] The Germans intended

---

[1] Selection by the governor from elected lists.   [2] Iliffe, *German rule*, ch. 9.
[3] TAA Executive Committee to Cohen, 21 May 1951, TNA 41736/1.

that alienation and population growth should force these peoples – the Bondei and their neighbours – to work on the plantations. In fact the reverse happened. In the late nineteenth century some Bondei did work for Europeans, but it quickly became clear that not enough were available. After a disastrous experiment with Chinese and Indonesian 'coolies', employers began in 1895 to recruit Nyamwezi and Sukuma workers from the western plateau. By 1900 some 4,000–5,000 were working on plantations in the north-east. Bondei had exported food to Zanzibar in the nineteenth century. Now they fed the plantation workers, some even hiring Nyamwezi immigrants. But the Nyamwezi too could take advantage of the new opportunities. By 1900 many had settled in Bonde to grow food. Two years later they were employing labour and European planters were demanding their repatriation.[1] Meanwhile the Europeans continued to need workers. Economic pressure having proved inadequate, political means were employed. The area was divided into labour divisions, each attached to a plantation to which the headman had to supply workers. Rechenberg forbade this in 1910, however, so that the 14,000 workers on European plantations in Tanga district in 1910 included only 1,200 local men, the remainder being long-distance migrants.[2] The Bonde example shows how capitalist relations permeated a largely pre-capitalist economy, how political means were needed to bolster economic methods of obtaining labour, and how the burden came to rest on distant peoples rather than on the Bondei, who tended to become peasants. It is a revealing model, but a model against which to study variation.

West Usambara provides one contrast. The Shambaa had been less involved than the Bondei in the nineteenth-century economy. They were more easily exploited because they feared to leave the mountains, whose climate deterred immigrant workers. Usambara's European farms required less labour than Bonde's plantations and offered no market for African-grown food. These circumstances shaped economic relations. Their chief feature was extreme political compulsion to secure farm labour. Each settler entering Usambara in the late 1890s was allocated several villages whose headmen had to provide a fixed number of workers each day. This system helped to discredit Kilindi rule and induce Kinyashi to abdicate in 1902 for fear of assassination.

[1] *RTA*, 1900/2, no. 437, p. 2,917; Meyer to Government, 23 March 1905, RKA 118/176; *RTA*, 1907/9, no. 622, p. 3,697; *RTA*, 1909/11, no. 179, p. 408.
[2] Rechenberg to Tanga, 9 December 1910, RKA 122/223; *Die deutschen Schutzgebiete 1909–10*, I, 16.

It also produced such abuses that Götzen abolished it in 1904. Disaster
followed for the settlers. 'Not a worker can now be found', one
complained. In 1907 the district officer imposed a solution by issuing
each Shambaa with a card obliging him to work for a European for
thirty days every four months at a fixed wage, on pain of being
conscripted for public works. The system's advantage was to allow the
worker to choose his employer, and much as he disliked it even
Rechenberg allowed it to continue. The result was exceptionally low
wages for the Shambaa. In 1907 contract workers in Lushoto district
earned Shs. 20 for thirty days' work and local workers only Shs. 9–10,
whereas in Tanga the contract wage was lower (Shs. 13–16) and the
local wage higher (Shs. 12–15). Local workers far exceeded contract
labourers in Lushoto, the reverse of the situation in Tanga.[1]

Card systems quickly spread elsewhere, for they satisfied both
employers and administrators. The government tacitly accepted one
in Morogoro which was 'based on an arrangement between the
planters and the district office'.[2] In Upare the district officer banned
a private card system operated by the planters but was prepared to
consider a proper one. In Handeni, on the other hand, government
forbade a system whereby *akidas* supplied labourers who had to work
until they provided substitutes, while the district officer in Dar es
Salaam was transferred in 1914 at the Reichstag's insistence for
organising a card system. At that time government acknowledged that
compulsory labour existed in Lushoto, Dar es Salaam, Rufiji,
Morogoro, and Lindi districts. These were probably the main areas,
although much informal compulsion occurred elsewhere. It had
probably become more rather than less common as time passed.[3]

The local labour supply was especially contentious on Kilimanjaro.
Alienation created some land hunger in limited areas. Tax was an
effective stimulant, for alternative sources of cash were less available
here than in the lower Pangani valley. Yet the labour supply never
satisfied the settlers. Some recruited migrants, but most demanded a
card system. Government rejected this in 1908 for fear of violent
Chagga reaction but stationed troops on Kilimanjaro at that time to
compel those who refused plantation employment to labour on public

[1] Iliffe, *German rule*, pp. 135–6; Martienssen to Wilhelmstal, 11 January 1906, TNA LKV
Lushoto 77; list in RKA 122/143; Meyer to Government, 23 March 1905, RKA 118/176.
[2] 'Protokoll der Versammlung des Wirtschaftlichen Verbandes von Rufiji in
Mpanganya', 12 February 1911, TNA VIII/J/66/1.
[3] BA Lushoto to Rau, 24 February 1912, TNA Grants Lushoto 281/3; Tetzlaff,
Entwicklung, pp. 237, 247–8.

works.[1] Eventually the settlers had their way. 'It particularly saddens me', a missionary wrote in 1910,

that our people can no longer be regarded as free cultivators. They are all apportioned among the farmers and in some way dependent on them. If one walks through the fields, one meets mainly old people, women, and girls. The men and boys are away on the farms and at most come home on Sundays.[2]

Whatever the law, a settler observed in 1912, 'in practice no district officer can rule three months here unless he finds some way of driving the Chagga back into the plantations from time to time'.[3] In that year Schnee authorised a card system.

Meanwhile the Kilimanjaro situation was complicated by several Chagga who had themselves become coffee farmers. In most plantation areas enterprising Africans experimented with the new crops, but usually without success. A few Nyamwezi in the north-east tried sisal, but it came to nothing. Small rubber plantations owned by Africans in Tanga and Bagamoyo either were sold to Europeans or collapsed in the crash of 1913.[4] Settlers always protested at these experiments, but the government refused to forbid them. 'The supply of raw materials to Germany...is the object', Rechenberg insisted, '...and whether it is achieved through plantation agriculture or native cultivation is a secondary consideration.'[5] He refused to discourage Chagga coffee-growers. The earliest were catechists who obtained seed from their respective missions during the 1890s, but the first entrepreneur was one of Marealle's advisors, Sawaya Mawalla, who in 1900 established a sizeable coffee plot on open land with seed obtained from an Italian settler. Marealle and other chiefs quickly followed his example. In 1913 the authorities reckoned that six Chagga had over a thousand bushes each and others had several hundred.[6] The growers came from 'the more intelligent, propertied class (chiefs, akidas [advisors], and the like), for they alone possess enough cattle [for manure] and land'.[7] Their emergence complicated the labour problem. They were apparently exempted from plantation labour but

[1] Winterfeld to Methner, 8 February 1908, TNA IV/O/3/1; *Deutsches Kolonialblatt*, 15 August 1909.
[2] Jensen, quoted in Schanz, *Am Fusse*, p. 134.
[3] Förster in *Usambara-Post*, 25 May 1912.
[4] Bald, *Deutsch-Ostafrika*, p. 153; *RTA*, 1907/9, no. 622, p. 3,701; Rohde to Government, 11 October 1913, TNA G8/176/21.
[5] Rechenberg to Methner, 24 October 1907, RKA 120/105.
[6] Kieran, 'Holy Ghost Fathers', p. 253; Pennington, 'KNPA' [February 1931] TNA 13060/203; Bald, *Deutsch-Ostafrika*, p. 154 n. 46.
[7] Förster in *Deutsch-Ostafrikanische Zeitung*, 21 August 1909.

prohibited from employing Chagga on the same terms as European employers. Since, according to a missionary, 'people here work for fellow-tribesmen only reluctantly', this situation threatened to inter-dict African capitalism:

There are really industrious cultivators in the area who lay out small coffee plots for themselves and would enlarge these if they had more land and workers. At present they are almost entirely dependent on the help of their wives, who have quite sufficient to do without this.[1]

'We don't need black capitalists, we need black workers', a settler insisted at this time.[2] In fact very few black capitalists emerged, for the Africans who exploited labour were chiefly those who controlled it by political means and could throw the risks on to their dependents. 'This year', it was reported from Shirati in 1912, 'the sultans have made their people hurry to cultivate large cotton plots.'[3] 'Individual natives got nothing', a British investigator explained, 'and the cash for cotton was largely taken by the chiefs. . . Every chief had his large patch, which was cultivated by free labour.'[4] On the other side of Lake Victoria the Chief of Missenyi's greed destroyed cotton-growing entirely.[5] In Usukuma cotton was introduced into the Nera chiefdom as a cash crop in 1902 by an eccentric German whose share-cropping system benefited the headmen but was so unprofitable to the people that by 1909 the undertaking was collapsing. The district officer, Gunzert, then compelled lakeshore Sukuma to grow cotton:

> The drum of the chief calls to plant cotton.
> Gird up your loins, clean the fields,
> Then even the European will not be angry.[6]

Between 1909 and 1913 Mwanza's exports of cotton lint rose from 123 to 3,735 bales.[7] Its profitability became evident:

About 1910 cotton cultivation was introduced first in the Nassa chiefdom. Gunsrat brought seed to Simba who was then chief and ordered him to distribute it and force each able-bodied man to plant a certain acreage. That year they had a wonderful crop. . . People in other chiefdoms seeing the profit in it also began to demand seed.[8]

[1] Schöne [?] to Moshi, 15 February 1913, TNA G44/6.
[2] Eismann to Government, 30 September 1912, TNA VIII/J/52a/1.
[3] *Kiongozi*, June 1912.
[4] 'Report on Schirati district by Major Hastings Horne', 8 January 1921, CO 691/51/279.
[5] Monthly report on Bukoba district for July 1918 by D. L. Baines, Cory papers, ULD.
[6] Sukuma song in Hans Cory [Koritschoner], 'Some East African native songs', *TNR*, IV (1937), 62. For Sukuma cotton-growing, see Austen, *Northwest Tanzania*, pp. 97–100.
[7] 1 bale = 181 kg. See Austen, *Northwest Tanzania*, p. 271.
[8] MacGillivray, 'History. . . through the eyes of Kiyumbi', in Maswa district book, TNA.

The total crop was small, but together with cash earnings from hides, rice, and groundnuts it enabled some Sukuma to abandon labour migration.[1]

The triangular competition for labour was best illustrated in Buhaya. The Haya had long grown and traded robusta coffee. When the Uganda railway reached Lake Victoria in 1901 the local officer encouraged production. Between 1906 and 1912 exports grew from 214,552 to 681,245 kg.[2] The main beneficiaries were the chiefs, especially the two most powerful and energetic, Kahigi of Kianja and Mutahangarwa of Kiziba. 'Mutahangarwa planted coffee', it was recalled, 'without listening to the warnings of the old people about what the spirit world (*okuzimu*) would say.'[3] He and Kahigi used tributary labour to grow coffee. From their subjects' plots they claimed the product of one coffee tree in fifty. They extended the *nyarubanja* land tenure system to include many areas either planted with or suitable for coffee. Thus ancient agricultural skills and pre-capitalist forms of exploitation were absorbed intact into the colonial structure. It was common knowledge that the only way to obtain porters in Buhaya was to pay the chief for them. Missionaries believed that the Haya cultivators' status deteriorated sharply under German rule, and there are indications of popular discontent.[4] A few European settlers also entered Buhaya. Kahigi opposed every form of European intrusion and finally persuaded the Germans to close Kianja to settlement in 1913, but in Kiziba the literate and ambitious Mutahangarwa sold tributary labour to settlers and even sought an open partnership. 'The three of us want to establish a plantation', he wrote. 'Bwana H. Rehse and Bwana Weber will each contribute £1,500. I myself shall not contribute anything because I shall supply workers until the plantation is ready.'[5] The three would share the profits equally. The government vetoed this scheme, but it reinforced the point that Africans, like Europeans, commonly needed political as well as economic resources in order to command local labour.

European labour requirements grew rapidly. In 1906 plantations employed an estimated 20,000 men; in 1912, 91,892, of whom 61,211

[1] *Die deutschen Schutzgebiete 1910/11*, I, 15.
[2] Austen, *Northwest Tanzania*, p. 270.
[3] F. X. Lwamugira, quoted in Carl-J. Hellberg, *Missions on a colonial frontier west of Lake Victoria* (trans. E. Sharpe, Lund, 1965), p. 72 n. 40.
[4] Stuemer to Mutahangarwa, 6 June 1914, TNA 215/50; Hirth to Government, 15 November 1903, TNA G9/19/153; Haber, 'Die innerpolitischen Verhältnisse im Bezirke Bukoba', 30 June 1904, RKA 1029/97.
[5] Mutahangarwa to Stuemer, 15 July 1907, TNA G34/5.

were concentrated in five north-eastern districts. In 1913 the total in paid employment of all kinds was 172,100, possibly some twenty per cent of German East Africa's available labour force.[1] It is estimated that twenty per cent of Tanganyika's adult males were working for wages in 1957,[2] but the intensity of labour demand in German times was probably exceptional because of the period's transitional character, with local porterage still absorbing much energy at the same time as plantation enterprise developed.

Table 1. *Unskilled wages in shillings per working month, selected districts, 1888–1913*

	Tanga contract	Tanga local	Pangani contract	Lushoto contract	Lushoto local	DSM general
1888	12½ᵃ					
1890						8½ᵇ
1891	12½ᶜ		12½ᶜ			12ᵈ
1895						9¼–12½ᵉ
1896			13⅓ᶠ			
1901	16–17⅓ᵍ		16–17⅓ᵍ		10ʰ	
1903	9⅓–16ʲ			16–20ʲ		10⅔–18⅔ʲ
1906	12–14⅔ᵏ	10⅔–13⅓ᵏ		16ᵏ	8–8⅔ᵏ	12–17⅓ᵏ
1907	13⅓–16ᵏ	12–14⅔ᵏ	16ᵏ	20ᵏ	9⅓–10ᵏ	12–17⅓ᵏ
1912	16–20ˡ		16ˡ	16ˡ	8–13⅓ˡ	13½–16ˡ
1913	20ᵐ					

SOURCES: a: Baumann, *Aufstand*, p. 42; b: Sicard, *Lutheran church*, p. 77; c: Baumann, 'Vorläufiges Bemerkungen über das Usambara-Bahn Projekt' [1891] TNA G12/1/16; d: *Deutsches Kolonialblatt*, 1 October 1891; e: *RTA*, 1895/7, no. 88, p. 893; f: *RTA*, 1895/7, no. 624, p. 2,973; g: *RTA*, 1900/2, no. 437, p. 2,917; h: Hohman to Wilhelmstal, 24 March 1901, TNA G54/33/342; j: Stuhlmann to AAKA, 31 March 1903, RKA 118/144; k: List in RKA 122/143; l: *Die deutschen Schutzgebiete 1912/13*, II, 79; m: Tetzlaff, *Entwicklung*, p. 269.

The plantations had more difficulty than other enterprises in attracting labour. Only during the Maji Maji rebellion was there a labour shortage on the central railway, but in the years 1904–6 and 1910–12 there were widespread shortages on the plantations. Nyamwezi

[1] List in RKA 122/139; *Die deutschen Schutzgebiete 1912/13*, II, 79; Tetzlaff, *Entwicklung*, p. 194.
[2] C. W. Guillebaud, *An economic survey of the sisal industry of Tanganyika* (2nd edn, Welwyn, 1958), p. 62.

always preferred porterage or railway work. For this there were probably several reasons. Perhaps the tedious familiarity of unskilled agricultural labour was less attractive than the more mobile and unfamiliar work of the porter or construction worker. Supervision and discipline were probably harsher on the plantations, and plantation workers were probably paid less and treated worse than most other employees. Table 1 lists money wages in plantation agriculture and unskilled urban employment, calculated as earnings for a working month (i.e. thirty days worked) in forms of employment where no food allowance was given. The figures suggest a slight upward trend over the German period, especially in its last years. They need to be compared with changing price levels, but fragmentary data make these most difficult to calculate. Between 1897 and 1912 the customs value per unit of imported cotton cloth, rice, and sugar rose by 44, 32, and 3 per cent respectively.[1] Cattle prices appear to have risen faster, often by 50–100 per cent between 1900 and 1914.[2] Grain prices presently available are too fragmentary to use. Pending the construction of a much-needed price index, it seems unlikely that plantation wages outstripped prices in German times. Earnings in railway construction were higher than on the plantations: Shs. 11–18 plus a food allowance of Shs. 6–7 during the period 1909–12.[3] Porters were paid by the journey, but if their earnings are recalculated as monthly rates according to official journey times, they range from Shs. 13 between Mwanza and Tabora in 1908 and Shs. 19 between Bagamoyo and Tabora in 1899 to a record figure of Shs. 33 per working month between Mahenge and Songea in 1909.[4] The plantation labourer's work was more regular and probably less strenuous, but it was also worse paid.

Plantation conditions were another deterrent. There were manifest abuses: brutality, flogging, bad housing, hunger, overwork, disease,

[1] *RTA*, 1900/2, no. 152, p. 952; *Die deutschen Schutzgebiete 1912/13*, II, 130–55, 180–203.

[2] 'The autobiography of Alfred Claude Hollis' (typescript, n.d.), II, 28a (Hollis papers, RH); 'Notizen über die Landwirtschaft in und bei Iringa' [1902] TNA G8/17; Prittwitz, 'Jahresbericht des Bezirksamt Tabora 1908–9', and Grawert, 'Jahresbericht der Militärstation Mahenge für das Etatsjahr 1909', TNA G1/6; Styx, 'Jahresbericht des Militärbezirks Iringa für das Berichtsjahr 1910/1911', TNA G1/7; Schaele, 'Die Rinder des Muansa- und Tabora-Bezirkes', *Der Pflanzer*, IX (1913), 117; Lichtenheld, 'Rinderrassen', p. 273.

[3] *Deutsches Kolonialblatt*, 1 June 1909; *Die deutschen Schutzgebiete 1912/13*, II, 79; Tetzlaff, *Entwicklung*, p. 269.

[4] *RTA*, 1907/9, no. 1,106, p. 6,552; Leue to Government, 11 February 1899, TNA G1/35/122; Grawert, 'Jahresbericht der Militärstation Mahenge für das Etatsjahr 1909', TNA G1/6; *Landesgesetzgebung*, II, 86–7.

and death. In 1888 the whole labour force at Lewa deserted a sadistic manager. During thirty months of 1909–11 the Dar es Salaam Provincial Court *convicted* 27 Europeans of brutality against Africans.[1] Plantation areas exported many diseases – notably syphilis and intestinal worms – to labour-supplying regions. A third of the Maji Maji captives sent to work in the north-east became infested with intestinal worms. To these disgusting conditions were added the planters' use of the wage system as a disciplinary weapon. In the early 1890s they tried to require their employees to work a fixed number of hours, usually ten, for six (or sometimes seven) days a week. This failed. Instead the plantations adopted a piecework or 'task' system: so many leaves cut or rows weeded were a day's task which, once completed, freed the worker either for rest or for a second task. The worker was contracted to complete a specified number of tasks, usually 180, either within a fixed period, often 270 days, or at his convenience. Each task was marked on a card. The system was universal by 1897.[2] It gave migrants without wives time to cook food. It allowed for illness, exhaustion, and sheer boredom. It approximated to the work patterns of peasant agriculture, the caravan trade, and the nineteenth-century slave plantations, just as caravan precedents led food allowances to be paid separately from wages. Most important, the employer could minimise his supervision costs, lay off his men cheaply when work was short, and yet know that a worker who failed to complete his contract could be flogged and spend six months in gaol. Abuse was easy. To set the task above the men's capacity was self-defeating, but tasks completed could be erased from the card as a punishment, or simply never entered. Workers were often not paid until they completed the full 180 days. Sometimes they were not paid until they accepted a new contract. Accused of these practices, a manager observed, 'That's how we've always done it.'[3]

Workers replied by self-protection. They commonly gave false names when enrolled. They tried to insist on their contract terms. 'My niggers are very particular about doing no work on Sundays! Yet they want their posho', an engineer noted.[4] The most common protest was 'desertion', normally individual but occasionally collective. Some 220 contract workers simultaneously quitted the Schuberthof plantation

[1] Müller, *Deutschland*, p. 243; Rechenberg to RKA, 21 June 1911, RKA 237/93.
[2] *RTA*, 1897/8, no. 94, p. 949.
[3] Bald, *Deutsch-Ostafrika*, p. 182. Generally, see Tetzlaff, *Entwicklung*, part 3; Iliffe, *German rule*, pp. 64–8, 103–8, 134–9.
[4] Gillman diary, 19 November 1905, RH. Posho = ration.

on the Rufiji when ill-treated.[1] Yet no true strike is known from this period. Indeed, labour action seems to have been less confident and co-ordinated than in the caravan trade, presumably because the colonial state weakened the workers' bargaining power and because plantation workers had not yet formed traditions of solidarity and protest to match those of the more professional porters.

Although the government greatly aided employers to obtain local workers, it refused to recruit long-distance migrants for them. They had to organise this themselves. Recruiting agents began to operate in the early 1890s in Unyamwezi, Usukuma, the south, and even in Mozambique, where men were hired to help build the northern railway. Attempts to create a single recruiting syndicate failed through undercapitalisation, inefficiency, and tension between large and small employers. Agents therefore flooded the countryside. There were said to be a thousand in Tabora district alone in 1913.[2] Some migrants welcomed recruitment because it guaranteed railway transport to the workplace. Others were deceived into contracts, often believing they were hired for light work until they found themselves with the hated task of cutting sisal. Some recruiters had semi-formal agreements with chiefs. Mtinginya of Usongo was under contract to supply a trading firm with porters. Threats were used in Iringa district, bribes in Songea, and whole cases of schnapps in Unyamwezi. 'Wanted to buy, 20 Nyamwezi, only good men', ran a newspaper advertisement.[3] Believing that Africans who were paid more would work less, employers needing labour invested in recruiting rather than higher wages. In 1912 one rubber company spent £2,880 on wages, £2,113 on food, and £2,188 on recruiting.[4]

There were three phases of labour migration in German East Africa. The first, covering the 1890s, was dominated by the 'Nyamwezi', a loose term embracing almost anyone from the western plateau. They moved quickly from caravan porterage through casual employment on the coast to regular plantation work. Sukuma were being engaged as plantation workers in 1896, while by 1903 there were some 4,000

[1] Tetzlaff, *Entwicklung*, p. 251.
[2] 'Verhandlungen des Gouvernementsrats des deutsch-ostafrikanischen Schutzgebiets vom 20. bis 23. Januar 1913', RKA 813/227. Generally, see Iliffe, *German rule*, pp. 67–8, 80, 91, 103–8, 133–9, 203.
[3] Meyer to Government, 2 April 1906, TNA G1/96; Styx, 'Jahresbericht des Militärbezirks Iringa für das Berichtsjahr 1910/1911', TNA G1/7; Peramiho mission diary, 14 May 1910, Peramiho archives; *Usambara-Post*, 19 June 1909.
[4] H. Waltz, 'Die Pflanzungen der Europäer in unseren tropischen Kolonien im Jahre 1913', *Jahrbuch über die deutschen Kolonien*, VI (1913), 206.

'Nyamwezi' in the north-east.[1] Among other Tanganyikan peoples migration was not yet an established pattern of life but rather the personal choice of individuals. In 1894 a survey of Dar es Salaam showed that of every 100 unskilled workers 47 were Zaramo and 23 'Swahili' – both from the immediate vicinity – while 10 were Sagara, 7 'Nyamwezi', 5 Shambaa, 3 Masai, 2 Gogo, 2 'Mahenge' (presumably Mbunga), and 1 'Manyema' of Congolese origin.[2]

During the second phase of migration, from 1900 to roughly 1908, the 'Nyamwezi' still dominated the labour market – in 1905, 27 per cent of Dar es Salaam's Africans were 'Nyamwezi'[3] – and most societies still supplied only occasional individuals, but tax pressed certain peoples into a more regular migration. This was clearest in the south. Soon after 1900 tax forced many Ngoni to work as caravan porters, and by 1910 some 6,000 were leaving for the coast each year. In 1905, 12 per cent of Dar es Salaam's Africans were said to come from the south. The Maji Maji rebellion brought certain peoples into the labour market, notably those of the Rufiji valley, who began to work in Dar es Salaam during the famine of 1906.[4]

The great expansion of migration began around 1908 and continued until the war. There were several reasons for it. The supply of Nyamwezi and Sukuma diminished. Recruiting extended rapidly. Tax was collected more widely and systematically: between 1906 and 1912 total hut tax revenue rose from £96,248 to £254,809.[5] Asian storekeepers – the best recruiters – were establishing themselves inland. The central railway brought many peoples along its route into the labour market. For all these reasons migration extended rapidly. In 1909 many Iramba, pressed by tax and famine, began to work on the northern railway and the plantations of Moshi and Arusha, where they and their neighbours later became the core of the labour force. Tax and famine brought the Bena of the Southern Highlands into the labour market in 1908–9, initially as railway navvies and then as sisal workers. As the central railway crossed the country, schools stood empty in Uzaramo, the Nyamwezi 'seemed to have no thought for anything else but the earning of money', and the first Kimbu, Gogo, Ha, Fipa, and Vinza sought employment with Europeans, although

[1] Herrmann to Government, 1 August 1896, RKA 287/146; Meyer to Government, 25 January 1905, RKA 118/207.
[2] *RTA*, 1895/7, no. 88, p. 893.   [3] Sicard, *Lutheran church*, p. 171 n. 6.
[4] Peramiho mission diary, 8 June 1911, Peramiho archives; Sicard, *Lutheran church*, p. 171 n. 6; Grass to Government, 10 December 1906, TNA iv/H/1/ii.
[5] *Die deutschen Schutzgebiete 1910/11*, ii, 333; *ibid. 1912/13*, ii, 408.

of these only the Fipa visited the plantations before 1914. A list of householders living in 1910 in the Pangani South native reserve, a dormitory settlement for sisal estates, shows members of 52 different tribes, including 236 'Nyamwezi', 79 'Swahili', 42 Ngoni, 24 Yao, 23 Ngulu, and 21 Manyema. Also listed are peoples as distant as the 'Kavirondo' (Luo or Luyia) from Kenya, Bemba and Bisa from Northern Rhodesia, Rundi, Nyasa, Mambwe from the Tanganyika-Northern Rhodesia border, and Makua from the Tanganyika-Mozambique border.[1]

So wide was the migration network by 1914 that the illuminating question is which peoples were *not* involved. There were those living in areas of intensive German enterprise or cash-crop development (Zaramo, Bondei, Shambaa, Pare, Chagga, Meru, Arusha, and Haya). There were pastoralists (Masai and Tatoga). There were agriculturalists with many cattle (Iraqw, Hehe, and Gogo). There were those who could earn cash from forest produce (notably Ngindo). There were remote peoples still largely untaxed (Nyakyusa, Ha, Hangaza, the peoples east of Lake Victoria). It is difficult to think of others. The list reveals two points.

First, labour migration was one economic activity where nineteenth-century patterns survived into the colonial period. Of the peoples who did not supply migrants in 1914, not one had been deeply involved in the caravan trade, while all the six peoples most strongly represented in the Pangani South native reserve had been so involved. For Nyamwezi, especially, the colonial economy initially enlarged employment opportunities. By 1908 Nyamwezi were working not only on both railway projects, on the north-eastern plantations, in Dar es Salaam, and as caravan porters, but for the Mombasa and Kisumu ports, the Uganda railway, the Kenya police, British safari firms, Kenyan farms, Zanzibar clove estates, and even the Rand.[2] 'We know every kind of work', they boasted:

From long ago we have carried the white men's boxes in every direction. When the coastal people, through their idleness, failed to build the railway and lay

---

[1] BNS Mkalama to Kondoa, 5 December 1912, TNA G9/48/144; James D. Graham, 'Changing patterns of wage labor in Tanzania: a history of the relations between African labor and European capitalism in Njombe district, 1931–1961', Ph.D. thesis, Northwestern University, 1968, p. 35; Sicard, *Lutheran church*, p. 195; 'Moravian church: extracts', September 1913; Shorter, *Chiefship*, pp. 340–1; Bückner to Eisenbahnkommissar, 22 May 1909, TNA G17/66; Hoffmann to Eisenbahnkommissar, 20 July and 20 August 1912, TNA G17/123; list in TNA LKV Pangani 37.

[2] Meyer to Government, 2 April 1906, TNA G1/96; Siegel, 'Reisebericht' [c. November 1908] RKA 278/97.

the rails, we took up our hoes and pick-axes, we broke the rocks and the hills, and soon the job was finished. Now the locomotive has arrived in Tabora. Soon we shall send it on to Ujiji. Do you see?[1]

The second generalisation is that the crucial determinants of labour migration were the need for cash and the alternative means available for earning it. Bondei did not need to migrate because they could sell food to plantations, Ngindo because they could collect rubber, pastoral peoples because cattle were mobile. Once railway transport enabled them to market their crops, even Sukuma began to abandon migration.[2]

The ecological catastrophe

Labour migration was the point at which the creation of the colonial economy interacted with the natural disasters of the 1890s to bring about an ecological catastrophe fundamental to Tanganyika's twentieth-century history. The nature of the interaction needs much research, but its effects on the ground were simple and dramatic. From the turn of the century many woodland savannah peoples suffered plagues of bush pigs and baboons which ruined their crops. Shortly afterwards lions and other predators multiplied, forcing the people to retreat from the forest fringes. The deserted fields relapsed to bush, soon infested by tsetse flies. Cattle began to die of trypanosomiasis and men of a disease which developed from fever and lassitude to coma and death. Men and livestock retreated further. Pigs, lions, bush, and tsetse followed them. Nature was reconquering the land.[3]

The *Grenzwildnisse* grew at astonishing speed. By 1911 Unyamwezi contained only four sizeable fly-free areas. Lions infested the Shinyanga region of southern Usukuma about 1909 and tsetse flies were advancing there in 1913. Within another decade the Sukuma abandoned a large proportion of their cultivated land.[4] Tsetse entered northern Karagwe by 1913 and within a decade occupied most of its former pastures. 'The sultanate resembles an immense desert', a missionary wrote in the 1930s. 'Signs of game are constantly present

---

[1] Paulo Kondemzigo, 'Sifa ya Wanyamwezi', *Rafiki yangu*, October 1912.
[2] Above, p. 156.
[3] See the description in C. F. M. Swynnerton, 'An experiment in control of tsetse-flies at Shinyanga', *Bulletin of entomological research*, xv (1924–5), 318.
[4] Wölfel, 'Beitrag zur Kenntnis der Tsetse (Glossina morsitans) und der Trypanosomiasis', *Der Pflanzer*, vii (1911), 397, 404; Swynnerton, 'Experiment', p. 318; Ford, *Trypanosomiases*, chs. 11–13.

and the fertile banana groves are abandoned.'[1] Eastern Tanganyika experienced the same disaster. In 1907 a missionary visiting Uzigua noted that 'great numbers of cattle have died in the last year or two from cattle disease, and I nowhere saw the vast herds which used to be such a striking feature of the Zigua country'. Twenty years later cattle had almost disappeared from Uzigua and trypanosomiasis was endemic.[2] Similar disasters occurred on the coast, in the Pangani valley, and in parts of the north-central highlands, while the devastation following the Maji Maji rebellion enabled tsetse to spread in the south.[3] In 1913 the Germans estimated that one-third of German East Africa was infested by tsetse. Numerous cattle survived only in four regions: the Southern Highlands; central Ugogo and the north-central highlands; the Masai plain; and central Usukuma – a belt running north to south through the centre of Tanganyika.[4]

Tsetse flies had long existed in the *Grenzwildnisse*, but whether they had previously carried trypanosomes which infected human beings with sleeping sickness is disputed. Some believe that sleeping sickness was a West African disease which entered East Africa around 1900 in two forms: Gambian sleeping sickness, first diagnosed on the Uganda shore of Lake Victoria in 1900 and at Shirati in Tanganyika in 1902, and Rhodesian sleeping sickness, first diagnosed in Tanganyika at the River Ruvuma in 1910. Others hold that the Gambian variety, at least, may have existed much longer in the *Grenzwildnisse*. The issue is vital to an understanding of the twentieth-century catastrophe, but it is at present unresolved. What is certain is that sleeping sickness quickly assumed epidemic proportions in the lake areas: 1,405 cases around Lake Victoria in 1909, 3,300 around Lake Tanganyika in 1913.[5]

The most powerful explanation of the spread of tsetse is Dr Ford's contention that it resulted chiefly from the natural disasters of the 1890s, exacerbated by German military actions and by administrative

[1] Ford, *Trypanosomiases*, chs. 7–8; Césard, 'Le Muhaya', p. 90.
[2] *Central Africa*, May 1907; C. F. M. Swynnerton, 'The tsetse flies of East Africa', *Transactions of the Royal Entomological Society of London*, LXXXIV (1936), 348–51.
[3] S. Napier Bax, 'Notes on the presence of tsetse fly, between 1857 and 1915, in the Dar es Salaam area', *TNR*, XVI (1943), 45–8; H. Morstatt, 'Bericht über eine Reise in den Bezirk Moschi', *Der Pflanzer*, VI (1910), 226; Ruff to Kilimatinde, 24 March 1910, TNA MPG 9138; below, p. 202.
[4] Lichtenheld, 'Rinderrassen', p. 261.
[5] See C. G. Knight, 'The ecology of African sleeping sickness', *Annals of the Association of American Geographers*, LXI (1971), 24–6; Ford, *Trypanosomiases*, pp. 242–3; Kjekshus, *Ecology control*, pp. 165–8; David F. Clyde, *History of the medical services of Tanganyika* (Dar es Salaam, 1962), pp. 28–32.

policies which, for example, tried to stop Africans killing game. Rinderpest, especially, destroyed the cattle whose browsing had controlled the bush. Rinderpest also killed game, but game recovered more quickly than cattle and occupied former pasture. Germans believed that the cattle herds recovered by 1901, but this was improbable. It is unlikely that they ever recovered in German times.[1]

Alongside the decline in the cattle herds there went, most probably, a falling human population. The first useful estimate of Tanganyika's total population was slightly over four million in 1911,[2] and later figures support its broad accuracy. Although Kuczynski excluded German East Africa from his study of East Africa's demographic history, his reasons for thinking that Kenya's population fell between 1895 and 1920 applied equally to German East Africa.[3] Famine caused appalling losses during the 1890s and in the south after Maji Maji. Tanga district's population was said to have fallen between 1897 and 1899 from 123,308 to 61,328. One observer guessed that more than 750,000 people died of hunger in the whole country between 1894 and 1899. How many died as a result of Maji Maji is unknown, but it may have been 200,000 or more. There are strong indications of population decline in the Rufiji valley.[4] Missionaries alleged enormous population losses in Unyamwezi and its environs: that Usumbwa lost half its people between 1892 and 1913 and Unyamwezi a third or a quarter; that between 1908 and 1914 the population of Tabora and its environs fell from 80,000 to 40,000.[5] Doctors produced fragmentary data: that 519 Nyamwezi women examined had only 360 living children; that 179 Sukuma women had only 128 living children; that Bukoba district contained 110,000 women but only 84,000 children.[6] Such figures are unreliable and, in this crude form, unhelpful. The only systematic study was made in Ulanga district in the 1930s. It suggested that even in areas which had not fought against the Germans during Maji Maji women at bearing age during the German period had not borne

[1] Ford, *Trypanosomiases, passim*; *RTA*, 1900/2, no. 814, p. 5,267.
[2] *Die deutschen Schutzgebiete 1911/12*, II, 34.
[3] R. R. Kuczynski, *Demographic survey of the British colonial empire*, II (London, 1949), pp. 118–25.
[4] *RTA*, 1898/1900, no. 518, p. 2,884; Kjekshus, *Ecology control*, p. 142; below, p. 200; Clarke Brooke, 'Types of food shortages in Tanzania', *Geographical review*, LVII (1967), 346.
[5] J. M. M. Van der Burgt, 'Zur Entvölkerungsfrage Unjamwesis und Usumbwas', *Koloniale Rundschau*, V (1913), 705–28; Tetzlaff, *Entwicklung*, p. 252.
[6] Tetzlaff, *Entwicklung*, pp. 257–8.

enough children to prevent population decline, and that it was not until the 1930s that the population began to reproduce itself.[1] Taken with the other data, this makes it likely that Tanganyika's total population fell, perhaps substantially, during the German period and did not increase again until perhaps 1925.[2]

To obtain a full picture of the ecological catastrophe, however, the effects of natural disaster must also be set in a wider context. An earlier chapter suggested that after 1860 the withdrawal of labour for porterage and the relocation of settlements for military defence may have caused tsetse to advance on the western plateau.[3] Comparable changes occurred under the Germans. Their arrival reversed the trend towards concentrated settlement. Field guns and disciplined askari could penetrate the strongest boma. Victorious Germans destroyed fortifications, while the ending of local wars made them less necessary. Concentration now made people vulnerable to tax and labour demands. Many peoples disliked living in large villages which impeded cultivation and restricted personal freedom. Settlements therefore broke up under the Germans in many areas.[4] They tried to set minimum sizes for villages – fifteen huts in South Pare, thirty on the Makonde plateau – but with little effect.[5] Zinza were returning to resettle the forest clearings when tsetse drove them out again. In Usukuma 'the bush is said to have taken on [a] chequered appearance, broken by fields and patches of open grazing'.[6] By 1914 most peoples were scattered in woodland settlements as before the coming of firearms, but now with fewer cattle and at greater risk from game and tsetse. Some Germans believed that this interpenetration of natural and managed ecosystems favoured the spread of tsetse. Travelling in Usumbwa during 1913, an observer became convinced that both tsetse's expansion and the false impression of depopulation were due to dispersal into forest clearings. Others held that those who abandoned Usumbwa and western Unyamwezi settled instead in Unyanyembe and south-eastern Unyamwezi, thus continuing

---

[1] A. T. and G. M. Culwick, 'A study of population in Ulanga', *Sociological review*, xxx (1938), 365–79, and xxxi (1939), 25–43.

[2] Kuczynski suggested 1925: *Demographic survey*, II, 399.

[3] Above, p. 76.

[4] *Deutsches Kolonialblatt*, 15 May 1907; *Central Africa*, August 1904; Kigonsera mission diary, 15 September 1902, Peramiho archives; Haber to Government, 12 January 1905, RKA 118/174.

[5] Schanz, *Am Fusse*, p. 198; Zache, 'Reisebericht', 23 January 1900, RKA 220/14.

[6] Kollmann, *Victoria Nyanza*, p. 106; Swynnerton, 'Experiment', p. 317.

a nineteenth-century trend.[1] Yet those who bewailed the depopulation of the western plateau blamed not rinderpest but labour migration.[2] Unlike much caravan porterage, plantation work kept the men away during the planting season. The cultivated area probably declined in most labour-exporting regions, so that bush and tsetse flies reclaimed deserted fields while men cleared land for rubber and sisal in the north-east. In this way the ecological catastrophe was part of the entire process of Tanganyika's integration into a larger world.

[1] Charisius in *Deutsches Kolonialblatt*, 15 May 1907; Gillman diary, 28 March, 25 May, and 11 August 1913, RH.
[2] Van der Burgt, 'Zur Entvölkerungsfrage', *passim*; Tetzlaff, *Entwicklung*, pp. 252–9.

CHAPTER 6

The Maji Maji rebellion, 1905–7

Outbreak

On a morning late in July 1905 the men of Nandete climbed a path towards a field of ripening cotton which they had cultivated. When they reached it their leaders, Ngulumbalyo Mandai and Lindimyo Machela, stepped forward and pulled three plants out of the ground. They did this in order to declare war on the German Empire.[1]

The Maji Maji rebellion was an explosion of African hatred of European rule. It was a final attempt by Tanganyika's old societies to destroy the colonial order by force, and its failure made the passing of the old societies inevitable. It is therefore a last opportunity to study the workings of those societies amidst an incomparably vivid crisis for which there exists detailed evidence unmatched for earlier periods or other parts of Africa. The rebellion began among the stateless peoples of the south-east and extended to the newly created states of the Southern Highlands. It took place at the moment of transition from the nineteenth-century economy to the colonial order and it began as a movement of highlanders and frontiersmen resisting incorporation into the colonial economy and reduction to peasant status. To uproot cotton was therefore an apt ultimatum. To the men of Nandete, in the Matumbi highlands north-west of Kilwa, cotton symbolised the foreign penetration and control which had followed defeat in the 'war of the pumpkins' seven years earlier.[2] An Arab *akida* (government agent) ruled them from Kibata. Five penniless Germans grew cotton in the foothills where the Matumbi had to work for five cents a day under harsh discipline and to the detriment of their fields. In 1903, when the colony's economy was most depressed, government required *akidas* and headmen in the southern

[1] Gwassa, 'Outbreak', p. 209.
[2] Above, p. 133.

coastal districts to establish cotton plots worked by communal labour. Earnings from them were negligible.[1] As a stateless people the Matumbi resented all authority. By 1904 they longed to destroy German control. Yet this presented great difficulties. The Matumbi had resisted Ngoni, Arabs, and Germans, but they were not a militarised people. In order to fight they had to be attacked. This was why they uprooted cotton. They also needed to ensure that every clan would join the rebellion and to find an answer to German firepower. 'They waited for a long period because they were afraid', it was remembered. '...Who would start?...While there were no superior weapons should the people not fear? Everywhere elders were busy thinking, "What should we do?"'[2]

These questions were answered by a prophet named Kinjikitile Ngwale.[3] He lived at Ngarambe, below the western slopes of Matumbi, and held no position of authority until mid 1904, when Hongo possessed him. Hongo was a spirit subordinate to Bokero, the chief deity venerated at Kibesa on the Rufiji, one of the territorial shrines of southern Tanganyika.[4] It was said in the 1960s that 'Hongo was to Bokero as Jesus is to God'. From the little that is known of the cult it appears that Bokero's prestige extended south towards the Mwera plateau and west to the Luwegu, while the related shrines of Kolelo carried the cult's influence northwards into Uluguru, Uzaramo, Ungulu, and Uzigua. Bokero communicated with men by possessing a medium and Kinjikitile's experience was remembered in the imagery commonly used to describe possession:

He was taken by an evil spirit one day...They saw him go on his belly, his hands stretched out before him...Then he disappeared in the pool of water...Those who knew how to swim [i.e. to exorcise by entering a trance] dived down into the pool but they did not see anything...The following morning...he emerged unhurt with his clothes dry and as he had tucked them the previous day. After returning from there he began talking of prophetic matters. He said, 'All dead ancestors will come back; they are at Bokero's in Rufiji Ruhingo. No lion or leopard will eat men. We are all the Sayyid Said's, the Sayyid's alone.' The song ran: 'We are the Sayyid's family alone. Be it a Pogoro, Kichi, or Matumbi, we are all the Sayyid Said's.'[5]

[1] John Iliffe, 'The organization of the Maji Maji rebellion', *JAH*, VIII (1967), 497–500.
[2] Gwassa and Iliffe, *Records*, pp. 8–9.
[3] The following account is based on Gwassa in Ranger and Kimambo, *Historical study*, pp. 202–17.
[4] Above, p. 29.
[5] Gwassa and Iliffe, *Records*, p. 9. For possession, see Swantz, *Ritual*, pp. 210–11, 398–9; Gwassa, 'Outbreak', pp. 201–2; Hatfield, 'The *nfumu*', p. 160.

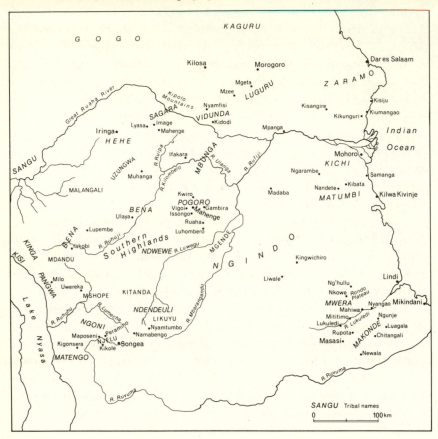

II   The Maji Maji rebellion

As 'the Sayyid Said's' men were one and free. Kinjikitile built a huge
spirit-hut where all could communicate with their ancestors. He
distributed a medicine – the *maji* (water) of the rebellion's name – to
protect men against European bullets. He took local beliefs in
divinity, possession, and medicines and amalgamated them into a new,
dynamic synthesis which promised the people unity, leadership, and
protection. By combining territorial authority and divine possession,
the Bokero cult possessed exactly the qualities needed to inspire
widespread popular rebellion.[1]

   Pilgrims visited Ngarambe openly in crowds, 'like a wedding
procession', but their secret object was to obtain war medicine against
the Germans. Kinjikitile took the title Bokero and employed assistants

[1] See Ranger in Ranger and Kimambo, *Historical study*, pp. 19–20.

called *hongo*. He faced enormous organisational problems. His secret mass movement – almost a contradiction in terms – required complete discipline and patience until he ordered a general uprising, but late in 1904 the rains cut communications with Ngarambe. Kinjikitile sent agents to command each area, but real control passed to local leaders.[1] Ngarambe was a meeting-point of peoples and was increasingly frequented at this time of economic expansion.[2] By mid 1905 most Matumbi and their Kichi neighbours were committed to Kinjikitile's movement. The Ngindo of Liwale sent to Ngarambe for medicine, while those of Madaba received it from Ngameya, an exorcist of the Bokero cult who became Kinjikitile's brother-in-law and established a distribution centre in northern Ungindo. Yet as Kinjikitile delayed his declaration of war the Matumbi lost patience. When the headman of Nandete ordered men to carry his tax chest to Kilwa, they decided, without consulting Kinjikitile, to declare war by uprooting cotton. The *akida* of Kibata, Sefu bin Amri, sent agents to investigate. Firing broke out. The Matumbi of Nandete beat the war drum to summon their neighbours and surrounded Sefu's house. He fled at night. Rebellion had begun.[3]

On 30 July 1905 the Matumbi found Sefu's house deserted. After sacking Kibata, each clan attacked the centre of German influence nearest its home. While the Kichi leader, Mkechekeche Kyuta, expelled *akidas* and assembled his forces close to Mohoro district office, most Matumbi made for Samanga on the coast, led by Ngogota Mhiwa. Wearing the dark *kaniki* cloth favoured by Bokero and with millet-stalks strung around their foreheads, they entered Samanga on 31 July, uprooted cotton on a hated plantation, and burned the Asian trading settlement before retiring to the mountains.[4]

The attack on Samanga alerted the German authorities, who had neglected Sefu's nervous warnings. Governor Götzen had only 588 askari and 458 police in the south. He sent nearly 200 to Kilwa, assuming that the Matumbi were responsible for a purely local affray. Pushing into Matumbi, Lieutenant Lincke was ambushed by the rebels and realised 'that an unusual morale animated the attackers'. On 8 August the Germans reached Kibata and started combing the

[1] See G. C. K. Gwassa, 'African methods of warfare during the Maji Maji war 1905–1907', in Ogot, *War*, pp. 123–48.
[2] Above, p. 130.
[3] Gwassa, 'Outbreak', pp. 220–47; Ambrosius Mayer, 'Wie 1905 in Matumbi der Aufstand begann', *Missions-Blätter der St Benediktus-Genossenschaft*, May 1914.
[4] G. A. von Götzen, *Deutsch-Ostafrika im Aufstand 1905–6* (Berlin, 1909), pp. 52–6; Gwassa in Ogot, *War*, p. 141.

mountains while the Matumbi hid their women and children, posted look-outs in the treetops, and ambushed patrols.[1]

Kinjikitile was hanged at Mohoro on 4 August, declaring from the scaffold that his medicine had already reached Kilosa and Mahenge.[2] News of war in Matumbi had already activated his organisation. The Ngindo were the first to move and became the most committed of all the rebel peoples.[3] Unwarlike and stateless, they shared the Matumbi's distaste for government, which consisted of a thatched boma at Liwale whence an N.C.O. ruled through a handful of brutal askari. The rebellion had two centres in Ungindo. One was in the north at Madaba, close to Ngameya's headquarters. When news of war in Matumbi arrived late in July, Ngameya ordered mobilisation and the Madaba trading settlement was sacked. The other centre was closer to Liwale. Here the key figure was Abdallah Mapanda of Kingwichiro, a man of important family, a famous hunter, an outlaw, and a natural war leader. During July 1905 he visited Ngarambe to 'see' his ancestors and obtain *maji*. Returning, he was met by three askari sent from Liwale to investigate. Abdallah plied them with beer and cut their throats. Next morning he organised his forces, distributed *kaniki*, and summonded surrounding headmen. All arrived save one, who sent his brother.

At dawn on 13 August 1905 the Ngindo attacked Liwale boma from three directions. Burning arrows ignited the thatched roof and everyone inside was killed. Next day an Ngindo force stumbled on a party of Benedictine missionaries led by Bishop Spiss and shot them as they tried to explain that they were men of peace. Abdallah Mapanda ambushed German troops from the coast and compelled them to withdraw. For the next three months power in Ungindo lay with a council which met under his chairmanship at Kingwichiro. The *maji* teaching was elaborated, both through the emergence of extremists who behaved extravagantly in the idiom of spirit possession and through the introduction of certain Islamic practices probably designed to make *maji* more acceptable to those Ngindo

[1] Götzen, *Aufstand*, pp. 50, 54, 58–63.
[2] 'Kriegstagebuch der Oberlt. z.S. Paasche', 6 August 1905, BA-M; Götzen, *Aufstand*, pp. 63–4.
[3] The following account is based on Gwassa, 'Outbreak', pp. 70–1, 81–3, 201–4, 261–78; Götzen, *Aufstand*, pp. 66–74; R. M. Bell, 'The Maji-Maji rebellion in the Liwale district', *TNR*, XXVIII (1950), 38–57; Crosse-Upcott, 'Social structure', pp. 151–2, 467, 481–8; Larson, 'History', pp. 259–65; Hofmann to Kilwa, 5 December 1912, TNA G9/48/93.

influenced by Islam through the rubber trade with the coast. The militants' most important action was to extend the rebellion to the Ngoni, whose military prowess was engraved in Ngindo minds. For this they chose Omari Kinjala, an Ngindo who had married Mkomanile, a female *nduna* of the Mshope chiefdom in Ungoni. Originally opposed to the rebellion, Kinjala was sentenced to death by the council but reprieved on condition that he carried *maji* to Mshope. By 26 August he had reached Ungoni's eastern border.

News of rebellion was meanwhile spreading northwards across the Rufiji to the hinterland of Dar es Salaam, where the Zaramo, another stateless people, were much angered by compulsory cotton growing. They had not visited Ngarambe, but in August 1905 two *hongo* brought *maji*. Uzaramo acknowledged the Kolelo shrine in Uluguru. Kolelo's officers probably took no part in the rising, but the *hongo* claimed Kolelo's authority and the cult's existence probably facilitated understanding of Kinjikitile's message. The *hongo* went first to Kisangire, a remote area populated by hunters, escaped slaves, and the like, under the leadership of Digalu Kibasila. The moment was propitious. In June 1905 government had caught up with Kibasila and imprisoned him for not making his people grow cotton. He had only just regained Kisangire when the *hongo* arrived to say that his dead father had sent them to tell him to accept *maji*. Kibasila began to distribute it to Zaramo from other villages. By 12 August many were killing and eating their livestock, believing that Kolelo had ordered this – an indication that as the movement spread further from Ngarambe it was acquiring a stronger millennial content, including the belief that the God who had sent Kolelo was himself about to appear. 'He will change this world and it will be new', it was said. 'His rule will be one of marvels.' Kibasila remained on the defensive until an *akida* arrested those who were taking money to Kisangire to buy *maji*. Kibasila's men freed them and then ambushed and shot an interpreter sent by the district officer to investigate. By the end of August most of the southern half of Dar es Salaam district was in revolt.[1]

The rebellion had also spread southwards to the Mwera plateau. The

[1] Martin Klamroth, 'Beiträge zum Verständnis der religiösen Vorstellungen der Saramo im Bezirk Daressalam', *Zeitschrift für Kolonialsprachen*, I (1910–11), 37–70, 118–53, 189–223; Sicard, *Lutheran church*, pp. 186–8; Tuheri Abraham Beho, 'Majimaji ao Kalava Dikono', manuscript, Lutheran church, Maneromango; Haber and Vincenti, 'Betr. Ursachen des Aufstandes im Bezirk Daressalam', 17 January 1906, RKA 726/109; correspondence in TNA G35/7.

stateless Mwera had not taken part in Kinjikitile's movement. Instead *maji*, news of war, and war itself reached them almost simultaneously and from several directions. Ngindo salt traders gave a garbled version of Kinjikitile's teaching to Selemani Mamba of Nkowe, a leading headman who promptly set off for Ngarambe. Other Ngindo arrived with *maji* and news of Liwale's capture, while a *hongo* from Ngarambe also brought *maji*. Again fervour increased with distance from Ngarambe. 'This is not war', Selemani Mamba told his men. 'We shall not die. We shall only kill.'[1] 'They took part in the rising', Mr Kalembo has written, 'with a full belief that the maji from Ngarambe could liquify a German bullet.'[2] Each clan head who accepted *maji* was known as a *hongo* and distributed medicine to his men, although there were also specialist *hongo* from Ungindo and Ngarambe as well as Ngindo warriors and Mwera 'militants', 'very lawless men...whose job it was to rid the warriors of their fear of dying'.[3]

The Mwera movement was strongest on the western plateau, close to Ungindo, but weaker in the east and in the Lukuledi valley to the south, where German influence was stronger and Benedictine missions existed at Lukuledi and Nyangao. During August two main Mwera leaders emerged: Selemani Mamba and Jumbe Gabriel Mbuu of Rupota. Both advanced on the mission stations in the valley, compelling reluctant villagers to join them. On his way to Nyangao, Selemani Mamba paused at Mahiwa, capital of the Makua chief, Hatia IV. Hatia was a man of peace, but he had many Mwera followers and was overawed by the rebels. Having kept the *maji* secretly for days, he now distributed it. Reinforcements reached Mahiwa from other Mwera regions and even from the Makonde plateau on the other side of the Lukuledi. Ngindo, Mwera, Makua, and Makonde were impressed by their own unity. 'Truly we were firmly united', one remembered. 'There was no tribalism in obeying the leaders.'[4]

The delay at Mahiwa enabled the missionaries at Nyangao to escape into the bush. When Selemani Mamba reached the mission on 28 August he found it deserted. His men destroyed it and forced its servants to reveal the missionaries' hiding-place. Encircled, the

[1] P. M. Libaba, 'The Maji Maji rising in the Lindi district', MMRP 7/68/2/1.
[2] A. K. Kalembo, 'An account of the Maji Maji rising in the Lukuledi valley', MMRP 7/68/1/1.
[3] 'Notes on the Maji Maji rising collected by Thomas Rashidi Kambona', MMRP 7/68/1/3/17.
[4] Abdala Undi in MMRP 7/68/2/3/1.

Fathers shot two *hongo* and escaped to Lindi, losing touch with a nun who was later discovered and killed. The death of the *hongo* shook Mwera confidence. Mounted on a looted donkey and carrying the church bell, Selemani Mamba led his men back to the plateau, silent and thoughtful. The *maji* had failed.[1]

Jumbe Mbuu's forces moved on Lukuledi. At Mititimo (later Ndanda) they forced Jumbe Mchekenje to accept and distribute *maji*. Delay again enabled the missionaries to escape. They reached Masasi, collected the staff of the Anglican mission, and the whole party walked the 190 kilometres to Mikindani in four days.[2] The rebels sacked Lukuledi and moved on towards Masasi, but here they met resistance. Masasi was a long-established mission. The local Yao and Makua were enemies of the Mwera and, not having received *maji*, saw the rebellion as a Mwera invasion. Resistance was led by the *akida*, Mursal, a Sudanese ex-askari who swore that if his rifle could produce only water he would kill himself. He shot several leading rebels before the others withdrew towards the plateau, leaving behind 27 dead men and numerous medicine bottles.[3]

Although the *maji* had again failed, it had meanwhile drawn the Makonde people into rebellion. The medicine had been fetched from Mititimo by Hamadi Pandamutwe of Ngunje and was accepted by the northern Makonde of the Luagala area, probably through the influence of those of Machemba's followers who still occupied Luagala. By contrast the southern Makonde rejected *maji* because they were influenced by the loyalist Yao chief of Newala, Matola II.[4]

News of the destruction of the missions reached Götzen on 31 August. Lack of troops compelled him to abandon the Mwera area temporarily. A fortnight earlier he had realised that the rebellion was more than a Matumbi affray. He had telegraphed for 150 European troops and the white personnel to command 600 extra askari. European troops were refused – to recall the Reichstag would have embarrassed the government's foreign policy – but the Kaiser ordered two cruisers and their marine complements from China and the Pacific to Dar es

[1] Libaba, 'Lindi district', MMRP 7/68/2/1; Lang, 'Bericht von der Zerstörung der Nyangao-Mission', 9 September 1905, RKA 723/48.

[2] Kalembo, 'Lukuledi valley', MMRP 7/68/1/1; Spreiter, 'Bericht über die Zerstörung der Kath. Missionsstation Lukuledi', 9 September 1905, RKA 723/43; *Central Africa*, November 1905.

[3] Z. R. J. Mchawala, 'Masasi documents', MMRP M/Ma/1/69; *Central Africa*, November 1905; 'Reminiscences of the Revd. Canon Kolumba Yohana Msigala...started in July, 1955', UMCA D/3.

[4] M. O. Namnauka, 'Maji Maji research in Newala', MMRP M/N/2/69.

Salaam.[1] In the capital 'a fear bordering on panic'[2] reigned and European volunteers drilled each evening outside the railway station. 'All the natives in and about the town are ready to rise – if they dared', an African priest reported. A district officer urged that the River Pangani should be defended to protect the settlers in the north-east.[3] Götzen had more pressing worries. On 5 September he received the news he most feared. A fugitive askari had reached Kilosa and reported that the Mbunga had taken Ifakara and threatened the key military stations at Mahenge and Iringa.[4] The movement was spreading to the Southern Highlands.

In fact Ifakara had fallen on 16 August. *Maji* and a *hongo* had reached Umbunga from Ngameya at the request of the Mbunga Chief Kindunda of Ifakara and his aunt, Mkihu, who had Ngindo affinities. The Bokero cult probably had no authority in Umbunga, but war medicines were familiar and the powerful military hierarchy used *maji* to mount a partially independent Mbunga uprising. Although the older men who had experienced German power in the 1890s argued against revolt, the younger generation, including Kindunda, outweighed them and *maji* was distributed. Here everyone who took it was called a *hongo*, greeted others with the title 'Saidi', and elaborated the password and slogan in question-and-answer form first used in Matumbi: 'Hongo or the European, which is the stronger?' 'Hongo!' It is said that anyone not wearing insignia of castor seeds and maize and millet stalks was speared to death. At midnight on 16 August the Mbunga overran the thirteen askari at Ifakara and replaced the German flag by the N.C.O.'s head. Then they crossed the Kilombero and climbed the escarpment towards the military station at Mahenge. But they were already betrayed. Kalimoto, an unimportant sub-chief, had opposed revolt and fled to Mahenge to escape death.[5]

When Captain Hassel heard Kalimoto's news he had already been at war for four days. On 19 August an *akida* from the south of Mahenge district had reported that the local Ngindo were in revolt, having received *maji* from another of Ngameya's *hongo* who had then

[1] Götzen, *Aufstand*, pp. 74, 89, 95; Bülow to AAKA, 21 August 1905, RKA 721/113.
[2] Götzen to AAKA, 26 August 1905, RKA 722/107.
[3] J. B. Mdoe, quoted in Hine to Travers, 9 September 1905, UMCA A/1/xiii; Wilhelm Methner, *Unter drei Gouverneuren* (Breslau, 1938), p. 80.
[4] Götzen, *Aufstand*, p. 94.
[5] O. Almasi, 'The Maji Maji rebellion in the Mbunga area south of Ifakara', MMRP 9/68/1/1; J. F. Kilato, 'An account of the Maji Maji rising in Ifakara township', MMRP 9/68/2/1; Joseph Henninger (ed.), *P. Aquilin Engelbergers Wapogoro-Tagebuch*, Micro-Bibliotheca Anthropos no. 13 (Freiburg, Schweiz, 1954), pp. 399–402.

continued into Upogoro. Pogoro military experience and political organisation were weak and the *maji* inspired a fervent and millennial belief:

In every village they [the *hongo*] reached they advised people to go to Mahenge to rob the white men of their property and women. Wherever they advised the people, they were asked, 'Can you really do it?' And they replied, 'We have our medicine which will change the Europeans' bullets into water.' And the people believed them and followed them.[1]

Yet in contrast to the Ngindo not all Pogoro accepted *maji*. In the south those of the Ruaha area apparently killed a *hongo*. Timiliasi of Isongo in central Upogoro refused *maji* because he had already experienced German firepower. Further north, the most powerful headman, Mlolere Liukawantu of Vigoi, ordered his elders to refuse the medicine, and generally the highland Pogoro were hostile.[2]

When Hassel learned of the Ngindo revolt on 19 August he marched southwards and hanged the headman of Luhombero. Hastening back to Mahenge on 23 August, he found the market deserted and the Benedictine missionaries from nearby Kwiro ensconced in the boma and dividing their time between compiling a Pogoro grammar and oiling their rifles. Kalimoto's news arrived that night. Hassel took sixty men to meet the Mbunga and walked straight into an ambush. German firepower carried the day against 'stubborn and fanatical resistance', killing 150 Mbunga. Returning to Mahenge, Hassel hastily fortified his ill-constructed boma, hanged suspected rebel sympathisers to the cheers of the crowds, and at each alarm climbed with four askari up a retractable ladder into a wooden tower fortified with a machine-gun and several cases of wine and tinned food.[3]

On 25 August Mahenge was reinforced by the arrival of Kiwanga, chief of lowland Ubena. After fifteen years of autocracy, Kiwanga was frightened. At his capital at Ulaya ('Europe') he wore European clothes, had his sons taught to read and write, grew rich on the rubber trade, and mercilessly exploited his subjects. Then in August 1905 the *maji* came, entering lowland Ubena from several directions. In the

[1] Athuman Manjawa in MMRP 9/68/1/3/10.

[2] Götzen, *Aufstand*, p. 106; Kwiro mission diary, preface, Kwiro archives; G. G. M. Ituga, 'The Maji Maji war in Ruaha and Mahenge areas', MMRP M/MH/2/69; E. E. Kazimoto, 'The assault on Mahenge boma', MMRP 8/68/1/1; Johann Mlolere, 'Hadithi ya utuwa wa akina Mlolere', typescript, Cory papers, ULD; Larson, 'History', pp. 116–18.

[3] Götzen, *Aufstand*, pp. 106–8; Kwiro mission diary, preface and 15 September 1905, Kwiro archives.

south, people of Ndwewe origin accepted *maji*, apparently from the Mbunga. They kept the movement secret from Kiwanga but unwisely took it to his Ngoni ally, Mpepo:

Mpepo accompanied the. . .*hongo* along the road. When they arrived at the place where his warriors had hidden themselves. . .the warriors came out and attacked the *hongo*. Fifteen *hongo* were killed and ten taken prisoner. . .

Mpepo informed Kiwanga I that the *maji* was a mere lie and that he had tested it thoroughly.[1]

Another account claims that Mpepo sent *hongo* to Kiwanga with the suggestion that he try shooting them, and certainly Kiwanga did execute several. Meanwhile *maji* also arrived from Ungindo and reached the Ndamba. Still graver for Kiwanga was division within his family. His elder half-brother, Magwira, lived with the Mbunga and brought *maji* to Kiwanga, urging him to rebel. Several sub-chiefs agreed. Kiwanga resorted to divination. It was his prerogative to consult *linautwa*, a ritual drum which only the ruling chief and his sons might see. Unsurprisingly, *linautwa* warned against *maji*. Kiwanga boarded his canoe, travelled down the Kilombero and climbed the plateau to Mahenge, whence he ordered each of his sub-chiefs to bring 200 men to the boma. The threat was open and the sub-chiefs obeyed. By 30 August Kiwanga's men were flocking into Mahenge.[2]

That morning, shortly after dawn, the rebel forces from southern Mahenge converged on the boma. One column, largely Ngindo, approached from the south. The other, composed of several groups, came from the east. Both were led by their *hongo*. 'All those who took the *maji* united as if they were of one clan', it was remembered.[3] Provided they did not turn their backs, they were assured, German bullets could not harm them. Faith reached its climax:

Two machine-guns, Europeans, and soldiers rained death and destruction among the ranks of the advancing enemy. Although we saw the ranks thin, the survivors maintained order for about a quarter of an hour, marching closer amidst a hail of bullets. But then the ranks broke apart and took cover behind the numerous small rocks. Now and again a group rushed out on to the road, lifted one of the fallen, and quickly fled again behind the rocks. Scurrying from rock to rock they made their retreat. Then suddenly the cry rang out: 'New enemy on the Gambira [eastern] side!' Everyone looked in that

[1] Kombo Ngalipa in MMRP M/MH/3/69/4a.
[2] J. A. Kayera, 'Maji Maji war in Mtimbira area', MMRP M/MH/3/69; Kwiro mission diary, 25 and 30 August 1905, Kwiro archives; information from Mr Kayera; *Deutsches Kolonialblatt*, 1 March 1906; Blasius Undole, 'Habari za Wandamba', typescript, 1965 (copy in my possession); Culwick, *Ubena*, p. 109; Larson, 'History', pp. 113–16.
[3] Claud Mkamati in MMRP 8/68/1/4/15.

direction, and there...a second column of at least 1,200 men was advancing towards us. Fire was opened upon them immediately. The enemy sought to reach Mahenge village at the double. There they were hidden by the houses and stormed up the road towards the boma. As soon as they reappeared within range they were met by deafening fire. The first attackers were only three paces from the firing line when they sank to the ground, struck by deadly bullets. Those behind them lost courage, turned, and scattered...When no more enemy could be seen, the Station Commander climbed down from the top of the boma tower...and distributed champagne.[1]

The leading *hongo*, killed at the gate of the *boma*, carried a millet stalk 'with which to beat the Germans'.[2] The Mbunga took no part in this attack and there is no evidence that they were in touch with Ngindo and Pogoro. Mbunga forces advanced to Mahenge on 1 September. But they were experienced in war, and while thousands watched, one man moved forward. He was shot down, a few others were killed, and the Mbunga withdrew to besiege rather than storm the boma.[3]

It is well to pause on the morrow of the assault on Mahenge – the climax of the first phase of the rebellion – and to consider how the movement had developed. The most important of Kinjikitile's teachings was multi-tribal unity, which differentiated the rebellion from such earlier uprisings as Kiva.[4] The assault on Mahenge expressed this unity most dramatically, but many indications appeared elsewhere, as when Mwera, Ngindo, Makonde, and Makua joined to attack Nyangao. Although the peoples of the south-east and the Southern Highlands belonged to different linguistic and cultural groups, they were nevertheless much mingled through trade, migration, marriage, and the exchange of ideas, while centres of German power like Mohoro and Mahenge were targets common to several peoples. Yet the unity achieved was normally multi-tribal rather than non-tribal. 'There was no tribalism in obeying the leaders', it has been said of the Mwera movement, 'but it is true that the men of an area stayed together.' In Matumbi '*litapos* [military groups] charged and retreated as clans'.[5] The rebellion possessed two potentially conflicting patterns of authority and leadership: the religious network of Kinjikitile and his *hongo*, a centripetal force, and the local military and political leaders, usually a centrifugal force.[6] The Matumbi declared war without even

[1] Kwiro mission diary, 31 August 1905, Kwiro archives.
[2] Kazimoto, 'Assault on Mahenge', MMRP 8/68/1/1.
[3] *Missions-Blätter der St Benediktus-Genossenschaft*, December 1905; Kwiro mission diary, 1 September 1905, Kwiro archives; Kilato, 'Ifakara township', MMRP 9/68/2/1.
[4] Above, pp. 65–6.
[5] Abdala Undi in MMRP 7/68/2/3/1; Gwassa, 'Outbreak', p. 277.
[6] See Gwassa in Ogot, *War*, pp. 123–48.

consulting Kinjikitile's representative and then fought as a coalition of clans under their natural military leaders. Among Ngindo, Mwera, and Zaramo, *hongo* normally stood alongside military leaders. In Ulanga the tension was resolved in two different ways, for local leaders controlled the Mbunga movement while in the Ngindo and Pogoro assault on Mahenge *hongo* apparently provided military as well as spiritual leadership. The failure to coordinate Mbunga and Ngindo action, together with Kiwanga's opposition to the war, accelerated the centrifugal trend. Although much inter-tribal cooperation continued, there was a definite tendency for the movement to become 'tribalised' after the end of August.

This trend was paralleled by the changing role of the *maji*. Those who visited Kinjikitile accepted it as part of a synthesis of existing beliefs. Nobody in that area appears to have tested the medicine by some superior authority, as Kiwanga did. When *maji* spread into areas where Hongo, Bokero, and even Kinjikitile himself were unknown, its meaning changed. At Ngarambe, Hongo was the spirit possessing Kinjikitile; later, *hongo* was used as his assistants' title. In Ungindo *hongo* meant any specialist who brought and distributed *maji*. In Umwera it meant anyone, including local headmen, who distributed *maji*. In Umbunga *honga* meant any warrior who took *maji*. In Uzungwa the whole rebellion was known as *pahonga*. Later still, in Kilosa, the original meaning was entirely lost and the movement was known as *homa-homa* from the local word for stabbing.[1] It no longer mattered, for *maji* had become a war medicine to be tested by its efficacy rather than its spiritual authority. And once efficacy became the test, it needed only time before rumours of the *maji*'s failure overtook it. By the end of August that failure was clear. It had failed to win over Christians or Muslims, who expelled a *hongo* from Kilwa.[2] Above all, *maji* had failed on the battlefield. At Mahenge the transition from confidence to doubt was illustrated by the three successive columns, the first marching straight at the machine-guns, the second using cover, and the third sending forward a single warrior.

To understand the changing character of the rebellion it is best to think of several impulses spreading inland. There were rumours of war. There were *hongo* with bottles of *maji* and stories of strange gods.

[1] C. J. Ngalalekumtwa, 'Maji Maji in Uzungwa', and D. L. Chipindulla, 'Maji Maji rising in Kilosa town', MMRP 3/68/2/1 and 2/68/1/1.

[2] G. C. K. Gwassa, 'A report on a research project in Kilwa district', typescript, 1966, in my possession.

There were rebel warriors, with bizarre uniforms, menacing behaviour, and tales of victory. There were rumours of disaster, rumours that *maji* was a lie. There were German messages passing along telegraph wires. And there were German troops. What happened in each area depended substantially on the sequence in which these impulses arrived, and that sequence changed with time and distance. Ngindo received *maji* and news of war before the Germans were alerted. Mwera received news, *maji*, and Ngindo warriors almost simultaneously. Masasi received Mwera warriors before *maji*, and resisted. Kiwanga received news of failure before he received *maji*, and joined the Germans. Time was against the rebels. Eventually *hongo* found the Germans waiting for them and the people convinced that *maji* was worthless. Then the rebels resorted to terror and the movement died.

Moreover, the rebellion was entering regions whose social and political organisation differed radically from Matumbi's. Maji Maji is the supreme example in Tanganyika's history of the interplay between stateless peoples and states. It began as a movement of colonists, highlanders, and incipient peasants, the most turbulent of rural peoples, hostile to all government, relatively undifferentiated, ignorant of war. All this changed when the rebellion entered the Southern Highlands. Here warfare and government were familiar and the interests of rulers and ruled often diverged. Kiwanga's calculations had to include the antipathy of conquered subjects, rivalry for his throne, historically-determined relations with neighbouring leaders, and fifteen years' experience of the Germans. In the Southern Highlands *maji* was not merely a weapon against Europeans but a potential catalyst of social upheaval.

Expansion

As the dry season of 1905 advanced, the rebellion spread into the Southern Highlands along two routes. One was the work of the Mbunga. After they had taken Ifakara on 16 August, Mkihu despatched *hongo* and warriors westwards and northwards into the highlands.[1] Late in August they entered Uzungwa, the mountain range which divided the Kilombero valley from Uhehe and had once been Mkwawa's refuge. When its headmen hesitated, the *vahonga* grew threatening:

[1] C. J. Ngalalekumtwa, 'Iringa documents', MMRP I/IR/2/69.

They carried spears, shields, and bottles, and they cried menacingly, 'Honga, Honga'. They danced in every kind of way. Some wore bells, others castor-seeds around their necks and foreheads, and many other things...One of them came and stood before us and asked us, 'Honga or the European, which is good?' We just kept quiet...We were totally bewildered. They told us a second time, 'When we say, "Honga or the European, which is good?" you answer, "Honga is good".'[1]

Many saw their property looted or destroyed, among them Panga-masasi Mwamsuva, headman of Muhanga. He sent men to Iringa for German protection.

Pangamasasi's messengers reached Captain Nigmann on 1 September. His command was the most important outside the capital, for his 117 askari included many experienced Sudanese, while his subjects, the Hehe, were the colony's most dangerous warrior people. When Nigmann heard of the revolt on 24 August from traders fleeing Ifakara, he realised that if he could restrain the Hehe he could prevent the rebellion spreading to the western plateau. Pangamasasi's message gave him the direction, and simultaneously he heard of the assault on Mahenge. On 3 September Nigmann set out with 75 askari, having ordered 150 Hehe leaders to meet him on the road to Uzungwa. He intended to show them that the *maji* was false and to force them to take his side before they could join the rebels.[2] Whether any Hehe received *maji* is uncertain, but none rebelled. They knew the reality of German firepower. European administration made only limited demands on them. They despised the rebel peoples. Above all, with Mkwawa's sons in exile they were leaderless: 'The Hehe had no chief to give them the medicine.'[3] Instead the rebellion lapped at the edges of Uhehe. Nigmann relieved Pangamasasi on 5 September. Descending into the Kilombero valley he found the Mbunga retreating towards Ifakara and followed, thus commencing a march which took him to Mahenge and Songea before he regained Iringa on 17 November. This expedition is considered later.[4] For the present, Nigmann's absence enabled Mbunga emissaries to win support in the north of Iringa district among the Sagara.

[1] Sigfridus Kupelsues, 'Mwanzo wa hongahonga katika Lulanga katika mwaka 1905', *Rafiki yangu*, January 1914. For events in Uzungwa, see Ngalalekumtwa, 'Uzungwa' and 'Iringa', MMRP 3/68/2/1 and I/IR/2/69.
[2] Götzen, *Aufstand*, pp. 110–12.
[3] *Deutsches Kolonialblatt*, 1 March 1906. See also P. T. V. N. Mhongole, 'The Hehe and the Maji Maji rebellion', MMRP 3/68/1/1; *Missions-Blätter der St Benediktus-Genossenschaft*, April 1906 and November 1907.
[4] Below, pp. 187, 196.

Stateless highlanders, the Sagara had been tributary to the Hehe state, combining profound respect for Mkwawa with hatred of his agents. When news of war arrived, the headman bordering Uzungwa, Godigodi Lihoha of Mahenge, investigated and returned with *maji* and Mbunga 'advisers'. His followers took the medicine and ate the government cattle entrusted to his care. The nearest Hehe sub-chief, Jumbe Mvinge of Image, reported this *lèse majesté* to Iringa, where Nigmann's deputy, lacking troops, replied, 'Let them eat and grow fat.' Mvinge was furious. He knew how to handle Sagara 'manioc-eaters':

Mvinge said, 'What can these weak and coward Sagara do?'
So Mvinge decided to go alone to fight the Sagara with his Image people, without the reinforcement of the German soldiers. Mvinge travelled on a white donkey which was for the members of the...noble class. He was a well-built, handsome, courageous, proud man and a great warrior.[1]

They met at Mahenge. Stiffened by *maji* and Mbunga advisers, the Sagara smashed the Hehe force, cutting off Mvinge's head and holding manioc to its lips. Other Sagara hastened to join Lihoha's movement. Faith was complete. 'They were just throwing themselves on the enemy after using the *maji*.'[2] By late September the Sagara were united as never before.

Meanwhile two further *hongo* of Mbunga origin were organising revolt on the northern bank of the Great Ruaha. Seeking notables with support across lineage boundaries, they recruited Chitalika of Nyamfisi near Kidodi, a Nyamwezi who had been both a government headman and a slave trader, had fought both for and against Mkwawa, and had recently emerged from prison with a bitter hatred of Germans. Chitalika arranged the distribution of *maji* in the valley while the *hongo* turned to the Vidunda mountains. Unlike other highlanders, the Vidunda had a chief, Ngwira, and he refused *maji*:

Ngwira told him that he had travelled to Kilosa, Morogoro, he had seen the ocean, he had walked to Tanga, Dar es Salaam and Tabora and everywhere he had seen the strength of the Europeans. Hongo must be driven right away before he could destroy the country.[3]

[1] Mhongole, 'Hehe', MMRP 3/68/1/1. See also *idem*, 'The Maji Maji war in Usagara', MMRP I/IR/1/69.
[2] Soliyambingu Mwachonya in MMRP 3/68/1/3/13.
[3] T. Schaegelen, 'The ethnology of the Vidunda tribe', in Kilosa district book, TNA. See also Anne V. Akeroyd, 'Bitterness in defeat: memories of the Maji-Maji rising in Uvidunda', seminar paper, University College, Dar es Salaam, 1969; I. A. S. Mananga, 'Morogoro documents', MMRP M/MOR/1/69.

Yet Ngwira's followers wanted *maji*. His kinsman Muhale Ciwaji was keen to lead them. Ngwira was powerless, and without his control the movement took an unusually radical form. The *hongo* ordered everyone to take *maji* on pain of death. Reversing the normal appeal to Muslims they declared that meat must be slaughtered by a man who had taken *maji*. They killed men for errors in performing the *maji* ritual. They ordered that witchcraft must end and its implements be burned. Then, having generated great excitement, they led their forces towards the German post at Kilosa, the *hongo* marching in front waving the whisks with which they administered *maji*, while their followers swayed their heads as they walked to rattle the millet stems which ringed their foreheads.

At Kilosa the rebels recruited townsmen until they reached a headman who was also the district officer's cook and who refused to join. This precipitated a quarrel which alerted the Germans. After forcing other townsmen to take *maji* at spearpoint, the rebels sacked the Asian shops and retired to their camp to celebrate for 24 hours, perhaps working up courage to storm the fortified boma. The Germans summoned reinforcements and advanced. The rebels moved out to meet them, ignoring warning shots and chanting, 'Homa! Homa! Maji! Maji! Germans? Cut their stomachs open!' Many died and the remainder fled back towards Kidodi.[1]

Back on the Ruaha the rebels rallied to face the pursuing Germans, who withdrew after confused fighting. The *hongo* claimed victory and revitalised their followers, who had begun to break the taboos. Reinforcements arrived from Uluguru[2] and Chitalika ordered a new advance towards Morogoro, compelling villagers along the route to join the column. On the way he ambushed a German force at Mzee, below the western face of the Uluguru mountains, but machine-gun fire dispersed the rebels in all directions. The leading *hongo*, it is said, hid in a tree and was never seen again. Chitalika was drowned. The Vidunda ran for their homes:

Makanyhanga returned with a bullet in his leg from which he limped all his life; Ciwaji was badly hurt and his companions said it would be better to finish him off as they would only slash him with pangas... Dalo was badly wounded and returned homewards alone, sobbing with pain and stumbling along with

---

[1] Chipindulla, 'Kilosa town', MMRP 2/68/1/1.
[2] These were followers of Mbagha Mwana Ng'asakwa of Mgeta. They were forced into revolt by German actions on hearing that *maji* had reached Mgeta. See J. T. Mkoba, 'The Maji Maji rising in Mgeta area', MMRP 1/68/1/1.

frequent halts...Those who reached Uvidunda fled up through the hills...
to hide in the forest and the mountain caves.[1]

The defeat at Mzee on 31 December 1905 ended the northern
expansion of the rebellion. Meanwhile Ngindo emissaries were
spreading the medicine further south. After taking Liwale on 13
August the Ngindo militants had compelled Omari Kinjala to carry
maji to Ungoni. His mission was formidable, for Ngoni aristocrats
despised unorganised and unwarlike Ngindo. Yet Kinjala had advantages. For the Ngoni, unlike other rebels, Maji Maji was a delayed
resistance.[2] Warned by Mkwawa's fate, recognising German firepower,
and not fully appreciating what foreign rule would entail, they had
not resisted German occupation in 1897. Now warfare and raiding
were banned, taxation symbolised subjection, aristocrats found their
control of commoners weakening, and the Benedictine missionaries
established at Peramiho since 1898 offended conservatives. Moreover,
the rebellion reached Ungoni at the peak of success. Liwale had fallen,
all Europeans were said to be dead, and strange spirits were
approaching to lead the uprising.[3] Amidst this excitement Kinjala's
men annihilated a police detachment from Songea on 26 August,
which greatly impressed Ngoni military leaders. Kinjala first approached the northern chiefdom, Mshope, choosing the Likuyu sub-
chiefdom inhabited by Ndendeuli subject peoples closely related to
the Ngindo. They readily accepted his teaching. Having left the
outbreak area early in the rebellion, Kinjala taught a purer version of
Kinjikitile's message than the Mbunga. He claimed divine authority,
dressed like Kinjikitile's assistants, experienced possession, and held
aloof from ordinary men:

He was a young man and had as his clothing nothing except a white loincloth
held together with a white girdle. He [the witness] could see him only from
a distance, however, for Kinjala did not mix with common people. The Ngoni
spoke of him only in secret, that he was God or actually the Son of God.[4]

When Kinjala entered Likuyu, news of *maji* had already reached
Uwereka, the capital of Chabruma, Chief of Mshope. Chabruma sent
a kinsman to investigate. Meanwhile Kinjala moved on to Kitanda

[1] Akeroyd, 'Bitterness'.
[2] See O. B. Mapunda and G. P. Mpangara, *The Maji Maji war in Ungoni* (Nairobi, 1969), *passim*; P. M. Redmond, 'Maji Maji in Ungoni', *IJAHS*, VIII (1975), 407-24; S. S. Kusilawe, 'The Maji Maji war for freedom in the Namtumbo area', MMRP R/S/1/69.
[3] Kigonsera mission diary, 21 and 25 August 1905, Peramiho archives; Cyrillus Wehrmeister, *Vor dem Sturm* (St Ottilien, 1906), pp. 136, 184-9.
[4] *Missions-Blätter der St Benediktus-Genossenschaft*, November 1906.

where his wife Mkomanile was sub-chief. She took him to Parangu, Chabruma's brother and rival, who passed him on to the chief, recommending acceptance. Chabruma hesitated. A great traditional chief, he avoided Europeans and bitterly resented German constraints on his independence. He possessed the most powerful military organisation surviving in Tanganyika. Yet he hesitated. He feared German firepower. His uncle, Mpepo, warned that the *maji* was a fraud. There is no evidence that Chabruma considered the medicine's religious origins. Instead he employed a ruler's devices. He consulted his war-diviner, who counselled acceptance. It is said that Chabruma tested the medicine, first on a dog and then on a criminal. When it failed, Kinjala said it was effective only against Germans and their allies. Finally, pressed by his advisers, Chabruma accepted *maji* and ordered its distribution. None refused. 'You could not object to what Chabruma had accepted.'[1]

Late in August the district officer in Songea, Captain Richter, learned that Chabruma had chosen war. Richter reached Uwereka on 3 September with 31 askari and 25 auxiliaries. His arrival surprised Chabruma, who was still distributing medicine and had at the capital only the 500 young men of his standing regiment. Armed with stabbing-spears, these untested warriors charged Richter's force in regimental formation and lost 200 dead before they withdrew, having killed a single askari. The *maji* had failed, but Kinjala assured Chabruma that the warriors must have broken the taboo against sexual intercourse. It no longer mattered. Chabruma was committed.

Richter returned immediately to Songea. For six weeks he remained on the defensive while the rebellion spread southwards into the Njelu chiefdom. Here the political situation was complicated. The chief, Mputa, had acceded six years earlier with majority support among the aristocrats but at the expense of a previous chief's young son, Usangila. Now Usangila's partisans opposed the war and took refuge in Songea boma. Moreover, Mputa had little authority even over his supporters, for Njelu had been disintegrating for several decades and *Nduna* Songea, the hero of the Hehe wars, commanded quite as much loyalty as his chief. This shaped the *maji*'s impact in Njelu. Mputa received it first, visiting Uwereka at Chabruma's invitation and returning with medicine and *hongo*. He summoned his sub-chiefs to his capital at Maposeni. They were divided, the younger war-leaders demanding action while elders advised caution; commoners were

---

[1] Quoted in Mapunda and Mpangara, *Ungoni*, p. 18.

probably less enthusiastic than aristocrats. Finally, and most uncertainly, they decided to fight. 'Let us drink the maji maji medicine so that we may all perish', Songea is said to have remarked.[1] The sub-chiefs distributed *maji* at their headquarters. Many commoners hesitated and force was used to compel acceptance, especially among the Christians of Peramiho, seven of whom were killed. 'Everything will now follow Ngoni custom', they were warned. 'They will kill everyone they find with European clothes.'[2]

Early in September Mputa's men unsuccessfully attacked an Arab trading settlement at Kikole and destroyed the missions at Peramiho and Kigonsera. But the crucial task was to capture Songea boma. For this the Ngoni must unite, and bringing them together for the first time since 1881 was the *maji*'s most important achievement in this area. Chabruma advanced towards Songea soon after the engagement at Uwereka. His Ndendeuli subjects camped at Namabengo, near the crossing of the River Lumecha with the Songea-Kilwa road. There Chabruma, Mputa, and Kinjala joined them. Warriors were already deserting, for many regiments had suffered casualties and lost faith in *maji*. Kinjala claimed that the dead had broken taboos or would rise again. He explained that a new *hongo* from Liwale had brought even stronger medicine. It was administered at the Lumecha, the uniform and prohibitions being varied slightly to emphasise a fresh start.[3] The warriors, some 5,000 strong, remained at Namabengo for a month preparing to assault the boma. But delay again aided the Germans. At dawn on 17 October Captain Nigmann reached Songea with his company. The Ngoni camp was asleep, with no outposts, when the Germans approached on 21 October. Mounting machine-guns on a hill, Nigmann opened fire at first light and the Ngoni fled in all directions without thought of defence. Few died, but their unity was broken.[4]

Before their rout at the Lumecha the Ngoni had tried to draw their neighbours into rebellion. Several former enemies refused. Few Matengo or Nyasa joined their persecutors.[5] The Yao Chief Mataka

[1] G. P. Mpangara, 'Songea Mbano', seminar paper, University College, Dar es Salaam, 1966.
[2] Joseph Sihaba, 'Bericht über die letzten Tage von Peramiho', in Wehrmeister, *Vor dem Sturm*, p. 186.
[3] *Missions-Blätter der St Benediktus-Genossenschaft*, October and November 1906.
[4] Götzen, *Aufstand*, pp. 124-5.
[5] Kigonsera mission diary, 12 and 24 September and 11 December 1905, Peramiho archives; Charles Mbungonji, 'Historia ya nchi kando ya Ziwa Nyasa toka Manda hata Chiwindi', UMCA Milo records, MUL.

in Mozambique plundered coastal traders but soon assured the Germans of his friendship.[1] Among the Pangwa and Bena of the Southern Highlands, however, Ngoni overtures were more successful. An Ngindo *hongo* reached the Pangwa early in September from Chabruma, their former overlord. He exploited Chabruma's authority, resentment of taxation, and experience of the *mwavi* poison ordeal:

When the mwavi expert arrived at some headman's, he was obliged to send people thought to be witches to go and take the medicine. Very often the medicine was very effective. The witches died and those who were not witches survived. For this reason, when *Hongo*'s medicine came and was distributed, it was difficult for people to refuse it.[2]

When most headmen had accepted *maji*, the Pangwa, like other highlanders, concentrated on removing aliens. Alerted by the murder of tax-collectors, the Lutheran missionary at Milo fled early in September. He was robbed but allowed to go free because 'he is innocent, he has no quarrel with us',[3] although his station was destroyed. The Pangwa then attacked recalcitrant headmen and the Kisi people on the Lake Nyasa shore who refused *maji*. The Pangwa may also have spread *maji* to their neighbours in Bukinga, where the most isolated of the four chiefdoms joined the rebellion. The Pangwa then dispersed to their homes until January 1906, when they were recalled to action by their Bena neighbours.[4]

Losers in the nineteenth-century struggle for the Southern Highlands, the Bena were divided into small chiefdoms disputed among the neighbouring Hehe, Sangu, and Ngoni, most of the north having paid tribute to Mkwawa and the south to Chabruma. The most powerful southern leader was Mbeyela, whose chiefdom, centred on Mdandu, had adopted elements of Ngoni military organisation. Chabruma naturally sent *maji* to Mbeyela, who may also have received it from Mbunga emissaries. Mbeyela summoned his councillors. Initially a German ally, he was too old for war and relied on his sons, Ngozingozi and Mpangire. Ngozingozi, the elder, was absent answering Nigmann's summons to Iringa. Instead the meeting was dominated by Mpangire, a firebrand already determined on war. Against Mbeyela's doubts the meeting ordered each headman to bring

[1] Ewerbeck to Government, 2 May 1906, RKA 700/202.
[2] Joseph Mtimavali in MMRP I/N/5/69/4.
[3] Zacharia Chaula in MMRP 4/68/4/3.
[4] C. K. Mbeya, 'Maji Maji war in Upangwa', MMRP I/N/5/69; Park in Swartz, *Political anthropology*, p. 234.

his men to Mdandu, where they accepted *maji* with enthusiasm. The meeting also decided to attack immediately without waiting to win other Bena. This made the rebellion a Bena civil war, with Chabruma's allies pitted against those linked to Hehe and Sangu. One of Mpangire's targets was the Lutheran mission station at Yakobi. Originally welcomed as allies, the missionaries had become closely associated with government in Bena eyes. On 19 September 1905 Mpangire led some 3,000 men towards Yakobi, each wearing red cloth on his right arm. They lost thirty men trying to overrun the strongly-defended mission house before retiring. Next day the Christians withdrew to Lupembe, singing 'A mighty fortress is our God'. A long and bitter war followed. Mbeyela and Ngozingozi destroyed the deserted Yakobi, killed several Christians, and ravaged neighbouring Bena chiefdoms, even killing rather than capturing women. As in Ungoni a new medicine was administered because the first was the wrong mixture.[1]

Early in October the Bena movement was checked by the arrival of Merere of Usangu with 1,500 followers. His appearance alarmed both sides, for neither knew which he supported. After Chabruma, Merere was the most powerful ruler in southern Tanganyika, and he was in a dilemma. His father had often allied with Chabruma and Mbeyela while fighting the Hehe, but the Sangu had also profited from cooperation with the Germans, who had restored their homeland. When Mbeyela sent *maji* to Usangu early in September, Merere faced an agonising choice. A relatively young man, he had ruled for twelve years but had never been a truly independent sovereign. Something of a moderniser, he nevertheless resented interference by administrators and missionaries. When *maji* arrived he apparently accepted it himself and administered it to close followers. But this news leaked to his kinsmen, notably his mother and his older half-brother, Mhavanginonya. As members of the older generation they had experienced the years of exile and had engineered the German alliance. Within days Merere found almost complete opposition among the Sangu 'establishment'. In their difficulties Kiwanga and Chabruma had resorted to divination. Merere had to do the same: he could not declare war without consulting the oracle *lihomelo*. But whereas Kiwanga consulted his own oracle, *lihomelo* was tended by priests

[1] P. Gröschel, *Zehn Jahre christlicher Kulturarbeit in Deutsch-Ostafrika* (Berlin, 1911), pp. 141–63; Mwenda, 'Ubena', pp. 113–17; J. M. Makwetta, 'Maji Maji in Ubena', MMRP 4/68/1/1; A. Z. Mhemedzi, 'The Majimaji rising in Kidugala', MMRP 4/68/4/1.

belonging to the establishment. As Mr Ndikwege has put it, in Usangu *vox dei* was often *vox veterani*. So it was now: *lihomelo* shed tears of blood and declared against the war. Merere next sought to remain neutral, but even this was impossible, for Nigmann ordered him to bring warriors to Ubena. On 22 September Merere acquiesced, destroyed his bottles of medicine, and assembled his men, allegedly intending to change sides if the *maji* worked in battle. He had no chance. Nigmann kept him under guard throughout the campaign and gave command of the Sangu forces to Mhavanginonya.[1]

Merere's decision to join Nigmann ended the expansion which the Ngindo militants had set in train a month earlier. *Maji* may have spread later into the Malangali area of southern Uhehe, but no fighting resulted.[2] Elsewhere there was no insurrection but widespread tension. A cruiser demonstrated outside Sadani when a nervous official detected unrest among the Zigua. The district officer in Pangani burned a black flag which he believed to be an invitation to join the revolt. Some Kaguru sympathised with the rebellion, but no *maji* arrived and a council of elders resolved to reject any rebel advances. In Ugogo there were rumours that people near Mvumi had accepted *maji*, but there was no serious fighting and other warriors mobilised to oppose rebel advances.[3] Still further to the west, *hongo* probably entered Unyamwezi. The Germans ascribed a caravan robbery in Ikungu to rebel incitement, while the commander in Tabora believed that many people in Unyanyembe received *maji* but were deterred from revolt by Chieftainess Karunde's hostility and his own threat to raze the town if they joined.[4] Panic spread to Mwanza, where European officers carried arms into their mess, locally-recruited askari were disarmed and sent to the coast, and Chief Makongoro was attacked and exiled for supposedly mobilising his warriors.[5] Tension

[1] M. S. Ndikwege, 'Chief Merere and the Maji Maji uprising', MMRP 5/68/1/1.
[2] A. P. Mahiga, 'Maji Maji in Mufindi area', MMRP 3/68/3/1.
[3] Back to Admiralty, 25 October 1905, Aelteste Offizier, Geheim-Akten, BA-M; Theodor Gunzert, 'Service in German East Africa and German Foreign Office 1902–33', microfilm, RH; J. R. Mlahagwa, 'The Maji Maji rebellion and Ukaguru', MMRP 2/68/2/1; Peel to Hirsch, 6 December 1905, TNA G36/14.
[4] Götzen to AAKA, 20 October 1905, RKA 723/38; White Fathers' mission diary, Tabora, 23 October 1905 (I owe this reference to Dr A. E. M. Shorter); 'S. M. S. Thetis: Kriegstagebuch', 26 October and 10 November 1905, BA-M; Glatzel to Götzen, 26 October 1905, Kriegstagebuch Thetis, Anlageband II, BA-M.
[5] 'S.M.S. Thetis: Kriegstagebuch', 30 October and 1 December 1905, BA-M; 'Die Tätigkeit der Marine während der Niederwerfung des Eingeborenen-Aufstandes in Ostafrika 1905/06', *Beiheft zur Marine-Rundschau* (Berlin, 1907), pp. 47–8; 'Kriegstagebuch des Lt. v. Milczewski Detachement Muansa', BA-M; Schleinitz, report, 1 June 1907, BA-M ADMB VII/1/5a/II.

was reported from Musoma, while Chief Kahigi sent 200 men from Buhaya to strengthen Mwanza's garrison. The rebellion was discussed in Bonde and Ufipa. Cloths with a design known as 'Bokero's eyes' were on sale in Dar es Salaam in December 1905 and a Maji Maji dance was popular in the south soon afterwards.[1] Maji Maji was Tanganyika's first collective political experience.

Expansion did not destroy the rebellion's multi-tribal character, either in areas of weak political authority, such as provided Chitalika's heterogeneous following, or in the powerful chiefdoms of the Southern Highlands, as is indicated by communication between Chabruma, Mbeyela, and Merere. Yet in these regions acceptance of *maji* and leadership in battle increasingly followed established patterns of statecraft and authority. Sangu commoners had no influence on their leaders' decision. What Chabruma accepted no subject dared refuse. Without a chief the Hehe did not rebel. Ngoni or Bena were not led into battle by *hongo*, as the Pogoro had been at Mahenge. Instead, Kinjala's role in Ungoni was much like that of previous war doctors. With traditional forms went traditional antipathies and the use of force to overcome them, as occurred when Mbunga compelled allegiance in Uzungwa and Vidunda in Uluguru. Kinjikitile's name meant nothing in the Southern Highlands.

Yet that is the problem. Given that Kinjikitile's name meant nothing to those outside the range of the Bokero cult, one must ask why they put any faith in *maji*, why Ngoni rulers listened to Kinjala. It is not enough to say that *maji* was not taken seriously but used merely as a source of unity. The Ngoni had been deterred from resistance in 1897 by German firepower and were no less familiar with it in 1905. Moreover, on occasion – at Yakobi and Kilosa – men demonstrated faith in *maji* by open assault on well-armed adversaries.

One answer is to suggest that *hongo* were believed because they operated within an existing religious tradition.[2] This explanation rests on two considerations. One is an account of the *hongo*'s activities in Uvidunda which suggests that *maji* was seen to be aimed not only against external enemies but also against internal danger in the shape of witchcraft:

Hongo gave orders that every man must anoint himself with his Usinga medicine; anyone who refused was to be caught and killed. People began to

---

[1] 'S.M.S. Thetis: Kriegstagebuch', 15 November 1905, BA-M; Austen, *Northwest Tanzania*, p. 60; *Habari za mwezi*, October 1905; *Chronique trimestrielle*, June 1906; *Deutsch-Ostafrikanische Zeitung*, 30 December 1905; Weule, *Native life*, pp. 354–5.
[2] See Iliffe, 'Organization', p. 508. I no longer believe this.

fear that they would be called witches and all of the people of Kidodi and the people of Jumbe Kulumzima went to Hongo to receive his medicine...

Then Hongo expounded his taboos which were as follows: No white magic or witchcraft was to be performed, no charms or medicines of any kind must be kept in their houses but all destroyed by fire.[1]

The second consideration is that after the rebellion southern Tanganyika experienced numerous witchcraft eradication movements which displayed many similarities to Maji Maji.[2] A practitioner would tour the region, enter villages, and announce that if the people destroyed all existing medicines and accepted his new medicine, nobody would subsequently suffer from witchcraft and anyone practising it would himself die. Such movements claimed to eradicate evil and death except through the natural process of ageing. So similar were they to the rebellion that it has been suggested that Maji Maji followed a tradition of witchcraft eradication which gave the *hongo* their authority.

Present evidence does not support this hypothesis. When interviewed, few survivors connected the rebellion with witchcraft eradication; more indignantly denied it. Research in Uvidunda has not confirmed the *maji*'s anti-witchcraft implications.[3] Most important, research has not revealed eradication movements antecedent to Maji Maji in the rebel area. What it has revealed are witch-*finding* movements – which lack eradication's millennial implications – both in the outbreak area[4] and through the widespread use of *mwavi* in the Southern Highlands.[5] Witchcraft eradication was probably invented later, when European governments forbade the identification and killing of witches.[6] German rule was not sufficiently intensive to have necessitated that change in southern Tanganyika by 1905. The connections between the different movements were probably more subtle. When witchcraft eradication emerged in this area after the First World War it drew heavily on memories of Maji Maji.[7] The rebellion itself, by contrast, drew both on witch-finding and on many other local religious ideas. *Hongo* sometimes banned other medicines. The *mwavi* tradition made it 'difficult' for people to refuse *maji*. Many *hongo*, like Ngameya, had previously been diviners or exorcists. The scale and

[1] Schaegelen in Kilosa district book, TNA.
[2] T. O. Ranger, 'Witchcraft eradication movements in central and southern Tanzania and their connection with the Maji Maji rising', seminar paper, University College, Dar es Salaam, 1966.
[3] Akeroyd, 'Bitterness'.
[4] Gwassa, 'Outbreak', pp. 512–14.
[5] Above, p. 188.
[6] Below, p. 207.
[7] Below, p. 367.

passion of the rebellion reshaped old ideas into a synthesis used by later eradicators. But present evidence suggests that acceptance of *maji* outside Bokero's sphere of authority depended on local circumstances and beliefs rather than on any common religious tradition.

Repression

When reinforcements arrived late in October 1905 Götzen could at last begin to suppress the rebellion systematically. Three expeditions moved inland. Captain Wangenheim reached Mahenge on 9 March 1906 via Kilosa and Iringa. Major Schleinitz occupied the Vidunda mountains. Major Johannes reached Songea on 29 November to operate against Ngoni, Bena, and Pangwa.[1] Their object was to compel the rebels to submit by surrendering weapons and 'ringleaders and witchdoctors' (who were normally executed), paying an idemnity of four shillings per man, and providing labour.[2] Submission was compelled by patrol warfare in which military engagements were secondary to seizure of food and destruction of crops. 'In my view', Wangenheim reported on 22 October, 'only hunger and want can bring about a final submission. Military actions alone will remain more or less a drop in the ocean.' Götzen had already decided to create a famine throughout the rebel area.[3] The rebels, for their part, seized food from loyalists and sought safe bases in which to cultivate. By 1906 their object was to avoid contact with the Germans. Famine, floods, and dreadful cruelty on both sides had by then made most rank-and-file rebels anxious to submit, but the hard core of *hongo* and military leaders, for whom surrender meant death, could be captured only by constant patrols and pressure on the civilian population. Such a guerrilla war is extraordinarily difficult to reconstruct, especially where the guerrillas were illiterate. It is best to take the major regions in the order in which they submitted, concentrating on the activities of the main leaders.

The Zaramo surrendered first. After shooting the interpreter on 19 August, Kibasila evaded punitive expeditions and withdrew towards the Rufiji, where he joined up with a Matumbi band. Others maintained resistance in Kisangire, while another Zaramo headman, Kulinani of Kikunguri, sacked Kiumangao and Kisiju early in

---

[1] Götzen, *Aufstand*, pp. 146–51, 167–73, 187–91, 200–19.
[2] Götzen, 'Befehl an die Truppenführer', 11 November 1905, TNA III/F/20/1.
[3] Götzen, *Aufstand*, p. 149; 'S.M.S. Thetis: Kriegstagebuch', 30 September 1905, BA-M.

October, carrying a black flag and shouting 'Mfaume Maji Maji'. Yet this was the last important rebel action in Uzaramo. Captain Fonck devastated Kisangire while the district officer dispersed Kulinani's following. By 18 November the Zaramo revolt was over, although Kibasila was not captured until March 1906. He was hanged from a mango tree in Dar es Salaam.[1]

Further south, along the Lukuledi valley, warfare was more protracted. Mwera, Makua, and Makonde confidence had been shaken by the *maji*'s failure when attacking the mission stations. The Makua chief, Hatia, had joined the revolt unwillingly and soon abandoned it. 'Am I a Mwera?' he asked, telling a clan meeting that he intended to make peace.[2] Many of his Mwera subjects remained with the rebels, but the Makua accepted terms in October 1905 and Hatia, 'a broken man', eventually regained his chiefdom.[3] The Makonde were the next to surrender. After attacking the mission stations they lost contact with their Mwera allies and fought a defensive war in the impenetrable bush of their plateau:

The Wamakonde are to the north of Chitangali river; they have rebelled again in these days, and the fighting is there. I think it will be many days before the fighting ceases, for the rebels on every side would rather die than be under the Germans, and many of them have died and their wives and children have been taken for spoil, but they will not leave off fighting.[4]

Their leader, Hamadi, was betrayed while crossing the Ruvuma. His execution ended the Makonde rebellion and left the Mwera fully exposed to German reprisals. Loyalist Yao chiefs, Nakaam and Matola, were delighted to seize captives and property from long-standing enemies. The Mwera forces united against them at Namitende but they were dispersed. They came together again on 1 December to attack a German camp at Ng'hullu. Daring leaders penetrated the camp at night and began to kill sleeping askari with their knives. When the askari counter-attacked, the 2,000 Mwera encircling the camp charged the stockade repeatedly until driven off with bayonets, leaving 81 dead. The survivors fled to the Rondo plateau and adopted guerrilla tactics. A fortnight after Ng'hullu no important Mwera leader had yet

[1] Mfaume = king. See 'Amtliche Nachrichten des Gouvernements aus den unruhigen Gebieten vom 14. Oktober 1905' and Boeder to Government, 9 October 1905, Kriegstagebuch Thetis, Anlageband 1, BA-M; Sicard, *Lutheran church*, p. 188.
[2] 'Notes...collected by Thomas Rashidi Kambona', MMRP 7/68/1/3/17.
[3] Weule, *Native life*, p. 54.
[4] Yustino Mkandu to Hine, 31 December 1905, in *Central Africa*, April 1906. See also Namnauka, 'Newala', MMRP M/N/2/69.

submitted, but in January 1906 Selemani Mamba sought peace. He was shot. Jumbe Mbuu surprisingly persuaded the Germans to free him. Mchekenje – whose real role remains unclear – died in prison. On 29 January 1906 the Germans could claim that the rebellion in Lindi district was over.[1]

It was also ending further north, in Kichi and Matumbi. The Kichi forces which concentrated near Mohoro on 7 August were dispersed by a naval detachment under Lieutenant Paasche, who thereafter fought a savage guerrilla campaign along the Rufiji against Kichi and other groups seeking food in the fertile valley. By October 1905 many Kichi had surrendered and the hard core had largely withdrawn into the mountains to join the Matumbi. On 27 October and 14 November their joint force attacked the German camp at Kibata. In the second assault over a thousand men encircled the camp under the eyes of its marine guard who thought they were askari returning from patrol:

They surrounded the German stockade in many files...Then at five in the morning the European ordered his askari to fire as the Matumbi tried to break into the stockade. Oh so many people died that day! For they had not known what a machine-gun was. They thought that the Germans had run out of ammunition and were beating empty tins to frighten them away...From then on they fought in small groups, waylaying the German askari.[2]

A blundering war for food and self-preservation followed in the forests:

At 2.30 a.m. we left the pacified area and pressed on towards the village with the greatest difficulty, partly in the rain, on narrow native paths through reeds taller than a man, and mostly through forest over deep elephant traps[3] invisible in the darkness...On the edge of the village the auxiliaries who were in the lead fired on some villagers who were gathering bananas, so that the planned surprise was out of the question. Although the village was immediately stormed at the run, all the huts were found abandoned...The inhabitants had taken only their guns and a few spears with them; fire was still burning in nearly every hut...Pursuit was out of the question...All the huts – about sixty – were burned, the food destroyed, and the fields destroyed so far as time allowed.[4]

---

[1] Kalembo, 'Lukuledi valley', and Libaba, 'Lindi', MMRP 7/68/1/1 and 7/68/2/1; Götzen to AAKA, 11 December 1905, Aelteste Offizier, Geheim-Akten Thetis I, BA-M; Seyfried to Kommando, 29 January 1906, Kriegstagebuch Thetis, Anlageband III, BA-M.

[2] Gwassa and Iliffe, *Records*, p. 21. See also 'Kriegstagebuch des Seesoldatendetachements Kibata bezw. Mtingi', 27 October and 14 November 1905, BA-M.

[3] The manuscript is barely legible here.

[4] 'Kriegstagebuch der Stabsarzt Dr zur Verth, Det. Mohoro', 19–20 December 1905, BA-M.

Gradually exhaustion, hunger, and despair compelled surrender. 'We had no stronghold, no place to stay in to do this or that', survivors recalled. 'We lived in *pori*. Nobody could dare walk along the road, never.'[1] Militants sustained morale by further elaborating the *maji* beliefs. In November Paasche found a *maji*-distribution centre above the Mpanga falls with 'a tiny hut with flasks, ground sand, and a gnu's tail, with coloured cloths as a flag in front of it'. In December he reported – how accurately one cannot tell – that one headman had obtained new *maji* from Ungindo, introduced human sacrifice into the ritual, and assembled his men to march on Mohoro and Dar es Salaam.[2] But gradually the hard core was tracked down. Mkechekeche surrendered on 27 January. Ngogota was captured early in March and the Matumbi rebellion collapsed.

Mahenge witnessed fighting on a larger scale. The Pogoro dispersed after attacking the boma and concentrated on avoiding punitive expeditions, but the Mbunga, with their powerful military system and extraordinary indifference to casualties, still expected victory. They spread the movement into Uzungwa, Usagara, and Uvidunda. They probed Hassel's beleaguered garrison at Mahenge. And they ambushed Nigmann's relief force early in September, preventing it crossing the Kilombero at Ifakara. Nigmann retraced his steps, crossed the river in Kiwanga's country, and reached Mahenge on 20 September, having marched from Ifakara in the regulation time for postal runners. Encamped to the north of Mahenge, the Mbunga were outflanked and unprepared for Nigmann's attack on 23 September. When the machine-guns sprayed their camp with bullets at dawn the Mbunga fled, pursued by Kiwanga's auxiliaries.[3] Nigmann left Mahenge three days later. The boma was still isolated: its only communication with the outside world between August and November was a birthday telegram from Hassel's fiancée. When Kiwanga left for his capital, the Mbunga followed, surrounded, and killed him on 19 October. Hastening to Ulaya to attend his ally's funeral, Hassel installed the chosen son Soliambingo, executed Bena leaders whose loyalty Kiwanga had doubted, and then advanced down the Kilombero

---

[1] Pori = bush. See Gwassa, 'Outbreak', p. 348.

[2] 'Bericht der Oberleutnant z. See Paasche über die Tätigkeit des Rufiyi-Expeditionsabt. v. 25. Oktober bis 23. November 1905' and Paasche to Glatzel, 23 December 1905, Kriegstagebuch Thetis, Anlageband III, BA-M; Glatzel to Kaiser, 7 January 1906, Aelteste Offizier, Geheim-Akten Thetis I, BA-M. For a general account, see Hans Paasche, *Im Morgenlicht: Kriegs-, Jagd- und Reise-Erlebnisse in Ostafrika* (2nd edn, Berlin, 1907).

[3] Götzen, *Aufstand*, pp. 112–15; Kilato, 'Ifakara township', MMRP 9/68/2/1.

into Umbunga to begin systematic repression. On 18 November the greatest pitched battle of the war took place at the Ruipa. Two thousand Mbunga warriors, in the regimental formation inherited from Shaka, charged almost up to the muzzles of Hassel's machine-guns before the loss of 300 shot and many drowned forced them to retreat. In March 1906 Wangenheim's expeditionary force reached Mahenge. Two months later the last rebel headman surrendered, after the Mbunga had handed over several *hongo*.[1]

Repression was also under way in the north-west. At Mzee, on 31 December 1905, Chitalika's forces failed to check a German column advancing towards the Vidunda mountains. After scaling the slopes, half-frozen and totally lost in enveloping mist, Schleinitz's men built a stockade at Ngwira's village, destroyed everything they could find, and prevented the Vidunda building or cultivating until total submission was achieved. Not until July 1906 were troops withdrawn from Uvidunda.[2] The Sagara experienced a similar fate. After defeating Mvinge in September 1905 the newly-united Sagara, with their *hongo* and Mbunga advisers, advanced to attack Iringa. Askari surprised them at Lyasa. The Sagara fled northwards into the forests of the Kipolo mountains. There, under appalling conditions, they remained undetected for several months, attempting to cultivate and debating whether to seek peace. At last, when only a single headman remained alive at Kipolo, they surrendered and returned to their devastated homes.[3]

Captain Johannes was meanwhile advancing inland towards Ungoni. After their defeat at Namabengo on 21 October the Ngoni forces dispersed. Mputa withdrew to his capital. When the Germans destroyed it on 2 November he hid near the River Lumecha, whence he ambushed several German patrols. Johannes reached Songea on 29 November and implemented Götzen's 'famine strategy', which achieved its goal when Mputa was captured on 10 January. In Mshope the resistance was more effective. Chabruma retreated northwards after Namabengo and took to the bush, where he inspired such fear and respect that none betrayed him. His aim, it appears, was to find a gap in the German forces through which he could cross the Ruvuma

[1] Götzen, *Aufstand*, pp. 139, 173–9; Culwick, *Ubena*, pp. 54–6; Kayera, 'Mtimbira', MMRP M/MH/3/69.

[2] Methner, *Unter drei Gouverneuren*, pp. 89–97; Götzen, *Aufstand*, pp. 190–1; Akeroyd, 'Bitterness'.

[3] Mhongole, 'Hehe' and 'Usagara', MMRP 3/68/1/1 and I/IR/1/69; Götzen, *Aufstand*, pp. 191–3.

into Mozambique. In January he entered Upangwa, probably hoping to make contact with the recently rejuvenated Bena and Pangwa movements.[1]

On 6 January 1906 Mbeyela's Bena ambushed and annihilated a German column crossing the Ruhuji. This success revived the rebellion in the Southern Highlands. Pangwa who participated in the ambush returned home singing their *hongo*'s praises. Chabruma made for the Pangwa mountains. But German forces also hastened to the scene, including Johannes from Songea, and the Bena leaders retreated towards Upangwa. By mid March all the hard core leaders in the Southern Highlands were there except Chabruma's brother, Parangu, who had already escaped eastwards to Mgende. There was little communication among them – Chabruma and Mbeyela never made contact – and little time for it, for, as Chabruma soon realised, Upangwa was a trap. With Lake Nyasa blocking escape to the west, the Germans could surround three sides of the mountains and gradually close in. On 2 April 1906 Johannes ordered a concentric advance by 300 askari and some 2,500 auxiliaries. They met at Milo on 21 April, empty-handed. Mbeyela had died of exhaustion, but Ngozingozi apparently escaped detection, Mpangire slipped through the German lines to Ubena, and Chabruma broke through eastwards to Mgende, probably taking Kinjala with him. The askari took a terrible revenge on the Pangwa highlanders.[2]

Mgende was a tangled, waterless *Grenzwildnis* between the Luwegu and Mbarangandu, and its few inhabitants were renowned for witchcraft. Ngoni raiders and their Ngindo allies had made it their base when raiding the coast. Now both Chabruma and the surviving Ngindo leaders took refuge there. German forces had converged on 'free Ungindo' late in 1905. Ngameya was captured on 15 December and hanged, but Kapolo of Madaba and Abdallah Mapanda retreated into Mgende. On 11 June 1906 the 500 askari who encircled their refuge moved forward. Once more they lost their quarry. A patrol stumbled on Chabruma's camp and wounded him, but he escaped up the Luwegu, 'passed right through Nyamtumbo outside the camp of the German soldiers at night and the soldiers were fast asleep', crossed the Ruvuma, and took refuge in Mozambique with Mataka, who feared

[1] Mapunda and Mpangara, *Ungoni*, pp. 23–5; *Deutsches Kolonialblatt*, 15 September 1906.
[2] Götzen, *Aufstand*, pp. 211–19; Gröschel, *Zehn Jahre*, pp. 175–7; *Deutsches Kolonialblatt*, 15 April 1907; Makwetta, 'Ubena', MMRP 4/68/1/1; Msemakweli Kitanji in MMRP I/N/5/69/1/b.

his ambition and soon had him murdered.[1] Omari Kinjala failed to cross the Ruvuma and returned to Ungindo, where he was captured by Ngindo loyalists and poisoned himself. Abdallah Mapanda, 'the most energetic and personally the bravest of all the rebel leaders',[2] survived longest. Some say he was never captured, but the Germans believed he was shot on 16 January 1907 by a patrol which cut off his right hand – distinctively mutilated in a hunting accident – and displayed it at Liwale.[3]

Only Ngozingozi and Mpangire still held out in the forests of Upangwa and southern Ubena. They survived for two years, evading or occasionally ambushing German patrols before both were betrayed, located, and shot, Ngozingozi in May 1908 and Mpangire on 18 July.[4] It was three years almost to the day since the men of Nandete had uprooted cotton.

Aftermath

Famine covered the land, a famine that killed. The greatest suffering was in Ungoni and the highlands. While Chabruma remained free, Captain Richter in Songea prevented cultivation and appropriated all food for his troops. 'The fellows can just starve', he declared. Not until April 1908 was food generally available again in Ungoni.[5] Southern Usagara was described late in 1906 as wholly depopulated. Uvidunda was thought to have lost half its population. 'What shall I rule?' Ngwira asked when he returned from prison. Götzen thought more than half the Matumbi died in the revolt. A missionary reckoned that more than three-quarters of the Pangwa perished.[6] A careful study of Ulanga made in the 1930s concluded that in the rebel areas, in addition to immediate deaths, 'the famine reduced the average fertility of the

---

[1] Larson, 'History', p. 106; Schönberg to Kommando, 15 December 1905, Kriegstagebuch Thetis, Anlageband III, BA-M; *Deutsches Kolonialblatt*, 15 April 1907; Mzee Kawalika in MMRP R/S/1/69/2/b; Rechenberg to RKA, 24 May 1907, RKA 701/16.

[2] Götzen, *Aufstand*, p. 231.

[3] Bell, 'Maji-Maji', pp. 20–1; Gwassa, 'Outbreak', p. 358; Rechenberg to RKA, 30 January 1907, RKA 725/26.

[4] Makwetta, 'Ubena', and Mhemedzi, 'Kidugala', MMRP 4/68/1/1 and 4/68/4/1; Keudel to Government, 5 May and 25 July 1908, RKA 701/177–9.

[5] Kigonsera mission diary, 7 February 1906, and Peramiho mission diary, 6 April 1908, Peramiho archives.

[6] Paul Fuchs, *Wirtschaftliche Eisenbahn-Erkundungen im mittleren und nördlichen Deutsch-Ostafrikas* (Berlin, 1907), p. 89; Lambrecht to Government, 14 November 1907, TNA III/N/10/I; Akeroyd, 'Bitterness'; Götzen, *Aufstand*, p. 159; Hans Stirnimann, 'Forschungen unter den Pangwa im Livingstone-Gebirge', *Anthropos*, LXI (1966), 805.

surviving women by over 25 per cent'.[1] Total deaths in Maji Maji and its aftermath are unknown. Dr Gwassa estimates them at 250,000–300,000, or perhaps one-third of the area's total population, and he may be right.[2] In return the rebels killed 15 Europeans, 73 askari, and 316 auxiliaries.[3]

The rebellion transformed political relationships throughout the south. Normally its immediate effect was chaos. Nearly a hundred Ngoni aristocrats were hanged, including Mputa and Songea.[4] 'The people are becoming barbarised', missionaries reported from Ungoni; '...where there are no chiefs and headmen, every man lives by his own law'.[5] In time new leaders emerged. Where rebellion had been almost unanimous, they were often necessarily from rebel families. In Ungoni both Chabruma and Songea were succeeded by youthful sons, but although it was important that aristocrats retained office at all, the new rulers never exercised their fathers' authority. Maji Maji finally destroyed Ngoni military society, wiping out a 'lost generation' of leaders and partly breaking down the status distinction between aristocrats and subjects.[6] Elsewhere loyalists inherited power. Kalimoto, who had betrayed the Mbunga rebellion, became a leading chief of Umbunga and married a sister of Mlolere, the most prominent Pogoro loyalist. Loyalty rehabilitated the Hehe, who regained control of Usagara and parts of Usangu and the Ulanga valley. In 1912 the Germans even contemplated restoring Mkwawa's dynasty, although they finally lost their nerve. Men who had had good wars gained advancement. Loyalist irregular leaders gained posts as *liwalis* and *akidas*. Enriched by booty, the Ngindo musketeers of Usangu became chief-makers. Yet such were the passions and uncertainties of the rebellion that even loyalty did not guarantee survival. Kiwanga's successor dared not keep a standing army at his capital and the Germans took the opportunity to devolve power on his headmen.[7]

The rebellion's long-term effects also varied. The fact that many Ngoni chiefs accepted baptism before execution[8] might suggest that

---

[1] Culwick, 'Population', p. 355.
[2] Gwassa, 'Outbreak', p. 389. The official figure of 75,000 (Gleim, 'Vermerk', 4 July 1912, RKA 725/63) originally referred only to those who died between July 1906 and June 1907 (*RTA*, 1907/9, no. 622, p. 3,693).
[3] *Deutsches Kolonialblatt*, 15 April 1907.
[4] See the vivid description in Gwassa and Iliffe, *Records*, pp. 25–6.
[5] *Missions-Blätter der St Benediktus-Genossenschaft*, July 1907.
[6] P. H. Gulliver, 'An administrative survey of the Ngoni and Ndendeuli', typescript, 1954, Cory papers, ULD; Redmond, 'Political history', p. 281.
[7] Iliffe, *German rule*, pp. 152–6, 184–5; Ndikwege, 'Merere', MMRP 5/68/1/1.
[8] Gwassa and Iliffe, *Records*, pp. 25–6.

the *maji*'s failure destroyed the credibility of indigenous faiths. Five hundred people attended the returning missionary's first service at Milo, and Christianity's rapid growth in Ungoni and the Southern Highlands after 1907 was widely ascribed to the abandoning of discredited beliefs.[1] Yet reality was more complicated. Among the Ngindo the crisis may have facilitated the acceptance of Islam. The Zaramo subsequently turned to Islam, as did both Ndendeuli and Mwera[2] – indeed, the events of August 1905 created a lasting barrier between Mwera and missionaries.[3] Moreover, indigenous beliefs did not simply fall before the machine-guns, as the vitality of witchcraft eradication movements shows. Long-term political consequences were also complicated. Kinjikitile taught the peoples unity and they often achieved it, but their object was to return to small-scale independence – each attacked its local boma rather than the capital – and defeat left lasting bitterness. Matumbi came to see Maji Maji as an Ngindo foolishness, while Ngindo blamed Matumbi, and everyone else blamed both. Even in the 1930s men from Kilwa district were refused hospitality on the road to Dar es Salaam because they were 'Maji Maji people'.[4] Most educated men took the German side and saw the rebellion as a hideous lesson in European strength. 'In truth they have learned that the power of the German government is very great', the *liwali* of Songea reflected. 'We *washenzi* are wholly incapable of driving out the Europeans.'[5] Uneducated men drew the same conclusion. Never again did any of the rebel peoples challenge German power. In July 1908 Mwera reported Islamic propaganda, saying, 'We are much afraid because two years ago very many of us died because of intrigue like this.'[6] Yet fear was not acceptance. During 1906 Matumbi refused to work on cotton plantations, declaring 'they would rather die of starvation in the bush than work for Europeans'. During the First World War the Mwera betrayed German positions at Mahiwa to the British in revenge for Maji Maji. In the 1950s a man who refused *maji* was still the butt of an Ngindo exorcism song.[7]

One point remains. When the survivors returned they found forest encroaching on their fields and game reoccupying cultivated land.

---

[1] *Jahresbericht der Gesellschaft zur Beförderung der evangelischen Missionen unter den Heiden zu Berlin. Für das Jahr 1906* (Berlin, 1907), p. 118.
[2] See below, p. 257.   [3] This is a personal impression.
[4] Gwassa, 'Outbreak', p. 401; below, pp. 519–20.
[5] Mzee bin Ramazani in *Usambara-Post*, 29 December 1906.
[6] Wendt to Government, 3 August 1908, TNA G9/46.
[7] Minutes, Bezirksrat Kilwa, 28 June 1906, TNA IV/F/8/III; Libaba, 'Lindi', MMRP 7/68/2/1; Crosse-Upcott, 'Social structure', p. 484.

'Not many tall trees are to be seen', a missionary wrote of Matumbi in 1910, 'for in the old days before the Maji Maji war there were many people... Now the people have become fewer; some have died in the war, others have since died from famine, many from cold and sickness and even from the wild animals.'[1] By 1921 elephants were entering Matumbi for the first time in living memory. Tsetse appeared simultaneously. In Ungindo the British created the largest game park in the world.[2] The people of southern Tanganyika had lost not only a hope of regaining freedom. They had lost a battle in their long war with nature.

[1] *Rafiki yangu*, April 1910.
[2] DPO Kilwa to Game Warden, 14 November 1921, CO 691/62/166; Gwassa, 'Outbreak', p. 393; Kjekshus, *Ecology control*, pp. 72–4.

CHAPTER 7

Religious and cultural change before 1914

As colonial rule became increasingly pervasive, so Tanganyika witnessed accelerated interaction among its indigenous religions, Islam,
and Christianity. This interaction is best analysed by distinguishing
between the function of religion as a means of countering evil and its
function as an intellectual system charting and explaining the world.[1]
Indigeneous religions continued to offer remedies for ancient evils but
were ill-equipped to explain or control the larger colonial world. Islam
provided solutions at both levels but continued to experience
contradiction between its world-view and its problem-solving techniques. Christianity was best able to explain the larger world, but
mission Christianity was ill-equipped to combat misfortune. The
varied resources and inadequacies of different religions led to
interaction among them. Extensive documentation (chiefly from
mission sources) makes religious change easier to identify than other
cultural and intellectual developments, but Tanganyika's early colonial
experience is also illuminated by dance.

Indigenous religions

Throughout the German period most men probably sought remedies
for evil in inherited beliefs and institutions. They consulted diviners,
made offerings for ancestral spirits, countered witches, employed
medicines. They visited rain-makers, propitiated nature spirits, made
pilgrimage to Kolelo, were possessed by Lyangombe. These practices
were sufficiently entrenched to survive the relatively light German
impact. Yet the European presence created new problems, enlarged
the world in which men lived, and provided motives and opportunities

[1] Many of the ideas in this chapter are taken from Robin Horton, 'African conversion',
Africa, XLI (1971), 85–108; Keith Thomas, *Religion and the decline of magic* (reprinted,
Harmondsworth, 1973).

for religious innovation. Four relationships between indigenous religions and the colonial order can be identified.

First, indigenous religions frequently inspired and provided organisation for resistance. Their roles in the Maji Maji rebellion have been described so fully that other examples need only be mentioned. In 1897 Nyakyusa and Kinga leaders 'came together at Lwembe's territorial shrine before a violent confrontation with the Germans.[1] Eleven years later invulnerability medicine distributed at the Tiita shrine in Unyaturu and obtained from Gidamausa of Dongobesh, the greatest of Tatoga rainmakers, brought Iramba, Mbugwe, and Turu into an abortive multi-tribal uprising.[2] Their organisations and supra-ethnic authority gave territorial cults and rain shrines special capacity to coordinate armed rebellion, but other religious institutions were involved in non-violent resistance. In the hope of expelling all Europeans the Safwa killed their male animals during 1901 at the supposed orders of a reincarnated ancestor-hero. A similar movement took place three years later in several western districts on the instructions of Katavi, spirit of Lake Tanganyika.[3] The *kubandwa* cult led opposition to Christianity in Buhaya and Usumbwa. Kimbu chiefs used the *uwuxala* society to organise covert resistance to Christianity.[4] The natural disasters of the 1890s stimulated anxious searches for spiritual aid. Katavi's association with epidemics may have expanded his cult greatly at this time. Famine stimulated the Shambaa spirit possession cult. Both in South Pare and Unyakyusa religious leaders blamed rinderpest on newly arrived missionaries, and the Germans were probably often thought to have caused the natural disasters.[5] Nyamwezi held Europeans responsible for drought, while Sukuma conservatives blamed religious innovation:

> We see the clouds but they move away.
> God hides the water and lets us die...
> What is our crime, O God? Men arrived
> Who taught us lies, not to make the right sacrifices.[6]

[1] Wright in Ranger and Kimambo, *Historical study*, pp. 164–7; Elpons to Kommando, 4 December 1897, RKA 289/11.
[2] Marguerite Jellicoe, 'The Turu resistance movement', *TNR*, LXX (1969), 1–12; correspondence in TNA G55/25.
[3] Kootz-Kretschmer, *Safwa*, II, 304–6; *Chronique trimestrielle*, October 1904; P. Fromm, 'Ufipa – Land und Leute', *MDS*, XXV (1912), 99–100; Blohm, *Nyamwezi*, II, 181.
[4] Nicholas Mugongo, 'Les mémoires d'un catéchiste noir', manuscript, n.d., Kipalapala archives; information from Fr Nolan; Shorter, *Chiefship*, p. 141.
[5] Blohm, *Nyamwezi*, II, 179–85; Ekemode, 'German rule', p. 209; Kimambo, *Political history*, pp. 216–19; S. R. Charsley, *The princes of Nyakyusa* (Nairobi, 1969), pp. 7–16.
[6] Text in Cory papers (file 167), ULD. See also Blohm, *Nyamwezi*, I, 173–4.

A prophet warned the Luo that they would die of smallpox unless they ousted the white men. Other prophets foretold the imminent departure of Europeans from Unyakyusa and Usukuma.[1]

Apart from inspiring opposition to Europeans, indigenous religious resources could help men to comprehend their new situation. One resource was the tradition of prophecy. Many peoples spoke of prophets who had foretold the coming of Europeans. In different ways these stories seem designed to demonstrate that because colonial innovations had been foreseen they were somehow controllable and did not discredit old beliefs.[2] Some stories suggested that past African heroes had actually created the Europeans. 'One evening', ran an Iramba tale, 'the Rainmaker killed a perfectly white goat and cut it in pieces and covered the pieces up till morning. In the morning he awoke early and uncovered the meat and there were the Europeans.'[3] Other stories justified African reactions to conquest. The Ngoni had submitted in 1897, it was claimed, because Mharule had warned them not to fight the white, transparent men who would come from the east. When Nyakyusa Christians told of prophecies that white men from the lake would bring peace and a new religion, they stifled some of their unease at abandoning the past.[4] Some versions were critiques of the colonial order:

> Kaswa said: 'A person will clothe his whole body,
> Even his eyes.
> Everything will have its price: grass and the very earth itself.
> Those born in that time will be mannerless boors,
> Unusued to civilised converse.
> The strangers come in flying machines with popping eyes,
> Purging fire from their arses.
> They bring the millipede [train] and the tortoise [car].[5]

Other versions promised that European control would be transient. A Chagga prophecy told that the Europeans would depart, to be followed by a plague of wild animals. The great Masai *laibon*, Mbatyan, supposedly foretold that rinderpest, civil war, and 'a white bird' would 'bring us to the verge of ruin' before the Masai regained their power.[6] Another method of absorbing change was to attribute

[1] Raum in Harlow and Chilver, *History*, II, 181–2; Holmes, 'Bakwimba', pp. 196–7.
[2] See the analogy in Thomas, *Religion*, pp. 503–7.
[3] Yakobo Ntundu, 'The position of rainmaker among the Wanyiramba', *TNR*, VII (1939), 86.
[4] Joseph Masiha in MMRP 6/68/6/4/1; Wilson, *Communal rituals*, pp. 16, 72.
[5] Willis, 'Kaswa', p. 253. See also R. G. Willis, 'The indigenous critique of colonialism', in Talal Asad (ed.), *Anthropology and the colonial encounter* (London, 1973), pp. 245–56.
[6] Gutmann, *Dschaggaland*, p. 33; Moritz Merker, *Die Masai* (Berlin, 1904), p. 339.

tensions to possession by the spirits of Europeans or their artefacts –
as previously of Arabs or alien Africans – which could be exorcised
by rites imitating their behaviour. Shambaa adopted a German spirit
and that of the railway train. The Bondei *mzungu* (white man's) spirit
'treads on fire, and likes rice and white clothing'. Zaramo exorcised
European spirits by imitating a military band, while on Mafia Island
it required eating at a table with knife and fork. When the Germans
tried to ban exorcism dances in 1910, Zaramo warned that 'many
people will die'.[1]

Three innovations in indigenous religions appear to have taken
place in German times. One was a continued 'vulgarisation' of
religious activities hitherto confined to specialists, much as *kubandwa*
had been vulgarised into *buswezi* in Unyamwezi. In Ufipa the
possession cult stimulated by Ngoni invasion subsequently fused with
divination and herbalism, so that by the 1920s spirit-medium and
magician-doctor were commonly the same person.[2] Local possession
cults increasingly intermingled. *Vutambo*, a variant of *kubandwa*,
penetrated as far south as Usafwa, while by the 1920s the *rungu* spirit
originating from Kolelo was experienced in Usambara.[3] Another area
of innovation was probably defence against witchcraft. Poison ordeals
continued to be used in German times. Several Chagga chiefs made
their followers drink a medicine called *uri* after declaring, 'If I should
practise sorcery against man or animal, may this drink kill me.'[4] In
some areas the Germans were remembered for dealing remorselessly
with witches, but they were equally ruthless towards those who sought
to counter witchcraft by employing ordeals. Mutitimia of Nkokolo in
Ukimbu died in custody after killing ten men by *mwavi*. In 1899 the
Germans hanged a chief near Masasi for killing a witch. In Tabora
they hanged several diviners.[5] The result was a search for alternative
techniques. Safwa drew on other religious resources, welcoming a
witch-finder who called himself Katavi and claimed to be sent by God.[6]
Another technique, in one area at least, was witchcraft eradication.

---

[1] Feierman, *Shambaa kingdom*, p. 202; Dale, 'Account', p. 222; Swantz, 'Medicine man',
     p. 84; Ann P. Caplan, 'Non-unilineal kinship on Mafia Island', Ph.D. thesis,
     University of London, 1968, p. 186; *Kiongozi*, January 1911.
[2] Willis, 'Changes', pp. 140, 146, 156 n. 29.
[3] Kootz-Kretschmer, *Safwa*, I, 241–4; E. Johanssen, *Führung und Erfahrung in 40 jährigem
     Missionsdienst* (3 vols, Bethel bei Bielefeld, n.d.), III, 57.
[4] Widenmann, *Kilimandscharo-Bevölkerung*, pp. 34–5.
[5] Paul Puritt, 'The Meru of Tanzania', Ph.D. thesis, University of Illinois, 1970, p. 154;
     Shorter, *Chiefship*, pp. 330–1; *Central Africa*, August 1899; Tabora mission diary, 8
     January 1901 and 18 July 1903 (references from Dr Shorter).
[6] Kootz-Kretschmer, *Safwa*, I, 7.

Unlike a witch-finder, an eradicator – if practising the craft in a pure form – sought not to identify and destroy witches but to treat whole communities with medicine which made their members invulnerable to witchcraft and killed any recipient who subsequently practised it. A less simple and direct technique than witch-finding, eradication required more faith, possibly gave less emotional satisfaction, and was probably not used where witch-finding could be practised. Significantly, Tanganyika's earliest known eradication movements took place between 1906 and 1910 in the north-east, the rural area under closest European control. In Usambara these movements followed a German ban on Shambaa courts hearing witchcraft cases. The most important eradicator was Majio, who distributed medicine in Usambara during 1908. He was a Segeju from Vanga who inherited his medicine from his grandfather. As guest of the old Kilindi chief, Kibanga, Majio sold for twenty cents a medicine said to protect men from witchcraft and kill witches who took it. He also chose local agents who later established their own practices. His career was similar to those of the eradicators later common in Tanganyika, except that his medicine was supposed to kill witches, which suggests a still uncompleted transition from witch-finding. There is no evidence of eradication movements elsewhere in German times.[1]

The third religious innovation was reformulation of beliefs, perhaps by emphasising God's intervention in human affairs as against the activities of subordinate spirits. Such reformulation logically accompanied enlargement of scale, for subordinate spirits were less relevant than God to the larger world. Hongo's possession of Kinjikitile has been interpreted in this light, while divine intervention against witches in Usafwa is another example.[2] Further evidence is sparse, but missionary work probably led some non-Christians to ascribe attributes of the Christian God to their own deities. This happened in Usafwa and lowland Ubena. In Unyamwezi the missionaries' identification of Katavi with Satan may have aided the growth of his cult.[3]

Occasionally the European presence positively benefited indigenous practices. Mkwawa's fall made Chanzi's shrine again a place of

[1] Correspondence in TNA G54/1; Feierman, 'Concepts', p. 315. For eradication movements on the Kenya coast at this time, see Cynthia Brantley, 'An historical perspective of the Giriama and witchcraft control', typescript, n.d., in Dr Brantley's possession.

[2] Robin Horton, 'On the rationality of conversion', *Africa*, XLV (1975), 230–1; above, p. 206.

[3] Alan Harwood, *Witchcraft, sorcery, and social categories among the Safwa* (London, 1970), p. 35 n. 2; Culwick, *Ubena*, pp. 100–1; Blohm, *Nyamwezi*, II, 180.

pilgrimage.[1] But this was exceptional. The predominant tendency was for indigenous religions to lose authority and vitality, especially during the final years of German rule. The last multi-chiefdom sacrifice in central Kilimanjaro took place in 1912, probably a few years after the last forest circumcision ceremony there. When Lwembe's priest died shortly before 1914 no Nyakyusa could be compelled to accept the office's obligatory seclusion. The rain shrine at Tiita ceased to 'sing' when violated by a German officer.[2] Tanganyika's indigenous religions, like its societies, were exceptionally small in scale, while world religions were available with unusual ease. For those – and they were probably still a minority – who wished to understand and participate in the colonial world, to adapt indigenous religions was often less satisfying than to adopt elements of a new faith.

Islam

It was vital to Tanganyika's later history that after defeating Abushiri the Germans made allies of the coastal Muslims rather than establishing a new power centre inland, as did the British in Kenya. It was equally important that coastal society contained men willing to learn western skills, serve western masters, and create a place for Muslims in colonial Tanganyika. These men came from two sections of coastal society. One was the Omani aristocracy which had served the Sayyid. Its members generally led the peace parties which negotiated with Wissmann. The most prominent was Wissmann's friend and agent, Suleiman bin Nasor, *liwali* successively of Pangani, Bagamoyo, and Dar es Salaam, and regarded by other Arabs as 'more German than the Germans'.[3] Some resistance leaders also rehabilitated themselves, notably the learned Omari bin Jamaliddini, *kadhi*[4] of Lindi from before the German invasion until 1945. The other group to serve the Germans contained younger men from lower social strata who took advantage of German education.

Germany had a tradition of secular state education. Tanganyika's first governor, Soden, wanted to restrict administration to the coast and establish commercial relations with the interior, using the coastal peoples and their Swahili language as his intermediaries. Secular,

[2] Clemm, 'White mountain', pp. 75, 208; Wilson, *Communal rituals*, p. 28; Jellicoe, 'Turu resistance', pp. 4–5.
[3] Euan Smith to Salisbury, 25 September 1890, FO 84/2064/258; Iliffe, *German rule*, p. 192.
[4] Islamic magistrate.

Swahili-speaking government schools in coastal towns were central to this programme. Soden opened the first at Tanga in 1892. By 1911 government was operating 83 schools with 4,312 pupils. Tanga School by then included a post-primary section with pupils from many parts of the country. In 1912–13 the school produced 192 graduates.[1] They were trained as cheap subordinate administrators:

The aims are to develop character towards obedience, tidiness, punctuality, conscientiousness, and a sense of duty. The curriculum of the second year also includes drafting letters, short reports, receipts, and so on. Important forms and documents are shown, also tax procedure and simple accounting ...Important government regulations and the basic principles of German law are the final subjects of study.[2]

Mdachi ('the German') Sharifu was a good example of Tanga's products. A Segeju born near Tanga, he studied and taught there before being posted to Songea, first as schoolteacher and then as acting *liwali*, eventually travelling to Germany to teach Swahili.[3] The state schools were thus the foundation of a territorial civil service whose members – among whom coastal men predominated – were transferred throughout the country. The lowest post was schoolteacher; the highest was *liwali*. The main intermediate grade was *akida*.

Borrowing the title and functions from the Sayyid's administration, the Germans appointed *akidas* throughout the coastal districts during the 1890s:

The *liwalis*, mostly of Arab blood, assist the administration at district headquarters. They are assessors at court hearings and advisers on local law and custom. Because of the absence of respected chiefs in the coastal districts, so-called *akidas*, trained in the government schools, have been installed over whole divisions. A few of the more important chiefs also hold this title. Under the *akidas* stand the elders of the smaller areas or villages – the so-called *jumbes*. *Liwalis* and *akidas* are paid by the government; the office of *jumbe* is an unpaid, honorary office.[4]

Because of its relative efficiency where chiefs were lacking, the *akida* system was extended to three inland districts. Between 1898 and 1903 *akidas* supplanted the disintegrating Kilindi administration in Lushoto district. Mpwapwa district recruited *akidas* in 1907 and

[1] Wright, 'Local roots', pp. 623–5; George Hornsby, 'A brief history of Tanga school up to 1914', *TNR*, LVIII (1962), 148–50; *Die deutschen Schutzgebiete 1912/13*, I, 17.
[2] Heinke (1900), quoted in George Hornsby, 'German educational achievement in East Africa', *TNR*, LXII (1964), 90.
[3] *Kiongozi*, February 1910 and April 1913; Isherwood to PC Eastern, 15 August 1930, TNA 61/207/1/24.
[4] *RTA*, 1900/2, no. 814, p. 5,260.

Morogoro in 1913; both were areas with innumerable minor headmen. No other inland district relied principally on *akidas*. Meanwhile the *akidas* themselves changed, with graduates of government schools gradually ousting the Arabs and African chiefs who had initially served alongside them.[1] Thus the Germans created a territorial civil service open to talent. Its consequences ramified through later history until the nationalist movement.

The official language of German district administration was Swahili. It was adopted for administrative convenience and subsequently defended against missionary enthusiasts for tribal languages and patriotic enthusiasts for German.[2] Roman Catholic and Anglican missions generally used Swahili, except in Buhaya where Africans objected strongly, but German Protestants frequently insisted on tribal vernaculars. In most regions Swahili became a language of intertribal communication in German times, rather than merely the means of communication with coastal people. The administration often rejected chiefs or headmen ignorant of Swahili. Ambitious Pare sent their sons to learn it in the trading villages below the mountains.[3] Doubtless most Africans remained ignorant of the language. Few inland women can have understood it. Iraqw elders objected when young men tried to learn Swahili. In 1908 not a word of it was spoken in Tukuyu district, where resistance to coastal culture was especially strong, and Swahili was rare in Upogoro, the southern hinterland, and doubtless other remote regions. Yet even Protestant missionaries acknowledged by 1914 that resistance was vain.[4] Wider communications made a *lingua franca* essential and the coast's prestige survived.

Many sections of coastal society suffered under colonial rule. Arabs, like Asians, were 'natives' under German law. By 1893 government had forbidden Pangani's Arabs to wear their prized daggers for fear of clashes with African police. The decline of slavery ruined many aristocrats and created delicate problems of social adjustment. Zaramo abandoned lavish installation rites for headmen who no longer received dues from inland caravans. Small ports withered as railways drew trade to Tanga and Dar es Salaam. Asian competition forced

---

[1] Iliffe, *German rule*, pp. 180–6.
[2] See Marcia Wright, 'Swahili language policy, 1890–1940', *Swahili*, xxxv (1965), 40–8.
[3] Shorter, *Chiefship*, p. 334; Kimambo, *Political history*, pp. 188–9.
[4] *Central Africa*, December 1924; Toshinao Yoneyama, 'The life and society of the Iraqw', *KUAS*, iv (1969), 79; Hardy to Government, 10 January 1908, TNA iv/L/2/ii; *Deutsche Kolonialzeitung*, 16 February 1907; 'Grundzüge für die Einrichtung und Leitung der Schulen in Deutsch-Ostafrika' [1904] TNA ix/B/i/iv; Axenfeld to Dernburg, 15 February 1909, RKA 820/14.

many Arabs and Swahili out of business.[1] Moreover, not all welcomed western education. 'The sons of the better Swahili and Arab families are only seldom to be found in the government schools', an observer declared. Kilwa's notables sent their slaves' children to German schools while Koran schools flourished there, although they had disappeared from Tanga by 1904.[2] The divisions brought by German conquest surfaced in 1908 with the arrival, supposedly from Mecca, of Arabic letters warning that the Day of Judgment was imminent. The letters were sent to Tanganyika by Rumaliza, once the predominant slave trader along Lake Tanganyika. They first reached Lindi and were denounced by the *kadhi*, Omari bin Jamaliddini. In Bagamoyo the letters were propagated by a *mwalimu* (teacher) and *imamu* (prayer-leader) named Abu Bakr bin Taha, who had thrice made the Pilgrimage. He was denounced by the *liwali*, Amur bin Nasor, a westerniser who had taught Swahili in Germany. In Tabora the pattern was different. There Arabs blamed acceptance of the letters on Zahor bin Mohamed, a radical *mwalimu* whose following was chiefly among Manyema freedmen. Like Abu Bakr he belonged to the Qadiriyya brotherhood.[3]

The Qadiriyya was partly responsible for the Islamic revival on the coast in German times.[4] The brotherhood was the oldest and largest of Islam's many orders. A brotherhood (*tariqa*) was founded by disciples of a mystic who taught an esoteric ritual (*dhikr*) which the brotherhood practised. Each lodge had a leader (*khalifa*) empowered to create other leaders by giving them a licence (*ijaza*). Brotherhoods were characteristically 'second-stage' organisations deepening the faith of existing Muslims, much like revival movements in Protestant Christianity, although in Tanganyika – again like Christian revivals – they also proselytised among followers of indigenous religions. Individual Qadiris had probably lived in East Africa for centuries, but three men pioneered Qadiriyya organisation. Sheikh Husein bin

[1] Dietert to Government, 21 April 1893, TNA G1/14/150; above, pp. 132, 137, 141; Swantz, *Ritual*, p. 157.

[2] F. O. Karstedt, 'Zur Beurteilung des Islam in Deutsch-Ostafrika', *Koloniale Rundschau*, v (1913), 734; P. Lienhardt, introduction to Hassan bin Ismail, *The medicine man: swifa ya Nguvumali* (Oxford, 1968), p. 10; Lorenz to Government, 12 September 1912, TNA IX/B/9/1; Blank to Tanga, 13 January 1904, TNA G9/56/68.

[3] Iliffe, *German rule*, pp. 189–99; Martin, 'Muslim politics', pp. 476–86.

[4] The following account is based on August H. Nimtz, 'The role of the Muslim Sufi order in political change', Ph.D. thesis, Indiana University, 1973, *passim*; Martin, 'Muslim politics', pp. 471–86; Martin, *Muslim brotherhoods*, pp. 152–77; Esmail M. Choka, 'A biography of Sheikh Yahya bin Abdallah l'Qadiriyya, known as Sheikh Ramiya', seminar paper, University College, Dar es Salaam, 1969.

Abdallah brought one branch of the brotherhood to Zanzibar from Mecca in about 1880. It reached the mainland late in German times and subsequently expanded inland, especially in the Rufiji area and around Lake Victoria. Meanwhile a second branch reached Zanzibar around 1883–4 from Somalia. Its *khalifa* was Uways bin Muhammad al-Barawi, 'Standard Bearer of the Qadiri Army', who is said to have made 520 *khulafa* during his lifetime. Sheikh Uways established his organisation on the coast, especially among fellow 'Barawi' from Somalia. Among his *khulafa* was Zahor bin Mohamed, who in 1894 carried the *tariqa* to Tabora, whence it spread to Ujiji and the Manyema. The third branch of the Qadiriyya was introduced to Baga-moyo in about 1905 by Muhammad bin Husein al-Lughani, who gave the *ijaza* to a Manyema freed slave known as Sheikh Ramiya. A man of great magnetism and piety, Ramiya attracted a following by perform-ing the *dhikr* alone outside his house. He taught disciples, institutional-ised the brotherhood, and initiated an annual Maulidi ceremony which made Bagamoyo a centre of learning and pilgrimage from all parts of Tanganyika. Another brotherhood, the Shadhiliyya, was brought from the Comoros Islands by Muhammad Ma'ruf around 1900. He gave the *ijaza* to Husein bin Mahmud of Kilwa, which became the brotherhood's Tanganyikan headquarters. As Bagamoyo and Kilwa decayed econ-omically, so their religious importance grew, a tendency accentuated by the mainland's gradual intellectual emancipation from Zanzibar.

The zeal of Muslim teachers, especially Qadiri *khulafa*, was one reason why the German period saw the first extensive acceptance of Islam by inland peoples. Previously there were Muslim nuclei in trading settlements and among such hinterland peoples as Bondei and Zigua, while two or three inland rulers had become Muslims and certain others had adopted a veneer of Islamic culture. In German times the impact went deeper in three directions.

One breakthrough was in the northern hinterland. The Segeju were overwhelmingly Muslim by 1914, while the Bondei appear to have been divided between Christians and Muslims, with the latter especially numerous in the east. Many Kilindi accepted Islam as their power collapsed in Usambara. By 1913 both Shambaa and coastal *waalimu* were active there.[1] Zigua conversion is associated with Omari Mgaza, a Zigua Qadiri trained at Bagamoyo. Probably most Zigua were at least nominal Muslims by 1914 and the *dhikr* was performed in quite remote

---

[1] *Central Africa*, March 1910; Wohlrab and Gleiss to Wilhelmstal, 22 September and 4 December 1912, TNA G9/48/136 and 139.

villages.[1] Further south a district officer reckoned in 1913 that half the Zaramo were Muslims. Proselytisation had come both from the coast and northwards from the Rufiji, whence Zaramo traced the boys' *jando* initiation rite which played a large part in Islam's expansion.[2]

Islam's history in southern Tanganyika took a slightly different course owing to the conversion of the Yao of Mozambique during the late nineteenth century, partly in response to the increasing Portuguese pressure which subsequently forced many Yao across the Ruvuma into Tanganyika, culminating in 1912 when Mataka settled near Tunduru.[3] The Yao proselytised vigorously among their neighbours. 'Here at Makochera, in the wilds of Rovuma, amidst utter heathendom, I find a small colony keeping a Moslem feast', a traveller wrote in 1909, 'and from this point to Songea Islam is a very powerful force.' Songea's successor became a Muslim in 1910 and when Likotiko became Chief of Mshope in 1914 he renamed his capital Zanzibari.[4] Nearer the southern coast Islam was accepted by many headmen in the years following Maji Maji. In 1913 fifteen of Ungindo's nineteen headmen were said to be Muslims. In lowland Ubena several of Kiwanga's sons became Muslims, as did several Pogoro and Mbunga leaders. By 1910 every village on the Makonde and Mwera plateaux was said to have a *mwalimu*.[5]

The third kind of Islamic expansion was personal adherence by individuals in contact with the coast or inland trading settlements. The most influential settlement was probably Kondoa-Irangi: 33 of the 147 headmen in its vicinity were said to be Muslims in 1913.[6] Islam's pioneers in Buhaya were Ganda refugees who converted Haya fellow-traders from a base at Kyaka, where a Zanzibar-trained Ganda, Sheikh Abdallah Musa, established his headquarters.[7] Most Muslims

1 Choka, 'Sheikh Ramiya'; Vogel [?] and Reutter to Government, 6 August and 3 June 1913, TNA G9/48/78 and 81; *Kiongozi*, January 1910; *Central Africa*, October 1904, May 1907, November 1910, April 1913.
2 Eggebrecht to Government, 14 May 1913, TNA G9/48/82; Swantz, *Ritual*, pp. 164–71, 298, 340.
3 Edward A. Alpers, 'Towards a history of the expansion of Islam in East Africa: the matrilineal peoples of the southern interior', in Ranger and Kimambo, *Historical study*, pp. 172–201.
4 Weston to Committee, 21 August [1909?] UMCA A/1/xvii; Nordeck to Government, 23 January 1913, TNA G9/48/122; Gallagher, 'Islam', p. 116.
5 Auracher to Government, 7 January 1913, TNA G9/48/85; Larson, 'History', pp. 259–65; Einsiedel to Government, 13 December 1912, TNA G9/48/164; Künster, 'Aufstands-Gefahr im Hinterlande von Lindi' [1910] RKA 702/50.
6 Grass to Government, 17 January 1913, TNA G9/48/140.
7 K. Mayanja Kiwanuka, 'The politics of Islam in Bukoba district', B.A. thesis, University of Dar es Salaam, 1973, pp. 19–20.

in Ujiji and Tabora were Manyema freedmen, although most *waalimu* were from the coast. Apart from certain chiefs, Nyamwezi remained generally indifferent to Islam. Those in Dar es Salaam apparently first observed Ramadhan in 1904, but when Nyamwezi returned home they often abandoned Islamic practices. Sukuma chiefs apparently expelled subjects who became Muslims.[1]

Apart from proselytisation, four main circumstances seem to have influenced responses to Islam. One was simply the extent of contact with Muslims, for Islam was not only a faith but a culture and a legal code, so that adherence meant gradual assimilation into an existing Islamic community. The first adherents were frequently traders or migrant labourers who were absent for unusually long periods. They had obvious material reasons for becoming Muslims. A Haya trader found that a friend would lend him money only if he became a Muslim, 'since he could not trust a non-Muslim'.[2] Moreover, Islamic culture still to some extent represented modernity. Unable to attract a Christian missionary, the modernising Chief Makwaia of Busiha in southern Usukuma employed a coastal teacher and became a Muslim. An official at Kondoa remarked 'the endeavour especially of the better-situated Rangi and the younger generation to shed the despised status of the *mshenzi* and even to be admitted into the *waungwana* caste'.[3] The defence force, government schools, and civil service were all predominantly Islamic institutions. In Uzaramo Muslim *akidas* introduced Islamic law and 'people understood the will of the Government to be that they become Muslims'.[4]

Yet contact and material interest were not alone sufficient. The Yao had visited the coast for 300 years before accepting Islam, and when they did so it was as a result of rapid change: the emergence of powerful chieftainships and the growing Portuguese threat. Dr Alpers suggests that both these changes were examples of enlargement of scale, a new emphasis on macrocosm which made indigenous Yao religion inadequate.[5] 'Enlargement of scale' embraces most circumstances under which men became Muslims in German times. It

[1] Schippel, 'Vom Islam im westlichen Teile von Deutsch-Ostafrika', *Die Welt des Islams*, II (1914), 6–8; Sicard, *Lutheran church*, p. 178 n. 26; Proempeler to Government, 24 January 1913, Höntsch to Tabora, 8 January 1913, and Kirsch [?] to Government, 7 March 1913, TNA G9/48/125, 129, 113.
[2] G. R. Mutahaba, *Portrait of a nationalist: the life of Ali Migeyo* (Nairobi, 1969), p. 13.
[3] Austen, *Northwest Tanzania*, p. 58; Thiesen to Government, 11 July 1909, TNA G36/13.
[4] Swantz, *Ritual*, p. 103.
[5] Alpers in Ranger and Kimambo, *Historical study*, pp. 195–6.

embraces traders and migrant workers. It embraces those whose contact with the nearby coast was making them peasants. It embraces those seeking to attach their small-scale societies to Islam's universal history, as Zigua claimed descent from Harun al-Rashid's soldiers or dynasties in the Southern Highlands claimed Arab ancestry.[1] And it embraces the political leaders who were often Muslim pioneers, for they had most dealings with the larger world and were most exposed to its dangers. Yet these reasons do not fully explain responses to Islam. Long contact with Muslims, material interest, proselytisation, military conquest, and enlargement of scale did not make most Nyamwezi receptive. Explanation must also consider the indigenous resources available to Africans facing the new world, and even then no satisfactory answer may appear.

In 1912 the governor reckoned that Tanganyika contained 300,000–500,000 Muslims.[2] Their levels of commitment varied widely. The coastal revival had probably deepened many faiths. Pilgrimage probably became more common, for several references survive, apart from Abu Bakr's three journeys.[3] Paradoxically, imperialism integrated Tanganyika more fully into the Islamic world. Educated Muslims were deeply interested in the Turko-Italian war. Millennial expectations were common. New Islamic books from Cairo, Mecca, and Jakarta arrived, although Europeans were uncertain how far they were understood.[4] By contrast, many long-distance migrants to the coast were doubtless only superficially Islamised. Among these the cult of *jini* flourished and Islamic magic was the *mwalimu*'s main function. Faced by the government's ban on killing witches, coastal Muslims employed a quasi-Islamic rite, *halubadili*, wherein the angels who had won the Battle of Badr for Muhammad's followers were invoked to make all participants in the rite immune to witchcraft and to kill those who practised it.[5] How far Islam could be adapted to African beliefs and cultures – through magic, by using drums and dance, or by encouraging female participation – divided Muslims throughout the

---

[1] Correspondence in TNA 3455/12; Culwick, *Ubena*, p. 57; 'A history of Usangu, related by the Wazee of Utengule', in Mbeya district book, TNA.

[2] Heinrich Schnee, *Deutsch-Ostafrika im Weltkriege* (Leipzig, 1919), p. 135.

[3] E.g. Nötzel to Government, 26 November 1908, and Sperling to Government, 23 February 1909, TNA G9/46.

[4] Herrmann, memorandum, 19 July 1912, TNA G9/48/9; *Kiongozi*, February 1913; *Central Africa*, April 1914; C. H. Becker, 'Materials for the understanding of Islam in German East Africa' (trans. B. G. Martin), *TNR*, LXVIII (1968), 31–61; Martin Klamroth, 'Der literarische Charakter des ostafrikanischen Islams', *Die Welt des Islams*, I (1913), 21–31.

[5] Swantz, 'Medicine man', p. 244.

colonial period. Orthodox Islam's dilemma was to be wholly a religion of the macrocosm, providing few humanly satisfying remedies for evil:

> If an ill fortune befalls you,
> [if you lose] your mother or father,
> or the child of your love,
> the best thing is to be patient.[1]

'Islam is a hard religion', said the Haya,[2] and that hardness (rather than Islam's laxity, as European observers assumed) gave rise to the popular cult. Yet orthodoxy slowly gained. Yao and Zaramo began to circumcise in the Islamic manner. The only Shambaa to refuse Majio's medicine were Muslims. Some German administrators believed that most Tanganyikans would soon embrace Islam.[3] But Muslims were probably less sanguine. They knew that Islam found increasing difficulty in presenting itself as the modern faith:

One day we Christians of Ushirombo went to the boma to pay tax...The clerks could not write us down quickly...Our teachers first wrote down the mission people, then they wrote down the cultivators...We heard the Muslim leader say, 'Let us Muslims take heed. Today these mission people have worked at the boma, but now, this very year, I want all Swahili to be taught to read and write in the European manner. Look here, we have been beaten by the unbelievers from the mission!'[4]

Christianity

Christianity both profited and suffered from its association with the new order. Some sought in it solutions to the new problems of the colonial period, while hoping to continue to solve older problems by inherited means. Others went further and also sought in Christianity new solutions to old problems. Some adopted it as supplement, others as substitute. Both were often disappointed, for Christianity proved both incompatible with old faiths and incapable of solving old problems.

Mission work expanded after German conquest.[5] Of the five societies already established, the oldest, the Holy Ghost Fathers,

[1] Quoted in Knappert, *Traditional poetry*, p. 28.
[2] Josiah M. Kibira, 'A study of Christianity among the Bahaya tribe', M.S.T. thesis, Boston University, 1964, p. 41.
[3] Rechenberg, memorandum, 24 March 1910, RKA 702/39.
[4] Hermann Shamba in *Rafiki yangu*, February 1914.
[5] For an outline, see Oliver, *Missionary factor*, ch. 4.

extended its work from the hinterland of Bagamoyo to Kilimanjaro (1891), Usambara (1907), and Ugogo (1910). The White Fathers spread outwards from early bases in Karema, Tabora, and Bukumbi, occupying the Rukwa basin, Usumbwa, and Buhaya during the 1890s and in the next decade expanding to Ufipa, Buha, Mbulu, and towards Lake Nyasa. Protestant societies moved more slowly. The UMCA extended its work from Bonde to Uzigua. The CMS concentrated on Uganda, abandoning its station on Kilimanjaro and retaining only an isolated sphere in Ukaguru and Ugogo. The LMS, after 29 years of failure at Urambo, handed over to the Moravians in 1897 and withdrew. Meanwhile German rule stimulated several German missions to undertake work. Among Roman Catholics, the Benedictines of St Ottilien, a monastic order formed for mission work in 1884, accepted responsibility for the south, founding stations at Lukuledi in 1895, Madibira (in Usangu) in 1896, Peramiho in 1898, and Kwiro in 1902. German Protestant activity was fragmented by long conflict between Lutherans and Calvinists. The first society in the field was the Bethel mission, created by DOAG supporters and drawing on the Evangelical-Lutheran state church of Prussia. It established itself in Usambara in 1891 and Buhaya in 1911. The older Berlin Mission, embodying a broad and inclusive Lutheranism, sought maximum independence of the colonial authorities by starting work in Unyakyusa in 1891, later expanding into Ubena, Uhehe, and Uzaramo. Unyakyusa also attracted the Moravians, heirs of the sixteenth-century Hussite movement in Czechoslovakia. The Leipzig mission, an orthodox Lutheran body, took over CMS work on Kilimanjaro in 1892 and later evangelised Upare and Iramba. Many smaller societies also entered the colony, including Adventists who settled in Musoma and Upare and the American-based Africa Inland Mission which chose Usukuma.

These missions represented the divisions of European society and churchmanship. University gentlemen from Oxford or Leipzig coexisted with Bavarian smallholders and Congregationalist artisans. Benedictine monks and Moravians from 'saved' communities were interspersed with Anglican revivalists and Lavigerie's ultra-mobile White Fathers. Yet by 1914 almost every society employed the same evangelistic approach, working in an extensive manner, building networks of schools and catechists, and encouraging converts to abandon old beliefs. For many societies this meant a reversal of policy. The Holy Ghost Fathers abandoned closed mission villages. Moravian brethren and Benedictine monks found themselves touring out-schools. The change of policy owed something to mission theory. By the 1880s missionaries were questioning earlier assumptions that Christianity must be accompanied by general socio-economic change – the view which had led them to send promising pupils to Europe for education. Instead, many feared that European training alienated African clergy from their flocks and bred unwelcome independence of mind. The missionaries' new ideal was Buganda, which seemed to prove that an African society could be converted from the top downwards as a unit. Increasingly fashionable racial theory suggested that every human group had a distinctive culture to which Christianity should be adapted. A German theologian, Gustav Warneck, system-atised these trends in his theory of *Volksmission*.[1] It attracted mission-aries who, regardless of social origins, hoped to find in Africa the organic social unity which a rapidly secularising Europe had lost. Lavigerie instructed White Fathers to find and convert powerful chiefs in order to create organic Christian kingdoms. The Abbot of St Ottilien ordered his monks to lead *peoples* to Christ, not merely particular classes. A UMCA synod resolved in 1893 'strenuously [to] discourage all Europeanisms'.[2] Theory and experience were rein-forced by necessity. In East Africa missionaries agreed they were competing with an expanding Islam. They were also competing with each other. Urgency demanded extensive evangelisation and an adaptive approach rather than laborious creation of closed com-munities. 'Our principal duty at present', Bishop Vogt of the Holy Ghost Fathers wrote in 1912, 'is to occupy the country by rural schools, in order to close it to Islam and the Protestants'.[3]

Conversion from the top downwards was tried in several areas. In Ungoni the Benedictines first adopted a language spoken only by aristocrats.[4] In Ukerewe the White Fathers supported a successful contender for the throne and the Father Superior fulfilled the missionary's dream of becoming archbishop of a Christian kingdom:

Before he began to rule, this king asked the fathers of the Catholic mission if he could receive the blessing of the Catholic Church for his work in the sight of all the people...When he reached the church door the Father

[1] Wright, *German missions*, ch. 1.
[2] J. Bouniol (ed.), *The White Fathers and their missions* (London, 1929), p. 82; Frumentius Renner (ed.), *Der fünfarmige Leuchter: Beiträge zum Werden und Wirken der Benediktinerkongregation von St Ottilien* (2 vols, St Ottilien, 1971), II, 136; *Diocese of Zanzibar: Acts of the Synods, 1884–1903* (n.p., n.d.), p. 18.
[3] Kieran, 'Holy Ghost Fathers', p. 195.
[4] Wehrmeister, *Vor dem Sturm*, p. 118.

Superior asperged the king and together they went to the altar...The Father Superior asked the king: 'From whom have you received the dignity of kingship?' The king replied before all the people: 'I have received the dignity of kingship from God'. 'Why have you received this dignity?' 'That I may rule my people with justice and so care for them that they may gain heaven.'...Then the Father Superior blessed the king.[1]

Yet this experience was rare. Whatever their devotion to *Volksmission*, most missionaries found themselves assaulting the established order of African societies. One reason was the difficulty of adapting Christian teaching to religions without sacred books or systematic theologies. Lavigerie told the White Fathers not to attack indigenous customs but added that they 'would have to deal with simple, unprejudiced negroes, to whom they were to preach the Gospel plainly, dwelling on the miraculous proofs of Christianity, and speaking always with authority, without unnecessary arguments and explanations'. In Ufipa his missionaries systematically destroyed shrines and shot sacred pythons.[2] Moreover, the circumstances of mission work made almost impossible the patient study which adaptation required. Sickness and death were too close. The average age of the first five Holy Ghost brothers to die at Bagamoyo was 25.[3] Tanganyika's was 'a brash, vigorous, insensitive evangelisation'.[4] Few introspective men could sustain the loneliness, deprivation, and frustration of mission life. 'I felt a sense of desolation unlike any I had ever before experienced', wrote J. P. Farler when he was the sole European at Magila.[5] Isolated missionaries drew strength from strict adherence to church law, which since the European Reformation had rigidly regulated matters such as marriage and the training of priests which had previously been treated more flexibly. And whatever the communitarian theories of *Volksmission*, the supremacy of individual conscience was the hallmark of nineteenth-century European Christianity. 'Truly, we don't want to Europeanize our Christians', the Anglo-Catholic Bishop Weston explained, 'but we do require, we must require that what is Christian in our European conscience be taken over into the African conscience, to individualize and purify it.'[6]

The reasons for a radical rather than adaptive approach to African societies are best illustrated by marriage. To demand monogamy was

---

[1] *Rafiki yangu*, January 1910.
[2] Bouniol, *White Fathers*, p. 93; Willis, 'Changes', p. 150.
[3] Versteijnen, *Bagamoyo*, s.v. 1877.
[4] R. E. S. Tanner, *Transition in African beliefs* (Maryknoll, 1967), p. 188.
[5] J. P. Farler, *The work of Christ in Central Africa* (London, 1878), p. 9.
[6] *Central Africa*, August 1908.

to set church law against the custom of most African societies and especially against the indigenous leaders who were commonly the polygynists but whose adherence was essential if societies were to be converted as units. One mission, the Moravians, made temporary concessions, but other missionaries decided, after much heart-searching, not to baptise polygynists and to urge them to put away multiple wives where this was possible without injustice, thus in effect denying that African marriages were binding. Bishop Smythies rejected the request of Tanganyika's first African priest to baptise the wives of polygynists, explaining, 'I knew it was hard, and might cause trouble, but our Lord Jesus Christ had told us that He came to cause trouble.'[1] Missionaries were appalled by the open sexuality of African marriage customs: 'too filthy to be described', according to the sympathetic Smythies.[2] At a time when Christians everywhere were clinging grimly to inherited authority, missionaries felt obliged, and perhaps relieved, to obey what had been the church's law throughout most of its known history. As Smythies put it, 'The Church must not be depressed to a lower level to meet half-way the heathenism of Africa.'[3] Moreover, the sacrifice required by monogamy enabled missionaries to test their converts' sincerity. 'They want to be Christians without *giving up anything*', one bewailed.[4] To impose this test, obey church law, and teach what they believed to be the true Gospel the missionaries destroyed all hope of *Volksmission*.

Yet *Volksmission* failed not only because missionaries did not practise it, but also because Africans did not want it. Tanganyikan societies were not the stable, homogeneous unities which Warneck's theory predicated, and where Christianity could be adapted to indigenous religions there was no reason why the indigenous religions should not be adapted instead. Most Tanganyikan converts accepted Christianity chiefly for what was new and different about it. They thereby determined that it should be established through conflict. This was true both of societies and of individuals.

Some strongly organised societies continued to find missionaries valuable as experts. The Holy Ghost Fathers were allowed into the Kilema chiefdom of Kilimanjaro only on condition that they opened schools. When Lutherans reached Unyakyusa they were welcomed by highland chiefs because they brought trade previously available only

---

[1] *Ibid.*, April 1894. [2] *Ibid.*, May 1887.
[3] Quoted in A. E. M. Anderson-Morshead, *The history of the Universities Mission to Central Africa, I: 1859–1909* (6th edn, London, 1955), p. 263.
[4] *Central Africa*, October 1896.

to the lakeshore peoples, because they might offer protection from Ngoni raids, and because they could be used as arbitrators.[1] Yet persecuted and destructured societies generally responded more enthusiastically than locally dominant peoples. Hehe and Sangu showed little interest in missionaries, but their Bena, Nyiha, and Safwa dependents proved more hospitable.[2] Bethel missionaries were welcomed to Usambara by the sub-chief of Mlalo, who had gained near-autonomy during the chaos of *pato*. 'Rev. Döring', it was recalled, 'prayed that there would be no war in Ushambaa; people should increase and that Mlalo should be independent.' By contrast, when the missionaries visited Vugha the king had them escorted back to Mlalo. By 1906 Mlalo had 468 of the 867 baptised Lutherans in Usambara.[3]

Shambaa kings drew much strength from ritual authority, and the nature of existing religious institutions clearly influenced collective responses to Christianity. In the coastal area and its hinterland Islam generally prevented effective mission work. Zaramo indifference led the Benedictines to transfer their activities inland.[4] Such indigenous religious institutions as the *kubandwa* cult and *uwuxala* society provided resources for resistance. Yet long-settled peoples were not necessarily hostile to Christianity. The Fipa experienced early and unusually widespread conversion, a process which needs study but was possibly aided by village organisation, an emphasis on individuality and rationality, and experience of Islam without commitment to it.[5] Moreover, certain aspects of indigenous religions facilitated acceptance of Christianity. Matola and Nakaam used Christianity to free themselves from ritual subordination to Makua headmen. Matola expected his first missionary to extirpate witchcraft. At Father Dupont's invitation many Fipa burned protective medicines during 1894. 'At that time many women were possessed', an early Shambaa pastor recalled, 'but after accepting Christianity they were not possessed.'[6] Conquest generally strengthened belief in the superior

[1] G. Nevil Shann, 'The educational development of the Chagga tribe', *Overseas education*, XXVI (1954), 51; Merensky, *Deutsche Arbeit*, p. 200; Charsley, *Princes*, pp. 102–3.
[2] Wright, *German missions*, chs. 3–4.
[3] Timilai H. I. Guga, 'Research into the history of the Usambara-Digo Church', typescript (trans. M. H. K. Mbwana), 1965, MUL; Johanssen, *Führung*, I, 53–5, 188–9, 217.
[4] Lambert Dörr, 'Afrikaner und Missionar', in Renner, *Leuchter*, II, 203.
[5] See Willis, *Man and beast*, pp. 10, 102–10.
[6] Terence Ranger, 'Missionary adaptation of African religious institutions: the Masasi case', in Ranger and Kimambo, *Historical study*, p. 226; T. O. Ranger, *The African churches of Tanzania* (Nairobi, n.d.), p. 7; Guga, 'Research'.

power of Europeans and their religion. There were exceptions – defeat seems initially to have hardened Hehe resistance to Christianity[1] – but they were rare. 'Today belongs to the Europeans', a Makua headman declared:

Look, there was...Machemba...He said, 'I am master; I do not fear the Europeans and do not accept their flag.' But when they came he fell down before them and gave them his gun and his powder...Yes, anyone who does not understand that the present days belong to the Europeans has the understanding of a child. Therefore I say my children can come to you and learn in the European fashion; I shall not stop them.[2]

On the only occasion when the Benedictines tried to precede German troops they met much hostility in Upogoro in 1897, but on returning in 1902, after German rule had become effective, they could almost immediately insist that villagers should build schools at their own expense.[3]

For all these reasons the radical rather than the adaptive aspects of mission work attracted most African societies, whose response then shaped the missionaries' behaviour. The tendency was even stronger at the level of individual adherence. Missionaries rarely found their first followers among established leaders. There were exceptions. The ruling Yao families provided most of the UMCA's first teachers and priests in Masasi. Many early Catholics in Buhaya came from the Ziba aristocracy. There were also areas such as Kilimanjaro where the first Christians came from all social groups.[4] But in Tanganyika generally, as so often before, the Christian Church found its first members chiefly among marginal people.

In many areas the first Christians were freedmen, even after the slave trade ended. Finding no powerful and compliant chief near Lake Tanganyika, the White Fathers formed congregations of freed Manyema slaves, who became their first catechists. Most of the first hearers at Tosamaganga were *vafugwa*, the servile group within the Hehe state. At Mtae in Usambara the first two converts were lepers and 'those who had twins and children born with teeth (vigego) made the mission their place of refuge'. The great Chagga teacher, Filipo Njau, went to the mission because he was the second

[1] Dörr in Renner, *Leuchter*, II, 208–9.
[2] *Ibid.*, pp. 204–5.
[3] Kwiro mission diary, preface, Kwiro archives; Larson, 'History', pp. 63–4.
[4] Iliffe, *German rule*, pp. 174, 177; Susan G. Rogers, 'The search for political focus on Kilimanjaro: a history of Chagga politics, 1916–1952', Ph.D. thesis, University of Dar es Salaam, 1972, p. 159.

of three sons and therefore, under Chagga law, inherited little property.[1] Many early priests and catechists were the sons of ritual experts, the intellectuals of pre-colonial societies who formed a rare profession open to talent, with special awareness of spiritual matters, unusual opportunity for travel, and a custom of ritual apprenticeship. John Saidi, the Bondei apostle to the Zigua, was the son of an exorcist. Kolumba Msigala, who took Christianity to the Yao, was the son of a herbalist. Ambilishye, the profoundly spiritual Moravian evangelist at the Nyamwanga court, had been an itinerant diviner whose travels brought him into contact with Christian teaching.[2] Mobility also characterised traders. Tanganyika's most remarkable Christian congregation was created by Haya traders who visited Buganda in the 1890s, accepted Protestant teaching, and returned to worship secretly each Sunday in a cave on the shore of Lake Victoria for fear of persecution by the chiefs, a decade before the first Protestant missionary settled in Buhaya.[3]

Those least committed to the existing order are the young, and their response to mission teaching gave the early church in Tanganyika – the Church of the Fathers – its special character and historical direction. This can best be seen in the history of the German Protestant societies. In 1911 the Bethel mission had 2,894 pupils in its schools; the Berlin mission, 3,573; the Moravians, 5,226; and the Leipzig mission, 6,059.[4] These figures accurately measured the extent to which each society had abandoned its original plans in favour of concentrating on the young. The Bethel missionaries were the most hostile to literary education, preferring craft training and teaching Swahili only in one evangelists' school. The Berlin Lutherans intended to provide schools only for children of Christians, but, as their historian explained:

In East Africa the awakening hunger for education which the permeation of European civilisation stimulated among the natives, the competition with Catholic missions which principally built their work on schools, and the threat of Islam (against which Christian mission schools are an effective means of evangelisation) caused schooling to take on a remarkable impetus.[5]

[1] Renault, *Lavigerie*, I, 179–84, 412–20; Melicho Mbamila in MMRP 3/68/1/3/2; Guga, 'Research'; Filipo Njau, *Aus meinem Leben* (trans. B. Gutmann, Erlangen, 1960), p. 35.

[2] *Central Africa*, July 1909; Msigala, 'Reminiscences', UMCA D/3; Bachmann, 'Ambilishye', pp. 10–11.

[3] Hellberg, *Missions*, pp. 84–7.

[4] Johanna Eggert, *Missionsschule und sozialer Wandel in Ostafrika* (Bielefeld, 1970), p. 272. This paragraph is based on Dr Eggert's book.

[5] Julius Richter, *Geschichte der Berliner Missionsgesellschaft 1824–1924* (Berlin, 1924), pp. 658–9.

The Moravians came to terms with reality rather sooner. When they took over Urambo from the LMS in 1897 they immediately concentrated on schools. The Leipzig missionaries on Kilimanjaro favoured broad popular education as the basis for a *Volkskirche* which would be progressive rather than fossilising the old order. They planned to work first among adults, but while learning the language they found so many children demanding teaching that they set up a school system and soon operated the most efficient in the colony. Their success was probably due in part to the vigorous competition between Protestant and Roman Catholic missions on Kilimanjaro.

During the last ten years of German rule primary schooling expanded greatly in almost every region where missionaries worked. The expansion accompanied incorporation into the colonial economy and encouragement for schooling – sometimes verging on compulsion – by the increasingly confident government. After 28 unrewarding years the CMS was considering abandoning its stations in Ukaguru and Ugogo when they experienced 'a great wave of interest and inquiry', manifested chiefly in demand for schools and probably due to the central railway's approach. Between 1910 and 1913 CMS pupils increased from 3,989 to 17,202.[1] Missions established late in the German period frequently met an immediate demand for education quite different from the slow beginnings made elsewhere. The Leipzig missionaries who entered South Pare in 1904 had this experience.[2] In all, by 1912 the great rush for education had increased the number of pupils in primary schools to 101,035, perhaps a quarter of all children of school age.[3]

The appeal of education to the young was to a large extent material. The first Nyakyusa pupils left when the missionaries refused to pay them. 'The first advantage was the joy and hope of going to heaven', declared Amandus Motela of Kilimanjaro, 'the second was to know the craft of carpentry.'[4] Yet young people were not moved solely by material motives. The novelty of education fascinated many:

Next morning I saw the other children gathered in a large hut, saying together 'A, B, C, D...' over and over again with an older boy in front leading them. I was attracted and thought it was a song – but actually it was the first school in our Diocese.[5]

[1] Oliver, *Missionary factor*, p. 198; Gordon Hewitt, *The problems of success: a history of the Church Missionary Society 1910–1942*, I (London, 1971), p. 183.
[2] Schanz, *Am Fusse*, p. 194.   [3] Schnee, *Lexicon*, s.v. Missionsschulwesen.
[4] Information from Fr Henry Zawadi.   [5] Msigala, 'Reminiscences', UMCA D/3.

The example of children who had already learned to read was especially powerful:

At the pastures one of them began teaching another to write, and I watched them idly. After a while I began to think about what they were learning, and said, 'I too am going to try to put something down on paper'. They said, 'Yes, come and try'. By-and-by I wrote many letters on paper. And at last my teacher said, 'These are all the letters. You have finished.' That day my love of learning began.[1]

Adolescence is the most common time to accept new beliefs. This was true of indigenous religions: the possession experiences which made people diviners or *kubandwa* mediums usually took place in youth.[2] Similarly, many young people accepted Christianity during schooling:

Many boys came to instruction, to learn to read and write, things to their advantage. Then behold! In the midst of their craving to read and write, the Word of God in their reading books overwhelmed them...They became Christians, saved by Jesus, children of God. So it was with me.[3]

Concern with Christianity was sometimes an anxiety to acquire whatever magical power its mysteries provided. In Bonde and Masasi many 'converts' ceased to attend church once confirmed.[4] Literacy itself had an almost magical quality. As a young catechist locked in combat with the *kubandwa* mediums of Buhaya, Nicholas Mugongo was taught to read by Christ in a vision:

'Courage', the vision then told me, 'henceforth you will no longer need to learn from books; in three days you will know how to decipher all of them.' I believed it.

Next morning I described the dream to the catechumens. Some of them had learned to read elsewhere; they mocked me. 'Give me a book', I said. Someone handed me a bible. I saw only white and black. Next day the same failure. At last the third day arrived. I took the book, made a large sign of the cross, and read fluently.[5]

Literacy gave Christianity authority, apparent rationality, and explanatory capacity which unwritten indigenous religions lacked. For Matayo Leveriya Kaaya 'the missionaries had been able to answer certain fundamental questions which his parents had failed to answer to his satisfaction. These included the problem of creation, the

[1] Elise Kootz-Kretschmer (ed.), *Ways I have trodden: the experiences of a teacher in Tanganyika* [*Msaturwa Mwachitete*] (trans. M. Bryan, London, 1932), p. 30.
[2] Hatfield, 'The *nfumu*', pp. 147–50; *Rafiki yangu*, June 1913; A. G. Ishumi, 'Embandwa cult in Buhaya: a socio-historical study', typescript, 1970, in Mr Ishumi's possession.
[3] Njau, *Aus meinem Leben*, p. 13.   [4] *Central Africa*, March 1893 and May 1899.
[5] Mugongo, 'Mémoires'.

purpose of man on earth, and the ultimate end of man.'[1] The sense of purpose – markedly absent from indigenous religions – attracted many ambitious young people. Fiwombe Malakilindu, a man of this type, chose a baptismal name meaning 'I must get God's things done'.[2] Literacy made even Christianity's traditions appear rational:

I met an old man...[who] asked me, 'Teacher, have you no taboo?' I said, 'Surely, these things: I do not eat meat on Fridays...it is a taboo to speak lies...or murder, or worship spirits, or...but let us not waste words. What sort of taboo do you mean, father?' Lowering his voice, he replied, 'Inside here there is a sick child. If your wife is pregnant, it is bad to come here and talk.' I said, 'What is this? Look, father, I have no taboo like this.'...They only replied, 'These are the customs of our ancestors, and we are bound to follow their example, although we do not know the reason.'[3]

The spiritual and intellectual power of the Christian story when preached for the first time must not be underestimated. Death was an immediate reality. Through ancestral veneration it dominated indigenous religions, and it dominated the writings of early Christians.[4] Lacking notions of rewards and punishments in an after-life, most indigenous religions left men naked before evil. Christian teachings of heaven and hell veiled that nakedness and gave a new urgency to religious choice. Hell was commonly translated by words for 'fire':

In the year 1906 the missionary Johannes Kretschmer sent evangelists all over the country... The evangelists went into all the villages...and said: 'Take heed ...Consider that God will send fire to burn us all, all the men in the world!' ...When this message was proclaimed my parents fled with me to Kukwe.[5]

Thirty years later a social anthropologist heard Christian women demanding of Nyakyusa villagers, 'Do you want to burn?'[6] Nicholas Mugongo was baptised after dreaming vividly of hell. Ambilishye had a similar experience:

Suddenly there appeared to me an angel of the Lord in a dream. I sat in a hollow tree, in the darkness of the devil, and the angel called me. When I heard the angel's call, I left the hollow tree, the dark cavity, and came forth into the open air.[7]

[1] A. S. Mbise, 'The evangelist: Matayo Leveriya Kaaya', in John Iliffe (ed.), *Modern Tanzanians* (Nairobi, 1973), p. 31.
[2] Oskar Gemuseus and Joseph Busse, *Ein Gebundener Jesu Christi: das Lebensbild des Fiwombe Malakilindu* (Hamburg, 1950), p. 55.
[3] Yohanes Ibrahimu in *Rafiki yangu*, January 1914.
[4] The Swahili mission newspapers are full of stories of death.
[5] Joseph Busse, 'Aus dem Leben von Asyukile Malango', ZES, xxxv (1949–50), 205–6.
[6] Monica Wilson, 'An African Christian morality', *Africa*, x (1937), 281.
[7] Bachmann, 'Ambilishiye', p. 11.

Against the fear of hell were set the equally novel conceptions of heaven and an incarnate, personal saviour. 'The Resurrection, I find, always secures their attention if nothing else will', an early missionary noted. 'It is just the kind of thing to interest this wonder loving people with their ideas of magic, witchcraft and rain-making.'[1] Fifty years later a social anthropologist made the same observation more sympathetically:

The supreme attraction, mentioned again and again as the reason for conversion, is: 'There is life'...and it is life in a world to come rather than 'more abundant life' here and now that is spoken of. The contrast is between heaven above and the shadowy world 'beneath' of pagan thought, or a fearful fiery hell in which most Christians believe and to which, some think, all pagans are condemned. Constantly in sermons by Nyakyusa preachers there was stress on life, resurrection, and on the rewards and punishments of the future life, and this theme recurs again and again in the dreams of Christians.[2]

The person of Christ, not the Christian God, caught the imagination of deeply convinced converts. The first Moravian convert at Kiwele 'repeatedly dreamed about Jesus'. 'I loved Him long before I was baptised', wrote Ambilishye.[3]

A powerful strand in the converts' thinking was a Manichean view of the world as a struggle between light and darkness. They often condemned non-Christian customs more rigorously than did the missionaries. When a conference of African Christians met at Magila in 1895, members who advocated 'greater laxity then could possibly be allowed' were sternly restrained by the African clergy. This and two later conferences, attended only by Africans, outlawed Bondei initiation, marriage, and burial rites, abortion, medicines, agricultural charms, observance of clan taboos, and Sunday markets.[4] Bondei leaders later rejected a proposal to invent a Christian substitute for initiation. In 1913 church leaders in Masasi advised Bishop Weston to ban all initiation rites.[5] The radical impact of Christianity was epitomised in Nicholas Mugongo's struggle with a medium of the *kubandwa* cult which was so deeply embedded in Haya history. 'I had come to destroy all that he wished to conserve', Mugongo wrote, and he saw it as a confrontation not only between Christianity and paganism but between young and old. 'Their assemblies', he wrote

[1] J. C. Price, 1881, quoted in Oded, *Islam*, pp. 60–1.
[2] Wilson, *Communal rituals*, p. 187.
[3] 'Moravian church: extracts', September 1903; Bachmann, 'Ambilishiye', p. 26.
[4] *Central Africa*, January 1896; Magila mission diary, September 1895, 28 August 1896, 30 August 1897, TNA.
[5] *Central Africa*, October 1937; Masasi mission diary, 18 April 1913, ULD.

of his enemies, 'were merely clubs of malcontents and reactionaries, just as my house was the meeting-place of the young, of eager and simple hopes for a better future.'[1] As the basis of the elders' power – their superior agricultural experience – became less essential to survival, so the young struggled to break their long dependence. Whereas indigenous religions and Islam were predominantly religions of the old, Christianity harnessed the energy released by generational conflict.

The Church of the Fathers was a church militant. Its vanguard was the village catechist. His was a new ministry devised specifically for the African situation, with its emphasis on rapid and extensive evangelisation mainly among the young. He was, first, the village school-teacher, teaching 'religion and the three Rs, with a spice of singing and drill thrown in for amusement'.[2] His school was also the church and his duties might include ringing the bell seven times a day, visiting the sick and those who missed church or school, preparing the church for services, leading the congregational worship, preaching if necessary, and bringing his flock to the mission to receive the sacraments.[3] The first catechists were freed slaves. Hilarion and his wife began work for the Holy Ghost Fathers at Mhonda in 1877, and almost simultaneously the UMCA introduced the system at Magila. By 1911 there were 1,105 'native teachers' in mission elementary schools and probably about the same number of catechists.[4] The system did not work equally well in all circumstances. The White Fathers found the catechist an ideal agent in the large and distinct Fipa villages, but he was less useful in densely-peopled Buhaya (where the missionary could make more effective contact) and largely useless among scattered Sukuma homesteads.[5] Yet the catechist was an anomalous minister. 'It does not follow', a missionary wrote, 'that the man who can teach children in school is also suited to the work of evangelist.' Lutheran missionaries on Kilimanjaro made teaching and evangelism separate careers, but they were apparently alone in this.[6]

The Holy Ghost Fathers' initial attempt to create an indigenous priesthood collapsed in 1877 when Latin was abandoned at the

---

[1] Mugongo, 'Mémoires'.   [2] *Central Africa*, July 1913.
[3] See the list of c. 1933 in Masasi mission diary, ULD.
[4] Francis Nolan, 'History of the catechist in eastern Africa', in Aylward Shorter and Eugene Kataza (ed.), *Missionaries to yourselves* (London, 1972), p. 3; Albert F. Calvert, *German East Africa* (London, 1917), p. 100.
[5] B. Joinet, 'Three case histories from Tanzania', in Shorter and Kataza, *Missionaries*, pp. 161–80.
[6] *Central Africa*, May 1911; Eggert, *Missionsschule*, p. 186.

Bagamoyo seminary. Thirty-six years later Bishop Munsch reported that 'it is still not possible to dream of an indigenous clergy'.[1] Benedictine experience was similar. One of their catechists, Paul Holola, taught at Chabruma's capital for six years before Maji Maji and felt a strong vocation for the priesthood, but when the missionaries concluded that this would be premature he decided to marry.[2] The White Fathers were more successful. Although insisting on the full eighteen years of training before ordination, their seminary at Rubya in Buhaya produced the territory's first two Roman Catholic priests in 1917.[3] Tanganyika was only the second colony (after Uganda) to establish an African Roman Catholic priesthood. It was the first to create an African sisterhood: the Sisters of Our Lady Queen of Africa, founded at Karema in 1907.[4]

Although their educational qualifications were lower, only one Protestant society ordained African ministers before the First World War. In 1869 the UMCA opened a school for freed slaves at Kiungani in Zanzibar. From the twelve of its pupils who had received further education in England by 1893 came Tanganyika's first indigenous Christian ministers. The first deacon, an Ngindo freed slave named John Swedi, was ordained in 1879 but never raised to the priesthood. He was followed by a Yao freedman, Cecil Majaliwa, who in 1890 became Tanganyika's first African priest. The second, in 1894, was Petro Limo, a Kilindi of Bonde, and the third, in 1896, was a Bondei, Samuel Sehoza. By the First World War the UMCA had ordained 22 deacons of Tanganyikan origin, of whom 8 had become priests. They were the best-educated Tanganyikans of the time.[5]

Cecil Majaliwa's career epitomises the work and trials of the African priests and catechists who evangelised Tanganyika. Sold in the Zanzibar slave market at the age of six, he was educated at Kiungani and St Augustine's College, Canterbury. Made deacon in 1886, Majaliwa was posted to Barnaba Nakaam's village at Chitangali, whose chief, educated at Kiungani, was the only Christian. Majaliwa was to be his spiritual aide in creating a Christian community. Nakaam forbade his followers to become Christians without his permission and kept firm control of Majaliwa's work. The experiment succeeded. After six years there were 69 baptised Christians in Chitangali, 143 hearers and catechumens, and 86 pupils at school. 'I like being here

---

[1] Kieran, 'Holy Ghost Fathers', p. 138.
[2] Dörr in Renner, *Leuchter*, II, 220.   [3] Bouniol, *White Fathers*, p. 117.
[4] Information from Dr J. M. Waliggo.
[5] D. Y. Mills, *The backbone of the mission* (Westminster, n.d.), *passim*; above, p. 85.

with Padre Cecil Majaliwa very much', wrote Bishop Smythies. 'The religion of the people seems so real.'[1] Of Majaliwa's pupils, no less than 6 later became priests and another 2 became deacons. Yet Majaliwa experienced strain and depression. He had forgotten his childhood language and was at first intensely lonely. 'I am left alone in the midst of the heathen', he wrote, 'like a cottage in the middle of a forest.'[2] His knowledge of English faded. Life at Chitangali was desperately insecure. Soon after arrival Majaliwa hid in the bush for a month to escape an Ngoni raid. His wife, a freed slave, pined for Zanzibar, and they wanted to bring up their children in what they regarded as a civilized environment. Majaliwa endured Chitangali for eleven years before demanding to return to Zanzibar. There he lived at odds with the mission, periodically in disgrace and suspended from orders.[3]

It is often revealing to ask of early African converts what their consciences inspired them to do beyond the missionaries' direct requirements. In Tanganyika the answer was generally to spread their new faith. By 1881 Bondei converts were independently organising preaching parties and prayer meetings. A Yao aristocrat, Yohana Abdallah – who knew English, Greek, and Arabic – devoted his life to the conversion of the Nyasa whom he despised. A West African doctor-catechist, Adrien Atiman, ministered at Karema from 1889 to 1956. Nyakyusa evangelists worked in Upangwa before missionaries arrived there, as did Nyiha evangelists in Unyamwanga. Hermann Kanafunzi worked alone for twenty years among his fellow Masai.[4] In 1910 the Roman Catholic community at Ilonga sent 8 teachers to Uvidunda. The next year they sent 39 Christians to start a mission at Kibakwe, and in 1912 another 14 went to teach in Ugogo. The proselytisation of Ugogo showed the catechist's full value. The Roman Catholic mission there was opened in 1909 and catechists were recruited from all the older mission centres in the colony. After only five years they had opened 91 schools with 4,000 pupils.[5]

According to one calculation, by 1913 some 80,598 Tanganyikans had been baptised, 19,463 by Protestant and 61,135 by Roman Catholic missions (including 33,685 by the White Fathers).[6] Only 2 per cent of

[1] Smythies to Travers, 4 December 1893, Smythies letters IX, UMCA. See also *Central Africa*, September 1892; Msigala, 'Reminiscences', UMCA D/3.
[2] *Central Africa*, November 1886.   [3] *Ibid.*, April 1933.
[4] Farler to Penney, 4 October 1881, UMCA A/1/VI/364; *Central Africa*, August 1924; R. Fouquer, *Le Docteur Adrien Atiman* (n.p., 1964); Richter, *Geschichte*, p. 642; Bachmann, 'Ambilishiye', pp. 57–65; *Maisha ya Hermann Kanafunzi* (Soni, 1960).
[5] *Rafiki yangu*, October 1912; Nolan in Shorter and Kataza, *Missionaries*, p. 15.
[6] Julius Richter, *Das deutsche Kolonialreich und die Mission* (Basle, 1914), *passim*.

the country's population had been baptised, even including dead Christians in the calculation. Early mission areas had experienced nearly forty years of work while other regions – Buha, Matumbi, Musoma, Iramba – were only just being pioneered and many, notably around the rift valley and in the southern hinterland, had seen no mission work whatever. Christian communities varied greatly in size and character. In long-proselytised Bonde Bishop Weston noted in 1914 'a very remarkable awakening of heathen adults, many of whom have received the Cross' – a sign that conversion was entering a new phase.[1] Yet success brought problems. A missionary complained in 1907 that Christianity in Machame 'was becoming a pleasantly approved social custom, lacking all the ardour and conviction shown by the first converts'.[2] By contrast, in late-proselytised areas such as Ugogo churches tended to grow rapidly and concentrate even more exclusively than before on the young.

Relations between Christians and the larger community also varied. At Mandera in Uzigua, after nearly forty years of work, the Holy Ghost Fathers could still convert only outcasts.[3] In Ubena the Lutherans had deliberately established Christian villages on mission land to isolate them from the rest of society. The Moravians tried to avoid this, but Nyakyusa practice was for groups of friends to build together, so that 'the new people', as converts were known, did form distinct communities.[4] In Usambara the corporate solidarity of villages, the hostility of extended families to converts, and the fact that many Christians were marginal people led them to withdraw into hilltop villages where alcohol and coastal hairstyles were banned and a 10.00 p.m. curfew was enforced by communal action. 'They led a different life from their relatives', it was remembered. 'They were regarded as *dead* by their parents and relatives...They lived together and this resulted in small villages with Biblical names' – Ararat, Sinai, Betania, Tariso. 'The first congregation [in Mtae] was very strong', it was said, 'because the Holy Spirit had helped the people to co-operate in different difficulties. If a Christian had done something wrong, another Christian went and counselled him without necessarily telling the pastor. They worked together, helped the sick, received and cared for strangers. They lived as one family, full of obedience, love and

---

[1] *Central Africa*, April 1914.
[2] Quoted in Anza A. Lema, 'The impact of the Leipzig Lutheran mission on the people of Kilimanjaro 1893–1920', Ph.D. thesis, University of Dar es Salaam, 1973, p. 189.
[3] Reutter to Government, 3 June 1913, TNA G9/48/81.
[4] Wright, *German missions*, pp. 79–84, 88–92; Wilson, *Communal rituals*, pp. 166–74.

service.'[1] In the other Bethel mission field in Bukoba, by contrast, separate Christian villages were not formed – they would have meant abandoning valuable, long-cultivated land – but the Christians within a village formed a social group with special mutual loyalties, much like initiates of the *kubandwa* cult.[2] The pattern on Kilimanjaro was similar. There the first Christians were known as 'people who have two cloths' and by 1912 chiefs were beginning to resent the fact 'that from among the previously poor people a more elevated stratum is working its way up, which...through industry, greater job opportunity, and intelligence is able to achieve a position which puts it alongside the stratum of chiefs and rich men'.[3] Elsewhere even chiefs accepted Christian teaching. As his subjects rapidly became a Christian people, Kilatu of Ufipa put his regalia up for sale.[4]

The new men's position was anxious and ambiguous. Opinion among Europeans hardened against them. 'Remember the fate of Zelewski's expedition which was betrayed by German-speaking boys', ran the entirely baseless gossip of the Tanga hotel.[5] As colonial society became more firmly entrenched, its attitudes permeated missionary thought. The missionaries who worked in Tanganyika before German occupation did not generally want colonial rule. They certainly did not want *German* rule, but the Holy Ghost Fathers also opposed French involvement because of their government's anti-clericalism, while the UMCA generally sought to avoid political entanglement.[6] When the Germans invaded, missionary attitudes became more mixed. The Holy Ghost Fathers initially welcomed the news cautiously but were soon disillusioned and sympathised with the coastal resistance.[7] The German societies which began work after 1885 also had diverse views. The Bethel mission was openly allied to the DOAG, but the Benedictines hoped to 'protect the aboriginees from encroachment and exploitation by white traders', while both the Berlin Lutherans and the quietist Moravians chose to work as far as possible from Dar es Salaam.[8] Yet whatever their suspicions of the colonial regime, missionaries were white. When the shooting started they were on the German side. 'Whatever their sympathies and reasoning might indicate as the origins of any quarrel leading to a political struggle

[1] Guga, 'Research'; Johanssen, *Führung*, I, 125–6, and III, 61.
[2] Hellberg, *Missions*, pp. 156–8.   [3] Quoted in Eggert, *Missionsschule*, p. 194.
[4] D. H. A. Bell (1944) in Sumbawanga district book, TNA.
[5] Hermann Consten, *Und ich weine um dich, Deutsch-Afrika* (Stuttgart, 1926), p. 65.
[6] Kieran, 'Holy Ghost Fathers', pp. 264–73, 286; *Central Africa*, November 1888.
[7] Kieran, 'Holy Ghost Fathers', pp. 287–92.
[8] Oliver, *Missionary factor*, pp. 96, 165–6; Renner, *Leuchter*, I, 95.

between European and African', Dr Kieran has written of the Holy
Ghost Fathers, 'their prejudices and fears swamped their original
convictions and led them to support the European administration.'
Despite their early sympathy with Abushiri, violence drove the
Fathers to support Wissmann, who used their converts to spy on
Abushiri's camp.[1] 'They are beasts are these Germans...My sympathies are all with the rebels', the UMCA bishop wrote in November
1905 while his converts were fighting the Mwera.[2] As their spiritual
and educational work grew, so missionaries became more enmeshed
with the regime and tension with their more sophisticated converts
increased. When UMCA missionaries abandoned Masasi during Maji
Maji their followers were left to their own resources: 'Our leaders had
left us without a word or even a good-bye.'[3] Subsequent conflict with
the returning missionaries was inevitable. The priest who had
maintained the mission's work during the rebellion, Daudi Machina,
'resents interference of any kind' and was suspended in 1913,
following accusations of debt and immorality.[4] A similar conflict occurred at Magila when schoolboys from Kiungani rejected
missionary control during holidays. In Ubena the Lutherans refused
to extend their educational system lest their teachers assert themselves as they had in South Africa, while Nyakyusa evangelists
expressed resentment at mission constraints on their advancement.[5]

The 'new people' were not challenging the missionaries' framework
of thought. Rather, they wanted a larger part in implementing it. It
was most important to Tanganyika's history that missionaries – and
indeed the colonial regime – could find allies among men, especially
freed slaves, rebelling against the nineteenth-century social order
which had oppressed them. A freedman named Martin Ganisya, the
leading Lutheran evangelist in Uzaramo, expressed their view of the
country's past:

Its condition was formerly one of injustice...You could not make a journey
of four or five days alone without being seized...But now, what is the
condition of the country today?...Now you can make a journey of three or

[1] Kieran, 'Holy Ghost Fathers', pp. 336, 295–7.
[2] Hine to Travers, 3 November 1905, UMCA A/1/xiii.
[3] Msigala, 'Reminiscences', UMCA D/3.
[4] Hine to Travers, 14 February 1908, UMCA A/1/xiii; T. O. Ranger, 'The apostle:
Kolumba Msigala', in Iliffe, *Tanzanians*, pp. 14–16.
[5] Magila mission diary, 25 May and 3 June 1908, TNA; Eggert, *Missionsschule*, p. 112;
Wright, *German missions*, p. 101.

four months without a weapon...Now there is peace everywhere; there is none who terrorises, for all are under the Kaiser's rule.[1]

The view was not confined to freedmen. 'People of Africa!' Samuel Sehoza proclaimed to the boys of Kiungani:

We were born in different parts and belong to different tribes, but we were all living in darkness and in the shadow of death. God led us through many hardships, by long journeys, through hunger and thirst, and even death, without our understanding that it was the good hand of our God upon us leading us in love. But today we understand the reason why we left home – today we have learnt and we know that Almighty God loved us, and when we were far away He remembered us. So when we think of our past dangers and our present prosperity, we give our thanks to God.[2]

Other educated men were more ambivalent. The surviving Swahili poetry of the German period – much of it written under European patronage – falls into two main categories: fulsome and generally worthless eulogies of the Germans, and epics of armed resistance.[3] The epics are strikingly ambivalent as they try to reconcile admiration of bravery with recognition of German power, generally by stressing the supposedly innate foolishness of *washenzi* in contrast to the wisdom but effeminacy of *waungwana*. Abdulkarim bin Jamaliddini wrote both an eulogy of the Germans and a mildly sympathetic account of Maji Maji, was brother of the loyalist *kadhi* of Lindi, and died in a German gaol while awaiting trial for sedition by means of Islamic radicalism.[4]

A similar ambivalence and range of opinion marked the new people's political thinking. Christians were vividly aware that they had joined a wider society. Although Kiungani's pupils 'were born in different parts and belong to different tribes', to Sehoza they were 'People of Africa'. To Ganisya, German East Africa was 'our land, the land of the black people'. For some this sense of supra-tribal unity began at mission boarding schools, for others at freed slave settlements, for others again in evangelical work far from their homes.[5] Whereas non-Christian Nyakyusa stressed the obligation to feed

---

[1] Ganisya in *Pwani na bara*, January 1910 (copy in TNA green 789), translated in K. Axenfeld, 'Geistige Kämpfe in der Eingeborenenbevölkerung an der Küste Ostafrikas', *Koloniale Rundschau*, v (1913), 670–2.

[2] *Central Africa*, February 1908.

[3] Examples are Ramazan Saidi, 'Sifa ya Wadachi', *Kiongozi*, June 1913, and Hemedi bin Abdallah, *Utenzi*.

[4] Abdulkarim bin Jamaliddini, *Utenzi wa vita vya Maji-Maji* (trans. W. H. Whiteley, Kampala, 1957); *idem*, 'Shairi la dola jermani', in Velten, 'Gedichte', pp. 174–80; Iliffe, *German rule*, pp. 195–6.

[5] Yohana Abdalla to Isobel Hall, 2 January 1894, UMCA A/5; *Rafiki yangu*, March and November 1913.

neighbours, Christians emphasised the duty of feeding strangers.[1] Educated men showed keen interest in the outside world. Nakaam interrogated a visitor to Newala about the implications of the Russo-Japanese war.[2] But alongside their broad but vague concerns the new people still put greater emphasis on their small communities. Kiungani's multi-tribal character impressed its Yao and Bondei pupils, but they never intermarried. Martin Ganisya visited Nyasaland to regain contact with his kinsmen.[3] Respect for hereditary authority remained strong. The first Roman Catholic converts in Buhaya often entered the chiefs' service. Alienation from chiefs who rejected mission teaching saddened many Christian commoners, but they were nevertheless sometimes willing to oppose exploitative chiefs. In 1914 two Pogoro visited Dar es Salaam to protest about a new tribute system.[4] Although new people were conscious of local communities and of vague identities as Africans, black people, Christians, and Muslims, there is little evidence that they were aware of an identity as people of German East Africa[5] or of the importance for them of the struggle for control between settlers and government. Perhaps at Rechenberg's instance, the old loyalist, Suleiman bin Nasor, warned acquaintances in Europe in 1908 that 'there will be hostility between the Government and the people of East Africa, for the people of East Africa now begin to understand political affairs and after ten years they will understand more, and if the people of Germany follow the words of von Roy and others like him then the whole colony will be spoiled'.[6] A mission employee in Usambara collected newspaper cuttings about native policy.[7] If later patterns are a guide, settler newspapers will have reached a wide African audience. Yet nothing written by an African at this time refers to major policy issues. For the new people, territorial politics still lay in the future.

The new people were marked out principally by literacy. It carried great prestige. Ceremonial public reading of the Koran crowned a Muslim boy's education. Nicholas Mugongo believed that he learned to read by a miracle. And literacy gave enormous advantages. Its

[1] Wilson, *Communal rituals*, p. 201.   [2] Weule, *Native life*, p. 125.
[3] He found they had become Muslims. See Sicard, *Lutheran church*, p. 191.
[4] Iliffe, *German rule*, p. 174; Franz Gleiss, *Nicht so sicher! Helle und dunkle Bilder aus dem Leben des Lazarus Schauli* (Bethel bei Bielefeld, 1926), p. 26; Larson, 'History', pp. 167–8.
[5] The drawing of territorial borders impressed itself strongly on coastal traders. See Velten, 'Gedichte', pp. 84, 179.
[6] Suleiman bin Nasor to Velten, 14 November 1908, Swahili manuscript collection no. 181, ULD. I owe this reference to Mr M. M. R. Alidina. Von Roy edited the *Deutsch-Ostafrikanische Zeitung*.
[7] Winzer to Wilhelmstal, 18 October 1908, TNA G54/1/22.

235

association with profitable employment antedated German rule. 'Where there are ink and paper there is wealth', ran a caravan song. To possess a written *Jumbenschein* declared a man a government-recognised headman. Mpangile of Uhehe was one of many anxious to read and write in order to handle official documents, while Mutahangarwa summoned experts and had his scribes write down Kiziba's history in his presence.[1] In the long term literacy brought greater rationality and reflective thought, and the codification of ideas and customs which in pre-literate societies had remained undogmatic and eclectic.[2] But in the short term literacy remained linked at many points to older ways of thought. Since Mutahangarwa's written history codified the version which successive chiefs appear to have imposed over rival accounts, the result was not necessarily greater truth.[3] The common practice of learning by rote suggested a transitional phase when literacy remained an adjunct to oral communication. Koran school pupils learned the Koran in Arabic without understanding its meaning, and it was said in 1912 that only eleven of the 150–200 *waalimu* in Uzaramo could interpret the Koran rather than recite it.[4] Literacy often merged into magic. Reading aloud the whole Koran was a means of remembering ancestors or cleansing a village. A Koranic verse was a common amulet and the ink dissolved in water was a common medicine. In lowland Ubena in the 1930s one diviner's equipment included a tattered breviary, while pencil, mirror, and cup were added to Nyakyusa grave goods.[5]

The early converts' Christianity often contained many ambiguities. Whether men accepted the faith as supplement or substitute, they generally expected it to solve problems beyond the capacity of indigenous religions. Yet mission Christianity was nineteenth-century European Christianity, an individualised, intellectualised faith which regarded many human problems – sickness and misfortune and death – either as soluble only by faith and prayer or as beyond the scope of religion and explicable only by science or chance. Indigenous religions were markedly this-worldly. Mission Christianity, like orthodox Islam, was markedly other-worldly. As converts slowly grasped

[1] Gallagher, 'Islam', p. 473; Mugongo, 'Mémoires'; Becker, *La vie*, II, 237; Adams, *Im Dienste*, p. 55; Schmidt, 'Investigation', p. 66.

[2] See Jack Goody (ed.), *Literacy in traditional societies* (Cambridge, 1968), pp. 1–68, 199–241.

[3] Schmidt, 'Investigation', chs. 4–5.

[4] Klamroth, 'Literarische Charakter', p. 22; Eggebrecht to Government, 14 May 1913, TNA G9/48/82.

[5] Caplan, *Choice*, p. 90; J. S. Trimingham, *Islam in East Africa* (Oxford, 1964), pp. 122–3; Culwick, *Ubena*, p. 117; Wilson, *Rituals of kinship*, p. 16.

this, they entered a situation much like that which the Protestant reformers had created in sixteenth-century England when they had tried to take the magic out of religion and ordinary people had felt compelled to put it back.[1] In Tanganyika the result was commonly eclecticism as individuals selected advantageous elements from different faiths and reinterpreted one religion in terms of another. Ambiguity existed at the beginning, when Kimweri of Usambara asked a missionary for charms against witchcraft and was told instead to pray. It still existed in 1918, when the Chief of Ihangiro in Buhaya interrupted his preparation for baptism owing to a break in the rains.[2] The intervening forty years were fertile of ambiguity. Farler rejoiced when his converts replaced their charms by small ivory crosses which they would not let non-Christians touch. Asyukile Malango, while believing firmly in witchcraft, believed also that baptism immunised him against it. A Bena congregation insisted that a newly-admitted diviner should sit apart. When Ambilishye's pupils failed to answer his questions in school, he concluded that one of them must be in a state of sin and demanded (and obtained) a confession. In 1912 Deacon Benedict Njewa of Masasi, believing himself bewitched but anxious not to disgrace his cloth, went to the local boma, removed his cassock and girdle, 'folded them up, and asked that they might be sent to the Mission, and then instantly became insane and violent'. Two years later a Pimbwe headman suspected that the Christian God might be responsible for his illness and dedicated to Him a tree beneath which villagers met each evening to say what they knew of Christian prayers.[3] There was ambiguity in all these beliefs, but no absurdity. They indicated the complexity and personal cost of religious change.

Dance

The ceremony that epitomised German rule was the annual cele-bration of the Kaiser's birthday.[4] At every district office the askari paraded before a massive crowd. After inspection and drill, the senior German official addressed the gathering, extolling his emperor's

---

[1] Thomas, *Religion, passim,* esp. p. 87.

[2] Anderson-Morshead, *History,* I, 42; Baines, report on Bukoba, May 1918, Cory papers, ULD.

[3] Farler to Steere, 30 September 1876, UMCA A/1/VI/398; Busse, 'Asyukile Malango', p. 194; Wright, *German missions,* p. 102; Bachmann, 'Ambilishiye', p. 93; Ranger in Ranger and Kimambo, *Historical study,* p. 233; M. Maurice, 'La religion des Bapimbwe', *Bibliotheca Africana,* III (1929–30), 289–90.

[4] This section is based chiefly on descriptions of celebrations in many issues of *Kiongozi.*

virtues and leading a threefold 'Hurrah!' for Kaiser and Reich. And then the people danced, in circles strewn across the parade ground.

One circle danced *kigoma*. All were Luguru, for, like many of the dances on the eve of the First World War, *kigoma* was a 'tribal' dance.[1] As men of many origins interacted in town or workplace, so they became identified by tribal names, and often one of the many dances which each group performed at home became known as its tribal dance. Workers on the central railway always danced in tribal groups.[2] Yet tribe was not the only category emphasised in colonial society. A circle of women danced *lelemama*. Its origins are uncertain, but *lelemama* was the most popular women's dance, the dance of towns and caravan routes, the dance of 'emancipated' women. When Chieftainess Karunde of Unyanyembe visited Dar es Salaam in 1912, the Manyema, Ndengereko, Matumbi, and Swahili women joined to greet her with *lelemama*.[3] More spectacular was *uyeye*, the dance of the Nyamwezi snake-handlers, whose society had spread along caravan paths and migration routes until *uyeye* was danced at Tanga in 1911 and at Moshi in 1913. Nyamwezi 'secret' societies had long danced for public entertainment, so that no vulgarisation took place when *uyeye* was performed on the Kaiser's birthday. But that was not true of the Manyema – probably former slaves and now Muslims – who danced *kisonge*, an exorcism dance from the Congo comparable to the rites of Lyangombe.[4]

All these dances were probably old, but others were innovations danced by the multi-tribal status groups of colonial society. One circle performed *robota*, a dance from the north-east which imitated the actions of decorticating and baling sisal.[5] Another danced *bom* – from the Swahili *bombom* for a cannon or machine-gun – which was doubtless one of the many dances imitating German military drill. It was danced in the Kaiser's honour at Sadani in 1911 by *ngoma ya kihuni*. This, 'the hooligan's dance society', was almost certainly the most recent of the competitive societies formed by low-class, up-country immigrants to coastal towns. In Bagamoyo the distinction in German times was between the old-fashioned Gaboreni (muzzle-loader) society, probably favoured by the Shomvi, and the 'modern' Seneda (breech-loader).[6] It was a variant on the traditional polarisation of the coastal

[1] Cory, 'Native songs', p. 63. [2] Gillman diary, 26 November 1905, RH.
[3] *Kiongozi*, October 1912.
[4] Cory, 'Native songs', p. 63; Saada Salim bin Omar, 'The Swahili life', *TNR*, IX (1940), 25.
[5] H. E. Lambert, 'The beni dance songs', *Swahili*, XXXIII (1962), 20–1.
[6] Nimtz, 'Sufi order', pp. 300–2.

towns, a polarisation increasingly along 'class' lines. *Ngoma ya kihuni*, which may have been confined to Sadani, clearly fitted this pattern:

Ngoma ya kihuni have recently slaughtered cattle. First they paraded through the town with their goods for the feast, carrying four flags. In the evening they went into the countryside, and there they held their feast. They returned in great triumph, dancing *bom* for their friends as they passed to show them the things they had done, and singing riddling songs all the time.[1]

Devotees of *bom* stood at the opposite end of the colonial social scale from those who invariably celebrated the Kaiser's birthday with *chapaulinge*. This was the dance of the clerks and teachers and domestic servants who formed a distinct, multi-tribal community at every district centre. In 1910 those of Lushoto celebrated Idd:

At 9.00 p.m. all the young men made their feast, clerks and domestic servants. They gathered together in Salimu Abdallah's house. His house is furnished in the European style and they admired it greatly. Every European who passed by was delighted at the character of his furniture. Well, they had a feast of rice and meat, and they relaxed. Afterwards they had a feast of tea with milk, bananas, *vibibi*, macaroni, bread, and sherbet. And at the end of the feast they said 'Hurrah!' three times.[2]

No description of *chapaulinge* survives, but by analogy with later dances it will have had the smartness and decorum of the newly important.

If he were fortunate and observant, a spectator at the Kaiser's birthday celebrations could see *kigoma* and *uyeye*, *lelemama* and *robota*, *bom* and *chapaulinge* performed simultaneously. He could see the changes of the German period re-enacted before his eyes.

[1] *Kiongozi*, October 1913. [2] *Ibid.*, November 1910.

CHAPTER 8

Fortunes of war

In a global perspective the First World War was both the culmination of European imperialism and the beginning of its decline.[1] To win the war, colonial powers tightened control over subject peoples and increased demands upon them. To restore their economies and prevent future wars, the victors sought to give their empires defensible frontiers and organise their resources more efficiently. At the same time the demands and opportunities of war stimulated political awareness and organisation amongst subject peoples.

Tanganyika was conquered late in imperial history and its full crisis came with the Second World War, but it experienced shock-waves from the earlier cataclysm. On the one hand, the East African campaign demonstrated African helplessness before European power. On the other, never were Europeans so dependent on Africans for survival. The transfer to British control gave Africans a brief opportunity to reshape the colonial relationship. African soldiers acquired new organisational skills. The collapse of mission work created opportunities for African Christians and Muslims. A new administration offered advancement to men excluded by the old. Amid famine and disease were new economic opportunities.

The war was an ordeal, but also an opportunity. When it ended, Tanganyika was subtly changed. The balance among its constituent elements had shifted and its future was set in a new direction.

The campaign and its outcome

When news of the European crisis reached East Africa on 30 July 1914, the German authorities were divided. They commanded 218 Europeans and 2,542 askari of the Defence Force, supplemented by 2,219 police, some 3,000 European residents, and innumerable

---

[1] Here and elsewhere I have borrowed many ideas from Professor J. A. Gallagher.

potential African recruits. They were surrounded by likely enemies. The British commanded 73 Europeans and 2,325 askari of the King's African Rifles (KAR) in Kenya, Uganda, and Nyasaland; some 2,000 European civilians in the same territories; and 800 police in Northern Rhodesia. In the Belgian Congo the ill-trained Force Publique and other units numbered 15,200 men. Perhaps 4,000 Portuguese and African troops were available in Mozambique, although their role was unpredictable. German plans assumed that in a world war the colonies' fate would be settled on European battlefields. Warships based in East Africa had standing orders to put to sea if war were declared. The Congo Act of 1885 contained provisions for neutralising African territories during a European war.[1]

Governor Heinrich Schnee hoped to preserve neutrality, for he regarded the colony as indefensible, feared African rebellion, and wished to spare his subjects the horrors of war. But in holding to the best traditions of the civilian regime he was opposed by an older, military tradition of colonialism, represented by the Defence Force commander, Colonel Paul von Lettow-Vorbeck. For Lettow-Vorbeck East Africa's interests were of no consequence. Its purpose was to serve Germany by attracting as many enemy troops as possible away from more important theatres. The Germans must therefore provoke and prolong full-scale war in East Africa.[2] This view eventually prevailed and Lettow-Vorbeck fought a guerrilla campaign of supreme military skill, but it was also a campaign of supreme ruthlessness where a small, well-armed force extorted supplies from civilians to whom it felt no responsibility. Lettow-Vorbeck's brilliant campaign was the climax of Africa's exploitation: its use as a mere battlefield.

The conflict between these views was resolved by British intervention. For Britain, East Africa was merely an outpost of the Indian empire. On 5 August 1914 the Committee of Imperial Defence defined three objectives. One was to prevent German East Africa's ports from acting as bases for German commerce-raiders in the Indian Ocean. A wireless station near Dar es Salaam was therefore shelled on 8 August. This shattered Schnee's hopes of neutrality and led him to declare Dar es Salaam and Tanga open towns, an 'act of treason' which determined Lettow-Vorbeck to ignore the governor's orders and

[1] Ludwig Boell, *Die Operationen in Ost-Afrika: Weltkrieg 1914–1918* (Hamburg, 1951), pp. 22–3, 28–32; Hordern, *Operations*, pp. 15, 559; Schnee, *Deutsch-Ostafrika*, p. 32.
[2] Schnee, *Deutsch-Ostafrika*, pp. 23–44; Paul von Lettow-Vorbeck, *My reminiscences of East Africa* (English translation, 2nd edn, London, n.d.), chs. 1–2.

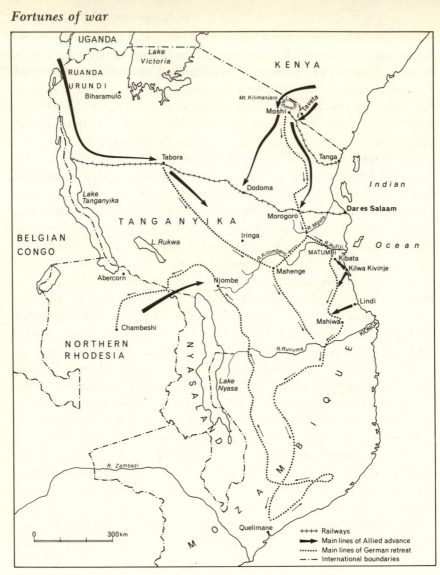

III   The East African campaign

concentrate his forces around Kilimanjaro, whence on 15 August they
entered Kenya and seized Taveta in the first major engagement on
land. Meanwhile the British had gained their second aim by seizing
naval control of the East African lakes. The third objective was for
the Indian army to occupy Dar es Salaam. An expeditionary force
assembled from its less reliable units sailed on 16 October with orders
'to bring the whole of German East Africa under British authority',

starting with a landing at Tanga. Anticipating this, Lettow-Vorbeck held 1,500 men ready along the northern railway.[1]

The landing at Tanga on 2 November 1914 was a disaster.[2] The Indian troops were exhausted, ill-trained, and absurdly sure of their ability to 'make short work of a lot of niggers'.[3] Machine-guns checked them and a reckless counter-attack led by Tom von Prince forced them to re-embark, leaving 359 dead against 51 on the German side. This action shaped the whole course of the war. It left Lettow-Vorbeck the undisputed German leader and made his guerrilla campaign morally possible. It stimulated recruiting to the Defence Force, which numbered 3,007 Europeans and 12,100 Africans at its peak in March 1916. It forced the British on to the defensive for sixteen months, yet made it morally impossible to escape Lettow-Vorbeck's trap by eschewing operations in East Africa. And it meant that they eventually attacked with such caution that the Germans escaped encirclement.[4]

The stalemate which followed Tanga was broken by German surrender in South-West Africa on 9 July 1915. This released South African troops and the settlers from Central Africa who took responsibility for German East Africa's south-western border and thus freed the Force Publique to invade from the west. In December 1915 the British Cabinet ordered 'the conquest of this German colony with as little delay as possible'.[5] General Smuts was appointed to command the imperial forces. By March 1916 he had 27,575 British and South African troops, 14,300 Indians, 6,875 KAR askaris, 580 Europeans and 14,000 Africans of the Force Publique, and (notionally) 10,000 men in Mozambique – 73,330 men against Lettow-Vorbeck's 15,017.[6]

Smuts planned to envelop the Germans by advancing on either side of Kilimanjaro, but when his troops reached Moshi on 14 March 1916 the Germans were already withdrawing towards the central railway. To divide them from other German forces in Tabora, Smuts pushed mounted troops forward to Dodoma on 29 July, while the Force Publique advanced from the west and reached Tabora on 19 September. Tabora's German garrison escaped south-eastwards, passed through a British force under General Northey which had

[1] Hordern, *Operations*, pp. 23, 29–31, 60–6; Boell, *Operationen*, chs. 2–3.
[2] Hordern, *Operations*, chs. 5–6; Boell, *Operationen*, ch. 4.
[3] General Aitken, quoted in R. Meinertzhagen, *Army diary 1899–1926* (Edinburgh, 1960), p. 105.
[4] 'Private diary of von Lettow', CO 691/27/187; Boell, *Operationen*, p. 158.
[5] Hordern, *Operations*, p. 212.
[6] Boell, *Operationen*, p. 158. These are ration strengths, higher than effectives.

invaded from the south-west and taken Iringa on 29 August, and took station at Mahenge alongside Lettow-Vorbeck. The German commander had meanwhile avoided Smuts' attempt 'to bottle the enemy up in Morogoro' and had stabilised his position on the River Mgeta. Here, on 26 September 1916, Smuts was forced to halt the advance southwards which had begun in March. He now attempted to encircle the Germans by taking Kilwa and advancing inland to Matumbi to cut off their retreat. Lettow-Vorbeck checked this advance at Kibata during December. A month earlier he had thrown back across the Ruvuma a Portuguese force seeking to close the ring from the south.[1]

By December 1916 German forces were concentrated on Mahenge and the Rufiji valley, with their retreat southwards to Mozambique still open. Their numbers had fallen since March from 15,107 to 11,000, of whom 3,400 were unfit. Against them the Allies had 98,800 men,[2] but this was delusive. The Belgians were disengaged. The Portuguese had fallen back in disorder. British, South African, and Indian troops had suffered severely. Of 1,600 Royal Fusiliers who had arrived in May 1915, less than 200 were fit for service in July 1916. The 9th South African Infantry lost 90 per cent of its effectives between February and October 1916.[3] The reasons were malaria, dysentery, tsetse, rain, mud, and shortage of food and supplies due to communications which stretched back hundreds of miles and depended on African porters. 'We lay there in the mud and retched from the stench of the dead animals and watched the rats crawl over us', a soldier wrote of the advance to Dodoma.[4] Ahead lay the Kilombero, Mgeta, and Rufiji valleys, the colony's most difficult country for military operations. Smuts sent home his European and Indian troops as quickly as he could replace them by West Africans and recruits to the KAR, whose numbers increased from 4,338 at the beginning of 1916 to 35,424 at the end of the war.[5] He also handed over command to General Hoskins, who organised a simultaneous advance from Kilwa and Lindi to encircle Lettow-Vorbeck from the south. When it began in July 1917 the German commander had already abandoned the Rufiji and moved southwards to face the British forces approaching from the east.

The British were now desperate to end a campaign which absorbed

---

[1] Hordern, *Operations*, chs. 7, 13, 15–21, 24–6, 28, and pp. 232–3, 374, 386–9; Boell, *Operationen*, chs. 10–15, 17–18, and pp. 244–6; H. Moyse-Bartlett, *The King's African Rifles* (Aldershot, 1956), pp. 336–43.

[2] Boell, *Operationen*, p. 300; Hordern, *Operations*, p. 514.

[3] Hordern, *Operations*, pp. 520–1.

[4] Quoted in Leonard Mosley, *Duel for Kilimanjaro* (London, 1963), p. 132.

[5] Hordern, *Operations*, p. 575.

precious shipping.[1] Belgian forces were persuaded to intervene again and took Mahenge on 9 October. Hoskins was replaced by an Afrikaner general, Van Deventer, who launched a frontal attack by the column advancing from Lindi. On 15–18 October 1917 this column met Lettow-Vorbeck's main force at Mahiwa on the south-western face of the Mwera Plateau in the most violent battle of the campaign. Deventer was checked, while Lettow-Vorbeck, his ammunition exhausted, crossed the Ruvuma into Mozambique on 25 November 1917. The force from Mahenge surrendered to avert starvation.[2]

For another year British forces – now almost entirely KAR – pursued Lettow-Vorbeck through Mozambique, where evasion was easier than eating:

The enemy never stopped to fight in force, always clearing at the last moment, only putting up small rearguard actions to delay us: he is again getting far away, and, as always, we have to follow him up through a country denuded of foodstuffs. It is the time of heaviest rains and there is much sickness (dysentery, malaria and pneumonia) among both Europeans and natives: but... we keep knocking little bits off the enemy, a few killed or wounded, small patrols captured, deserters rounded up.[3]

The Germans moved southwards until in July 1918 they threatened the port of Quelimane. Deventer transferred his reserves from the Ruvuma to defend the Mozambique coastline. Lettow-Vorbeck doubled back northwards, penetrated the British lines, and crossed the almost undefended Ruvuma on 28 September 1918. Three weeks later he was in Njombe. Convinced he was heading for Tabora, Deventer regrouped on the central railway. But it was only a feint. On 19 October Lettow-Vorbeck turned back south-westwards into Northern Rhodesia. At Chambeshi on 13 November 1918 he heard that Germany was defeated.[4] Twelve days later he led his men into Abercorn to surrender. He had 155 Europeans, 1,168 askari, 1,522 porters, and 1,726 other followers, including 427 women:

The long motley column, Europeans and askari, all veterans of a hundred fights, the latter clothed with every kind of headgear, women who had stuck to their husbands through all these years of hardships, carrying huge loads, some with children born during the campaign, carriers coming in singing with undisguised joy at the thought that their labours were ended at last.[5]

[1] CIGS to Deventer, 22 May 1917, CO 691/10/290.
[2] Boell, *Operationen*, pp. 372–7, 380–6, 399–400, and ch. 25; Moyse-Bartlett, *KAR*, pp. 367–88.
[3] 'War diary of Maj.-Gen. E. Northey', February 1918, CO 691/14/297.
[4] Boell, *Operationen*, chs. 26–7; Moyse-Bartlett, *KAR*, ch. 13.
[5] *Bulawayo chronicle*, quoted in Mosley, *Duel*, p. 223. For strengths, see Boell, *Operationen*, p. 424.

Many advantages had aided Lettow-Vorbeck's skill: the size of the country; the bush which made the campaign 'a huge night operation';[1] human and animal diseases; the lack of motorable roads; the absence of railway lines from north to south; the machine-gun which gave advantage to the defence in this as other theatres; and especially the availability of food and labour from a defenceless and unregarded population. The campaign had employed between 210,000 and 240,000 Allied troops, roughly half of them Africans. British imperial forces had lost 3,443 men killed or fatally wounded and 6,558 dead of disease. The equivalent Belgian figures were 683 and 1,300. The Portuguese had lost 1,734 Europeans and an unknown number of Africans. The German Defence Force had lost 734 Europeans and some 1,798 Africans dead.[2]

The victors divided the spoils.[3] Fear that submarines – the deadly new weapons of the war – might act against imperial communications from bases in German East Africa led imperialists in the British Cabinet to favour annexation. They were supported by South Africans anxious to give the southern half of Tanganyika to Portugal in exchange for southern Mozambique, which would be added to the Union. Wartime propaganda had stressed German colonial brutality and made annexation acceptable to humanitarians. This and a desire to control communications through eastern Africa from north to south led the British Colonial Office to favour annexation. Opposition came chiefly from the Belgians, whose concern was to occupy territory either as a bargaining counter with Germany in Europe (should the war end in stalemate) or (if the Allies won) to compensate the British for giving southern Tanganyika to Portugal in exchange for the transfer of the southern bank of the lower Congo from Portuguese Angola to the Belgian Congo. The situation was further complicated by America's entry into the war. Since Americans opposed annexation, British annexationists borrowed from liberal intellectuals the idea that former German colonies should be administered as 'Mandated Territories' under loose supervision by the proposed League of Nations. Imperial security was thereby reconciled with idealism.

When the Peace Conference met in January 1919, Belgian troops occupied Rwanda, Burundi, Biharamulo, and the north-eastern shore

[1] Hordern, *Operations*, p. 513.   [2] Boell, *Operationen*, pp. 427–8.
[3] The following account is based on W. Roger Louis, *Great Britain and Germany's lost colonies 1914–1919* (Oxford, 1967), *passim; idem, Ruanda-Urundi 1884–1919* (Oxford, 1963), chs. 20–1; Ronald Hyam, *The failure of South African expansion 1908–1948* (London, 1972), pp. 28–33; Milner to Hollis, 22 October 1919, CO 691/27/376.

of Lake Tanganyika. The Portuguese occupied a tiny enclave known as the Kionga Triangle south of the Ruvuma estuary. The remainder of German East Africa was under British occupation. The conference largely confirmed this division. After much confusion, British and Belgian negotiators agreed that Belgium should retain Rwanda and Burundi while abandoning the eastern shore of Lake Tanganyika and the western shore of Lake Victoria, thus giving Britain 'the great lines of communications both from East to West, and from North to South'.[1] Since the Portuguese refused to abandon southern Mozambique or the lower Congo, Belgians and South Africans were thwarted. Belgium gained a mandated territory she did not want and Tanganyika gained the boundaries she retained until 1964.

The British Mandate, as agreed in July 1922, gave Britain 'full powers of legislation and administration', while binding her to promote 'the material and moral well-being and the social progress of [the] inhabitants', specifically by banning slavery, forced labour for private advantage, the arms and liquor trades, and abuse of African land rights. Citizens of all member states of the League had the same rights as British citizens in the territory. Provided the Mandate's other terms were not infringed, the territory could be incorporated into 'a customs, fiscal and administrative union or federation'. Generally the Mandate was an old-fashioned document embodying pre-war safeguards against colonial abuses but containing no provision for enforcement against a recalcitrant mandatory.[2]

The final problem was to name the territory. The Colonial Office enjoyed this. Smutsland was dismissed as inelegant, Eburnea[3] and Azania as pedantic. New Maryland, Windsorland, and Victoria were vetoed by the Colonial Secretary's insistence on 'a native name prominently associated with the territory'. He considered Kilimanjaro and Tabora before settling on 'The Tanganyika Protectorate', as proposed by his deputy undersecretary. A junior official suggested that 'Territory' was more in accordance with the Mandate, and on 1 February 1920 the Tanganyika Territory took its anomalous place in the British Empire.[4]

---

[1] Milner to Clement-Ives [?] 1 June 1919, CO 691/27/367.
[2] Text in Harlow and Chilver, *History*, II, 690–5.   [3] From the Latin for ivory.
[4] Correspondence in CO 691/25, 29, and 30.

Survival and opportunity

Those whose status was most dramatically reversed by the war were the askari of the German Defence Force. Highly paid by local standards, they had served the Germans with the loyalty of a mercenary elite. While normally obedient, they had threatened mutiny when a commander planned to abandon their wives, and they had surrendered only when guaranteed that they would be exempt from the despised work of porters.[1] As mercenaries they had changed employers in peacetime or when decisively defeated in war. Early in the war many prisoners captured by the British had joined the KAR, where they had won a reputation for efficiency on parade and violence and indiscipline off-duty. Some 2,847 of Lettow-Vorbeck's 13,430 askari had deserted.[2] In the last stage of the campaign they had longed for peace. 'In contrast to the Europeans', Schnee noted on 15 November 1918, 'great joy reigns among our coloured men about returning home. Dances are taking place at night.'[3] Yet the askari also feared for the future. Lettow-Vorbeck was deeply relieved when they agreed to lay down their arms. 'It will be impressed on them', the British fatuously decreed, 'that they have been defeated by the power of British arms', and the askari were furious when treated as prisoners of war.[4] Not all would acknowledge their new masters. Early in 1919 numbers were still in Mozambique 'living a freelance existence in a series of miniature native republics'.[5] Those who returned found an outlet for the frustrations of defeat in *beni* dance societies.[6] Invented on the Kenya coast during the 1890s, this dance reached Tanganyika either shortly before or during the war and soon followed the pattern of earlier dances on the coast by dividing into high-status Marini and low-status Arinoti societies. During the war *beni* became the fashionable dance of both armies. Askari joined the Marini, porters the Arinoti. Both societies adopted military ranks, uniforms, and drill steps. By 1919 there were branches in every important East African town, often led by war veterans. The most remarkable was a former teacher and *akida*, Saleh bin Mpangile, Mkwawa's German-educated nephew. As 'Bismarck' of the Marini, Saleh supervised the society's welfare functions from Iringa, issuing

---

[1] Boell, *Operationen*, pp. 396–7; Northey, 'War diary', November 1916, CO 691/1/203.
[2] Boell, *Operationen*, p. 427.   [3] Quoted in Bald, *Deutsch-Ostafrika*, p. 26 n. 1.
[4] WO to CO, 16 November 1918, CO 691/19/545; Mosley, *Duel*, pp. 222–4.
[5] Orde Browne to SA, 8 February 1919, CO 691/21/254.
[6] This account is based on Ranger, *Dance*, chs 1–2.

orders to branches as distant as Kismayu in Kenya, exercising a wider geographical influence than any previous Tanganyikan, and organising in Iringa elaborate war-games in which the Marini always defeated the ritually inferior Arinoti. The societies modelled their organisation on European imperial structures, as earlier Nyamwezi dance societies had imitated chiefdom organisation. In this way the war was a lesson in organisation.

It was fitting that porters joined the Arinoti, for they were the human misery on which rested the edifice of European fear and greed. At their peak in March 1916 German forces employed some 45,000 carriers and auxiliaries,[1] but German needs were insignificant when compared with those of the Allied forces. Early in the war the British formed a Carrier Corps in Kenya which was soon imitated in the Congo and Central Africa. By 1917 Tanganyika itself provided most of the porters. Administrative chaos and the discretion exercised by sub-ordinate commanders make it impossible to know the number of porters employed by the Allies. The Governor later stated that Kenya supplied 201,431.[2] According to its commander, the Carrier Corps recruited 403,504, excluding Northey's carriers, 'a large number of casuals', and those employed by Belgians and Portuguese.[3] The Force Publique recruited 260,000.[4] In March 1917 the British commander-in-chief controlled some 125,000 porters, 44,000 of them from Kenya and 81,000 from German East Africa. The highest number in any month was 140,122 in August 1917. In April 1918 the number was still 124,447.[5] The Colonial Office guessed that between half and three-quarters of a million 'native non-combatants' participated in the campaign. A German estimate suggested that the Allies used nearly a million porters and labourers, and that may be the best figure for both sides.[6]

The porters' experience was terrible. Deaths in action were rare – 376 on the British side, by one account[7] – but deaths from disease,

---

[1] Boell, *Operationen*, p. 148.

[2] A. H. le Q. Clayton, 'Labour in the East Africa Protectorate 1895–1918', Ph.D. thesis, University of St Andrews [1970?] p. 261; Donald C. Savage and J. Forbes Munro, 'Carrier Corps recruitment in the British East Africa Protectorate 1914–1918', *JAH*, VII (1966), 313–42.

[3] Information from Mr D. M. Feldman.

[4] Crawford Young, *Politics in the Congo* (Princeton, 1965), p. 219.

[5] Hoskins to WO, 17 March 1917, CO 691/9/345; *Report on medical and sanitary matters in German East Africa 1917* (Nairobi, 1918), in CO 691/19/286; Boell, *Operationen*, p. 407 n. 2.

[6] Mächtig, 'East African campaign', 18 December 1918, CO691/19/621; Boell, *Operationen*, p. 429.   [7] Boell, *Operationen*, p. 428.

malnutrition, exhaustion, and sheer nameless brutality were appalling. The official British figure was 44,911 dead of disease, or four times as many as the troops of all armies who died from all causes during the campaign.[1] Yet this figure probably covered only the official Carrier Corps, and even for that was probably underestimated. In the second half of 1917 *recorded* deaths were over 2 per cent per *month* and 'wastage' – including every kind of incapacitation and desertion – was reckoned at 15 per cent per month.[2] If these figures are meaningful, and if nearly a million porters were employed, total deaths must have exceeded 100,000, and may have been two or three times that figure. At best the porter's ration contained only some 3,500 calories a day, compared with 4,500 for British soldiers.[3] At worst, if the carrier ate anything it was mouldy maize meal ill-cooked in filthy water, for it was generally assumed that Africans could drink anything. Dysentery killed the most porters, followed by malaria, for although quinine was generally compulsory for soldiers it was not issued to porters.[4] Sheer cold killed many carriers in the Livingstone Mountains, whose inhabitants, by contrast, died of fever in the plains. Alongside these horrors was the hopelessness of men conscripted for the duration of a meaningless campaign, often shot if they tried to desert, always at the mercy of their guards. 'Another two porters' corpses on the road! Shot by the soldiers detailed to guard them', a Belgian officer observed. 'Not a day passes without one or more of these unfortunates paying with their lives for their love of freedom.'[5]

Of the Tanganyikan porters' response we know only three things. We know that whenever possible they fled: they deserted the columns, abandoned their loads, and took to the bush as the troops approached. We know that they remembered: when Europeans launched their next war, Tanganyikan labourers deserted en masse for fear of a new carrier corps – some indeed deserted as early as October 1938.[6] And we know that they danced: along the supply routes, in the camps, and home again in the villages, as members of the Arinoti or local *ngoma*, they danced with the astonishing resilience of Africans.[7]

[1] *Ibid.*

[2] *Report on medical and sanitary matters 1917*, CO 691/19/286; Hoskins to WO, 17 March 1917, CO 691/9/345.

[3] Note for parliamentary question, 19 July 1917, CO 691/9/35.

[4] *Report on medical and sanitary matters 1917*, CO 691/19/286.

[5] Emmanuel Muller, *Les troupes du Katanga et les campagnes d'Afrique 1914–1918* (Bruxelles, 1937), p. 89.

[6] Jerrard, inspection report on Mwera Estate, 12 October 1938, TNA 25908/1/224.

[7] Ranger, *Dance*, p. 76.

For civilians the primary emotion was fear. In the 1960s Zaramo maturity rites still included a dance imitating fear of aeroplanes, first seen during this war.[1] Every army looted, but the most feared was the Force Publique, widely believed by Tanganyikans (and many Europeans) to consist of cannibals. Living off the land, and with bitter memories of Nyamwezi slave-raiders, Belgian troops created utter terror in the Tabora region. 'It is like proceeding through a deserted plague stricken land', wrote an observer, and householders along routes frequented by the Force Publique took to putting their empty tin trunks outside their doors to show that nothing remained to loot.[2] Danger existed for the civilian because his labour, food, and local knowledge were needed by two armies both determined to commit him to their side but neither able to guarantee the protection which made commitment safe. Early in the war the British forced Sonjo villagers on the Kenya border to aid an attack on a German patrol. The Germans devastated the villages in reprisal. Kerewe were terrified lest the British, having once occupied the island, should withdraw. During 1917 a German column broke northwards in search of food and created appalling problems for civilians who had accepted British rule. In the Ututwa chiefdom of Usukuma, for example, the chief welcomed the party and then had to leave with it, while Asian traders accused by a headman of refusing to sell goods for worthless German banknotes were forced to do so at gunpoint. The British later arrested the headman.[3]

The peoples of southern Tanganyika were generally more hostile to the Germans than those of the north. This was doubtless largely because the fighting in the south took place when the Germans were weaker, but memories of German oppression may also have been more bitter there. Mwera revenged Maji Maji by betraying German positions at Mahiwa. The Ngoni and Ndendeuli of Chabruma's former chiefdom 'aided the enemy not only by information and by betraying German patrols, but even by attacks on German lines of communication during subsequent operations'. Another group victimised in Maji Maji, the Pangwa, were notably helpful to the British.[4] The Hehe turned actively against the Germans as early as June 1916.

[1] Swantz, *Ritual*, p. 373 n. 13.
[2] Owen to Wilkinson, 1 October 1916, and Handley to O/C Uganda Police Battalion, 30 September 1916, CO 691/10/594 and 604.
[3] Boell, *Operationen*, pp. 55 n. 1, 155; Hordern, *Operations*, pp. 159, 413 n. 1; Tufnell, 'Extract from monthly report for June 1917 by DPO Mwanza', CO 691/5/618.
[4] Libaba, 'Lindi', MMRP 7/68/2/1; Boell, *Operationen*, p. 155; APO Milo to Songea, 30 January 1919, CO 691/29/145.

'They would rise at once if they thought they could help us drive the enemy out', Northey reported, and the German garrison from Tabora looted Hehe cattle in reprisal as it passed through late in 1916.[1] In the north the Masai had suffered most from German rule. Early in the war Masai spied for both sides and were alleged to meet and exchange information, but as the Germans retreated the Masai openly took the British side. They also seized the chance to escape the hated reserve into which the Germans had penned them. By 1917 Masai had regained most of their pastures north to the Kenya border, just as Chagga, Meru, and Arusha occupied abandoned European farms and cut into forest reserves.[2] Chaos enabled pastoralists to regain military dominance over agricultural neighbours. Masai seized the herds which Iloikop, Mbugwe, and Iraqw had built up under European protection. Tatoga launched cattle raids into Unyaturu even before the Germans left. The British officer who took over Mbulu in May 1916 was 'for a time fully occupied in dealing with unrest and cattle-raiding among the native tribes'.[3] The withdrawal of European control obliged African leaders to seek security by other means. Early in 1916 Chagga chiefs resumed diplomatic relations with the Masai, made blood-brotherhood among themselves, and turned to indigenous religious experts for support. But when the British arrived they were persuaded by Roman Catholic converts and missionaries that the chiefs were organising an anti-European uprising. The district officer deported 36 chiefs and headmen, and not until 1919 was the mistake discovered.[4]

'The native', Lettow-Vorbeck reflected, 'has a fine sense of the transfer of real power from one hand to the other.'[5] For men of ambition and nerve, wartime chaos offered superb opportunities for the intrigue which had been common during the German conquest but had lost efficacy under more systematic administration. Few sub-imperialisms survived the war. Kiwanga's son Soliambingo, accused by rivals of communicating with the British, was shot by the

---

[1] Northey, 'War diary', July 1916, CO 691/1/10; Schnee, *Deutsch-Ostafrika*, p. 237.

[2] Schnee, *Deutsch-Ostafrika*, p. 86; H. A. Fosbrooke, 'An administrative survey of the Masai social system', *TNR*, XXVI (1948), 7–11; Eva Stuart-Watt, *Africa's dome of mystery* (London, 1929), p. 110; Kitching, 'Native land in the Arusha district', 3 December 1930, CO 691/114.

[3] Boell, *Operationen*, pp. 180, 187 n. 3; Schnee, *Deutsch-Ostafrika*, pp. 221–2; Hordern, *Operations*, p. 283.

[4] Hollis to Milner, 17 July 1919, and Dundas to SA, 21 August 1919, CO 691/23/70 and 598; Rogers, 'Political focus', pp. 195–216.

[5] Lettow-Vorbeck, *Reminiscences*, p. 33.

Germans in 1917.[1] Loyalists who had gained power after Maji Maji lost it again to the descendants of rebels. In Ubena the British found Chief Masasi to be 'loathed and detested by all Wabena' and quickly replaced him by Mbeyela's surviving son Pangamahuti.[2] By 1919 Sapi bin Mkwawa ruled Uhehe. It was a world turned upside down once more.

Haya chiefs had long been masters of intrigue. Their border location, long contact with Uganda, and experience of exploiting external aid all guaranteed that not only Europeans would participate in the 'transfer of real power'. In 1914 the dominant chief was still Kahigi of Kianja. His domain incorporated sections of Bukara and Kyamutwara, while his brother-in-law Kyobya ruled Karagwe, nominally on behalf of its young Chief Ntare. Kahigi saw the war as a new opportunity. Ntare either appealed for British aid or was successfully accused of doing so; in either event the Germans hanged him. After the British raided Bukoba in June 1915 the returning Germans learned that loot could be found in the house of Kahigi's old enemy, Muntu of Kyamutwara. Search revealed a German officer's uniform. Muntu was deposed. Yet Kianja paid for Kahigi's loyalty to the Germans. In 1916 the British invaded Buhaya and the Germans hastily withdrew, warning the chiefs not to resist. The chiefs had no intention of resisting: they had better ways of handling these situations. Kahigi had not lost his touch. At his first meeting with a British officer he secured a promise to continue the large tax rebate which the Germans paid to Haya chiefs. But later in the year Kahigi died and his sub-imperialism, so brilliantly sustained, collapsed overnight. Bukara regained independence for services to British Intelligence. Kyobya was replaced by Ntare's young son Daudi Rumanyika. The Kiziba chiefdom was given a portion of Kyamutwara. Kahigi's successor reportedly carried a revolver, employed a guard of spearmen, and had all his food tasted in his presence. When the German interpreter and agent, Francis Lwamugira, returned from accompanying the German forces to Tabora, it needed all his courtly diplomacy to win British favour. Lwamugira 'replied with a smile that everyone was now in favour of the British', the district officer noted in December 1918, and a few months later the chiefs contemplated an appeal to the Peace Conference to ensure that Buhaya remained British. The new administration welcomed this tribute. Perhaps the chiefs also reflected that the war had restored the relative equality

[1] Culwick, *Ubena*, pp. 90–1.
[2] APO Milo to Songea, 30 January 1919, CO 691/29/145; Songea district book, TNA.

among them which Kahigi's long alliance with the Germans had destroyed.[1]

The change of masters generally restored older political relations which the Germans had distorted. In Ungoni, where chieftainship still retained prestige, two years of disorder and European weakness enabled the chiefs to regain much power lost after Maji Maji.[2] Artificial chieftainships created for administrative convenience rarely survived. In the Musoma region almost every 'chief' either left with the Germans or was expelled by his 'subjects', the one major exception being the only hereditary ruler, Ruhaga of Ushashi.[3] 'Re-traditionalisation' can be seen also in the restoration of Hehe chieftainship and the collapse of sub-imperialisms. The war largely wiped out the political changes which the Germans had imposed. In doing so it facilitated the Indirect Rule policies which the British introduced in 1925 and perhaps dissolved some of the antagonism felt in other colonies towards the original European conquerors, just as mobility of leadership minimised the conflict of political generations which was so much more apparent in Kenya and Uganda than in Tanganyika during the 1920s.

Yet just as the 'collapse of the local compromise' in late German times often brought ancillary structural change, so 're-traditionalis-ation' often incorporated European innovations. In 1914 no Haya chief was a Christian, but a decade later eight of the nine chiefs were, 'for people said, "The British will not have anybody as a chief who is not a Christian."'[4] Literacy was rarely more valuable than in communicating with the 'enemy'. The Germans wrote Masanja of Nera in Usukuma a letter of recommendation to the British, whom he served for many years. A Tatoga orphan who had been German interpreter in Singida and headman of central Unyaturu, Mgeni ('the Stranger'), changed sides at so precisely the right moment in 1916 and made his linguistic skills so useful both to Turu and British that by 1924 he was paramount chief.[5] Moreover, the British introduced many alien Africans as their agents, especially around Lake Victoria where

---

[1] Austen, *Northwest Tanzania*, pp. 112–29; Katoke, *Karagwe*, pp. 128–30, 175–7; Baines to CS, 3 January 1923, TNA 215/50/2; Carl Jungblut, *Vierzig Jahre Afrika* (3rd edn, Berlin, 1941), p. 191; Baines, note, 6 December 1918, Cory papers, ULD; Hollis to Milner, 24 April 1919, CO 691/22/55.

[2] Redmond, 'Political history', p. 298.

[3] Hans Cory, 'The Musoma pre-European tribal system', typescript, 1945, Cory papers, ULD.

[4] C.-J. Hellberg, 'Andrea Kajerero: the man and his church', typescript, 1957, MUL. See also Austen, *Northwest Tanzania*, p. 135.

[5] Austen, *Northwest Tanzania*, p. 117; below, p. 327.

Ugandan models predominated. Jaffari Mukasa in Missenyi (northern Buhaya), Izake Kyakwambala and Alexi Munanya in Karagwe, and Alexander in Karumo (Buzinza) were all employed during or shortly after the war to train Tanganyikans in administrative virtues, while a Ziba aristocrat, Mapera Kyaruzi, performed the same duty in Bugufi.[1]

For the supple and the shrewd war was an opportunity. But most Tanganyikans were neither shrewd nor supple. For them war was an ordeal, the object survival, the method evasion or acquiescence. Experienced German administrators expected Africans to take advantage of the war to rebel, but no rebellion occurred. The British collected tax from 1916 without difficulty, often exceeding the highest German collections.[2] Yet few welcomed the British as deliverers. Had the conquerors hoped for that, their need for porters and supplies precluded it. In some regions recruiting of carriers 'brought the remaining native population to the verge of open resistance'.[3] In Buhaya, where few porters were recruited, deep anger was shown when news of Carrier Corps casualties became public.[4]

Perhaps religion embodied the paradox of war most clearly. For Christian missions it was a catastrophe. Early in the war the Germans arrested British missionaries and many of their converts. Teachers from Magila suffered dreadfully as porters and labourers on the supply route from Morogoro to Korogwe. Later, like the staff from Masasi, they were interned. Deacon Paul Kasinde of Luatala and four teachers 'died in chains at Lukuledi for being English-made Christians', as did at least twelve teachers from Magila.[5] Petro Mzaba, once head prefect at Kiungani, carried a load with Lettow-Vorbeck's troops throughout the war. Andrea Mwaka, senior CMS teacher in Dodoma, was beaten up by German troops. The venerable Canon Petro Limo returned from his ordeal as overseer on the Handeni road with his right arm paralysed and deaf in one ear, 'because we had a German who treated me like animal he some kick me about or strike me in my head'. 'I became very poor since the war', he explained sadly, 'I came back and found even my house and church was broken down.' His first sermon urged his congregation not to hate Germans.[6]

---

[1] Austen, *Northwest Tanzania*, p. 131; Mapera Kyaruzi's service record in TNA 197/1/3.
[2] C. P. Fendall, *The East African Force 1915–1919* (London, 1921), p. 179.
[3] Byatt to Long, 22 March 1918, CO 691/14/406.
[4] Baines, monthly reports on Bukoba, August and September 1918, Cory papers, ULD.
[5] *Central Africa*, April 1918 and May 1917.
[6] Limo to Travers, 2 April 1922, UMCA A/5; *Central Africa*, April 1946.

German missionaries and their converts also suffered. 'There was no longer any differentiation between Christian, heathen and Mohammedan', one wrote of Dar es Salaam under British occupation, 'but it was only between Germans and English.' By the end of 1919 the Benedictines (whose lay brothers joined the German army) had seen 131 of their 134 personnel deported.[1] The British expelled German missionaries remorselessly. The last left in 1922. None returned until 1925. Roman Catholic missions generally secured skeleton staffs of French or Swiss priests. Protestants had greater difficulty. Some work was taken over temporarily by British societies, but elsewhere there were no missionaries for several years.

The missionaries' absence disrupted many fledgling Christian communities. 'Christianity in Mkalama has completely died out', the district officer reported early in 1923. 'In August the last two remaining Christians informed me that they had followed the rest of the Lutheran flock, and had reverted to paganism.' Only 200 of Kwiro's 3,000 'converts' continued to practise.[2] 'The Berlin missionaries were forbidden to return', it is told of Upangwa:

As a result their Christians remained alone without a single shepherd. After a while all the Christians at that time returned to their pagan practices. They began again to marry several wives, they consulted diviners, they venerated the ancestors, they made offerings to the spirits, and the like. They behaved as did the Israelites when Moses went up into the mountain...At that time almost every teacher abandoned religion for a long period. Only one remained faithful: Mwalimu Yoheli Mung'ong'o. And even he married two wives.[3]

In these circumstances indigenous religions probably revived, but little evidence survives. On Kilimanjaro, it is said, ritual leaders predicted the imminent end of European rule and some mission teachers returned to the old faith.[4] It was undoubtedly a time of great Islamic expansion. In the coastal hinterland many peoples – Ngindo, Zaramo, Zigua – had been much influenced by Islam before 1914; now the region finally became predominantly Islamic, except for Masasi and parts of Bonde (with long mission experience) and to some extent Matumbi.[5] In the north the destruction of Lutheran work removed the last obstacle to the Islamisation of the Digo. In the south many

[1] Translation of Berlin mission journal, June 1919, CO 691/24/544; Renner, *Leuchter*, II, 139–43. For this period, see Wright, *German missions*, ch. 7.
[2] Bagshawe, Kondoa DAR 1922, TNA 1733/22/14; Larson, 'History', pp. 252–3.
[3] Anonymous history of Milo, UMCA Milo papers, MUL.
[4] Ekemode, 'German rule', p. 329.
[5] See especially Larson, 'History', pp. 259–65.

256

Mwera and Makua abandoned Christian practices, so that when mission work resumed, polygynous marriages and other obstacles prevented many converts from returning, with the result that Islam became the predominant religion of the area.[1] In the early 1920s proselytisation by coastal and Zigua *waalimu* established the first Christian communities in Upare and Kilimanjaro, where it was said that 'Islam came in with British troops.'[2] A missionary returning to Usambara in 1925 took it for granted that 'all important people are Mohamedans'.[3] Islam also became established in two inland regions. One was Unyanyembe, where a Muslim chief acceded in 1917. The other was Undendeuli, where Islamic proselytisers – Arab and Ngindo traders, Yao *waalimu*, Ndendeuli migrant labourers, askari, government agents – found success in a region neglected by missionaries. The first mosques were built in Undendeuli in the 1920s, the *jando* circumcision ceremony was introduced, and the Qadiriyya order was established.[4] Islam's impetus survived until the late 1920s, and then, with the re-establishment of stable colonial rule and mission work, it returned to a barely perceptible permeation.

Yet for Christianity the ordeal of war was also a strengthening. As missionary control lapsed, so African Christians gained a responsibility which they could not otherwise have acquired at this time. The war consolidated power in the hands of the Fathers, the first generation of African Christians, with their revolutionary view of Christianity. As revolutionaries come to power, they imposed this pattern on Tanganyikan Christianity, not only giving it a distinctive and lasting character, but also shaping the next generation's protest. Martin Ganisya's experience was symptomatic. Before the war he was an obedient evangelist, holding as a freedman that Europe had redeemed Africa from anarchy. Now his mentors hastily ordained him as they went into exile. In their absence Ganisya held together his congregation of 100–150 Lutherans in Dar es Salaam, refusing to merge it with the triumphant Anglicans and becoming 'a serious problem' to the

---

[1] Waltenberg, pastoral letter, 1962, in M. H. Y. Kaniki (ed.), 'The Lutheran Church in Usambara', duplicated, n.d., University College, Dar es Salaam, p. 136; Viktor Haelg, 'Islam und christliche Missionsarbeit an der ostafrikanischen Küste', in Renner, *Leuchter*, II, 166.

[2] G. N. Shann, 'The early development of education among the Chagga', *TNR*, XLV (1956), 30. See also I. N. Kimambo (ed.), 'The history of the Pare to 1900: oral texts', duplicated, n.d., University College, Dar es Salaam, pp. 16, 41; Rogers, 'Political focus', pp. 217–18.

[3] Johanssen, *Führung*, III, 43.

[4] Gallagher, 'Islam', pp. 121–2, 131–4.

authorities. The congregation welcomed Lutheran migrants, one of whom, an ex-soldier named Yohane Nyagava, was so impressed by Ganisya that when missionaries were again expelled in 1939 he tried to take control of a whole diocese.[1] As the only African Lutheran pastor, Ganisya also visited Usambara to baptise and celebrate the Eucharist. 'We told each other', wrote one who met him, 'how the Kingdom of God is going forward in Dar es Salaam, Uzaramo, in Tanga and in Digoland, in Usambara and on Kilimanjaro. We listened and sang hymns, we praised and thanked God for the great deeds he has done for us.'[2]

In Usambara the departing missionaries considered ordaining an African pastor, but, regarding this as hasty, instead selected seven teachers as 'shepherds'. One embezzled the group's finances, but the others ran the Shambaa church from 1920 to 1925 with astonishing success:

Because of the rumours of war many left Christianity thinking that the Christians were not wanted. But when one congregation started inviting others during festivals, the fire was re-kindled and many came back to the congregation and were baptised...The word of God was further spread when the church was being run by natives. There was no opposition. Only a few individuals forbade their children to go to Church. Those who accepted Christianity were helped by the Holy Spirit and had a burning zeal without being forced by any circumstance. It was never because of poverty that they accepted Christianity. During that time there was a true manifestation of Love. At festivals many came from far and sang hymns and played trumpets.[3]

Such exaltation among small communities in a hostile world was experienced elsewhere when missionaries left. Lutheran teachers on Kilimanjaro worked unpaid for six years. Filipo Njau remembered them as years of intense satisfaction. His chiefdom, Moshi, had a new, literate ruler anxious for Christian progress. Schools were built, Sunday markets forbidden, and Njau was encouraged to preach at the chief's *baraza*.[4] In Ugweno, Andrea Msechu was left to protect his people from the British soldiery. 'He rang the Church bell', he later recalled, 'and people came to pray for their survival so that God could

[1] Sicard, *Lutheran church*, p. 214; *Central Africa*, June 1922; A. L. Sakafu, 'The pastor: Yohane Nyagava', in Iliffe, *Tanzanians*, pp. 197–8.
[2] Jakobo Ngombe to Delius, 13 September 1924, in Franz Gleiss (ed.), *An meinen Hirten! Was Negerchristen in Usambara und Tanga an ihren Hirten in der Notzeit 1922–25 zu schreiben hatten* (Bethel bei Bielefeld, 1926), p. 16.
[3] Guga, 'Research'.
[4] Njau, *Aus meinem Leben*, pp. 37–41; Bruno Gutmann (ed.), *Briefe aus Afrika* (Leipzig, 1925), pp. 14, 18, 20.

receive their souls if the British were coming to kill them for their association with the Germans.'[1]

The war committed the Fathers more deeply to their denominations. Hitherto these had often meant little. 'When you white men have gone we shall agree', Cecil Majaliwa once declared. 'You argue and talk and we have to listen, but when you have gone we shall remember that for all of us Africans the difference is the darkness out of which we came and the light in which we are.'[2] Now responsibility made the Fathers jealous of their inheritance. 'We have celebrated Christmas Eve as hitherto and introduced no new customs', Filipo Njau assured his mentors.[3] Rival missionary societies sought to absorb the German congregations. Cassian Homahoma refused to let Benedictine converts on the Nyasa lakeshore be absorbed by Anglicans. 'If we do not receive priests to lead us', he warned the Roman Catholic authorities,

we shall write a letter to the Holy Father, that he may send us priests. We feel deep resentment because we have no priests...Our mission is experiencing much difficulty from the UMCA. Time and again our Christians are receiving gifts of money from the UMCA. They are trying to cheat us, and they say, 'It is the end of your mission now, for you no longer receive your priests.'[4]

Such men were delighted when missionaries returned. 'Love came out of hearts and overflowed into hands, faces and mouths', one wrote of the return to Usambara. '...The children have seen their father who has been released from prison.'[5] Then difficulties began. Men who had borne responsibility did not easily resubmit to mission discipline. 'When the missionaries came back', a Shambaa historian explained, 'there were signs that the Holy Spirit had left for the desire to co-operate to work for the Lord was no more seen. Trouble started when they started grading workers. Hatred started.'[6] Even more difficult was the relationship between African church leaders and new missionary societies made responsible for them by some remote authority in Europe. When Lutheran missionaries left Buhaya, their followers – many of them originally baptised in Uganda – eagerly welcomed the CMS, but when the latter handed over to South African Wesleyans

[1] N. M. Banduka, 'Life history of Reverend Andrew M. Msechu', seminar paper, University of Dar es Salaam, 1971.
[2] *Central Africa*, July 1940.
[3] Filipo Njau to Gutmann, 20 February 1922, in Gutmann, *Briefe*, p. 12.
[4] I owe this quotation to Fr J. Baur.
[5] Jakobo Ngombe to Gleiss, 14 and 29 March 1925, in Gleiss, *An meinen Hirten*, pp. 62, 67.
[6] Guga, 'Research'.

without consulting the Haya, the result was crisis. The Wesleyans, it was alleged, turned their churches into cinemas, gave Communion to those under church discipline, and made baptismal candidates declare, 'I wish to be a member of John Wesley's church'. The Haya concluded that they were false prophets. Led by an evangelist named Andrea Kajerero, they boycotted the mission and there were violent disputes about property. Forbidden by the administration to form an independent church, Kajerero instead appealed to the Lutherans, who returned in 1927. At first those baptised by the Wesleyans rejected the Lutherans, but the schism was finally healed in 1932.[1]

The first African pastor ordained in Buhaya, in 1929, was Andrea Kajerero. The first African ministers ordained in the Leipzig field – Andrea Msechu in Ugweno, Solomon Nkya in Machame, and Lazarus Laiser in Arusha – had all led their churches during the missionaries' absence. When the Lutherans ordained the first eight pastors in Ubena in 1934, seven had spent part of the war in British prisons. In 1917 the White Fathers ordained the first two Tanganyikan priests of the Roman Catholic Church. The Benedictines of Kwiro admitted their first two African lay brothers in 1925. And Bishop Weston of the UMCA celebrated his teachers' faithfulness by making nine priests and fifteen deacons in the first four years after the war, at such speed that Canon Samuel Sehoza protested.[2]

In the long run the war also led to great numerical growth in areas where the church was already firmly established. In part this merely continued the trend of the last years of German rule. Perhaps war also enlarged men's experience and awareness of European power. Perhaps peace demonstrated that European rulers might change but European domination continued. At all events, almost every well-established mission experienced massive post-war demand for instruction. The White Fathers who briefly ran Peramiho baptised 800 and made over 2,000 catechumens. 'Ungoni is a second Uganda', one commented.[3] In 1913 Magila had 450 Christmas communicants; in 1916, 256; in 1919, 700. 'There were more Catechumens and more Confirmation candidates than could possibly be taught', a visitor

[1] Hellberg, 'Kajerero', ch. 5; Johanssen, *Führung*, III, 134–6, 167–8, 176, 203, 209, 252, 258, 331; Austen, *Northwest Tanzania*, p. 166.
[2] Hellberg, 'Kajerero', p. vi; Henrik Smedjebacka, *Lutheran church autonomy in northern Tanzania 1940–1963* (Åbo, 1973), pp. 41, 48; Wright, *German missions*, pp. 191–2; Bouniol, *White Fathers*, p. 117; Kwiro mission diary, 4 October and 19 November 1925, Kwiro archives; Spanton to Travers, 9 April 1918, UMCA D/3/i.
[3] I owe this information to Fr Baur.

observed in 1920.[1] When missionaries at Kwiro were forbidden in 1924 to baptise further catechumens because they could not care for them, Father Superior disobeyed as a matter of conscience, baptised over 450 children, and died a month later.[2] Between 1916 and 1924 the number of baptised Protestants in Bukoba increased from 100 to over 2,000. 'Every village has its School and Mission Teacher', the provincial commissioner noticed in Ufipa in 1926. 'Practically every child in each village attends school.'[3] Distinct areas of the country were becoming predominantly Christian, just as others were becoming specifically Muslim. The war widened the distinction between them. Tanganyika's new shape was crystallising. In 1919 Kahigi's successor celebrated his conversion to Christianity by burning the *kubandwa* cult's main local shrine at Butakia and dispersing the priests who had been rivals of royal power since Hinda chiefs first ruled Buhaya.[4] War had brought forth its victors.

The British regime and its beneficiaries

Tanganyika had been Germany's most valued colony. The British wanted only to deny it to others. Britain had long been incapable of developing all her possessions. Now the empire was even larger and the metropolitan economy terribly weakened. At no time between the wars did the volume of Britain's exports exceed 81 per cent of their 1913 level. During the 1930s Britain was a net importer of capital and migrants.[5] Of course, even Britain's waning economic vigour could have transformed Tanganyika had the territory possessed any economic attraction, but it offered nothing to compare with South African gold, Middle Eastern oil, or Malayan tin and rubber. Continuing poverty was British Tanganyika's leading characteristic.

Britain's economic interest in Tanganyika was confined to imperial firms which took the pickings of the old regime. When ex-German sisal estates were auctioned, British investors bought only the most profitable. The two main buyers epitomised the imperial connection, for Wigglesworth and Company were London's leading sisal brokers and Bird and Company were a subsidiary of a powerful Anglo-Indian

---

[1] Magila mission diary, TNA; *Central Africa*, August 1920.
[2] Kwiro mission diary, 9 December 1924–20 February 1925, Kwiro archives.
[3] Johanssen, *Führung*, III, 134; Bagenal, Kigoma PAR 1926, TNA 1733/5/55/1.
[4] SC Bukoba, monthly report, September 1922, TNA 19303/73.
[5] London and Cambridge Economic Service, *The British economy: key statistics, 1900–1966* (London, 1967), table K; D. H. Aldcroft, *The inter-war economy* (London, 1970), pp. 224, 262 (I owe this reference to Professor Gallagher).

concern. As early as 1916 the National Bank of India became government bankers in Dar es Salaam, later giving way to the Standard Bank of South Africa. In 1916 lighterage companies based in Mombasa and Durban took over Dar es Salaam port and ran it in the interests of the imperial shipping lines, Union-Castle and British-India.[1] The latter's agents, Smith Mackenzie, became a leading import-export firm, as did Dalgety and Company whose main interests were in Australia and New Zealand. These firms were not innovators but inheritors.

Yet there were advantages in being the runt of the litter. The British Colonial Office had much experience of protecting native interests against European encroachment. Its officials held that Tanganyika should follow the 'west coast' policy of primarily African development which Rechenberg had unsuccessfully advocated. The key official, Sir Charles Strachey, urged in 1921 that Tanganyika must be 'primarily a Black man's country' and his permanent secretary, 'needless to say', agreed, especially in view of the Mandate. A year later Strachey drafted a Tanganyikan land law based on Nigerian models. In 1924 he urged that the Nigerian policy of indirect rule should be introduced, and this was done in the next year by a governor with Nigerian experience. Despite vicissitudes, Tanganyika never lost the direction given in these years.[2]

The virtues of British policy were negative, and this was especially true of Sir Horace Byatt, the colonial official who headed Tanganyika's administration from 1917 to 1924. He was a narrowly competent man, unimaginative, unpopular, and unwell, but he shared the good intentions of the Colonial Office.[3] Byatt had three main aims. One was to destroy the German presence, and he ruthlessly deported settlers and missionaries. When the last Germans left in 1922, Tanganyika's European population was only half its pre-war figure. Byatt's second aim was to discourage new settlers because there was insufficient African labour and the territory should follow west coast models. His third aim was to re-establish order. This he achieved by staffing the

---

[1] Wynne to CO, 19 September 1922, CO 691/61/337; Smuts to Bonar Law, 14 December 1916, CO 691/1/231; John Iliffe, 'A history of the dockworkers of Dar es Salaam', *TNR*, LXXI (1970), 121–2.

[2] Strachey to Read, 5 August 1921, and Fiddes to Wood, 18 July 1921, CO 691/52/259–60; Strachey, 'Land policy in Tanganyika', 29 April 1922, CO 691/60/148; below, p. 320. For Strachey's left-wing affinities, see P. S. Gupta, *Imperialism and the British labour movement 1914–1964* (London, 1975), pp. 74–5.

[3] The best accounts are Hollis, 'Autobiography', v, RH; Margaret L. Bates, 'Tanganyika under British administration 1920-1955', D.Phil. thesis, Oxford University, 1957, ch. 3.

German administrative machinery with recruits from neighbouring colonies and the British forces – many lacking administrative experience – with consequent diversity of administrative practice and absence of central policy. Believing that German rule had been brutal, Byatt reorganised the police force and abolished slavery and racial distinctions in the legal system, introducing the Indian Penal Code. But he admired German social services and sought especially to revive the state education system, partly because he loathed missionaries. Nevertheless, the chief feature of his governorship was economic stagnation owing to worldwide depression, Treasury parsimony, and his own lethargy.

The regime's first beneficiaries were Asians. They had suffered severely during the war, being very vulnerable. When German forces abandoned Musoma in 1916 the local people entirely destroyed the Asian bazaar.[1] Asians were also the chief victims of wartime commercial collapse, which was so complete that domestic industries revived in several regions and even slave-trading was alleged in remote areas.[2] Not until 1924 did Tanganyika's external trade regain its 1912 level, even ignoring intervening inflation. Many Asians lost heavily from valueless German notes (redeemed at 1½ per cent of face value) and exchange fluctuations between sterling and rupees consequent on Britain's wartime inflation. Yet once peace returned the Asian position rapidly improved. Needing English-speaking subordinates, the British recruited clerks and artisans from India. Protected by the Mandate, immigration swelled the Asian population from 8,698 in 1912 to 25,144 in 1931.[3] Asians were no longer legally natives. New communities took shape, notably that of the Sikh entrepreneurs and artisans who built their first temple in Dar es Salaam in 1918.[4] Most Asians – 56 per cent of adult males in 1932 – were engaged in commerce,[5] but the most successful businessmen were diversifying out of trade into landownership, agriculture, and industry. Most large ex-German plantations were bought by European companies and many mixed farms went to British settlers, but medium-sized properties – characteristically urban

---

[1] Byatt to Long, 7 June 1917, CO 691/5/306.
[2] Barnes, 'Safari report. Abolition of various small Wasumbwa sultanates' [1921] Barnes papers III, RH.
[3] *Die deutschen Schutzgebiete 1912/13*, II, 38–9; Robert G. Gregory, *India and East Africa 1890–1939* (Oxford, 1971), p. 387.
[4] G. S. Bhavra, 'The Sikhs in East Africa', B.A. thesis, University College, Dar es Salaam, 1968.
[5] Gregory, *India*, pp. 388–9.

estate and the smaller sisal and coffee plantations – were often sold
at low prices to Asian merchants. The most successful were the
Karimjee Jivanjee family, whose founding ancestor had reached
Zanzibar in 1819. They bought sisal, coconut, and coffee plantations,
then diversified into cotton ginning, oil and soap manufacture,
milling, and the sale and maintenance of motor vehicles.[1] Hitherto
unprivileged European groups also benefited. Among the Greeks the
most successful was George Arnautoglu, former manager of the
Burgerhof in Dar es Salaam, whose connections enabled him to
affiliate with German interests returning to Tanganyika. Besides
creating his own sisal empire he became a director of the Usagara
Company, formed in 1925 as successor to the DOAG. By the 1950s
Arnautoglu was among Tanganyika's wealthiest men.[2]

British rule also gave Asians political opportunity. The use of Asian
troops in East Africa stimulated suggestions that the conquered
territory should become an Indian colony.[3] The idea was championed
by Britain's Secretary of State for India, who hoped it would 'settle
the question of Indian emigration' then troubling Kenya, South
Africa, and Australia. Indian National Congress leaders also toyed
with the idea until Gandhi vetoed it. The plan finally collapsed in
August 1920 when an Indian Government representative reported that
Tanganyika was thoroughly unsuitable for Asian settlement, but the
campaign stimulated the formation of an Indian Association in Dar
es Salaam in 1918.[4] This arranged meetings and formed branches in
several towns. Among its first presidents were Karmali Daya and
Ghulamali Damji, both merchants, while other early leaders included
two lawyers, S. N. Ghose (later the first Asian Legislative Councillor)
and K. A. Master (a Parsee), as well as M. O. Abbasi, a journalist and
Muslim extremist. Conflict between more radical professional men and
respectable community leaders was an enduring feature of Asian
politics in Tanganyika and soon appeared within the Indian
Association.

When Gandhi was sentenced to six years imprisonment in March
1922 the Indian Association imitated his tactics and called a one-day
hartal or closure of shops, appealing to Asians to use Indian-made

[1] Abdulla Saleh al-Farsy, *Seyyid Said bin Sultan* (Zanzibar, n.d.), p. 55; *Dar es Salaam Times*, 19 November 1921; M. and C. Booth, 'Directory of business names for Dar es Salaam township, 1920–1950', typescript, 1970, in my possession.
[2] Wolfgang Hinnenberg, *Die deutschen Bestrebungen zur wirtschaftlichen Durchdringung Tanganyikas 1925 bis 1933* (Hamburg, 1973), pp. 71–2.
[3] See Gregory, *India*, ch. 5.
[4] *Ibid.*, p. 382; Jadab to Indian Association Nairobi, 13 November 1918, CO 691/16/544.

goods and join Congress.[1] The radicals were apparently gaining influence, but they needed to break the political inertia of the numerically preponderant shopkeepers. In 1923 Byatt gave them an opportunity. His Profits Tax Ordinance required shopkeepers to pay a licence fee and a profits tax assessed by an official commission. At the suggestion of the European Chamber of Commerce, Asian businessmen were required also to keep their books in English or Swahili or provide a translation from Gujarati. Asians had opposed a similar plan in German times, for good reason. Many shopkeepers were illiterate, few knew English, most kept their accounts in their heads, and all depended on credit-worthiness whose real status would now be known to officials. The proposal appeared discriminatory, contrary to the Mandate, and a deliberate attack on the Gujarati language. Radicals saw it as a move towards introducing Kenya's anti-Asian policies into Tanganyika.[2] In March 1923, after consulting the branches, radical leaders drawn from several rival communities overcame the opposition of conservative merchants and called a *hartal* until the new ordinance was repealed. Asian and Arab shops remained closed throughout the territory for 54 days. Government claimed that permission to reopen was joyfully received by shop-keepers who had obeyed only lest non-observance should 'result in local traders obtaining no subsequent consignments of goods from Dar es Salaam and thus cause their ruin'.[3] Doubtless there was truth in this, but the issue deeply concerned the shopkeepers and there is no indication that anyone broke the *hartal*. Forty-four Asians in Lindi preferred prison to fines and went on hunger strike.[4] The decision to reopen shops was taken only after a delegation to London, including Yusufali Karimjee Jivanjee, received a promise to consider amendment from the Colonial Office.[5]

The most important effect of Asian political activity was to stimulate African awareness. The war's chief African beneficiaries were English-speaking adherents of British missions, especially those educated at Kiungani. From all over eastern Africa they flocked to serve the new regime. Samwil Chiponde, a defrocked priest, left Zanzibar to become High Court interpreter in Dar es Salaam. His brother, Leslie Matola,

[1] *Dar es Salaam Times*, March–April 1922.
[2] Correspondence in TNA 7090; Smith to Salisbury, 16 July 1891, FO 84/2148/294; Iliffe, *German rule*, pp. 85–6; Byatt to Devonshire, 2 April 1923, and Nalid Adat to Byatt, 21 March 1923, CO 691/62/388 and 395; Gregory, *India*, pp. 381–4.
[3] Watts, Rungwe DAR 1923, TNA library.
[4] Byatt to Devonshire, 18 April 1923, CO 691/62/475.
[5] Devonshire to Byatt, 24 May 1923, CO 691/68/73.

who had previously taught in Pemba, joined the Dar es Salaam government school, together with another brother, Cecil Matola, formerly a carpenter on a Kenyan estate. Benedict Madalito, a Makua educated in Zanzibar, became senior African clerk in the Dar es Salaam district office. His counterpart in Tanga was Martin Kayamba, who was a great-grandson of Kimweri ya Nyumbai and had served the British in Kenya and Uganda. The Kiungani men were rivalled by products of the CMS school at Mombasa, notably Edwin Brenn (senior clerk in the Education Department) and Rawson Watts (who worked in the Secretariat). Further inland, British occupation attracted educated Africans from Nyasaland, Northern Rhodesia, and Uganda. In 1926 men born outside Tanganyika held 31 of the 45 top posts in the African civil service.[1]

These men pioneered modern African politics in Tanganyika. They did not oppose the British. Rather, because they were committed to the regime and confident of its benevolence they organised themselves to participate in the expected advancement. Their ideas were profoundly British. 'People can say what they want', Chiponde once declared, 'but to the African mind, to imitate Europeans is civilization.'[2] They were ambitious, self-interested men, proud of their skills and contemptuous of less 'civilised' Africans. They had strong racial attitudes, especially towards Asians who often held coveted middle-grade civil service posts. They were also men of wide experience with a sense of Tanganyika as a unit transcending ethnic divisions. They worked in a mobile, territorial bureaucracy. Tanganyika's wartime experience and mandatory status made it more obviously a unit than most other territories. It is not surprising that the civil servants saw themselves as leaders and spokesmen for Tanganyika's Africans.

Two stimuli brought the civil servants into territorial politics. One was the plan to make Tanganyika an Indian colony. When African leaders in Tanga – the territory's educational centre – learned that local Asians planned a meeting to support the proposal on 19 December 1918, they organised a meeting two days earlier to oppose it – 'a spontaneous meeting of protest', according to Byatt.[3] They stated three objections to Asian rule:

[1] Correspondence in TNA 3715; *Mambo leo*, August–September 1929; 'The story of Martin Kayamba', in Margery Perham (ed.), *Ten Africans* (2nd edn, London, 1963), pp. 195–8; John Iliffe, 'The spokesman: Martin Kayamba', in Iliffe, *Tanzanians*, pp. 71–3.
[2] Quoted in R. A. Austen, 'Notes on the pre-history of TANU', *Makerere journal*, IX (1964), 2.
[3] Byatt to Long, 21 December 1918, CO 691/16/540.

(a) We East Africans need the control and care of Europeans for the development of ourselves, our country, and our children.

(b) We have been looking forward to being governed by the British in order that we might enjoy greater justice, better education, and more liberty than under the past régime.

(c) Although only in a small degree we and our brethren have helped the British, and sacrificed ourselves in fighting this war, that we might be redeemed by the British.[1]

The signatories were Muslim notables led by the pro-British *liwali*, Ali bin Diwani, and English-educated civil servants headed by Martin Kayamba. This coalition was the basis of subsequent political organisation in Tanga.

The second motive for action was the group interest of civil servants, again threatened by Asian gains. In August 1921 Chiponde, Madalito, and Cecil Matola protested to the Chief Secretary on behalf of forty African clerks at the 'great distinction made by the Government in several matters between Asiatic clerks and Native clerks', especially regarding salaries, housing allowances, and leave arrangements.[2] Meanwhile both European and Asian civil servants had formed associations, while a Kenya African Civil Servants Association existed by 1920. These models probably encouraged Africans in Tanganyika to create a similar body. While those in Dar es Salaam discussed plans, their counterparts in Tanga decided on 24 March 1922 to form the Tanganyika Territory African Civil Services Association, the territory's first known African organisation of a modern kind.[3] TTACSA's president was Kayamba and its members were English-speaking Christians working in Tanga district office and Swahili-speaking Muslims who staffed the local field administration. The association ran a library and a football team, collected money for a club house, and held evening classes in English, geography, and history. Its combination of mutual improvement and elite unity exactly expressed Kayamba's thinking. 'It is said – Unity is strength – and unless Africans sooner or later come to realise this their future is dark and gloomy', he wrote at this time. 'Our Association gives these advantages to every African Civil Servant who joins: (a) Close fellowship (b) Free reading and social advancement in accordance with the ethics of the present civilization (c) Sportsman-

[1] Ali bin Diwani and others to Byatt, 17 December 1918, CO 691/16/546.
[2] Chiponde and others to CS, 23 August 1921, TNA 11051/I/A.1.
[3] *Mambo leo*, March–April 1923; Kayamba and Alkhidhri bin Likhidhri to CS, 5 April 1922, TNA 3715/1.

ship.'[1] He had found a new means of harnessing the energy of the young.

The civil servants intended that bodies similar to TTACSA should be formed elsewhere and federated into a territorial organisation. One was formed during 1923 as the Pangani Sports Club. Kilwa decided to form a welfare association, but it is not clear whether anything came of this or of an 'African Association Service Club' in Mikindani designed to rival the Indian Association. Far away in Bukoba educated Haya formed the Bukoba Bahaya Union in 1924 in imitation of Kayamba's organisation. A TTACSA branch was established in Tukuyu, where Nyasa clerks predominated, and still existed in 1932. The Tanga branch survived until 1945, chiefly as a club for the Kayamba circle. Leadership had long passed to Dar es Salaam. There, with some seventy members, TTACSA developed during 1925–7 in a trade union direction.[2]

The civil servants demanded higher salaries, housing allowances, and the like on the grounds that as the vanguard of civilisation they must earn enough to lead suitably respectable lives. When Governor Cameron arrived from Nigeria in 1925 they wrote:

As your Excellency had been in West Africa, you are well convinced of what a Black educated person can do if properly taught and given a chance to improve himself...The world is civilizing no doubt; and civilization means one to have enough money to meet his ends...just to keep him up to date in the class and company he belongs to...We fail to understand why we are given deck passages...and 3rd class in the trains...Our civilization doesn't permit us to mingle with our respectable wives and children on decks of ships and in 3rd Class coaches.[3]

TTACSA also demanded parity with Asians. As the climax of their campaign the civil servants petitioned the Colonial Office in 1927 for the same terms of service as obtained for Africans in Kenya and Zanzibar, a carefully documented protest which bought a curt reply and ended an unsuccessful agitation which nevertheless provided valuable experience for later political organisation.[4]

---

[1] Kayamba, 'Report of the Tanganyika Territory African Civil Service Association, Tanga, for 1922', TNA 3715/4.

[2] *Mambo leo*, September and December 1923, March and June 1924; Brett to CS, 18 August 1924, TNA 215/21; Madalito to CS, 18 March 1927, TNA 11051/1/A.26; SG TTACSA Tukuyu to Symes, 24 August 1932, TNA 10849/2; Ngumia to AA Dodoma, 9 March 1945, Suleiman papers, TNA; Madalito and Brenn to CS, 21 September 1926, TNA 11051/I/A.17.

[3] Madalito and Brenn to Cameron, 11 September 1925, TNA 11051/I/A.7.

[4] Madalito and Brenn to CS, 24 August 1927, and Ormsby-Gore to Cameron, 18 November 1927, TNA 11051/I/1 and 11; below, p. 407.

The Great War for Civilisation[1]

The famine was one enduring collective memory of the war. Early in the campaign food was short in towns as imports ceased, military requirements grew, and prices rose. During 1915 requisitioning and drought produced localised famine in the north-east, Ufiome, parts of Ugogo, Ulanga, and the Makonde plateau. Conditions in these areas deteriorated during 1916. Some 800 people died in that year around Luatala in the Masasi region.[2] As the demand for porters grew, so labour to cultivate land decreased. By 1917 both sides were seizing cattle at will and destroying whatever grain they could not consume. Altogether they may have commandeered about a quarter of Tanganyika's famine reserve of four million cattle.[3] As Lettow-Vorbeck withdrew from the Rufiji valley, Mahenge, and the south during 1917 he left famine behind. Yet this was only the prelude to catastrophe. It came in 1918 and was worst in Dodoma, Kondoa, and Singida, notoriously the areas most susceptible to famine. 'The whole District has been ransacked for cattle', the British district officer in Dodoma reported in December 1916. The Germans had taken 26,000 beasts, while in five months the British had procured another 5,659, plus 24,000 porters and nearly 100 tonnes of flour.[4] Requisitioning continued throughout 1917, but local officers dismissed rumours of impending disaster. Food was being collected forcibly because Gogo had no use for money, it was explained, but people were 'merely resigned' and famine was unlikely.[5] Then in November 1917 the rains failed and the whole central region, its reserves exhausted, experienced three years of *mutunya*, 'the scramble for food', the worst famine in human memory. One estimate put deaths in Dodoma district alone at 30,000, or about one person in five. Thousands emigrated. Others sold starving cattle for a shilling each in Dodoma market.[6]

'The Christians and Catechumens who survived the famine of 1915', it was reported from the Makonde plateau, 'perished of the smallpox and the coughing.'[7] Smallpox was widespread when the

[1] The phrase inscribed on First World War medals. See Ranger, *Dance*, p. 45.
[2] *Central Africa*, January 1919.
[3] McCall, 'A memorandum on the Veterinary Department', 3 November 1919, CO 691/24/306.
[4] DPO Dodoma to CPO, 28 December 1916, TNA 46/2/1; Monson, 'Memorandum on the administration of occupied territory', 1 December 1916, CO 691/4/26; DPO Dodoma to Staff Officer for Political Affairs, 15 April 1917, TNA library.
[5] DPO Dodoma to Staff Officer for Political Affairs, 29 June 1917, TNA library.
[6] Rigby, *Cattle*, pp. 21-2; Hignell, Dodoma DAR 1924, TNA library.
[7] Silvano Ngaweje in *Central Africa*, July 1929.

war ended. 'Coughing' was a Spanish influenza pandemic which killed an estimated 50,000–80,000 people in Tanganyika between 1918 and 1920.[1] Of the 1,168 askari who surrendered with Lettow-Vorbeck, 162 died of influenza. Special cemeteries were opened in Dar es Salaam. In Masasi 'every hut possessed its sufferers'. Some 15,000–20,000 people may have died in central Tukuyu district during 1918–19; the whole district contained about 180,000. The district officer tried fifteen witchcraft cases attributed to the epidemic and noted that headmen were again administering *mwavi*.[2]

The expansion of tsetse antedated the war but was doubtless accelerated by the removal of labour for porterage, the dispersal of population to escape military exactions, and the demographic consequences of war, famine, and influenza. Tsetse spread chiefly in four regions once the war ended. On the western plateau it expanded southwards into Ukimbu and converged from east and west to narrow the corridor of cultivation stretching southwards from Mwanza to Tabora. Here at Shinyanga in 1921 the British tsetse expert, C. F. M. Swynnerton, found the population 'on the run' and launched an anti-tsetse campaign.[3] The second area of expansion was the north-west. Highland Buha was taxed, drawn into the colonial economy, and led to supply migrant labour during the 1920s. Tsetse entered the area in the late 1920s. The Bugufi chiefdom, densely populated by men and cattle, was free of tsetse until rinderpest reduced its herds from 14,721 in 1928 to 5,562 in 1937. Tsetse quickly followed.[4] The third region of expansion was the north-east, where, besides continuing to spread through Uzigua and the Pangani valley, tsetse also penetrated the Masai plain.[5] The fourth and most important inter-war expansion began in the early 1920s in that central region which suffered so severely from post-war famine. 'The present position', it was reported in 1934, 'is that the comparatively small central belt of *morsitans* in Kondoa–Irangi and Singida is spreading southwards and westwards towards the great westerly fly belt, which is advancing east to meet it. The gap between is lessening year by year.' The long-established Sandawe, whose language had no word for tsetse, claimed that the

[1] Tanganyika, *Annual report of the Medical Department 1920*, p. 80.
[2] Boell, *Operationen*, p. 424; Barnes, safari diary, 5 June 1919, Barnes papers, RH; Wells, Rungwe DAR 1918–19, TNA library.
[3] Swynnerton, 'Experiment', p. 318.
[4] Veterinary report 1927, CO 691/99; Ngara district book, TNA.
[5] Sheedy to SA, 7 February 1920, CO 691/34/220.

insect was 'brought in by the English'.[1] In 1913 the Germans had estimated that one-third of German East Africa was infested; in 1924 the British set the figure at two-thirds of Tanganyika.[2]

Sleeping sickness followed a decade or two behind. In 1914 it was confined to the upper Ruvuma valley and the shores of Lakes Victoria and Tanganyika. Only a handful of men contracted the disease during the war.[3] But it was identified in Maswa in 1922,[4] Ufipa and Ungindo in 1924, southern Unyamwezi in 1925, Ukimbu in 1927, Buha in 1931, and Mkalama in 1936. Between 1922 and 1946, 23,955 cases were diagnosed in Tanganyika.[5]

In the early 1920s British authorities initiated serious measures against tsetse, rather than merely treating sleeping sickness as hitherto. The tsetse problem depended on the conjunction of men, trypanosomes, tsetse, and game which harboured flies. Theoretically the problem could be attacked at any of these four points, but drugs to combat trypanosomes were not yet available. Some, especially medical men, proposed to destroy game by letting Africans hunt freely, but critics denied (quite mistakenly) that game harboured trypanosomes dangerous to men and urged that wildlife extermination was both impossible and indefensible.[6] Others proposed to move men into settlements large enough to prevent bush regeneration, leaving the remaining land to tsetse until natural population growth permitted recolonisation. This policy was adopted when sleeping sickness epidemics occurred, but critics complained that soil erosion made concentrated settlements untenable and that they were a despairing 'trench warfare' which made ultimate recolonisation unnecessarily difficult.[7] The predominant inter-war approach, advocated by Swynnerton with vigorous support from scientists and colonial secretaries in Britain, aimed to attack the flies by 'ecological

[1] 'A further account of the anti-tsetse campaign in Tanganyika Territory' [1934] CO 691/136; Newman, *Sandawe*, p. 136.

[2] Above, p. 164; Swynnerton to CS, 20 August 1924, CO 691/72/245.

[3] *Report on medical and sanitary matters 1917*, CO 691/19/286; M. Taute, 'A German account of the medical side of the war in East Africa', *TNR*, VIII (1939), 14.

[4] And possibly in Mwanza in 1917: H. L. Duke, 'An enquiry into an outbreak of human trypanosomiasis in a *morsitans* belt to the east of Mwanza' [1922] CO 691/58/125.

[5] Ford, *Trypanosomiases*, pp. 194, 476; Clyde, *History*, pp. 122–6; Buckley, Tabora DAR 1925, TNA 1733/20/105/108; Owen, Manyoni DAR 1927, TNA library.

[6] Davey, 'Memorandum on game preservation', 16 October 1922, CO 691/57/555; Swynnerton to CO, 11 March 1923, CO 691/67/203.

[7] George Maclean, 'The relationship between economic development and Rhodesian sleeping sickness in Tanganyika Territory', *Annals of tropical medicine and parasitology*, XXIII (1929), 37–46; Swynnerton, 'Memorandum on tsetse research', February 1933, CO 691/128.

intervention'. This included experiments with grass burning, selective destruction of vegetation, and various kinds of barriers. In response to immediate tsetse expansion, Swynnerton and district officers mobilised millions of man-days of compulsory labour to cut and burn barriers in the bush. The policy had many opponents in Tanganyika. It may have checked tsetse slightly in certain areas, but their vast expansion elsewhere demonstrates its general failure.[1]

Yet for African cultivators – as for chiefs and Christians, Asians and Anglophiles – war was not only an ordeal but an opportunity. For if in his struggle with nature the cultivator had lost a battle, the European settler had lost a campaign. The bush encroaching on Shinyanga's fields already choked the north-eastern plantations. For a spell – a brief, vital spell – Tanganyika's productive economy was again in African hands.

[1] Swynnerton, 'The ecological study and control of the East African species of tsetse fly' [1935] CO 691/149 (and other papers in this file); John J. McKelvey, *Man against tsetse* (Ithaca, 1973), pp. 134–56.

CHAPTER 9

The origins of rural capitalism

Two connected processes dominated Tanganyika's economic history between the wars. One was the continuing integration of local economies into the international economy, until capitalist relationships among Africans appeared and peasant societies emerged in certain areas. The other process was regional differentiation.

It was a peculiarity of sub-Saharan Africa that capitalism and peasant societies evolved together. Peasants live in small communities, cultivate land they own or control, rely chiefly on family labour, and produce their own subsistence while also supplying larger economic systems which include non-peasants. Characteristically, peasants belong to states which exploit them, and they practise a rustic variant of their rulers' high culture.[1] Simultaneous involvement in local community and wider state distinguishes peasants both from tribesmen, whose societies are more exclusively local, and from farmers, who employ non-family labour and are chiefly concerned with the wider market. A peasant society is a society most of whose members are peasants. By this definition the coastal peoples were probably Tanganyika's only peasants before European invasion, although they retained much political autonomy. European control, taxation, acceptance of world religions, and production for the market began to extend peasant status in German times, but it was in the 1920s that peasant societies appeared inland, notably in Kilimanjaro and Buhaya. These two societies differed, because – as is the nature of peasant societies – each contained non-peasants who gave it a distinctive shape: African farmers in Kilimanjaro, African landlords and traders in Buhaya. Yet their similarities were more striking. 'Peasantisation' was a once-for-all transformation comparable in impact to industrialisa-

[1] For definitions, see John S. Saul and Roger Woods, 'African peasantries', and Robert Redfield and Milton B. Singer, 'City and countryside', in Teodor Shanin (ed.), *Peasants and peasant societies* (Harmondsworth, 1971), pp. 103–14, 337–65.

tion. Among its consequences were the new forms of political action which occurred at this time in Kilimanjaro and Buhaya. Political eruptions consequent on the successive peasantisation of Tanganyika's societies powered much of the country's political development.

Cash-crop areas joined towns and European plantations as the regions most fully integrated into the world economy. They in turn drew resources from peripheral regions supplying migrant labour and from intermediate regions supplying food and other services. This tripartite relationship supplanted Tanganyika's old division into geographical regions and remained its basic economic structure until Independence. By stimulating inter-regional exchange and rivalry, it was another source of political action.

This chapter first describes the emergence of peasant societies in Kilimanjaro and Buhaya, Tanganyika's growth points in the 1920s. After discussing other cash-crop areas and plantation agriculture, it considers labour-exporting and food-producing regions. British records are the chief sources, but literacy and political activism make contemporary African sources more widely available than before.

The emergence of peasant societies

During the 1920s coffee-growing transformed the Chagga into peasants. Kilimanjaro's volcanic soil and highland climate favoured coffee. Its sophisticated agriculture provided surplus labour. Railway transport was available, European plantations existed as a model, and coffee was an ideal peasant crop because its returns varied directly with the labour invested. Chagga pioneers had grown coffee in German times. In 1916 they owned some 100,000 trees. Rising prices after 1921 caused them to clean their plots and sell seedlings to imitators. Ideas passed quickly among close-packed Chagga homesteads. By 1925 there were 6,716 Chagga coffee growers with 987,175 trees. Five years later there were nearly six million trees.[1]

Coffee-growing divided the Chagga. Rombo, on the eastern slopes, was too dry for optimum production and supplied agricultural labour after other Chagga ceased to work for Europeans. Certain chiefdoms adopted coffee more enthusiastically than others. Possibly because of missionary discouragement, the average coffee plot in Moshi, a

[1] Above, p. 154; Dundas, 'Native coffee cultivation on Kilimanjaro', 12 May 1924, CO 691/70/379; Clark, Moshi DAR 1925, TNA 1733/14/92/5; Pennington to PC Northern, 23 September 1930, TNA 13060/100.

pioneer area, was only 500 square metres in 1930, while in Kibosho, where land was short and coffee scarcely grown before 1920, it was 4,600 square metres.[1] Differentiation among individuals also resulted. In 1930 only one man in three grew coffee. Of those who did, 96 per cent owned less than a thousand coffee trees, normally planted among the bananas in their *vihamba*. The remainder – probably less than 500 men – owned nearly a hectare or more of coffee, often growing it in distinct plantations with hired labour.[2] These emerging capitalists belonged to two groups. Some were established leaders. Chiefs inherited large landholdings and in the early 1920s commanded tributary labour. Shangali Ndeserua, retired Chief of Machame, was among the largest growers in 1932, with 12,682 trees.[3] Other prominent men possessed several *vihamba* where personal retainers had previously lived. These could be planted with coffee. The second group of farmers were educated Christians like Joseph Merinyo, the district office interpreter who popularised coffee-growing in the 1920s.[4] Christians had access to European aid and were often receptive to change, while some planted coffee on spare *vihamba* inherited from polygynous fathers.

Coffee-growing bred tension and conflict. Unwritten Chagga law was vague, contentious, and mutable. It assumed that every married man should have a *kihamba* for each wife. Most men inherited *vihamba* on clan land, but in German times chiefs had acquired power to allocate unoccupied *vihamba*. Coffee farmers rarely acquired land by allocation. Instead they encroached on their neighbours' uncultivated plots, enclosed and cultivated theoretically communal pasture, opened new land on the cold upper slopes, or planted grain on lower *shamba* land to free *vihamba* for coffee. Around 1927 they began to buy and sell land, demanding written titles and claiming that freehold tenure was Chagga 'tradition'.[5] As land values increased and the law became a lottery, ambitious men realised that unless they grabbed a share immediately none would be left. Disputes multiplied in local courts.[6] Other changes exacerbated tension. Before 1914 one Chagga had rarely worked for another unless he owed him political allegiance, but in the 1920s capitalist relations became increasingly common.

[1] Pennington to PC Northern, 23 September 1930, TNA 13060/100.
[2] A. W. M. Griffith, 'Chagga land tenure report', typescript, 1930, Cory papers, ULD.
[3] *Uremi*, August 1932.   [4] Rogers, 'Political focus', pp. 235–9.
[5] See Griffith, 'Chagga land tenure'; Clemm, 'White mountain', ch. 15.
[6] Merinyo to Hilton Young Commission, 23 February 1928, TNA 11200/18; P. S. Maro, 'Population and land resources in northern Tanzania: the dynamics of change 1920–1970', Ph.D. thesis, University of Minnesota, 1974, p. 174.

'Important men are no longer prepared to give anything to help the weak as they once were', Filipo Njau complained, 'for they see that amongst the weak every man relies on his employer, be he white or black.'[1] Local trade flourished. 'Everywhere along the road one saw small shops where tea or coffee were supplied, fresh meat sold, or ripe fruit offered for purchase', a visitor wrote in 1925, the year when Chagga traders began to form a Native Shopkeepers Association.[2] Moreover, the Chagga were becoming peasants in a political and cultural sense through subordination to government and acceptance of world religions. There were 10,980 professing Christians on Kilimanjaro in 1922. A missionary noticed children dressed in mock surplices playing at preaching, baptising, and hymn-singing.[3]

This ferment took place while chiefs, whom peace had freed from the democratic restraints of age-grade organisation, still had power to whip their subjects. It also occurred when European settlers were still consolidating their influence. Purchasers of former German farms faced angry disputes over boundaries and wartime encroachments. They loudly demanded further alienation and Kilimanjaro's transfer to European-dominated Kenya. Coffee-growing increased these antagonisms. Settlers protested that African coffee would spread disease, devalue the local product, and encourage theft from European farms. Privately they feared that it would harm their labour supply. In 1923 they formed a Kilimanjaro Planters Association and demanded that Chagga should be forbidden to grow coffee.[4]

To allay European fears, the district officer suggested that the growers should combine to buy spraying equipment. Merinyo championed the idea and a *wakili* was selected in each chiefdom to list coffee-growers in an exercise book and collect an annual shilling from each. Needing a central body to manage the funds, the *wakili* met on 15 January 1925 and formed the Kilimanjaro Native Planters Association. Merinyo soon became president and Stefano Lema secretary. To bypass Asian buyers the *wakili* began to collect and bulk coffee for shipment to Britain, where a European firm marketed it on commission, paying a 50 per cent advance on the anticipated price and a

---

[1] Filipo Njau to Gutmann, 3 April 1921, in Gutmann, *Briefe*, p. 10.
[2] Johanssen, *Führung*, iii, 96; Rogers, 'Political focus', p. 289.
[3] Dundas, Moshi DAR 1922, TNA 1733/22/1; Raum, *Childhood*, pp. 257–8.
[4] Stuart-Watt, *Dome of mystery*, pp. 110, 129; Rydon to Baldwin, 11 November 1924, CO 691/75/258; Pennington, 'KNPA' [February 1931] TNA 13060/203.

second payment after sale. By 1927 the KNPA had become the nucleus of a marketing cooperative.[1]

Since crop marketing is a peasant society's main connection with the larger polity and market of which it is part, the marketing system often forms an important framework for political organisation. This is a recurrent distinction between peasant and tribal societies and is one reason why cash-crop agriculture was so important to Tanganyika's political history. The KNPA quickly evolved into a new kind of political body. Its leaders were chiefly coffee farmers. Merinyo was a large grower, as was the chairman, Joseph Maliti of Machame. Stefano Lema owned a lorry in which coffee was transported, while committee members included Sawaya Mawalla of Marangu, the pioneer who in 1930 owned twenty hectares of coffee.[2] The farmers' interests brought them into conflict with the coalition of administrators, settlers, and chiefs who controlled Moshi district. In 1927, under settler pressure, government decided to discourage African cultivation of arabica coffee. This policy was not fully implemented on Kilimanjaro, but food crops were given priority there and an unsuccessful attempt was made to limit individual holdings to a thousand trees, 'to encourage a small peasant proprietor class in preference to one of native employers'.[3] Moreover, a new district officer with a South African background, Captain Hallier, regarded the KNPA as corrupt and pretentious and sought an opportunity to destroy it. Tension now escalated. Early in 1928 a commision visited Moshi to investigate the possibility of uniting the three East African territories. It met the KNPA and revived fears of settler domination. Later in 1928 government reopened Kilimanjaro's lower slopes to alienation. These issues became linked with growing competition for land. Early in 1927, it appears, Chagga farmers began to buy and sell coffee land. The chiefs urged Hallier to ban land sales. He agreed, but added that allotments to young men should in future be accurately demarcated. Claiming that landholdings were to be measured and restricted, KNPA leaders roused clan elders who resented the chiefs' control of land. 'Even in regard to future holdings', government later explained, 'there was strong opposition among the Elders to what they under-

[1] Minutes in R. J. M. Swynnerton and A. L. B. Bennett, *All about 'KNCU' coffee* (Moshi, 1948), p. 11; Pennington, 'KNPA' [February 1931] TNA 13060/203.

[2] 'Mkutano wa K.N.P.A. ulikuwa hapa Moshi siku ya 8th June [19]30', TNA 19126/1/3; Hallier to PC Northern, 10 October 1928, TNA 12809/22; Griffith, 'Chagga land tenure'.

[3] Clark, Moshi DAR 1925, TNA 1733/14/92/5.

stood was a proposal actually to measure an allotment to be made. To the other misconceptions of the tribesmen was added the mistaken belief that land was to be taken from individuals and restored to the Chiefs.'[1] During October 1928 there were noisy meetings where KNPA activists led crowds in shouting down the chiefs' henchmen. This enabled Hallier to demand the KNPA's abolition as 'a redundant body and potentially a political danger' profiting only the 'Young Chagga Planters...[who] wish to set up their own authority to suit their own ends and grab all the land they can'. The provincial commissioner confirmed that 'The Association is undermining the authority of the Native Authorities and...two powers exist in the land. I consider therefore that the KNPA should cease to exist forthwith.'[2] The settlers noisily agreed, while a KNPA mass meeting discussed a boycott of settler farms. 'It is like the maji-maji rebellion', Samwil Chiponde reported.[3]

Heads were cooler in Dar es Salaam. 'Largely a creation of Capt. Hallier's mind', the Governor observed.[4] Anxious to keep the chiefs out of coffee marketing and to use the KNPA to combat disease and settler attacks, he replaced Hallier and ordered that KNPA and chiefs should be reconciled. This proved delusively easy: farmers affirmed their loyalty while chiefs temporarily abandoned any hopes of taking over the KNPA.[5] It was a political victory for the association. 'Continuous opposition has developed in the members a strong corporate spirit', an official wrote two years later. '...There is no doubt that the vast majority of the individual native coffee growers feel that but for the existence of the KNPA they would have been forbidden to grow coffee long ago.' 'Not that this is a feeling to which I should take exception', the Governor noted.[6]

Yet the KNPA did not long survive its victory. First it was reorganised in April 1929 at government insistence. Membership was made compulsory for coffee growers in order to facilitate the registration of plots, but members were not obliged to sell through the association. Subscriptions were replaced by a levy which proved difficult to collect and undermined the KNPA's finances. Thus weakened, the association was then destroyed during a new crisis.

[1] CS to de la Mothe, 4 January 1929, in *Tanganyika Times*, 12 January 1929.
[2] Hallier to PC Northern, 10 October 1928, and Webster to CS, 20 October 1928, TNA 12809/22 and 16.
[3] Quoted in Dundas, minute, 8 November 1928, TNA 12809/54.
[4] Cameron, minute, 12 November 1928, TNA 12809/57.
[5] Dundas to CS, 27 November 1928, TNA 13060/8.
[6] Pennington to PC Northern, 23 October 1930, and Cameron on this, TNA 13060/125.

Coffee had tied the Chagga to the fluctuations of the world market. In 1929 it collapsed during the international depression. Between 1929 and 1931 Chagga coffee fell from £70 to £29 per tonne. The initial collapse occurred after KNPA members had received their first payment for the 1929–30 crop. When the final price proved less than the first payment, the KNPA became indebted to its London agents when its finances were already in disarray. A levy was imposed on members to cover the debt, but meanwhile the association lost any bargaining power with the agents. This further reduced prices, so that in 1931 growers sold much coffee to private Chagga and Asian businessmen. Still embittered by defeat in 1928, local administrators seized the opportunity to 'discredit J[oseph] M[erinyo] in the eyes of the Chagga'.[1] Investigation provided evidence that Merinyo had embezzled KNPA funds. During his imprisonment the government transformed the association into Tanganyika's first cooperative society, the Kilimanjaro Native Cooperative Union.[2]

Although the KNCU later became a model of African progress for people throughout Tanganyika, its early years were racked by controversy. Unlike the KNPA it was at first seen by the Chagga as a government institution. It was accused of Roman Catholic domination, it was closely supervised by an official registrar, it had a European manager, it was deliberately decentralised and depoliticised, and it was commonly thought to be controlled by chiefs, especially by Chief Abdiel Shangali of Machame, whose energy, progressive aims, and government favour made him the spearhead of the official campaign to control the emerging Chagga capitalists. Moreover, the KNCU monopolised the Chagga coffee crop on the insecure legal foundation of a rule made by the chiefs under the Native Authority Ordinance. It was a natural target for hostility from growers angered by low prices and from Asian and African traders.[3]

In 1935 these discontents coalesced into a new crisis. It again began with a fall in world coffee prices, caused by Brazil flooding the market. When the KNCU made no second payment during 1935 growers accused it of mismanagement, corruption, and extravagance. Late in that year several primary societies tried to elect new officers, notably in Machame where the dissident leaders were personal opponents of Chief Abdiel. These 'ringleaders' were generally substantial coffee

[1] PC Northern to CS, 25 August 1931, TNA 26034/39.
[2] Susan G. Rogers, 'The Kilimanjaro Native Planters Association', *TJH*, IV (1974), 101–9.
[3] *Ibid.*, pp. 109–11; Griffith, 'Chagga land tenure'.

growers who had other occupations as teachers, masons, carpenters, tailors, shopkeepers, or lorry-owners – the last two categories being especially hostile to the KNCU's policies of bulking the crop at chiefdom level and then giving the transport contract to an Asian. Late in 1935 agitation crystallised into a demand to abolish the cooperative's monopoly and 'to be allowed to sell their coffee as they like'.[1] On Merinyo's advice the dissidents hired a lawyer. Quasi-secret meetings collected funds and much small-scale intimidation took place. In May 1936 government and chiefs began to arrest dissidents for holding unauthorised meetings. A few 'ringleaders' were deported. In July 1937 the Acting Governor visited Moshi, threatened the dissidents, but insisted that the KNCU belonged to the Chagga to make or break.

When the High Court dismissed the dissidents' case in September 1937 they responded by attempting to close, and if necessary destroy, the primary societies' premises:

The agitators...said that if they will not be allowed to close their Societies, they will later demolish them at all. They went back to Machame and break almost all Societies buildings...Mr. Miler was sent over with some asikaris from Police Moshi. They went, when they arrived at Machame they saw big crowd of the people about 5,000, singing hymns it was bad confusion...it was funny and foolish act, for they wouldn't say why they had broken those go downs, nor could they express their feelings. They brought their children and wives put them in front and asked the Provincial Commissioner to fire them up. They behaved like mad people...On the 18/9/37 at 4.30 a.m. news came that the East Marangu Co-operative Society has been broken...we found that the house has been hammered properly balance shattered to bits, but safe with 2000/- was safe...My nephew is at Machame with Mr. Miler to fight the rebels.[2]

That day two R.A.F. aeroplanes flew over Marangu. Government and chiefs pursued 'ringleaders' remorselessly. Thirteen were deported by the end of October. 'We feel', the Acting Governor reported, 'that the real interests of the progressive and politically minded Chagga will best be served if no consideration is shown to those who attempt to foment trouble behind closed doors and we hope to check with every means at our disposal the intrusion of European ideas in so far as these encourage the formation of political or semi-political associations.'[3]

The crisis of 1937 was not only a vivid example of peasant action,

[1] *A report on the Kilimanjaro Native Cooperative Union* (Legislative Council sessional paper no. 4 of 1937), p. 9. See also Atkinson and others to Macdonald, 3 October 1938, CO 691/168; Rogers, 'Political focus', pp. 580–8, 603–7, 620–31, 652.
[2] Petro Itosi Marealle to Vickers-Haviland, 12 October 1937, Vickers-Haviland papers, RH.
[3] Kennedy to Bottomley, 15 April 1937, CO 691/156.

but in Tanganyika's wider history it was both the nadir of African impotence and an important advance in political consciousness. Gone was the inter-chiefdom intrigue of German times. Instead the chiefs of Machame and Marangu, ancient rivals, allied against 'rebels' whose experience of lawyers, courts, and public subscriptions was to be passed on to a sequence of later political actions.[1] But gone too was any hope of defeating the colonial regime. The rebels of 1905 had still hoped to destroy their rulers, even if they needed *maji* to do it, but the dissidents of 1937 launched a self-sacrificial protest to persuade their rulers. They 'brought their children and wives...and asked the Provincial Commissioner to fire them up'. As peasants, the Chagga had become more dependent than their fathers, but also more realistic. Yet like other peasants they only partly comprehended the source of their wrongs, attacking the local institutions which they could reach rather than the government or the world market which they either could not touch or did not understand. It was a 'funny and foolish act' indeed, for the demonstrators unwittingly acted against their own real interests and chiefly to the advantage of their non-peasant leaders. When in doing so they also sang hymns, they behaved as a peasantry. Coffee trees and catechists had made them so.

Buhaya also witnessed riots during 1937. Fundamentally similar in origin to those on Kilimanjaro, they were nevertheless subtly different in character. Haya remembered the 1920s as the *otandibatira*, the years of 'do not tread on', meaning 'do not tread on my land or my coffee'.[2] Two million coffee trees were planted during 1923 alone,[3] and after 1925, when prices reached new heights, coffee planting became a collective obsession. A missionary observed that Haya men had never worked so hard before.[4] By 1928 more than half the 80,000 taxpayers in Bukoba district grew coffee. Their 7,973 tonnes exported entirely dwarfed the 314 tonnes sold by the Chagga.[5] In the lakeshore chiefdoms near Bukoba the land available was almost entirely occupied, but motor transport enabled coffee-growing to spread southwards into Ihangiro and, to a small extent, westwards into the highlands of Karagwe. By 1936 several major coffee areas were no longer self-sufficient in bananas. The period brought great prosperity.

---

[1] Below, p. 490.   [2] Information from Mr K. M. Kiwanuka.
[3] McMillen, Bukoba DAR 1923, TNA 215/77/6.
[4] Césard, 'Le Muhaya' (1936), p. 97.
[5] O'Brien to DA, 13 January 1928, TNA 11969/I/3; Austen, *Northwest Tanzania*, p. 271; *Kilimanjaro Native Cooperative Union Limited: twenty-ninth annual report 1960–1961* (Moshi, 1961).

'A better dressed crowd I never saw in Africa', an experienced official observed after attending a ceremony there.[1] Education, Islam, and Christianity also spread rapidly. In 1921 there were 12,383 baptised Roman Catholics in the Bukoba diocese; in 1936, 53,445.[2] The Haya had become a peasantry.

Yet Buhaya's peasant society differed from Kilimanjaro's, for three reasons. First, wage-labour was more common in Buhaya, because, unlike the Chagga, the Haya were surrounded by remote, impoverished, overpopulated regions whose inhabitants accepted wages so low that even small producers could afford them. By 1924 at least 20,000 *bashuti* from Burundi, Bugufi, Biharamulo, and Karagwe worked on Haya coffee farms. They earned only four shillings a month, plus food, but relations with their employers were some way from the impersonal cash-nexus of European plantations, for they lived as squatters in the banana groves, often ate food cooked by their employers' wives, and were free to leave at will. They cultivated land, cut firewood, peeled bananas, picked coffee, carried it to buying centres, and even carried their employers to church on Sundays.[3] Twenty years earlier many Haya had worked for Ganda masters. Now they were themselves the masters. Partly as a result, large coffee farmers were more numerous in Buhaya than Kilimanjaro. By 1935 especially wealthy growers might produce three tonnes a year. Land sales had also advanced further in Buhaya, for they were common by 1924.[4] This rural capitalism contrasted sharply with the pre-war situation, when normally only political power had commanded labour. The contrast had two facets. On the one hand, capitalist relations were accompanied and made possible by the weakening of quasi-feudal relationships previously existing between aristocrats and commoners. On the other, emerging capitalism was strongly coloured by pre-capitalist survivals. The coffee-grower borne to church on his *mushuti*'s shoulders might once have borne his chief on his own shoulders.

Quasi-feudal relations were weakened by the abolition of tribute. As agriculture was commercialised, the tribute paid to Haya chiefs became less a redistribution system and more a source of personal wealth. An investigation in 1920 showed that each subject was

---

[1] Mitchell to Cameron, 5 June 1930, TNA 13284/14.
[2] Baines, Bukoba DAR 1921, TNA 215/77/5; Donald Attwater, *The White Fathers in Africa* (London, 1937), p. 112.
[3] Kitching, Biharamulo DAR 1924, TNA 215/77/13.
[4] Northcote, 'Report on Bukoba coffee marketing', October 1936, TNA 215/1410; White to CS, 15 November 1928, TNA 11884/1/21.

required to supply the produce of one coffee tree, loads of groundnuts and beans and grain, bananas selected by the chief's cook, pepper and barkcloth and beer, and a month's work each year.[1] Chiefs also received a proportion of the tax they collected. In 1925 government replaced tributary labour by an obligation to work on undertakings of public utility, and tribute in kind by increased tax. The chiefs still benefited enormously. In 1927 Kalemera of Kianja, with only 20,000–25,000 taxpaying subjects but an income of £2,773 a year, earned more than the Kabaka of Buganda. 'Their extravagance is deplorable and futile', an official complained; 'large automobiles, expensive lounge suits and Paris dresses for their wives, large households and lavish largess and gifts to favourites'.[2] But direct control of labour was broken. Meanwhile *nyarubanja* land tenure was also changing. When the first British officials ordered all such holdings to be listed, pen and paper as usual distorted unwritten custom in favour of the literate. Chiefs who compiled the registers included as their *nyarubanja* tenants many who subsequently claimed to have been free cultivators. By 1922 the registers showed 2,139 *nyarubanja* owners and 9,605 tenants, the bulk being in Kianja and Kiziba, the pioneer coffee areas. Thereafter the spread of coffee-growing and the abolition of tribute made *nyarubanja* a subject of intense conflict. In 1925 the British freed tenants from tributary labour but forbade owners to evict those who did not work for them. Tenants promptly refused to work and *nyarubanja* owners protested vociferously. Four years later the governor imposed a settlement. The owner was to pay government between five and twenty shillings each year and receive a share of his tenants' bananas and coffee, but no free labour was to be demanded and no new *nyarubanja* created. New registers compiled in 1938 reduced the number of owners to 1,718 and tenants to 6,821. The settlement improved the lot of the tenants, but conflict between them and landlords festered throughout British rule.[3]

Thus Buhaya's hierarchical traditions made its peasant society more sharply differentiated than Kilimanjaro's and its internal conflicts more intense. Another feature differentiating the regions was that there were no European settlers in Buhaya, so that its coffee did not

[1] McMillen to Bakama, 4 February 1920, TNA 215/50.
[2] Dundas to Cameron [1927?] TNA 10952/1.
[3] J. L. Fairclough, 'Nyarubanja in the Bukoba district. Historical note' (1938), in Bukoba district book, TNA; correspondence in TNA 11884/1–11; Cameron to Amery, 18 May 1929, CO 691/104; J. L. Fairclough, 'Report on nyarubanja system of land tenure in the Bukoba district', typescript [1937?] Cory papers, ULD.

need the protection against European opposition which led the
Chagga to form the KNPA. Lack of a communal marketing organisation meant that individual Haya traders became the agents or
competitors of Asian merchants. When a politico-commercial organisation was eventually formed, therefore, it embraced not producers
but traders. Haya coffee-marketing was a remarkable undertaking.
Robusta – later used for powdered instant coffee – was a low-quality
product consumed chiefly in the Middle East. It was sold through
Mombasa by Asian and European firms with agents in Bukoba who
employed hundreds of small shopkeepers and itinerant traders to
collect coffee from growers. As elsewhere in Tanganyika these petty
traders were known as *wachuruzi*, 'tricklers', a word with the
implication of blood seeping from a wound. They bought on
commission or credit. One practice was to slaughter a cow in a village
and sell the joints for parcels of coffee. The price was the same
whatever the quality. Good coffee was adulterated to increase its
weight, although this was seldom necessary because much was hulled
by grinding on rocky outcrops. There were between five and seven
thousand *wachuruzi* in Buhaya in the 1920s, most of them also coffee
growers.[1] Mobile, often Muslim, dependent on official policy for their
livelihood, and in antagonistic relations with Asians, they were natural
political pioneers:

It was...in these circumstances, Ali [Migeyo] thinks, that his awareness of
politics was born...One day Ali was called by Omwami Kaishemuntu, the local
headman, and told that he would not be allowed to buy the coffee from the
people that day. The Mukungu brought his chair and sat exactly at the spot
where Ali had slaughtered his cow...Ali decided to take the matter up with
Suedi Kagasheki, who was running a teahouse in Bukoba Town. There...he
came to learn of the existence of the Bukoba Bahaya Union as an association
which could help him.[2]

The Bukoba Bahaya Union had been formed by Haya clerks in 1924
in imitation of TTACSA. It opposed the chiefs on the *nyarubanja* issue
and demanded an educated paramount chief to unify Buhaya as the
Kabaka unified Buganda. By the 1930s the association was dominated
by traders, either Muslims like Suedi Kagasheki who had prospered
in the *otandibatira* or clerks who had invested their savings in business.
One of the latter was the leading figure, Clemens Kiiza, who in 1931
built a coffee-hulling factory in Kyamutwara. For this he needed a

[1] Northcote, 'Report on Bukoba coffee marketing', October 1936, TNA 215/1410; SAO
Northwest to DA, 15 January 1929, TNA 215/71/A/50.
[2] Mutahaba, *Portrait*, p. 16.

regular supply of coffee, so in 1935 he used the Bukoba Bahaya Union as the nucleus of a Native Growers Association to supply coffee.[1]

When riots took place in Buhaya in 1937, government blamed them squarely on the traders who led the Bukoba Bahaya Union (then known as the African Association) and there is little reason to dispute this, although other members of the association disowned the radicals. To their demands for a paramount chief, more education, and the abolition of *nyarubanja* were added government's refusal to assist the Native Growers Association, attempts to rationalise coffee-trading by reducing licensed African traders from 5,600 in 1929 to 800 in 1936, and official acquiescence in the direct coffee-buying from peasants by Asian lorry-owners which began in 1936.[2] The opportunity for protest was given by new coffee rules which the administration forced on the chiefs and began to implement in January 1937. At a meeting at the native authority headquarters in Rwamishenye a crowd chose eight representatives who were arrested for shouting down the chiefs explaining the rules. Their trial a fortnight later was broken up by several hundred armed men who 'did not wish the accused persons to be tried as they had represented the people'. Protests reaching government concentrated on two points. First, the new rules threatened agricultural prosperity by empowering agricultural officers to order the cutting of banana plants or coffee trees, by forbidding the planting of coffee without the chief's permission, and by ordering that diseased coffee trees should be burned. 'We do not plant coffee for fire but to get profit', the protesters insisted, 'and burning is not the cure of coffee plant disease... We did not grow coffee to become afterwards as a trap to fall in but we grow it on the sake of getting profit and become rich and prosperous... We do not need to be taught how to grow coffee or banana trees or to stop from growing anything on our shambas or on our soil.' The dissidents' second claim was that by accepting the rules without consulting the people the chiefs had again demonstrated the need for more representative government. When the administration decided to force entry into coffee plots in Bukara, an African Association agent from Kianja, Eustace Bagwarwa, organised resistance by a crowd armed with spears. The police dispersed them and arrested the leaders. A week later Chief Kalemera of Kianja was jeered by an audience at the notoriously dissident

---

[1] Austen, *Northwest Tanzania*, pp. 163–5, 216–24; Philibert Rwehumbiza, 'Clemens Kiiza', seminar paper, University of Dar es Salaam, 1970.
[2] Northcote, 'Report', October 1936, TNA 215/1410.

trading settlement in Kamachumu. Next day a police baton charge dispersed a crowd there.[1] Thereafter protests quickly subsided. A few African Association members spent brief spells in gaol. The association went underground for several years. The Native Growers Association collapsed and Kiiza lost his hulling licence. Chiefs also suffered. The two worst were deposed, while others, notably Kalemera, survived only a few more years. Yet chieftainship itself was strengthened. 'The Haya were again required to perform unpaid labor', Dr Austen explains, 'and the new Provincial Commissioner was happy to witness the reintroduction of bowing and saluting during his tour of the district.'[2]

Buhaya's riots differed from Kilimanjaro's. In Buhaya there was no cooperative organisation to attract discontent, and local property was not attacked. Instead, in Buhaya's hierarchical society protest quickly crystallised into a direct assault on the chiefs' acquiescence in government measures. Yet despite this difference the riots bore the marks of peasant action in their concern for the inviolability of holdings, their reliance on rumour, their determination to prevent the victimisation of spokesmen, their indifference to old political boundaries, their organisation along lines of social division, their orientation towards the interests of the non-peasant members of society, and their quality as demonstrations rather than serious contests of power. Much indeed had changed in the forty years since Kiziba's warriors had died defending their chief's palace against German troops.[3]

Cash crops and social change

Although peasant societies evolved most fully in Kilimanjaro and Buhaya during the 1920s, that decade saw the beginnings of African export production in several other regions. Crops introduced in German times spread again once markets were reopened. In 1923 Sukuma cotton production first exceeded its 1913 figure of 3,714 bales.[4] Coffee was the boom crop of the period. After 1926 it spread among the Nyakyusa, who had grown very small quantities in German times. Meru and Arusha began to cultivate coffee in the early 1920s, Shambaa around 1921, the Hangaza of Bugufi in 1924–5, the Nyiha

---

[1] Flynn to PC Lake, 18 February and 8 March 1937, and 'The native coffee growers of Bukoba district' to MacMichael, 4 March 1937, TNA 215/1445/1, 10, 60.

[2] Austen, *Northwest Tanzania*, p. 229.

[3] Kalben, 'Gefechtsbericht über das Gefecht mit Sultan Mutatembwa von Kisiba am 18. Juli 1895', RKA 286/154.

[4] Austen, *Northwest Tanzania*, pp. 271–2.

and Matengo by 1928.[1] Tobacco was also pioneered in this period in Ungoni (1928) and Buzinza (1931).[2]

There were five main reasons why these innovations succeeded while others failed. First, the environment obviously had to suit the crop. Well-watered highlands generally proved most suitable, so that economic growth points moved back from the plains – through which the nineteenth-century trade routes had run – to older regions of cultural leadership. Status reversal followed in several areas. Men from Karagwe worked on Haya coffee estates, while Ngoni cultivated coffee for formerly dependent Matengo.[3] But not all highland areas prospered. Coffee grew better in volcanic soils – even the wind-blown volcanic ash of Mbozi – than in the shallow, acidic soil of Usambara. Cash crops also required surplus labour and land so that they would not interfere unduly with the subsistence economy. Labour was most easily available where the staple crop was bananas. Cotton was hampered in Sukumaland by needing to be planted at the same time as grain. Land was generally easily available at this time, although shortage was beginning to constrain cash-crop production in Meru and Bugufi as well as Kilimanjaro and Buhaya.[4]

The third determinant of cash-crop success was the availability of transport. The Uganda railway carried Haya coffee and Sukuma cotton, while the Tanga line served the Shambaa, Chagga, Meru, and Arusha coffee crops. By contrast, to transport coffee from Mbinga to the coast cost twice as much as shipping it thence to Europe.[5] The crucial interwar innovation was motor transport. For this, as the figures in table 11 show, the 1920s were the take-off years. By 1926 head porterage had almost disappeared from Tanga, Tabora, Singida, and Mwanza districts.[6] Tanganyika's first African lorry owners were the

[1] Tetzlaff, *Entwicklung*, p. 274; Thompson to CS, 29 August 1929, TNA 13205/1/48; Kirby to CS, 28 March and 14 April 1928, TNA 11160/24 and 29; McMillen to CS, 12 February 1924, TNA 215/21/3; Haarer to DA, 10 December 1928, TNA 13205/1/3; Matengo tour book p. 249, TNA 155/1.

[2] Northcote and McGregor, 'Report on the Songea tobacco industry', 12 August 1940, TNA 155/COOP/27; CS to PC Iringa, 4 January 1935, TNA 77/2/44/10.

[3] McMillen, Bukoba DAR 1923, TNA 215/77/6; John B. M. Newa, 'The Ndendeule struggle against Ngoni feudalism and British imperialism', B.A. thesis, University College, Dar es Salaam, 1970, p. 94.

[4] 'Memorandum by the Tanganyika African Association Arusha on the proposed redistribution of land in Arusha district' [October 1946] TNA 69/913/110; Brett to SAO Mwanza, 1 March 1936, TNA 197/5/3/298.

[5] Matengo tour book p. 252, TNA 155/1.

[6] Harrington, Tanga DAR 1926, TNA library; Buckley, Tabora PAR 1926, TNA 1733/9/69/7; Flynn, Singida DAR 1927, TNA library; Stiebel, Mwanza PAR 1926, TNA 1733/11/80/1.

The origins of rural capitalism

chiefs of Kibosho and Keni on Kilimanjaro and Clemens Kiiza and another entrepreneur in Buhaya, who all bought vehicles in 1926.[1] Lorries greatly extended the area in which cash crops could be grown profitably. Small coffee crops in Bugufi and Mbinga became barely viable. Cotton-growing spread along the newly-built roads of Sukumaland. Toy cars and lorries became the craze among Chagga children.[2] Just as the porter had carried the caravan trade on his shoulders and the railway had drawn the colonial economy behind it, so in the late 1920s the peasant came to Tanganyika on the back of a lorry.

Table 11. *Value of motor spirit imports, selected years, 1920–48*

1920	£12,328
1923	£8,778
1929	£150,197
1938	£175,583
1948	£591,481

SOURCES: Tanganyika, *Blue books*, 1922, p. 70; 1923, pp. 78–9; 1929, p. 110; 1938, pp. 166–7; 1948, pp. 218–19.

The fourth element in cash-crop success was the role of Europeans, Asians, and Africans from more developed regions. Private Europeans were important chiefly as models to imitate and as suppliers of seed. Missionaries gave Nyakyusa their first coffee seed. Together with European settlers they also provided the seed for pioneer Chagga and Shambaa coffee-growers. Meru first cultivated coffee on European estates regained after the First World War. An Asian settler first grew cotton in the Musoma area, while an Arab, Salim bin Najum, was the first large-scale rice planter in Rungwe,[3] but the Asians' normal role was to stimulate new crops by buying them. Successful African planters also acted as models. The first non-European coffee growers in Arusha were Somali traders. The Pare adopted coffee from the

[1] Rogers, 'Political focus', p. 330; Vickers-Haviland, Bukoba DAR 1926, TNA 215/77/A/4.
[2] Longland, 'Report on native labour in gold mining areas: interim report no. 2', 4 December 1935, TNA 23047/1; Raum, *Childhood*, p. 284.
[3] 'Rungwe Cooperative Union, Ltd: first annual report 1949–50', TNA 176/47/17/II/244; above, p. 154; Bruce to DA, 20 March 1930, TNA 18996/1k; Sturdy to SAO Northeast, 26 November 1930, TNA 472/ASS/12/1; *RTA*, 1907/9, no. 622, p. 3,703; *RTA*, 1897/8, no. 94, p. 946.

288

Chagga, as did the Matengo, while Chagga instructors encouraged coffee-growing in Bugufi.[1]

The colonial governments' attitude to cash-crop growing varied in different situations. The British followed German practice in strongly pressing the Sukuma to grow cotton. They also encouraged tobacco in Songea and Biharamulo. The desire to end labour migration led officials in Bugufi to enforce coffee cultivation so strongly that many Hangaza long believed that the government owned their coffee trees.[2] Yet such vigorous encouragement was not universal. Policy was first to prevent famine by insisting on adequate food cultivation and then 'to induce the native to become a producer directly or indirectly, that is, to produce or to assist in producing something more than the crop of local foodstuffs that he requires for the sustenance of himself and his family'.[3] Africans were to choose whether to produce a food surplus, a cash crop , or to work for an employer. The administration was theoretically neutral, but in practice neutrality was rarely possible, for employers clamoured for labour while African cultivators clamoured for assistance. In the north-east government made a 'gentleman's agreement' with sisal planters not to encourage cash crops in order to safeguard the supply of food and labour.[4] The dilemma was especially difficult with regard to coffee, for most African growers (except in Buhaya) were highlanders in close proximity to Europeans who insisted, as on Kilimanjaro, that African coffee would spread disease, impair quality, encourage theft, and reduce the labour supply. From 1927 to 1932 government encouraged robusta but refused to assist Africans to grow arabica except on Kilimanjaro, where it was already established.[5] Government therefore pressed robusta in Bugufi, Rungwe, Mbinga, and Buha where arabica was better suited and more desired by the people. In 1926 the governor undertook to 'throw cold water' on the endeavours of Meru and Arusha to grow arabica. 'A policy of non-encouragement...without prohibition' was also followed in Usambara. 'Coffee: Policy, not to encourage it. Ngaka Society (still unregistered) to be abolished', an official

---

1 Rohde to Government, 11 October 1913, TNA G8/176/21; Dundas, 1 February 1926, on Clark, Moshi DAR 1925, TNA 1733/14/92/5; Matengo tour book p. 249, TNA 155/1; Brett to SAO Mwanza, 13 December 1934, TNA 197/5/3/316.
2 Hill to Biharamulo, 28 April 1936, TNA 197/5/3/307.
3 Cameron, 'Agriculture and labour', 5 September 1926, TNA 215/121/48.
4 Scupham to Tanga, December 1938, TNA 26298/v/1/4; E. K. Lumley, *Forgotten Mandate: a British district officer in Tanganyika* (London, 1976), pp. 68–70.
5 CS to PCs, 20 December 1927, TNA 11160/15a.

noted in Mbinga.[1] In Buha and Upare complete disapproval was shown:

An Agricultural Officer from Same came to North Pare in about 1935 and ordered the uprooting of coffee and destruction of nurseries. He and his instructors destroyed all nurseries, and a lot of bearing coffee trees were uprooted all over the coffee growing areas. To those whom he felt sympathy with their shambas he ordered them to pay Shs. 1/-. . . The growers were not told the reason for doing so.[2]

Yet the fact that this complaint came from Pare coffee growers shows that government policy was rarely decisive in determining success or failure. 'The trouble is that native coffee needs no encouragement', an agricultural officer complained. '. . . The area of Native coffee in Arusha is increasing against all the discouragement it is possible for my Department to give.' His colleague in Mbinga had the same problem: 'Whether Government assists, "discourages" or ignores coffee they are determined to plant coffee, and to plant Arabica coffee.'[3] And plant it they did. The trees multiplied. The Ngaka Society flourished.

For as in Buhaya and Kilimanjaro a powerful thrust of indigenous entrepreneurship lay behind cash-crop growing. Entrepreneurs are men who change methods of production or distribution to meet or stimulate changes in demand. They need vision and the resources to put it into practice. Although this deserves further study, Tanganyika's cash-crop entrepreneurs probably fell into three broad categories, all possessing unusual vision: political leaders, who often had exceptional experience of the outside world; those who had travelled widely, often as traders or migrant labourers; and those who had somehow detached themselves partly from society, perhaps through education or acceptance of Christianity or Islam. Of course, not every chief or migrant or Christian was an entrepreneur, but it was from these categories that entrepreneurs came.

Chiefs might be well placed to innovate. With superior access to information, they could often introduce innovations successful elsewhere. Two chiefs pioneered Nyakyusa rice-growing with seed

[1] 'Note taken at a meeting at Arusha on 25th July, 1929', TNA 13742/6; Baines to CS, 3 September 1927, TNA 18996/1a; Large, memorandum, 10 December 1938, TNA 155/COOP/27/II/125.
[2] Senzighe to Same, 17 January 1953, TNA 4/8/36/188.
[3] Haarer to PC Northern, 10 July 1928, TNA 11160/66; Latham to DA, 7 July 1932, TNA 16/15/46/4.

obtained from coastal traders living in Malawi.[1] Chiefs also benefited from contacts with Europeans. Marealle of Marangu obtained coffee seed from European settlers. Government favoured chiefs when introducing new crops, hoping thereby to diffuse the innovation. When introducing coffee into Bugufi, the British gave 1,182 trees to the chief, 1,500 to the leading sub-chief, and smaller numbers to each headman.[2] Chiefs commanded the land and labour needed to innovate and could transfer the attendant risk to their subjects. Some 76 per cent of the cotton grown in Shinyanga district in 1923 was produced by chiefs using tributary labour.[3] Chiefs often patronised embryonic associations of cash-crop growers. After failing to prevent one, the Chief of Usambara joined it and occasionally presided over meetings.[4] Yet chiefs found difficulty in controlling commercial agriculture even when they had helped to introduce it, and many showed little interest in agricultural innovation, for they were seldom practising cultivators, they lacked the concern with agricultural technique which marked the dedicated entrepreneur, and some showed an aristocratic disdain for cultivation.

Personal inclination was also essential among those entrepreneurs whose perception was sharpened by travel. Hangaza migrants working in Uganda and Buhaya introduced arabica coffee to Bugufi. Matengo labourers brought coffee seed home with them from Arusha and Moshi, many having refused to work anywhere but on a coffee estate where they could learn the techniques of cultivation.[5] The leading Matengo entrepreneur was Chrisostomus Makita, a young, educated member of a family which had dominated central Umatengo in German times but had lost favour with the British. In 1924 he worked as a clerk on a sisal plantation where 'he learned to appreciate what nature can give to a man. He became aware of the great wealth which is locked up in the land, and he returned home determined to develop new sorts of agriculture.'[6] Chrisostomus toured the mountains creating coffee nurseries, distributing seedlings, and supervising

---

[1] 'The Rungwe Cooperative Union, Ltd: first annual report 1949–50', TNA 176/47/17/II/244.
[2] Young to Ngara, 31 March 1931, TNA 11969/I/85.
[3] Isherwood, Tabora DAR 1923, TNA 1733/21/1.
[4] Hartnoll to Tanga, 28 May 1931, TNA 304/8/2/1/52; 'Minutes of the inaugural meeting – Usambara Native Coffee Growers Cooperative Society (in formation). Held at the Sultani's court Vuga on 21/5/51', TNA 72/3/6/B/I/110l.
[5] O'Brien to DA, 6 March 1929, TNA 11969/I/46; Matengo tour book p. 249, TNA 155/I.
[6] G. S. Haule, 'The entrepreneur: Chrisostomus Makita', in Iliffe, *Tanzanians*, pp. 161–2.

planting, while extending his own plantation and organising growers into groups which later formed the nuclei of cooperative societies.

Since personal ambition is the essence of entrepreneurship, many Tanganyikan innovators of this period were 'new people' from mission schools. Christianity gave access to European sources of seed, implements, and ideas. It provided opportunities for salaried employment which enabled entrepreneurs to 'work under shade'. It emancipated men from customary restraints surrounding agriculture and created minorities whose cohesion formed the basis of entrepreneurial groups much like the Asian communities. In Rungwe, for example, Christian congregations established the first African-owned coffee plots to support the sick and aged. In Usambara the first African-owned coffee was planted shortly after the war to support church activities by Christian congregations left without missionaries. The pioneer was one of the first African pastors, Luka Jang'andu, who also initiated the Usambara Native Coffee Growers Association. Most early Shambaa coffee growers were Christians, although some were Muslim traders from Mlalo.[1] Matengo Christians, political leaders, and migrants formed a single entrepreneurial group:

Most of these early coffee-growers were older than Chrisostomus himself: young people seldom took up coffee growing. The majority were Christians with at least some formal education. Many were either Chrisostomus's own relations – sometimes very distant relations – or were his schoolfellows, or were court elders who were his agents in persuading the people to grow coffee. A number had also been migrant labourers. Thus the great majority of the early coffee-growers were men who in one way or another had experience wider than that of ordinary people.[2]

Since entrepreneurship originated among specific groups, a specific pattern of regional and social differentiation emerged in cash-crop areas. Nyiha coffee farmers clustered around the mission station, the chief's headquarters, and the European farms. The first Shambaa coffee plots were mainly in Vugha and Mlalo, but concentration later shifted to Bumbuli as land became scarce in the pioneer regions. Nyakyusa grew rice in the lakeshore plains and coffee in the highlands further north, leaving the intervening middle belt without a cash crop.[3] Social differentiation was also clearly marked. Cash crops

[1] Tetzlaff, *Entwicklung*, p. 274; Guga, 'Research'; Taylor to DAO Lushoto, 19 May 1930, TNA 18996/6b.
[2] Haule in Iliffe, *Tanzanians*, p. 163.
[3] Eustace, Tukuyu monthly agricultural report, December 1933, TNA 77/2/19/68; C. Gregory Knight, *Ecology and change* (New York, 1974), p. 222; Taylor to DAO Lushoto, 19 May 1930, TNA 18996/6b; Bennett, note, 5 September 1949, TNA

were a minority interest in all these areas before the Second World
War. Whereas most Haya produced coffee in the 1930s, only one Ngoni
taxpayer in five cultivated tobacco in 1937, and the numbers elsewhere
were even smaller: 286 coffee growers in Mbozi in 1937, 743 in Mbinga,
some 7,000 in Rungwe, and a quarter of the Meru in 1938.[1] Among
the growers a very few capitalist farmers, often drawn from the
original entrepreneurs, were distinguished from the great majority of
producers who had merely added a few trees or plants to their food
crops. Sheer agricultural skill partly accounted for this, for not
everyone was a keen or efficient cultivator, but the pattern of
entrepreneurship reinforced the tendency. In 1937 four-fifths of
Matengo coffee was produced by four of the 743 growers. Of the 35,324
bearing coffee trees owned by Africans in Usambara in 1930, 20,788
belonged to five of the 250 growers, all living in Vugha. Tobacco
growers in Songea were also differentiated – in 1939–40, 5,987 members of the cooperative each grew less than 200 kg. while 88 members
each grew more than 300 kg. – but tobacco was less profitable than
coffee, so that the range of wealth was smaller.[2] The emerging
farmers commonly employed seasonal labour. It was reported from
Mbozi in 1944 that '45% of the growers employ labour, varying on an
average from one to twelve men or *watoto* [children] per month'.
Nyakyusa chiefs and rice growers first employed poor young men for
wages in the 1930s. Thousands of Ha and Rundi worked for the
townsmen of Ujiji in the rice fields of the Luiche delta.[3]

The plough was the key innovation of the interwar years and the
chosen implement of the emerging farmer. Probably the expansion
of markets by motor transport made ploughing profitable for the first
time. German experiments had failed entirely, but by 1931, with the
Lupa goldfield providing the Nyakyusa with a market for lakeshore
rice, 'the natives in the area are keenly interested in the plough', and
fifteen years later more than 700 were in use on rice fields, although

72/3/6/B/1/49; P. H. Gulliver, *Land tenure and social change among the Nyakyusa* (Kampala, 1958), p. 47.

[1] Large, note, 31 July 1937, TNA 155/AGR/1/18/b/II/150; Agricultural Assistant Tukuyu to Mbeya, 3 February 1944, TNA 33/A/3/13/615; Matengo tour book p. 254, TNA 155/1; Dashwood to PC Southern Highlands, 8 February 1938, TNA 77/26/24/14; Hartley, 'A brief note on the Meru people with special reference to their expansion problem', February 1938, TNA 69/602/7.
[2] Large, memorandum [July 1938?] TNA 155/A/3/22/293; Taylor to DAO Lushoto, 19 May 1930, TNA 18996/6b; Northcote and McGregor, 'Report on the Songea tobacco industry', 12 August 1940, TNA 155/COOP/27.
[3] Agricultural Assistant Tukuyu to Mbeya, 3 February 1944, TNA 33/A/3/13/615; Wilson, *Good company*, pp. 56, 63; Robertson, Ujiji DAR 1925, TNA 1733/7/62/63.

digging sticks were still common in more remote areas.[1] Ploughing experiments in Usukuma came to little until the late 1930s, when ploughs were widely adopted on the eastern shore of Lake Victoria under the stimulus of the food demands of local gold mines and the arrival of Luo entrepreneurs from Kenya who grew maize on a large scale. Nyiha entrepreneurs began to use ploughs in 1934 because they were cheaper than hiring additional labour.[2] The farmers made other innovations. Early Nyiha coffee growers bought pulpers, fermenting tanks, and drying trays, and profited by selling seedlings to later growers. Three-fifths of Haya coffee was processed in wooden hullers devised by Roman Catholic missionaries and made by local craftsmen. In 1938 a group of Arusha wheat-growers bought a petrol-driven threshing machine. The prosperous Kerewe bought some 2,000 bicycles during 1935 and a handful of entrepreneurs owned lorries.[3] But the sophistication of this early rural capitalism should not be exaggerated, for the simplicity of its innovations distinguished it from the more spectacular entrepreneurship which followed the Second World War. Nyakyusa processed their coffee by chewing it and grew rice on the same fields every year, without rotation, manure, or irrigation, harvesting it with knives.[4] There is no evidence that cash-crop innovations led to any change in subsistence cultivation.

As on Kilimanjaro, peasants needed to cooperate in order to prevent crop disease, facilitate marketing, and generally advance their group interests. Their organisations varied. The Usambara Native Coffee Growers Association, formed in 1931, was much like the original KNPA, building stores, buying sprays and insecticides, and negotiating an overall price at which individual growers sold to a single buyer. Nyiha coffee growers built a central store in 1934 and sold at a fixed rate to a single purchaser.[5] Matengo chose local chairmen in

[1] *RTA*, 1897/8, no. 94, p. 946; Davies, Tukuyu monthly agricultural report, December 1931, TNA 77/2/19/23; Agricultural Assistant Tukuyu to SAO Iringa, 1 August 1946, TNA 139/9/3/102; Wilson, *Social change*, p. 33.

[2] Wakefield, 'Maize production in North Mara' [August 1937?] TNA 215/1474/I/4; Agricultural Assistant Tukuyu to Mbeya, 3 February 1944, TNA 33/A/3/13/615.

[3] Eustace to DAO Tukuyu, 31 October 1934, TNA 77/2/10/A; Northcote, 'Report on Bukoba coffee marketing', October 1936, TNA 215/1410; Tanganyika, *Department of Agriculture: annual report [Agriculture report] 1938*, p. 35; Kayamba, 'Notes on Ukerewe – Mwanza district', 13 April 1936, TNA 23567/1.

[4] DO Tukuyu to PC Southern Highlands, 9 February 1938, TNA 138/2/3/228; Lemke to Government, 5 May 1902, TNA G8/17; Eccles, 'Proposals for future development', 15 August 1947, TNA 139/9/3/118.

[5] 'Minutes of the inaugural meeting – Usambara Native Coffee Growers Cooperative Society', 21 May 1951, TNA 72/3/6/B/I/110l; Eustace to DAO Tukuyu, 31 October 1934, TNA 77/2/10/A/208.

1934 and these later formed the Ngaka Coffee Society, which sold coffee through the Ngoni-Matengo Cooperative Union (Ngomat), an organisation chiefly concerned with the Songea tobacco crop. Similar groups in Rungwe marketed coffee through the native treasury.[1] All these organisations were chiefly designed to protect prices against Asian buyers who tried to form rings and deal with individual growers. The organisations were usually founded by early entrepreneurs who held office for many years. Luka Jang'andu was still chairman of the Usambara association in 1948. So long as associations confined themselves to combating disease and organising sales the government generally aided them, but it refused to let them develop into full-scale cooperative societies, partly because of unhappy experience with the KNCU and partly because associations generally lacked the capital to finance the crop between delivery at their stores and sale in Europe. Officials feared cooperatives as potentially 'disruptive of tribal discipline based on the authority of the Chiefs'. 'A rich grower is inclined to be swollen-headed', one district officer pronounced. 'Vis-à-vis the Native Authorities and Courts he is the same as the poorest native...A society should not have a better office than the Native Authorities. It should be smaller, for one thing: and not of brick unless the Native Authority buildings are of brick.'[2]

Organisation was more difficult where crops other than coffee were grown. Sukuma cotton growers failed to create any organisation during the inter-war period, although desire for cooperatives was evident in Kwimba as early as 1932 and four years later the growers organised a successful hold-up there, refusing to sell their cotton until prices rose.[3] More dispersed than highlanders who grew coffee, the cotton growers presumably found association more difficult, and cotton needed less elaborate protection against disease. Most important, Asian businessmen controlled the ginning industry, and ginners, buying at prices fixed by the government, dominated cotton marketing. Not until Sukuma traders tried to break this monopoly in the later 1940s did cooperative organisation come to Sukumaland.

There were three exceptions to these generalisations about marketing organisations. In Bugufi the government created an agricultural society to market coffee as early as 1932, largely to prevent a

[1] Matengo tour book p. 251, TNA 155/1; Thomas to DA, 10 December 1934, TNA 77/2/10/A/212.
[2] MacMichael, note on the Pim report, 1938, CO 691/158; Matengo tour book p. 262, TNA 155/1.
[3] Diary of Sir Philip Mitchell, 26 June 1932, RH; Holmes, 'Bakwimba', p. 459.

disturbing influx of *wachuruzi* from Buhaya. In 1936 this society became an unregistered and ineffective cooperative.[1] The authorities also created an agricultural society in Biharamulo to handle tobacco, while in Songea government formed a full-scale cooperative society, Ngomat, to market the tobacco crop, whose processing was beyond the individual grower's means. The society was established in 1936 without consulting the growers and with a strong desire to assert official control. In 1940 an investigator recorded this conversation:

Do you hoe tobacco? – Yes.
Where do you sell it? – To the Chama [Union].
Did you join of your own free will? – Yes.
Who elect the committee? – The Government.
How often is it elected? – They were put in in 1936 and they have never changed.
Do you think the Chama is a good thing? – Do I not get money from it?[2]

In Buhaya and Kilimanjaro the marketing system formed the basis of peasant politics. This did not happen elsewhere. There were no coffee riots in Usambara or Rungwe. Several marketing organisations were too obviously government bodies, and in any case the entrepreneurs who led them were still small minorities. Where most cultivators had become peasants growing cash crops, as in Buhaya and Kilimanjaro, entrepreneurs could mobilise them for political purposes. But the handful of Shambaa or Matengo growers had no such purchase on the population. Chiefs who felt their authority threatened were able to frustrate attempts to sell land or encourage smallholder farming in Usukuma in the 1930s,[3] for Usukuma had not yet experienced its *otandibatira* and was not yet ripe for peasant politics.

Yet this did not mean that cash crops left societies unchanged. The entrepreneurs' ambitions challenged inherited law and relationships. The common belief that colonialism imposed law and order on Africa needs always to be weighed against its tendency to disrupt the legal mechanisms of small societies. Nyakyusa were unsure whether a man's coffee trees could be re-allocated by his headman if the original owner moved to another village – a frequent occurrence where witchcraft accusations were common – until their chiefs decreed in 1935 'that all

---

[1] Richards to Kitching, 22 September 1930, TNA 215/71/C/2; minute, 3 March 1938, TNA 23556/I/133.
[2] Northcote and McGregor, 'Report on the Songea tobacco industry', 12 August 1940, TNA 155/COOP/27. See also P. M. Redmond, 'The NMCMU and tobacco production in Songea', *TNR*, LXXIX (1976), 65–98.
[3] *Agriculture report*, 1938, p. 12; T. M. Revington, 'The pain of individualism', *TNR*, III (1937), 121.

coffee trees and other trees of a cash value shall in future be the absolute property of the owner even if he migrates to another area'. In Mbozi the same dilemma produced the rule that the coffee trees could be claimed by the emigrant's family – an indication that commercial agriculture could strengthen kinship ties as well as loosening them.[1] From here it was a short step to the commercialisation of land. Coffee plots were bought and sold in Unyakyusa in the late 1930s, while pasture was enclosed on Meru and the Nyasa lakeshore.[2] Meanwhile legal uncertainty extended more widely. In 1939 the chiefs of Mwanza district 'decided by a small majority...that female children cannot inherit property'.[3] Patrilineal Islamic law brought confusion to newly-Islamised matrilineal peoples, while Christian monogamy wrought chaos elsewhere.[4] Generally men tried to keep old and new separate. A Nyamwezi had no right to sell an abandoned house built with communal labour, but in 1931 a chief ruled that 'Natives who build in brick *with paid labour* should naturally be considered the owners of such houses.' Neighbourly cooperation in producing food was rarely extended to coffee or rice in Unyakyusa, nor was the notion that everyone should hoe at the same time and not 'overstep' his neighbours.[5] Successful entrepreneurs were commonly suspected of witchcraft. The most successful African trader in the Selya area of Unyakyusa was 'said to use the *inyifwila* medicine employed by chiefs, while Sukuma still remembered forty years later the successful farmers of the 1920s who had made zombies cultivate their land for them.[6] 'Is there any law to break up the African custom, which are necessary to the country?' Nyakyusa dissidents demanded in 1937:

Should only money destroy the manners or languages of the country which God created for the human beings, namely the black people?

What kind of authority can direct the country without following the native custom and their manners concerning their black colour, which cannot either be changed or washed away with a soap, or by any valuable clothing?

The tribal law which God gave to us is being destroyed completely,

---

[1] 'Minutes of the meeting of the Council held on 8th and 9th of May 1935', TNA 77/26/24/3; DO Mbeya to PC Southern Highlands, 20 January 1938, TNA 77/26/24/10.
[2] T. Sankey Mwanjisi to DO Tukuyu, 4 December 1939, TNA 138/2/3/376; *Agriculture report*, 1936, p. 44; Eccles, 'Proposals for future development', 15 August 1947, TNA 139/9/3/118.
[3] Minutes of chiefs' meeting, 10 July 1939, in Mwanza district book, TNA.
[4] Below, pp. 299–300.
[5] Gordon to PC Tabora, 18 June 1931, TNA 20239/10; Wilson, *Good company*, pp. 55–6.
[6] Wilson, *Good company*, p. 59; R. E. S. Tanner, 'The sorcerer in northern Sukumaland', *Southwestern journal of anthropology*, XII (1966), 439.

therefore the hearts of the people on our side are very sad...Money destroys the ranks and those who have been chosen and salaried are happy, thus they despise their unfortunate friends of the same rank. In the old days, when there was no money, there was no killing each other, no jealousy, or falsehoods; while in these present days all these have happened simply because the new customs have upset the old ones, in nothing save in money alone.[1]

The direction in which Tanganyika's more developed rural areas were moving was best illustrated by its oldest peasant society, that of the coastal villages.[2] There the units of society were individuals and villages rather than kinship groups. 'Individual responsibility', Dr Wijeyewardene has written, 'is...the basis of Swahili social behaviour.'[3] The village ethos was egalitarian except in its main cash-earning activity, fishing, where boats were owned by capitalists and captains exercised an authority unthinkable on dry land. Membership of a village required acceptance of Islam. It was a rustic variety – while Muslim law deprecated marriage among kin, villagers favoured it – but Islam linked the village to the larger world. The chief Islamic ceremony was the *Maulidi* reading which each village performed every few years to celebrate the Prophet's birthday. The ceremony involved the men of each village as rival groups, and as contacts with other villages and the larger world increased *Maulidi* grew in popularity and elaboration. It embodied the simultaneous involvement in local community and wider society which characterised peasant status.

Elsewhere peasanthood brought not *Maulidi* but 'the era of the dance'. Dr Hartwig has shown[4] that whereas each status group in nineteenth-century Ukerewe had monopolised specific musical forms and instruments, the colonial period untuned the string of degree. Young men sang to the *enanga* zither. Dance groups (*bangoma*) multiplied, each with its eye-catching mascot and fame-hungry lead singer judged by originality rather than musical skill, each using magic to trounce its rivals, each performing to hitherto forbidden drums. Ceremony changed into entertainment, ascribed status into public competition, regalia into ornament, ritual into magic. Four forces were at work. Colonial rule 'made all things small',[5] reducing the

---

[1] Mwafilombe s/o Kalindwana and others to PC Southern Highlands [1937] TNA 77/26/24/7.

[2] This paragraph is based on G. E. T. Wijeyewardene, 'Some aspects of village solidarity in Ki-Swahili speaking coastal communities of Kenya and Tanganyika', Ph.D. thesis, Cambridge University, 1961. Although this refers to the late 1950s, its main findings are probably valid for the 1930s.

[3] *Idem*, 'Kinship and ritual in the Swahili community', EAISR conference paper, 1959.

[4] Hartwig, 'Historical and social role', pp. 48–55.

[5] The phrase was Sukarno's.

significance of status in the Kerewe hierarchy and opening Ukerewe to the competitive dance traditions of egalitarian Usukuma. Cotton-growing enabled individuals to earn wealth regardless of their social status, and yet left time for dancing. Christianity undermined parental control. And the chief – that Gabriel Ruhumbika whom the Father Superior had blessed – patronised the *bangoma*. While Chagga demonstrated, Kerewe danced. Around Lake Victoria men who were young in this period remembered the intensely competitive era of the dance in which they first displayed their talents.[1] Yet *bangoma* did not destroy Kerewe society. Rather, they reintegrated it, weakening distinctions between Sese aristocrats, Jita commoners, Kara labourers, and Ruri slaves. When intermarriage started in the 1930s, a distinct Kerewe people began to emerge. While conservatives bewailed irreligion and disorder, a new society took shape on the dancing-fields of Nansio.

Social ambiguity and legal uncertainty characterised marriage and the status of women. In Unyakyusa in the 1930s Professor Wilson found great confusion.[2] Nyakyusa lived in virilocal[3] age villages where women had probably always had low status because they lacked solidarity and had no senior kinsmen to protect their interests. Moreover, Nyakyusa attached great importance to cattle which were given in bridewealth and were controlled by older men, so that polygyny had probably been unusually common and men had married so late that adultery, divorce, litigation, and marital instability were probably very widespread, as the first missionaries reported. In the 1930s the coexistence of inherited values with new sources of wealth generally exacerbated these problems. Some 70 per cent of Nyakyusa women and 28 per cent of men belonged to polygynous families, women marrying perhaps a decade younger than men. Nyakyusa believed that polygyny had increased during 'European times' because chiefs and leading men earned salaries while government banned cattle raiding and supported the authority of the old. Bridewealth had doubled or trebled since the 1890s, encouraging fathers to reduce the marriage age of non-Christian women, more than half of whom had been divorced. Three-quarters of the cases in local courts were marital disputes. Marriage by labour service, formerly practised by the poor, had given way entirely to bridewealth in cattle,

---

[1] .Iliffe, *Tanzanians*, pp. 176–8, 211.
[2] This paragraph is based on Wilson, 'Zig-zag change', pp. 399–409.
[3] In virilocal marriage the couple go to live at the husband's residence.

which young men had to earn through migrant labour, whose profits thus went chiefly to the old. Yet the colonial situation also had positive consequences. By paying cattle earned through migrant labour a man secured rights over his wife's children, who in labour-service marriage had belonged to their mother's kinsmen. Christians were prohibited from polygyny, and although they insisted on paying bridewealth, their example combined with government pressure to enable some brave young women to refuse marriage with polygynists. By the late 1930s some European observers thought that polygyny was at last waning, an observation strengthened by increasing employment of hired labour in place of plural wives.

Although an extreme case, the Nyakyusa experience of economic change exaggerating old marital patterns while intellectual change undermined them was probably fairly common. Bridewealth payments generally increased substantially. In Usambara, for example, the payment to the bride's father around 1900 was beer or a goat; by 1946 it was beer and two bulls.[1] Rather than an exchange between kin groups, bridewealth became increasingly a personal payment from groom to bride's father, and hence approximated more to a price. There is no evidence from outside Unyakyusa to show whether polygyny was becoming more common, but on Kilimanjaro the age at marriage fell markedly.[2]

Other changes in female status seem to have worked in contradictory directions. Women were often excluded from such innovations as cash-crop farming – almost invariably a male occupation – and western education. Yet educated African men were often keen advocates of female education, and the few educated women, predominantly Christians, prefigured an elevation in female status. As elsewhere in eastern Africa, missionaries found it relatively easy to establish African sisterhoods, which may indicate low female status but certainly elevated it. On the other hand, the colonial world was a man's world and women probably took less part in political leadership than before, while several matrilineal societies moved towards patriliny.[3] Islam often depressed women's status, especially in matrilineal areas,[4] but towns probably elevated it, chiefly by freeing women from

[1] Feierman, 'Concepts', p. 112. Among many other examples, see Joseph Busse, 'Lambya-Texte', *ZES*, xxx (1940), 263–4. For exceptions, see Rigby, *Cattle*, p. 229; Culwick, *Ubena*, p. 320.
[2] Gutmann, *Recht*, p. 79.
[3] Culwick, *Ubena*, pp. 138–9; Beidelman in Middleton and Winter, *Witchcraft*, p. 60.
[4] Swantz, *Ritual*, p. 298.

agricultural drudgery. The urban prostitution which began between the wars and obsessed African men after 1945 was probably in part an escape from the relative decline in women's status in cash-crop areas. But these are subjects needing much further research.

European enterprise and African labour

An overview of Tanganyika's interwar economy shows stagnation following the war, quite rapid growth in the later 1920s, collapse between 1929 and 1932, and then faltering recovery. Analysis of the territory's exports shows two important changes. In the early 1920s peasant production gained over the plantation crops and forest produce which had predominated in German times. Then the later 1920s and the 1930s saw the revival of plantation enterprise, now almost wholly devoted to sisal. The European share of export production, which in 1912 was roughly 60 per cent, fell by 1923 to 40 per cent, but then rose again by 1929 to around 55 per cent.[1] The early 1920s belonged to the peasant, the 1930s to the sisal planter.

None of these changes significantly altered Tanganyika's economic structure. As elsewhere in Africa at this time, Britain failed to dominate the territory's economy. Whereas in 1912 some 56 per cent of German East Africa's exports had gone to Germany, the highest proportion which Tanganyika exported direct to Britain between the wars was 27 per cent in 1925, although exports to Britain via Kenya may have raised the highest figure to around 32 per cent. The proportion of imports drawn from Britain was high after the war – 65 per cent in 1925 – but by 1938 had fallen to only 27 per cent.[2] Britain's economic vigour was waning and Tanganyika lacked economic attraction to compare with other parts of Britain's overgrown empire. The Mandate prohibited Britain from favouring her own nationals in Tanganyika. Officials did not seek to stimulate structural change in the territorial economy. In the 1930s subsidiaries of Kenya's nascent manufacturing industries – Unga Ltd (millers), East African Breweries, the Bata Shoe Company – established themselves in Dar es Salaam to process local products for internal consumption, but the governor – partly for financial reasons – discouraged a textile mill and Japanese plans to manufacture matches in Tanganyika from

[1] Arning, *Deutsch Ostafrika*, p. 339; E. A. Brett, *Colonialism and underdevelopment in East Africa* (London, 1973), p. 222.
[2] Tanganyika, *Blue book*, 1925, p. 86; Brett, *Colonialism*, p. 153.

imported materials, while the Colonial Secretary vetoed an attempt to export sisal twine manufactured in Tanganyika when Britain's sisal spinners boycotted Tanganyikan sisal in protest.[1] On balance, Tanganyika invested in Britain. Between 1938 and 1948 Tanganyikan bank deposits rose from £1,800,000 to £17,950,000, while bank lending increased only from £1,550,000 to £1,800,000. The balance went to London. In 1927 Tanganyika was forced into a customs union with Kenya and a growing proportion of its trade – between 17 and 24 per cent of imports in the 1930s – passed through Nairobi.[2]

Tanganyika was at the bottom of the imperial pecking order. Its status was in question throughout the interwar period. British imperialists insisted on its retention and German imperialists demanded its return, but statesmen on both sides saw it as a bargaining counter. In sanguine moments British leaders hoped that colonial concessions might help to secure European peace. 'I don't believe myself that we could purchase peace and a lasting settlement by handing over Tanganyika to the Germans', a British Prime Minister wrote, 'but if I did, I would not hesitate for a moment.'[3] Hitler's obsession was mastery of central and eastern Europe, for which he sought Britain's friendship or neutrality. Until 1936 he tried to buy this by repudiating colonies. Thereafter he tried to coerce it by threats which included allusions to colonial restitution, but colonies ranked low in his long-term plans.[4] Neither side thought African territories important; both exaggerated their importance to the other. Naturally no bargain resulted, but the consequence for Tanganyika was extreme uncertainty as Britain used 'every sort of verbal *chinoiserie* to get out of making...an announcement that Tanganyika will remain under British administration'.[5] In 1933, 1936, and 1938 businessmen interested in Tanganyika panicked, and it was widely held that uncertainty deterred investors. Yet in any case few investors were interested in Tanganyika during the 1930s. The constraints which the depression imposed were clearly illustrated by railway policy. Having acquired German assets without compensation, Byatt and his successor

---

[1] Booth, 'Business names'; Cameron to Passfield, 10 June 1930, CO 691/112; Cameron to Bottomley, 29 June 1928, CO 691/99; Cunliffe-Lister, minute, 28 July 1934, CO 691/135; Mitchell diary, 28 February 1935, RH.

[2] Justinian Rweyemamu, *Underdevelopment and industrialization in Tanzania* (Nairobi, 1973), p. 35; Brett, *Colonialism*, pp. 100–6.

[3] Keith Feiling, *The life of Neville Chamberlain* (new edn, London, 1970), p. 300.

[4] Klaus Hildebrand, *Vom Reich zum Weltreich: Hitler, NSDAP und koloniale Frage 1919–45* (München, 1969), ch. 6.

[5] Dawe, minute, 19 January 1940, CO 822/103.

could afford loans from the Treasury and the London capital market, borrowing some £8,693,350 between 1921 and 1932.[1] This was spent on public buildings, renovating German railways, and a mistaken programme of branch lines which extended the northern railway to Arusha in 1930 and built branches from the central railway to Mwanza in 1928 and Kinyangiri (in Unyaturu) in 1932, but more ambitious plans for a branch line from the central railway to Northern Rhodesia were destroyed by the unlikelihood of attracting the copper traffic and by the depression, which ended borrowing and all serious public investment for a decade.[2]

Thus British rule brought no major structural change except African cash-crop farming. European settlement showed the continuity with German times. Deportation of Germans reduced the white population between 1913 and 1921 from 4,998 to 2,447.[3] After 1921 British settlers bought ex-enemy properties, often as speculations, but no new land was alienated. Official views on settlement became more sympathetic in the late 1920s. Restoration of normal relations with Germany in 1925 made it impossible to exclude German settlers, who had the incentive of Germany's economic distress and found Tanganyika more attractive than did British emigrants with access to many other territories. To admit Germans also meant encouraging British settlers to balance them. In June 1939 there were 6,514 European unofficials in Tanganyika, including 2,100 Britons and 2,729 Germans.[4] Most Germans were small farmers, often financed indirectly by the Reich. They regained much land on Kilimanjaro and also predominated in new settlement areas in the Southern Highlands and at Oldeani in Mbulu district. Altogether the period added nearly 400,000 hectares of newly alienated land, bringing the total to a peak of 1,157,246 hectares in 1937,[5] but this was only 1.31 per cent of the country. All the new land was alienated on rights of occupancy for up to 99 years. In view of the Mandate, German settlement, and the official view that Tanganyika must be predominantly an African territory, government gave less indirect aid to settlement – through freight rates, technical assistance, and the like – than had the Germans.

---

[1] Tanganyika, *Blue book*, 1932, p. 70.
[2] C. Gillman, 'A short history of the Tanganyika railways', *TNR*, XIII (1942), 45–53; Symes to Cunliffe-Lister, 21 December 1931, CO 691/120.
[3] *Die deutschen Schutzgebiete 1912/13*, II, 10–11; Ernst Weigt, *Europäer in Ostafrika* (Köln, 1955), p. 48.
[4] Young to Macdonald, 10 June 1939, CO 691/171.
[5] Tanganyika, *Blue books*, 1921, p. 125, 1937, p. 263. The best survey of settlement is Weigt, *Europäer*.

Between the wars sisal became Tanganyika's chief export crop. Exports rose between 1912 and 1938 from 17,057 to 103,428 tonnes.[1] Sisal was only one of several hard fibres, although the highest in quality. Its chief competitors, Mexican henequen and Manila hemp (grown by Philippino peasants) both experienced disaster between the wars, Manila because it was uncompetitive and henequen because of agrarian reforms in Mexico after 1934. Sisal's share of the hard-fibre market consequently rose between the early 1920s and the late 1930s from 16 to 47 per cent, while world sisal production increased between 1923 and 1935–8 from 50,000 to 258,000 tonnes. Tanganyika's share of this increased production rose in the same period from 27 to 36 per cent.[2] Even international depression scarcely interrupted expansion. One reason was that many estates were controlled by sisal merchants who could balance losses on production by agency profits on larger quantities. A more important reason was the sheer inelasticity of supply of a crop needing seven years to mature. Having planted sisal in the prosperous 1920s, one could only cut it in the 1930s.

Despite marketing campaigns, in 1936–8 only 27 per cent of sisal exports went to Britain. Twice as much went to Continental Europe – Antwerp was the main entrepôt – and the remainder to North America.[3] In April 1934 Germans owned 40 sisal estates, Greeks 29, Britons 24, and Asians 22.[4] British plantations were usually large and externally owned, while Greek and Asian estates were locally financed – a distinction between metropolitan and local capital which later gained political significance. In 1940 the largest sisal producer (10,966 tonnes) was Karimjee Jivanjee. The other major Asian firm, with 7,167 tonnes, was Taibali Essaji Sachak and Company, founded by a Bohra merchant who reached Tanganyika in 1910. Among European interests the largest on the eve of war was the Usagara Company, the quasi-governmental German enterprise, with 10,459 tonnes. Amboni Estates Limited, financed jointly by Swiss businessmen and Wigglesworth and Company, the London merchants, produced 9,643 tonnes. No individual planter could match these interests. The most important was probably Major Sir William Lead, founder and president of the Tanganyika Sisal Growers Association, leader of the unofficial side of

---

[1] *Die deutschen Schutzgebiete 1912/13*, II, 158–73; Tanganyika, *Blue book*, 1938, pp. 167–8.
[2] C. W. Guillebaud, *An economic survey of the sisal industry of Tanganyika* (3rd edn, Welwyn, 1966), pp. 1, 5.
[3] [Hitchcock?] to Bretherton, 28 May 1947, TNA 29513/II/188.
[4] Mitchell to Cunliffe-Lister, 25 April 1934, CO 691/135.

the Legislative Council, and half-owner of a sisal estate producing 2,469 tonnes.[1]

Since the sisal planter's rule of thumb was that one man working for one year produced one tonne of fibre on one hectare of land, an increase in output from 10,000 to 100,000 tonnes had dramatic implications for the labour market. Nor was it alone. European farming expanded into the Southern Highlands. African entrepreneurs became significant employers. Gold mining boomed during the depression. The African population of Dar es Salaam increased between 1914 and 1939 from some 20,000 to over 30,000.[2] Altogether the Germans had estimated in 1912 that 139,515 Africans were in wage employment. The figure fell after the war and probably declined temporarily in the early 1930s, but by 1937 it had risen to some 244,000, excluding those working for Africans.[3]

Before the war the general trend had been away from local labour, except where it could be compelled by political means, and towards greater reliance on long-distance migrants from peripheral areas unable to meet cash needs by marketing crops or cattle. The interwar period intensified this trend. Early in the 1920s the largest groups of migrants were still Nyamwezi, Sumbwa, and Sukuma, but during the depression many Sukuma became cotton-growers and much of Unyamwezi was closed to recruiting because of sleeping-sickness, so that a century of Nyamwezi migration at last faded away.[4] Instead, migrants came increasingly from remote, peripheral regions. The proportion of Bena taxpayers absent from home rose between 1926 and 1945 from 20 to 45 per cent.[5] Most estate workers in Arusha and Moshi came from impoverished areas of Central Province, notably Kondoa, Mkalama, and Singida. These patterns had been established before the war, but new groups were also drawn in. Many Nyakyusa travelled to the north-east in the 1920s until the Lupa goldfield offered a closer market for food and labour. The most important new group were the Ha, who began travelling to work in Ujiji when slavery died away before the First World War and were then driven to the north-eastern plantations around 1925 by higher tax and active recruiting. They often worked as sisal-cutters, a task also accepted by

[1] 'List of registered sisal estates', 1940, TNA 29113/57D.
[2] J. E. G. Sutton, 'Dar es Salaam: a sketch of a hundred years', *TNR*, LXXI (1970), 19.
[3] *Die deutschen Schutzgebiete 1912/13*, II, 79; Tanganyika, *Report of the committee... on... native labour* (Dar es Salaam, 1938), p. 9.
[4] Wyatt, Tanga DAR 1922, TNA 1733/22/8; Wakefield to CS, 7 December 1937, TNA 215/1047/1/205; Government notice 132 of 1933.
[5] Graham, 'Wage labor', pp. 60, 89.

Makonde and Makua immigrants from Mozambique, by Rundi, and by Mambwe and Bemba from Zambia. In 1937 there were some 45,000 immigrants working in Tanganyika.[1]

New migrations were chiefly stimulated by tax, whose receipts increased between 1912 and 1939 by 155 per cent as against an increase in total government revenue of only 120 per cent,[2] but established migrants sought cash also for imported goods, school fees, cattle for bridewealth, and investment. Scarcely any society was yet bound to labour migration by land shortage.[3] When profitable crops, transport facilities, or markets became available, men usually abandoned labour migration, as did Sukuma cotton growers, Ndendeuli tobacco producers, and Matengo coffee planters. Hopes of relatively high wages might encourage educated men to migrate, but among the unskilled it was the poor who left their homes. 'All. . . Nyamwezi who live on the coast as workers belong to the lowest classes', a German observer stated.[4] The feeling was embodied in the common word for migrants: *manamba*, 'numbers'. Most were young men who lacked family responsibilities and needed capital to establish homesteads, but there were areas – Bugufi, Buha, Ubena – where men might have to migrate several times, even after marriage. One symptom was that in the 1920s men first took their families to the plantations. In 1928, 4 per cent of migrants were thought to be accompanied by their wives. Men also stayed longer, expecially when wages were low during the 1930s.[5] All the evidence suggests that economic need was the overwhelming motive for migration. Non-economic circumstances were usually only 'final straws' impelling particular individuals. Migration earned no prestige; that came from not having to migrate. Nor did the 'bright lights' of employment areas attract many, for a sisal estate's kerosene lamps were not especially luminous. Some deliberately chose isolated plantations where there was little inducement to fritter away their earnings.[6]

[1] Shunya Hino, 'Social stratification of a Swahili town', *KUAS*, II (1968), 58, 62–3; Laurent Sago, 'A history of labour migration in Kasulu district Tanzania, 1928–1960', M.A. thesis, University of Dar es Salaam, 1974, ch. 1; Tanganyika, *Report. . .on. . .native labour*, p. 8.
[2] *Die deutschen Schutzgebiete 1912/13*, II, 408; Tanganyika, *Blue book*, 1939, pp. 14–16.
[3] Majita and Ukara may have been exceptions.
[4] Meyer to Government, 11 May 1906, TNA G1/96.
[5] Note for Legislative Council reply, May 1928, TNA 11625/1/51; Graham, 'Wage labor', p. 73.
[6] See especially P. H. Gulliver, *Labour migration in a rural economy: a study of the Ngoni and Ndendeuli* (Kampala, 1955); idem, 'Nyakyusa labour migration', *Rhodes-Livingstone journal*, XXI (1957), 32–63.

Migration had its positive consequences. Matengo and Hangaza migrants pioneered coffee growing. Migration encouraged the adoption of Islam in Unyamwezi, Undendeuli, Kondoa, and elsewhere. European fears that migrants would return with seditious notions were exaggerated – there were not many seditious notions to learn on sisal estates – but many tribal unions important to later politics originated at distant workplaces.[1] Generally the effects of migration depended on its articulation with indigenous economies. Fertile Unyakyusa, with much surplus labour, could supply many migrants without damaging its agriculture – although also, of course, without improving it.[2] Where agriculture was a seasonal occupation, as in Central Province, migrants could travel fairly short distances after harvest, work for four or five months, and return to plant their crops.[3] But distant areas whose agriculture was not markedly seasonal suffered very seriously. The best example is Bugufi. When tax stimulated massive labour migration from the area in the early 1920s, officials hoped that coffee-growing might prove an alternative source of cash which would also emancipate the Hangaza from subservience to Tusi chiefs who lived on their tribute. In 1944 a social anthropologist found that exactly the opposite had happened.[4] Tusi power had grown; Hangaza office-holders had been reduced by half between 1931 and 1940. Tribute had risen sharply, the fee paid when seeking land had increased, and the cultivator's tenure had become even less secure. Coffee was bitterly unpopular because transport difficulties kept prices low, much work was involved, and the men's absence forced women to cultivate a crop whose sparse profits belonged to their husbands. Bugufi's aristocratic reaction had many causes. Extensive immigration from overpopulated and reactionary Burundi enabled Tusi to extract larger tribute from tenants and reduced living standards to Burundi's appalling levels. With government recognition, Tusi headmen could ignore their subjects' interests. But much responsibility lay with labour migration, which made the cultivators' tenure even less secure, weakened their capacity to defend corporate interests, and provided income which aristocrats could extort without bothering to establish coffee plantations. In 1944 landowners devoted even smaller propor-

[1] Below, pp. 389, 490.
[2] Gulliver, 'Nyakyusa migration', p. 60.
[3] Oldaker, Kondoa DAR 1933, TNA library.
[4] Richards to Kitching, 22 September 1930, TNA 215/71/C/2; Hans Cory, 'Report on land tenure in Bugufi' and 'Survey of the utwaliates of Bugufi', typescripts, 1944, Cory papers, ULD; R. de Z. Hall and H. Cory, 'A study of land tenure in Bugufi 1925–1944', *TNR*, XXIV (1947), 28–45.

tions of their land to coffee than did squatters. Yet even fleas have smaller fleas. Absent Hangaza often hired Rundi to look after their fields.

Hangaza normally left for Uganda in teams of three or four. For them, as for most *manamba*, migration was a communal enterprise. Men gathered experience gradually. Ha teenagers normally went no further than Ujiji. Later, on their first visit to the north-east, they undertook low-paid cultivation work, graduating to sisal cutting only on their second trip. Past the age of 45 they again confined their journeys to Ujiji.[1] *Manamba* had to choose whether to walk or to seek a recruiter to provide a ticket to the closed goods or cattle wagons in which the Ha travelled their hated 'middle passage' along the central railway.[2] Each job had its drawbacks. Underground mining paid good wages but was dangerous, unfamiliar, exhausting, and cursed with overbearing foremen. The Lupa's alluvial diggings were less disciplined and offered rich pickings, but the water was foul, the food expensive, the working conditions unhealthy, crime and violence common, and wages often unpaid. Towns were exciting but vicious and expensive, and with 25 per cent unemployment they were for the tough and ambitious. It was not surprising that men walked a thousand kilometres to the ill-paid but secure and familiar work of a sisal estate, or that Mambwe discouraged young men from visiting the Copperbelt until they had proved themselves on a plantation.[3]

Since workers were migrants or local peasants, sisal plantations were never the disciplined, totalitarian institutions described in the West Indies and elsewhere, but they were nevertheless social units as well as enterprises.[4] A few followed advanced principles of industrial welfare. Amboni boasted three schoolrooms, two churches, a mosque, market house, tea room, brewery, butchery, and hospital. Other estates were notorious for squalid rows of hovels, each housing up to a dozen migrants, but most were laid out more casually, with workers' huts and fields scattered in tribal clusters where newcomers could join their countrymen, and only the office and factory acting as a central focus. Much of an estate's life took place around its edges

[1] Sago, 'Labour migration', p. 49.
[2] Anse Tambila, 'A history of the Tanga sisal labour force: 1936–1964', M.A. thesis, University of Dar es Salaam, 1974, p. 26.
[3] Montague, 'Report on visit of inspection to Kentan Gold Areas Ltd., Sagagura', May 1936, TNA 12019/1/95; 'Report by Mr J. L. Berne, Ag P.C., on Lupa gold field', 12 July 1932, TNA 13555/1/20; below, pp. 352–4; William Watson, *Tribal cohesion in a money economy* (Manchester, 1958), p. 52.
[4] See the vivid account in Tambila, 'History'.

– *mwisho ya shamba*, as these areas were known – where lived the *walowezi*, the migrants who had somehow never gone home, where traders built stores, cultivators sold food, beer was brewed and prostitutes lived and – in time – politics were discussed and strikes were planned. The names of these settlements revealed their origins: Chumbageni ('the aliens' place'), Ugogoni, Ubena, Unyanyembe.[1]

Sisal workers formed distinct categories. The aristocrats were clerks, dressers, schoolteachers, and the like who commonly came from early educational centres like Bonde. The most influential manual workers were headmen, overseers, and factory workers who often spent their working lives on one estate. By contrast, the heavy work of cutting was usually done by gangs of migrants who cultivated the brash virility expected of up-country men. Cutting had low status on the estates, but it was esteemed in Buha because it paid relatively well and demonstrated toughness.[2] Cutters worked to a *kipande* of thirty 'tasks' – so many leaves cut, bundled, and stacked. Inter-war tasks were relatively small – usually about 2,000 leaves – and strong men often completed two in a day. The worst-paid work – clearing, planting, hoeing – was left to local casual labour or women and children.

Plantation labourers expressed their ideas and experiences most vividly in their forms of protest. The least sophisticated form of action was intertribal fighting, invariably among migrants and usually involving Nyakyusa. This could escalate into a labour dispute, as at Kidifu in 1938 when Makonde workers beat up a non-Makonde headman who refused to sign their wives' *vipande*,[3] but it normally lacked the essential quality of industrial action. The most common form of protest remained desertion. Anonymous *manamba* could move so easily between estates or lose themselves so thoroughly in Tanga's slums or the *mwisho ya shamba* that an altered task or brutal overseer could disperse a labour force overnight. Government treated desertion from contract as a criminal offence, but labour officers also tried to hold employers to their contracts. During the 1930s workers often called in labour officers to weigh rations, measure tasks, or check wage records. A frequent response to breach of contract was to down tools, and this was the reason for most of the sisal strikes which became common in the 1930s.[4] The biggest of these commonly took a form

[1] S. Ndawula-Kajumba, 'A sociological description of the Tanzanian sisal industry', UEASSC paper, 1970.
[2] Sago, 'Labour migration', pp. 52–3.
[3] Jerrard to Chief Inspector of Labour, 15 August 1938, TNA 25908/1/41.
[4] For the economic background, see below, pp. 352–3.

observed on plantations elsewhere and already familiar in nineteenth-century caravans.[1] To avoid victimisation, protest had to be an anonymous demonstration by a crowd from which individuals could not be picked out as 'ringleaders'. Consequently, inter-war labour action, although far from spontaneous, was characteristically, even deliberately, leaderless. Leadership required sufficient solidarity to ensure that the leader's personal vulnerability was balanced by his followers' willingness to protect him by collective action, and equally to ensure that the 'leader' did not sell out to management. Given the migrant workers' concern for quick earnings, their divisions of tribe and status, their ignorance and inexperience and fear – given all these, the solidarity necessary for leadership did not yet exist. A slightly later incident illustrated this vividly. Accused of stabbing his plantation manager, a Rundi cutter called another Rundi as his first witness, only to hear him declare:

I do not know the accused. I have never seen him before. I used to work at Hassani Sisal estate. I am now in prison. I was arrested...during a labour disturbance...I did not do anything and have no idea what the disturbance is about.[2]

Like Kilimanjaro's peasant demonstration, the anonymous and often riotous sisal strikes of this period were recognitions of real weakness.

Yet there was one partial exception to this generalisation. Appropriately it happened in August 1939 at Amboni, the most progressive estate, and resulted from urban labour's first impact on plantation action. In August 1939 Tanga's dockworkers struck and sent emissaries to Amboni, just outside the town, to seek support. The cutters responded, attacked and halted the factory, and set out for Tanga. After a short distance enthusiasm ebbed and they returned, demanding thirty shillings for thirty tasks, 'the old rate of pay before the depression in the sisal industry'. They eventually resumed work with nothing gained. The strike displayed features customary on sisal estates in the 1930s: leaderlessness, the crowd's protective anonymity, intimidation to secure solidarity, hostility between cutters and permanent employees, and cautious deference to Europeans. But it also marked an advance in its connections with urban protest and, especially, in its demand for a return to pre-depression wages, for

[1] See Chandra Jayawardena, *Conflict and solidarity in a Guianese plantation* (London, 1963), ch. 4; above, p. 46.
[2] 'In the Resident Magistrate's court of Tanga, criminal case no. 2 of 1948. Rex versus Sumuni s/o Ngoi', 14 September 1948, TNA 37687/19A.

this implied a collective memory and identity as sisal workers quite different from the consciousness underlying momentary and defensive stoppages. Perhaps such collective memory existed at Amboni because it had a more stable labour force than other plantations. Pre-depression wages were also the aim of the dockworkers' strikes in Tanga and Dar es Salaam in 1939. At Amboni, coast and hinterland, town and country joined fleetingly in common action for the first time since Abushiri's resistance.[1]

Regional differentiation and food production

By the 1930s a new pattern of regional differentiation was replacing Tanganyika's old division into purely geographical regions. Certain favourably situated areas – plantations, towns, cash-crop regions – specialised in export production, around which the whole pattern focussed. The most remote and least favoured regions supplied them with migrant labour. Between the two were regions which supplied the export-producing areas with food and other services. The categories were not wholly exclusive. Unyakyusa exported coffee while supplying both food and labour to the Lupa goldfield. Nor were specialisations immutable: Ulanga switched from collecting rubber to growing rice when rubber prices fell and Kilosa's railway line and sisal estates opened just before the First World War.[2] Yet each region normally specialised in one activity, and specialisations changed rather little before Independence.

The best way to picture regional differentiation is through the eyes of a consumer, perhaps a Dar es Salaam stevedore. When in funds at the beginning of the month his favourite food was rice. Much was imported, chiefly from Burma, but quantities also travelled along the central railway from the Luiche delta, arrived by lorry from the Kilombero and Rufiji valleys, or were carried into the town by the 500 or so residents who cultivated the surrounding creeks.[3] A stevedore's pay bought only a day or two of rice before he turned to millet and maize. Quantities trickled into the market from surrounding villages, but much millet came by dhow from the south, for Kilwa, Lindi, and

---

[1] 'Report of the proceedings of the meeting with the Provincial Commissioner, Tanga', 11 August 1939, TNA 304/959/1/28; Tanganyika, *Report of the commission...into the disturbances...in...Tanga during...August 1939* (Dar es Salaam, 1940).

[2] Larson, 'History', pp. 136–7.

[3] H. H. McCleery, 'Report of an enquiry into landownership in Dar es Salaam', typescript, 1939, ULD.

their hinterlands had been the coast's granary since German times. At the month's end the stevedore ate manioc from Uzaramo. For his relish he drew on the whole of the capital's hinterland. Dried shark, a favourite delicacy, was produced locally, as were many fruits and vegetables. Each region along the central railway supplied its speciality. Kigoma sent *dagaa*, the sun-dried whitebait from Lake Tanganyika which had reached the coast since the nineteenth century. Uvinza supplied salt, Tabora produced groundnuts, Ugogo sent cattle, Usagara and Ukhutu were renowned for tobacco, Uluguru had been the capital's main source of vegetables since the railway reached it in German times, and Uzaramo supplied the charcoal – thousands of tons of it – on which Dar es Salaam cooked. Yet, situated on the coast of a vast country, the capital never dominated Tanganyika's economy as Nairobi dominated Kenya's. Instead Tanganyika had a polycentric economy, with each export-producing region acting as a focus of exchange. North-eastern estates drew maize and fruit from Bonde, vegetables and tobacco from Usambara, and meat from Mbulu, Kondoa, Singida, Masailand, and Usukuma. Coffee-rich Buhaya bought the cattle of Sukumaland and Rwanda, the fish of Lake Victoria, and the tobacco of Biharamulo. These regional economies were as yet scarcely integrated into a territorial economy.

Since tsetse had made two-thirds of the territory unsuitable for cattle, continued ability to breed them enabled fortunate societies to satisfy their cash needs without producing cash crops or exporting labour, so that they could escape the social changes which those activities entailed. This advantage was probably the chief reason for the 'conservatism' of cattle-keeping peoples. Cultural conservatism indeed there was among Masai and Tatoga pastoralists and among agriculturalists like the Arusha and Sukuma who still possessed valuable herds. Few amongst them welcomed education or alien religions. But cultural conservatism was made possible by willingness to exploit their herds as economic assets. The Masai clung to pastoral life, but projects to increase pastoral efficiency found ready support. 'They are wealthy', their most knowledgeable British observer explained, 'and, fully alive to the advantages to be derived from modern scientific improvements, are prepared to spend money on measures to improve and conserve their stock. In this respect they are somewhat in advance of other native tribes.'[1] Pastoralists, like cash-crop growers, were highly differentiated, and the more important cattle

[1] Hollis to Milner, 16 February 1921, CO 691/43/85.

were to an economy, the more unequally they were owned. In productive agricultural regions like Rungwe and Singida cattle were relatively evenly distributed, but in the more arid country of the Irangi less than a third of homesteads owned cattle in 1933. Later investigation showed that cattle were the least evenly distributed form of wealth in Usukuma, while Masailand's inequalities were evident even in the nineteenth century.[1] Differentiation shaped the pattern of cattle sales. In normal years a steady supply of surplus male animals reached the market from large owners who obtained their cash needs in this manner, while poorer men sold crops or labour and tried to earn sufficient to build up a herd. A year of drought or depression, by contrast, flooded the markets with low-priced, half-starved beasts.[2]

This pattern helps to explain the economics of food supply in general. Again there was a continuum. At one pole stood the cultivator who marketed his 'normal surplus': the excess over subsistence needs which he produced in a normal or good year by planting enough to supply his homestead should the season prove subnormal. At the other pole stood the food planter employing labour to produce what was essentially a cash crop. Between these poles most food producers occupied intermediate positions, planning perhaps to market a surplus even in a bad year, or employing labour for transport but not cultivation. The possibilities were infinite. They ranged from the capitalist rice growers of Ujiji, through Ngindo who abandoned bushland homes to grow rice in river valleys, to Nyamwezi who produced groundnuts to cover taxes and Makonde who marketed surplus manioc in favourable years.[3]

Beneath ephemeral market responses more fundamental agricultural changes took place. The most important was the continuing adoption of American crops to supplement or supersede millets and bananas. Maize and British administration reached Bugufi almost simultaneously. In southern Sukumaland and many other regions maize spread because its taste was preferred to millet, it produced higher yields, it was easier to store, and it was simpler to prepare for village women or men returning from work. Maize required less

---

[1] DO Tukuyu to PC Southern Highlands, February 1942, TNA 25827/11/3B; Armstrong, Singida DAR 1934, TNA library; Oldaker, Kondoa DAR 1933, TNA library; John Sender, 'Some preliminary notes on the political economy of rural development in Tanzania', seminar paper, University of Dar es Salaam, 1973; Fischer, *Massai-Land*, p. 29.

[2] See, for example, the cattle sales listed in Maswa district book, TNA.

[3] Robertson, Ujiji DAR 1925, TNA 1733/7/62/63; Crosse-Upcott, 'Social structure', p. 35; *Agriculture report*, 1936, p. 79.

communal labour – an advantage where communities were dispersing – and it is noteworthy that the regions where millet survived best, especially Ufipa and Buha, were those where communal labour remained most common. Maize was an individualistic crop suited to an increasingly individualistic and competitive society. Its greater susceptibility to drought mattered less where a colonial government provided aid during famine.[1] Manioc was adopted for mixed reasons, for although few preferred its flavour it was highly productive, resistant to drought and locusts, and pressed relentlessly by government as an anti-famine measure. Although American crops were ever more widely grown, millet retained its ritual associations. Maji Maji rebels had worn millet stalks and abused Mvinge for calling them manioc-eaters.

A more complicated and still unstudied exchange of varieties also took place. The Germans had introduced new manioc strains from Madagascar which gradually replaced indigenous varieties. In the late 1920s South African maize very widely superseded less productive local varieties. American groundnuts began to supplant the indigenous strains.[2] Not all the new strains were imported. Millet from Sukumaland became popular in Uzigua, and doubtless many similar innovations left no trace. Sometimes a new variety began with an act of entrepreneurship comparable with those which brought coffee to Kilimanjaro or Mbinga. Abdulrahman Saidi Mboga, a Zaramo migrant labourer, was remembered for bringing better strains of rice and techniques of irrigation to South Pare.[3] Yet there was an important difference between export-producing and food-producing regions: the profits from food were simply much lower than those available to export-producers, because transport costs were so high for bulky products. Bondei or Kaguru who supplied plantations with grain could earn enough to escape wage-labour but not enough to make Bonde or Ukaguru as prosperous as Buhaya or Kilimanjaro. Food-producing areas occupied a middle place in the regional hierarchy and social formations consequently differed there. In Buhaya men often abandoned salaried employment for trade and agriculture; in Bonde or Ukaguru salaried employment remained

[1] McMillen, Lukira DAR 1923, TNA 215/77/6; Rounce, *Cultivation steppe*, p. 31; Latham to DA, 10 December 1930, CO 691/117; R. G. Abrahams, *The political organization of Unyamwezi* (Cambridge, 1967), pp. 167–8; Willis in Roberts, *Tanzania*, pp. 83–4.
[2] *RTA*, 1903/5, no. 54, p. 91; *RTA*, 1907/9, no. 622, p. 3,703; *Agriculture report*, 1928–9, 1, 6; *ibid.*, 1929–30, 1, 4; *ibid.*, 1930, 1, 4, 23.
[3] S. E. Manongi, 'The biography of an important Kihurio farmer', seminar paper, University of Dar es Salaam, 1970.

the preferred career, so that local leadership remained with official elites. There were no demonstrations in food-growing regions in the 1930s.

Agricultural change and regional differentiation became enmeshed with deep-rooted themes of Tanganyikan history. One was famine. No general famine took place between the wars to rival those of the late 1890s or 1919. Instead famines appear to have been localised in two kinds of region. One category contained areas which 'experienced isolated calamities. They included Mbozi (1924), the Tanga hinterland (1925 and 1933), Bugufi (1929), Tunduru (1930–2), and Unyamwezi (1938–9).[1] The other category embraced two areas, Central Province (especially Ugogo) and Uzigua, which experienced repeated famines. Ugogo suffered food shortage in 1919–21, 1925–6, 1928–30, 1932–5, 1937, and 1939,[2] Uzigua in 1925, 1926, 1930, 1933, and 1934.[3] The chief reason in both areas was drought, exacerbated by annual locust invasions during the 1930s. Ugogo and Uzigua shared long histories of famine, exceptionally unreliable rainfall, the capacity to export grain in good years, and inability or unwillingness to cultivate drought-resistant crops like manioc. Uzigua had in addition lost its cattle reserve to tsetse, while Ugogo was threatened by tsetse and deliberately isolated from territorial affairs by a reactionary provincial commissioner. It is probably significant that neither area exported much labour except in extreme hardship, for elsewhere the pattern of the inter-war years seems to have been a growing freedom from famine due to improved communications, the government's growing capacity to intervene, the spread of drought-resistant crops, and wider participation in the commercial economy which provided a certain protection against bad years, even if it was only through labour migration.

As the dismal peaks of famine became less frequent and widespread, Tanganyika's population decline was reversed. Kuczynski put the turning-point in the mid 1920s. He estimated that the territory's population in 1931 was between 4,500,000 and 5,200,000; in 1939 it was between 4,600,000 and 5,500,000.[4] The increase probably began first

---

[1] Knight, *Ecology and change*, p. 78; Barnes, safari diary, 1 July 1925, RH; D. B. Wilson, *Report of the malaria unit, Tanga, 1933–34* (Dar es Salaam, 1936), p. 28; Lumley, *Forgotten Mandate*, pp. 36–42, 54–6; Jardine to Cunliffe-Lister, 19 October 1933, CO 691/133; Kennedy to Macdonald, 23 February 1939, CO 691/170.

[2] Brooke, 'Heritage', pp. 21–2; Rigby, *Cattle*, p. 21.

[3] *Central Africa*, December 1925, February 1926, December 1933; *Agriculture reports*, 1930, p. 17, 1933, p. 25, 1934, p. 28.

[4] Kuczynski, *Demographic survey*, II, 98, 399.

in high-rainfall areas.[1] Pressed partly by increasing numbers, recolonisation began. Haya pioneers from coffee-growing lakeshore chiefdoms colonised southwards into Ihangiro, westwards into Karagwe, northwards into Missenye. In the 1930s far-seeing Meru and Arusha entrepreneurs acquired large areas of the plains below Mount Meru in a genuine land-rush. Coffee-growing forced many Chagga out into open fields in the *shamba* land of the foothills. Luo colonists from the overpopulated Nyanza province of Kenya continued to press southwards into the Mara region, bringing ploughs to cultivate maize for nearby gold mines.[2] By 1930 some 600 Nyakyusa families had settled in Mbeya district, partly driven by localised land shortage but much more attracted by ample land and the market for crops at the Lupa goldfield. Another 2,400 families followed them during the 1930s.[3]

These pioneers came from high-rainfall areas and produced for the market. After bringing a generation or more of disaster and retreat, Tanganyika's integration with the world economy now stimulated a counter-attack. The process was best seen in Sukumaland. Government regarded Usukuma as the danger point in the expansion of tsetse and concentrated its remedial measures there. Between 1924 and 1939 some 2,000 square kilometres of Sukumaland were cleared under official supervision. But between 1924 and 1947 not less than 8,000 square kilometres of Sukumaland were reopened to human settlement. The balance was cleared by peasant colonists.[4] Their main achievement was in Geita, whose recolonisation began around 1931 as Sukuma settled first on the lake shore and gradually pushed inland. By 1936 some 3,000–4,000 people had entered Geita. Both 'push' and 'pull' factors had brought them. The main 'push' was shortage of land in Mwanza and Kwimba districts, whose population density was estimated in 1934 at 49 per square kilometre. The loss of land to tsetse, the recovery of herds from rinderpest, and the expansion of cotton growing due to motor transport in the 1920s all put pressure on land. It was exacerbated by the depression, which discouraged labour migration and led government to institute a 'plant more crops' campaign. The combination of pressures impelled newly-married Sukuma to emi-

---

[1] Between 1914 and 1930 Chagga numbers may have increased from some 100,000 to 150,000. See Haber to Government, 5 March 1905, RKA 700/93; Dundas to Scott [1925] TNA 11147/2; Bone, Moshi DAR 1948, TNA 69/63/16/1.

[2] J. L. Fairclough, 'Notes on land problems in Bukoba' [March 1938] TNA 11884/11/200/42; Gulliver, 'Interim report', p. 1; Clemm, 'White mountain', p. 318; Wakefield, 'Maize production in North Mara' [August 1937?] TNA 215/1474/1/4.

[3] R. de Z. Hall, 'Local migration in Tanganyika', *African studies*, IV (1945), 53–69.

[4] Ford, *Trypanosomiases*, pp. 198–200.

grate, but what attracted them specifically to Geita was the high cotton yield of its lakeshore land, twice that obtained in Sukumaland.[1] 'A class of native farmer is growing up', the Director of Agriculture wrote in 1933. '...The tendency of the more educated natives to drift to the towns has been checked by the depression and lack of employment, and a large number of natives formerly employed in Government service and by commercial firms have been forced to return to the land...not as a means of subsistence but as a livelihood.'[2] The emergence of rural capitalism had differentiated Tanganyika's peoples and converted some into peasants. Now it provided the energy for a counter-attack against nature.

[1] Rounce, 'Observations...on...the possibilities of settlement in Uzinza', 1934, TNA 215/1047/1/2; Lamb to PC Lake, 30 May 1936, TNA 215/1047/1/88.
[2] *Agriculture report*, 1933, pp. 51–3.

CHAPTER 10

The creation of tribes

In pre-colonial Tanganyika each individual had belonged to several social groups: nuclear family and extended family, lineage and chiefdom, and perhaps clan and tribe. Circumstances had led some to emphasise one identity. Successful warfare had stimulated consciousness of Hehe identity, travel had taught others that strangers called them Nyamwezi, and Shambaa clans had atrophied under unified Kilindi rule. Yet groups and identities had remained so amorphous that to write of them is to oversimplify them.

The colonial period further complicated identities and loyalties. Men might now think of themselves as also being Muslims or Christians, Protestants or Catholics, clerks or workers, Africans, or even Tanganyikans. Again circumstances largely determined which identity they emphasised. Men deeply involved in colonial society formed the Tanganyika Territory African Civil Services Association, while the deprived often stressed parochial identities. But between the wars the chief emphasis was on tribal identity. Men devoted as much energy to consolidating and advancing tribes as their children would later devote to creating a nation. The subject has been little studied, but it is clear that emphasis on tribe rather than other identities resulted from socio-economic change and government policy. The policy was indirect rule. Although conservative in origin it was radical in effect because it rested on historical misunderstanding. The British wrongly believed that Tanganyikans belonged to tribes; Tanganyikans created tribes to function within the colonial framework.

The adoption of indirect rule

The motives for introducing indirect rule were mixed. One was administrative efficiency. Until 1925 Governor Byatt preserved the German administrative structure, with 22 district officers reporting to

318

the secretariat in Dar es Salaam and using chiefs or *akidas* as agents. Either these agents or the district office staff collected tax, while many chiefs continued to receive tribute from their subjects. Although many political units remained unchanged since German times, some district officers made their own innovations. These varied from introducing *akidas* into districts where there had been none before the war, as in Kigoma, to merging small chiefdoms into large ones in an attempt to create 'reunited tribes', as in Tabora.[1] Byatt had little interest in district administration and left district officers to their own devices. By 1924 administration faced serious difficulties. The secretariat was overburdened and wished to decentralise by creating provinces, a proposal equally welcome to district officers who wanted less detailed interference and more general guidance. Tribute was increasingly resented as commercial agriculture developed. When the Treasury insisted that he increase taxation to meet Tanganyika's continuing deficits, Byatt proposed in March 1924 that he should at the same time replace the chiefs' tribute by salaries from government funds.[2]

The Colonial Office greeted Byatt's proposal as 'a step in the direction of..."indirect rule"' and replied with a selection of papers on that policy in Nigeria.[3] Devised twenty years earlier by Sir Frederick Lugard as an expedient method of governing Nigeria's newly-conquered Muslim emirates, indirect rule had developed into a doctrine. Its essence was the complete integration of indigenous political systems into the colonial administration so that 'there are not two sets of rulers – British and Native – working either separately or in co-operation, but a single Government'.[4] The system differed both from direct rule (as in Byatt's Tanganyika) where native authorities needed no indigenous status, and from a 'native state' (as broadly in Buganda) where relations between European and African rulers were fixed by treaty. Under indirect rule a native administration consisted of three parts: a native authority – chief, council, or some combination of these – with legislative and executive powers; native courts; and a native treasury, which collected all taxes, remitting a percentage to central government and retaining the rest to pay the native authority

[1] Bagenal, Kigoma DAR 1924, TNA 1733/3/45/1; Isherwood, Tabora DAR 1923, TNA 1733/21/1; Stiebel, Tabora DAR 1925, TNA 1733/4/52/1.
[2] Byatt to Thomas, 27 March 1924, CO 691/69/352. Generally, see Ralph A. Austen, 'The official mind of indirect rule: British policy in Tanganyika, 1916–1939', in Gifford and Louis, *Britain and Germany*, pp. 577–606.
[3] Strachey to Read, 23 June 1924, CO 691/69/351.
[4] Lugard, quoted in A. H. M. Kirk-Greene (ed.), *The principles of native administration in Nigeria* (London, 1965), p. 71.

and finance local works and services. The European officer's normal role was to supervise and educate, but if necessary he could issue orders to the native administration. This policy was admired by many officials anxious to bring Tanganyika into the mainstream of colonial government. Late in 1924 a conference of district officers unanimously recommended decentralisation through provinces, commutation of tribute, and the establishment in each area of 'an autonomous local native Government having its own legislation, treasury and authorities'.[1]

Early in 1925 Sir Donald Cameron arrived in Tanganyika as Governor. After seventeen years in Nigeria he had been appointed by a Labour government as a man of liberal views, administrative efficiency, and personal dynamism. He later denied that he reached Tanganyika itching to introduce indirect rule,[2] but his letters belie this. On arrival he was appalled by the lack of administrative policy. 'I found each District Officer doing just as he pleased', he told Lugard in September 1925:

There are no general instructions on any question of native policy... Administrative Officers are engaged in every task except Political work which is neglected...Indirect rule is a fiction...The people are out of hand because the Chiefs can no longer punish them.[3]

Cameron had to decide immediately whether chiefs should be paid by central government or local native administrations when tribute was commuted. He chose the latter and thereby committed himself to indirect rule. In July 1925 he outlined its broad principles and six months later ordered the investigations and negotiations needed to establish native administrations.[4] Provinces were established at the same time. Native courts were regularised in 1929. When Cameron left Tanganyika in 1931 almost the whole country was covered by native administrations.

Alongside administrative motives for indirect rule were broader considerations. A West Indian creole, Cameron shared the period's widespread scepticism of the desirability of assimilating non-Europeans to European culture. *Volksmission* theory was one expression of this scepticism. Indirect rule was its political counterpart, and it was reinforced by post-war despair with European values, especially

[1] Tanganyika, *Administrative conference, 1924* (Dar es Salaam, 1924), p. 12.
[2] Sir Donald Cameron, *My Tanganyika service, and some Nigeria* (London, 1939), p. 34.
[3] Cameron to Lugard, 12 September 1925, in Bates, 'British administration', p. 62 n. 2.
[4] Cameron to Amery, 10 July 1925, CO 691/78/94; Cameron, 'Native administration', 16 July 1925, TNA 7777/20; Cameron, *Tanganyika service*, pp. 22–4, 31–4.

among conservative Englishmen. Intellectuals seriously feared that Africans, like Australian aboriginees, might die out unless their institutions were deliberately preserved. Cameron was too robust to accept all the implications of this view, but his creole background, Nigerian experience, and contacts with *Volksmission* theorists in London convinced him of its central point. 'It is our duty', he wrote soon after reaching Tanganyika,

> to do everything in our power to develop the native on lines which will not Westernise him and turn him into a bad imitation of a European – our whole Education policy is directed to that end. We want to make him a good African...We must not...destroy the African atmosphere, the African mind, the whole foundations of his race, and we shall certainly do this if we sweep away all his tribal organisations.[1]

For Cameron, indirect rule was also a political calculation. European settlers in Kenya and their Conservative sympathisers in Britain were urging Tanganyika into a 'closer union' with Kenya and Uganda. The campaign collapsed in the early 1930s, largely because the settlers wanted only a union they controlled, other parties made rejection of settler control their precondition, and the Government of India was powerful enough to veto the scheme.[2] During the late 1920s Cameron openly opposed the plan, partly because it threatened his own power but also because he believed that it would sacrifice Africans to Europeans. Yet he recognized that European settlers were a permanency and sought to improve his strained relations with them by creating a Legislative Council with European and Asian unofficial members in 1926. Since Cameron held that Africans were not yet ready to join this council, he sought by means of indirect rule to create areas of limited African self-government outside settler influence as training grounds and power bases for future African political participation, thereby 'preparing a place in the political world for the native'.[3]

Yet for which native? Alongside its idealism, indirect rule contained much conservative self-interest. In the early 1920s Britain experienced the strength of nationalism in Ireland, India, and Egypt. Lugard had devised indirect rule partly as a counterweight to the 'Europeanised Africans' of Lagos. Cameron also saw it in these terms. 'If we set up merely a European form of administration', he warned,

---

[1] Cameron, 'Native administration', 16 July 1925, TNA 7777/20.
[2] See Robert G. Gregory, *Sidney Webb and East Africa* (Berkeley, 1962), *passim*; Gupta, *Imperialism*, pp. 129 n. 209, 180–6.
[3] Great Britain, *Joint select committee on closer union in East Africa: II: minutes of evidence* (London, 1931), para. 1,816.

the day will come when the people of the Territory will demand that the British form of administration shall pass into their hands – we have India at our doors as an object lesson. If we aim at indirect administration through the appropriate Native Authority – Chief or Council – founded on the people's own traditions and preserving their own tribal organisation, their own laws and customs purged of anything that is 'repugnant to justice and morality' we shall be building an edifice with some foundation to it, capable of standing the shock which will inevitably come when the educated native seeks to gain possession of the machinery of Government and to run it on Western lines... If we treat them properly, moreover, we shall have the members of the Native Administration on our side.[1]

Indirect rule was not simply 'divide and rule': it had more positive goals than that, and its more intelligent proponents denied any wish 'to use the old fashioned savage to bottle up the progressives'.[2] But it was, in Professor Austen's phrase, 'a safely non-nationalist basis for African political development'.[3]

In adopting indirect rule Tanganyika followed general British practice in inter-war Africa, but Tanganyika's peculiarity was that it had been a German colony. All colonial regimes had short memories, but British memories in Tanganyika were especially brief. Convinced by their own propaganda, most British officers believed that the Germans had sought 'to crush the existing social system by methods of violence and completely destroy the power of the chiefs', appointing alien *akidas*.[4] Consequently indirect rule did not mean incorporating existing institutions into the colonial structure – as Lugard had done in Northern Nigeria – but reconstructing the institutions existing before the disaster of German rule. 'The difficulty after a period of disintegration', Cameron told a visitor, 'is to find out what their system was. *They* know perfectly well but, for one reason or other, they may not tell you.'[5] Others were more confident:

The form of government best suited to African Natives at their present stage of development has been definitely decided and all efforts have been directed towards evolving a system for the native of the Dar es Salaam District compatible with the accepted policy of Indirect Rule through Native Authorities.

Such a system must obviously be a normal evolution of whatever form of tribal government exists, or existed prior to the introduction by Europeans in 1888 of disruptive influences, and later the considered policy of the late

[1] Cameron, minute, 24 April 1925, TNA 7777/3.
[2] Mitchell diary, 23 December 1930, RH.
[3] Austen in Gifford and Louis, *Britain and Germany*, pp. 593–4.
[4] Byatt to Long, 7 June 1917, CO 691/5/306.
[5] Quoted in Margery Perham, *East African journey* (London, 1976), p. 43.

German Government to weaken tribal cohesion and break down tribal government. It is therefore essential to obtain a true appreciation of the existing conditions and forms of government immediately prior to German occupation and rule, for certainly there was some form of government, and up to that date tribal Government had evolved upon normal lines, and that date marks the point in Zaramu tribal history when further evolution of purely tribal Government ceased.[1]

Since establishment of native administrations was as much a historical as a political exercise, its outcome depended heavily on the historical views current among administrators or plausibly advocated by interested Africans. Much effort was devoted to 'finding the chief' by recording the genealogies which African contestants invented. 'Each tribe must be considered as a distinct unit...Each tribe must be under a chief', one provincial commissioner told his staff in 1926.[2] But most administrators knew that many peoples had no chiefs, and the construction of conciliar systems for stateless peoples was Cameron's chief contribution to indirect rule. Consequently, when an official proposed to subordinate lesser Nyakyusa chiefs to more powerful ones, a superior quickly pointed out that the object was not to 'manufacture paramount chiefs'. 'We don't want to know what he can devise so much as what the Natives devised long ago', another added, and Cameron summarised the whole policy by explaining that 'Mr Thompson must take the *tribal* unit'.[3]

The notion of tribe lay at the heart of indirect rule in Tanganyika. Refining the racial thinking common in German times, administrators believed that every African belonged to a tribe, just as every European belonged to a nation. The idea doubtless owed much to the Old Testament, to Tacitus and Caesar, to academic distinctions between tribal societies based on status and modern societies based on contract, and to post-war anthropologists who preferred 'tribal' to the more pejorative word 'savage'.[4] Tribes were seen as cultural units 'possessing a common language, a single social system, and an established customary law'.[5] Their political and social systems rested on kinship. Tribal membership was hereditary. Different tribes were

[1] Anonymous memorandum, March 1930, in Kisarawe district book, TNA.
[2] Quoted in James D. Graham, 'Indirect rule: the establishment of "chiefs" and "tribes" in Cameron's Tanganyika', *TNR*, LXXVII (1976), 4.
[3] Minutes by Mitchell, Dundas, and Cameron, October 1925, on Thompson to CS, 15 September 1925, TNA 2724/31.
[4] As in Bronislaw Malinowski, *Argonauts of the western Pacific* (London, 1922: reprinted, 1972), pp. 10–11.
[5] Tanganyika, *Native administration memorandum no. 11: native courts* (2nd edn, Dar es Salaam, 1930), p. 1.

related genealogically, so that Africa's history was a vast family tree of tribes. Small tribes were offshoots of big ones and might therefore be reunited. Whole tribes migrated in *Völkerwanderungen*, recalling places of origin and routes of migration. Chieftainship emerged when 'the peaceful home Bantu peoples' were dominated by Hamitic immigrants, 'just by being superior'.[1]

As unusually well-informed officials knew,[2] this stereotype bore little relation to Tanganyika's kaleidoscopic history, but it was the shifting sand on which Cameron and his disciples erected indirect rule by 'taking the *tribal* unit'. They had the power and they created a new political geography. This would have been transient, however, had it not coincided with similar trends among Africans. They too had to live amidst bewildering social complexity, which they ordered in kinship terms and buttressed with invented history. Moreover, Africans wanted effective units of action just as officials wanted effective units of government. Many Africans had strong personal motives for creating new units which they could lead. Europeans believed Africans belonged to tribes; Africans built tribes to belong to.

During the twenty years after 1925 Tanganyika experienced a vast social reorganisation in which Europeans and Africans combined to create a new political order based on mythical history. 'Assuming that the Germans had never occupied the country these Pazi [headmen] or their descendants would still be in power', a district officer explained, adding that the people had enthusiastically chosen the appropriate descendants. His successor described those selected as 'the imbecile, the leper, the syphilitic, ex-convicts, ex-ricksha boys, ex-domestic servants and so on. Any one in fact who was incapable or unlikely to exercise authority.'[3] 'A large portion of the district easily and naturally falls back into the state in which it was some 70 years ago', an officer reported from Songea.[4] 'You have given our country back to us', wrote the Nyakyusa paramount chief shortly after his invention in 1926.[5] Yet it would be wrong to be cynical. The effort to create a Nyakyusa tribe was as honest and constructive as the essentially similar effort forty years later to create a Tanganyikan

[1] CS to SCs, 5 February 1926, TNA 4/6/5; Cory, 'Land tenure in Bugufi', p. 14.
[2] Notably Dundas. See Graham, 'Indirect rule', p. 5.
[3] Fryer, Dar es Salaam DAR 1929, TNA 54/3; Ronayne, 'The district of Dar es Salaam: handing-over report, October 1935', TNA 61/161/A/1/50.
[4] Longland, 1925, quoted in Gallagher, 'Islam', p. 306.
[5] MacAllan, Rungwe DAR 1926, TNA library.

nation. Both were attempts to build societies in which men could live well in the modern world.

The implementation of indirect rule

'Paradoxical as it may seem', Cameron observed in 1928 after touring Sukumaland,

although indirect has replaced direct administration there is a great deal more administration than there was before. The peasant of remote Meatu, on the shores of Lake Eyassi, is now linked up to his Headman, the Headman to the Sub-Chief, the Sub-Chief to the Chief, and the Chief to the District Office. The Provincial Commissioner can be aware of what is happening throughout his Province as he certainly was not aware before.[1]

This was true. Until 1925 district administration was largely confined to building, punishing violence, collecting tax, hearing those cases brought to the boma, establishing relationships with local rulers, and touring sufficiently for each village to glimpse an official every few years. Indirect rule marked a second stage of European control, a deeper penetration of society by the state, and a most important standardisation of Tanganyikan life.[2]

Standardised government needed standardised administrators. Before 1914 British colonial officials were recruited *ad hoc* from untrained applicants, often with military backgrounds, but during the 1920s the Colonial Office began to recruit administrators chiefly from Oxford and Cambridge. Holding that government must be learned through experience, the recruiters sought men who were – in a favourite phrase – 'chiefs in their own country', with good general educations and strong moral qualities. Unlike the Home and Indian civil services there were no written examinations, but applicants were screened by references and interviews designed to identify 'those qualities of character and personality so essential in dealing with native peoples'.[3] Their backgrounds have not been studied systematically, but most administrators probably came from upper middle class families with traditions of authority and service. Many were probably escaping the class-ridden tedium of inter-war Britain. They romanticised their work, especially in retrospect,[4] but most were honest, just, energetic

[1] Cameron, 'Tour through Mwanza Province', 18 August 1928, TNA 12662/14.
[2] See the analysis in Larson, 'History', ch. 5.
[3] Ralph Furse, *Aucuparius: recollections of a recruiting officer* (London, 1962), p. 122. See also Robert Heussler, *Yesterday's rulers: the making of the British colonial service* (London, 1963).   [4] Lumley, *Forgotten Mandate*, is a good example.

officials, less colourful but more humane than their predecessors and working as interchangeable parts in an administration notorious for rapid movement of staff. 'You will ask what of the native – Is he any happier or better off?' an official mused:

Well, Sir, we have tried to make the King's Writ run in Dodoma and put redress for wrong within the reach of all...At the Baraza Court at Dodoma alone 701 natives have stated their wrongs and been judged by their peers before the Bwana Shauri [district officer]. Often a chief has to step down from the dais to answer a charge brought against him by one of his people ...We have given them schools for their children and hospitals for their sick...It is our job of work and we should have to do it whatever the view the native might take as to our motives. But...the one refrain you can recognize coming from any ngoma in the district is the refrain of the song they sing to celebrate the end of famine...: 'Food came from the coast, there is always rain there. A Whiteman brought it we don't know his name'.[1]

Many district officers laboured in this way to ameliorate evils which were in part – but only in part – the consequences of the colonial system which they served. They cared for the virtues of an ordered rural society and provided it with schools and courts, with roads and creameries and 'the unspeakable benefit of justice'.[2] But they also believed it their duty to protect society from disruptive change and to safeguard their own rule on which collective welfare seemed to depend. Peasants were encouraged to grow coffee, but coffee farmers were 'swollen-headed' and subversive. The 'natural African' was 'the man in the blanket',[3] while towns were alien and dangerous. District reports show that after 1925 concern with economic development was swamped by interest in administrative structure – it was in 1926 that officers first declared the Gogo uninterested in progress.[4] Indirect rule became a means of social control rather than social progress. Officials came to assume that a native authority could order its subjects to do anything. By the late 1930s native authorities, instructed by European 'advisers', were ordering men to quit homes in the interests of soil conservation, to destroy herds in the interests of balanced stock-keeping, to uproot coffee trees in the interests of improved husbandry. Behind the whole structure, latent and rarely visible, was the underlying violence of colonial government. It was no accident that

[1] Hignell, Dodoma DAR 1920–1, TNA library.
[2] Cameron, 'Native administration', 3 November 1925, TNA 7777/57B.
[3] Furse, *Aucuparius*, p. 264.
[4] Hartnoll, Dodoma DAR 1926, TNA library.

lawyers were the Europeans most critical of 'the oppressive and static qualities of indirect rule'.[1]

Analysing the system, one officer concluded that its main supporters were the progressive chiefs.[2] Although their lives remain to be written, it is clear that they were the key figures in indirect rule. Its chief virtue was indeed to release their energies. Perhaps the most remarkable was Mgeni of the Turu. With 200,000 subjects he was Tanganyika's most powerful chief, and most administrators thought he was its best. He had no hereditary status, for the Turu had been stateless, but he had risen through diplomatic skill and European favour during the war, and became paramount chief in 1924. A Muslim, fluent in Swahili but barely literate, obsequious towards Europeans but popular with his subjects, he was exactly the government-appointed intermediary acceptable and necessary to a stateless people compelled to deal with a colonial government and anxious for the leadership needed to enact new laws and organise development. Mgeni was famed for justice in court, but he also encouraged education, ploughing, famine crops, and all the rural improvements at a progressive chief's command. Although rich in cattle, his salary was relatively small and he refused the motor car which was normally the progressive chief's status symbol. 'Met Chief Mgeni', was a district officer's first diary entry on reaching Singida, and thereafter he rarely communicated with the Turu except through the chief.[3] Among Mgeni's contemporaries and counterparts might be listed Minja of Ugweno, Abdiel Shangali of Machame, Gabriel Ruhumbika of Ukerewe, Dominikus Chabruma of Mshope, and many others who recreated the tradition of progressive chieftainship stretching back to Rindi and Mirambo.

Although some Europeans feared that the bureaucratic aspects of indirect rule might weaken the chiefs' authority, this was largely because they listened to the chiefs' complaints and exaggerated pre-colonial harmony and authority. In reality, as many officials realised, whether the new system strengthened an individual chief depended largely on how effectively he exploited it, and there was a general tendency to level out the chiefs' power, reducing that of a

[1] Bushe to Dawe, 10 March 1939, CO 691/168. Bushe was Legal Adviser to the Colonial Office.
[2] A. T. and G. M. Culwick, 'What the Wabena think of indirect rule', *Journal of the Royal African Society*, xxxvi (1937), 186–8.
[3] Diary of F. C. Hallier, 3 May 1931, RH. See also Sick, 'Waniaturu', p. 1; Singida district book, TNA; Singida DARs 1919–27, TNA library; Marguerite R. Jellicoe, 'Social change in Singida', M.A. thesis, Makerere University College, 1967, p. 125.

Merere or Kalemera while increasing that exercised in more egalitarian societies. 'Before you Europeans came', Nyakyusa told a social anthropologist, 'the chiefs like Mwaipopo were not awe-inspiring, they feared the commoners very much...It is you Europeans who have created chieftainship and awe.'[1] Official salaries made chiefs much richer than their subjects. Native treasuries kept less than a third of the tax they collected, and more than 60 per cent of their income during the 1930s was absorbed by recurrent costs of administration, notably the chiefs' salaries.[2] In 1927 the eight Haya chiefs received about half the native treasury's income of £19,860, while Kasusura of Rusubi was paid £960 from a native treasury income of £1,383 and continued to collect tribute as though it had never been commuted. His chiefdom's extraordinary expenditure in 1927 was nil.[3] Other benefits also accrued to native authorities. Saidi Fundikira of Unyanyembe embezzled over £10,000 of tax before discovery.[4] Besides his 40 wives and 160 children, Makongoro of Ikizu employed his subjects to pick his cotton and induced them to buy him a car.[5] When Tabora school was opened in 1925 it initially admitted only chiefs' relatives. The leading native authority school in Unyakyusa, a district officer complained in 1938, 'is an aristocratic school, confined to the sons of Government and Native Authority employees and of a few rich men...with the result that a far greater disparity is growing up between them and the rest of the community than existed under primitive tribal conditions'.[6]

Only in areas of exceptional education and wealth did chiefs yet meet serious opposition from educated subjects. The Bukoba and Kilimanjaro riots of 1937 had no counterparts elsewhere. Where education was less widely available, opposition came mainly from the chiefs' conservative kinsmen, for the native administrations employed many members of the local elite, who were also often the chiefs' relatives. Usukuma's native administrations were increasingly controlled by their educated clerks and treasurers during the 1930s,[7] and this may have been true of other native administrations, but historians

---

[1] Wilson, *Communal rituals*, p. 13.
[2] Bates, 'British administration', p. 96.
[3] Dundas to Cameron [1927?] TNA 10952/1; Vickers-Haviland, Biharamulo DAR 1927, TNA 215/77/A/2.
[4] Cameron, 'Malversation of public funds by Chief Saidi of Unyanyembe', 9 July 1929, CO 691/105.
[5] E. B. Moronda, 'Chief Makongoro', typescript [1967?] in Mr Moronda's possession.
[6] Hall, minute, 15 September 1938, and Hall to PC Southern Highlands, 5 October 1938, TNA 18/12/11/120 and 122.
[7] Austen, *Northwest Tanzania*, pp. 238–40.

have not yet begun to examine their records. Even educated men without native administration posts generally acknowledged hereditary authority. TTACSA applauded indirect rule, while Martin Kayamba prided himself on descent from Kimweri ya Nyumbai and was happiest when visiting native authorities to discuss education and rural advancement. In return many chiefs welcomed educated guidance. In 1934 Towegale of lowland Ubena visited Dar es Salaam and stayed in Kayamba's house:

> The meeting made a profound impression, and he came away convinced that the policy of Government was not directed towards the everlasting subordination of his race...Motor roads and ferries, markets, brick buildings – houses, dispensaries, and a school – are the immediate outcome, and what is even more valuable, the will to learn to shoulder more and more responsibility.[1]

The outstanding exponent of progressive traditionalism was Francis Lwamugira of Buhaya. A mission-educated courtier from Kiziba, Lwamugira so impressed the British that when a single native administration was created for the eight Haya chiefdoms in 1926 he became its secretary. For the next nineteen years he ran the most elaborate bureaucracy in African hands. All administrative posts were in his gift and tended to go to men from Kiziba, whose early educational lead provided trained recruits. His control of funds and council business, his experience and ability, and the knowledge that the British took his advice when appointing chiefs won him the title of 'the ninth Mukama' and the hatred of the younger chiefs, despite his outward deference. Lwamugira forced through the building of schools and dispensaries and roads, compelled parents to educate their children, and supported any project of economic development unless it threatened the established order. Rioters stoned him in 1937, but to the British he was 'the most perfect native gentleman'.[2]

Indirect rule encouraged the crystallisation of African social organisation into a tribal mould. The most blatant tribe-maker was H. C. Stiebel. Trained in the Transvaal, he believed that Africans belonged by nature and history to 'tribal nations' which had been broken up by recent change but could be reunited with ethnological and administrative advantage, preferably under paramount chiefs, 'until ultimately unions are formed which will not be far short of

[1] Culwick, 'Indirect rule', p. 190.
[2] Fairclough, Bukoba DAR 1932, TNA 251/1138. See I. K. Katoke and P. Rwehumbiza, 'The administrator: Francis Lwamugira', in Iliffe, *Tanzanians*, pp. 43–65; Austen, *Northwest Tanzania*, pp. 89–90, 162–3, 173–4.

nationalities'.[1] In Tabora district he subordinated smaller chiefdoms to Unyanyembe – perhaps the best example of the British favouring those who had resisted the Germans, especially after 1929 when Isike's descendants displaced the now discredited line of Bibi Nyaso. Stiebel also sought to reconstruct the Usongo hegemony which the Germans had deliberately destroyed after Mtinginya's death. Further north his success varied, but by his departure in 1929 there were paramount chiefs in Usumbwa, Kwimba, and Buzinza, while the Binza and Shinyanga chiefdoms were federated and three amalgamations existed in Mwanza district. The paramountcies later gave way to looser federations, but the policy of amalgamating the small chiefdoms of the western plateau into larger units survived the Second World War. 'Sukuma' had once been simply the Nyamwezi word for 'north', but in 1945 a Sukuma Union was formed.[2]

The chief obstacles to Cameron's social engineering were stateless peoples. Nobody doubted that councils were less efficient and convenient than paramount chiefs. If a chief like Mgeni could be induced to emerge, this was the ideal solution. Where none appeared, one alternative was to subordinate a stateless people to a neighbouring chiefdom, so that indirect rule contained a distinct bias against stateless societies. The Sagara, for example, remained under the Hehe sub-chiefs imposed on them after Maji Maji, but these were now subordinate to Mkwawa's son and the Sagara were more fully integrated into the Hehe state than ever before.[3] Religious leaders were converted into administrative chiefs in Uluguru and Iramba, while the *laibon* was recognised as paramount chief of the Masai.[4] Another approach was to elevate the most prominent local headmen into chiefs, but this was almost always a disaster. Attempts to administer the Makonde through headmen descended from pioneer settlers were unconvincing:

The somewhat primitive minded headmen...generally reply *iko* (there is) to any query concerning administration or procedure, but give the same old man a complicated inheritance case to decide, involving barter, gift and levy in items varying from drums to dried fish, he will ascend the family tree and descend it by 9 branches and 13 collaterals and a bend sinister to deliver a perfectly

---

[1] Dundas to Cameron [1927?] TNA 10952/1; Stiebel, Tabora DAR 1925, TNA 1733/4/52/1; Austen, *Northwest Tanzania*, pp. 182–6.
[2] Below, p. 487.
[3] Northcote to CS, 3 May 1928, TNA 11414/1/7.
[4] Roland Young and Henry Fosbrooke, *Land and politics among the Luguru of Tanganyika* (London, 1960), p. 84; Flynn, Singida DAR 1927, TNA library; Jacobs, 'Pastoral Masai', p. 107.

equitable judgment in terms of beeswax without looking up from his matutinal porridge; ask him how many court receipts have been issued and he will probably say *iko*.[1]

Most Makonde headmen were abandoned as hopeless in 1937 and *liwalis* were appointed on the German model. Moreover, Cameron never understood that while many stateless peoples recognised the advantages of a central authority, they nevertheless often preferred to remain stateless, at least in their internal relations, and were chiefly concerned that the agents of the alien administration should themselves be aliens so that they could not jeopardise the internal egalitarianism which was central to the group's identity and ideology. Such jealously egalitarian peoples as the Matumbi failed to produce any native authority. An attempted Pangwa paramountcy 'foundered on the mountaineers' individualism and lust for independence'. The Segeju refused to elect a senior headman and preferred an official nominee provided that he remained an *akida* rather than a native authority – with the implication that he could then have no claim to legitimacy within Segeju society.[2]

Historians have neglected the process of tribal aggregation. It could be conservative. A remarkable ritual leader, Nade Bea, appears to have sanctioned the very striking unification and geographical expansion of the Iraqw people which took place in the twentieth century.[3] But aggregation was often encouraged by social change. The KNPA was the first organisation to override Kilimanjaro's chiefdom rivalries, for example, and its success led Chagga chiefs to unite in a council to defend hereditary authority. As one said of the coffee farmers, 'These people's influence is over the whole tribe whereas our influence is only in our own sections of the mountain.'[4] By 1934 Chagga chiefs were discussing the selection of a paramount, although they were discussing it in Swahili because their dialects were mutually unintelligible. Among the Kerewe the *bangoma* broke down status divisions and helped to create a single tribe, and a trend towards specifically tribal dances was a general consequence of intermingling in the early colonial period. Urbanisation also encouraged tribal aggregation.[5] The most spectacular new tribe were the Nyakyusa. In the nineteenth century their

[1] Tanganyika, *Annual reports of the Provincial Commissioners*, 1929, p. 36.
[2] *Ibid.*, 1932, p. 10; Stirnimann, 'Zur Gesellschaftsordnung', p. 395; Harrington, Tanga DAR 1926, TNA library.
[3] Yoneyama, 'Life and society', p. 109.
[4] PC Northern to CS, 25 August 1931, TNA 26034/39.
[5] Above, pp. 238, 299; below, pp. 389–91.

name described only inhabitants of certain lakeshore chiefdoms. Some German observers and early British officials extended it to embrace also the Kukwe and Selya further north, their culture being broadly similar. After failing to impose paramounts on this essentially stateless people, the British established a council of chiefs in 1933 and described it as the tribal system. Buttressed by distinctive culture, common language, and sheer isolation, the newly-invented Nyakyusa tribe soon became an effective political unit. In 1942 a Nyakyusa Union was formed 'to preserve the good customs and habits of the tribe'.[1]

One example of tribal aggregation so completely illustrates the process that it deserves more extensive treatment: the introduction of indirect rule into the region surrounding the lower Pangani. This began in 1925 when the British rediscovered the Shambaa kingdom, whose institutions had been supplanted by *akidas* since Kinyashi's abdication in 1902. Before Kinyashi was restored to power in 1926 the rains broke and a lion entered Vugha for the first time in years,[2] but to recreate the Shambaa state was also to recreate the conflicts which had brought 'the time of rapacity'. The one indubitably traditional thing about the kingdom was that its power relations were contentious. Kinyashi represented only one of the parties which had fought for Kimweri ya Nyumbai's inheritance. An elderly, frail, introspective, and superstitious man, he was terrified of witchcraft, convinced that Vugha would be as fatal to him as to his father and grandfather, and so aware that he reigned by British favour that he apparently hoarded his salary in order to return it when he was deposed.[3] In 1929 he abdicated a second time, and in his place the British turned to the rival faction, installing successively two grandsons of Semboja. Moreover, recreating the kingdom also revived the old dispute over the extent of the king's control over provincial sub-chiefs. After twelve years of resistance, the sub-chief of long-independent Mlalo was deposed for insubordination in 1942, the district officer having decided to his own satisfaction that 'the chief and elders [of Vugha]...have the right to turn out an unsuitable sub-chief'.[4]

Since the most dramatic incident of the Shambaa civil war had been

[1] Wilson, *Good company*, p. 2 n. 2; Helmuth von Trotha, 'Begleitworte zu der Garnison-Umgebungs-Karte von Massoko', *MDS*, XXVI (1913), 344; Tukuyu district book, TNA; 'Sheria zilizotungwa na kuthubutishwa na Umoja wa Wanyakyusa wa Mbeya' [1942?] TNA 33/A/6/35.
[2] Barnes to CS, 27 January 1926, Barnes papers V, RH. For the background, see above, pp. 65–6.
[3] Feierman, 'Concepts', p. 398.
[4] E. B. Dobson, 'Land tenure of the Wasambaa', *TNR*, x (1940), 7.

the Kiva uprising by which the Bondei regained independence, restoration of the kingdom naturally alarmed the Bondei. A resolutely stateless people, the Bondei could not accept any of their number as leader, since the head of any one family inevitably aroused the opposition of all other families. The Germans met this difficulty by appointing an alien *akida*, as did the early British regime, but Cameron's obsessive hatred of *akidas* made it necessary to convert the *akida* into an elected *jumbe mkuu* (superior headman). At the first election in November 1925 the two candidates were the serving *akida*, John Juma, son of a Kilindi man and a Bondei woman, and Geldart Mhina, a Christian Bondei clerk and founder of TTACSA. According to the provincial commissioner, 95 per cent of the elders and headmen chose John Juma, although all would have preferred him to be *akida*.[1] The defeated party saw the choice of a part-Kilindi as a restoration of Kilindi hegemony:

Bondeis will not prosper, nor advance, they will live in ignorance and barbarity if they do not accept a Sultan. The Government should enforce this matter whether the Bondei like it or not: they must have an Mbondei Sultan, like other tribes...

The Government should find a good and intelligent man, who understands to read, a middle-aged man, and a pure Bondei who will be able to look after and lead his brothers and tribe according to law and justice.[2]

Twice more between the wars – in 1930 and 1934 – Bondei elders were unable to agree on the choice of a *jumbe mkuu* and had to accept the government's nomination of men with Kilindi affiliations.[3] In the interim Bondei learned to couch political claims in historical language. While Geldart Mhina protested that he was the last survivor of Bonde's ancient rulers, his supporters claimed that the massacre of Kilindi during Kiva returned to their minds 'whenever we see on the throne a Kilindi'. When, they demanded, would Bonde be granted indirect rule?[4] Their notion of a 'pure Bondei' came strangely from that section of the Shambaa-Zigua linguistic group living 'in the valley'.

The final consequence of restoring the Shambaa kingdom was to revive the ancient dispute about its borders. The British held that it had 'dominated the whole of the Usambara District with the

---

[1] Baines to CS, 4 November 1925, and White to SC Tanga, 20 November 1925, TNA 4/6/1/1/21 and 33.
[2] Mdoe to Tanga, 8 November 1925, TNA 4/6/1/1/27.
[3] Baines to CS, 27 November 1930, TNA 4/6/1/11/19; Grierson to CS, 13 October 1934, TNA 26162/22.
[4] 'The Bondeis' to MacMichael, 4 October 1934, and 'Wazee wa inchi, Wabondei' to MacMichael, 23 October 1934, TNA 26162/13 and 26.

exception of the South Pare mountains', including the valley below
the southern mountain face whose Zigua inhabitants, so the British
claimed, had acknowledged the king at Vugha 'as their Overlord or
Paramount Chief'.[1] The previously independent Zigua headman was
therefore incorporated into the Shambaa native administration. In the
meantime, however, the bulk of the Zigua, who lived in other districts,
were consolidated into a tribal federation in 1928. 'It was not as in olden
days of our ancestors when they met with furious faces ready for war',
one rejoiced. 'I hope our fellow Zigua people in various countries will
hear that now Zigua has united into one nation, therefore let all the
Zigua descendants return and enter into the unity and become a
nation.'[2] Thus inspired, the Zigua under Kilindi rule formed an
association 'to protect their interests in the country of their adoption'.
In 1943 they petitioned for the return of the valley lands, claiming that
these had been part of Uzigua before the German invasion. Advised
by a scarcely disinterested missionary in Mlalo, the British rejected the
petition on historical grounds. In fact the Zigua were entirely right,
for their ancestors had seized the valley during Kimweri ya Nyumbai's
dotage. Continuing Zigua irredentism was to have an important
influence on responses to nationalism in this area in the 1950s.[3] Thus,
as in Usambara and Bonde, old conflicts, much transformed, were
carried into modern politics, while African political thought and
organisation adopted the framework of colonial administration.

The ideology of indirect rule

Just as later nationalists sought to create a national culture, so those
who built modern tribes emphasised tribal cultures. In each case
educated men took the lead. Between the wars their attitudes to
indigenous cultures were varied and ambiguous. The freed slaves like
Martin Ganisya who had turned their backs on the past were aging.
Their uncritical westernisation – Ganisya held that Africans did not
want to preserve their cultures[4] – might still be found among young
townsmen, and many educated men like Martin Kayamba affected
European clothes and displayed a sense of cultural inferiority, but
Kayamba was also an ardent tribal historian who believed that 'there

[1] Barnes, Usambara DAR 1925, TNA 1733/11/79/3.
[2] Enclosed in PC Tanga to CS, 9 April 1928, TNA 11412.
[3] DC Korogwe, 'Report on Zigua agitation', 1 June 1943, and Bonavia to CS, 9 June 1943, TNA 31515/15A and 15; above, p. 65; below, p. 528.
[4] Eggert, *Missionsschule*, p. 235.

was much to be praised in [Africa's] earlier forms of government'.[1]
Such men sought to reconcile the old and new societies. Their
solutions were often highly personal. Kayamba, the master of
compromise, believed, for example, that Africans had built Zimbabwe
for non-Africans. The Nyakyusa pastor Lazarus Mwanjisi rarely wore
European clothes but resigned his teaching post at Rungwe for a
better-paid government appointment. 'I wish I could tear off this black
skin of mine. We are every whit as good as the whiteman and as fit
to control our own country,' declared a Chagga teacher, Petro Njau,
who was later a prominent neo-traditionalist politician.[2] The problem
was to synthesise, to 'pick out what is best from [European culture]
and dilute it with what we hold'.[3] In doing so, educated men naturally
reformulated the past, so that their syntheses were actually new
creations.

One area of rethinking was an interest among African Christians
in the indigenous religions against which early converts had often
reacted violently. As early as 1904 a teacher wrote a treatise on
indigenous medicines for his colleagues,[4] but it was not until
missionaries studied African religions carefully during the 1920s that
most Africans dared to reconsider their attitudes publicly. Michael
Kikurwe, a Zigua teacher and cultural tribalist, envisaged a golden age
of traditional African society:

In each district men and women were busy to help one another, they taught
their children the same laws and traditions. Every Chief tried as much as he
could to help and please his people, and likewise his people did the same in
turn, they all knew what was lawful and unlawful, and they knew that there
is a powerful God in heaven, and they had many ways of worshipping him.[5]

Samuel Sehoza pioneered the idea that indigenous religious beliefs had
prefigured Christianity.[6] 'In their minds', he wrote of Bondei
mourning ceremonies, 'there is a part of human nature which does
not share the death or the decay of the body...Surely it is the
soul.' His disciples developed his ideas vigorously. Quoting a phrase
sung in Shambaa sacrifices – 'But I kill on this log' – a teacher
commented: 'A log means a dry tree. Who was slain on a dry tree?'[7]

[1] H. M. T. Kayamba, *African problems* (London, 1948), p. 19.
[2] *Ibid.*, p. 81; Gemuseus and Busse, *Ein Gebundener*, pp. 92–3; Stuart-Watt, *Dome of mystery*, p. 199; below, pp. 492–3.
[3] Kayamba, *Problems*, p. 23.   [4] *Central Africa*, July 1904.
[5] Kikurwe to PC Tanga, 11 June 1947, TNA 6/A/6/2/43b.
[6] In *Central Africa*, August 1929 – March 1930.
[7] Mwalimu Yoswa in *ibid.*, May 1937.

Studying the *galo* initiation ceremony, another Bondei teacher, John Sepeku – later Tanganyika's first Anglican archbishop – found 'signs' prefiguring confession, original sin, guardian angels, hell, and several commandments.[1] African schoolteachers were often interested in pre-colonial education.[2]

These ideas coincided neatly with European concern to revive indigenous institutions or adapt Christianity to indigenous societies according to *Volksmission* principles. Yet missionary adaptation, like indirect rule, produced neither a revival of indigenous rituals and institutions nor exactly the Christianised forms of them which the missionaries desired, but instead created essentially new forms shaped chiefly by the Africans who gained control of the adaptation process. In his study of Bishop Lucas's attempt to create Christian initiation rites in Masasi, Professor Ranger has shown that African priests and teachers cooperated because they gained two important advantages. They were genuinely interested in adaptation, for it met their need for an accommodation between African cultures and their new faith, and they were able to enhance their status as against both the local chiefs who had previously controlled initiation and the missionaries who were inhibited from interfering too deeply.[3] By contrast, unwillingness to meet the political and intellectual interests of African leaders hampered the adaptation experiment conducted on Kilimanjaro by the Lutheran missionary, Bruno Gutmann. Disillusioned with European civilisation and appalled by the materialism of Kilimanjaro's emerging peasant society, Gutmann insisted that Africans must never be treated as individuals but always as members of organic groups based on 'primordial social ties'. He sought to incorporate these groups – clans, age sets, elders – into church organisation. He opposed both the KNPA and the ordination of educated Chagga, and he failed. Legend has it that a campaign led by Joseph Merinyo culminated in an all-night confrontation between Merinyo and Gutmann during which the missionary was persuaded to accept an African clergy.[4]

Inter-war history-writing reveals a similar combination of intellectual ambivalence, political self-seeking, and creative energy. Like later nationalism, cultural tribalism led men to collect or invent traditions. Kayamba spent his accumulated leave writing Shambaa history and studying Digo customs. That busy bureaucrat Francis Lwamugira

---

[1] *Ibid.*, October 1937.   [2] E.g. Yonathan Madengelo in *Mwanafunzi*, March 1939.
[3] Ranger in Ranger and Kimambo, *Historical study*, pp. 225–47.
[4] Rogers, 'Political focus', pp. 436–49. Gutmann's basic work is *Gemeindeaufbau aus dem Evangelium* (Leipzig, 1925).

planned a compilation of Haya traditions so vast that he could not afford to publish it. J. M. Kadaso in Bukwimba, Nathanael Mtui on Kilimanjaro, Dominikus Chabruma in Mshope, and many lesser men filled countless exercise books with local traditions.[1] Many were self-interested. A Chagga dissident of 1937 wrote a history of Kilimanjaro aimed against chiefly authority:

The Mangi relied on the united opinion of all the aboriginal inhabitants...The Wamangi did the manual work by the effort of their own hands...The Wachagga say in reality that the former Chiefs had less power and they were more or less like mere clerks.[2]

More commonly history buttressed a claim to rule. 'I have thought it well to claim the chieftainship of this country', a Pare aspirant blandly explained, 'for it has been my family's inheritance for many years and so in 1943 I wrote a "history" which established that the chieftainship of the Pare District was mine.'[3] Another motive was a real desire to define oneself and one's tribe by its origins, experience, and culture. The Safwa antiquarian, Johannes Syavana Zambi, was bitterly disappointed that when he asked elders to speak the true Safwa language, each elder produced a different version.[4] Their history-writing probably best illustrates the educated men's thinking. Each of their works concerned one tribe or smaller unit, unlike the larger canvas of coastal writers using an Islamic framework. Like their informants, tribal historians were obsessed with origins, migrations, and genealogies. Their histories were accounts of conflict between powerful individuals: migration leaders, warrior rulers, individual European officers or missionaries, great contemporary chiefs. Neither the heroes' motives nor the forces acting on them were normally considered, for this was the thinking of men born in small-scale, personalised societies and subject to the whims of an alien regime. Tusi, Kilindi, or other immigrants were the only source of positive or extensive change. The only possible kind of enduring autochthonous

---

[1] Kayamba to PC Tanga, 5 July 1930, TNA 304/874/181/7; Kayamba, 'Wadigo'; Katoke and Rwehumbiza in Iliffe, *Tanzanians*, p. 63; J. M. Kadaso Mange, 'Mfumo ya Bukwimba: the origin of Bukwimba' (trans. E. S. Kadaso), *IJAHS*, IV (1971), 115–38 (and several typescripts in ULD); Nathanael Mtui in *Mambo leo*, October 1923 *et seq.*; Dominikus Chabruma, 'Habari na hadisi za asili za Wangoni', typescript, ULD.

[2] H. E. Reuben, 'The history of the Wachagga', in *Kwetu*, 4 and 23 August and 13 December 1940, 18 January 1941. Another example is Augustiny, 'Geschichte'.

[3] Emmanuel Sebughe to Jackson, 26 October 1944, TNA 32702/3A.

[4] Elise Kootz-Kretschmer, 'Safwa-Texte in Briefen geschrieben von Johannes Syavana Zambi in den Jahren von 1926–1929', *ZES*, XXXIII (1942–3), 136–7.

change was degeneration. In this, as in much else, African and European thinking converged.

The most important embodiment of indirect rule ideology was education policy. Here, as in mission strategy and administrative theory, men had to choose or compromise between an assimilative approach, emphasising the inculcation of European skills and values, and an adaptive approach building on indigenous practices. Broadly speaking, German education had been assimilative, especially in the state schools, which Byatt's administration sought to revive. However, this approach was out of key with educational thought in Europe and America which reached Tanganyika through the Colonial Office Advisory Committee on Native Education and the Phelps-Stokes Fund, an American educational foundation which in 1924 investigated East African schooling. Behind the new thinking lay psychological and racial theories, white fears of black Americans, middle-class fears of working-class Europeans, anxiety to perpetuate Christian principles, unhappy experience of Indian education, and a host of other reasons and prejudices.[1] The outcome was emphasis on adaptation. 'The modern conception of education', the Phelps-Stokes commission declared, 'is that of guiding and training natural individual growth rather than of giving formal instruction...It must be a vital education fitted to the needs of those who seek it, so as to make them useful members in their own community life.'[2] The commission recognised the need to give some Africans professional skills and a knowledge of European languages, but its bias was towards adaptation. It suggested that Tanganyika was backward in this and criticised the government's failure to cooperate with missionaries. The Colonial Office committee produced a policy statement on the same lines in 1925 with a deliberately anti-nationalist intent.[3] Cameron implemented this policy and established a partnership between government and missions under which Government subsidised mission schools which met its standards with regard to syllabuses and teachers' qualifications, while missions gained the right to consultation. However, Government maintained its English-language central schools to train teachers, clerks, and chiefs, and during the 1930s Tabora school in particular evolved into the equivalent of an English public school open to entry by competitive examination. Government also insisted that Swahili

[1] See Kenneth J. King, *Pan-Africanism and education* (Oxford, 1971).
[2] Thomas Jesse Jones, *Education in East Africa* (New York, n.d.), p. xvi.
[3] *Education policy in British tropical Africa* (Cmd 2374 of 1925); Gupta, *Imperialism*, p. 127.

338

must be the language of education in recognised schools, refusing to subsidise the hundreds of vernacular 'bush schools' where village catechists inculcated rudimentary Christianity and literacy. The new policy was a compromise between assimilation and adaptation, but weighted increasingly towards the latter as time passed.[1]

At its simplest, adaptive education often meant little more than organising a school's houses by 'tribes', but it could have more serious implications. Among missionaries, some extreme proponents of *Volksmission* opposed any education in English lest it should produce an alienated elite which might flock to the towns and leave the rural areas to stagnate. On these grounds the Moravians closed the English class at their seminary in Rungwe.[2] The government's most remarkable attempt at adaptation was the 'tribal school' created at Malangali after 1928 by W. B. Mumford. Imitating the education of pages at the Hehe and Sangu courts, Mumford used elders as moral tutors to students who themselves wore 'traditional' (late nineteenth-century) dress, lived in *tembe* dormitories, exercised themselves by spear-throwing and tribal dances rather than football, and learned tribal history and handicrafts before the alien skills of literacy. Mumford's motives were mixed. 'I do want to help them to keep a belief in themselves and to feel they can be people of whom their ancestors would be proud', he explained, but he was also anxious to counteract 'the immigration to the towns and the growth of the over-dressed and self-opinionated clerical type'.[3] Cameron's realism and faith in progress allowed him little confidence in Malangali. 'We aim at making a good African and not a cheap imitation of a European', he explained; 'but in saying that I do not think that I have ever intended that we wanted the native to continue to *think*, for the greater part, as an African.' His successor wrote more bluntly that Malangali 'could be expected to survive neither in the Africa of today nor of tomorrow'.[4]

Advocates of adaptation realised that the crux was to incorporate agricultural training into the timetable.[5] In 1933 it was agreed that all schools should have an agricultural bias, but little was achieved. Some

[1] See A. R. Thompson, 'Partnership in education in Tanganyika 1919–1961', M.A. thesis, University of London, 1965.
[2] Wright, *German missions*, pp. 194–6.
[3] *Ibid.*, p. 170; Tanganyika, *Educational Department: annual report for the year 1924*, p. 29; W. B. Mumford, 'Malangali school', *Africa*, III (1930), 265–92.
[4] Cameron on Mumford, 'Memorandum on education and the social adjustment of the primitive peoples of Africa to European culture' [1927?] TNA 11570/42; Stewart Symes, *Tour of duty* (London, 1946), p. 168.
[5] See Pat Saul, 'Agricultural education in Tanganyika 1925–1955', East African Academy sixth annual symposium paper, n.d.

primary schools were surrounded by untidy plots of manioc, zealous missionaries herded resentful pupils to daily spells of weeding, and economy gave four central schools new syllabuses with large elements of agriculture. Scarcely any European educator knew anything about agriculture or how to integrate it into school activities. African teachers, who did know something about agriculture, knew no more than their pupils' parents and resented becoming part-time peasants. The Agricultural Department had some useful knowledge but no time or staff to teach children. Much talk about making agriculture the core of the curriculum was hypocritical, for educators assumed in practice that farming was for children who were no good at school, and the whole career and earnings structure of the colonial economy was biassed against it. Moreover, few Africans wanted agricultural education. African members of the Advisory Committee on Native Education – nearly all from Kiungani – paid occasional lip-service to agricultural training but protested vigorously at any suggestion that existing schools should be given an agricultural bias.[1] This attitude extended to the whole field of educational adaptation. What Africans wanted, at this time and throughout the colonial period, was literary, assimilative education in a European language, for this was seen as the route to high wages, equality, and power. As Kayamba explained, 'The Africans think that without literary education their present rate of progress will be very slow indeed and unnecessarily slow...Those who think that literary education is unsuitable for Africans...deny the Africans the very means of progress.'[2] In 1939 the Education Department reported that 'African elders throughout the Territory, from regions as far apart as Songea and Moshi, have sent appeals for higher standards of education, particularly in English'. Nine years earlier even the deferential Lwamugira had complained 'that Europeans were purposely not teaching Africans beyond a certain standard to suit their own ends'.[3]

The height of ambition for African schoolboys was Makerere College. Founded at Kampala in Uganda in 1922, Makerere developed as a professional and liberal arts college, introducing school certificate courses in 1933.[4] At first the Tanganyika Government discouraged its

---

[1] 'Proceedings of the Advisory Committee on African Education', 28 March 1933, TNA 19484/1/59.
[2] Perham, *Ten Africans*, pp. 247–8.
[3] O. W. Furley and T. Watson, 'Education in Tanganyika between the wars', *South Atlantic quarterly*, LXV (1966), 490; Austen, *Northwest Tanzania*, p. 177.
[4] See Margaret MacPherson, *They built for the future* (Cambridge, 1964).

subjects from going there lest they become 'political agitators',[1] while in any case Makerere admitted students after Standard VIII, which no Tanganyikan school taught until 1933. In practice the first Tanganyikan entered Makerere in 1930 and a handful more gained admission by 1934 after completing their schooling in Kenya, Uganda, or Zanzibar. They were much poorer than other students and worked as labourers to earn pocket money. From 1934 a regular six or seven Tanganyikans won places each year, so that by 1939 nearly fifty Tanganyikans had entered, mostly on government grants.[2] A plan to develop Makerere to university status was accepted in 1938 but not implemented until after the war. It obliged the Tanganyika Government to upgrade Tabora school towards full secondary status.[3]

Makerere was a vital counterweight to 'adaptive' education. It was anti-tribal and meritocratic, taking most students by competitive examination regardless of social origin. Tanganyikan entrants were almost equally divided between sons of chiefs, children of highly-educated fathers, and students lacking those advantages. The first Tanganyikan entrant was Martin Kayamba's son, Hugh Godfrey.[4] Other sons of Kiungani men who followed him in the 1930s included Augustine Makame (grandson of Samuel Sehoza) and Matthew Ramadhani (son of the former senior African teacher at Kiungani). Among hereditary aristocrats were Adam Sapi Mkwawa of Uhehe, Msabila Lugusha of Nzega, and Joseph Mutahangarwa of Kiziba (the first Tanganyikan to obtain a medical license). Ten of the first 33 came from the small but educationally advanced area of Bonde, while Haya and Nyakyusa were also prominent.[5] Makerere's teaching was deliberately assimilationist. Visiting the college in 1936, East Africa's Directors of Education regretted 'the almost entire absence of anything African within the whole range of student activities'.[6] It was an odd comment, but entirely characteristic of the ideology of indirect rule.

[1] Isherwood to CS, 15 April 1932, TNA 13658/1/75.
[2] DE to CS, 20 June 1941, TNA 25103/1/19.
[3] DE to CS, 12 December 1938, TNA 26255/1/102.
[4] Mitchell to DCS, 4 February 1930, TNA 13658/1/23.
[5] J. E. Goldthorpe, *An African elite: Makerere College students 1922–1960* (Nairobi, 1965), pp. 27–31.
[6] 'Report on the inspection of Makerere College', February 1936, TNA 23820/23.

CHAPTER 11

The crisis of colonial society, 1929–45

These years were the pivot of Tanganyika's modern history. They saw the transition from the creation of colonial society to the beginning of its dissolution. The transition coincided with the crisis of western capitalism during the international depression and the Second World War, when Britain exploited her empire in a manner which some realised must make its eventual loss inevitable. A new colonial initiative after the war briefly concealed the crisis but ultimately deepened it.

The crisis contained five elements.[1] First, the restructuring of economy and society into a colonial mould slowed down. Although the structures of colonial society subsequently became more elaborate, they did not fundamentally change. Tanganyika's economic structure in 1961 was essentially the same as in 1939. Second, and related to this, colonial society and economy produced diminishing returns. Each investment of effort brought a smaller reward. Economic growth and social advancement only intensified the problems they sought to solve. The third element of crisis was that both colonisers and colonised lost faith in the colonisers' vision of the future. Europeans doubted whether their aims were attainable; Africans doubted whether they were desirable. Consequently – and this is the fourth point – the colonial regime became increasingly conservative and repressive as it defended earlier achievements. The final element of crisis followed: responsibility for the future passed into the minds and hands of the colonised. Liberation became the dynamic of change.

The loss of creative energy

From their epicentre in New York in October 1929 the shockwaves of the depression spread out to penetrate Tanganyika, revealing its

[1] The starting-point for this analysis has been Berque, *French North Africa.*

342

Table III. *Capacity utilisation in the U.S. economy and Tanganyika sisal prices, 1929–39*

	U.S. capacity utilisation (per cent)	Sisal prices (£ per tonne)
1929	83	31
1930	66	22
1931	53	13
1932	42	11
1933	52	13
1934	58	12
1935	68	14
1936	80	22
1937	83	22
1938	60	14
1939	72	13

SOURCES: Paul A. Baran and Paul M. Sweezy, *Monopoly capital* (reprinted, Harmondsworth, 1968), pp. 232, 237; Tanganyika, *Blue books*, 1929–39, *passim*.

structures and lines of weakness as though testing it for metal fatigue. They showed an economy dependent on the industrial nations. This appeared most clearly in collapsing export prices. Between 1929 and 1931 Bukoba's coffee export prices fell from £59 to £20 a tonne and the price of seed cotton to the Sukuma grower fell from 40 to 12 cents per kilogram.[1] As table III shows, the price of sisal followed American economic trends exactly. War intensified dependence as Britain's colonies were 'welded into one vast machine for the defence of liberty'.[2] Sisal experienced the most marked fluctuations. Germany's declaration of war and occupation of France deprived East Africa of more than half its sisal market. The growers responded by persuading the Tanganyika Government to impose production quotas. Then Japanese occupation of Indonesia and the Philippines in 1941 deprived the United States of binder twine. Sisal became a high-priority dollar-earner and Africans were conscripted for sisal work. Between 1938 and 1948 Tanganyika's proportion of world sisal production rose

[1] Northcote, 'Report on Bukoba coffee marketing', October 1936, TNA 215/1410; *Agriculture report*, 1929–30, I, 24; *ibid.*, 1931, p. 15.
[2] Cranborne, 1945, quoted in J. F. A. Ajayi and M. Crowder (ed.), *History of West Africa*, II (London, 1974), p. 623.

from 36 to 47 per cent. The chief beneficiary was Britain's exchequer. In 1942 the United States bought sisal from the British Government at over twice the price paid to Tanganyika. When price controls ended in 1948 the sisal growers had lost an estimated eleven million pounds available on a free market.[1] Other exporters had similar experiences. In 1940 Britain had over two years' coffee stocks. Chagga coffee prices fell between 1938–9 and 1940–1 from £45 to £31 per tonne. By 1943, however, coffee was again scarce and government compelled the KNCU to sell its crop to the Ministry of Food at substantially less than free market prices. Moreover, to prevent inflation and aid Britain, growers' prices were depressed and the balance invested in war bonds, so that in 1950 government still held some £633,675 belonging to Haya coffee-growers.[2]

Crisis also highlighted the uneven development of export-producing, food-producing, and labour-exporting regions. Since Tanganyika's economy focussed on export production, falling export prices reverberated along the lines of regional exchange. As sisal planters laid off workers, food prices in Tanga district fell by almost 75 per cent during 1930. Millet prices in the south were so low that producers could not afford motor transport and reverted to porterage. 'We scan the sisal prices anxiously each week', the district officer wrote from Kondoa, where cattle prices fell from Shs. 49.00 per head in 1928 to Shs. 10.84 in 1934 and migrant labourers returned without finding jobs.[3] Such peoples were soon unable to pay tax. Vigorous tax drives during 1932 collected 82 per cent of tax due in Tanga province but only 18 per cent in the south. Together with declining customs income this reduced government revenue by a quarter between 1929–30 and 1933.[4] At the cost of re-imposed Treasury control Tanganyika obtained an imperial loan of £500,000 in 1932[5] but avoided bankruptcy only by cutting staff and services and abandoning development works for a decade. This policy favoured prosperous areas: agricultural staff, for example, were withdrawn from Central and Southern provinces to more productive regions. Other types of differentiation also

[1] Correspondence in TNA 29513/1; below, pp. 371–2; Guillebaud, *Economic survey* (1966 edn), pp. 5, 35; Bonavia on Jerrard to LC, 18 November 1942, TNA 4/652/12/52.
[2] *KNCU annual report 1960–1*; 'Minute of meeting of the Coffee Board of Tanganyika', 9 October 1943, TNA 77/2/10/A/315; Surridge to Twining, 21 October 1950, TNA 37576/1/183.
[3] Ransome, Tanga DAR 1930, TNA library; Barnes to PC Southern, 30 July 1931, Barnes papers v, RH; Kondoa DAR 1928, 1931, 1934, TNA library.
[4] Hucks, note on taxes paid during 1931–2, TNA 15304/57; Tanganyika, *Blue books*, 1929, pp. 48–9, 1933, pp. 68–9.
[5] CO to Treasury, 30 April 1932, CO 691/123.

hardened. The territory's division into broadly Christian or Muslim regions remained substantially unchanged after 1930, while the social distance between Christians, Muslims, and adherents of indigenous religions widened. In this period, it seems, Islam finally lost its claim to modernity, partly because government refused to incorporate Koran schools into the subsidised educational system. Conscious of deprivation, Muslims attempted to found modern Islamic schools by private subscription.[1] Regional inequalities in education remained striking. In 1939 the proportion of boys of school age at vernacular primary schools ranged from 27 per cent in Tanga province to only 3 per cent in the Southern Highlands.[2]

Another symptom of waning developmental energy was defensive consolidation of vested interests. The sisal planters responded to depression in December 1930 by forming an employers' organisation, the Tanganyika Sisal Growers Association, which organised concerted wage cuts, maintained control of estate wages and conditions for nearly thirty years, and in 1944 formed a single recruiting agency, the Sisal Labour Bureau (Silabu).[3] Its plans for cooperative marketing failed, however, because several large estates, like many coffee plantations, were financed by produce merchants in London who naturally insisted on marketing their sisal themselves. Even when wartime control ended in 1948, 22.5 per cent of TSGA members (producing 41.5 per cent of tonnage) defeated proposals for a cooperative marketing agency, although this time the locally-financed growers, led by Abdallah Karimjee, formed their own Tanganyika Sisal Marketing Association and certain foreign-based firms joined it.[4] Powerful interests also consolidated their hold on the marketing of African crops. When cotton ginners claimed that if they and the cotton crop were to survive the depression they must monopolise cotton buying, government took powers to grant exclusive trading licences and began to 'zone' cotton-growing areas to particular ginneries. Meanwhile depression helped to destroy the KNPA and necessitated cooperative

[1] J. Cameron and W. A. Dodd, *Society, schools and progress in Tanzania* (Oxford, 1970), pp. 50–2, 56, 75; Daisy Sykes Buruku, 'The townsman: Kleist Sykes', in Iliffe, *Tanzanians*, pp. 106–7.

[2] Tanganyika, *Report of the Central Education Committee, 1939* (Dar es Salaam, 1943), p. 17.

[3] Correspondence in TNA 11475/I and 29513/I.

[4] Baines to CS, 19 September 1931, TNA 11475/I/239; PC Northern to CS, 12 May 1933, TNA 11681/27; minutes of TSGA special general meeting, 31 May 1948, TNA 29513/III/213; *Annual report of the East African sisal industry, 1948* (Tanga, 1949); Eldred Hitchcock, 'The sisal industry of East Africa', *TNR*, LII (1959), 9.

legislation, later reinforced by powers to create marketing boards with monopoly rights.[1]

As Asian shopkeepers found themselves squeezed between collective marketing and wealthy capitalists, their leaders diagnosed a concerted campaign to protect European interests amidst increased competition. 'We are not only not wanted', one protested in 1935, 'but we are harassed in a thousand ways so that we may leave the country.'[2] Radical protest had lapsed after the *hartal* of 1923 but reappeared in 1929 and 1930, when the Indian Association organised opposition to closer union proposals and the arrest of Congress leaders in India, collecting funds and apparently enlisting volunteers to join Gandhi's civil disobedience campaign. This activity expanded during 1932 to include trade grievances, and it emerged again to oppose the Produce Marketing Bill of 1937, when cables once again reached Congress and the Government of India.[3] The 'crystallization of trade channels'[4] during the depression made the small shopkeeper's position increasingly difficult. Ismaili Khojas responded most effectively. 'Their first need', the Aga Khan realised, 'is to learn to co-operate in their thrift and self-help, to extend what they practise in their families and as individuals to the community as a whole.'[5] His Golden Jubilee in 1937 was celebrated by establishing the Jubilee Insurance Company to make loans to small businessmen, thus preventing the community from stagnating, increasing its leaders' administrative power, and perhaps reducing the social tensions apparent in all Asian communities.[6] In 1937 Dar es Salaam's first important strike was organised by an Asiatic Labour Union chiefly composed of Sikh carpenters whose wages, reduced during the depression, were not keeping pace with reflation.[7] Beneath the formidable solidarity of the Asian communities the tensions of crisis were apparent.

For Africans the crisis years brought a narrowing of opportunity. Again small traders were badly affected. Although figures are scarce, the number of African traders had probably increased substantially during the prosperous 1920s, especially in fields such as hotel-keeping where Asians had no special access to supplies and in areas like Upare where concerted resistance appears to have ousted Asian

[1] Brett, *Colonialism*, p. 260.
[2] D. K. Patel, quoted in *Tanganyika herald*, 9 August 1935.
[3] Gregory, *India*, pp. 376–93, 476–86; correspondence in CO 691/112, 114, 159.
[4] Quoted in Walji, 'History', p. 173.
[5] *The memoirs of Aga Khan: world enough and time* (London, 1954), p. 288.
[6] Walji, 'History', pp. 166–71.   [7] Papers in TNA 24829.

traders.[1] Thereafter, however, depression and restrictive legislation made it especially difficult to establish new businesses. Traders led the riots of 1937 in Buhaya and were involved in the disturbances on Kilimanjaro. The Tanganyika African Welfare and Commercial Association, which sought to organise the African traders of Dar es Salaam, joined the opposition to the Produce Marketing Bill of 1937 (as did the Arab Association).[2] Dr Larson has shown that large-scale, export-orientated Asian trade expanded in Ulanga during the depression at the expense of local African commerce.[3] The African share of Tanganyika's retail trade probably declined during the depression. War was even more crippling to African businessmen. Since quotas of imported goods were allocated in proportion to pre-war turnover, new businesses could not be established. Tanganyika's leading African businessman, Ramadhani Bikola of Ujiji, died in 1942. A Manyema from the Congo, barely literate, he owned fifteen shops, employed an Asian accountant, and left £7,500. Within five years his numerous heirs dissipated the inheritance, the chief heir was imprisoned, and rain washed away all trace of the main shop.[4] No comparable entrepreneur emerged before Independence. The structures of colonial society had become too rigid.

Diminishing returns

Between 1929 and 1945 an agricultural crisis took shape. It had four main causes: the concentration of economic activity in export-producing areas; changing European perceptions of African agriculture; continuing ecological change; and the special pressures of depression and war.

Export-producing regions experienced land shortage as population grew and European and African planters sought to expand holdings. Several Europeans in Usambara survived the depression by renting surplus land to Africans. On Kilimanjaro many settlers allowed Chagga to use virgin land for a year in return for clearing it.[5] While Chagga protests against land shortage mounted, the courts increasingly held that *vihamba* were private property, and those granted to

[1] Beatrice Omari, 'Pottery production and marketing 1936–1975: Usangi Pare case study', M.A. thesis, University of Dar es Salaam, 1975, pp. 47–8; *Kwetu*, 26 December 1941.
[2] *Tanganyika herald*, 30 September 1937; below, pp. 393–5.
[3] Larson, 'History', ch. 5.
[4] *Kwetu*, 31 March 1944; correspondence in TNA 180/D/1/21/I and II.
[5] Callaghan, inspection report on Mbugai estate, 8 July 1932, TNA 21192/29; Latham to PC Northern, 9 September 1937, TNA 11774/65.

newly-married men steadily grew smaller. 'In the last four or five years', it was reported in 1948, 'there have been severe shortages of bananas and it has been only the increased planting of maize in the lowlands for the war effort that has averted serious food shortages.' There was also evidence that coffee yields were falling.[1] Meanwhile land hunger appeared in new areas. In the Masanze chiefdom of Kilosa district – the heart of the central line sisal region – the number of land cases heard by native courts increased between 1933 and 1941 from two to fourteen. 'The first thing I learnt about Kilosa was the land hunger of Africans', an official wrote in 1942. Here also yields were said to be falling.[2] Luguru colonists expanded into the plains below their mountains, while by 1938 many were renting land from missions and other proprietors.[3] The Haya coffee crop of 1935 was only twice exceeded during the next 25 years because the land suitable for coffee had been taken up and population growth necessitated the replacement of coffee by bananas, whose yields also declined.[4] The *otandibatira* was over.

European thinking about African agriculture was also changing. During the 1920s agricultural experts developed systematic extension techniques, emphasised the virtues of mixed farming, and became obsessed with soil erosion. Erosion first attracted official attention in Shinyanga in 1924. Cameron saw the danger in 1929 and the Colonial Office in 1930.[5] In that year floods which destroyed stretches of the central railway were ascribed to more rapid run-off following deforestation by feckless Africans. The Director of Veterinary Services warned the first meeting of the Standing Committee on Soil Erosion in June 1931 that overstocking would produce desert conditions in Sukumaland within twenty years.[6] Some agriculturalists began to encourage such anti-erosion measures as contour-planting, hedging, and trash-bunding. But then the urgency faded. The Standing

[1] R. W. James, *Land tenure and policy in Tanzania* (Dar es Salaam, 1971), p. 63; Johnston, 'Land tenure', p. 1; Swynnerton and Bennett, '*KNCU*' *coffee*, p. 24; *Agriculture report*, 1937, II, 29.

[2] Coke to PC Eastern, 19 December 1941, TNA 2/13/18/1; Dickson to Kilosa, 24 February 1942, TNA 61/14/5/V/1231.

[3] Gillman diary, 5 December 1920, RH; *Agriculture report*, 1938, p. 11.

[4] Coffee export figures in Bukoba district book, TNA; Hall to Private Secretary, 6 July 1948, TNA 41011/1; Karl-Heinz Friedrich, 'Coffee-banana holdings at Bukoba', in Hans Ruthenberg (ed.), *Smallholder farming and smallholder development in Tanzania* (München, 1968), p. 178; *Agriculture report*, 1952, p. 36.

[5] Stiebel to CS, 28 April 1924, CO 691/70/317; *Tanganyika Times*, 15 June 1929; Symes to Cunliffe-Lister, 2 November 1932, CO 691/124.

[6] 'Minutes of the first meeting of the standing committee on soil erosion', 15 June 1931, TNA 77/2/33/2.

Committee met in February 1932 and then adjourned for nearly six years. The Director of Agriculture's circulars adopted a cautionary tone. Reclamation, he warned, was costly and economically disappointing. 'Too much engrossment with the subject of soil erosion', the Director of Veterinary Services warned, 'is liable to upset mental balance.'[1] There were probably two reasons for this reversal. One was lack of money and staff during the depression. The other was that panic over erosion conflicted with government's need of revenue, which late in 1931 produced a campaign to 'plant more crops'. 'Whatever the price', government ordered, 'a tonnage for export is to be aimed at as a duty.'[2] The campaign chiefly affected Sukumaland, where it multiplied cotton output five times between 1932 and 1936.[3] It was intensely controversial. Provincial commissioners in Dodoma and Lindi thought it a blatant exploitation of Africans, which was why agricultural staff left their provinces. One observer called it the 'destroy your Land Policy' and blamed it for obscuring the erosion problem.[4] This recaptured attention in the 1940s. 'Soil conservation is the most important and the most urgent problem facing this Territory', a new Director of Veterinary Services declared in 1944, 'and...should form the first and paramount consideration in our post-war planning...remedial measures on a scale so far undreamt of, will be necessary.'[5] The lines of postwar action were thus laid during the crisis.

In retrospect the soil erosion problem was less cataclysmic than the colonial government's short memory suggested. Sukumaland was not approaching desert conditions in 1951, but was on the eve of its greatest economic prosperity.[6] Seen in perspective, the flooding of the central railway was not simply the result of recent deforestation in Uluguru, for a similar flood had destroyed a walled settlement at Simbamwene sixty years earlier and the Germans had noticed overpopulation and forest destruction in Uluguru in the 1890s.[7] Much the same was true of West Usambara, where many bewailed the declining fertility of the Mlalo Basin. 'The whole region', the Director of Agriculture reported in 1945, 'has reached a very low level of

[1] Harrison, 'Memorandum on soil erosion', 25 August 1937, TNA 77/2/33/74a.
[2] McElderry to PCs, 14 October 1931, TNA 215/155/8.
[3] Austen, *Northwest Tanzania*, pp. 240–1, 272.   [4] Gillman diary, 7 May 1935, RH.
[5] Lowe to Veterinary Officer Mwanza, 28 January 1944, TNA 30580/17.
[6] Below, p. 454.
[7] Young and Fosbrooke, *Land and politics*, pp. 25, 143–4; 'Bericht über die Expedition des Leutnants v. Grawert auf der Ostseite des Uruguru-Gebirges', 1 April 1895, RKA 286/49.

fertility owing to over-cultivation, over-grazing and failure to manure the land', but he added that Mlalo had looked equally bad twenty years earlier, while the Chief of Usambara denied that it had ever been especially fertile and local elders claimed that the situation had not changed significantly within human memory, Mlalo's prosperity varying with the rains.[1] Yet erosion was undoubtedly becoming serious in several limited areas. What was probably happening was that Europeans were becoming aware of the more obvious effects of the profound, long-term changes acting on Tanganyika's ecology. In Usambara, for example, all figures suggest that population roughly doubled between 1914 and 1948.[2] By 1947 the average family's landholding in the Mlalo Basin was only 1.39 hectares, while half had less than 0.82 hectares.[3] The proportion of fallow had fallen since German times. 'The land where bananas thrive' had exchanged its staple crop for maize, while poor families were turning increasingly to high-yielding but low-protein manioc. Usambara was experiencing 'a slow process of pauperisation'.[4] No comparable evidence is available for Uluguru, but involution was probably characteristic of mountain areas with limited cultivable land and no valuable cash crop.

Yet such regions were exceptional. On the open plateau the crucial reason for agricultural crisis was the restriction of the cultivable area imposed by the expansion of the natural ecosystem.[5] This was probably Sukumaland's problem, although it was intensified by extended cotton-growing during the 'plant more crops' campaign. The territory's worst erosion, on the Irangi plateau of Kondoa district, was due partly to withdrawing cattle from plains which tsetse infested in the late 1920s, although the plateau had been eroded even in the nineteenth century.[6] Similar pressures caused Turu and Iramba to withdraw outlying settlements and concentrate around Singida and Mkalama. But the most vivid example was Mbulu. Until the late

[1] *Agriculture report*, 1945, p. 121; Miller, minute, 10 December 1945, TNA 33049/1; Cory to PC Tanga, 31 August 1946, TNA 4/269/5/I/158.
[2] Eggert, *Missionsschule*, p. 150; Barnes, Usambara DAR 1925, TNA 1733/11/79/3; Tanganyika, *African census report 1957* (Dar es Salaam, 1963), p. 42.
[3] Clegg to Development Commission, 29 October 1949, TNA 4/269/6/145.
[4] Manfred Attems, 'Permanent cropping in the Usambara mountains', in Ruthenberg, *Smallholder*, p. 140.
[5] Long-term climatic change might also repay study. There seems to be some evidence that the first half of the twentieth century was unusually dry in tropical Africa. See H. H. Lamb, 'Climate in the 1960s', *Geographical journal*, CXXXII (1966), 191–2, 210–11; A. T. Grove, 'Desertification in the African environment', *African affairs*, LXXIII (1974), 141–3. I owe these references to Mr Grove.
[6] Gerhard Liesegang, 'Some iron age wares from central Tanzania', *Azania*, X (1975), 93.

nineteenth century the Iraqw people had occupied a concentrated settlement at Kainam on the western rim of the rift valley. Prevented from expanding by Masai and Tatoga pastoralists, they had developed an intensive agriculture with manuring, soil conservation, private landownership, and extremely unequal possession of cattle. When rinderpest broke the pastoralists in the early 1890s the Iraqw expanded, at first cautiously and then with growing speed, taking Mbulu from the Tatoga, pushing northwards into Karatu, and even settling below the rift wall. In these areas herds increased quickly and the sophisticated agriculture of Kainam was abandoned. The Iraqw became a more pastoral people than before. But then came tsetse, reaching Mbulu from west and south by the 1930s and compelling a retreat which continued until 1948, when a barrier was cut along the whole western frontier of Iraqw settlement. In the meantime, however, more than three-fifths of Mbulu district had been infested by tsetse and hundreds of square kilometres of grazing – including even south-eastern Kainam – had been lost. Between 1941 and 1945 shortage of pasture and water reduced Iraqw herds by 20 per cent. Elders agreed that the size and milk-yields of cattle were falling. A survey made in 1950 showed that the average household possessed less than a hectare of arable land. Once a granary even in famine seasons, Mbulu experienced its first famine for many years in 1939.[1]

Famine was the point at which long-term ecological change met short-term crisis. Since the last general famine of 1919, serious dearth had occurred chiefly in limited areas of extreme aridity and economic stagnation, notably Uzigua and Ugogo. In 1943, however, Tanganyika again experienced territorial famine. As usual, it began in Ugogo and was chiefly due to drought, but drought causes famine when reserves are low, recuperative powers are weakened, outside relief is difficult to obtain, and transport and communications are defective. In all these ways the war generalised, intensified, and prolonged the famine. Government promoted the export of grain and cattle for military consumption and encouraged the production of drought-prone maize rather than resistant millet. Shipping was not available to import food. Tanganyika's normal supplier of rice, Burma, was in Japanese hands. Transport and administration were run down. From Britain's viewpoint, Tanganyika's chief wartime duty was to be quiet. So the famine

---

[1] Jürgen Schultz, *Agrarlandwirtschaftliche Veränderungen in Tanzania* (München, 1971), *passim*; Rowe, 'Five-years' development plan for northern Mbulu', 12 September 1945, TNA 69/868/1/30; Bell, 'Memorandum for the destocking of cattle in the Iraqw chiefdom', 12 December 1949, TNA 38504/1/81A.

had to be survived.[1] That deaths occurred only in Ugogo indicated the improvements in transport and administration which had taken place since 1919, but shortage and suffering were almost universal. In the first two months of 1943 some 3,000 people sought food at Kwiro mission. On sisal estates the optimum ration of nearly a kilogram of meal a day was reduced to 316 grams. Nyamwezi traders are said to have bought children for grain and cash in Usandawe, where the dearth was remembered as 'Europe's famine'. The number of murderers convicted in the territory, normally between 20 and 40 a year, rose in 1943 to 56.[2] Nor did 1944 bring respite, for Ugogo, Uzigua, Ukwere, and Usukuma were all famine-stricken. The Gogo suffered again in 1946. Next year their district officer reported, 'Morale is high and it is felt that now the war is over, the period of famine is over until the next war.'[3]

Famine lay deep in Tanganyika's collective unconscious, but colonial society also had new indicators of distress. One was the level of wages. Care is needed here. Money wages fell sharply during the depression. The average pay (per working month of 30 days) of a sisal cutter in Tanga district approached Shs. 30 in 1929; by 1935 it was Shs. 13–18; in 1944, Shs. 21; and in 1948, Shs. 38.[4] Yet these figures are misleading because they make no provision for free rations, the size of tasks, the cost of living, or unemployment. Available statistics suggest the following picture. The First World War was a disaster for workers, cutting money wages somewhat and stimulating a drastic price inflation.[5] During the 1920s prices remained relatively stable – those of imported goods falling slightly – while wages rose quickly to regain roughly their 1914 value.[6] The first four years of depression approximately halved money wages. They cut prices equally and perhaps even more dramatically, as food prices in Tanga indicate, but unemployment probably increased, although how much is difficult to say. In 1933–4 some 32 per cent of adult male Africans in Tanga were

[1] Larson, 'History', pp. 303–5; *Agriculture report*, 1950, p. 76; CS to all officers, 6 June 1940, TNA 176/1/25/2.
[2] Brooke, 'Heritage', p. 16; Kwiro mission diary, January–February 1945, Kwiro archives; Paton, 'Memorandum on the position of the sisal industry', 30 August 1943, TNA 29513/1/30; Newman, *Sandawe*, p. 79; ten Raa, 'Bush foraging', p. 38; CS to PCs, 12 July 1944, TNA 18/A/2/15/46.
[3] Brooke, 'Heritage', p. 22; Bagamoyo DAR 1944, TNA library; Gill, Mwanza DAR 1944, TNA 41/128/20/6; DC Dodoma to PC Central, 22 July 1947, TNA 46/2/13/35.
[4] Jerrard to Native Welfare Committee Tanga, 10 February 1941, TNA 4/652/12/31; *Tanganyika Times*, 2 November 1929; tabulation of sisal wages in TNA 24693/11/193.
[5] *Dar es Salaam Times*, 4 February and 8 April 1922.
[6] *Tanganyika Times*, 18 January 1930.

out of work; they are probably best seen as a burden on those who *were* employed.[1] Yet the real problem began in the later 1930s. As prices rose again there was little equivalent increase in wages. Unskilled rates in Dar es Salaam were lower in 1936 than in 1932. Sisal wages were increased in 1935 by a bonus for regular work, but the daily task was also augmented.[2] By 1939 sisal cutters were earning as much in real terms as ten years earlier, but were working harder for it.

Table IV. *Cost of living and wage indices, Dar es Salaam, 1939–51* (*1 Sept. 1939 = 100*)

Date	Cost of living index	Government daily rate, casual labour
1 Sept. 1939	100	100
Oct. 1940		160
Sept. 1942	122	
1 Jan. 1943	155	200
1 Jan. 1944	167	220
1 Jan. 1945	177	
1 Jan. 1946	184	260
1 March 1947	187	260
10 Sept. 1948	247	320
Sept. 1949	287	320
25 Oct. 1950	299	350
31 Dec. 1951	351	430

SOURCE: Iliffe, 'Dockworkers', p. 123.

War disorganised the whole wage structure. The price of imported goods soared as supplies and shipping became unavailable. In 1931 a pair of the khangas commonly worn by African women cost two or three shillings in Dar es Salaam, in 1939 five, and in 1942 eight, and other clothing prices rose even more steeply.[3] Then war demands, poor harvests, and rapid urbanisation inflated the prices of local products. Table IV shows that prices in Dar es Salaam nearly doubled

[1] Lists of wage rates in TNA 61/14/III/1; Iliffe, 'Dockworkers', p. 123; Wilson, *Malaria unit*, p. 15.
[2] Lists of wage rates in TNA 61/14/III/1/171 and 61/14/12/43; Jerrard to Native Welfare Committee Tanga, TNA 4/652/12/31.
[3] Hartnoll to DCs, 22 January 1943, TNA 61/295/2/1/13; 'Memorandum on rise in cost of living for Africans in Dar es Salaam township from 1st September, 1939, to December, 1942', TNA 61/295/2/1/98.

during the war, and since these were 'controlled' prices they probably underestimated the real increase, for much profiteering occurred. The table suggests that government unskilled labour earnings kept pace with, and perhaps outstripped, inflation, but an enquiry in 1942 reckoned that 'some 87 per cent of Government employees in Dar es Salaam are in receipt of a wage on which they cannot possibly subsist without getting into debt'.[1] Most other Africans fared worse. Skilled wages rose less quickly. Workers in the private sector, such as dockworkers, probably fell behind inflation.[2] If domestic servants' wages rose 60–70 per cent between 1939 and 1948,[3] this was only half the rate of inflation. The largest group of workers, in the sisal industry, suffered especially. Cutters' wages remained static from 1939 to 1943. Subsequent periodic increases fell behind the rate of inflation. In 1950 the index of sisal wages (1939 = 100) stood at 253, whereas the Dar es Salaam cost of living index stood at 299. A sisal worker's real wage was then lower than in 1929 and very probably lower than at any time for sixty years. In West Usambara estate labour earned less in 1948 than in 1929 even in money terms – Shs. 18 as against Shs. 15–30 a month.[4] The colonial economy was producing diminishing returns.

Two things made possible this decline in real wages. One was that an increasing proportion of men had become dependent on wages, especially in economically decaying areas like Usambara or isolated regions like Buha. The other was the employers' increased power. The TSGA fixed maximum sisal wages. Wartime conscription helped to keep earnings down: in February 1941 a labour officer reported that only fear of military conscription deterred sisal labourers from protesting.[5] Wages no longer followed broad economic trends. After the laissez-faire 1920s the European-controlled polity once more commanded the economy in its own interests.

Diminishing returns were especially marked in education. Between 1931–2 and 1938 government's annual educational expenditure fell from £122,666 to £97,862. Government central schools were reduced from eight to three, a measure which neatly matched the growing preference for adaptive rather than literary education. Only ten

---

[1] 'Report of enquiry into wages and cost of living of low grade African government employees in Dar es Salaam' [September 1942] TNA 30598/15.
[2] Iliffe, 'Dockworkers', pp. 123, 128–31.
[3] *Tanganyika standard*, 2 March 1948.
[4] Above, p. 158; Piggott, Lushoto DAR 1948, TNA 72/62/6/III/211; *Tanganyika Times*, 18 January 1930.
[5] Jerrard to Native Welfare Committee Tanga, 10 February 1941, TNA 4/652/12/31.

African women teachers were registered during the whole of the 1930s.[1] Mission subsidies and revenues also fell. The number of children at school consequently remained roughly constant throughout the 1930s at something under 100,000. As the financial situation improved, a ten-year development plan was devised in 1939 to increase the school population to 240,000 and raise the annual entry to Makerere to sixty.[2] Then war intervened. Some development did take place. Between 1939 and 1945 government educational spending increased by 126 per cent, the cost of living by only 77 per cent.[3] But the targets set in 1939 became chimerical, and in other directions the war disrupted education. When German missionaries were arrested in 1939, for example, their school systems again fell into disarray. 'The native intelligentsia', Usambara's district officer reported,

...are extremely disappointed in the educational facilities which have been granted them during the past twenty years; twice during that period they have experienced the total collapse of what they consider higher education, which was in the hands of German Missions...These natives maintain that the time is now ripe for their educational needs to be managed by their own Native Authority.[4]

Pare expressed a similar desire, while Chagga reactions inaugurated a new pattern of African education. Kilimanjaro was an area of vigorous competition between Lutherans and Roman Catholics. Christianity was entwined with local politics and missionaries were often resented as landowners. In the late 1930s educated Chagga leaders began to see sectarian competition as a threat to their authority and an obstacle to unity and progress. They were angry that Kilimanjaro had much primary education but no secondary school. Early in the war, government suggested that the native authority should control all primary schools as a secular local education authority – an issue then agitating relations between church and state in Britain. The Chagga Council welcomed the suggestion, and after much mission opposition a District Education Committee was established to run all schools in Kilimanjaro, the Council levying a two shilling rate to pay the 25 per cent of teachers' salaries previously

---

[1] Tanganyika, *Blue books*, 1931, p. 62, 1938, p. 79; *Memorandum on education in Tanganyika* (Legislative Council sessional paper no. 4 of 1934); Bates, 'British administration', p. 466.

[2] Isherwood, 'Memorandum on African education in Tanganyika', January 1933, TNA 61/67/I/56A; Jackson to Stanley, 20 December 1944, TNA 28867/II/82.

[3] Tanganyika, *Blue books*, 1939, p. 17, 1945, p. 81.

[4] Korogwe DAR 1942, TNA 72/62/6/II/146. See also Gustav Bernander, *Lutheran wartime assistance to Tanzanian churches 1940–1945* (Lund, 1968), pp. 45, 55–6, 72–7, 111–13, 141–2.

covered by school fees (the other 75 per cent being paid by government). It was an important increase in African power.[1]

The war's most disastrous educational impact was on entrance to Makerere. The plan of 1939 envisaged that 60 Tanganyikans would enter the College in 1949. In fact the *total* number of Tanganyikans there in 1949 was only 35. Entrants declined from 12 in 1940 to only 2 in 1946.[2] After every Tanganyikan candidate failed the entrance examination in 1945 it was explained that Makerere's standards were rising while plans to open additional forms in Tanganyikan schools were delayed by war. The Colonial Office thought, by contrast, 'that the Tanganyika Territory Education Department is rotten bad'. Educated Tanganyikans were reaching the same conclusion.[3]

A fading vision

As colonialism lost momentum, so the colonisers' vision of the future lost its credibility to themselves and their subjects. For the government, Tanganyika's future lay with indirect rule. To Cameron the policy was explicitly 'a means and not an end'. He saw the native administrations as foundations for wider African political organisation. This might be representation in Legislative Council, if Africans wanted it, but he preferred a pyramid of councils leading to 'a council for the whole of Tanganyika', in 'probably not less than three or four generations'.[4] After his departure, however, indirect rule stagnated. In 1932 his successor, Sir Stewart Symes – who was utterly bored by Tanganyika – ordered that native administrations must confine themselves to '*local* government' and eschew 'matters outside the proper sphere of a local authority'.[5] Indirect rule became an end and not a means.

Africans were increasingly frustrated with indirect rule and alienated from their chiefs. Native authorities, a critic wrote, 'make

[1] Petro Itosi Marealle to Vickers-Haviland, 12 October 1937, Vickers-Haviland papers, RH; correspondence in TNA 12844/II, 19484/II, 31723, 31889/I, 69/148/2, and 69/821; 'Pastoral letter from Bishop Byrne, read in the churches. Kilema, April 1943', FCB papers 122, RH; Rogers, 'Political focus', pp. 748–53.

[2] Attenborough to Wood, 23 May 1950, TNA 25401/IV/325; Goldthorpe, *Elite*, p. 26.

[3] Note for Legislative Council reply, 25 July 1946, TNA 26255/II/59; Clauson to Boyd, 11 August 1939, CO 691/175; 'Memorandum on matters for consideration' [1944–5] Suleiman papers, TNA.

[4] Cameron, *Tanganyika service*, p. 97; *Joint committee on closer union*, II, paras. 1,649, 1,993; *Native administration memorandum*, 1930, quoted in H. F. Morris and James S. Read, *Indirect rule and the search for justice* (Oxford, 1972), p. 259.

[5] Jardine to PCs, 6 September 1932, TNA 4/6/38.

judgement in order to revenge. They are exercising sweated labour. They are receiving bribes secretly . . . Many Government officers do not listen to what their subjects say, they just listen to the Native chiefs.'[1] Nor were chiefs themselves satisfied to be front men for British policies. In 1940 the German-educated Sapi bin Mkwawa of Uhehe was deposed for drunkenly assuring his district officer that 'If the Germans take Dar es Salaam I will take Iringa.'[2] The whole regime was tiring. While wartime conditions made chiefs more autocratic, European officials aged noticeably after depression checked recruitment and military circumstances made overseas leave impossible. In 1946 not one officer in Arusha district spent a single night on tour. A year earlier provincial commissioners had collectively refused to incorporate more educated Africans into native authority councils because 'in the great majority of areas in the Territory they would be alien to the ideas of the people, would not be acceptable to them and would derogate from the Chief's authority'.[3] Outside observers grew increasingly critical:

The Tanganyika Service includes an unusually high proportion of men who have written valuable memoranda and reports on the tribes of the Territory. There is among them an *esprit de corps* which is probably as high as that of any unit in the Colonial Empire. Nevertheless, the progress of the Territory as far as native affairs are concerned seems to have come to a standstill. Improvements continue to be made in the machinery, but as a whole, the machine does not seem to move forward.[4]

Crisis also shook British credibility in the eyes of educated Africans. In 1931 promotion of African clerks was suspended as an economy measure. When Martin Kayamba, sole African in the civil service's administrative grade, died in 1939 he was said to have been buried 'with the bag containing A.C.S. promotions to higher appointments. We understand that a kind coroner has ordered its exhumation and that it is to be formally opened immediately after the war!'[5] Yet even Kayamba, most Anglophile of Africans, lost faith in the vision of a Tanganyika modernised by African and European cooperation which had animated TTACSA. *African Problems*, which he wrote in the late 1930s, shows much disillusionment with colonial change. Colonialism

---

[1] Unpublished letter from K. Kitanuka of Moshi to *Kwetu*, c. December 1940, in TNA 23754/II/55.
[2] Young to Macdonald, 20 May 1940, CO 691/180.
[3] Surridge to PCs, 19 February 1947, TNA 33026.
[4] Lord Hailey, 1944, quoted by Austen in Gifford and Louis, *Britain and Germany*, p. 606.
[5] *Kwetu*, 5 February 1941.

had brought material benefits, he admitted, but its overall consequences were 'mixed and complex'. The missionaries had uprooted
valuable customs without replacing them. What Kayamba called
'industrialism' was making Africa 'a vast recruiting area' and
destroying family life. Land alienation and commercial agriculture
were breaking up villages as social units. Kayamba did not think the
old societies could be reconstructed. Instead he advocated new social
organisations: model villages, voluntary associations, the non-tribal
African solidarity embodied in Makerere. That these might require
the seizure of power was beyond his imagination, but that they could
be achieved by current methods was beyond his belief. If Kayamba,
of all men, was losing confidence in it, then the colonial vision was
indeed fading.[1]

Disillusionment was expressed most clearly in Christianity. While
numerical growth continued, the churches' character changed. They
had been created through conflict with African societies, generally by
appealing to the unprivileged, especially the young. By the 1930s this
relationship with society was changing and the mission churches were
becoming increasingly integrated with colonial society. They were
experiencing the problems of large organisations – authoritarianism,
bureaucracy, impersonality, specialisation – which Dr Taylor has
called 'disengagement'.[2] One reason was the policy of educational
partnership adopted in 1925. Apart from the Africa Inland Mission,
all societies became heavily dependent on state subsidies, which led
the CMS, for example, to increase its missionary strength in Africa
at the expense of Asia.[3] Mission schools multiplied. In the Masasi
diocese they increased between 1927 and 1936 from 89 to 237. 'The
school must always be in the foreground', the Apostolic Delegate told
Roman Catholic missionaries in 1928. 'If the question arises whether
to build a school or a new Church, the school should come first.'[4] This
meant that the village catechist and teacher, on whom Tanganyika's
churches had been built, lost status when the missions reclassified their
African staffs as either teachers or catechists, depending on whether
they could pass government examinations. Catechists were paid less
and inadequately trained, thus weakening the church at its roots. In
Usambara 'trouble started when they started grading workers. Hatred

[1] Kayamba, *Problems, passim.*
[2] John V. Taylor, *Processes of growth in an African church* (London, 1958), pp. 12–15.
[3] Hewitt, *Success*, I, xiv, 432.
[4] *Annual review of the work of the UMCA, 1936* (Westminster, 1937), p. 1; *Conference of the heads of Catholic missions in Tanganyika Territory, 1928* (Nyeri, 1929), p. 38.

started.' In their Tanganyika diocese the White Fathers sacked 68 of 100 catechists as inadequately trained. Teachers had hitherto assumed that their careers led upwards towards ordination, but from 1937 the UMCA (with government aid) paid teachers as much as priests.[1] Many missionaries doubted whether educational partnership benefited their work. Bondei parents said, 'My child is reading Government only'. 'It has strengthened the erroneous idea that Christianity is the Government religion', a missionary explained. '...Moslems in this particular district often state this as an objection to Christianity.'[2]

'God has nothing to do with organisations', Bruno Gutmann once wrote. 'He creates organisms.'[3] Between the wars mission churches increasingly became modern organisations. They experienced the growing income differentials of colonial society. Mission teachers no longer earned less than plantation labourers but belonged to the 'educated elite'. Church law became more rigid. No inter-war missionary suggested baptising polygynists. At Masasi missionaries refused Communion to parents whose children missed school. They made a practice of supporting parents against children, even when this prevented baptism.[4] The church itself was aging as the young rebels who had been early catechists became entrenched as Fathers. Most of Kwiro's leading laymen were drawn from less than a hundred schoolboys baptised before Maji Maji. Many of the UMCA's African leaders belonged to intermarried Christian families – Kayambas, Ramadhanis, Makames, Mang'enyas, Mwinyipembes, Mhinas, Chipondes – whose children dominated the senior forms at Minaki and the entrance examinations to Makerere.[5]

'The Church in Bonde', a missionary wrote in 1926, '...has passed from the pioneer or missionary stage to the pastoral. We no longer go out to preach to the heathen in the villages, for our whole work is to build up the Church and train the converts that the Church brings to us by her normal life.'[6] Although this was not true of newer mission areas, it was true of established churches. There missionaries rarely met 'heathens'. Like motorised district officers, they visited not homesteads but 'centres'. 'God blesses those who go on foot', the elderly Bishop Hirth grunted when a White Father displayed his new

[1] Guga, 'Research'; Nolan in Shorter and Kataza, *Missionaries*, p. 24; *Central Africa*, August 1949.
[2] *Central Africa*, March 1931.   [3] Gutmann, *Dschaggaland*, p. 109.
[4] Masasi mission diary, 7 March 1921 and 24 November 1940, ULD.
[5] L. E. Larson, 'The Kwiro mission, 1902–1912', duplicated paper, n.d., in my possession; Iliffe, *German rule*, p. 177 n. 1.
[6] *Central Africa*, February 1926.

bicycle.[1] Mission problems were increasingly those of established churches. In Liuli, where a thousand people were confirmed each year in the early 1930s and over three hundred adults were baptised at one Pentecost, two Christians in seven were under church discipline in 1944, largely for marital irregularities.[2] There the missionaries also faced the problem of elderly people left out when the young adopted the new religion, a problem troubling every mission. The African ministry also faced difficulties. Only severe pressure forced German Protestants to ordain Africans. Educated Chagga had to overcome Gutmann's opposition. For the Moravians the stimulus was a rival Pentecostal mission which ordained easily.[3] Although the UMCA had some fifty African priests in Tanganyika in 1938, they were in practice not allowed to head central missions or become archdeacons. 'African ministries of *today*', their bishop maintained, 'cannot be built up safely, soundly, satisfactorily, without European examples, sympathy, experience and oversight.'[4]

Mission churches were no longer the vanguards of progress. They were victims of the process whereby African advancement grew more complex and expensive – symbolised by Makerere's progress towards university status – while depression and war impoverished established institutions. Between 1931 and 1935 the central missionary funds of the Roman Catholic church were halved. CMS income fell by roughly a fifth. The Nazi regime forbade currency transfers to German missions except to pay European staff.[5] Missions responded by emphasising African 'self-support', which made it even more difficult to keep wages in line with secular employment. In 1948 the UMCA's African priests earned Shs. 65 a month while the recommended salary of first-grade African teachers was Shs. 300. Three seminarians left the mission for this reason in 1949. Between about 1930 and 1946 Kwiro lost a third of its teachers to government employment, including the senior African teacher at the central school, who resigned 'because they could not give me a salary adequate to support my growing family'.[6] Scarcely any Makerere graduate sought ordination. With

[1] Nolan in Shorter and Kataza, *Missionaries*, p. 8.
[2] A. G. Blood, *A new creation: a review of the work of the UMCA in 1944* (Westminster, 1945), p. 9.
[3] Above, p. 336; Wright, *German missions*, pp. 178–9.
[4] *Annual review of the work of the UMCA, 1935* (Westminster, 1936), p. 4.
[5] Oliver, *Missionary factor*, p. 232 n. 2; Hewitt, *Success*, I, 480–5; Wright, *German missions*, p. 186.
[6] A. G. Blood, *The King's business: a review of the work of the UMCA in 1948* (Westminster, 1949), pp. 5–6; *Central Africa*, August 1949; Larson, 'History', pp. 318–19.

difficulty (and large subsidies) each mission tried to maintain its secondary school, but even these pinnacles wobbled. Minaki, which had pioneered African medical training, closed its course for hospital assistants in 1951 because those it trained failed the government's increasingly difficult examinations.[1]

African response to disengagement is perhaps the best illustration of the dialectic between colonial crisis and African initiative. As the European vision of the future faded, so African Christians sought one for themselves. They chose three approaches: independency, revival, and eclecticism.

Only five independent churches were formed in Tanganyika at this time, and all were confined to border regions.[2] There were three main reasons for this. Independency flourishes in strongly Christian environments, which were rare in Tanganyika because mission work had been disrupted by war. The continuing (if waning) prestige of Swahili culture offered an alternative form of modernity to those rejecting mission control, especially in the towns. And few Tanga-nyikan Christians had access to a vernacular – as opposed to Swahili – bible, the chief source of independent Christian inspiration.[3]

The earliest of the five churches was the Watchtower movement, which originated in southern Africa and owed its ideas to the Watchtower and Bible Tract Society, the parent body of Jehovah's Witnesses. It foretold the imminent end of the world, the destruction of intrinsically evil earthly rulers, and the salvation of poor and oppressed believers. The movement was brought to Kasanga district in 1919 by Hanoc Sindano, a Mambwe from Tanganyika who had accepted Watchtower teachings while working in southern Africa. The movement spread no further. Watchtower followers in Kasanga built several villages called 'Jerusalems' designed as communities uncor-rupted by colonial society and combining Watchtower virtue with the solidarities of village life. Like the local congregations of other independent churches they were reactions against the enlargement of scale in African society.[4]

The African National Church was very different. Formed in

---

[1] *Central Africa*, April 1952.
[2] In addition there is mention of a syncretic sect on Kilimanjaro in Raum, *Childhood*, p. 291.
[3] T. O. Ranger, 'Christian independency in Tanzania', in David B. Barrett (ed.), *African initiatives in religion* (Nairobi, 1971), pp. 122–45; Barrett, *Schism and renewal in Africa* (Nairobi, 1968), pp. 129–34. Chagga Christians who became polygynists are said to have embraced Islam: Clemm, 'White mountain', p. 78.
[4] Ranger, *African churches*, pp. 12–16.

northern Malawi in 1928, it embodied the aims of educated Christians who had deserted mission churches either to become polygynists or to seek leadership. One, Paddy Nyasulu, brought the church's message into Unyakyusa, where he established schools (which soon failed) and gained several hundred followers. ANC teaching attacked the mission churches' elitism, their tendency to divide Africans and impose alien social concepts, and especially their exclusion of the old:

We believe the commission of the Christian Church to Africa was to impart Christ and education in such a way as to fit in with manners and customs of the people and not that it should impose on the African the unnecessary and impracticable methods of European countries, such as having one wife, etc., which have no biblical authority...

The aim of this Church is the uplifting of the African *en masse* taking in its rise the old people who are at present being left out by religions of the North and its civilization, as well as winning those who are considered bad because of polygamy and drink, and are refused any latent qualities for doing good any more, to try and restore an atmosphere of a deeply, naturally religious life as prevailed in the days of long ago.

While Watchtower was millennial, the ANC was modernist, concerned with education, politics, and macrocosmic problems. Yet it too held that colonial society was corrupted. 'We have done wrong in our village, Father', its general confession prayed:

Witchcraft, adultery, and hatred, all these are in our village...Our Chiefs do not love one another in their hearts...The old worship is broken down; we have come as wild animals which are without God. Call us again to worship, Father.[1]

The Last Church of God and His Christ, founded in Malawi in 1925 by Jordan Msumwa, also stressed village solidarity and the salvation of polygynists but appealed to less educated men. Jordan Msumwa himself worked in Mwanza and Shinyanga and tried to form a church there. 'Is it not fit', he wrote, 'for the black mankind, africa, a man of wives to praise God with his wives as holy men of God as our customs.'[2] This attempt failed, but another, by a Nyakyusa named Silwani Ngemela, introduced the church into Rungwe in 1930:

We don't preach to the Christians but to those whom does not know God, and Converting and burry men and women, in Jordan, which means we are Byptizing men, and women in any River...although a man having 10 wives, or 100, if he rempents and give his heart to Jesus, is to be Barried in Jordan...We dont count man's properties But we count the repented heart

[1] Wilson, *Communal rituals*, pp. 190–5; Ranger, *African churches*, pp. 16–20.
[2] Jordan Amsumba to Symes, 25 June 1932, TNA 19460/7.

of man...we realy teach the Ten Commandments, etc, but we dont prevent to marry wives...we dont like to Chase away men's wives, we are not, big enough.[1]

Ngemela dominated the church throughout the 1930s; a follower described him as 'our European'. By 1954 the church claimed over 10,000 members and was probably more popular, if less sophisticated, than the ANC.[2]

Extensively-evangelised Rungwe and Kasanga were Tanganyika's chief areas of independency between the wars,[3] but two churches were established near Lake Victoria. One was a branch of the Abamalaki – the Society of the One Almighty God – powerful in Uganda since before the First World War. This converted several Haya, probably while visiting Uganda, but they did not establish a permanent congregation. In 1924, however, an Abamalaki congregation was formed in the Nassa chiefdom of Sukumaland by a headman, Yohanna Mininga, who resented CMS plans to transfer local mission work to the Africa Inland Mission. Mininga's church – sometimes known as 'the polygynists' religion' – was a purely local organisation with a few score followers gradually declining with its founder's health until he died in 1967.[4] The other church was a branch of the Nomiya Luo Mission, formed in Kenya in 1918 by secession from the CMS and introduced into the Mara region of Tanganyika in 1929 by a Luo migrant who subsequently became its archbishop. Created in a less fully Christian environment than the other churches, Nomiya ('I have received') was highly syncretic, stressing dreams and spirit possession and apparently teaching that Jesus was only a prophet of equal standing to its founder, Johanes Oalo, who was called by God to lead the Luo to a heaven which they would share with Jews and Arabs. Nomiya exemplified the independent churches' attempts to chart and explain the larger colonial world from a specifically indigenous viewpoint.[5]

Far more important than independency to Tanganyika's history was

[1] T. K. M. Sankey to Mbeya, 8 September 1932, TNA 77/25/3/ir/58.
[2] Wilson, *Communal rituals*, pp. 172–3, 195–6, 213 n. 1; Ranger, *African churches*, pp. 20–2.
[3] For largely unsuccessful attempts to establish the African Methodist Episcopal Church in these districts, see Adrian Hastings, 'John Lester Membe', in T. O. Ranger and John Weller (ed.), *Themes in the Christian history of Central Africa* (London, 1975), pp. 186–91.
[4] Ranger, *African churches*, pp. 22–4; Hellberg, *Missions*, p. 82 n. 82; Austen, *Northwest Tanzania*, p. 143.
[5] Marie-France Perrin Jassy, *La communauté de base dans les églises africaines* (Bandundu, 1970), pp. 77, 86, 98, 105, 119, 179–81.

Revival. Evangelists and traders from Rwanda, where it originated, brought the movement to Bukoba in 1939. By 1946 *balokole* ('saved ones') were at work in Dodoma and during the next twenty years they influenced almost every Protestant church.[1] In Bukoba the movement took a classical revivalist form. Itinerant preachers demanded public confession of sins. Those 'saved' formed local cells which remained within the mission churches but met separately for prayer and fellowship and arranged public assemblies to testify and invite further confessions. Revival was a 'reaction against the factors of disengagement in the Church':[2]

It caught fire in a church where the idea of sin had been taken all too lightly, where drunkenness, heathenism, superstition, adultery, idleness, and levity flourished under the cloak of a nominal Christianity. One could no longer distinguish, by their behaviour, who was a Christian and who not. The church had become worldly, and the world churchly.[3]

Against worldliness and institutionalisation *balokole* set the anarchy of personal experience. The test of salvation was to 'shine', to feel cleansed and to testify from personal experience:

> Days are drawing nigh;
> When they come, those shall die
> Who never knew Jesus as their Physician...
>
> We may not meet again
> With these bodily eyes;
> Nevertheless, we the saved ones
> Shall meet in Zion.[4]

The fellowship of local cell and mass assembly created communities superseding family and clan. Fellowship was open even to Europeans who were 'saved' and abandoned pretensions to superiority. The movement spread chiefly by being fetched from village to village, much as villagers fetched *maji* or a witchcraft eradicator's medicine. *Balokole* prided themselves on lacking organisation and leaders: 'Who makes conclusions is Jesus – in one's heart.'[5] Such lack of structure was possible only because the movement was parasitic on the mission churches, much as earlier spirit cults had been parasitic on indigenous

[1] Max Warren, *Revival: an enquiry* (London, 1954), pp. 45, 53; Josiah Kibira, *Aus einer afrikanischen Kirche* (Bethel bei Bielefeld, 1963), pp. 31–3.
[2] Taylor, *Processes*, p. 15.
[3] Kibira, *Kirche*, pp. 32–3.
[4] An early *balokole* hymn, quoted in Ishumi, 'Embandwa'.
[5] Quoted from my notes of a talk on revival by Mr E. B. Kibira at the University College, Dar es Salaam, 10 September 1967.

religious systems. In Bukoba *balokole* criticised both the missionaries
– perhaps more profoundly challenged than any other Europeans of
this period – and the early converts who controlled the church. The
old men responded by excluding *balokole* from preaching or church
office. Andrea Kajerero, the church's champion after 1918 and its first
African pastor, moved from sympathy to antagonism:

They hopped and danced and despised those who had not yet been revived.
They refused to eat coffee-beans or groundnuts or to use ornaments and
spears. They soon started to have their own services and despised their former
friends saying 'You have not yet been saved'. In that way they refused to obey
their missionaries and pastors and they said to them: 'We have no fellowship
with you'.[1]

Kajerero's account is telescoped: fellowship was not finally broken
until the 1950s. Yet it reveals how a movement designed to overcome
divisions might itself become divisive. Another indication of ambiguity
appeared in confessions, which often emphasised the penitent's
unworthiness for an elite office. 'A district official stinking of beer?'
one reflected. 'I must get saved.'[2] A designedly egalitarian movement
might thus reinforce social distinctions. Unlike independents, *balokole*
were more hostile than missionaries to African culture, rejecting
secular dancing, alcohol, and polygyny, but further research might
show that the movement was deeply influenced by the *kubandwa* cult
within whose sphere it originated.

  The most common critique of mission Christianity was eclecticism.
Tanganyika's indigenous religions continued to decay. The rites which
suffered most were those surrounding the middle range of immaterial
forces – ancestors, heroes, nature spirits – and especially those rituals
which were communal. Such rites were increasingly difficult to
perform when members of the group were away at work or school,
or when some had become Christians or Muslims and neglected ritual
without apparently suffering harm. Rituals designed to meet
immediate disasters like drought often survived – in 1928 Kolelo
ordered elaborate cleansing of the harvest before it was eaten[3] – but
regular propitiation of household or chiefdom ancestors had apparently ceased in Usukuma by 1939 and was rare in Unyakyusa, where
annual new fire ceremonies lapsed and chiefs were reluctant to send

[1] Hellberg, 'Kajerero', p. 30.
[2] Kibira, *Kirche*, p. 46.
[3] H. Krelle, 'Beiträge zur Kenntnis der Saramoreligion', *Archiv für Anthropologie*, XXIII (1935), 229.

sacrificial beasts to Lwembe.[1] A similar trend occurred somewhat later in the Mara region:

Those [rites] which closely affect men and families preserve their immediacy, such as marriage, funerals, and the recurrent manifestations of magic and sorcery. By contrast, those which relate to the totality of the Luo people – to rhythms which are no longer fundamental to individual existence, to their physical environment which seems less remarkable today when compared with western civilisation's prodigies – are disappearing little by little.[2]

Dr Willis has analysed the impoverishment of Fipa religion in similar terms, adding that one of the first elements to disappear was specialisation in divination, sacrifice, exorcism, or healing, the various specialists giving way to general practitioners – a trend widely observed elsewhere.[3] Yet the problem of evil remained, and so did the assumption that religion must provide remedies for misfortune. Men therefore concentrated on the largest element in their religious systems, God, and the most immediate and personal: witchcraft, sorcery, and spirit possession.

Perhaps the most important religious innovations were more clearly defined notions of God and his active concern with human affairs. These ideas often drew on Muslim or Christian notions. Missionaries in Unyakyusa had used for God the name of a hero-divinity, Kyala. By the 1930s Kyala's name was venerated even at the shrines of other hero-divinities, and Kyala had become a unique creator even for non-Christians. Anthropologists heard a priest add Jesus and the Holy Spirit to the ancestors he invoked. Nyiha came to believe that God had an evil son named Shetani, whom they propitiated.[4] Yet God remained very distant and provided few satisfying answers to misfortune:

Once we were harvesting and started to argue as to whether witchcraft existed. I said it was just another form of human rottenness carried in the blood. They replied that witchcraft was the real cause of sickness and death. But for me everything is the consequence of the High God's actions. Then they asked why does a child die who cannot have known evil if the High God

---

[1] R. E. S. Tanner, 'The theory and practice of Sukuma spirit mediumship', in John Beattie and John Middleton (ed.), *Spirit mediumship and society in Africa* (London, 1969), p. 276; Busse, 'Asyukile Malango', p. 193; Wilson, *Communal rituals*, pp. 29, 102, 176–7.

[2] Perrin Jassy, *La communauté de base*, p. 46 (referring to the 1960s).

[3] Willis, 'Changes', pp. 143–53; Clemm, 'White mountain', p. 79; P. J. Imperato, 'Witchcraft and traditional medicine among the Luo of Tanzania', *TNR*, LXVI (1966), 198.

[4] Wilson, *Communal rituals*, pp. 16–18, 119; Beverley Brock, 'The Nyiha of Mbozi', *TNR*, LXV (1966), 19, 21, 24.

I

controls everything. I could only answer that the child's days were numbered from his birth and perhaps the High God does not want to show his power.[1]

Given this inadequacy, men often concentrated on the proximate causes of evil. The most enduring of these were witchcraft and sorcery. Whether belief in them increased is impossible to know, but it certainly flourished. In particular, the notion of sorcery – the procurement of evil by using material substances – had the intellectual advantage that it could be confused with poisoning and so reconciled with 'scientific' explanations of misfortune. Moreover, belief in witchcraft and sorcery was a socially relevant means of combating evil in an increasingly mobile and individualistic society, for the individual need not assemble scattered kin for some communal ritual. This was one reason why sorcery beliefs flourished in towns.[2]

Between the wars witchcraft eradication movements became an integral feature of Tanganyikan life. Their scale increased, probably as a result of motor transport, until they reached regional dimensions. No such movements are reported from the hierarchical north-west. In the north-east Majio's tradition survived. In the south-east the most famous eradicator was an Ngindo, Ngoja bin Kimeta, who in the 1920s headed a network of disciples throughout the area of the Maji Maji rebellion.[3] In the south-west the outstanding movement was *mchape*, which originated in Mozambique and Nyasaland and entered Tanganyika in 1933, penetrating northwards to Ufipa, Tabora, and Manyoni.[4] Both Ngoja and the *mchape* specialists were thought to use medicines to cure individuals of innate witchcraft and immunise men against it, but they worked within different cultural traditions. Ngoja's campaign drew on Islam and beliefs surrounding the Bokero cult, evoking memories of Maji Maji, whereas *mchape* originated in the Christian atmosphere of central Africa, used such symbols of modernity as mirrors and whistles, exploited the generational protest of the young, sometimes absorbed elements of Watchtower's millenarianism, and grew from mission Christianity's failure to combat witchcraft:

[1] Tanner, 'Sorcerer', p. 438.
[2] Willis, 'Changes', pp. 144–9; Busse, 'Asyukile Malango', p. 194; Wilson, *Good company*, p. 127; Swantz, 'Medicine man', pp. 289–93, 319–21.
[3] See correspondence in TNA 12333 and 45/218; Ranger, 'Witchcraft eradication'; Anthony A. Lee, 'Ngoja and six theories of witchcraft eradication', *Ufahamu*, VI (1976), 101–17.
[4] See correspondence in TNA 61/128/1, 18/A/2/15, and 16/5/7/11; Edward Shaba, 'A brief history of the proposed visit of the "Mchapi People"', 3 March 1934, TNA 180/C/24; Ranger, 'Witchcraft eradication'; R. G. Willis, 'Kamcape: an anti-sorcery movement in south-west Tanzania', *Africa*, XXXVIII (1968), 1–15.

Your Missionaries came in the country some 50 years ago. They tried with all their best to save people and teach you not to kill one another yet without success. But we feel sympathy with you for you have lost your dear friends, not because God took them away but by being poisoned by these wizards whom you will see today. We follow the Commandment of God which says '*Thou shalt not Kill*'. This commandment is being observed and fulfilled by us more than other religion. For they all fail to save people but we do.[1]

Even witchcraft eradication illustrated Tanganyika's growing regional differentiation.

Another flourishing antidote to misfortune was spirit exorcism. Again one cannot know whether it became more common, but there is no doubt of its vitality or of expansion, intermingling, and innovation among cults as transport improved, mobility increased, and dilemmas changed. After the First World War, for example, the *migawo* possession cult of Ufipa, centring on Katavi, spread into Ukimbu, incorporating elements from local rites, *kubandwa*, and coastal *shetani* possession rituals.[2] Such cults generally attracted the deprived. In a study of Kanga village on Mafia Island – made in 1965 but perhaps applicable to the previous generation – Dr Caplan analysed tension between the orthodox Islamic behaviour of high-status lineages and the life-style of low-status people who experienced possession by nature spirits. Whereas low-status people ascribed misfortune to the spirits, 'people of high religious status would say that sickness is caused by the will of God or "bad luck"'.[3] Thus religious affiliation was correlated with status in colonial society and with differing emphasis on microcosmic or macrocosmic agencies in explaining misfortune.

On the coast orthodox Islam had long opposed spirit possession. As Islam penetrated inland its dialectic with indigenous religions broadened. Superficially, Islam might seem immune to the strains affecting Christianity. It had no priesthood, no school system integrated with the state, and little external finance. Yet Islam did experience many strains of disengagement. One symptom was controversy over the permissible level of syncretism between Islam and indigenous practices – how far Islamic rites could be popularised by introducing drums or giving women a larger ritual role. Another symptom was rivalry between newly-converted Africans and the coastal peoples who had hitherto monopolised Islamic leadership.

[1] I owe this statement by a Nyasa clerk to Professor Ranger.
[2] Aylward Shorter, 'The *migawo*', *Anthropos*, LXV (1970), 117–25.
[3] Caplan, *Choice*, p. 109.

Often conflict crystallised into rivalry between *ulema* – the teachers, magistrates, and prayer-leaders of formal Islam, commonly of coastal origin – and leaders of brotherhoods, often Africans of recognised spirituality rather than formal learning. Such rivalry had existed in Tabora in German times. Now it became widespread. The best-documented case was Bagamoyo. Here the leading brotherhood, the Qadiriyya, was 'the brotherhood of up-country people'. Its founder, Sheikh Ramiya, was a freed slave from Zaire. By contrast, 25 of Bagamoyo's 32 leading *ulema* during the colonial period were either 'Shirazi' or Arabs. It is said that conflict culminated when Ramiya's son and successor, Sheikh Muhammad, declared in a mosque in 1938 that the Prophet had not been an Arab, meaning, as he apparently later explained, that the Prophet had been 'a personage of Arabs and Swahili and other peoples'. Profoundly offended, the Arabs appealed to jurists in Zanzibar, who supported them. When a rival brotherhood, the Ahmadiyya, reached Bagamoyo in the same year the Arabs and Shirazi joined it, causing it to be called 'the brotherhood of masters'.[1]

Its heritage of slavery sharpened Bagamoyo's rivalries, but similar tensions existed elsewhere. In Bukoba, for example, the Qadiriyya's arrival split the Islamic community. Predominantly rural, Qadiris used a drum called *dufu* in their ceremonies and admitted women. Their opponents were mostly townsmen led by coastal immigrants. In 1933 the town headman, an Arab, issued a proclamation countersigned by the district officer stating that '*duffu* is not *dhikr*'. 'The "Piga duffu" section', complained the district officer, 'base their actions upon the Koran and will not listen to the local Mohammedan leaders of different nationalities who are better informed than these Africans.' External authorities were consulted, but since most were *ulema* their learned opinions were generally unacceptable to dissidents.[2] Similar disputes occurred elsewhere. The Qadiriyya's arrival provoked conflict among Muslims in Songea. In Tabora two parties known as 'right hand' and 'left hand' quarrelled over whether women might enter the Friday mosque. In Tanga, after much dispute, the conservatives won and women were excluded from *dhikr* ceremonies. Lindi, Pangani, and Mkwaja all experienced dissension. In Dar es Salaam a noted Makua religious leader, Sheikh Idris bin Saad, was refused office in the

[1] Nimtz, 'Sufi order', chs. 7–8.
[2] Kiwanuka, 'Islam in Bukoba', *passim*; 'Tangazo kwa Waislam wote wa nchi ya Bukoba', 15 March 1933, TNA 285/155/1; Allsop to PC Lake, 31 May 1933, TNA 21447/6; Ali bin Hemed, 'Hukumu ya Duffu katika sharia ya Islamu', 21 July 1943, TNA 285/155/15.

Qadiriyya and founded a new *tariqa*, the Askariyya, which was the Islamic equivalent of an independent church.[1]

In Islam, even more than other spheres, government supported conservatism. In Bagamoyo the authorities supported Arab and Shirazi leaders against freedmen. In Bukoba they sought advice on *dufu* from conservative sheikhs. Nothing more clearly illustrated the logical connection between crisis and authoritarianism.

The spiral of repression

The depression only slightly increased governmental authoritarianism, chiefly through the 'plant more crops' campaign and agricultural regulations such as provoked the Buhaya riots of 1937. By contrast, war vastly extended regimentation. This time there was no fighting in Tanganyika. In Swahili the war was called *mpakani*, 'at the borders'. Tanganyikan askari campaigned against Italians in Somalia and Ethiopia, against pro-German French in Madagascar, and especially against Japanese in Burma, where the fighting was very severe. Of the 86,740 men enlisted from Tanganyika, 2,358 were killed or died on active service.[2] Compared with Kenyans they obtained less prestigious postings, nearly half serving as unskilled labourers in the pioneer corps or the hated military labour service. The largest contingent apparently came from Musoma, where Kuria and Luo had few other sources of income but were highly regarded as soldiers.[3] From 1940, when Italy declared war, all recruits were conscripted. In practice this meant arbitrary impressment. In Bagamoyo 'most of the male population took to the bush' and 'were afraid they would be impressed if they came near the town'. In Dar es Salaam tax defaulters were systematically conscripted. In Usambara the native administration supplied conscripts and was accused of favouring Kilindi, although Shambaa might have been mollified to know that their district officer had conscripted a troublesome Zigua irredentist. Early in 1945, 3,861 Tanganyikan Africans were absent without leave from the forces.[4]

[1] Abdallah Kayuni, quoted in Gallagher, 'Islam', p. 398; Little to CP, 8 February 1934, TNA 26105/6; Kayamba to Thornley, 21 March 1933, TNA 21447/4; *Provincial commissioners' reports*, 1934, p. 24, 1933, p. 66; Nimtz, 'Sufi order', pp. 78–9, 91–4.

[2] Moyse-Bartlett, *KAR*, part 5; *Annual report of the Labour Department [Labour report]* 1946, p. 48.

[3] CS (Governors Conference) to CS (Kenya), 14 October 1943, CO 822/117; list of family remittances, December 1942 – May 1943, TNA 31739/1.

[4] Pike, Bagamoyo DAR 1941, TNA library; Revington, Dar es Salaam DAR 1941, TNA 61/3/XVI/A/7; Korogwe DAR 1942, TNA 72/62/6/II/146; DC Korogwe, 'Report on Zigua agitation', 1 June 1943, TNA 31515/15A; 'African man power conference. Nairobi – 6th March, 1945', CO 822/117.

Greater discontent followed the conscription of labour for plantations. As a breach of fundamental policy, this decision – close to
temporary enslavement – reveals Britain's desperation. Requests for
large-scale conscription came in August 1943 from sisal growers
pressed for maximum production at minimum cost but convinced that
higher wages would produce less work. They asked for 16,000
workers, each for three years. The Colonial Office hesitated, but the
War Cabinet – at Churchill's personal insistence – authorised the
conscription of an initial 11,000 for not more than six (later twelve)
working months.[1] A district officer reported:

Conscription has had to develop into a cunning procedure on the part of both
the hunter and the hunted. A date is fixed with the Liwalis and any signs of
the impending action, such as the ordering of lorries for the transport of
recruits to Lindi and preparations of notices of selection, must be kept
secret...Then in the night preceding the fatal day a swoop is made and a
few of the weak, meek, and slow are gathered.[2]

Some from Central Province were 'aged and obviously unfit'. 'The
chief matter of concern for the natives of this district has been the fear
of conscription for sisal labour', Mwanza's district officer reported.[3]
Conditions were severe. Few estates were equipped for the influx, staff
and materials were unobtainable, and conscription made it unnecessary to attract workers by good conditions, although by 1945 labour
officers had learned to compel employers to improve conditions by
refusing them conscripts.[4] Workers returning from one estate declared that they had slept in the open, had not received firewood or
food when they were sick – rations were then less than half their
normal level – and had lost seven days work from their cards if they
missed a plant when cutting.[5] Sisal sores caused agony to men
unaccustomed and unfitted to cutting. While employers used conscription to hold down wages,[6] conscripts used their ingenuity to
escape. When Arusha district office conscripted 700 'semi-detribalised
loafers' they caused such trouble that local employers refused any

[1] TSGA executive committee minutes, 23 August and 11 November 1943, TNA
29513/1/30 and 31; 'Note on a meeting held in the Secretary of State's room on 12th
August 1943' and 'War Cabinet 129 (43): extract from conclusions', 20 September 1943,
CO 691/184.
[2] Newala DAR 1943, quoted in Liebenow, *Colonial rule*, p. 161.
[3] Hutt, Moshi DAR 1943, TNA 69/63/11/1; DC Mwanza to PC Lake, 16 October 1944, TNA
215/1603/A/119.
[4] Stewart, 'Annual report on labour, Tanga Province, 1945', TNA 304/962/9/1.
[5] DC Mwanza to PC Lake, 12 December 1944, and Stewart to LC, 23 January 1945, TNA
215/1603/A/133 and 145A.
[6] TSGA executive committee minutes, 11 November 1943, TNA 29513/1/31.

more, so the next batch were sent to Bonde, only for 140 of 594 to desert before the train arrived. Of 7,627 conscripts reaching rubber estates during 1945, 79 died and 512 deserted. Government ceased to send tax defaulters from Dar es Salaam to the north-east because they disappeared immediately into Tanga's backstreets.[1]

As the war progressed, discontent with shortages, inflation, and regimentation grew. Swollen town populations added housing shortages to low wages and bad food. By 1947 more than two-thirds of the houses in Dar es Salaam's African townships contravened the overcrowding rules.[2] Food rationing, introduced in 1942, largely failed. 'The price control regulations were like Hitler's Pacts', a Swahili newspaper protested, '...not worth the papers they were written on.... The letters FST (First, Second, Third) are now translated as *Fool* them, Swindle them, Twist their tails!'[3] The shortage and expense of cotton cloth were particularly resented. 'For the African', a district officer reported, 'the end of the war and a lavish supply of cotton piece goods were expected to be synonymous.'[4] They were disappointed. In August 1947 government organised a sale of black *kaniki* in Dar es Salaam. A queue nearly half a mile long formed before selling began; when it ended, the queue was still half a mile long.[5]

'It is most undesirable', Cameron had pronounced, 'that the Government should have trade relations with the natives.'[6] During the crisis this maxim was ignored and control of trade became part of the accelerating trend towards managerial government which brought a new level of state penetration into society and a new style of political action. As government took control of the economy, so Africans directed their grievances and misfortunes towards government. Protest which in 1937 was aimed against chiefs or cooperatives would in later years focus directly on the British. And since all Tanganyikans were subjects of the British, they would become increasingly aware of shared grievances and a common enemy. The trend towards big government in the crisis years was an important stimulus to nationalism.[7] Moreover, big government was conservative government. A

[1] Maddocks, Arusha DAR 1944, TNA 69/63/12/38; Maddocks, Arusha DAR 1945, TNA 69/63/13/28; Nelson, 'Annual report for 1945: Labour Officer, Muheza', TNA 304/962/9/14; Pike, 'Uzaramo district: report for the month of May 1944', TNA 57/1/17/57.
[2] MOH to MS, 15 April 1947, TNA 26693/II/45A.   [3] *Kwetu*, 3 April 1943.
[4] Malcolm to PC Lake, 22 December 1945, TNA 215/1603/A/185.
[5] *Tanganyika standard* (weekly), 30 August 1947.
[6] Cameron to Passfield, 7 May 1930, CO 691/111.
[7] This is a theme of later chapters.

feature of crisis was government's increasing alliance with the
conservative elements in society. Early colonial regimes were generally
concerned to maximise change and had little use for African
conservatives. They preferred Kiwanga to Chabruma, Ambilishye to
Gidamausa. But with its basic restructuring completed, government
came to prefer conservatives to progressives. This was true of Islam,
of indirect rule, and especially of relations between government and
the immigrant communities.

In the 1930s European settlers regained some of the influence they
had lost during the First World War. Several reasons explained this.
The total European population had grown from 2,447 in 1921 to 8,200
in 1931, compared with 4,998 in 1913.[1] The formation of a Legislative
Council in 1926 provided a forum. A Congress of Associations on the
Kenyan model met in 1928, and a European Association was formed
to coordinate local organisations.[2] Depression showed the value of
European agriculture as the prices of African export crops fell.
Government needed British settlers' support against the growing
German community. The formation of the TSGA in 1930 greatly
increased European strength. Its president, Sir William Lead, was also
the unofficials' leader in the Legislative Council and as dominant as
Feilke in German times. Although government never abandoned its
trusteeship for the African population, it nevertheless became increasingly sensitive to European opinion. In 1937 it appointed a
commission with a European unofficial majority to investigate labour
supply.[3] Next year it responded to Lead's agitation by appointing a
Central Development Committee of unofficial Legislative Councillors,
chaired by the Chief Secretary, to produce a territorial development
plan. Governor Sir Mark Young (1938–41) was unusually sympathetic
to settlers and encouraged this committee to stress European farming.
Its report marked a new high-point of European influence. It
recommended extensive white settlement in which 'the Government
itself should become a prime mover' by creating a Land Settlement
Board and a Land Bank. 'The stimulus provided by other races', the
committee declared, 'is essential to African development and the more
widespread this stimulus can be made the quicker must be its effects.'
War prevented implementation, but the report became the basis of

[1] Weigt, *Europäer*, p. 48; *Die deutschen Schutzgebiete 1912/13*, II, 10–11.
[2] 'Resolutions passed by the Tanganyika Congress of Associations', 24–6 October 1928,
CO 691/104; *Tanganyika Times*, 5 and 19 January and 23 March 1929.
[3] Tanganyika, *Report...on...native labour*.

Tanganyika's postwar planning.[1] Meanwhile Young appointed three European unofficials and one Asian to the Executive Council in 1939. When war began, Lead joined the government as Sisal Controller and other elderly, public-spirited men undertook voluntary duties. At this time of supreme crisis the British community consolidated.

Asians also played more part in government. Their Legislative Councillors were commonly wealthy professional or businessmen like A. A. Adamjee, a senior executive with Karimjee Jivanjee, V. M. Nazerali, a leading Dar es Salaam retailer who also owned sisal estates, and Dr S. B. Malik, who joined the Executive Council in 1939 and two years later became the first unofficial chairman of the Dar es Salaam township authority. The prosperous 1920s had produced a group of large-scale capitalists who gained power around 1930 and held it throughout the crisis. Dr Walji has shown that around 1930 eight of the eleven seats on the Ismaili Provincial Council for Tanganyika were taken over by the new businessmen, including Nazerali, Kassum Sunderji, and Habib Punja. Starting as retailers, these men were diversifying into service trades and processing industries. Habib Punja set up a soap factory in Dar es Salaam in 1933, moved into milling in 1941, and five years later obtained interests in building materials and urban property, while Kassum Sunderji owned a grocery chain in the capital, built its first cinema, and in 1948 started a fleet of taxis.[2] The war offered wealthy men many opportunities to invest in land and other property. These successful men were government's allies. Desiring to end the worst abuses of small-scale trade, Governor Symes

discussed the situation frankly with some of the leading Indians...I asked them if they could find means to curtail those practices and to deal with defaulters...In the course of two or three months, the results became apparent. District officials...reported that matters were improving, and mentioned instances of individual 'black sheep' who had either changed their fleeces or gone out of business.[3]

During the protests of 1937 Indian Association branches urged Asian Legislative Councillors to resign if the Native Produce Bill went through. Instead they amended it to the Native Coffee Bill, persuaded

[1] Tanganyika, *Report of the Central Development Committee* (Dar es Salaam, 1940); Young to Moyne, 22 July 1941, CO 691/184; below, p. 439.
[2] Shirin Walji, 'Business enterprise and leadership in the Ismaili community, 1914–1968', seminar paper, University of Dar es Salaam, 1970; Booth, 'Directory'.
[3] Symes, *Tour of duty*, pp. 173–4.

the Chief Secretary to apply it only to Kilimanjaro, and joined the unanimous vote in its favour.[1]

With growing Asian participation in territorial affairs went growing African resentment. Antagonism was always latent and it is remarkable that Asians suffered so little violence. Government certainly did little to prevent antagonism, refusing joint educational facilities for the two races lest Asians should transmit political ideas.[2] Hostility to Asians was particularly strong among African clerks and traders who competed with them. The crisis intensified antagonisms. Africans commonly blamed Asian traders for low prices. Business competition became more ruthless. Asian infiltration of African residential zones was strongly resented. 'Why the non-natives cannot go back to their proper place that is Zone II or to go back to their country', residents of the capital demanded.[3] Asian political influence was more unpopular than European. In 1938 the crowd attending a public meeting to oppose Tanganyika's return to Germany listened quietly to speeches in Swahili and English but shouted down a speaker who began in Gujarati.[4] War added new tensions. Mwanza experienced one riot in 1939 which threatened to loot Asian shops for profiteering, and another in 1946 possibly caused by African traders unable to obtain quotas of controlled goods.[5] Economic controls and rationing led to an increased categorisation which stimulated racial consciousness. While Arabs protested against their 'amphibian category of Asians and Africans at the same time',[6] urban Africans resented the inferior rations and cost-of-living bonuses which they received. 'Colour bar is now spreading like a forest fire and would contaminate every nook of this territory', one complained in 1945.[7] Having helped to create political tribes, government was helping to create political races.

[1] *Tanganyika herald*, 29 September 1937; Executive Council minutes, 28 September and 15 October 1937, CO 736/21; Legislative Council proceedings, October 1937, in TNA 25038/II/197.
[2] Rivers-Smith to CS, 24 July 1925, quoted in Walter Morris-Hale, *British administration in Tanganyika from 1920 to 1945* (Genève, 1969), p. 167.
[3] 'Native retail shops in Dar es Salaam', 27 December 1938, TNA 61/490/325.
[4] *Kwetu*, 22 November 1938.
[5] Gilbert, Mwanza DAR 1939, TNA 41/128/20/1; DC Mwanza to PC Lake, 29 October 1946, TNA 215/1603/A/227.
[6] Arab Association to Stanley, 8 October 1943, CO 691/181.
[7] G. G. Mhina to AA Dodoma, 16 March 1945, Suleiman papers, TNA.

Responsibility for the future

Between the wars educated Tanganyikans concentrated on improving their societies and themselves through education, economic advancement, and local government. Improvement was expected to be achieved gradually through self-help and cooperation with Europeans. The aim was embodied in TTACSA and the Bukoba Bahaya Union, in the work of Mgeni and Joseph Merinyo. Crisis changed this approach by infusing urgency. Nearly two decades of stagnation left men impatient of the colonial regime. Excited by talk of the brave new world to follow victory, and alarmed that Tanganyika's future was once more at issue, Africans began to demand a voice in post-war planning. They began to take upon themselves the responsibility for the future. Moreover, war brought greater awareness of external affairs: Britain's imperial strategies, African politics in Kenya and West Africa, white oppression in South Africa, Asian nationalism, Pan-Africanism, and communism.

The British knew that war must stimulate political awareness. They expected it chiefly among those who joined the forces, visited distant countries, learned to shoot white men, and might return with novel and seditious notions. A district officer stressed the need 'to inculcate a certain amount of "mind cleansing" into the mind of the native soldier on his return', and plans were made to minimise disruption.[1] Some African soldiers did experience a political awakening. Signing himself 'The Dreamer', a signaller wrote from India to advocate an African Continental Union rather than a purely territorial body. 'When will Tanganyika alone bring Africa freedom?' he asked:

I have now been two years and seven months in India...Once I made a very good friend who was a student at Muslim College Madras, and on another occasion by chance I made another who was at Calcutta University...

In many offices...you will see that the P.C. is an Indian and the D.C. a European. In many workshops they are mixed up; you do not see only Europeans in charge as they are in Africa. I asked them...Is this because of education, or for what reason? They told me: No, not at all; these things have come about because of the unity of the association of The All-Indians-Union...

Truly Indians have unity. It is not the union of a game alone, like drunkards or children, but a union with the power to lift up the whole of India...

I mourn for my own Africa. When shall we Africans be free like this?[2]

[1] DC Korogwe to PC Tanga, 15 May 1944, TNA 4/173/4/3; 'Employment of ex-servicemen. Meeting held on the 2nd August [1944]' TNA 171/76/10/9A.

[2] J. A. M. Ibrahim-Juma to AA Dodoma, 30 December 1945, Suleiman papers, TNA.

Recalling the battle of Kalewa in Burma, where KAR troops broke through after British and Americans had failed, a soldier remembered that 'we scorned the British, for we saw that a Briton's bragging was based on the deeds of others, especially we Africans. We saw that – given a rifle – we could be better than a European.'[1] One group with Asian experience was to be deeply involved in early nationalist politics in Dar es Salaam,[2] and several were to hold office in local branches of political associations. Generally, however, the soldiers' political contribution was surprisingly small. Their gratuities were commonly invested in cattle or lost in trade, while their military experience made more impact on conversation at village beer parties than on political organisation. It was no accident that many former sergeants made first-rate village headmen. 'They still tend to line up in the front row of the baraza and salute, as a separate body', a district officer reported, 'but I have noticed that after this demonstration they seem to have little to say. When their military clothing is finished the ex-askaris of this division will, I think, with a few exceptions, fade into their surroundings.'[3] He was right. 'It is impossible to tell an ex-askari from any other person', a nationalist organiser complained in the late 1950s. 'They went into the army as illiterates and they remained "empty-headed", forgetting everything but how to give a snappy salute and say "*Ndio, Bwana*".'[4]

Change in secular thought is the truly neglected area of Tanganyika's intellectual history, but it is clear that the war's chief impact was on men – especially educated men – who stayed at home. One way to observe it is to read the Swahili newspaper *Kwetu* from its first number in November 1937. Admittedly, it was not entirely typical. Its proprietor and editor, Erica Fiah, was a Ganda who had entered Tanganyika as a medical clerk during the First World War and had settled, working in clerical posts until he opened a shop in Dar es Salaam in 1932. He was a clever, quarrelsome, mercenary, unprincipled man in touch with elite politics in Buganda and thence with the pan-African writings of black Americans and West Indians like Marcus Garvey and George Padmore.[5] Yet *Kwetu* was open to literate Tanganyikans and vividly reveals their wartime intellectual awakening. It began in improving vein. Its sub-title was 'The key to

[1] Lotari Lupinda, quoted in Larson, 'History', pp. 329–30.
[2] Below, p. 507.   [3] Dobson to PC Lake, 7 November 1946, TNA 215/1603/A/231.
[4] 'Yes, Sir'. Quoted in Liebenow, *Colonial rule*, p. 162.
[5] 'Maisha ya mvumbuzi wa Kwetu', in *Kwetu*, February 1945. I am also indebted to Dr J. M. Lonsdale for notes of interviews with Erica Fiah during January 1965.

civilisation' and its aims were 'to spread knowledge among those sons of the soil who could read and write Kiswahili...to do social and humanitarian work and to establish a closer contact between the native and the non-native communities'.[1] With the approach of war and the danger of Tanganyika being given to Germany, *Kwetu* rallied to Britain. 'Any African favouring Hitler is the enemy of Africa', Fiah proclaimed. 'Every African ought to pray that Great Britain continues to rule over us for evermore.'[2] This was the general view of educated Africans; teachers at Minaki even urged that Tanganyika should become a colony in order to be securely British.[3] *Kwetu*'s tone began to change during 1941 and swung quickly in the next year with shortages and conscription. Allied victory was not questioned, but its value to Africans was. 'Who will deny', Fiah asked in August 1941,

...that Shs. 9/- is a low wage for a family man for 30 long days of a month, with bare maize flour and beans as the ration?...

Who will deny the sacrifices made by the African native in the last war, and what, in the name of Heaven, did he reap after that? He has remained a clerk for 20 long years...

Who will deny that there is no direct representation for us whatever?[4]

For Fiah, as for other educated Tanganyikans, the war opened the issue of the future. 'The African is awakening from his long slumber', a correspondent declared in December 1941.[5] During the next four years concern for the future increasingly dominated *Kwetu*. 'After the War, What?' it asked in May 1942:

Will the African native be allowed a better place and a little more voice and responsibility in the administration of his country, or will he continue to remain as a clerk, last on the list, as he has always been?[6]

The word *uhuru* became increasingly common. Originally meaning freedom as opposed to slavery, it was adopted by government to describe the Allies' 'war for freedom', *vita vya uhuru*. It did not yet have the specific sense of national independence but was used to mean almost any kind of increased liberty or opportunity. 'Everything is freedom these days', a correspondent observed in *Kwetu*, although Fiah warned that 'the African post-war freedom is only a mere joke'.[7] The idea of *uhuru* made a lasting impact. In 1947 an anonymous writer warned the Chief of Usambara, 'Now is the time for the British to fulfil

[1] *Kwetu*, 18 November 1937.   [2] *Ibid.*, 8 June 1939 and 29 June 1940.
[3] *Ibid.*, 16 April 1939.   [4] *Ibid.*, 1 August 1941.
[5] *Ibid.*, 26 December 1941.   [6] *Ibid.*, 1 May 1942.
[7] *Ibid.*, February 1945 and 22 September 1943.

their promise that when the war ended the world would be made new and all men would gain freedom.'[1] In *Kwetu*'s columns a rising politician struck a new note by urging that Africans should *regain* their former glory:

The line of progress must be planned not by the tutors alone, but by the cooperation of the tutors and the taught...Civilization started in Africa long before the other countries of the world awoke, but Africa's progress was retarded by the awakening of the other countries...Now she is awakening from her long siesta.[2]

A second area in which to see the wartime awakening is Swahili poetry. With rare exceptions[3] inter-war poetry was trite, moralising, or religious. The war brought change. It was most apparent in the work of Tanganyika's greatest poet, Shaaban Robert, the son of a Yao clerk at Amboni sisal estate. A Muslim civil servant who spent most of his life in Tanga and Pangani, Shaaban Robert's work still lacks adequate study, but he seems to have inherited many coastal values, notably pride of race, love of Islam and the Swahili language, and delight in moralising and verbal elaboration. Like most Tanganyikans he was not an especially political man. He valued rhyme above abstract principle and his opinions were confused and inconsistent. But he was remarkably sensitive to contemporary issues and could dramatise them in a literary form which established him as unofficial poet laureate and made his work a major historical source.

Shaaban Robert first wrote poetry in 1932. Seven years later he published a poem in praise of appeasement.[4] During the war he wrote 'a poem to celebrate the war of the whole world...the great event which happened in the world in my century'.[5] He called it *Utenzi wa vita vya uhuru*. After 1945 his writings caught post-war excitement. He eulogised the quasi-political African Association, of which he was an active member, celebrated the end of the war, and mourned the death of Gandhi.[6] And he wrote two major prose works, *Kufikirika*[7] and *Kusadikika*,[8] in which 'he began to search for social righteousness'.[9]

[1] 'Maulizo mbele ya bwana', anonymous document [1947] in TNA 72/43/3/83A.
[2] Petro C. Mntambo, 'The African at the road junction', in *Kwetu*, January 1948. Mntambo was a museum assistant.
[3] One is quoted below, p. 407.   [4] *Mambo leo*, January 1939.
[5] Shaaban bin Robert, *Maisha yangu na Baada ya miaka hamsini* (reprinted, London, 1966), pp. 67-8.
[6] 'Chama cha Waafrika' and 'Hitler' in *Pambo la lugha* (Johannesburg, 1948), pp. 9-10, 5-6; 'Mahatma Gandhi' in *Mwafrika aimba* (London, 1949), pp. 35-6.
[7] Reprinted, Nairobi, 1974.   [8] London, 1951.
[9] R. Ohly, 'Historical approach to Swahili literature', *Kiswahili*, XLIII (1973), 83.

Both concerned imaginary kingdoms. *Kusadikika* in particular was a utopian story about the contrast between existing injustice and the organisation of an ideal society. In it Shaaban Robert embodied both the concern with the future which pervaded post-war African thinking and the conflict between idealistic youth and cynical age which was another public issue of the day.[1] Yet it was symptomatic of his and the time's ideological limitations that *Kusadikika*'s conflict was resolved by the judgment of a wise king in the tradition of Islamic folktale. The crisis of colonial society had led Tanganyikans to reach for the control of their history, but it had not yet shown them how to win or use that control. Like *Kusadikika*, Tanganyikans remained utopian.

Kwetu's pages and Shaaban Robert's works reveal an intellectual awakening. To see that awakening taking place through action and experience – to see liberation becoming *in practice* the central theme of Tanganyika's history – one must turn to the actions of urban workers and of the educated men who created the African Association.

[1] Ahmed Mgeni, 'Recipe for a utopia', *Kiswahili*, XLI (1971), 91–4.

CHAPTER 12

Townsmen and workers

It was in the towns that Europeans first lost control of Africa. Depression and war had their greatest impact on Tanganyika's townsmen: on educated men who formed the African Association and on workers whose labour movement culminated in 1947 in a general strike which was both the climax of the colonial crisis and the first modern, popular, multi-tribal movement in Tanganyika's history. Both African Association and labour movement took much of their character from the social organisation of the capital, where each quarter had a particular social composition corresponding to a distinct phase in the country's history. To understand Dar es Salaam's particularity, however, it is first necessary to examine the social organisation of Tanganyika's towns in general – a difficult task where so little urban history has been written.

Urban diversity and social categories

Pre-colonial towns were located on the coast, along caravan routes, or at the capitals of powerful chiefs like Kimweri and Merere. With walls razed, rulers impoverished, and inhabitants dispersed, royal capitals disintegrated under German rule. Vugha burned down and was not rebuilt. Utengule Usafwa was deliberately destroyed by the Germans. Some commercial towns survived better, for the colonial economy was still based on the coast and on east-west lines of communication. Dar es Salaam, Tanga, and Lindi prospered as European administrative and commercial centres, but other ports decayed. Some inland trading settlements, such as Tabora, became administrative headquarters, but more were displaced by German stations on sites determined by transport, strategic and political considerations, and suitability for European habitation. At Moshi and Arusha, Iringa and Dodoma, planned settlements were built with straight roads and clear fields of fire.

At one end of the spectrum of urban change was the expanding capital; at the other was the port by-passed by modern communications. With declining trade and population, Bagamoyo illustrates the second experience. In the nineteenth century its inhabitants had formed three strata. Power was shared among Swahili-speaking *diwani* of Shomvi or Shirazi origin, immigrant Arabs including the Sayyid's *liwali,* and Asian merchants. Perhaps a third of the inhabitants were slaves, often from the Congo and known as Manyema. The remaining townsmen were free African fishermen, cultivators, or labourers.[1] Economic decline and colonial rule transformed relationships among these groups. Many Shomvi supported Abushiri's resistance and were killed or fled the town. Those who remained lost their slaves and sought to maintain an aristocratic life-style in reduced circumstances by selling land to Asian or African entrepreneurs. The Germans regarded Shomvi simply as Africans and replaced the previous diffusion of power by a hierarchy centring on their *liwali,* normally an Arab or Baluchi. The British preserved this system, regarding indirect rule as irrelevant to towns. The legacy of slavery left tensions expressed in the rivalry between the Qadiriyya brotherhood's Manyema leaders and the Arab or Shomvi *ulema.* Racial antagonism, on the other hand, cut across the division between former slaves and masters, for Manyema attended the Shomvi mosque, and when the African Association reached Bagamoyo in 1939 it sought to unite Shomvi and Manyema against the 'white people's' control of the town. The strength and complexity of racial tensions also affected tribal categorisation. A small town with no predominant ethnic group, Bagamoyo had gained from slavery and porterage an unusually diverse population, yet, paradoxically, few ethnic groups were generally recognised, each embracing people from a broad area. All men from the western plateau commonly called themselves Nyamwezi, for example, while social deprivation appears to have given the Manyema greater solidarity than they possessed in many other towns. There is no evidence of conflict *among* Manyema in Bagamoyo.[2]

In this Bagamoyo contrasted sharply with Ujiji. Another predominantly Islamic centre, deliberately imitating the coastal culture, Ujiji also had a very diverse African population and a legacy of slavery, and it experienced little twentieth-century growth, the population increasing between 1900 and 1957 from some 7,000 to only

[1] Brown, 'Pre-colonial history', chs. 4–6; Nimtz, 'Sufi order', chs. 4–6.
[2] Nimtz, 'Sufi order', chs. 5–7.

12,011.[1] Yet despite these similarities, Ujiji differed significantly from Bagamoyo. It was overwhelmingly African in composition, with few Asian traders and only a sprinkling of Arabs and coastal men after the ivory trade collapsed in the 1890s. Most Africans – 75 per cent in 1912, according to one estimate[2] – were Manyema from one or other shore of Lake Tanganyika. Once slavery was abolished, the Manyema left the town's menial work to immigrants from neighbouring Buha.[3] Moreover, Ujiji had no long-established urban aristocracy. Its control had been disputed since the nineteenth century between the townsmen and the neighbouring Jiji chief, Rusimbi, in whose territory the town stood. The Germans gave control to the Arabs, but Cameron transferred it to Rusimbi.[4] This encouraged the antagonism between Ujiji's two main factions: the Congo Arabiani and the Watanganyika. Although both were Manyema who spoke Swahili as their first language, their antagonism originated in slavery. The Arabiani were men (or descendants of men) who had served the Arabs and accepted coastal culture: 'a sort of old guard who carry on the tradition of the Arab regime, the older men, sons of caravan overseers, ruga-ruga, slaves'.[5] By contrast, the Watanganyika were drawn from the peoples who lived around the lake and fished its waters. They tended to be younger – often the sons of men who had resisted slave raiders – and considerably more numerous than the Arabiani because their numbers were swollen by immigrants. Although the Watanganyika were slowly being acculturated, the nineteenth-century antagonism between those who had accepted coastal culture and those who had rejected it survived in bitter rivalry. 'The Wa-Tanganyika used to tell Kongo Arabians, "You are slaves". And the latter used to tell the former, "You are still very uncivilised".'[6] Following Cameron's decision to subordinate the town to Rusimbi, an Arabiani was killed with a knife and several men were seriously wounded in street fighting during April 1932.[7]

The contrast between conflict in Ujiji and Manyema unity in

---

[1] 'Auszug aus dem Grenzbericht des Hauptzollamts-Vorsteher Ewerbeck', 22 July – 19 August 1900, RKA 640/83; Tanzania, *Recorded population changes 1948–1967* (Dar es Salaam, 1968), table 5.

[2] F. O. Karstedt, *Beiträge zur Praxis der Eingeborenenrechtssprechung in Deutsch-Ostafrika* (Dar es Salaam, 1912), p. 55.

[3] Hino, 'Social stratification', p. 63.

[4] Mitchell to Symes, 5 May 1932, TNA 20797/1/6.

[5] Longland to CS, 13 April 1932, TNA 180/196/21/1.

[6] A. Kabembo, 'African politics in Ujiji', duplicated paper, 1969, in my possession.

[7] F. Amani Karonda, 'Mazungumzo ya vita vya Ujiji bayna ya taifa mbili hizi Wamanyema na Watanganyika, siku ya 3rd April, 1932', typescript, 1932, copy in my possession.

Bagamoyo shows how a town's social categories and tensions depended on its history and socio-economic structure. In place of their multiple pre-colonial identities, urban immigrants adopted a set of categories appropriate to their particular town. Men who were predominantly Manyema in Bagamoyo might be predominantly Arabiani in Ujiji. This was one aspect of the phenomenon which social anthropologists called situationalism, meaning that an African's identity often varied depending on the situation in which he found himself.[1] In one form this affected even Tanganyika's Asians, whose castes lost their exclusive association with particular occupations and some of their hierarchical relationships to one another, but survived as endogamous groups and social categories with such differentiating characteristics as personality stereotypes and food preferences.[2] Situationalism also led to the emergence in inland townships of a category of people – normally Muslim, Swahili-speaking townsmen – who remembered their ethnic origins but regarded themselves as Swahili in contrast to the surrounding 'tribesmen'.[3] And most important for the present purpose, situationalism enabled the system of categories peculiar to a particular town – the capital – to shape the development of African political organisation throughout the territory.

Dar es Salaam

As the rings of a tree reveal ecological change, so each phase of Tanganyika's modern history was embodied in the human geography of its capital.[4] The town grew up around a crescent-shaped bay facing north-eastwards towards Zanzibar. Near the southern arm of the crescent an inlet led into an inner bay which became the harbour. In 1865 Sayyid Majid began to build a town around the inner bay, perhaps to escape Zanzibar's feuds, control the coast more directly,

[1] The anthropologists add that one man may stress different identities in different situations in the same town. See J. C. Mitchell, *The Kalela dance*, Rhodes-Livingstone paper no. 27 (Manchester, 1956); A. L. Epstein, *Politics in an urban African community* (Manchester, 1958).

[2] Pocock, '"Difference"', pp. 290–8; Agehananda Bharati, *The Asians in East Africa* (Chicago, 1972), ch. 2; Anne K. Fleuret, 'Social organization and adaptation among Sikhs in Tanzania', Ph.D. thesis, University of California at Santa Barbara, 1975, ch. 5.

[3] W. Arens, 'Tribalism and the poly-ethnic rural community', *Man*, VIII (1973), 441–50; *idem*, 'The *Waswahili*', *Africa*, XLV (1975), 426–38; Naomichi Ishige, 'On Swahilization', *KUAS*, III (1969), 93–108.

[4] This account is based on C. Gillman, 'Dar es Salaam, 1860 to 1940', *TNR*, XX (1945), 1–23; Sutton, 'Dar es Salaam', pp. 1–19; Leslie, *Survey*, *passim*.

and forestall Britain's expected prohibition of slave exports. Building stopped when he died in 1870, leaving a few stone houses around the inner bay and 200,000 coconut palms covering the whole site. In 1886 some 5,000 people lived there. Five years later the Germans made it their capital because of its sheltered deep-water harbour. Offices, European houses, and the port were built around the inner bay, with the commercial area of Asian shops and houses slightly to the west. African settlements fringed the European and Asian quarters. One of the earliest housed Sudanese and Shangaan askari, who were among Dar es Salaam's first permanent townsmen. Another early group were Manyema freedmen, 'the citizens of Dar es Salaam *par excellence*',[1] but most African inhabitants at this time were either Zaramo from the neighbouring countryside or long-distance migrants who settled together along the roads leading from their homelands. Each Asian community occupied a section of the commercial area, clustering around its mosque or temple or meeting-house, although these groupings were partially obscured by the town's growth. Each Christian mission also had its settlement: Roman Catholics at Kurasini, Anglicans at Kichwele, and Lutherans at Ng'ambo.

To prevent racial intermingling, the Germans began in 1912 to divide the town into three racial 'building zones'. The British completed the scheme after 1918, locating the African zone west of the commercial centre at Kariakoo, where their Carrier Corps had camped. In Kariakoo individual Africans leased plots from government and built their own houses. Most were single-storey structures with mangrove-pole frames, mud walls, and palm-frond roofs. The owner occupied one room and rented out the other five. He was known in Swahili slang as *fadhahausi*.[2] 'The great aim of the urbanised African', an official explained, 'is to buy or build a house in the Township as a safeguard against indigence in his old age.'[3] Thus emerged a politically important group of African landlords rare in colonial towns. Built in the 1920s, Kariakoo became the core of the African town and the nearest thing Tanganyika had to a territorial focus. It was a place of sand and puddles, of verandahs by day and pressure-lamps by night, of smells and prayers and rumours. In the 1930s the older African settlements were destroyed and another new suburb built at Ilala, south-west of Kariakoo. Thus as Dar es Salaam grew, Africans were gradually pushed further from its centre.

[1] Leslie, *Survey*, p. 49.   [2] Father of the house.
[3] Baker to CS, 5 October 1943, TNA 31751/2.

The Germans administered the town's Africans through a *liwali*. The British first created a Township Authority of nominated Asians and Europeans and then experimented with a succession of 'native administrations'. These included making a Zaramo headman the chief of the whole township; creating a council of six elders, each representing a grouping of tribes from one direction; making the town a separate district and dividing it into six wards, one under each elder; and finally in 1941 giving the Township Authority a native affairs sub-committee and its first African members.[1] Administrative chaos worsened the misery and insecurity of the depression. In 1939 an investigation suggested that 60 per cent of employed Africans earned less than 15 shillings a month.[2] Another survey found that one African man in three was unemployed.[3] Malaria increased with distance from the town centre, while tuberculosis, the scourge of the world's slums, went almost unchecked. Yet these conditions were only a prelude to the disaster of the Second World War. Between 1939 and 1948 the town's African population increased from some 25,000 to 50,765.[4] Malaria increased markedly. Rationing collapsed. In July 1944 only 24 street lights and 16 water kiosks served the African townships. With building materials almost unobtainable, the number of houses in the African zone actually fell slightly during the war.[5] A survey made in 1950 showed that the larger his family, the less a man paid in rent.[6]

Population growth changed the whole character of Dar es Salaam. The immigrants built shanty towns which absorbed many Zaramo villages, notably Buguruni. Government itself began to provide housing, especially at Magomeni, north-west of Kariakoo, but in 1950 only 15 per cent of African households lived in publicly owned houses, for most construction in the new suburbs was by Africans who leased plots and built houses for both residence and letting. Of the first 500 plots at Magomeni, 150 were acquired by people who owned houses elsewhere. 'It is often said', an observer noted, 'that it is the first house which is difficult to build.'[7] Kariakoo's urban capitalism was thus exported to the new suburbs, but in other ways the town's character changed fundamentally. It was partly a matter of size. Magomeni was

[1] Correspondence in TNA 61/1/A and 61/207/I–III.
[2] Pike, 'Report on native affairs in Dar es Salaam township', 5 June 1939, TNA 61/207/II/220.
[3] McCleery, 'Landownership'.   [4] Sutton, 'Dar es Salaam', p. 19.
[5] *Medical report*, 1943, p. 8; above, p. 372; Pike to Postwar Planning Committee, 13 July 1944, TNA 33024/1/75; Pike, 'Report on native affairs', 5 June 1939, TNA 61/207/II/220.
[6] *Labour report*, 1951, p. 95.   [7] Leslie, *Survey*, p. 167.

a suburb as Kariakoo had never been: its residents did much of their shopping in the Kariakoo market. Rickshaws disappeared from the streets in the late 1940s, making room for buses carrying suburbanites to work. Serious industrial development began in 1947 to the south of Ilala.[1] The building labourer replaced the domestic servant as Dar es Salaam's typical worker. In 1949 the town became a municipality, each racial group providing four nominated town councillors who elected a mayor. Africans felt increasingly alienated. 'The Municipality', a newspaper complained, 'is busy cleaning the town by demolishing the older African houses in order that multi-storeyed houses may be built reaching to the skies, without considering the suffering caused to Africans compelled to move because they are powerless.'[2]

Each section of Dar es Salaam housed certain categories of men. The categories were in part tribal. Magomeni had more than twice the normal density of Nyamwezi, while Buguruni in the extreme west merged into the countryside and housed many Zaramo.[3] Yet residential patterns owed even more to the zoning system. Since most Africans worked in the commercial zone but lived in the African zone to the west, the most desirable residential area was the eastern section of Kariakoo from which the walk to work was shortest. Consequently, eastern Kariakoo housed many of the better-paid Africans who were educated and politically aware, and its most easterly road, New Street (later Lumumba Street), was the organisational centre of Tanganyika's African politics. For Africans, clerical work was the chief source of wealth. The number of successful African shopkeepers – often retired civil servants – was very small: only 43 belonged to the African Retailers Association in 1947.[4] The core of urban capitalists were the houseowners – probably about 3,000 in 1939, or one townsman in five – but their earnings were much less than those of a well-educated clerk and they formed the middle stratum of the African population. A survey in 1956 showed that most houses had been built with the savings of artisans or small-scale traders. It also showed that certain ethnic groups owned many houses, notably the Manyema, Yao, and Makonde who were among the town's earliest settlers.[5] Significantly, however, neither Shomvi nor Zaramo owned much property, for Dar

[1] Below, p. 447.   [2] *Zuhra*, 15 February 1952.
[3] Leslie, *Survey*, pp. 38, 259.
[4] Page-Jones to CS, 25 September 1947, TNA 16756/14.
[5] Pike, 'Report on native affairs', 5 June 1939, TNA 61/207/II/220; Leslie, *Survey*, pp. 169, 178.

es Salaam's rapid growth from small beginnings had swamped these indigenous groups. Both Shomvi and Zaramo periodically claimed to 'own' the town, but nobody took them seriously. Shomvi were chiefly fishermen, while Zaramo, from an educationally backward area, were 'very submerged' – a fact which distinguished Dar es Salaam from East Africa's other capitals. An alternative source of leadership might have been religious authority. Little is known of this, but sheikhs, imams, and *waalimu* clearly enjoyed considerable prestige before and during the Second World War. There were sixteen mosques in the town in 1904 and seventeen in Kariakoo alone in 1941, so it appears.[1] The older mosques possessed considerable *waqf* property: in 1948 the Friday Mosque of the Sunni community owned an agricultural plot and six houses, drawing an annual income of £550.[2] Brotherhoods also owned property. Yet probably only a minority of townsmen, chiefly permanent residents, seriously recognised religious leadership. This was so in the mid 1950s[3] and probably earlier. Dar es Salaam was nominally a Muslim town, where Christians were an out-group and many immigrants adopted coastal dress and a Muslim name as easily as they adopted the Swahili language. In 1932 only 2.8 per cent of Africans wore western dress.[4] But the capital was too big, too diverse, too shifting in composition, too secular and eclectic in culture for religious leaders to dominate it. As a nationalist orator later declared, 'Dar es Salaam is everybody's town.'[5]

Some townsmen accepted no authority at all. Probably at an early date, and certainly by the 1930s, they practised what Professor Lewis has called a culture of poverty.[6] It was the life of the unorganised and insecure, who took no part in town institutions and gained nothing from them, but lived from day to day, almost permanently in debt, incapable of planning for the future. Their domestic unions were often casual, their enemies were police and authorities, their heroes were the *wanaharamu* ('sons of sin') or smart guys of the town, their faith was application to a diviner in personal misfortune. This was not the normal pattern of life in Dar es Salaam – only research in police records will show how common it was – but it was one pattern of life. It included the thousand or so young boys at work in the 1930s, many

[1] Sicard, *Lutheran church*, p. 177; *Kwetu*, 7 September 1941.
[2] List of *waqf* property, 23 November 1948, TNA 27123/65.
[3] Leslie, *Survey*, pp. 210–18.
[4] *Colonial development fund (malaria research scheme): report on work done at Dar es Salaam during the period January 1932 – January 1934* (London, 1935), p. 5.
[5] G. P. Kunambi, in notes of a meeting, 1955 [?] TANU 49.
[6] Oscar Lewis, 'The culture of poverty', *Scientific American*, ccxv (1966), 19–25.

as domestic servants in Asian households but others in any 'employ-ment' which turned up, from collecting scrap or selling oranges to touting for brothels. It included the 'Compania Zinzia' – almost literally 'street-corner boys' – a gang of fourteen teenagers who had amassed 58 convictions when dispersed in 1938.[1] It included many young men who sat on pavements waiting for the chance to unload a lorry or thronged the dock gates at dawn when the harbour was crowded. It included many regular dockworkers, who cultivated a carefree toughness. There was an underlying violence in Dar es Salaam. It lived in the constant presence of the police, who questioned any African found on the streets after 10.00 p.m.[2] It lived in the crowd which collected when an Asian shopkeeper quarrelled with a customer. It lived in the popular belief that witchcraft flourished in the slums.[3] It lived in the minds of men who lived in New Street.

For many respectable long-distance migrants the leadership vacuum was filled until the 1940s by the tribal elders. They had official administrative functions and also led the profusion of tribal associa-tions. Not only did immigrants look to fellow-tribesmen for jobs and accommodation, but some needs could be satisfied only by fellow-tribesmen – a man's funeral, for example, if he died in the town. The first known African organisations in Dar es Salaam were tribal associations formed when the Germans ordered that tribes should bury their members dying in hospital. A resulting Pogoro Association apparently dated from 1912, while the Bisa of Northern Rhodesia and the Chagga claimed to have founded associations in 1919.[4] Perhaps the best example of these organisations was 'The New Wanyamwezi Association – Dar es Salaam', founded in 1936. With their long hostility to coastal culture, Nyamwezi were temporary, unskilled, long-distance migrants *par excellence* – in 1956 they had a lower pro-portion of long-term residents in the town than any other tribe.[5] Aiming 'to join together and concern ourselves with every sort of human problem for the whole Wanyamwezi nation (*taifa*)', their association was open to Nyamwezi 'of any religion: Muslims, Chris-tians, pagans, drinkers, dancers, etc.'[6] Each was to contribute ten cents whenever a Nyamwezi was sick and thirty cents whenever one died,

[1] Pike, 'Report on native affairs', 5 June 1939, TNA 61/207/II/220; CP to CS, 2 June 1938, TNA 21963/I/55.
[2] SP Eastern to CP, 13 July 1934, TNA 21963/I/7.
[3] Swantz, 'Medicine man', p. 94. [4] Leslie, *Survey*, pp. 37, 51–4.
[5] *Ibid.*, p. 258.
[6] 'The New Wanyamwezi Association – Dar es Salaam', enclosed in Northcote to PC Eastern, 8 May 1936, TNA 61/450/40.

in addition to a subscription of fifty cents a month. There was a fixed scale of aid to distressed members. The president was Juma Sultani, their recognised headman. Other offices were shared between elders and educated young men: the young men wrote the letters while the elders arranged the funerals. As in Bagamoyo, the New Wanyamwezi Association was open to Sumbwa and Sukuma as well as 'Nyamwezi proper', for in Dar es Salaam the basic category among migrants was the 'supertribe' of men from the same broad region. An example was the Ukami Union, formed in 1938 to embrace Luguru, Kami, Doe, Zigua, Kwere, Khutu, Vidunda, and Sagara 'for unity as in the past'.[1] More distant peoples formed even larger units. The Buganda and Bukoba Natives Association Dar es Salaam came to embrace anyone from Uganda or Kenya, and a Nyasaland and Northern Rhodesia Association also existed.[2] This flexibility of categories was best illustrated by Sudanese and Manyema. Descendants of Sudanese askari formed something approaching a new tribe, although speaking Swahili and having little knowledge of their ethnic origins. The Sudanese Association, formed in 1931, claimed affiliation to an organisation in Khartoum, registered every Sudanese in the territory, and demanded representation on the Dar es Salaam native court.[3] Manyema, by contrast, were torn between the unity they possessed in Bagamoyo and the divisions which troubled them in Ujiji. In 1923 they split into Arabian Congo and Belgian Congo factions. These were superseded in the 1930s by conflict between other Manyema and the Kusu, the dominant ethnic group in the Manyema who claimed priority of settlement in Dar es Salaam and ownership of the community mosque. Then in the late 1930s all eighteen 'tribes' of Manyema from both sides of Lake Tanganyika established the Congo Union Association, which later formed branches throughout the territory, outlawed competitive dancing as divisive, and subsidised the schooling of Manyema boys.[4]

Manyema experience shows that ethnic categorisation varied with different periods as well as different towns. By 1956 large-scale tribal associations like the Nyamwezi's had been swamped by the town's

[1] Mohamed Kawambwa and others to PC Eastern, 20 May 1944, TNA 61/561/1/1.
[2] *Kwetu*, 13 April 1938 and 4 August 1940; PC Central to CS, 15 March 1940, TNA 46/44/8/2.
[3] Issa Makki to PC Eastern, 25 August 1945, TNA 61/1/A/IV/23.
[4] D. A. Sykes, 'The life of Mzee bin Sudi', seminar paper, University College, Dar es Salaam, 1969; Fikirini Masanga and others to PC Eastern, 12 October 1938, TNA 61/280/42; Pike to Baker, 28 February 1941, TNA 61/725/15; Hassan Juma to CS, 9 March 1945, TNA 61/815/1; *Rules and regulations of the Congo Union Association, 1946* (Dar es Salaam, 1946), in TNA 32891/11A.

growth, which made effective organisation on that scale almost impossible, but 51 'ethnic' associations registered their existence when required to do so in 1954. Most averaged only about 75 members. Many were groups with few townsmen like the predominantly skilled and Christian Fipa, whose tribal union was formed in 1953, or sub-ethnic groups like the Mbaha Union which brought together men from one section of the Lake Nyasa shore. Some older societies like the Pogoro Union had been taken over by young educated men.[1] Apart from urban welfare, the associations of the 1950s were much concerned with rural improvement. The best example was the Wazaramo Union. Living so close to the town, Zaramo did not need an association to bury or care for them. Yet in 1955 some 3,500 of the 6,500 members of registered tribal unions in Dar es Salaam belonged to the Wazaramo Union. Its chief concern was the advancement of rural Uzaramo. 'The object of this Union', its secretary explained, 'is to construct the "UNITY, BESTIR LIFT UP" the Wazaramo and their country in the essential matters.' To this end it bought and operated two lorries to carry passengers and agricultural produce between town and countryside, founded nine branches in the tribal area, and campaigned against 'the old out of date Wakilis' recognised by government, urging instead a paramount chief to lead the Zaramo towards progress.[2] Urban ethnicity was not simply a survival but a positive attempt to create units to function effectively in colonial society.

Ethnicity was only one means of urban identification. As usual, dance revealed the diversity of social categories. In German times the predominant modes were 'tribal' or 'supertribal'. These modes continued to attract women and a few resolutely migrant peoples like the Nyamwezi until Independence, while 'traditional' dancing remained a popular means of exorcism. Of 58 African dance societies seeking registration in Dar es Salaam during eleven months after June 1954, most were *lelemama* (i.e. women's) or exorcism societies, but only six were specifically tribal groups.[3] The first major enemies of tribal modes had been the *beni* societies with their proud modernity and multi-tribalism, but *beni* itself passed out of fashion during the 1930s. Although a derivative, *mganda*, became the modern dance of Christians around Lake Nyasa, elsewhere *beni* became increasingly the

[1] Leslie, *Survey*, pp. 32, 38–9, 43–5, 52, 55–6; DC Dar es Salaam to PC Eastern, 11 May 1955, TNA 61/A/6/12/I/78.
[2] Mohamed Juma to Secretary for African Affairs, 9 September 1948, and to PC Eastern, 6 March 1952, TNA 26027/37 and 74.
[3] DC Dar es Salaam to PC Eastern, 11 May 1955, TNA 61/A/6/12/I/78.

dance of men in deprived rural areas who aspired to be modern.[1] New Street followed another fashion, *dansi*, the international, individual-istic ballroom dancing whose personalised sexuality shocked the elderly. Like *beni* it apparently originated around Mombasa and entered Tanganyika through Tanga, whence it was probably brought to Dar es Salaam in the early 1930s by the *avant-garde* of the Tanga Young Comrades Club and was popularised by branches of the New Generation Club formed in several towns later in the decade. With their 'kings' and 'queens' adopted from the *beni* societies, their female sections composed chiefly of nursemaids, and their insatiable thirst for tea and soft drinks, New Generation Clubs epitomised the *dansi* mode.[2] *Kwetu* complained in the early 1940s that 'the young men have taken up *dansi* in place of *beni*', that 'the African has little taste for his tribal dances. He has taken a fancy to the European one.' 'The dances held are mainly European type', it was said of Dar es Salaam in 1944, 'but an occasional native women's dance takes place.'[3]

Dansi added a new layer to Tanganyika's cultural differentiation and complexity, and this time it was a symptom of growing cultural dependence on the outside world. Together with it went a craze for foreign music. While some favoured 'Bantu' music from South Africa,[4] more were enraptured by Latin American modes. At least one jazz band existed in the capital in 1939, probably the Dar es Salaam Jazz Band which inspired Salum Abdallah to seek a ship for South America and induced Ally Sykes to run away from home to learn music in the army.[5] Philomoni Hasani Namkina, Ulanga's finest post-war guitarist, was taught by Italian prisoners in Nairobi, while Kanyama Chiume learned the guitar during the war at Dar es Salaam government school.[6]

Between Ally Sykes's samba and the *madogoli* of a sick Zaramo woman there was a gulf as wide as that between New Street and Buguruni. Another indicator of social distance was football, whose growing popularity absorbed much of the youthful aggression which

[1] Ranger, *Dance*, chs. 3–5.
[2] *Ibid.*, pp. 15–16; 'The list of the New Generation Club members during the year 1938' (and other papers), TANU 2.
[3] *Kwetu*, 7 June 1942 and November–December 1941; MS to CS, 27 July 1944, TNA 11205/IV/89.
[4] 'Bantu' records were advertised in *Kwetu*, 22 November 1938.
[5] 'The UMCA Dance Club Dar es Salaam', 4 February 1939, TANU 2; Jumaa R. R. Mkabarah, *Mwanamuziki wa Tanzania: Salum Abdallah* (Dar es Salaam, 1972), pp. 11–12; Sykes Buruku in Iliffe, *Tanzanians*, p. 113.
[6] Larson, 'History', p. 332; M. W. Kanyama Chiume, *Kwacha: an autobiography* (Nairobi, 1975), p. 17.

pre-colonial societies had encouraged. Introduced by English missionaries – on 17 September 1884 Magila and Mkuzi drew Tanganyika's
first recorded match[1] – football was popularised in the 1920s by young
men from Kiungani. Thirty years later the Dar es Salaam league had
38 registered clubs whose membership mirrored the town's social
structure.[2] While many were tribal, there were also works or departmental teams such as the police or the dockworkers' team which
developed into the powerful Cosmopolitans club. Cosmopolitans had
two main rivals, Young Africans and Sunderland. These two sides were
found in every coastal town in the 1950s.[3] Broadly speaking, Young
Africans were then a blue-collar team supported by unskilled workers,
while Sunderland attracted clerks, but this had not always been so. The
history of football clubs remains unwritten, but like modes of dance
they apparently rose and declined with each generation. The Young
Africans club subsequently dated its origin to 1926.[4] In Dodoma it was
founded ten years later when the fashionable side was the New Strong
Team, which apparently drew support from the same kind of
educated young men as danced with the Tanga Young Comrades.[5]
Young Africans became prominent in the late 1930s, and at least until
the mid 1940s it was a club for educated men.[6] It probably superseded
the New Strong Team and was then itself challenged by Sunderland.
The pattern of rise and fall suggests the extensive social leadership
which educated men exercised, at least among younger townsmen.
Football also shows how emerging economic divisions were still
partially obscured by tribal, occupational, and generational differences. Dar es Salaam's Africans were still far from being divided on class
lines.

Among the capital's occupational groups, the best organised in the
1930s were traders. Their society, the African Commercial Association,
was founded in 1934 by Erica Fiah. Its first members were 16
shopkeepers and 32 petty traders anxious to resist Asian competition
and the Township Authority's increasingly irksome restraints. They

[1] Magila mission diary, 17 September 1884, TNA.
[2] DC Dar es Salaam to PC Eastern, 11 May 1955, TNA 61/A/6/12/1/78.
[3] Lienhardt in Hassan bin Ismail, *Medicine man*, p. 16.
[4] *Sunday nation*, 11 January 1976.
[5] Mwangosi, 'Ilani', 18 October 1936, Suleiman papers, TNA; Farahan bin Fereji
   and others, 'Tuliotendewa na tulioyaona Wa-African Sports', 2 August 1935,
   TANU 52. There are many reports of football clubs and matches in *Mwanafunzi*.
[6] *Kwetu*, 21 February 1939; 'Yaliyosemwa katika mkutano wa African Association,
   jumatano Februari 21, 1945', TANU 7.

also urged townsmen to 'buy African'. The association's 'by-laws' of 1935 declared that 'all of the members must prefer the native shops to others', promised welfare benefits in case of death, and proposed to open branches.[1] Shortly afterwards Fiah discovered the remains of Marcus Garvey's Universal Negro Improvement Association, the Harlem-based Pan-African organisation which still produced a flood of radical literature. Under its influence he renamed his organisation the Tanganyika African Welfare and Commercial Association in January 1936.[2] The new TAWCA undertook to bury any African who died without relatives in Dar es Salaam, and did indeed bury 54 people before its funds gave out. It planned to care for orphans and provide schooling for children. It sought representation on the Township Authority because 'Dar es Salaam has no chiefs such as up countries to plead for our petty matters'.[3] It even claimed to represent all Tanganyika Africans:

Since the Africans are not represented in the Legislative Council, this Association, as the Central body, looking after the welfare of all Africans in Tanganyika Territory, would always watch carefully any laws proposed by the Government which may affect Africans and after proper consideration, would make such representations to Government, and Members of Legislative Council, as the Association consider proper...

Every African is bound to obey the Association, whether he is contributing or not, just as much as he obeys the Government.[4]

Fiah represented the radical side of African thinking, but his ambition, greed, and dangerous opinions made him unpopular with educated men. *Kwetu* had great influence on African political thinking, but TAWCA failed. Antagonised by its extravagant claims, government gave Fiah a warning which brought less ambitious by-laws and assurances that TAWCA was 'a merely praying Association'.[5] Fiah soon lost interest in the organisation, which apparently lapsed about 1942. Its impact outside the capital was limited. Branches were opened at Iringa, Mwanza, and Singida in 1937, the last of these surviving, as the Singida African Committee, to provide one local nucleus for nationalism in the 1950s. Another branch opened at Kisiju in 1939,

---

[1] 'The by-laws of the African Commercial Association' [1935] TNA 22444/I/31.
[2] CP to CS, 27 March 1936, TNA 22444/I/45; 'The proposed by-laws of the Tanganyika African Welfare and Commercial Association', enclosed in Fiah to Northcote, 16 March 1936, TNA 22444/I/46.
[3] Fiah to CS, 14 July 1936, TNA 22444/I/76.
[4] 'Proposed by-laws' [1936] TNA 22444/I/46.
[5] Idi Salim to CS, 9 August 1936, TNA 22444/I/96.

while a cattle trader who had belonged to the Dar es Salaam association founded a branch at Uvinza in 1946.[1]

In terms of the capital's social geography, TAWCA represented the politics of the Kariakoo market. By contrast, the politics of New Street – of educated civil servants and the leading *fadhahausi* – were embodied in the African Association. This organisation was the most important contribution which Dar es Salaam's distinctive social structure made to Tanganyika's political evolution, but before introducing it we must note one other pattern of organisation and action which the capital extended throughout the territory. This was labour organisation.

The labour movement

While desertion had been the most common form of labour protest in caravans and early plantations, workers had also mounted strikes and demonstrations which had been ostensibly anonymous and leaderless. Between 1929 and 1947 urban workers advanced beyond this level of consciousness and action in three directions. Leaders appeared who were publicly responsible for organising workers over a period rather than 'emerging' as spokesmen in particular protests. Group solidarity increased among workers in particular enterprises and industries, and was occasionally expressed in permanent trade unions. Finally, at the end of the period there were indications of collective workers' consciousness transcending particular occupations. These advances were made by workers themselves learning from industrial experience, but consciousness and organisation advanced unevenly among different groups. Since Tanganyika had a colonial economy, its sequence of labour organisation was the reverse of a metropolitan country's. British labour organisation, for example, began in skilled trades and led through factory workers and transport industries to the service sector and finally to white-collar workers and civil servants. Tanganyika's sequence was almost exactly the reverse, beginning with civil servants and moving through service and transport sectors to reach industrial workers in the 1950s.[2] Conse-

[1] *Kwetu*, 7 December 1937 and 19 May 1942; above, p. 377 n. 5; AA Dar es Salaam to Singida, 22 October 1937, TNA 302/43/31/1/5; H. P. Diwani to PC Eastern, 25 January 1939, TNA 61/490/336; Mrisho Luhomwa to Kigoma, 6 November 1946, TNA 180/A/6/1/39.

[2] Agricultural workers were an exception. They were equally late to organise in both countries.

quently, Tanganyika's first labour organisations were in occupations especially difficult to organise, for it is easier to unionise a factory than scattered motor drivers. This gave the labour movement a distinctive character and explained many early difficulties.

The first African workers to organise were the civil servants who formed TTACSA in 1922. After lively but ineffective activity during the 1920s, this body was weakened in 1929 when many members joined the more broadly-based African Association.[1] Some branches maintained a shadowy existence during the 1930s, but serious trade union activity began in 1944, when the association was revived and renamed the Tanganyika African Government Servants Association. Its rules confined membership to clerks and skilled workers, excluded labourers, and claimed the same representative functions as Asian and European civil service associations.[2] Government acknowledged this. The immediate reason for revival was wartime austerity. In 1943 government awarded lower-paid employees a cost of living bonus but gave nothing to those earning over ninety shillings a month. Clerical workers responded by joining TAGSA. By October 1944 it claimed 1,820 members in Tanga, Mwanza, Arusha, and Dar es Salaam. By utilising government's communications network, another 23 branches were formed at district centres during the next year.[3]

TAGSA left copious records, but less is known of two other organisations of public employees. One was the African Teachers Association, formed in 1944 under the presidency of Paolo Mwinyi-pembe, a Makerere-trained teacher denied education in Britain. At the end of 1944 it claimed 210 members in 35 branches.[4] More important was the Railway African Association. Railway workers were relatively skilled and numerous, and their occupation provided a natural framework of organisation and communications. An organisation of railway workers may have existed as early as 1929,[5] but nothing more is heard of it until the Second World War. Then inflation caused discontent and frequent stoppages, so that the railway administration encouraged the formation of African staff associations.

[1] Above, pp. 267–8; below, p. 407.
[2] A. Shaba to CS, 11 August 1944, and Sandford to PCs, 8 November 1944, TNA 11051/11/18B and 42.
[3] TAGSA, 'Report and activities of the association for the year 1944', TNA 11051/11/63A; note by Administrative Secretary, 28 October 1944, J. Nyangarika to CS, 14 June 1945, and J. B. Matovu to CS, 13 May 1946, TNA 11051/11/34, 74, 98; E. B. Amos, 'The life of Elias Kisenge', seminar paper, University College, Dar es Salaam, 1968.
[4] Thompson, 'Partnership', p. 261.
[5] Sykes Buruku in Iliffe, *Tanzanians*, p. 108.

By 1945 the Railway African Association was the most powerful workers' organisation in the territory, with some 2,000 members under the presidency of a Kenyan named George Ogilo. It was very loosely organised, with the senior African at each station running his branch as a private empire and officers allegedly embezzling funds repeatedly, but its latent vitality was to appear in the general strike of 1947.[1]

Tanganyika's first trade unions – as opposed to staff associations – were formed in the 1930s by Asians.[2] The Union of Shop Assistants of Tanganyika was registered in 1933 and lapsed in 1940. The Asiatic Labour Union, composed of Sikh carpenters in Dar es Salaam, was formed in 1937 and organised the capital's first considerable strike before vanishing later in the year. The Labour Trade Union of East Africa, an Asian-sponsored organisation based in Nairobi, was registered in Tanganyika but had no impact there.[3] The first registered African trade union was the African Cooks, Washermen, and House Servants Association. The original *Chama cha Wapishi na Maboi* was formed in Dodoma in August 1939, 'on account of distresses and difficulties which frequently fall on us who work as cooks and servants in our duty'.[4] It was probably an offshoot of the lively local African Association. Two years later a similar body took shape in Dar es Salaam.[5] During 1943 domestic servants in the capital talked of striking unless they were assisted to obtain work and better wages. The rules of their association, drafted in January 1944, showed considerable solidarity. 'The decision of the Association to be acted upon in unanimity and at once', they decreed. 'Members should not cheapen themselves as regards wages paid to them by their employers; each man must remember what befalls another will react on him.'[6] Domestic servants were the capital's largest occupational group and the most difficult to organise. They first sought the provincial commissioner's intervention, but his refusal brought 'absolutely disappointment and murmuring'.[7] Instead they turned to Saleh bin Fundi, a Hehe resident of New Street who had almost certainly been (and perhaps still was) the capital's Arinoti leader.[8] Early in 1945 he

[1] *Labour report*, 1945, p. 11; Norman Pearson, 'Trade unionist on safari', typescript, 1949 [?] pp. 59, 113, 138, 140, 158, 210–13, Pearson papers, RH.
[2] The Tanganyika Railways Asiatic Union existed in 1925, probably as a staff association. See J. D. Jacobs and Dharam Paul to Amery, 4 February 1925, CO 691/76/429.
[3] Minute, 9 August 1933, TNA 19335/1/79; above, p. 346; *Labour report*, 1949, p. 28.
[4] Shabani Abdallah and others to AA Dodoma, 14 August 1939, TNA 46/A/6/3/1/35.
[5] Mohamed Radi, 'Hotuba', 24 April 1949, TNA 16/37/79/139.
[6] 'Hizi ndizo sheria za chama chetu cha maboi', 16 January 1944, TNA 61/679/1/15.
[7] Saidi Kupakupa and others to PC Eastern, 13 March 1944, TNA 61/679/1/18.
[8] Saleh bin Mkwawa to Mohamed bin Zuberi, 13 July 1920, TNA 075.

held three public meetings. The first sent a deputation to the Chief Secretary, who replied, according to Saleh,

'that Government agreed to their suggestions in principle, and that they would receive the assistance of a European who would act for them as Chairman and carry out their orders as directed and a special office would be opened for them in the boma to deal with matters concerning their affairs.'

Salehe continued by saying. 'Are you happy now?' 'We are happy', the crowd replied.

'Yes', retorted Salehe; 'the Serkali [government] have two ways of doing things, one good and one bad, and if they choose the latter and lock up all committee members next time they call us and tell us that we are teaching you wrongful ways, what are you going to do?'

'If that happens we shall refuse to work.'

'No', said Salehe, 'if you do not know, I will tell you.'

'In such a case, all of you, boys employed by Europeans as well as those employed by Indians, should go to the Chief Secretary and ask to be locked up.'[1]

Saleh bin Fundi was Tanganyika's first African labour leader. In contrast to the anonymous plantation strike or the cautious letter-writing of a TAGSA secretary, he deliberately made himself conspicuous, established a personal command through public meetings, and attempted to instil a solidarity sufficient to protect him from victimisation. His technique of passive protest may have been borrowed from a demonstration then taking place outside the district office at Same.[2] Recognising that a leader's best protection against victimisation was a trade union, Saleh was organising one of territorial scope. The first three branches, in the Southern Highlands, were formed by late 1944. The territorial body was registered on 28 August 1945. During the next three years branches opened at Dodoma, Kigoma, Chunya, Kilosa, Lindi, Singida, Tanga, and Korogwe. Yet so large an organisation in so unstructured an occupation proved impracticable. On 12 June 1949 the union was deregistered for persistently failing to comply with the demands of the Registrar of Trade Unions.[3]

Members of the *Chama cha Maboi* had distinctive conceptions of trade unionism coloured by the totalitarianism of village life. They assumed that concern with their collective welfare automatically entitled them to government's support and gave them the right to

---

[1] 'Meeting of native domestic servants at Mbuyuni wa Simba Mwene', 13 February 1945, TNA 61/679/1/32.

[2] Below, p. 495.

[3] Correspondence in TNA 134/LAB/63; *Labour reports*, 1945, p. 11, 1949, p. 28.

control labour. 'If a member is employed but does not follow his master's orders', one branch assumed, 'his master has right to accuse him before the Heads of the association who will take serious views and punish him.'[1] Similar ideas appeared in an attempt to organise motor drivers. African drivers in the Moshi area formed an association as early as 1927 and there was a society in Dar es Salaam in 1940, but the first well-documented organisation was created among drivers working for the railways in the Southern Highlands in 1944, the idea apparently having been learned in the army.[2] 'What we are after', the association explained, 'is nothing but good pays, taking into consideration the difficulties in life experienced by the present War Situation', but it hoped to prevent drivers working for employers who had dismissed other drivers unjustly and it shared the domestic servants' exaggerated notion of trade union powers, proposing that employers should recruit drivers only through the association and that non-members 'may be made to cease to work'.[3] Both drivers and domestic servants worked in quasi-skilled occupations where those with jobs feared to be swamped by massive urbanisation and demobilisation and were probably under special pressure to find work for relatives and clients, which helps to explain their desire for trade unions to control entry into their occupations. Drivers possessed excellent communications, so that union branches were formed in Dodoma, Western Province, Dar es Salaam, and probably elsewhere. But drivers were also excessively dispersed, mobile, and individualistic. The Amalgamated African Motor Drivers and Commercial Road Transport Workers Union, registered in August 1948 with 340 members, was deregistered two years later because it had no members at all.[4]

Effective trade unionism required concentrated groups of workers. They were found among dockworkers. In 1937 those of Tanga carried out the territory's first important strike by African townsmen, 250 men stopping work for two days.[5] Two years later another dock strike in Tanga developed into a serious riot, but of the anonymous type. As a detective explained, 'There could be found no isolated acts of incitement nor particular evidence of a ringleader. Apparently

---

[1] Paper signed by Ali Mwasokwa, 8 February 1945, TNA 134/LAB/63.
[2] Jardine to Cameron, 30 October 1930, TNA 19335/1/4; Baker to LC, 11 July 1940, TNA 61/14/22/1/11; Southern Highlands Province African Drivers Association to Mbeya, 28 September 1944, TNA 327/C/2/3/11/9.
[3] J. Mwalemba to LO Mbeya, 16 March 1945 and 10 October 1944, TNA 134/LAB/63/50 and 3.
[4] *Labour reports*, 1948, p. 119, 1950, p. 18.   [5] Tanga DAR 1937, TNA library.

there was no directing brain.'[1] More sophisticated organisation was pioneered by the dockworkers of the capital.[2] Dar es Salaam was a small port where the work available fluctuated with the arrival of ships. Cargo-handling companies consequently employed a few skilled men on permanent terms but hired most workers daily as needed. In the late 1920s these 'coolies' earned two shillings a day. This was reduced to Shs. 1.50 in 1931, and the companies attempted to stabilise their workforce by forming a registered pool of casual workers to receive preference over other applicants. In 1939 the port employed 307 permanent employees, including 24 headmen who led labour gangs; 360 registered casual labourers, divided into 8 gangs summoned to work in turn by their headmen touring the African township with a bellringer; and unregistered casuals to fill any vacancies. The dock-workers' initial problem was therefore to create a solidarity tran-scending status divisions. Given prevailing wages and unemployment levels they were already relatively privileged, so that strikes might be broken by the employers hiring new labour.

The first known dockworkers' organisation was the African Labour Union of 1937, presumably modelled on the Asian body of that year. In September 1937 it had forty members, three of whom had seen similar organisations in South Africa. Disclaiming aspirations to 'influence the employment and control of labour', it was essentially a friendly society. Its rules[3] declared membership open to any worker. A club house was to be built and meetings held twice a month. Procedure was laid down with the rigour characteristic of early labour associations. 'Matters which have already been decided at a meeting should not be discussed again', the rules insisted. 'Each member should talk by turn.' Officers were to subscribe Shs. 1.50 and ordinary members one shilling each month to help those sick or unemployed and to hire a teacher to teach all members to read and write. Every member was to pay his debts and taxes and open a savings account for his retirement. He was to 'implicitly obey his employer', be 'submissive and courteous to everyone', 'attend at his work before the prescribed time', and not 'leave his work before the proper time or without his employer's permission'. This concern with reliability and

---

[1] Tanganyika, *Report of the commission...into the disturbances...in...Tanga*, p. 10. See also the correspondence in TNA 27231/I-II.

[2] Save where stated, the remainder of this chapter is based on Iliffe, 'Dockworkers', pp. 119–38.

[3] 'The African Labour Union: Mmoja wa Wenyeji Watumishi wa Kazi, etc. Sheria na kanuni za chama' [1937] TNA 61/14/14/2.

punctuality expressed the countryman's determination to learn urban and industrial ways, and although the union disappeared from the records in December 1937 it illustrated the potential for disciplined action existing even among volatile dockworkers.

Between 1939 and 1947 Dar es Salaam's dockworkers organised three major strikes, each marking a stage in the growth of solidarity, organisation, and understanding of the economic and political system, until the last, in 1947, made the dockworkers the vanguard of Tanganyikan labour as a whole. The strike of July 1939 showed consciousness very similar to that in Tanga or the plantations. It was a defensive and backward-looking action demanding the restoration of the two shilling daily wage which had existed before the depression. Pickets were posted at the dock gates, but some men returned to work on the second day, so that solidarity was slight. Moreover, because only casual workers struck the employers could break the strike by threatening to recruit other unskilled labourers. The spokesmen – whose identity is unknown – did not call off the strike but removed their pickets on the fifth day, thereby allowing workers to trickle back. Casual workers gained nothing except a reduction of the registered pool so that work was available more regularly. The whole action showed little consciousness or solidarity, but it was a stage in the learning process which is the heart of a labour movement.

The contrast appeared in the second strike, which occurred in August 1943 and lasted ten days.[1] To the experience of disunity and failure in 1939 were added wartime grievances. These affected especially the permanent workers, whose wages were outpaced by inflation and did not benefit from the larger number of ships visiting the port. Consequently the strike for the first time involved permanent employees, and its demands for wage increases and other concessions would chiefly have benefited them. The strikers took an oath not to return until their demands were accepted. The only workers who did not join were headmen, although they acted as intermediaries at government's request and signed the letter stating the strikers' demands, showing that the line between workers and management was not yet clearly drawn and group solidarity was incomplete. Government refused to let the employers try to recruit new labour, but wartime necessity obliged it to ensure that ships were not delayed. It therefore appointed a tribunal of enquiry, declared the strike illegal under defence regulations, and arrested 142 permanent employees.

[1] Additional material is in CO 691/183.

Having hitherto maintained their solidarity, the workers now slowly returned. The tribunal awarded permanent workers limited wage increases, which taught them that government rather than the employers ultimately controlled wages. More important, the strike revealed the dockworkers' organisational weakness, for the employers dismissed several long-service workers identified as ringleaders. Lacking permanent organisation and legally prohibited from striking, their colleagues could not protect them. It illustrated Saleh bin Fundi's point that leadership, solidarity, and organisation were interdependent.

The third strike in the sequence occurred in 1947 and was quite different in character. Although started by the dockworkers it became a general strike, bringing together the traditions and organisations of different working groups and pitting them successfully against the colonial regime in Tanganyika's most widespread protest since the Maji Maji rebellion. The climax of the colonial crisis, the strike was generalised by common postwar grievances and was directed against the government rather than particular employers. It illustrated that aggregation of grievances against the regime which was the war's crucial political consequence.

On 6 September 1947 the Dar es Salaam dockworkers struck for higher wages to meet inflation. Headmen probably joined for the first time. Two days later the strike spread to other casual workers and some intimidation was reported. The crucial decision to join was taken on 10 September by the railway workers, whose communications stretched deep inland. On 11 September railway workers at Morogoro, Dodoma, and Tabora struck. Four days later those at Kigoma and Mwanza also came out. This rapid expansion led some to think that the strike was pre-arranged. There is evidence of widespread demand for a general wage increase, but no direct evidence of planning. Rather, wartime grievances, racial tension, and mass urbanisation enabled small groups of activists to mobilise large numbers of workers.

On 11 September 1947 Dar es Salaam was in ferment, with few Africans at work, picketing throughout the town, and widespread intimidation, although government later confessed that the stoppage had been supported by all sections of the African population. The authorities reacted vigorously. Forty-five people were arrested on 11 September and some were imprisoned for a year for intimidation. Several hundred special constables were enrolled and plans were made for European, Asian, and African volunteers to take over essential services. On 13 September, however, the strike began to break.

Lorries with police escorts toured the African township to transport those willing to work. Government threatened to dismiss civil servants who were not at work on 15 September. With funds running low, a mass meeting of dockworkers on 14 September was evenly divided on continuing the strike, but that afternoon the pickets were removed. Seventy per cent of the dockworkers reported for work on 15 September, most diehards being permanent workers.

Upcountry, however, the general strike was only beginning. In Morogoro railway staff spread the movement to other urban workers and then to surrounding sisal estates. It ended on 15 September when instructions to return reached the local secretary of the African Association from the railway workers in the capital.[1] At Tabora the long-standing bitterness among educated men appeared in two manifestos. One, on behalf of government servants, demanded immediate wage increases of 33–50 per cent, a programme to replace Asian officials by Africans, and one code of regulations for all races. 'We are now tired', it stated, 'with these zigzag regulations of our Tanganyika Government, equal pay for equal work is not recognised and this can easily be seen from our present salaries which have entirely been based on racial prejudice. Up to this time African is serving absolutely under colour bar system.'[2] The second document, produced by the Tabora branch of the Railway African Association, made similar demands. 'An African', it declared, 'has never been given a free opportunity to work independently and therefore his usefulness depends on an Indian Boss who gains full credit for all works done by him, thereby damaging his prospects. . . Time has now come when "EQUAL PAY FOR EQUAL WORK" is claimed.'[3] The strike was not merely a demand for higher pay, but for a larger place in the future. It gradually spread deeper inland. The railway workers who struck at Mwanza port on 15 September split into parties, armed themselves with sticks, and toured the town, entering offices and houses and summoning other workers to join them. Groundnut Scheme workers at Kongwa struck on 15 September and did not return until threatened with dismissal thirteen days later. 'Ringleaders' there were imprisoned. The final stoppage took place at the Uruwira lead mines in Mpanda on 6 October. The strike had taken a month to reach Mpanda.

[1] Mwinjuma to AA Dar es Salaam, 14 September 1947, TANU 7.
[2] A. J. Barnabas to PC Western, 20 September 1947, TNA 47/P/1/4/11.
[3] R. Gondwe to PC Western, 19 September 1947, TNA 47/P/1/4/12.

It was a frightening and exhilarating month. New Street was thoroughly alarmed. 'This misbehaviour [*uhuni*] was neither origin-ated nor incited by the African Association', its secretary insisted.[1] But African workers were triumphant, for the tribunal gave the dock-workers 40–50 per cent increases, which produced wage rises of a third or more in other sectors. Nevertheless, the strike showed that solidarity amongst workers was limited. Action was confined almost entirely to the central railway area and its feeders. No attempt was made to create a general trade union of the kind then being advocated in Kenya.[2] What was created was Tanganyika's first powerful trade union among the Dar es Salaam dockworkers. In 1943 they had been powerless to prevent the victimisation of leaders. This time experience led the informal committee which had organised the strike to transform itself into the nucleus of a trade union which was registered on 3 January 1948. Its original leaders were mostly headmen, for, as members explained, 'the men we trust have no education',[3] but as membership rose to a maximum of 2,259 late in 1949 they hired educated secretaries, first Abdulwahid Sykes from the ex-askari community and then the ubiquitous Erica Fiah. During stoppages in 1948–9 the union showed much solidarity, strengthened by its capacity to prevent non-members obtaining work in the port. Since dockworkers were now a highly privileged group, the union collaborated with a government scheme to register them and exclude other casual labourers from employment. By 1950 the union possessed £3,250, partly invested in a half-completed clubhouse.

That clubhouse symbolised the post-war experience of Tanganyika's townsmen and workers. It was built in what became Nkrumah Street, between Kariakoo and the port. In tribute to the rise of the working man, it was to be the first two-storey building erected and owned by Africans in Dar es Salaam, but the upper storey was never completed. In 1950 the union collapsed in the worst riot the capital experienced before Independence. With it ended a period of labour history. The foundations were laid, the ground floor was constructed – and there the half-completed building stood, to be finished in a different style by other hands. Why this was so, why the urban experience of the colonial crisis did not lead forward unbroken into the 1950s, must be considered later.[4]

[1] D. Mkande to Mfaume bin Mussa, 7 November 1947, TANU 7.
[2] A. H. Clayton and D. C. Savage, *Government and labour in Kenya* (London, 1974), pp. 276–83.
[3] Pearson, 'Trade unionist', p. 239, RH.   [4] Below, p. 537.

CHAPTER 13

The African Association, 1929–48

There are four reasons for treating the history of the African Association in special detail. First, it was the earliest African organisation for which much documentary evidence survives, the earliest to leave extensive contemporary records of what Africans were writing and saying to one another, although these documents often remain unstudied in private hands and need to be supplemented by systematic oral research. Second, the association's development was shaped by and illustrated the colonial crisis, especially its impact on the political consciousness of educated men. Third, the association's history illuminates Tanganyika's political dynamics: the interplay among regions and social groups; the relationships between town and country, capital and provinces; the cyclical pattern of political activity; and the collective learning which is the core of a people's political evolution.

Finally, the African Association was the institution through which many diverse ideas and ambitions were woven into political nationalism. The strands led back into the territory's special colonial experience, nineteenth-century change, and the character of pre-colonial societies. As the association grew it absorbed many local political aspirations while narrowing the ideas of educated men from a racial or continental to a territorial perspective. The association's structure eventually provided the framework for a unitary nationalist movement unique in East Africa. In 1954, when new leaders showed it the tactics necessary to regain independence, the association gave birth in a truly organic way to a nationalist movement. That final phase is described later.[1] This chapter deals with earlier periods: the association's formation in Dar es Salaam in 1929 and its experience there during the next decade; the formation of provincial branches; the amalgamation of those branches into a territorial organisation; and

[1] Below, ch. 15.

finally the loss of political momentum which affected educated men as well as urban workers in the late 1940s.

The association in Dar es Salaam, 1929–39

No record of the African Association's formation has been found, but it probably came into existence in Dar es Salaam late in 1929.[1] The immediate stimulus was controversy over the closer union of Tanganyika with Kenya and Uganda, which reached its peak in 1929. European settlers – who alone in Tanganyika supported closer union – formed a European Association in January 1929 and the Indian Association was reinvigorated.[2] The African Association was clearly modelled on these organisations and its formation probably had the approval of the government, which also opposed closer union.[3]

Just as the Indian Association claimed to speak for the whole Asian community, so the African Association aspired to be the sole representative of Africans. This was the basis of its programme and appeal throughout its history. It embodied African unity. It was *Chama cha Umoja wa Watu wa Afrika*, 'The Association of the Unity of the People of Africa'. Its founders conceived unity as continental rather than territorial. Their aim, they declared, was 'to safeguard the interests of Africans, not only in Tanganyika, but in the whole of Africa'.[4] The constitution stated that 'anyone who is an African may be a member', regardless of tribe, religion, or territorial origin. No boundary was set to the association's growth. 'The leaders of business in Dar es Salaam', the constitution stated, 'shall have the power to open this association in any town they wish.'[5] A later version was even more specific: 'Every association that is here in Africa, that is of the people of Africa, its father is the African Association.'[6] To understand this emphasis on unity, one must remember that urban tribalism and rural parochialism constantly reminded educated men of the divisions which they blamed for African weakness and colonial rule. Their conviction was expressed in the association's endlessly repeated motto, 'Unity is

---

[1] *Mambo leo*, September 1931.
[2] *Tanganyika Times*, 29 January 1929; above, pp. 346, 373.
[3] J. S. Chombo to PC Lake, 22 May 1939, Suleiman papers, TNA. It is unlikely that government initiated the association. Cameron knew little about it (Cameron to Passfield, 22 August 1930, TNA 19325/1/5) and Mitchell's diary (RH) is silent.
[4] Rawson Watts, quoted in *Tanganyika standard*, 20 October 1930.
[5] *The African Association: kanuni na sheria za Chama cha Umoja wa Watu wa Africa* (Dar es Salaam, 1933), para. 6 (in TNA 61/385/1/31).
[6] *The African Association: kanuni na sheria za Chama cha Umoja wa Watu wa Africa* (Zanzibar, 1935), para. 6a. I owe this source to Mr J. A. Ramadhani.

Strength'. It was emphasised in Swahili newspapers, in countless speeches, and occasionally in poetry:

> What I want to ask of all us Africans
> Is why we do not pull together, though one in origin?
> Our blackness is the same, even the hair of our heads:
> What is it hinders us, O Africans?...
>
> You may happen to see another African in trouble,
> Yet pass him by, saying, I am a freeman from Pangani,
> How can I know this man, a Makonde from Mikindani?
> What is it hinders us, O Africans?...
>
> Let us look at the Europeans: they do not all agree,
> But because of their unity, you find them round one table,
> The Englishman and the German, the Frenchman and the Italian,
> What is it hinders us, O Africans?
>
> Unity is the answer. We shall never again be weak
> When we have unity and strength, the very mosquitoes will
>   quit our houses,
> By God, the very bugs will scuttle from our beds.
> What is it hinders us, O Africans?[1]

The African Association's concern with unity arose from its founders' experience. Its first president was Mwalimu Cecil Matola, the aristocratic Yao teacher educated at Kiungani who had worked in Kenya before becoming a pioneer of TTACSA and senior African teacher at the Dar es Salaam government school, which made him almost *ex officio* leader of the capital's educated Africans. The association's inaugural meeting took place in his house and he remained its president until he died in March 1931.[2] Through him the African Association inherited Kiungani's supra-tribal unity and the predominance which its former pupils enjoyed during the 1920s. Their chief rivals, from the CMS establishment at Mombasa, were also represented among the association's founders, notably by the assistant secretary, Rawson Watts, a secretariat clerk who is reputed to have first suggested the association.[3] Matola and Watts were beneficiaries of the British administration's need for English-speaking staff. By 1929, however, some German-trained civil servants had learned English and rehabilitated themselves. Among the African Association's first committee members was Mdachi Sharifu, the Tanga-trained teacher

[1] N. E. G. Masudi, 'Lipi linalotudhuru sisi Waafrikani?' in *Kwetu*, June 1938. I owe the translation to Mr J. E. F. Mhina.

[2] *Mambo leo*, August and September 1929 and August 1931; Matola to CS, 21 April 1930, TNA 61/207/1/12; Sykes Buruku in Iliffe, *Tanzanians*, p. 102.

[3] Sykes Buruku in Iliffe, *Tanzanians*, p. 102. For Watts, see *Kwetu*, 14 July, 2 August, and 10 December 1938 and 14 January 1939; Stuart-Watt, *Dome of mystery*, p. 198.

and official who had spent the First World War in Germany and had since become president of TTACSA. Other early members included Akida Mambo, Ibrahim Hamisi, and Zibe Kidasi who, as compositors in the Government Printing Works, were in German times the capital's intellectual aristocrats. They had deeper roots in urban society than Matola or Watts. In the early 1920s, for example, Zibe Kidasi was Brigadier-General of the Arinoti in Dar es Salaam, with influence far beyond the civil service. Although TTACSA provided much of its core, the African Association was not simply a clerks' trade union. It was a deliberate attempt to unite civil servants with the leaders of other social groups.

The three leading groups of Africans in Dar es Salaam in the 1920s – former askari, Manyema, and Zaramo – were all represented among the African Association's first leaders. Its secretary, Kleist Sykes, had been brought up by the ex-askari community's former leader, Effendi Plantan.[1] Among the committee members was Mzee Sudi, son of slave parents, an important houseowner, and leader of the Belgian Congo branch of the Manyema.[2] The Zaramo provided two prominent leaders: Ali Saidi, a building inspector who was the association's treasurer during the 1930s, and Ramadhani Ali, the first vice-president, who was a trader. Both were later presidents of the Wazaramo Union, while Ramadhani Ali was also King of the Marini in Dar es Salaam and one of the most influential Africans in the town.[3] Such men had interests and ideas of unity very different from those of Watts or Matola. Throughout the 1930s the association was divided between those who favoured a territorial alliance of educated men and those who sought unity between different social strata in the capital.

The association's initial activities showed the diversity and imprecision of its aims. It recruited some 300 members by March 1931 and began to build a clubhouse – inevitably in New Street – on a plot apparently provided by the government.[4] The association did not provide welfare benefits. 'It is a duty to help in death or burial', the constitution stated, 'but not with the association's funds.' Membership was expensive: a five shilling entrance fee plus annual subscriptions of twenty shillings for leaders, ten for 'strong members', and five for junior members – a distinction common among African societies and symptomatic of hunger for leadership positions. The association

---

[1] Sykes Buruku in Iliffe, *Tanzanians*, pp. 95–105.
[2] Sykes, 'Mzee bin Sudi'.   [3] Ranger, *Dance*, p. 95.
[4] Helps, 'Administration of Dar es Salaam', 2 March 1931, TNA 10906/1/36; *Mambo leo*, September 1931.

enjoyed playing at government, adopting elaborate bureaucratic procedures and giving members the satisfaction of making and executing decisions rather than merely typing and filing. Its officers – Auditor, Chief Advisor, Personal Assistant to the President – resembled, in another idiom, the Kings and Nursing Sisters of the *beni* societies. Every branch had an 'office boy' whom everyone could order around. Members visiting another branch claimed hospitality and were treated like officials on tour. The association was also the counterpart of the European club found at every district headquarters. Branches held tea parties, built up libraries, and organised festivities. Yet the association also tried to intervene in politics at several levels. It petitioned for an African *kadhi* for Dar es Salaam. It invited chiefs to join, apparently without success. It sent its constitution and other documents to the KNPA, which was in disarray and did not reply.[1] And the association made its first, disastrous intervention in territorial politics.

By the time the association was ready to act on the closer union issue, the British government had declared itself opposed to settler ambitions. In July 1930, therefore, the association decided to thank the Colonial Secretary 'on behalf of the African Community' of Tanganyika for encouraging the African 'to stand for himself on the equality with the other Civilised Nations', and to urge him to resist contrary pressures.[2] Meeting no adverse reaction, the association was then emboldened to ask that Africans should be heard by the parliamentary committee appointed to investigate closer union. This request was encouraged by a friendly Asian lawyer, Ramakrishna Pillai, who probably hoped that African representation would strengthen the Asian case against closer union. On 12 October 1930 Pillai addressed the association, urging it to send a deputation to seek Cameron's aid in securing representation.[3] Pillai's speech, comparing Cameron with Abraham Lincoln as a champion of the oppressed, angered the immigrant communities. 'To flout their innocence and ignorance by talks of civil wars', the Indian Association protested, 'is something akin to agitating them without education', while the settler press denounced 'the combination of a propagandist of the Indian type and a party of half educated Africans'.[4]

[1] Matola to CS, 21 April 1930, TNA 61/207/1/12; *Tanganyika standard*, 14 October 1930; Matola to KNPA, 22 September 1930, TNA 19325/1/23.
[2] Matola and others to Passfield, 25 July 1930, TNA 19325/1/2.
[3] 'Mkutano wa siku ya jumaa pili mwezi 12–10–1930 katika African Association alio fika Bwana Ramakrishna Pillai', TNA 19325/1/13; *The Times*, 15 October 1930.
[4] *Tanganyika standard*, 17 and 20 October 1930.

Cameron apparently spoke bluntly to the deputation on 20 October 1930:

His Excellency is said to have warned the members that if the Association has anything to do with the political side as apart from social and economic problems it would be advisable for the Government servants to resign from the same as they are prohibited from taking any part in politics according to service regulations.[1]

Such fear did the colonial regime evoke that Cameron's warning nearly destroyed the African Association. Political aspirations were abandoned for a decade. In September 1931 the association asked for a European advisor. Three years later it invited the Governor to become patron, explaining that 'we feel that there are many persons in the Territory who would like to become members, but who are withheld from joining us by a fear that, despite our avowed intention of avoiding any interference in politics, the Government does not wholly approve of the Association'.[2] Other considerations encouraged timidity. The depression undermined optimistic hopes of improvement. Fear of unemployment inhibited political activity. The association's leadership weakened. Matola died in 1931 and subsequent presidents were of lesser quality. Watts moved to Tanga. Kleist Sykes resigned the secretaryship soon after Cameron's warning. In December 1932 Watts warned an ill-attended meeting that the association might 'go under'.[3] 'It is a long time now', Mzee Sudi wrote to Kleist Sykes three months later,

since you last involved yourself in the business of the Association, attended meetings or came to the office... We must remember that it is not for us to neglect this Association, for we have carried it thus far and we should not retire. Being the few who have the benefit of some education we are obliged to lead our less fortunate fellows.[4]

Such appeals had little effect. Instead the association fell into the hands of younger men chiefly concerned with *dansi* and civil service careers. 'The african association', critics complained in 1936, 'is not now representing Africans owing to insufficient members, hence the Africans have no reliance to that Association.'[5]

At this moment of weakness the association's legitimacy was

[1] *Tanganyika herald*, 28 October 1930.
[2] Saadal Omar to PC Eastern, 15 September 1931, TNA 61/385/1/15; Mzee Sudi to CS, 16 May 1934, TNA 19325/1/48.
[3] 'Mkutano mkuu uliokuwapo siku ya ijumaa-mosi 17th December 1932', TANU 7.
[4] Quoted by Sykes Buruku in Iliffe, *Tanzanians*, p. 104.
[5] Idi Salim to CS, 26 August 1936, TNA 22444/1/98.

challenged by Erica Fiah's Tanganyika African Welfare and Commercial Association. Its reorganisation in 1936 with Garveyite overtones and extensive political demands led government to ban civil servants from holding office in TAWCA. When Fiah sought official recognition, the Chief Secretary unwisely asked why Africans needed two associations.[1] Fiah promptly opened a campaign to amalgamate them. Two years of obscure and confused events followed. In July 1936 Mzee Sudi announced that the two bodies had merged and a new committee changed the African Association's rules to include welfare activities, but a general meeting reversed these decisions. Two years later civil servants were persuaded not to stand for office, Fiah became secretary, and the two bodies were again amalgamated until another general meeting of the African Association reasserted independence. Officials dismissed the dispute as a squabble over money and buildings. This was partly true: Fiah wanted the association's clubhouse and was later prosecuted for misappropriating its funds.[2] His unpopularity was an important element in the quarrel. Yet more was at stake. In origin it was a dispute between two broad social and ideological groups, with the traders and more radical civil servants led by Fiah pitted against most civil servants and a few urban notables who had helped to found the African Association. One issue was the African Association's elitism. 'This Association's work', *Kwetu* claimed, 'is to hold *ngoma* on festivals and to invite and to be invited to tea parties', whereas TAWCA's rules specified that 'no person should be refused through suspicion of his polite being bad'.[3] Another issue was whether the association was a European-style organisation of subscribing members or automatically embraced every African. The existing association, a critic complained, would be better named 'the Dar es Salaam African Members Association',[4] and the officers' attempt to exclude those who rarely attended meetings or paid subscriptions gave Fiah his initial support within the association. The squabble tarnished its legitimacy. Swahili newspapers of the late 1930s reveal growing disenchantment with the capital's factional politics:

Can we hope for any progress when we still have the African Association, the Welfare Association and the African Community functioning as separate

---

[1] *Ibid.*
[2] See the correspondence in TNA 19325/1, 22444/1, 61/385/1.
[3] *Kwetu*, 7 December 1937; 'The by-laws of the African Commercial Association' [1935] TNA 22444/1/31.
[4] *Kwetu*, 29 March 1939.

units...These hopeless bodies owing to their unfriendly situation and standing have lost all recognition from those living outside Dar es Salaam...These Associations have failed in their duty to the society to which they belong.[1]

At this nadir of its history the African Association was revitalised by its branches.

The association in the provinces, 1929–39

The formation of African Association branches during the 1930s illuminates Tanganyika's political dynamics. Only one of the ten branches was created by Dar es Salaam headquarters, whose normal role was confined to sending delegates who ceremonially 'opened' and legitimised existing branches, as the constitution required. The actual initiative usually came from a headquarters member moving to another town, someone from the provinces visiting Dar es Salaam or another branch and deciding to imitate it, or men who read about the association in a Swahili newspaper or the immense correspondence which passed among educated Africans. The desire to share in the association's promised unity was very strong, just as Christian or Muslim leaders – or even witchcraft eradicators – stressed the scale of their organisations. No branch felt secure until 'opened' by head-quarters, just as powerful chiefs installed their inferiors or one *khalifa* sought his *ijaza* from another in the true succession. The promise of the association's name seemed to offer aid with local problems and support for those factions within a local arena which affiliated to it. Political growth by recognition rather than initiation produced an organisation lacking programme or central direction, but it enabled each branch to adapt to the local situation, so that by 1939 the association embraced at least a small part of Tanganyika's diversity.

Two branches left little record. Of the Pemba branch nothing is known except its existence.[2] That at Kwimba in Sukumaland was opened in 1932 by M. B. Makeja, the Dar es Salaam secretary, at the request of his friend J. M. Kadaso, an avid correspondent and newspaper reader who headed the local native treasury.[3] The other eight branches are better known. The earliest was apparently at Dodoma. It opened on 26 April 1933 when Makeja was posted there

[1] *Ibid.*, 14 January 1939. The writer was probably Thomas Marealle.
[2] Seme Sindi to committees, 23 March 1939, TNA 46/A/6/3/1/32.
[3] *Mambo leo*, April 1934.

from Dar es Salaam.[1] He became treasurer of the branch, which had 87 members. Its other officers included Ali Maneno Ponda, a Manyema schoolteacher who became one of the association's most active leaders. The vice-president, Ibrahim Sururu, was a Sudanese trader, while the president, Ramadhani Sudi, was also a trader and probably a Manyema. Thus the branch combined civil servants and urban notables as in Dar es Salaam. Their views were joined in the branch's declared aims – 'Oneness of African', 'A betterness of African Race', 'And Africa to be rebuilt by degrees' – and in its demands:

African we came to understand that although the British Government had proclaimed wherever the flag is flying there is no slavery but we still under the Indian bondage, for an instants, Indian buys our foodstuff cultivated by our people in our Country for lowest price and sell same to us for highest price i.e. robbing father and son...

Unity is strength, the African being our cow it is lawful that we are the people of Africa as right to drink milk from our mother, that is to say cow and make our African fellow to wake up and think of progress of African brother in Negeria.[2]

As in Dar es Salaam, the alliance between traders and civil servants in Dodoma soon weakened. The town was a German creation and unusually isolated from the countryside. Its civil servants needed a social club, and this the association soon became. By 1936 all its officers save one were civil servants, the traders being relegated to a 'sub-committee'. According to the police, 'the Association...is a dance club which meets about once a week and the members endeavour to ape European methods of dancing and dressing'.[3] The association itself complained that non-members were breaking up its dances and admitted that 'our community is now disliked by many people in Dodoma'.[4] At this point, however, it was transformed by Edward Mwangosi, a clerk and compulsive organiser from Tukuyu district who played an important role in Tanganyika's political history. Having persuaded the provincial commissioner and town elders to attend a re-opening ceremony which restored local respectability, Mwangosi formulated plans to found sub-branches throughout Central Province and in Tabora, Mwanza, and Mbeya.[5] The first objective was soon

[1] This account is based on *Mambo leo*, December 1933; Ramadhani Sudi to PC Central, 2 May 1933, TNA 46/A/6/3/1/1; G. G. Hajivayanis and others, 'The politicians: Ali Ponda and Hassan Suleiman', in Iliffe, *Tanzanians*, pp. 234–40.
[2] Ramadhani Sudi to PC Central, 2 May 1933, TNA 46/A/6/3/1/1.
[3] SP Dodoma to CP, 17 October 1936, TNA 46/A/6/3/1/6.
[4] Amiri Saidi and T. E. J. N. Mwangosi to PC Central, 18 May 1937, TNA 19325/1/55.
[5] Mwangosi to Jabil bin Salim, 16 September 1936, Suleiman papers, TNA.

attained, following a request for a branch in Kondoa by a group of civil servants and notables led by the Kenya-born market master, Shariff Husein bin Omar. Founded in March 1937 with the aid of a band and dance team from Dodoma, this branch struggled for several years against degeneration into a purely local welfare society. It had its own sub-branch at Kwa Mtoro.[1] The branch at Mpwapwa was organised in 1937 by a court clerk named E. K. T. John White who was transferred from Dodoma.[2] In Singida, as in Mpwapwa, many initial contacts were made through dance societies, but the branch opened there in 1937 was led by traders who appointed agents in neighbouring trading centres, opened a Koran school, and displayed marked animosity to Asians.[3] Attempts to open branches in Manyoni or outside Central Province apparently failed, but Mwangosi's activism impressed the senior branches in Dar es Salaam and Zanzibar. Dar es Salaam sent its secretary, Nasoro Kiruka, to 'open' the Singida branch in July 1937 and he was followed in December by the secretary of the Zanzibar branch, Adrian Benjamin Boyd. In return Dodoma's officers visited Zanzibar and Dar es Salaam. Welcoming a group of chiefs in 1937, Ali Ponda explained:

The African Association is a union of the black people of Africa. Any black man of Africa can be a member of this association...For this association is not concerned with any one religion, or with any one tribe, or with wealth or indeed with poverty. This association is for men of any religion and any tribe and any condition, it is for the black people of Africa. Do not accuse us of belonging to this or that religion, this or that tribe, this or that condition. We have one father and one mother, and that indeed is AFRICA...We here have just opened branches in Kondoa-Irangi, Singida and Mpwapwa, and soon Korogwe will be opened.[4] We are receiving assistance from Zanzibar and Dar es Salaam.[5]

The branch established at this time in Bagamoyo reveals all the difference between a decaying slave port and a colonial administrative centre like Dodoma. In Bagamoyo's racially stratified society the *African* Association was an organisation of black men against immi-

---

[1] Abdurahamani bin Modu and others to AA Dodoma, 26 September 1936, and Mwangosi, 'Kufungua African Association – Kondoa Irangi. 7th March, 1937', Suleiman papers, TNA.

[2] E. K. T. J. White to Mwangosi, 30 April 1937, Suleiman papers, TNA.

[3] 'Memorandum concerning the opening of the African Association Singida', 26 July 1937, Suleiman papers, TNA; A. R. Abubakar to Singida, 18 February 1939, TNA 302/43/31/1/12; Abubakar, 'Monthly report 1937–1939. Singida African Association', Suleiman papers, TNA.

[4] It probably was not.

[5] Mwangosi to PC Central, 19 July 1937, TNA 46/A/6/3/1/20.

grants of other races. The black men were Manyema freedmen or déclassé Shomvi aristocrats with social backgrounds and political perspectives different from those of Dodoma's civil servants. The branch's initiator was a Manyema lorry driver, Mtumwa ('the slave') Makusudi, whose trips to Dar es Salaam put him in touch with the association. After consulting the Qadiri *khalifa*, Mtumwa persuaded Dar es Salaam to send delegates to 'open' the branch in June 1939, to the strains of the British national anthem. The branch's seven founders were all local men. Three were drivers, two cultivators, one a fisherman, and one owned a *hoteli*. Two were Manyema and three Shomvi: Mtumwa Makusudi explained that he asked the Shomvi to join because they were Bagamoyo's ancient rulers. The branch became increasingly associated with the Qadiriyya. In 1944 ten of the seventeen officers and 'strong members' were Qadiris. Two years later the brotherhood's *khalifa* became branch president. 'All of the *murids* [disciples] took part when they saw *me*', he later recalled. With such support, the branch's preoccupations were parochial: appointment of court elders, wartime food rationing, agricultural rules, and membership of the township authority. Grand statements of unity were not its style.[1]

During the 1930s the African Association was predominantly urban. Indeed, some believed it was solely for townsmen.[2] Educated townsmen needed a non-tribal association, and Cameron – with the colonial administrator's innate fear of urban-rural communication – warned its leaders in 1930 'to confine the Association to the towns in the first instance'.[3] Yet the one rural branch of this period again displayed the association's adaptability. It was in Bukoba, where the association, on the first of many occasions in its history, was drawn into the conflicts attending the emergence of peasant society. The branch's nucleus was the Bukoba Bahaya Union, formed in 1924, in imitation of TTACSA, chiefly by Ziba clerks and traders. Its transition into an African Association branch may have taken place gradually from the early 1930s, with the organisation preserving its old title for local affairs. Dodoma dated Bukoba's 'opening' to 1935 but was not asked to provide guidance until February 1938, following which the Bukoba branch apparently first made contact with Dar es Salaam. Yet it was not organisation but the idea of unity that tied the African Association

[1] Correspondence in TNA 7/3/2; Nimtz, 'Sufi order', pp. 465–82.
[2] 'Mkutano wa watu wote kufungulia office ya Umoja wa Kilimanjaro tarekh 7 Novemba 1948', TNA 5/583/820.
[3] Cameron, minute, 23 October 1930, TNA 19325/1/22.

together. Its members in Bukoba were known as *ab'obumoi,* 'members of unity'.[1]

In 1935 certain Bukoba leaders who were also traders formed the Native Growers Association which broadened into opposition to agricultural regulations and chiefs, culminating in the riots of 1937. The resulting repression lost the African Association much support, but it was not destroyed. Its troubles led it to contact the territorial organisation. It sent a delegate to the African Association's first territorial conference in 1939. Of the thirteen sub-branches formed in the Haya countryside during the campaign of 1935–7, one, at Nshamba in the Ihangiro chiefdom, struck permanent roots. Most of its members were enemies of the local chief. Many were probably *nyarubanja* tenants seeking enfranchisement. A vicious little conflict ensued. *Ab'obumoi* refused to undertake unpaid road work. The chief persecuted and imprisoned them. Finally in 1939 they were accused of burning his house and were severely assaulted by his followers. Their organisation went underground, but twenty years later the nationalist party's entire committee in Nshamba was drawn from the *ab'obumoi* of the 1930s.[2]

Although the Bagamoyo and Bukoba branches illustrate the African Association's capacity to penetrate local politics, they were scarcely a force in territorial affairs. The initiative which opened the next phase in the association's history came instead from Zanzibar. Here, it appears, the association was modelled on that of Dar es Salaam and grew out of the amalgamation of several football teams during 1933, following which 'the African Association's auspicion were taken up and formed a body of 25 people to stand and ask for it'.[3] These 25 men present at the first meeting on 7 May 1934 were mostly Christians from the mainland, including several freed slaves, who formed an unprivileged outgroup in the Arab sultanate. Their leader was Adrian Benjamin Boyd, of Mwera origin, enslaved in 1897, released by a British gunboat, and educated by American missionaries in Muscat and India, where he lived for 27 years, married an Indian,

---

[1] Above, p. 284; Austen, *Northwest Tanzania,* pp. 216–27; Göran Hydén, *Political development in rural Tanzania* (reprinted, Nairobi, 1974), pp. 207–12; Mwangosi to PC Central, 5 September 1938, and to AA Bukoba, 21 February 1938, Suleiman papers, TNA; *Kwetu,* 25 March 1938; Rwehumbiza, 'Clemens Kiiza'.

[2] Above, pp. 284–6; L. Ludovick to AA Dodoma, 4 March 1938, Suleiman papers, TNA; R. Gervas Byansheko, 'Hatua ya kudai uhuru', manuscript, 1959, in TANU 49; below, p. 533.

[3] Adrian Benjamin Boyd, note on visit to Singida, 30 December 1937, Suleiman papers, TNA. See also Augustine Ramadhani and others to AA Dodoma, 22 April 1937, TNA 46/A/6/3/1/15; M. Borafia to CS Zanzibar, 29 November 1945, TANU 48.

and worked as a carpenter until 'Indianisation' drove him to Zanzibar in 1929. His main collaborators were two young mission-educated men from the mainland: George Masudi, who was educated by the UMCA at Mkomaindo near Masasi, and Paul Seme Sindi, a Moravian-trained Ndali schoolteacher and friend of Edward Mwangosi who had wandered to Zanzibar in search of work.[1] They offered the branch's presidency to the recognised head of their Christian community, Augustine Ramadhani, formerly senior African teacher at Kiungani. Their constitution of 1935 showed their isolation and Christian origins by providing for welfare benefits and containing a long statement of progressive intentions like rooting out 'witchcraft and devils' and 'outmoded habits'.[2] In the 1940s the branch broadened to include Muslims and gained government recognition as spokesman for Africans from the mainland. In the 1930s, however, it remained predominantly Christian, and the millennial language of the anti-slavery campaign still inspired its manifestos:

Its main object is to supply the adequate measures for the people of Africa on the whole, because we were separated from one another and were not on equal basis, every one thought of himself better than the other... Now the sons and daughters of Africa are able to say to their mother that whatever thou listest that the sons and daughters may be for Thee, here we are and ask for forgiveness and say, 'We have sinned against thee and against heaven...'[3]

Beneath the language, however, was a political awareness sharpened by oppression and exclusion. Masudi wrote the poem on unity quoted earlier,[4] while Boyd's accounts of surviving African communities in India fascinated his audiences and strengthened their racial consciousness.[5] It was from this milieu that Seme Sindi invited the presidents of African Association branches to attend an 'East African President's Conference for the African Association' in Zanzibar on 6 May 1939.[6]

[1] Masasi mission diary, 18 February 1914, ULD; B. P. Venance, 'P. A. P. Seme Sindi', seminar paper, University of Dar es Salaam, 1970.
[2] Above, p. 406 n. 6.
[3] Augustine Ramadhani and others to AA Dodoma, 22 April 1937, TNA 46/A/6/3/1/15.
[4] Above, p. 407.
[5] Mwangosi to AA Bukoba, 21 February 1938, Suleiman papers, TNA.
[6] Seme Sindi to committees, 23 March 1939, TNA 46/A/6/3/1/32.

Popular organisation and pan-Africanism, 1939–45

Between 1939 and 1947 the African Association held five conferences of branch delegates. It also experienced wartime austerity, increased governmental controls, and access to radical ideas. Together these experiences elicited the association's first collective opinions, stated in conference resolutions. Its emerging programme centred on four points: greater African representation in territorial affairs; the association's expansion into a popular body through organisation directed from headquarters; increased awareness first of African unity and then of the particular identity of Tanganyika; and concern for the territory's future independence. This was not a nationalist programme, for it was a series of requests and aspirations and not a direct challenge to the regime, but it was an advance in political consciousness which could subsequently be passed on to a nationalist movement.

What contribution was made by the Zanzibar conference of May 1939 is unknown, for no record of its proceedings has been discovered. All that is known is that delegates attended from Zanzibar, Dar es Salaam, Dodoma, Kondoa, Mpwapwa, Singida, and Bukoba.[1] The conference made little public impact – *Kwetu* denounced the delegates for holding a 'secret meeting'[2] – but it impressed those who attended. 'When I reached Dodoma', wrote Singida's representative, 'I met the secretaries from Bukoba and Kondoa-Irangi, and the A.A. brotherhood (*Jamaa*) delighted me greatly.'[3] The conference also temporarily revitalised Dar es Salaam headquarters. Having attempted unsuccessfully to have the association registered as a cooperative society so that it would have monopoly control of African affairs,[4] Dar es Salaam called its own conference during 1940. Delegates came from Zanzibar, Pemba, Dodoma, Kondoa, Singida, and Bukoba, while Mzee Sudi took the chair and the secretary was Petro Charles Mntambo, a young museum assistant whose energy and political awareness probably contributed much to Dar es Salaam's temporary revival.[5] One of the conference's eight resolutions was especially interesting:

That His Majesty's Government should consider the possibilities of forming Provincial and Inter-Provincial Boards, where Africans could represent their

[1] *Kwetu*, 21 May 1939.   [2] *Ibid.*, 8 June 1939.
[3] A. R. Abubakar, 'Monthly report 1937–1939. Singida African Association', Suleiman papers, TNA.
[4] P. C. Mntambo to Young, 26 February 1940, TNA 19325/11/7.
[5] S. H. S. Omar, 'Riport ya safari ya conference' [1940] Suleiman papers, TNA.

own country. – In a word, we are now claiming for a voice in the Government. That is, the African now be given chance to speak on behalf of his country.[1]

Thus the association adopted the same demand for a territorial African forum as Cameron and Kayamba had proposed in 1931. It received the same response. To 'represent their own country', the Chief Secretary held, was the function of native authorities, not of an unrepresentative voluntary association.[2]

The Dar es Salaam meeting apparently decided that in 1941 the 'third headquarters' at Dodoma should arrange a conference, and the branch appointed officers to organise it. In fact it never took place, and plans for a conference in August 1942 were also cancelled.[3] With several leaders posted away, its president in the army, and a multitude of local wartime preoccupations, Dodoma lost some of its political momentum. A branch was opened in 1941 at Tukuyu, but others stagnated and Singida, by its own account, 'collapsed utterly'.[4] During 1943, however, Dodoma regained vitality. The reasons are obscure. One may have been wartime austerity. During 1943, for example, the branch issued over 2,500 ration permits on government's behalf. This may have extended its influence; the first African Association membership cards yet discovered were issued at Dodoma during 1943.[5] Moreover, earlier activity was still bearing fruit. During 1943 applications to form branches reached Dodoma from remote Mpanda and from Bahi and Kintinku in the Central Province, where Mwangosi resuscitated the Mpwapwa branch and a new one was formed at Mayamaya.[6] The revival accelerated during 1944. Early in the year Zanzibar's president visited Dodoma, probably to exchange criticisms of Dar es Salaam and to enquire when Dodoma's conference would meet. Shortly afterwards Dodoma's leadership was strengthened by the release from prison of Hassan Suleiman, a Yao clerk with an unusually searching, self-educated intelligence. He became Dodoma's 'Chief Adviser' and most active organiser. In April 1944 contact was

[1] Resolution in Mzee Sudi and P. C. Mntambo to Young, 3 August 1940, TNA 28944/1.
[2] Montague to AA Dar es Salaam, 8 August 1940, TNA 28944/2.
[3] *Tanganyika standard*, 14 February 1941; Mwangosi to AA Singida, 18 May 1942, and AA Dar es Salaam to AA Kondoa, 4 August 1942, Suleiman papers, TNA.
[4] 'The African Association, Dodoma. Annual report, 1942', TNA 46/A/6/3/1/60; T. M. Sankey to AA Dodoma, 16 August 1941, and A. R. Abubakar to AA Dodoma, 15 September 1942, Suleiman papers, TNA.
[5] 'African Association – Dodoma: annual report for the year 1943', and membership card of Idi Salum, dated 4 December 1943, Suleiman papers, TNA.
[6] R. T. K. Mwakasege to Mwangosi, 11 December 1943, and 'The African Association, Mpwapwa. Mkutano wa African Association siku ya 25/12/43', Suleiman papers, TNA.

made with Hugh Godfrey Kayamba, a Makerere-trained clerk working
in Mwanza. Mwangosi and Ali Ponda had visited Mwanza in December
1939 to form a branch there, but nothing resulted until Kayamba took
the initiative in 1943. During 1944 he also organised the recently
revived African Government Servants Association in the Lake Province, creating sections at every administrative centre. An arrogant,
embittered man, Kayamba was in touch with Kenyan politics and was
angrily impatient with the lack of African representatives on Tanganyika's Legislative Council. He pressed this and other demands on
the Dodoma leaders, who were now gathering together the elements
of a radical programme.[1] In May 1944 they gave the local provincial
commissioner a postwar reconstruction scheme which prefigured the
association's programme for the next three years.[2] Like Kayamba, they
emphasised education: compulsory primary schooling, a secondary
school in each province, expansion of girls' education to Makerere
entrance level, and scholarships to universities in Britain, South Africa,
and Egypt. Instead of spending money on European settlers, government should transform African agriculture by teaching ploughing.
Domestic industries should be encouraged. Above all, Africans should
have direct representation on the Legislative Council. Joseph Merinyo
and the Haya chiefs had suggested this during the closer union
controversy, *Kwetu* advocated it during 1943, and by 1944 it was a
widespread demand among educated Africans.[3]

Meanwhile Dodoma prepared its conference. Leaders wrote to
African societies throughout the territory, apparently using a list
obtained from the government's information officer. In August 1944
Zanzibar's secretary, Salehe Juma, visited Dodoma, helped to revive
the Kondoa branch and open one at Iringa,[4] and then travelled to Dar
es Salaam with Hassan Suleiman for a preliminary meeting, equipped
with plans 'to start African Associations everywhere'.[5] The meeting
took place in New Street during September.[6] Hassan Suleiman began
by asking 'why Dar es Salaam is going backwards', while Salehe Juma

[1] Mwangosi to Ludovick, 8 March 1940, and H. G. Kayamba to AA Dodoma, 21 April,
17 May, and 6 July 1944, Suleiman papers, TNA.
[2] Mohamed Kisome to PC Central, 28 May 1944, TNA 46/C/82/1/68.
[3] Rogers, 'Political focus', p. 410; Haya chiefs to Joint committee, 9 March 1931, TNA
19569/16; *Kwetu*, 13 January 1943; Petro C. Mntambo, 'The African and how to
promote his welfare', *TNR*, XVIII (1944), 6.
[4] 'Hotuba ya ufunguzi wa African Association Iringa', 12 August 1944, Suleiman papers,
TNA.
[5] Mwangosi to AA Dar es Salaam, 29 August 1944, Suleiman papers, TNA.
[6] 'Minutes za mkutano uliyofanyika katika nyumba ya African Association, tarehe 15
September, 1944 – 18–9–1944', Suleiman papers, TNA.

enquired, 'Is there an African Association in Dar es Salaam or has it died?' Mntambo indignantly denied the charges. Eventually it was agreed that branches should exchange monthly reports and that members visiting other towns might open branches there – Dar es Salaam thus renouncing its sole right to do so. Hassan Suleiman announced that he would visit Tabora, Kigoma, Mwanza, and Korogwe to form branches. At their final meeting the delegates were joined by leaders of the trade unions formed during the war: Yohana Mnkande and Fabian Mzoo of TAGSA, George Ogilo of the Tanganyika Railway African Employees Association, and Paolo Mwinyipembe of the Teachers Association. Hassan Suleiman asked why they were not members of the parent association and urged that it 'is not the enemy of the government', but they were not convinced.

Back in Dodoma, Hassan Suleiman and the other leaders strove to multiply the branches which could send delegates to make the forthcoming conference a success. New branches were formed in Central Province at Manyoni, Handali, Babayu, Kilema, and Itigi, the organiser of the last being the poet Mathias Mnyampala.[1] In December 1944 Hassan Suleiman visited Mwanza and urged a meeting to open an African Association branch 'with the object of UNITY regardless of differences of tribe or religion or rank'. By September 1945 this branch possessed nearly 200 members and a provincial and district organisation modelled on TAGSA.[2] Ali Ponda organised a branch at Ujiji in December 1944 with strong Muslim support and both Arabiani and Watanganyika members.[3] Activity in Tabora began in March 1944[4] when the African Association's president from Zanzibar addressed a meeting. This stimulated interest among members of the Combined Dancing Club, to one of whose meetings Dodoma sent M. J. Rupani, B.A., who was apparently an Afro-Asian teacher at a local secondary school. Ali Ponda and Hassan Suleiman both visited Tabora late in 1944 and the branch at last opened in March 1945. It included

[1] Mwangosi to Combined Dancing Club Tabora, 18 March 1944, Ali Ponda to AA Babayu, 2 August 1945, Mwangosi to Isa Kondo, 23 April 1946, and M. Mnyampala to AA Dodoma, 15 December 1944, Suleiman papers, TNA.

[2] H. G. Kayamba, 'Minutes za mikutano mitatu iliyofanya Mwanza tarehe 19–20, December, 1944', and I. A. Msowoya to AA Dodoma, 18 September 1945, Suleiman papers, TNA.

[3] Ali Ponda to AA Dodoma, 4 December 1944, Suleiman papers, TNA; K. O. Rajabu to Kigoma, 3 January 1945, TNA 180/A/6/1/2; Dean E. McHenry, 'A study of the rise of TANU and the demise of British rule in Kigoma region', *The African review*, III (1973), 406; Kabembo, 'African politics'.

[4] There is mention of branches in Tabora, Mwanza, and Mbeya in a note by PC Eastern, 8 May 1940, TNA 19325/II/9A.

several teachers trained at Makerere, notably Hamza Mwapachu and Andrew Tibandebage. They were the association's first important contacts among their generation.[1] At Makerere itself Tanganyikan students had formed a Tanganyika African Welfare Society, but on hearing of this Mwangosi told them of the African Association and in November 1945 they converted their organisation into a branch under the presidency of a Zanaki student named Julius Nyerere.[2] Mwangosi was delighted:

Educated Africans must not keep away from the rest of Africans because the latter are uneducated and illiterate...Do not feel uncomfortable when we tell you that the present President of the African Association does not speak English, and is only a humble citizen of Dodoma doing his private business. In fact the African Association has been started by people who had not received sufficient modern education. Generally they discussed only unimportant social matters up to now. It is only since 1944 that it has been possible to infuse a new spirit into the African Association. A strange thing here is that no highly educated Tanganyika Africans have yet been able to come out as leaders to lead the masses as they have in Kenya.[3] Our special efforts are directed towards attracting more and more educated Africans to the cause of African Association, so that some of well educated Africans will one day think it their duty to come out and lead the masses.[4]

The climax of Dodoma's activity was the conference which assembled there on 29 March 1945 with Boyd in the chair. Ali Ponda was secretary with Hassan Suleiman as his assistant and Rupani as an active participant. Zanzibar and Dar es Salaam sent their secretaries, Masudi and Mntambo. For the first time two trade unions were represented: the railway workers by Ogilo and TAGSA by Mzoo and its Ugandan secretary, F. B. E. Serinjogi. Mwanza and Ujiji sent delegates, as did the still 'unopened' Shinyanga branch and Dodoma's sub-branches at Singida, Kondoa, and Bahi. Tabora, Bukoba, Bagamoyo, and Mpwapwa were not represented. Eliud Mathu, M.L.C., was invited from Kenya but did not attend, and neither did expected delegates from Mombasa and the Kenya African Study Union. A conspicuous participant was the Superintendent of Police, who

[1] Mwangosi to Combined Dancing Club Tabora, 18 March and 20 May 1944, J. M. Kiruvugo to AA Dodoma, 28 June 1945, and 'African Association office bearers, 1945. Tabora', Suleiman papers, TNA.

[2] 'Minutes za mkutano wa kumkaribisha Bwana Nyerere', Dodoma, 23 April 1954, and Mwangosi to AA Makerere, 28 November 1945, Suleiman papers, TNA; Judith Listowel, *The making of Tanganyika* (London, 1965), pp. 182–5.

[3] Presumably a reference to Eliud Mathu, appointed to Kenya's Legislative Council in October 1944.

[4] Mwangosi to AA Makerere, 28 November 1945, Suleiman papers, TNA.

reported, however, that 'the Conference opened with expressions of loyalty to King and Government, and was conducted throughout with restraint and decorum'.[1]

Dodoma's activists plainly intended that the conference should press forward the association's expansion and politicisation. Invitations urged branches to send 'representatives who understand politics (*wajumbe wenye siasa*)'.[2] The agenda contained proposals for popular organisation ('That efforts be made to enrol all Africans, women and men, in the African Association') and representation on Legislative Council and all other official bodies, together with such issues as education, domestic industry, trade, European immigration, the Mandate, and closer union.[3] No record of the proceedings has been found, but the activists probably failed to press through the whole of their programme. A summary of conclusions[4] lists demands presented to the government, including compulsory education for all Africans, ending of conscription, continuance of the Mandate, 'that there shall be no East African Federation', and that Europeans 'should not come unless they are employed by Government'. Delegates also agreed to transfer the association's headquarters to Dodoma until the next conference, since Dar es Salaam's leaders 'were quite inability and...were sometimes trying to unite with the members of the Tanganyika African Government Servants Association whose object is for the social and not in matters relative to political purposes'.[5] Thus was Cameron's fifteen-year-old constraint abandoned. Another victory for the activists was to reduce the association's subscriptions. But the resolutions did not refer to popular organisation. The activists' views on that subject may have been too advanced for other members.

This inference is supported by a document which the Dodoma leaders sent to the government shortly after the conference.[6] Although described as the minutes of the meeting, it was not in the form of minutes but rather a working paper embodying the activists' views. The first section dealt with 'brotherhood (*umoja*)':

[1] 'Majina ya manaibu na walikotoka', TNA 19325/II/16A; H. Suleiman to TAGSA [1945] Suleiman papers, TNA; Director of Intelligence and Security, Dar es Salaam, to Director of Intelligence and Security, Nairobi, 12 May 1945, TNA 19325/II/16.
[2] H. Suleiman to TAGSA [1945] Suleiman papers, TNA.
[3] 'Draft of the agenda for the third conference of the African Association', TNA 19325/II/16B.
[4] Ali Ponda to branches [1945] TNA 19325/II/16C.
[5] Ali Ponda to CS, 15 June 1945, TNA 19325/II/17.
[6] 'Minutes of the African Association third conference held at Dodoma, Tanganyika Territory, on 29th March to 3rd April, 1945', TNA 19325/II/18A (largely reprinted in Morris-Hale, *British administration*, pp. 296–8).

It shall be the duty of each and every African to do away with all tribal, religious, sectarian, economical, political, cultural, educational, territorial, and other differences, and to work whole heartedly to foster and promote a sense of solid brotherhood of all Africans. Africans are first Africans. It is only after that that they are or may be any other things...

The cultured shall not look down on the uncultured...

The rich shall help the poor in their fight against poverty.

The educated shall not look down on the uneducated...

The politically advanced shall endeavour to teach his people what he knows and thereby help the political awakening and advancement of the whole nation.

The next section urged 'the establishment of African Associations everywhere':

Each Provincial Chief Town must have a strong African Association which shall act as Head-Quarters for its Province. It shall be its duty to open branches all over the province, in each district and town, and to help Associations already established...

African Associations shall always make it their policy to include in them and in their committees the Elders of their respective towns. A small group of educated persons who prefer to keep away from the elders and the masses cannot be truly strong and useful, nor can it expect to be able to represent the people in the true sense. Each African Association shall have the Elders and the masses as its backbone.

The memorandum then considered current issues. It condemned the Central Development Committee for encouraging white settlement, which 'has proved disastrous to Africans' in Kenya and southern Africa. It proposed to recruit Afro-American and South African teachers and cited the Soviet Union as a model of mass education. It urged modernisation of African agriculture, encouragement of domestic industry and trade unions, and continuance of the Mandate to prevent Tanganyika suffering Kenya's fate. Remarkably for this period, it warned against South African expansion northwards. While recognising Britain's ambivalence between support for European settlement and encouragement of African advancement, the memorandum urged that British control should remain. Nowhere did it mention independence, but there was a radical hope for the future. 'We are proud of our participation in the present war', the memorandum concluded, 'and expect we shall not be forgotten in the New World that is to come after the end of the war.'

As an expression of African political consciousness, this document was unprecedented in Tanganyika. Government suspected 'that some of the views and sentiments expressed and even the language in which they are couched originate from published literature rather than the minds of the members of our local African Association'.[1] Yet the document's detailed knowledge of Tanganyika shows that it was composed by men living there, while most of its ideas had been debated among the activists since 1944, were expressed then in their post-war development plan, and were outlined by Hassan Suleiman in his speech at Mwanza. The document testified to the political awakening among educated Africans during the war. But it may have been influenced by men whose presence in Dodoma is now unknown, and some of its language and wider ideas may have been drawn from pan-African propaganda.

The conference's mood was more pan-African than territorial. During 1942 the Dodoma branch had ceased to describe itself as 'the union of black people (African Association)' and instead as the 'African Association for the whole of Africa'.[2] In 1944 Hassan Suleiman proposed to form branches outside Tanganyika, and non-Tanganyikans were invited to the conference. 'The aim of this association', Mwangosi explained in February 1945, 'is to try to unite all the tribes of Tanganyika, and afterwards Kenya, Uganda, Nyasaland and Rhodesia'.[3] During 1945 he took leave in the Belgian Congo intending to propagandise for the association there.[4] Early in 1946 the association contacted George Padmore, secretary of the Pan-African Federation whose recent congress at Manchester had formulated the declaration: 'Today there is only one road to effective action – the organisation of the masses.'[5] Padmore's reply shows complete ignorance of the association,[6] but Dodoma's leaders were familiar with pan-African literature. Hassan Suleiman read Padmore's *African Sentinel*, which was advertised in *Kwetu* in 1938. Erica Fiah was in touch with Padmore and the Garveyite movement and possessed books from both sources, together with Gandhi's works and communist literature. In March 1942 he published a feature by Ladipo Solanke, president of the West African Students Union in London.[7] Moreover, educated Tanganyikans had access to pan-African thinking through Kenyans

[1] Administrative Secretary, minute on above, 14 October 1945, TNA 19325/II.
[2] I.e. *Umoja wa Watu Weusi (African Association)* gave way to *African Association Afrika Nzima*. See the membership application forms in Suleiman papers, TNA.
[3] Mwangosi to Bondei Welfare Association, 28 February 1945, Suleiman papers, TNA.
[4] Ali Ponda to AA Dar es Salaam, 4 June 1945, Suleiman papers, TNA.
[5] Quoted in Colin Legum, *Pan-Africanism* (London, 1962), p. 137.
[6] G. G. Hajivayanis, 'The life of Mzee Hassan Toufiq Suleiman', seminar paper, University of Dar es Salaam, 1970, appendices 1–2.
[7] *Ibid.*; *Kwetu*, 1 May 1938, November–December 1941, 26 March 1942.

and Ugandans working in Tanganyika, through the political hothouse at Makerere, and probably through the military. The Dodoma conference was the culmination of this influence and of the whole wartime political awakening.

Territorial consciousness and organisational collapse, 1945–8

The Dodoma conference revitalised Tanganyika's elite politics, but not as the activists intended. They visualised popular organisation under strong central control, but this proved beyond their capacity. Hassan Suleiman abandoned plans to 'open' new branches, and requests from Tanga, Upare, and elsewhere could not be met.[1] In April 1946 headquarters returned permanently to Dar es Salaam, to Dodoma's mingled regret and relief, for it 'has been defeated by lack of money for fares, since between 1944 and May 1946 it has spent Shs. 1,050/- on fares to send delegates here and there'. Dodoma's leaders suggested that 'each provincial headquarters must strive to open the African Association in every part of its districts'.[2] Four consequences followed. First, the association grew quickly between 1945 and 1948, when headquarters claimed 39 branches with 1,780 members.[3] Records suggest that 54 branches existed at some time before 1948, although all did not necessarily survive until that year.[4] With only slight exaggeration Mwangosi claimed in 1946 that 'there remain few areas of Tanganyika Territory without an African Association'.[5] As a second consequence these branches were more conscious than before of belonging to a single organisation. 'In the whole of Tanganyika we are using one method in the sections of the African Association', Bukoba's secretary wrote in 1946 when seeking approval to organise a cell in every Haya sub-chiefdom.[6] Third, the association's growth increased the centrifugal forces within it. Between 1945 and 1948, as

[1] Ali Ponda to AA Dar es Salaam, 24 January 1946, and Mwangosi to AA Usangi, 28 February 1946, TANU 26.
[2] Mohamed Johar to AA Tabora, 30 May 1946, TANU 26.
[3] UN, *Report of the United Nations visiting mission to East Africa on Tanganyika, 1948* (UNTC T/218), pp. 199–203.
[4] They were at Arusha, Babayu, Bagamoyo, Bahi, Biharamulo, Bukoba, Dar es Salaam, Dodoma, Handali, Ifakara, Ikizu, Itigi, Kibosho, Kidodi, Kilema, Kilosa, Kilwa, Kindi, Kondoa, Kwa Mtoro, Lindi, Machame, Mafia, Mahenge, Makerere, Manyoni, Mayamaya, Mbeya, Mbokomu, Mbulu, Missungwi, Mlingotini, Morogoro, Moshi, Mpwapwa, Mtimbira, Musoma, Mwanza, Ngudu, Nzega, Pangani, Pare, Pemba, Rufiji, Rungwe/Tukuyu, Sanya Chini, Shinyanga, Singida, Tabora, Tanga, Tarime, Ujiji, Ukerewe, and Zanzibar.
[5] Mwangosi to AA Makerere, 7 May 1946, TANU 26.
[6] AA Bukoba to DC Bukoba, 7 June 1946, TNA 215/1921/1/8.

in the 1930s, the association was regionalised. Yet – and this is the fourth point – regionalisation meant that its roots sank deeper into local societies, feeding their diverse energies into the central stem.

The association expanded in two main ways between 1945 and 1948. Certain existing branches were stimulated by the Dodoma conference. In 1945 the Bukoba branch consisted effectively of Ihangiro's tiny clique of dissidents, whose organisation had been broken up by the chief in 1943. Bukoba was not represented at territorial conferences after 1940. Its revival began when Mwanza became provincial head-quarters in 1945. By June 1946 Bukoba district claimed 622 members in six chiefdoms and was trying to create sub-branches.[1] Even more striking growth took place in Moshi. The branch was created by Joseph Kimalando, a Chagga civil servant active in the Dar es Salaam association in the late 1930s. Arriving home in 1940, Kimalando opened a tiny branch in Moshi but was soon posted away again. Returning in 1945 he had greater success, for two years later there were sub-branches at Sanya Chini and in the four mountain chiefdoms of Kibosho, Kindi, Machame, and Mbokomu. In Arusha, similarly, Kimalando failed to open a branch in 1941 but succeeded in 1945.[2]

Branches were also formed by members moving from one area to another. Husein Omar of Kondoa visited Pangani in 1946 and organised a branch there.[3] In Ifakara an embryonic traders' organ-isation, founded in 1945, was converted into an African Association branch two years later by educated men who had known the parent association in Dar es Salaam, the purpose of the change being to gain the official recognition which the association's long existence elsewhere was taken to imply.[4] In the Usangi chiefdom of North Pare the local clerks, traders, and schoolteachers had since 1935 belonged to the Usangi Sports and Welfare Club, which was interested in the area's general improvement. Early in 1946 a member named Juma Nyanga-rika returned from Dar es Salaam, where he had been an African Association activist. What happened next appears in the club's minute book:

[1] Gervas Byansheko to CS, 30 January 1947, and AA Bukoba to DC Bukoba, 7 June 1946, TNA 215/1921/1/12 and 8.
[2] Mwangosi to AA Mwanza, 16 August 1940, Suleiman papers, TNA; A. K. Mwakipesile to CS, 10 September 1947, TNA 19325/II/80; S. W. Frederick, 'The life of Joseph Kimalando', *TNR*, LXX (1969), 24–6; Rogers, 'Political focus', pp. 767–78.
[3] Hussein Omar, 'Report ya safari' [June 1946] Suleiman papers, TNA.
[4] Peter P. Mgohakamwali, 'Sub-branch of the African Association, Ifakara, Ulanga district. Special record', typescript, 1947 (copy in my possession); Larson, 'History', pp. 352–8.

Certain members had asked for a special general meeting [on 8 February 1946]
so that the members could be informed about an association of all Africans
– 'The African Association'...

Discussion: (a) Mr. Juma Nyangarika was requested to tell the meeting what
he knew about the Association...

(b) The whole constitution of the African Association was read...

The meeting agreed to give further consideration on that issue till 15/2/46,
so that those members who would join the African Association should fully
prepare themselves, so as not to bring shame to the nation.

They reassembled a week later:

The members met to...look for those members who were now prepared to
join the African Association...

[22 names follow]

The members of the Usangi Sports and Welfare Club have agreed to allow
the African Association to use one of its offices till the Association is strong
enough to have its own office, because almost all the members of the Usangi
Sports and Welfare Club are also members of the African Association.[1]

The association's dynamics are nowhere better illustrated: the returning migrant; the appeal of the association's claim to embrace 'all
Africans'; the seriousness, 'so as not to bring shame to the nation';
and finally the collective decision to link Usangi's aspirations with the
territory's.

Given their varied origins and environments, branches differed
greatly. A few were discussion clubs for educated men. Makerere was
one example, while the Mpwapwa branch came to be dominated by
instructors at the nearby Teachers' College.[2] Normally, however, civil
servants shared leadership with traders and urban notables. One of
Mwanza's first secretaries was Joseph Chombo, a Bondei clerk and
dansi enthusiast who had been secretary in Dar es Salaam in 1939, but
the president was Mwalimu Amri Mgeni, a shopkeeper, houseowner,
and Koran teacher. Relations between the two groups were often
strained. A civil servant in Mwanza complained of attacks at committee
meetings for not being 'a true native of Mwanza'.[3] In Tanga the initial
committee of 1945 chiefly contained townsmen – notably the 'Adviser',
a self-educated Muslim firewood-dealer named Maalim Kihere – but
later passed into the hands of Makerere-educated teachers and civil

[1] Usangi Sports and Welfare Club, minute book, 8 and 15 February 1946. I owe this
reference to Professor I. N. Kimambo and the translation to Dr G. C. K. Gwassa.

[2] Martha V. Mlagala, 'The traveller: Lulapangilo Zakaria Mhemedzi', in Iliffe, *Tanzanians*, p. 128.

[3] 'Minutes za mkutano wa tarehe 6 Januari 1945', Suleiman papers, TNA; G. A.
Maguire, *Toward 'Uhuru' in Tanzania* (Cambridge, 1969), p. 65; I. A. Msowoya to AA
Dodoma, 18 July 1945, Suleiman papers, TNA.

servants, not without friction.[1] In some small townships, by contrast, the traders dominated, and such branches often concentrated on distributing controlled goods among their members. The Ifakara branch almost collapsed in 1950 when such controls ended.[2]

Most branches were urban, but those with many traders often established strong rural ties. By 1946 the Ukerewe Island branch was weighing its members' cotton.[3] A few branches, like Usangi, were specifically rural. When Ulanga's traders organised after the war, the autocratic Chief Towegale of lowland Ubena formed an African Association branch of his own and persuaded the Dar es Salaam leaders to recognise it.[4] This illustrated the danger of fragmentation which faced the association, like the Maji Maji rebellion, as it expanded beyond its initial nuclei. Three branches were indeed entirely swamped by rural particularism. The Usangi branch lost ground to the Pare Union, of which Juma Nyangarika became secretary. The Moshi branch, having sought rural support, was taken over by rural politicians in 1948 and converted into an autonomous Kilimanjaro Union. The 'Usambara branch' founded independently was disowned by headquarters in 1947 when government proscribed it for subverting the native authority:

It was decided that the African Association may not enter into, or permit any entry whatever into, disputes concerning the choice of native authorities. Matters of this kind are solely for the people of the area to discuss with the government, according to the customs and practices of their area. Therefore your branch has no right to enter into or magnify local disorders, for that is not the association's aim.[5]

Danger as well as profit lurked in the countryside. The association's leaders accepted nationalist aims but not nationalist tactics. In disavowing the 'Usambara branch' they abandoned post-war activism.

Ironically, the association's growing territorial consciousness between 1945 and 1948 was accompanied by a waning political vitality. Four elements explain its growing concern with Tanganyika's future.

[1] Kombo Salim to AA Dodoma [1946] Suleiman papers, TNA; J. J. Mbuli, 'The Tanganyika African Association in Tanga', seminar paper, University of Dar es Salaam, 1970.
[2] Larson, 'History', pp. 360–1.
[3] Rounce to AA Mwanza, 13 May 1947, TNA 215/1921/1/16.
[4] 'Muhtasari wa mkutano wa ghafla wa halmashauri ulioitwa tarehe 21st June 1948', TANU 7.
[5] Abdiel Shangali to AA Usambara, 11 November 1947, TNA 4/6/2/385. Events in Upare, Kilimanjaro, and Usambara are described below, pp. 491–9.

One was branch expansion, for when delegates met in conference they realised that they formed a territorial organisation. Second, members from Makerere were more sharply aware of Tanganyika's international situation than older members. Third, war and official economic controls stimulated territorial consciousness as they also encouraged the advance from isolated stoppage to general strike. Finally, war made Tanganyika's future an urgent issue, and as in 1918 and 1929 debate about the territory's future stimulated African political consciousness. The three main post-war fears were summarised by the Mwanza branch in 1946: 'We do not want Tanganyika to be a colony...We do not want white settlement...The joining together of these three countries, we do not want it.'[1]

Hostility to European settlement was strongly expressed in the Dodoma memorandum of 1945 and was repeated in many of the association's later statements. Tanganyika's mandatory status became an issue through the collapse of the League of Nations. Under American pressure, Britain eventually agreed to administer Tanganyika under a trusteeship agreement with the newly-formed United Nations Organisation, an agreement which bound Britain to prepare the country for independence and empowered the U.N. Trusteeship Council to send a visiting mission every three years and to receive written and oral petitions from inhabitants.[2] These arrangements were not completed until 1947. Until then Tanganyika's future was uncertain. Africans universally desired that it should remain a Mandate or come under trusteeship. 'The Mandate affords some protection to the interests of Africans', the Dodoma memorandum explained. 'Conditions in Kenya clearly point out what a boon this Mandate has been.' Fear of Kenya grew when the British proposed late in 1945 to amalgamate the services common to the three East African territories under a Central Legislative Assembly with equal representation of Africans, Asians, and Europeans. Kenya's Europeans protested so violently that when the plan was implemented in 1948 racial parity was dropped. In the interim the settler campaign deeply alarmed Africans.[3]

The closer union issue led the African Association towards a specifically Tanganyikan identity. In January 1946 two leaders of the Kenya African Study Union, James Gichuru and Francis Khamisi,

[1] AA Mwanza to AA Dar es Salaam, 1 August 1946, in E. A. Lukwaro (ed.), 'Records of the African Association, Upare', duplicated paper, 1970, in my possession.
[2] See B. T. G. Chidzero, *Tanganyika and international trusteeship* (London, 1961), *passim*.
[3] See below, p. 475.

visited Tanganyika to propose a joint African response to British plans. Previous contact with Kenyan politicians, especially by the Chagga, had taught Tanganyikans to admire their militancy and fear their deprivations. In Moshi, chiefs and African Association leaders told Khamisi 'that in Kenya people had leprosy and for this reason we wouldn't unite with them. By this we meant that the Kenya Government was a colony.'[1] In Dar es Salaam the African Association committee held a preliminary meeting under the chairmanship of Chief Kidaha Makwaia of Shinyanga, recently appointed as one of the first two African members of the Legislative Council. The meeting decided to oppose amalgamation for fear of Kenya's oppressive regime.[2] When Gichuru and Khamisi met the committee on 18 January 1946 they found it unwilling even to consider the amalgamation question until Africans had equal and elective representation in all legislative bodies. The Kenyans' idea of an East African Congress was considered 'sound' but deferred to the African Association's next conference. Gichuru's proposal that KASU's projected delegation to the Colonial Office should also represent Tanganyika Africans was rejected. Much disappointed, Gichuru allegedly remarked that 'Tanganyikans are essentially a backward people.' Rather than encouraging East African unity, the meeting gave the African Association a defensive territorialism.[3]

The consequence was seen three months later at the association's conference in Dar es Salaam. No list of delegates has been found, although they included Chief Abdiel Shangali M.L.C., George Masudi from Zanzibar, Joseph Kimalando from Moshi, and Julius Nyerere from Tabora. If the Dodoma headquarters was represented, which is uncertain, it was outweighed by the predominance of civil servants from Dar es Salaam. Several resolutions suggest this.[4] Headquarters returned to Dar es Salaam 'permanently'. A proposal from Mwanza[5] that civil servants should not be African Association leaders was rejected and their right to office specifically affirmed. Routine resolutions on education, racial discrimination, urban affairs, and the like were passed. But the main business concerned Tanganyika's

[1] Kimalando, quoted in Rogers, 'Political focus', pp. 773–4.
[2] 'Minutes za standing committee juu ya inter-territorial organisation', 13 January 1946, TANU 7.
[3] Minutes, 18 January 1946, TNA 19325/II/35A; Hajivayanis and others in Iliffe, *Tanzanians*, p. 248.
[4] E. J. Kazi to CS, 4 May 1946, and enclosures, TNA 19325/II/41. The agenda is in Lukwaro, 'Records'.
[5] 'Mashauri...yamefikiriwa katika mkutano mkuu Mwanza tarehe 3/3/46', TANU 7.

future, and here there was a significant advance in political consciousness. One initiative came from Tabora and marked Julius
Nyerere's entry into territorial politics. Only 24 years old and
the Roman Catholic son of a Zanaki chief from east of Lake Victoria,
Nyerere had left Makerere in 1945 to teach at St. Mary's Secondary
School, Tabora. His contribution was a memorandum which he and
Andrew Tibandebage had persuaded the Tabora branch to place
on the conference agenda.[1] It became the basis of a conference resolution demanding constitutional advance by means of a
pyramid of elected councils leading upwards from townships and
chiefdoms through districts and provinces to a Legislative Council
with at least eight African members, one elected by each provincial
council. The memorandum also suggested that the association should
have a single treasury and a paid, full-time general secretary in
order to prevent a repetition of Dodoma's exhaustion, but this was
not implemented. On the main business the conference urged that
Tanganyika should come under trusteeship, with Britain undertaking
to develop it quickly 'until the Africans reach the point where
they can manage their own affairs'. Then, the conference added,
'the Trustee Power should grant them their independence without
any unnecessary delay':

Tanganyika Africans have always feared any contact that would lead to
political closer union with Kenya. Although the proposed unification is only
economic, this Conference believes that its ultimate result will be political closer
union...
   After the First Great War, Tanganyika was put under the protection of the
British Government by the League of Nations as a mandated territory. The
Africans of Tanganyika hope and believe that a day will come when they will
get their independence or self-government as Tanganyika Africans and not
as East Africans.[2]

Thus the conference retreated from the radicalism of 1945. Gone were
aggressive pan-Africanism and concern for popular organisation. In
their place was the defensive territorialism of the civil servants. Yet
the resolutions were also the association's first coherent demand that
the colonial territory of Tanganyika should become an independent
nation state. National consciousness – although not yet nationalism –
had entered the African Association's programme.
   The sharpening of territorial focus was sustained at the Zanzibar

[1] A. Tibandebage and J. K. Nyerere to AA Dodoma, 8 March 1946, TANU 6.
[2] 'Colonial paper no. 191', enclosed in Kazi to CS, 4 May 1946, TNA 19325/II/41.

conference of 1947.[1] Owing to recent expansion, this meeting was more representative than before, with 34 delegates from 17 branches. Benjamin Boyd and George Masudi were chairman and secretary. Three members attended from Dar es Salaam, two each from Pemba, Tanga (Maalim Kihere and Shaaban Robert), Pare (including Juma Nyangarika), and Morogoro, and one each from Pangani, Dodoma (Hassan Suleiman), Bagamoyo, Mlingotini, Tabora, Ujiji, Kondoa, Mwanza, Moshi (Joseph Kimalando), Singida, and Arusha. The main business apparently concerned African disabilities in Zanzibar[2] and Boyd's opening address was framed in pan-African terms, but the resolutions repeated the association's hostility to Kenya:

The Conference...recorded that it is not objected to unite No. 1 (Kenya) with No. 2 (Uganda), and No. 3 (Tanganyika) with No. 4 (Zanzibar). It went on to say that it is considered not advisable at present to have these four countries united together.

In other directions the conference continued the retreat from radicalism. Hassan Suleiman seemed a voice from the past when he unsuccessfully revived Nyerere's proposal to appoint paid officers.

The final step towards territorialism had an air of farce. The Zanzibar conference was embittered by jealousy between Zanzibar and Dar es Salaam. Early in 1948 Zanzibar's secretary sent the conference minutes direct to the Tanganyika Government. Understandably alarmed, Dar es Salaam's officers disowned them and in August 1948 severed relations with Zanzibar, renaming the association the *Tanganyika African Association*.[3]

TAA's birth coincided with political decline. The conference planned for 1948 in Dar es Salaam was cancelled. The secretary, R. K. Mziray, explained that government had not answered previous conference resolutions and that Dar es Salaam lacked funds and would wait until the association's finances were centralised. Mziray had taken over after the headquarters committee had scarcely met for several months. A civil servant best known for his book on letter-writing etiquette, Mziray addressed the branches in English – for the first time since the early 1930s – and planned to extend the association's welfare functions in the capital, only to be transferred in September.[4]

---

[1] 'Minutes of the 5th East African conference of the African Association held at Zanzibar on the 4th–7th April, 1947', TNA 19325/11/67A.
[2] Frederick, 'Kimalando', p. 25.
[3] R. R. K. Mziray to CS, 17 August 1948, TNA 19325/11/97.
[4] 'Muhtasari wa mkutano wa halmashauri uliyoitwa siku ya jumanne tarehe 25.5.1948', TANU 7; Mziray to branches, 31 May 1948, TANU 48; Mziray, 'The Tanganyika African Association' [1948] TANU 7.

Thereafter headquarters apparently collapsed entirely. There is only one indication of its existence during 1949.[1] One senses a general withdrawal from politics by civil servants, possibly influenced by experience during the general strike, the Usambara crisis, and their quarrel with Zanzibar. TAGSA also wilted at this time. TAA's evidence to the first U.N. Visiting Mission of 1948 was peculiarly parochial. 'Social conditions in suburbs and in the country are grand', headquarters blandly declared, 'but social conditions in the so-called African Zones in townships are mediocre'.[2] Yet decay was not confined to Dar es Salaam. The Pare and Moshi branches lapsed into parochialism. The Mwanza delegate's return from Zanzibar led to a large and lively provincial conference in May 1947, but thereafter the branch did little until the early 1950s.[3] Dodoma disappeared entirely from the records between 1948 and 1954. Only one branch of TAA showed any activity during 1949, and that was a small rural cell.[4]

Perhaps two reasons explain the universality of political decay. One was the end of wartime austerity. After the general strike, urban wages at last outpaced inflation, shortages eased, economic controls withered, export prices rose. With personnel and materials at last available, post-war development began. Establishment of the trusteeship system removed some anxiety about the future. The second reason was that in 1949 the British government seized the political initiative in Tanganyika for the first time since Cameron's departure and channelled politics into new directions.

Yet as so often in Tanganyika the disappearance of an institution or an idea from the records did not mean that it was dead but that it was germinating, to re-emerge later in new shape. By 1947 the African Association possessed all the elements of nationalism except the determination, the techniques, and the popular support to seize power. Its politics were only ideas and resolutions. Yet ideas matter. The association was itself the embodiment of an idea, and just as the collapse of territorial leadership in the 1930s had left that idea to work itself out in men's minds, in upcountry villages and schools and townships, so the idea of unity survived the new organisational collapse. In 1948, at the moment of decay, an uneducated Sukuma tailor explained the central idea to the people of Mwanza:

[1] *Tanganyika standard* (weekly), 9 July 1949.
[2] UN, *Report of the visiting mission, 1948*, pp. 199–203.
[3] 'The African Association provincial conference, Lake Province, Mwanza – 17th–18th May [1947]' TNA 215/1921/1/19.
[4] Busega in Usukuma. See Maguire, '*Uhuru*', pp. 113–22.

Since the war, wise Africans have established TAA branches in almost all the large towns of Tanganyika and Zanzibar...Every African is a child of TAA; there is no division of tribe or religion. TAA is to build unity, to speak out about our problems, to seek our rights. TAA is not for two days only or for two years. Those who come after us, being more knowledgeable, will build TAA better than we. Do not be discouraged even if the road is long and difficult. Let us begin now to fashion a path for our children.[1]

[1] Selemani Mahugi to 'all citizens', 5 June 1948, in *ibid.*, pp. 74–5.

CHAPTER 14

The new colonialism

The Second World War transformed Tanganyika's relationship with Britain. With an exhausted economy, colossal debts, and a disintegrating Asian empire, Britain at last needed even Tanganyika's meagre resources, if they could be extracted. The post-war decade therefore saw a 'second colonial occupation'[1] embodied in development planning and secondary industry, cash-crop expansion and agricultural improvement schemes, educational advance, constitutional progress, and local government reform. Yet as in earlier colonial empires,[2] increased imperial control antagonised subjects who had often acquiesced in lighter suzerainty. Active government created grievances to stimulate political activity and provided resources to make it effective. The new colonialism followed nearly twenty years of crisis, and although in the short term it checked African political development, in the long term it only accentuated the crisis, widening regional and social disparities, reinforcing the structural contradictions of colonial society rather than bringing structural change, and intensifying the process of uneven and combined development. Moreover, the new colonialism contained a contradiction, for while some expected it to restore Britain's power, others saw it as a means of creating friendly successor states. The balance between the views remains uncertain, however, for records are often closed after 1945 and we know progressively less about Tanganyika's history as we approach the present.

Post-war change created a more complicated country, widening the range of techniques, roles, interests, and aspirations. One result was a multitude of political associations embodying elements of the more complicated society. Another was the complex political movement of

[1] D. A. Low and J. M. Lonsdale, 'Introduction', in D. A. Low and Alison Smith (ed.), *History of East Africa*, III (Oxford, 1976), p. 12.
[2] The model is John Lynch, *Spanish colonial administration, 1782–1810* (London, 1958), esp. pp. 286–9.

nationalism. Yet simultaneously Africans were internalising colonial values, while at another level changing relationships among men went alongside human gains over nature. It is in these last years of colonial rule that the complexity of Tanganyika's history becomes most apparent.

Policy and planning

The new colonialism's manifesto was the Colonial Development and Welfare Act of 1940, which provided imperial finance for long-term colonial development plans. Its motives combined self-interest and altruism. The depression had shown that impoverished colonies were politically dangerous and could not buy British exports, preferring cheaper Japanese or Indian products. The Act countered German propaganda, helped appease American anti-imperialism, and encouraged colonial peoples to restrain their demands until the war ended. It also gave the Colonial Office greater authority over colonial economies, exercised through controls established during the war and matching the general trend of the time towards managerial government. Altruistic motives were equally important, for the depression had revealed the frailty of economies resting on export monocultures, while social anthropologists had anatomised poverty and malnutrition and many public men felt a responsibility to advance colonial development.[1]

Combined altruism and self-interest characterised Britain's whole post-war colonial policy. Both Conservative and Labour parties were committed 'to guide Colonial peoples along the road to self-government within the framework of the British Empire',[2] but the war and the loss of India appeared to give Africa new strategic and economic value. While a creative colonial secretary, Arthur Creech Jones, advocated economic development, social reform, and political advancement, other ministers either saw Africa in strategic terms or concentrated on its contribution to Britain's reconstruction. They resolved the contradiction by denying its existence. 'There is no conflict', the Foreign Secretary declared, 'between the social and economic development of these overseas territories to the advantage of their people, and their development as a source of supplies for Western Europe.'[3]

[1] I am indebted to Mr M. G. Oates for much information on colonial development and welfare.
[2] Stanley, 13 July 1943, quoted in David Goldsworthy, *Colonial issues in British politics 1945–1961* (Oxford, 1971), p. 12.
[3] Bevin, quoted in S. A. H. Haqqi, *The colonial policy of the Labour government (1945–51)* (Aligarh, 1960), p. 128.

Different government agencies consequently worked in contrary
directions. Led by Creech Jones and the dynamic head of its Africa
Division, Andrew Cohen, the traditionally liberal Colonial Office
concluded that the major African territories would probably govern
themselves within a generation, so that Britain must concentrate on
making them viable and friendly nation states by collaborating with,
and using, the educated nationalists who alone could govern them.[1]
Yet this strategy left three unresolved problems. One was to decide
when a territory was ready for self-government – the British generally
held that it must first have enough wealth, education, and experienced
administrators to govern itself well by British standards. The second
problem was the form of the successor states, for the new strategy
produced both Nkrumah's Ghana and the white-dominated Central
African Federation, while in East Africa – where black and white were
most evenly balanced – it produced fifteen years of conflict. The third
problem was that the Colonial Office was not the British government.
The much more powerful economic and service ministries had to be
convinced, and so did the great block of middle class interest and
opinion represented by the Conservative Party. Those battles were
fought in the 1950s. For the present, the new colonialism's virtue was
its ambiguity and its consequent acceptability to most shades of
opinion.

In Dar es Salaam the Colonial Development and Welfare Act
scarcely ruffled the leaves in Acacia Avenue. The African Association
demanded a voice in spending the money, but officials recognised
Britain's military peril and their own depleted numbers and concluded
that long-term planning was then merely an unpatriotic waste of
energy.[2] Pressure from London late in 1942 produced educational
plans, but government did not grasp the urgency of the issue until
April 1943, when the Financial Secretary warned that 'we must make
sure to open our mouths wide enough'. A development branch of the
Secretariat was set up and a planning committee produced an outline
scheme by the end of 1944.[3]

Haste, staff shortages, and basic incomprehension ruled out the
comprehensive plan concentrating on the 'improvement of productive

[1] See Ronald Robinson, 'The journal and the transfer of power 1947–51', *Journal of administration overseas*, XIII (1974), 256–7. I am also drawing on information from Professor Robinson.
[2] Mzee Sudi and P. C. Mntambo to Young, 3 August 1940, TNA 28944/1; Tanganyika, *An outline of post-war development proposals* (Dar es Salaam, 1944), p. 1.
[3] FS to CS, minute, 17 April 1943, TNA 28867/1; Tanganyika, *Outline*.

and earning power' which the Colonial Office demanded.[1] Instead
planners relied on two pre-war blueprints. *The Report of the Central
Education Committee* originated from a Colonial Office policy statement
of 1935 which marked the apogee of adaptive education for village life.[2]
The Report of the Central Development Committee of 1940 was designed
to please European settlers. Intending 'to make Tanganyika a
country', the development committee had proposed to spend 45 per
cent of planned expenditure on roads, 27 per cent on social services,
7 per cent on European settlement, and 5 per cent on African
agriculture (chiefly land rehabilitation schemes). The Colonial Office
had criticised the report's settler bias, but the planning committee
worked from it and from lists of departmental projects.[3] White
settlement was excluded because ex-German property had become
available, but the largest expenditure in the outline plan of 1944 was
£1,500,000 over seven years on roads, while £875,500 over five years
was earmarked for townships and £1,000,000 for government housing.
The total projected expenditure was £12,631,750 over ten years.[4]
Tanganyika was certainly opening its mouth wide enough, but
old-fashioned words were emerging. The Colonial Office intended
that plans should emphasise productive projects and 'modern'
activities like industry and secondary education. Tanganyika, by
contrast, emphasised infrastructural development, land rehabilitation,
and primary schooling, 'the necessary preliminaries to a policy of
productive expansion'.[5] The techniques of the new colonialism were
incorporated into the time-scale of the old.

Surprised by Japan's sudden surrender after Hiroshima, the
Colonial Office allocated Colonial Development and Welfare Funds
late in 1945. Tanganyika received £5,250,000 over ten years.[6] Colonial
Office pressure for productive investment instead of tarmac roads was
ineffective, but it insisted that another million pounds must be spent
on education.[7] As table v shows, however, Tanganyika still allocated
less to education and more to communications than other colonies.
Meanwhile 1947 had come and scarcely any development had

---

[1] Stanley to Jackson, 28 April 1944, TNA 33026/1.
[2] Great Britain, *Memorandum on the education of African communities* (Col. 103 of 1935).
[3] Above, p. 373; Tanganyika, *Central Development Committee*, pp. 7, 177–83; Cranborne
to Young, 7 April 1942, CO 691/181; Tanganyika, *Outline*, p. 1.
[4] Tanganyika, *Outline*, pp. 8–12.
[5] Marlow to Stanley, 6 January 1945, TNA 33048/1/25.
[6] Hall to governors, 12 November 1945, TNA 33048/II/65. Another £3,500,000 was
allocated for interterritorial schemes in East Africa.
[7] Creech Jones to Battershill, 29 January 1947, TNA 33062/I/115.

Table v. *Percentages of expenditure proposed in post-war development plans*

	Tanganyika	Nigeria	Kenya	Northern Rhodesia
Agriculture (incl. European)	8	6	37	18
Communications	39	23	12	17
Health	17	21	5	13
Education	11	16	14	12
Towns, etc.	18	17	20	13

SOURCE: Calculated from Haqqi, *Colonial policy*, p. 177.

happened. Staff and materials were scarce and Britain had first priority. District officers reported deep disillusionment with post-war development.[1] Yet in February 1947 men and equipment in vast quantities began to land at Dar es Salaam.

The frantic urgency of the Groundnut Scheme contrasted strangely with the leisured pace of post-war planning, but they both originated in Britain's post-war crisis. In 1947 only 60 per cent of the world's pre-war oils and fats entered international trade and a shortfall was predicted for ten or twenty years.[2] Early in 1946 a director of Unilever, a major producer of oils, toured Africa seeking new supplies. Tanganyika's Director of Agriculture suggested that Unilever should grow ground-nuts with machinery on some 40,000 hectares of tsetse-infested Western Province. Unilever proposed instead that government should itself cultivate a million hectares of groundnuts. Government sent A. J. Wakefield, formerly Tanganyika's Director of Agriculture, to investigate and select land. Wakefield spent six weeks flying over the bush. He proposed that government should take up some 1,300,000 hectares, three-quarters of it in Tanganyika at Nachingwea in Southern Province and at Kongwa and Urambo on the central railway. Since labour was scarce, every possible operation should be mechanised. The first 60,000 hectares were to be cleared in 1947. Wakefield estimated the capital cost at £24,000,000. The undertaking was feasible, he insisted, given 'the same determination...as was needed, and found, for the conduct of the major operations of the

[1] E.g. DC Kigoma to PC Western, 12 April 1946, TNA 180/D/2/2/26.
[2] Great Britain, *A plan for the mechanised production of groundnuts* (Cmd 7030 of 1947), p. 15.

war'. Once Britain's crisis was overcome, the scheme would be handed over to Tanganyika. Idealism and larger rations were a combination irresistible to Labour politicians. The Cabinet entrusted the plan's implementation to the Ministry of Food, judging the Colonial Office too conservative. Anxious to prove its virility, the Tanganyika Government overrode specialist warnings and supported the scheme warmly.[1]

Against the Tanganyika Government's advice, work began at Kongwa because the bush looked thinner there and port and railway facilities existed. Soon the operation acquired the ex-army-surplus quality which pervaded post-war Britain. Bulldozers were salvaged from Pacific islands. Even a few tanks were converted. Over 100,000 Britons applied for jobs.[2] Some 3,000 of them were eventually employed, together with African drivers and craftsmen equally delighted to return to service life. By December 1947 some 3,000 hectares had been cleared, compared with the intended 60,000. Undismayed, the commanders made 60,000 hectares the target for 1948. Only 20,000 were cleared. Early in 1949 expenditure was a million pounds a month, Conservatives were demanding blood, and the Treasury refused to raise the ceiling on total cost. More groundnuts had been bought as seed than had been harvested. Heavy equipment stood unserviceable while labourers gathered groundnuts by hand. A drought during 1949 ended the agony. Next year a commission recommended abandonment. £35,870,000 had been spent, equal to the Tanganyika Government's total expenditure between 1946 and 1950.

The mistakes were obvious in retrospect.[3] Despite expansive promises, the scheme ignored Tanganyika's views or interests. The Tanganyika Government was not even represented on the board of management. The operation was direct exploitation from London unique in Tanganyika's history. It assumed that machinery and willpower would triumph at Kongwa as at el-Alamein, neglecting any serious consideration of commercial viability and assuming that civilians could be only a nuisance. Since it was politically impossible to dispossess African cultivators, Wakefield argued that empty land

---

[1] Miller to Christie, 15 March 1946, TNA 38744/5; *Plan for mechanised production, passim* (quotation on p. 47); correspondence in TNA 35781.

[2] A. T. P. Seabrook, 'The groundnut scheme in retrospect', *TNR*, XLVII (1957), 88. This paragraph is based chiefly on Alan Wood, *The groundnut affair* (London, 1950).

[3] For a critique, see S. H. Frankel, *The economic impact on under-developed societies* (Oxford, 1953), ch. 8.

was a positive advantage. Sharing the prevailing impatience with peasant agriculture, he did not ask whether cultivators had reason to neglect these areas. Urgency precluded research or experimentation. Wakefield declared airily that 'in later years work. . . will be expanded to include more fundamental aspects'.[1] That Kongwa had enough rain was inferred from statistics for nearby Mpwapwa, but Mpwapwa was in the hills, its rainfall fluctuated widely, and local people knew Kongwa as 'the country of perpetual drought'. The scheme eventually foundered on drought, bush, and soil so hard that it disabled the decrepit machinery.

The scheme left few legacies. Cleared land was handed over for ranching, tobacco, or African smallholder farming. A small modern port was built at Mtwara. Negatively, development planning was somewhat distorted. Mtwara's construction delayed much-needed deep-water berths at Dar es Salaam, while hopes that the Mtwara-Nachingwea railway might continue to Lake Nyasa may have delayed other access routes to the Southern Highlands.[2] There is little evidence that the much-publicised disaster inhibited investment in Tanganyika,[3] for nothing suggests that much investment was ever contemplated, but the scheme may have inhibited constitutional planning between 1946 and 1949. Its real significance, however, lay elsewhere. The Groundnut Scheme was Europe's last major attempt to restructure Tanganyika's economy. Had it succeeded, this major imperial interest must have complicated decolonisation.

As the Groundnut Scheme's cost passed £25,000,000 in June 1949, Sir Edward Twining became Governor of Tanganyika. A big man, bluff and vital, humane, well-intentioned, and intellectually limited, he had made an undistinguished career until war and colonial development had catapulted him in ten years from deputy labour commissioner in Mauritius to the fourth most prestigious governorship in the colonial empire. Twining was a developer. Evidence is lacking, but Creech Jones and Cohen probably chose him as a blunt instrument to force Tanganyika into motion along the lines they had chosen. If so, it was a brilliant choice. Twining became Tanganyika's most important governor, and Britain lost Tanganyika.[4]

[1] *Plan for mechanised production*, p. 30.
[2] Minute to Governor, 18 November 1947, TNA 33042; Sir Edward Twining, 'The situation in Tanganyika', *African affairs*, LI (1951), 303.
[3] As argued in Cyril Ehrlich, 'Some aspects of economic policy in Tanganyika, 1945–60', *Journal of modern African studies*, II (1964), 267.
[4] Darrell Bates, *A gust of plumes: a biography of Lord Twining* (London, 1972).

Twining soon expanded development plans. Whereas the original plan allocated £19,186,000 over ten years from 1947, the new scheme of 1950 allocated £24,450,191 over seven years and was even more heavily orientated towards infrastructure, earmarking £8,783,000 for communications and £8,283,000 for townships, public works, and African housing.[1] The Colonial Office was soon warning Twining against inflation, in an unduly cautious and wholly ineffective manner. Roads, hospitals, public buildings, urban suburbs, schemes of all kinds marked Twining's governorship on a scale modest by other criteria but dramatic by Tanganyika's. Between 1949 and 1956 annual government expenditure rose from £8,700,000 to £22,600,000.[2] Such activity meant a new level of governmental penetration of society. By 1950 two-thirds of Tanganyika's administrative officers had been appointed since 1944 and Africans were protesting at the growing army of officials.[3] For government as for missions, expansion led to disengagement, to the detachment of decision-makers from popular feeling, to impersonal bureaucratic relationships, and to government by compulsion rather than persuasion. 'We are faced with a serious invasion, more serious, in fact, than the first world war', local politicians in Eastern Province protested in 1955. '...We are a poor people...and yet we are made poorer by demands of taxes and working for projects which make us no better.' It was in that year that the police first cost more than the provincial administration.[4] But officials and educated Africans shared an impatience with 'peasant conservatism'. The African Association rarely met without demanding compulsion in some field. A report on answers to the territorial standard VIII examination of 1950 observed that 'the word "force" was in the foreground, e.g. "force" should be applied in agriculture, "force" in education of boys and girls alike, "force" in preparing the Native rulers in their schooling to become leaders, "force" to return the girls from the groundnut area'.[5]

[1] *Ten year development and welfare plan for Tanganyika* (Legislative Council sessional paper no. 2 of 1950).
[2] Cyril Ehrlich, 'The poor country: the Tanganyika economy from 1945 to Independence', in Low and Smith, *History*, III, 291.
[3] Twining to Griffiths, 20 September 1950, Cadiz papers, RH; Tanganyika, 'Committee on constitutional development: evidence and memoranda submitted to the fact-finding sub-committee 1950' (duplicated), I, 115 (evidence of African Discussion Group, Tanga).
[4] Quoted in J. R. Mlahagwa, 'Agricultural change in the Uluguru mountains during the colonial period', M.A. thesis, University of Dar es Salaam, 1974, p. 45; Bates, 'British administration', p. 377.
[5] Quoted in Larson, 'History', pp. 335–8.

Apart from groundnuts, the most contentious area of post-war policy was education. Tanganyika's educational backwardness brought repeated criticism from London, but the ten-year plan approved in 1947 preserved the pre-war emphasis on primary schooling adapted to village life. 'Based on the existing structure with as little interference with it as possible',[1] the plan's chief aim was to increase school places, and in this it succeeded. Between 1948 and 1955 the proportion of government's recurrent expenditure which went on education rose from 6 to 14 per cent.[2] The problem was the type of schooling provided. The plan's central feature was a distinction between primary schools, providing four years of education, and middle schools which would take 20 per cent of primary school leavers and give them four further years of vernacular schooling with an agricultural bias in order to produce 'that rural middle class or yeoman type so necessary for any enduring improvement'.[3] Only the most able 20 per cent would pass on from middle school to a literary education in English. Each stage was to be as complete as possible and produce 'useful citizens...instead of potential malcontents'.[4] The plan contained four assumptions which proved false. One was that the wastage of primary pupils would continue high, for this determined the proportion leaving standard IV who would enter middle school. In fact primary school wastage fell so dramatically that the proportion of primary school leavers entering middle school declined between 1947 and 1957 from 40 to 13 per cent.[5] This undercut the further assumption that Africans would consider four years of primary schooling a useful education. The error was apparent even in 1950, when the ten European members of the advisory committee had to outvote the seven Africans who insisted that children leaving school after four years were not permanently literate and were too young to begin work.[6] The third mistaken assumption was that Africans wanted an education adapted to village life. And the fourth was that ample time remained for another ten-year plan to expand secondary schooling.

[1] 'Ten year plan for development of African education' [1947] TNA 41242/11.
[2] Tanganyika, *Blue book*, 1948, p. 85; Tanganyika, *Development plan for Tanganyika 1961/62 – 1963/64* (Dar es Salaam, 1962), p. 10.
[3] Jackson to Stanley, 21 December 1943, CO 691/189.
[4] Tanganyika, *Ten year plan for African education (scheme for revision)* (Dar es Salaam, 1950), p. 9.
[5] UN, *Visiting mission to trust territories in East Africa, 1957: report on the trust territory of Tanganyika* (UNTC T/1345), annex v.
[6] 'Minutes of the 17th meeting of the Advisory Committee on African Education', 5–6 June 1950, TNA 19484/11/69.

Educational planners also had to consider the diversity of provision and enthusiasm for education in different regions. In 1948 literacy among children between six and fifteen years old varied from 21 per cent in Tanga Province to 5 per cent in Central Province. Whereas in 1956 some 90 per cent of Chagga children were at school, the proportion among the neighbouring Meru three years later was 74 per cent and among the Arusha only 34 per cent.[1] Some Muslim regions still resisted European schooling, but most other backward areas strove to catch up with more fortunate neighbours who themselves strove, generally with greater success, to stay ahead, so that small tribes with early mission experience generally kept their educational lead over larger tribes – with important political repercussions. Amidst this competition, the lack of provision for 80 per cent of primary school leavers met violent criticism. Many demanded the old six-year primary course. Others wanted more middle schools. More often the whole middle school system was denounced. 'Middle Schools are for Africans only', it was protested, 'and the African "syllabus" is different from that of other races'.[2] The agricultural bias was particularly resented as an obstacle to wealth, equality, and power. 'We want our children to go on to higher education', Sukuma cotton growers insisted; 'they can't do that if they spend so much time on agriculture.'[3] The most widespread grievance was lack of secondary schools, especially in highly-educated regions. Visiting Kilimanjaro in 1950, Twining noted a fear 'that unless they had improved education "the Wachagga may not maintain their position as the premier tribe in Tanganyika"'.[4]

At Makerere the problem was not lack of places but lack of Tanganyikans to fill them, for as the college approached university status – its first degree examinations were in December 1953 – its entrance standards outpaced Tanganyikan schools. In 1950 only 41 Tanganyikans were at Makerere, or less than half the number planned five years earlier. Several were now Chagga, Zigua, or Sukuma, who took places alongside the Bondei, Haya, and Nyakyusa who had hitherto predominated, but most other areas were repre-

---

[1] DE to Member for Social Services, 26 November 1952, TNA 41242/II/103; Michael von Clemm, 'Agricultural productivity and sentiment on Kilimanjaro', *Economic botany*, XVIII (1964), 99; Snaith, Arusha DAR 1959, TNA 471/R/3/3/I/10.
[2] E. A. Kisenge to African MLCs, 25 April 1958, TANU 28.
[3] Quoted in Maguire, '*Uhuru*', p. 106.
[4] 'Note by H.E. the Governor on his visit to Moshi district, January 7–11, 1950', TNA 31723/84.

sented only by an occasional chief's son educated at Tabora.[1] In the early 1950s entrants increased as secondary schools were upgraded. In 1955 some 150 Tanganyikans were at Makerere, including four women. Government also recognised that future planning must emphasise higher education.[2] But at the same time the position of students leaving Makerere was becoming increasingly difficult. 'I can neither cope up with my own peoples life, nor that of a civilized man', one complained in 1943,[3] although his medical training made him one of those who gained employment and status most easily. Makerere's general courses were of lower quality than its professional training, while the education course contained many who lacked a teacher's vocation. These students were exposed to the radical ideas current among Ugandan and Kenyan students but found few employment opportunities. After the war Government decided to recruit experienced clerks rather than Makerere students into the administrative service, and when Makerere began to award pass degrees Government made an honours degree the necessary qualification for the political administration.[4] By the mid 1950s small groups of embittered clerks and teachers from Makerere existed in several towns.

The top of the educational ladder moved overseas. In the early mission years, and even in German times, several Tanganyikans had finished their education abroad, but British occupation ended this. One reason for developing Makerere was to prevent East Africans absorbing subversive ideas at foreign universities.[5] Only one Tanganyikan received a single term's education in Europe between the wars,[6] but it remained relatively common for West Africans, and the Colonial Development and Welfare Act provided funds for scholarships which were also available to Tanganyikans, especially before Makerere's degree courses were fully established. Perhaps a score of Tanganyikans studied in Britain after the war. A few belonged to prominent chiefly families. Thomas Marealle, grandson of the Germans' collaborator, studied at Cambridge and the London School

[1] Attenborough to Wood, 23 May 1950, TNA 25401/IV/325; Goldthorpe, *Elite*, pp. 27–31.
[2] Listowel, *Making*, p. 180; *Tanganyika standard*, 18 November 1953.
[3] Statement by E. F. Mwaisela [c. 1943] FCB papers 121, RH.
[4] Minute, 12 April 1951, TNA 25103/1; R. C. Pratt, *The critical phase in Tanzania 1945–1968* (Cambridge, 1976), p. 18.
[5] Cunliffe-Lister to MacMichael, 15 August 1934, and enclosure, TNA 13658/I/115; Mitchell to MacMichael, 1 November 1937, TNA 25401/I/5 (bound into 25401/III).
[6] Bonaventura Masanja, at Harper Adams Agricultural College. African Roman Catholic priests may have studied abroad.

of Economics, while Chief Kidaha Makwaia of Busiha spent a year at Oxford. More came from families educated by the UMCA. Matthew Ramadhani, whose degree from Sheffield was the first obtained by a Tanganyika African, was the son of Kiungani's senior African teacher, while Godfrey Kayamba's studies in London made him the third generation of his family to visit Britain. A third category contained men whose only claim was academic success, notably Julius Nyerere, the Zanaki schoolteacher who had been active in the African Association. Their foreign experience varied greatly. Several, especially from Anglican backgrounds, became Anglophiles. 'My visit to England was like a dream', wrote Justino Mponda, a Makonde schoolteacher.[1] Others were more unhappy, notably the arrogant and bitter Godfrey Kayamba. It was chiefly those already politically active who sharpened their specifically political awareness. Marealle, Nyerere, Hamza Mwapachu, and Dunstan Omari all established ties with the Fabian wing of the Labour Party,[2] but none seems to have been closely associated with more extreme groups. Their preoccupation with the Fabian issues of race, development, and constitutional advance was expressed in Nyerere's essay on 'The race problem in East Africa'.[3]

Apart from education, 'modernising imperialism' stressed industrial development as a means of diversifying colonial economies. Lacking Kenya's immigrant market or Uganda's forceful leadership, Tanganyika's industrial growth was almost confined to the Pugu Road area of Dar es Salaam. Many factories built there in the late 1940s produced furniture or supplied the expanding building trade. Other plants provided engineering services for the Groundnut Scheme and motor vehicles. Others again were processing industries: a subsidiary of the Metal Box Company (1947), the local licensee for Coca Cola (1950), important flour millers like Chande Brothers (1946), together with a brewery, paint factory, and the like. In 1956 Dar es Salaam's deep-water berths were opened. Factory textile production began in 1957. By then the banks were increasingly investing in local enterprise, and in 1955 the East African Currency Board was empowered to invest locally rather than in London. In 1958 manufacturing created less than 5 per cent of Tanganyika's gross domestic product

[1] Quoted in Jacob D. Iddi, 'The life of Justino Mponda', typescript, 1971, in my possession.
[2] There is much correspondence with and about them in FCB papers 121, RH.
[3] Extract in Julius K. Nyerere, *Freedom and unity* (Dar es Salaam, 1966), pp. 23–9.

447

and employed only 75,000 men, more than half of them in agricultural processing.[1]

Import substitution industries had few linkages with the indigenous economy, but general prosperity probably stimulated craft industries and small-scale trade. When figures first became available in 1969, 418,000 households participated in some way in craft production, 83 per cent of the labour force being family members. Crafts then provided 10 per cent of rural income.[2] Domestic weaving had almost disappeared and iron-smithing survived only as a local craft, but brewing flourished, areas renowned for pottery experienced considerable prosperity as road transport extended markets, and many new crafts grew up around the construction industry. 'Near Mlalo trading centre', a visitor to Usambara observed in 1946, 'whole villages are inhabited entirely by carpenters whose window frames and doors are sold within and without the District.' It was noteworthy that even the simplest of the new crafts, such as dressmaking or bicycle-repairing, remained the province of specialists.[3]

After the war, it appears, Africans at last made inroads into retail trade – as Asians were keenly aware. This owed little to war or to official policy. Many returning askari invested gratuities in trade and formed elaborate trading societies. Few survived the abolition of import controls, but individuals slowly made their way. In 1952 Africans owned some 27,000 licensed shops, Asians 7,500, and Arabs 3,500. There were also 8,000 licensed itinerant traders, probably mostly Africans, and doubtless many unlicensed pedlars.[4] Africans handled only a minority of business – less than a third in 1961[5] – but this, with its resultant discontents, increased the traders' importance as a group. In all but two regions African success varied with distance from railways. In 1961 Dar es Salaam's shops remained predominantly in Asian and Arab hands, while the proportion of shops owned by Africans was only 44 per cent in Shinyanga district, 49 in Mpwapwa, 53 in Dodoma and Tabora, 57 in Arusha, and 70 in Kigoma. By contrast, Africans owned 93 per cent of shops in Handeni district, 92

---

[1] Martha Honey, 'Asian industrial activities in Tanganyika', *TNR*, LXXIV (1974), 65–6; Rweyemamu, *Underdevelopment*, pp. 111–13; Booth, 'Business names'; Pratt, *Critical phase*, p. 20.

[2] Manuel Gottlieb, 'The extent and character of differentiation in Tanzanian agricultural and rural society 1967–1969', *The African review*, III (1973), 249.

[3] Cory to PC Tanga, 31 August 1946, TNA 4/269/5/1/158; Perrin Jassy, *La communauté*, p. 57.

[4] Wright, *Consumers*, pp. 39–41.

[5] H. C. G. Hawkins, *Wholesale and retail trade in Tanganyika* (New York, 1965), p. 150.

448

in Kasulu, 91 in Njombe, 90 in Lushoto, and 88 in Rungwe – all these being districts remote from railways. One exception was that the highest proportion of African-owned shops – 98 per cent – was in Same district, where the Pare had combined to oust Asian shopkeepers from the countryside. The other exception was Moshi district, where Africans owned 80 per cent of shops and were apparently in the process of forcing Asians to quit Kilimanjaro. In 1951 there were 3,000 Chagga traders in Moshi district.[1]

The Arab community survived almost entirely as a trading group: 84 per cent of adult male Arabs were traders in 1952. The figure for Asians was 51 per cent, only a modest decrease from the 56 per cent of 1932, despite a larger Asian population, African competition, cooperative development, and a more sophisticated capitalism.[2] Some Asian shopkeepers found openings in development areas like Mtwara, where the Ismaili Khoja community subsidised its members to establish themselves. In the late 1950s large Nairobi dealers took over much of Tanganyika's textile wholesaling, but other wholesale merchants cut deeply into European control of the export-import trade and profited from the general commercial expansion, while successful businessmen diversified into industry or real estate, where many fortunes were made during the post-war housing boom. Yet Asian leaders increasingly believed that education was the key to the community's future. Ismaili Khojas reached this conclusion in 1937, when their councils first encouraged young men to seek higher education in India. Between 1948 and 1961 Asian secondary school pupils increased nearly five-fold.[3] Asians increasingly entered the professions, which altered the structure of the community. Whereas most Ismaili Khoja councillors had hitherto been wealthy merchants, in the 1950s increasing numbers were professional men with university educations, often sons of the old councillors.[4] Such men pressed forward the Aga Khan's westernising policy. When the British Nationality Act of 1948 first enabled inhabitants of trust territories to seek naturalisation, most Ismaili Khojas sought British nationality, deliberately breaking their ties with India. Then at their Evian

[1] Wright, *Consumers*, p. 112; Leslie, *Survey*, p. 135; above, p. 346; S. J. Ntiro, *Desturi za Wachagga* (Dar es Salaam, 1953), pp. 47–8; Great Britain, *Report of the United Nations visiting mission to Tanganyika, 1954: observations of the administering authority* (Col. 935 of 1955), p. 18; Page-Jones to Member for Local Government, 8 December 1951, TNA 12844/III/398.

[2] Wright, *Consumers*, pp. 45–6.

[3] Walji, 'Ismailis', p. 108; Honey, 'Industrial activities', p. 67.

[4] Walji, 'Business enterprise'.

conference of 1952 Ismaili Khoja leaders decided that the community 'should in future look towards the West rather than towards the East, and that its members should identify themselves with the territories in which they reside'. English replaced Gujarati in Ismaili Khoja schools, women were encouraged to adopt western dress and allowed to seek employment as nurses or secretaries, civil law on matters like divorce and polygyny was brought closer to European models, and a new constitution was designed to perpetuate the Aga Khan's work after his death.[1] Other communities also emancipated themselves, although more slowly. A conference at Tanga in 1951 produced a constitution for the previously authoritarian Ismaili Bohra community, which even began to accept such innovations as the remarriage of widows.[2] Yet such steps contained dangers. Many Asian crafts – shoe-making, tailoring, tin-smithing – were collapsing under competition from international firms and mass-produced imports, while small rural shops lost much of their profitability as the rising African cooperatives gained monopolies of crop-buying.[3] Division between modernising leaders and the bulk of the community may have increased. Bohra *jamats* were commonly divided between progressive and traditionalist factions. The Indian Merchants Chamber of Dar es Salaam had to abandon a discussion of rent control 'since the Chamber was composed of both landlords and shop tenants', while a decision to oppose a bill threatening the interests of small millers led the representative of Chande Brothers to walk out.[4] Ismaili Khoja leaders had to ban conspicuous expenditure at marriages and other cere-monies. Such divisions were to affect Asian politics during the 1950s.

Outside the towns, post-war development gave a larger role to European settlement. As after the previous war, the deportation of Germans partly balanced increased British immigration. Between 1938 and 1948 the European population increased from 9,345 to 10,648, but during the next decade it doubled to 20,598.[5] Many were officials, commercial employees, or 'groundnutters', but there were also many settlers. The British authorities gave them more support than before,

[1] Bates, 'British administration', p. 275; Leslie to PCs, 29 November 1952, TNA 45/988/43; Walji, 'History', pp. 109–13, 208–33; Robert J. Bocock, 'The Ismailis in Tanzania', *British journal of sociology*, XXII (1971), 367.
[2] Amiji, 'Bohras', pp. 52–5.
[3] Adolfo C. Mascarenhas, 'Urban development in Dar es Salaam', M.A. thesis, University of California at Los Angeles, 1966, pp. 166–9; Hawkins, *Trade*, pp. 99, 103.
[4] Indian Merchants Chamber, Dar es Salaam, minutes, 13 April 1957 and 7 March 1959. I owe these references to Dr S. R. Walji.
[5] J. Clagett Taylor, *The political development of Tanganyika* (Stanford, 1963), pp. 27–8.

450

as one aspect of active government. The Colonial Office declared its policy in 1946. Government was to retain ultimate control of all land. None needed by Africans either currently or in the future might be alienated, and no compulsion might be used to evict Africans. European settlement was not to be subsidised. Within these limits, however, 'a limited amount of non-native settlement, by suitably selected persons of the right type and under conditions of proper Government control, is likely to be conducive to the economic development of the Territory'.[1] Most ex-enemy property was then re-alienated, initially on 33-year leases which were extended in 1950, under settler pressure, to the previous norm of 99 years. Between 1948 and 1959 the total amount of alienated land increased from 660,961 to 1,284,647 hectares.[2] The new guiding principle was how land could best be utilised for the territory's general benefit. The policy evoked greatest contention around Kilimanjaro and Meru. There the Germans had established a few European farms on the densely-peopled mountainsides, had drawn rings of alienated farms around the foothills, and had allowed Europeans to enclose most water sources in the plains. In the 1920s local settlers proposed to rationalise the situation by creating a homogeneous block of European land running from West Kilimanjaro across the Sanya Plain to East Meru. Originally there was talk that this block might secede to Kenya, but in 1940 the Central Development Committee adopted the plan as a means of creating a disease-free European ranching area. In 1946 Justice Mark Wilson investigated the problem and endorsed this proposal. The Chagga received 9,093 hectares of mainly ex-German land in the *vihamba* belt and southern foothills, while Kilimanjaro's western foothills were made available to Europeans. On Meru there was more difficulty, for the homogeneous European area in the eastern foothills meant moving Meru homesteads and cattle from two farms in Engare Nanyuki which Meru had bought back from Europeans between the wars. Their eviction in 1951 and the resulting 'Meru Lands Case' were direct results of land utilisation policy.[3]

The post-war decade greatly profited the sisal growers. During the war, with coffee and cotton markets depressed and Indonesian competition destroyed, they increasingly dominated the territorial

---

[1] Hall to Battershill, 21 February 1946, CO 691/186.
[2] Griffiths to Hinden, 10 October 1950, FCB papers 122, RH; Taylor, *Political development*, pp. 116–17, 210; Tanganyika, *Blue book*, 1948, p. 373.
[3] Above, p. 144; Tanganyika, *Central Development Committee*, p. 71; Tanganyika, *Report of the Arusha-Moshi lands commission* (Dar es Salaam, 1947), *passim*; below, pp. 499–503.

Table VI. *Tanganyika sisal exports, 1947–61: volume, value, and price per tonne*

Year	Tonnes (000)	Value (£000)	Price (£ per tonne)
1947	98	5,469	56
1948	119	8,930	75
1949	131	11,116	85
1950	120	11,962	100
1951	146	23,960	164
1952	163	21,708	133
1953	174	12,773	73
1954	172	10,902	63
1955	177	9,956	56
1956	190	10,823	57
1957	186	9,517	51
1958	205	10,479	51
1959	211	12,893	61
1960	205	15,027	73
1961	199	13,704	69

SOURCES: Tanganyika, *Blue books*, 1947, p. 211; 1948, p. 220; Guillebaud, *Economic survey* (1958 edn), p. 9; *ibid.* (1966 edn), p. 132.

economy. In 1948 they provided 55 per cent of export value and 47 per cent of world sisal output.[1] The subsequent boom is indicated by table VI. There were three reasons for it: post-war recovery in the industrial nations; the much slower recovery of the Indonesian sisal industry; and the Korean War of 1950, which provoked a scramble for strategic materials. The plantations enjoyed their only period of great profitability. In the peak year, 1951, the average profit of ten large and prosperous companies was 72 per cent. The same companies paid shareholders an average 37 per cent of profits over the next five years. At the same time, 27 per cent of profits were re-invested, which brought a greatly increased production after 1957. By 1958, some £20,000,000 was thought to be invested in the sisal industry.[2] Between the sisal magnate's prosperity and the poverty of Afrikaner farmers to the north of Meru was a gulf as wide as that between a Karimjee and a *dukawalla*.

[1] Tanganyika, *Blue book*, 1948, p. 220; Guillebaud, *Economic survey* (1966 edn), p. 5.
[2] Guillebaud, *Economic survey* (1958 edn), pp. 45, 48; *ibid.* (1966 edn), p. 64.

Development and deprivation in African rural societies

For African peasants the post-war period was dominated by the cash-crop boom of the early 1950s. Between 1948 and 1954 Kilimanjaro coffee prices rose from £128 to £582 per tonne and the price paid to Sukuma cotton growers increased from 53 to 132 cents per kg of seed cotton. Resulting production increases came too late to benefit fully from high prices, but agricultural export earnings rose between 1945 and 1960 from £6,215,000 to £41,000,000, the Chagga coffee crop trebled, and Sukuma cotton output multiplied five times.[1] Whereas in 1948 sisal provided 55 per cent of export earnings, by 1955 the proportion was only 28 per cent and coffee and cotton, predominantly African crops, had risen respectively from 5 to 19 and from 8 to 15 per cent of the total.[2] The scale of African commercial farming must not be exaggerated. In the early 1950s Ndendeuli tobacco growers earned 'enough for tax payment and an absolute minimum of cotton clothing of the cheapest kind', while coffee exports in 1954 were little more valuable than estimated African beer production.[3] Yet by Tanganyika's standards the cash-crop boom brought new levels of rural prosperity. Between 1933 and 1950 the average earnings of Chagga coffee growers rose from less than Shs. 100 to Shs. 750; by 1955 they were Shs. 1,600.[4] The boom was accompanied and made possible by improved transport, and specifically a massive expansion of motor traffic. Between 1943 and 1957 the number of licensed vehicles rose from 3,847 to 32,019. In 1947 Chagga owned more than 150 lorries, while four years later there were 1,400 professional Chagga drivers in Moshi district.[5] The penetration of mud roads and lorries to remote villages made possible Sukuma cotton expansion and many other agricultural developments. Reversing earlier trends, settlement increasingly concentrated along main roads.[6]

[1] *KNCU annual report 1960–1;* John C. de Wilde and others, *Experiences with agricultural development in tropical Africa* (2 vols, Baltimore, 1967), II, 427; N. R. Fuggles-Couchman, *Agricultural change in Tanganyika 1945–1960* (Stanford, 1964), p. 21.
[2] Tanganyika, *Blue book*, 1948, p. 220; *Agriculture report*, 1955, p. 44.
[3] Gulliver, *Neighbours*, p. 39; Ehrlich in Low and Smith, *History*, III, 292.
[4] Maro, 'Population', p. 83.
[5] J. R. Farquharson, *Tanganyika transport: a review* (Dar es Salaam, 1945), p. 17; John McKay, 'A guide to basic data on road transport in Tanzania', University of Dar es Salaam: Bureau of Resource Assessment and Land Use Planning, n.d., p. 18; Hill, 'Memorandum on Chagga native treasury' [July 1947] TNA 12844/II/99A; Page-Jones to Member for Local Government, 8 December 1951, TNA 12844/III/398.
[6] E.g. Eckhard Baum, 'Land use in the Kilombero valley', in Ruthenberg, *Smallholder*, p. 28.

The cash-crop boom partly blurred the distinction between export-producing, food-producing, and labour-supplying regions. Even hitherto marginal crops like Bugufi's coffee prospered during the Korean War, when coffee was adopted in such new areas as Upangwa and Ubena. In 1951 Bena, Nyiha, Nyakyusa, and other Southern Highlanders began to grow pyrethrum. The southern hinterland, the Cinderella region since Maji Maji, found a profitable crop in cashewnuts, exports from Southern Province rising between 1947 and 1960 from 1,312 to 41,288 tons.[1] Moreover, economic growth, urbanisation, and increasing export production in favoured regions stimulated the food-producing areas. Dar es Salaam's rapid growth benefited a hinterland stretching the full length of the central railway. In 1944 that weather-vane of Tanganyikan history, Erica Fiah, abandoned his editorial office in Kariakoo for rice fields at outlying Ukonga, where he inevitably organised the local food-producers into a Native Farmers Association.[2] Luguru supplied the capital with 600–700 tons of vegetables each year in the 1950s. At the end of the decade even remote Buha became a major supplier of marketed sorghum, beans, and cassava,[3] so that almost every region of Tanganyika had been drawn into commercial production by the end of the colonial period.

The most important agricultural development of the period was the new *otandibatira* in Sukumaland. Although the Lake Province was Tanganyika's main cotton producer in 1939, its 30,000 bales a year were insignificant when compared either with the area available or with Uganda's output. Sukumaland largely missed the cash-crop expansion of the 1920s because transporting a bulky product over its vast areas was so difficult. In the early 1950s relaxation of wartime price controls coincided with the cash-crop boom, cheaper motor transport, improved seed, official encouragement, and the beginnings of cooperative organisation to produce a dramatic expansion of production. In 1951 Sukumaland produced 40,669 bales of cotton; in 1954, 90,845; in 1957, 150,982.[4] Cotton became almost as central to the Sukuma economy as coffee to the Chagga or Haya, and because its expansion used more advanced technology, the results were perhaps more dramatic than in the *otandibatira* of the 1920s. The creation of a peasant society in

[1] *Agriculture reports*, 1947, p. 113, 1960, p. 32.
[2] A. Ramadhani to DA, 6 October 1947, TNA 36781/2.
[3] *Agriculture report*, 1961, p. 27.
[4] de Wilde, *Experiences*, II, 427.

Sukumaland was among Tanganyika's most important post-war developments.

Technological change accelerated after the war. Ox-drawn ploughs existed before 1939 in Sukumaland, Musoma, Arusha, and the Nyasa lakeshore, but thereafter they became increasingly common. Whereas in 1946 some 700 were in use in Rungwe, in 1958 they were generally used by rice growers there. Between 1952 and 1961 the number of ploughs employed in Sukumaland rose from some 5,000 to over 20,000.[1] Other technological innovations also spread. By 1958–9 there were 93 African-owned maize mills on Kilimanjaro, 40 in Mwanza district, and more than 30 in Tabora district.[2] Tanganyika's fertiliser imports increased nearly thirty-fold between 1945 and 1960.[3] Yet the crucial agricultural innovation was the tractor, which became an obsession with progressive farmers and was to be the true symbol of Tanganyika's first years of independence. Europeans set the example, both at Kongwa, among the large grain farmers of Northern Province, and in contract-ploughing schemes which the Agricultural Department operated in the late 1940s. In 1947 a group of Iraqw wheat growers bought a tractor,[4] and thereafter the numbers in African ownership increased rapidly. By 1958 there were 10 in the Southern Province and 71 on Kilimanjaro. Two years later 147 were engaged on contract-ploughing in Lake Province. Africans possessed some 40 in Mbulu district in 1961, and there were smaller numbers elsewhere.[5] The most striking example of mechanisation was around Mount Meru. Before the war, local entrepreneurs established small coffee plots on the mountainside. After 1945 they turned instead to the surrounding lowlands where wheat and maize could profit from government subsidies to large producers. Exploiting land tenure systems which allowed pioneers to own whatever they cleared, Arusha entrepreneurs carved out large holdings in the Musa area, while ambitious Meru soon followed their example in Kingori, Leguruki, and Mwakivaru. Initially they used ox-ploughs, but in the early 1950s they began to buy tractors. By 1958 some fifty Africans in Arusha district owned

[1] Agricultural Assistant Tukuyu to SAO Iringa, 1 August 1946, TNA 139/9/3/102; Gulliver, *Land tenure*, p. 13; *Agriculture reports*, 1952, p. 38, 1960, p. 20, 1961, p. 19.
[2] Divisional chiefs to Moshi, December 1958, TNA 5/1959/9–11; Mwanza rural DAR 1959, TNA library; Manson, Tabora DAR 1958, TNA 47/R/3/1/II/116.
[3] Fuggles-Couchman, *Agricultural change*, p. 31.
[4] Philip Raikes, 'Wheat production and the development of capitalism in north Iraqw', in Lionel Cliffe and others (ed.), *Rural cooperation in Tanzania* (Dar es Salaam, 1975), p. 91.
[5] *Agriculture reports*, 1958, p. 23, 1960, p. 20; divisional chiefs to Moshi, December 1958, TNA 5/1959/9–11; Schultz, *Veränderungen*, p. 254.

tractors, while two also possessed combine-harvesters. 'The old ox plough is slowly dying out', the district officer recorded.[1]

In the 1920s African entrepreneurs had chiefly been men with the vision to appreciate the potential profitability of relatively small changes in indigenous agriculture, often no more than planting coffee beneath bananas. Consequently the normal qualification for entrepreneurship had been the unusually wide experience and contacts available to chiefs, Christians, migrant labourers, and the like. This often remained true in the 1950s. The introduction of coffee into Upangwa in 1952 was like a repetition of what happened in other highland regions in the 1920s, with a schoolteacher fetching seeds from Umatengo and distributing them to Christians and former migrants.[2] Most large-scale cashewnut growers on the Makonde Plateau were Christians, several having previously held salaried native administration posts. Most pioneer Arusha grain-farmers were Christians from powerful families who used social influence to ensure control of their tracts of lowland.[3] Chiefs were admirably placed to benefit from contract-ploughing schemes. In 1950 Chief Towegale of lowland Ubena was laying out 160 hectares of contract-ploughed rice and pressing government for a combine-harvester. The first two tractor-owners in Buha were Chief Theresa Ntare and her sister Anna Gwassa.[4] Several chiefs contracted to plough their subjects' land. Yet despite these similarities, many entrepreneurs of the 1950s differed from the previous generation because innovation – especially where it meant tractors – was often far more expensive. Loans were rare, for few Africans could provide security. More common was hire purchase, often financed by contract-ploughing. Tractors were bought by public subscription in Upare, Singida, and Rufiji.[5] Sukumaland's cotton cooperatives also purchased machinery. Yet these collective undertakings were exceptional. Normally substantial savings had to be accumulated from other ventures.

Some entrepreneurs accumulated savings through rural activities. Among them were the wheat growers of the Karatu area in northern Mbulu – Nchi Mpya, 'the new country', to the Iraqw who opened this

---

[1] Arusha DARs 1953, 1955, 1958, TNA 471/R/3/3/I/1–8.
[2] M. M. Kihaule, 'Upangwa Farmers' Cooperative Society Ltd.', B.A. thesis, University of Dar es Salaam, 1974.
[3] Liebenow, *Colonial rule*, pp. 155–7, 329 n. 15; Arusha DAR 1953, TNA 471/R/3/3/I/1.
[4] *Agriculture report*, 1950, p. 4; Makinda, Kasulu DAR 1961, TNA library.
[5] Interview with Kinyasi Ngomoi in E. A. Lukwaro (ed.), 'Documents concerning the Wapare Union', typescript, 1970, in my possession; *Agriculture reports*, 1953, p. 25, 1955, p. 28.

area of fertile volcanic soil in the 1930s as pasture. Wheat was introduced by Afrikaner settlers. Following the famine of 1943, Iraqw imitated them, using ox-ploughs and sometimes hiring the Europeans' machinery. In 1947 Iraqw bought their first tractors and seven years later their output first exceeded 1,000 tons. The rust problem was solved in 1958 and increased production followed, until in the 1960s some Africans cultivated up to 400 hectares. Most entrepreneurs were Christians:

Few, if any, went straight into commercial wheat growing from subsistence farming. Some had been cattle-buyers, an extremely lucrative occupation in the boom conditions after the war, and others had grown onions as cash crop. Others again had worked for settlers, often as tractor drivers, and may have started as wheat farmers by taking part of their pay in cultivation of their shambas, now a common practice. Two important members of the group were government clerks, and the only ones who might be described as coming from the traditional environment were large cattle owners who thus had at their disposal a ready source of realisable capital.[1]

The other main source of capital was trade. Many tractor-owning cotton-farmers in Sukumaland had previously been shopkeepers or cattle dealers.[2] Another example was large-scale maize growing in Ismani, north of Iringa. To meet wartime food shortage government paid planting grants to European farmers who cultivated more than 10 hectares of grain. In 1947 it extended these grants to Africans. Two years later the first entrepreneurs moved into hitherto unoccupied Ismani. The pioneer, Celestino Fivawo, was a Hehe lorry-owner, while others were traders, drivers, or mechanics from Iringa town, together with some migrant farmers and native administration officials. They employed labourers, often from famine-stricken Ugogo, to cut and burn the bush and scatter maize seed broadcast on the land without any attempt at cultivation, abandoning the exhausted land after 3 annual crops. By 1951 a few maize-growers were earning up to £1,250 a year. Six years later over 16,000 hectares were under maize at Ismani. The 367 cultivators owning 4 hectares or more were drawn from thirty tribes. Twenty-nine farmers had over 40 hectares, the largest cultivating over 140 hectares. Several owned lorries. From 1955, when good harvests in Ugogo brought labour shortage, they also bought tractors.[3]

[1] Raikes in Cliffe, *Cooperation*, pp. 91–2. See also Schultz, *Veränderungen*, pp. 210–19.
[2] S. E. Migot-Adholla, 'The politics of a growers' cooperative organisation', in Cliffe, *Cooperation*, pp. 228–9.
[3] Correspondence in TNA 24/C/2/4 and 24/D/3/4; 'Ismani domesday book', typescript, 1957, TNA library; A. Awiti, 'Ismani and the rise of capitalism', in Cliffe, *Cooperation*, pp. 51–78.

Prosperous post-war societies displayed increasing signs of rural capitalism. Inequality resulted chiefly from ownership of land, control of labour, and access to the resources of the larger colonial society. Evidence of unequal land distribution abounded. A Chagga politician identified three classes on Kilimanjaro in 1949:

1. People who live on *vihamba* [home farms] and seek paid work every month;
2. People who live on *vihamba*, do not seek paid work every month, but simply remain on their *vihamba*;
3. People who live on *vihamba* and wish to have large grain farms as their own property.[1]

The third category was probably fairly small. One investigator found that 'a very few Chagga, probably mostly members of ruling clans...have single holdings of considerable size – 20–40 acres of coffee; 50–100 acres of lowland maize fields; 200–2,000 acres of grazing land'. A survey of Machame chiefdom in 1961 showed that *vihamba* varied from less than 4,000 square metres to four hectares, the average being slightly over one hectare.[2] At the other extreme, 6,615 Chagga were reckoned to be landless in 1949, but most of these were probably young men awaiting an inheritance, and an observer noted twelve years later that 'the Chagga without a *kihamba* is even today quite rare'.[3] Similar conditions existed in some other densely-populated areas. In 1967 there were thought to be 16,000 landless or almost landless Haya. In the rice-producing plain bordering Lake Nyasa the average holding in 1958 was 6,000–8,000 square metres, but a few powerful men owned 10–12 hectares. In the early 1960s many young Fipa could not obtain land within several kilometres of their villages.[4] In most areas land itself was not scarce, but the best land was. The swamp land essential for dry season grazing in Unyaturu was owned by only the oldest lineages, who commonly rented it to others. In one Lambya village in the 1960s, 10 per cent of peasant families owned 45 per cent of the best riverain land, while 34 per cent had none.[5]

---

[1] P. M. Njau, 'Kilimanjaro Chagga Union, amezaliwa Moshi' [July 1949] TNA 5/584/29.
[2] Clemm, 'Productivity', p. 104; Roy S. Beck, 'An economic study of coffee-banana farms in the Machame central area', duplicated, Dar es Salaam, 1963, p. 1.
[3] Maro, 'Population', p. 130; Clemm, 'White mountain', p. 45.
[4] B. B. Bakula, 'The effect of traditionalism on rural development', B.A. thesis, University College, Dar es Salaam, 1969, p. 19; Gulliver, *Land tenure*, pp. 16–17; Willis, 'Kamcape', p. 193.
[5] Jellicoe, 'Social change', p. 181; P. M. Van Hekken and H. U. E. Thoden van Velzen, *Land scarcity and rural inequality in Tanzania* (The Hague, 1972), pp. 20–1.

Where land was scarce it was often marketable. On Kilimanjaro, freehold ownership, which chiefs had tried to deny to coffee farmers in the 1920s, was universally accepted by 1960, to the point where land was mortgaged, sold over the owner's head by foreclosing creditors, bequeathed at the testator's discretion, and used as security for government loans. In 1946 the Chagga Council formally declared that a *kihamba* 'is a freehold property with which the owner can do whatever he likes'. Fifteen years later freehold rights were being asserted even over *shamba* land, especially by tractor farmers.[1] In Buhaya, similarly, the reallocation of land had passed from the chiefs to the market. A study suggested that over a quarter of the land under bananas in the 1960s had been purchased.[2] Enclosure of common lands for private arable farming was virtually complete on Kilimanjaro, was proceeding apace in Meru and Rungwe, and was beginning even in remote Buha and Mara once commercial crops became common. During the 1950s a meeting of farmers and headmen in Mbozi arranged a 'mutual delimitation of boundaries of land holdings', although land did not become marketable there until the 1960s.[3]

This picture of triumphant rural capitalism must be qualified, however, because capitalism met powerful resistance from older ideas and institutions. Most commercial farmers still grew their own food. Both Haya and Chagga gave bananas preference over coffee in their farming systems, and even an enthusiast for modern farming was horrified that Chagga 'might if we went on specializing in coffee come to a point where we shall have to import our food!'[4] Iraqw wheat farmers ate wheat only when they were short of other grain. There 'one may see farmers who own their own tractors and machinery hoeing maize by hand or even cultivating with a *jembe* [hoe]'.[5] In relatively highly commercialised Buhaya only an estimated 39 per cent of agricultural produce was sold in the 1960s. Most peasants planted food before cash crops lest the rains should be early and brief, although by the late 1950s some Sukuma planted maize, then cotton, and then other food crops, while a very few grew only cotton.

[1] 'A memorandum to the commissioner, Moshi-Arusha land commission, by a committee appointed by the Chagga Chiefs Council' [1946] TNA 69/913/54; Clemm, 'White mountain', ch. 15.
[2] Reining, 'Haya', pp. 247–50, 272; Friedrich in Ruthenberg, *Smallholder*, p. 181.
[3] Knight, *Ecology and change*, pp. 132, 58–9.
[4] P. M. Njau, 'A full report on recent tour of the mountain', 29 October 1952, TNA 5/25/26/128. See also Hydén, *Political development*, pp. 186–7; Clemm, 'White mountain', p. 281.
[5] Raikes in Cliffe, *Cooperation*, p. 82.

'Innovations have "added" to African agriculture', one observer commented, 'but they have not generally transformed it.'[1]

In another sense, too, older social patterns resisted capitalism. Evidence of unequal ownership might suggest that land was increasingly concentrated in capitalist hands, while others were expropriated and proletarianised. The subject needs further study, but concentration of ownership may rather have occurred only where ploughs required large holdings, while where the hoe was used the tendency was towards fragmentation through population growth. Concentration took place in the Rungwe lake plain, which produced grain by plough cultivation, and in Ismani and Karatu, where capitalists even rented land from poorer neighbours.[2] On Kilimanjaro the large farmers were those who 'wish to have large *grain* farms', for after the war Chagga entrepreneurs concentrated less on growing coffee on the mountainside than on rearing cattle or growing maize with machinery in the lowlands. Intensive hoe-cultivation probably encouraged the sub-division of holdings on Kilimanjaro, where the rapidly growing Chagga population was with difficulty accommodated in this way. There, as in Buhaya, actual fragmentation was rare – even in 1972 only 2 per cent of Chagga owned more than one piece of *kihamba* land – but in ancient areas of dense settlement fragmentation reached extraordinary levels. Some plots in Kainam were less than 1,000 square metres, while in 1934 the average Kara taxpayer owned fifteen plots of which some were only a few square metres.[3]

Many pressures encouraged sub-division and fragmentation in densely-settled areas. One was the deeply-rooted notion that every householder had a right to land. 'A Chagga without a *kihamba* is not a social being', an observer commented, and chiefs distributed plots as small as one hundred square metres to newly-married subjects.[4] Kinship also pressed wealthy landowners to make land available to poorer neighbours, as did the need for labour and clients. In the densely-populated Arusha chiefdom every householder possessed land, although 25 per cent had sub-economic holdings and 15 per cent were tenants, usually holding from kinsmen and paying no cash rent.

[1] Friedrich in Ruthenberg, *Smallholder*, p. 199; Hans Ruthenberg, *Agricultural development in Tanganyika* (Berlin, 1964), p. 22; de Wilde, *Experiences*, 1, 25.
[2] Gulliver, *Land tenure*, pp. 16–17; Rayah Feldman, 'Custom and capitalism: changes in the basis of land tenure in Ismani', *Journal of development studies*, x (1974), 313; Rweyemamu, *Underdevelopment*, p. 56.
[3] Maro, 'Population', ch. 4 (esp. p. 123); Reining, 'Haya', pp. 224–6; Schultz, *Veränderungen*, p. 74; Malcolm, 'Ukara' [1934] CO 691/141.
[4] Clemm, 'White mountain', p. 324; Johnston, 'Land tenure', p. 2.

In 1969 only 1.5 per cent of Tanganyika's householders declared that they paid any rent, although Kerewe landowners had rented land and even auctioned annual tenancies in the mid 1950s.[1] Kinship groups tried to prevent the sale of land. Land was scarce in Uluguru but little commercial development took place because lineages kept tight corporate control over property and deliberately preserved land for food-growing. In Ukara land had apparently been sold for generations but was still sold only to other Kara. In 1969 80 per cent of agricultural loans were between kin. Haya clans had no legal rights over land but exerted pressure to keep it in the clan; many clan associations had formal rules restricting land sales. Yet these were rearguard actions. Chagga clans are said to have lost all control over land by 1961.[2]

The capitalists' ambitions were resisted also by their neighbours. Nyakyusa were among many said to ostracise 'progressive' farmers who adopted soil conservation measures. In North Mara there was strong resistance to enclosures; Mrs Ogot's tale of colonisation there turns on the use of witchcraft to curb too eager entrepreneurship.[3] In societies whose structure rested on gradual transfer of land between generations, scarcity provoked intense rivalry between brothers, between sisters-in-law, between fathers and sons. In Unyakyusa it ended the formation of separate young men's villages and the resolution of disputes by migration to another village, thus confining conflict within the small community. An observer estimated in 1961 that whereas educated Chagga men commonly married at about 25, the normal age for peasants whose economic independence was at their fathers' mercy was around 30. Litigation over land on Kilimanjaro reached its peak in the mid 1950s.[4] Tanganyika's developed areas once more experienced the tensions which had marked nineteenth-century defensive settlements.

In several areas cash crops produced diminishing returns on ever smaller parcels of exhausted land. As Buhaya's slowly accumulated

---

[1] Gulliver, 'Interim report', pp. 11, 57–60; Gottlieb, 'Differentiation', p. 253; E. B. Dobson, 'Comparative land tenure of ten African tribes', *TNR*, xxxviii (1955), 36.

[2] James L. Brain, 'Ancestors as elders in Africa – further thoughts', *Africa*, xliii (1973), 128; Ludwig in Ruthenberg, *Smallholder*, pp. 129–30; Gottlieb, 'Differentiation', p. 250; Reining, 'Haya', pp. 275–80; proposed rules of 'Umoja wa ukoo wa Bakoba' [1957?] TNA 71/A/6/1/C/51; Clemm, 'White mountain', p. 316.

[3] *Agriculture report*, 1958, p. 20; Grace Ogot, *The promised land* (Nairobi, 1966).

[4] Gulliver, 'Interim report', p. 32; Sally F. Moore, 'Selection for failure in a small social field: ritual concord and fraternal strife among the Chagga', in S. F. Moore and B. G. Myerhoff (ed.), *Symbol and politics in communal ideology* (Ithaca, 1975), pp. 109–43; Wilson, *Communal rituals*, p. 206; Clemm, 'White mountain', p. 132; Maro, 'Population', p. 174.

fertility was depleted, banana yields fell and only in one post-war year did coffee exports exceed their level of 1935. Ukerewe's cotton output was maintained only by greater labour and by supplanting preferred maize and millet by increasing reliance on high-yielding but less appetising and nutritious manioc. As the Nyiha dedicated their best land and much labour to coffee they too increasingly ate manioc, supplementing its nutritional deficiencies by meat bought with coffee earnings. The growing Chagga population relied increasingly on maize from the lower mountain slopes, while coffee-growing areas almost ceased to produce finger millet for brewing and instead imported it.[1]

Yet involution was only one response to land shortage. A comparison of farm surveys in central Sukumaland in 1945 and 1962 shows that Sukuma responded to population growth by reducing livestock, abandoning millet and sorghum, growing larger acreages of maize and cotton, and exporting men and cattle to colonise new areas.[2] This contrast reinforces the distinction between two kinds of rural capitalism. One was longer-established and wealthier, but used the hoe to cultivate permanent crops on limited areas of especially well-watered land and tended to suffer involution through population growth. The other was only just establishing cash crops and was less prosperous, but used ploughs to cultivate larger farms in ample savannah land. In reality the situation was more complicated, for many peoples combined both types of farming, as did Chagga and Arusha pioneers who lived on the mountainsides but farmed the lowlands. Moreover, the contrast was obscured by the second aspect of rural capitalism: the incidence of hired labour. Both types of farming made limited use of wage-labour, chiefly at peak seasons, but it was less common in the more densely populated areas, regardless of whether plough or hoe was used, because family labour commonly took its place there. The distinction appeared in a survey of Lake Province cotton growers in 1963. In overpopulated Ukerewe the average grower spent only nine shillings a year on wages. In Kwimba population was moderately dense and each grower spent Shs. 32 on wages. In Shinyanga, however, population density was only half Kwimba's and farmers averaged Shs. 110 on wages, while in Geita, where Kwimba's hoe-cultivation had been

---

[1] *Agriculture report*, 1952, p. 36; Dietrich von Rotenhan, 'Cotton farming in Sukumaland', in Ruthenberg, *Smallholder*, p. 77; Knight, *Ecology and change*, pp. 138–42; Clemm, 'White mountain', pp. 299–300.

[2] M. P. Collinson, 'The economic characteristics of the Sukuma farming system', seminar paper, University of Dar es Salaam, 1972.

exported to a less densely-populated area, hired labour was again common.[1] In Buhaya wage-labour seems to have been more common in the more recently opened coffee regions of Ihangiro than in the longer-established areas, where only 6 per cent of agricultural labour was hired (at a cost of twenty or thirty shillings) during 1964 and peasants rarely cultivated for more than two or three hours a day.[2] The most extensive use of hired labour was naturally in the new areas of large-scale commercial farming. Of African farmers regularly employing labour in 1967, 31 per cent grew cotton, 15 per cent cereals, and only 13 per cent coffee or tea.[3] Tanganyika's most prosperous capitalist farmers grew tobacco at Urambo under a scheme supervised and initially financed by the East African Tobacco Company. In 1963–4 each of the larger mechanised holdings there paid an average of Shs. 4,040 in wages. Ismani showed comparable patterns, while several Makonde pioneers had 60–80 hectares of cashew trees worked by immigrant labourers from Mozambique. 'Anyone who can afford it hires labourers', Dr Swantz has written of Uzaramo, '...and as the cashew nut season approaches extra labour is hired for clearing the underbush and later for picking the cashew...A man can be a good farmer only if he is in a position to hire labourers.'[4]

Thus the paradox of rural capitalism was that what caused land scarcity and freehold ownership also made it possible to use family rather than hired labour, thereby revitalising the pre-capitalist lineage mode of production. In Ukerewe land was scarce but family labour sufficed, whereas in Shinyanga labour was hired but land was not yet marketable. This lack of correlation retarded the development of capitalism on classical lines, so that rich farmers remained rare and politically weak in Tanganyika – a fact of great political significance.[5] It ensured that rural societies remained complex and still largely uninvestigated amalgams of kinship and the cash nexus: that the new did not replace the old but mingled with it. Before analysing the resulting hybrid, however, it is necessary to examine a third disparity: unequal access to the resources of the larger colonial society. This is

[1] Rotenhan in Ruthenberg, *Smallholder*, p. 55; Kenneth R. M. Anthony and V. C. Uchendu, *Agricultural change in Geita district* (Nairobi, 1974), p. 20.
[2] Jørgen and Karen Rald, *Rural organization in Bukoba district* (Uppsala, 1975), pp. 47, 70; Friedrich in Ruthenberg, *Smallholder*, pp. 198, 206; Reining, 'Haya', p. 132.
[3] Gottlieb, 'Differentiation', p. 247.
[4] Walter Scheffler, 'Tobacco schemes in the central region', in Ruthenberg, *Smallholder*, p. 293; Liebenow, *Colonial rule*, p. 39; Swantz, *Ritual*, pp. 68, 102.
[5] See Issa G. Shivji, *Class struggles in Tanzania* (London, 1976), pp. 50–2.

best approached by examining an area of rural activity where its effects were especially clear: the cooperative movement.[1]

In 1944 Tanganyika possessed three cooperative unions: the largely autonomous KNCU and the Ngoni-Matengo and Bugufi cooperatives which were mainly front organisations enabling the Agricultural Department to control local tobacco and coffee crops. Expansion waited on the ending of wartime marketing controls in the late 1940s, for cooperatives were pointless while prices were fixed. Subsequent growth – from 79 registered societies with 60,445 members in 1949 to 691 societies with 326,211 members in 1960[2] – made Tanganyika's cooperative movement the largest in tropical Africa. Cooperatives were usually tribal. Their grandiose headquarters at Moshi, Mwanza, Tukuyu, Same, and elsewhere were status symbols in a growing inter-tribal competition. Envy of existing societies was a common motive for cooperation. 'My friends', a Haya wrote in 1939, 'do you not know that the Asians' object is to close our path and to make us their servants?...We shall be fools to be beaten even by the Warundi of Bugufi, who have succeeded in selling their coffee together and obtaining good prices.'[3] This appeal shows that cooperation was also a response to African traders' failure to wrest the produce trade from Asian control, itself partly a consequence of the territory's poverty and the economic discontinuity of the early twentieth century. Where African traders were most successful, cooperation faced greatest difficulty. In Bukoba most coffee growers favoured cooperation and a union was constructed between 1949 and 1954, but it was strongly opposed by the numerous African coffee traders.[4] Yet this was untypical. More significant was the fact that largely unsuccessful African traders themselves took the lead in forming the Sukuma cotton cooperatives which composed the Victoria Federation of Cooperative Unions, the biggest cooperative organisation in Africa.

The Sukuma cooperative movement emerged from antagonism to Asian cotton buyers. In 1946 several growers in Ukerewe bought scales, 'constituted themselves as unofficial weighers and in some instances collected cotton from growers and sold in bulk to the cotton buyers'.[5] The practice spread into the Mwanza and Geita districts, but

[1] The following analysis derives from John S. Saul, 'Marketing cooperatives in a developing country: the Tanzanian case', in Lionel Cliffe and J. S. Saul (ed.), *Socialism in Tanzania* (2 vols, Nairobi, 1972–3), II, 141–52.
[2] Fuggles-Couchman, *Agricultural change*, p. 48.
[3] B. Rutahiwa in *Kwetu*, 3 August 1939.
[4] H. Rugizibwa to Bukoba, 3 July 1956, TNA 71/A/6/16/47.
[5] Russell, Mwanza DAR 1946, TNA 41/128/20/8.

grievances remained because the merchants had a monopoly and could refuse to buy except on their own terms. Two initiatives came from men with experience wider than the ordinary peasant's. In July 1950 progressive farmers in Geita district formed the Buchosa Farmers Union (later the Mweli Farmers Union), its five leaders being a former sisal estate clerk, a fisherman, an ex-military signaller, a former agricultural instructor, and a retired policeman.[1] The other initiative came from African traders in Mwanza town who had failed to break Asian control of cotton-buying.[2] The key figure was the secretary of the traders' association, Paul Bomani, the son of a Sukuma Adventist preacher. In December 1950 Bomani arranged meetings in Ukerewe and Mwanza districts to discuss cooperation, playing on Asian unscrupulousness and contrasting conditions in Buhaya and Kilimanjaro. 'We want unity', one meeting resolved; 'we are tired of doing our work for the Asians.' Nothing concrete resulted until 1952, when Bomani studied cooperation in Uganda, toured Sukumaland collecting funds, founded the Lake Province Growers Association, and obtained government recognition. Three years later the primary societies were amalgamated into the VFCU. By 1959 this handled the whole crop and was also gaining control of ginning.

Many Sukuma grew cotton and the cooperative primary societies were genuine community enterprises. At its higher levels, however, VFCU leaders were overwhelmingly those whom Mr Saul has aptly called 'activists' in contrast to 'parochials', activists being characterised by literacy, education, employment or trading experience outside the locality, and often large-scale agricultural enterprise.[3] The VFCU's first president was Masanja Shija, the former sisal estate clerk who had led the Mweli Farmers, while an early vice-president was Daudi Kabeya Murangira from Majita, who had sold his fishing boats to grow cotton.[4] Bomani himself was general manager. Such activists commonly led cooperatives. The Ismani African Maize Growers Cooperative Society developed from an informal association of large maize-growers, each with a Shs. 100 share, who continued to dominate the larger organisation. The Kasulu Coffee Cooperative Society was organised by large growers led by the husband of Mwami Theresa Ntare, the most powerful chief in the territory. The Nguu Coffee Growers Cooperative Society had a Legislative Councillor as its secretary, drew

[1] Correspondence in TNA 251/30/1.   [2] Maguire, '*Uhuru*', pp. 83–99.
[3] Saul in Cliffe and Saul, *Socialism*, II, 143. See also Rayah Feldman, 'Ismani', in F. G. Bailey (ed.), *Debate and compromise* (Oxford, 1973), pp. 280–308.
[4] Magoti in Iliffe, *Tanzanians*, pp. 183–8.

465

most members from Dar es Salaam, and aimed 'to enable members to own farms without working on them themselves'.[1]

Post-war Tanganyika's wealthier areas were in an early stage of class formation. Unequal access to land, labour, and external resources was producing a class of capitalist farmers seeking to accumulate their communities' resources and monopolise their external relations, but the trend was retarded and obscured by older attitudes and relations of production. Kinship obligations often bound rich and poor together. Since each community stood in opposition to the colonial regime, local capitalist became local champion when, for example, a cooperative society sought official recognition. Students of rural societies in the 1950s and 1960s – a time of extreme social mobility – generally reported a lack of overt class hostility even in highly differentiated areas.[2] Perhaps the only overt class conflict among rural Africans in colonial Tanganyika was between *nyarubanja* owners and tenants.[3] Class consciousness usually develops first among the rich, but the rich lacked political power and often subordinated their collective interests to competition with each other.

The predominant social pattern in peasant societies was neither class nor kinship but clientage – a transitional pattern appropriate to the peasant's transitional status.[4] Poor men lined up behind wealthy men who provided work and land and leadership in return for labour and deference and political support. The nucleus of a clientage was often a powerful lineage, so that economic and kinship ties were inextricably fused. In Unyaturu the patrons were owners of marshland grazing who used this scarce resource to oblige other members of supposedly cooperative herding groups to look after their cattle for them. In Rungwe wealthy men were commonly from the families of chiefs or headmen and were elder sons.[5] There communal work parties often consisted of a powerful man's clients working on his behalf, although in less developed areas communal work remained more egalitarian.[6]

---

[1] Kasambala, 'Report on a visit to Iringa proposed maize growers cooperative society' [October 1952] TNA 24/C/2/4/98; Mitchell, Kasulu DAR 1959, TNA library; DC Handeni to RG, 2 July 1954, TNA 6/A/6/1/18.

[2] Gulliver, *Land tenure*, p. 17; Van Hekken and Thoden van Velzen, *Land scarcity*, p. 14; Schultz, *Veränderungen*, p. 256.　　　　　　　　　[3] Below, p. 506.

[4] This paragraph is based chiefly on Van Hekken and Thoden van Velzen, *Land scarcity*, *passim*.

[5] Harold K. Schneider, *The Wahi Wanyaturu* (Chicago, 1970), p. 30; H. A. Luning and others, 'A farm economic survey in Rungwe district', duplicated, Leyden, 1969, p. 87.

[6] Van Hekken and Thoden van Velzen, *Land scarcity*, p. 34; Rigby, *Cattle*, pp. 38–40; Gulliver, *Neighbours*, ch. 6.

Corruption and nepotism – normal accompaniments of clientage – were probably widespread in native administrations and cooperatives.[1] Above all, political action in peasant societies – as on Kilimanjaro in the 1930s – was the work of coalitions, of groups of clientages. This pattern characterised post-war Tanganyika's rural protests and that greatest of coalitions, the nationalist movement.

Regional disparity remained much more striking than social differentiation. Developed peasant societies had been profoundly transformed by production for the market and by state power, literacy, and world religions. Dr von Clemm's study of the Lyamungo area of Kilimanjaro in 1960–1 provides an illustration.[2] Land remained the basis of Lyamungo's peasant society; it was unevenly distributed and enviously coveted, but most men still possessed the plot which made them social beings, although perhaps a third supplemented their incomes by wages. Three homesteads in five had concrete houses. Bananas remained the preferred food, supplemented by lowland maize, and meat was eaten almost daily. Virtually all Chagga – men, women and children – drank beer and tea, although seldom coffee. Many peasants wore secondhand clothes imported from America. Beneath overt egalitarianism, peasant society was innovative and ruthlessly competitive. One object of competition was education, valued almost entirely in terms of money and power. Land, agricultural machinery, motor vehicles, and commercial success were also coveted. Branches of the major banks existed on the mountainside, while numerous moneylenders charged interest of twenty per cent or more each month. Men disguised their wealth, many, including some chiefs, posting 'Private. Keep Out!' notices around their modern houses. Yet the capitalist ethic was so universal that little class conflict was evident. Clans and extended families had limited influence, but nuclear families were tight-knit property-holding groups often subject to much internal tension. Over eighty per cent of Chagga were Christians and their attitudes dominated public opinion. Western medicine was highly valued. Indigenous rituals seldom took place. Muslims formed a tight-knit outgroup, but the few followers of indigenous religions were viewed with embarrassment.

Kilimanjaro was at one end of the spectrum of Tanganyika's

[1] Norman N. Miller, 'Village leadership and modernization in Tanzania: rural politics among the Nyamwezi', Ph.D. thesis, Indiana University, 1966, p. 114; Young, Kasulu DAR 1947, TNA library; Allan to Provincial Agricultural Officer Southern Highlands, 5 February 1957, TNA 33/A/3/35/36; Feldman in Bailey, *Debate*, p. 299.
[2] Clemm, 'White mountain', *passim*. He chose Lyamungo as an area of maximum change.

societies. Close to the other end was Buha. Remote from territorial communications, invaded by tsetse, and subject to a reactionary Tusi regime, Buha remained a labour reservoir, recruitment reaching its peak in 1952. 'Bring WAHA BACHELORS', a sisal planter instructed his recruiter, '. . . they can live four or five in a house.'[1] Between the wars the British sporadically attempted to establish cash crops in Buha, but depression prices discouraged them and gradually the labour reservoir stereotype became fixed in British minds. In 1952 government promised employers not to 'press' established migrants to grow high-priced cash crops, while the local provincial commissioner said bluntly that Buha's function was to supply labour.[2] A district officer described Tusi rule as a thinly-veiled welter of blood, corruption, and intrigue, adding, however, that the people 'give no indication of dissatisfaction' with it.[3] Crime was widespread. The *bateko* clan heads who had allocated land and been a partial counterweight to Tusi chiefs had been abolished as corrupt. In 1959–60 all sub-chiefs were Tusi except one commoner married to a Tusi. Powerful Tusi commanded hundreds of clients through cattle loans.[4] Many Ha still wore skins, barkcloth, or sacking. 'The height of a man's ambition', wrote a district officer, 'would appear to be the ownership of an umbrella.'[5] Only food exports in the late 1950s began to relieve this poverty.

Although high export prices tended to even out regional inequalities, post-war development generally benefited more developed areas. 'Up to now', Hamza Mwapachu complained in 1950, 'it is everything in Dar es Salaam to the neglect and expense to the other centres in the territory.' The plan of 1946 proposed to spend £4.56 per person in Northern Province and £4.13 in Eastern (including Dar es Salaam), but only £0.87 in Central Province and £0.66 in Western – in close proportion to existing wealth.[6] Mechanisation accentuated the tendency. A survey in the early 1960s showed annual farm returns ranging from £640 on mechanised tobacco farms at Urambo to £35 in a remote part of Usambara. The degree of commercialisation in the two areas was ninety and four per cent.[7] In 1961 monetary income

[1] Quoted in Tambila, 'History', p. 32.
[2] Sago, 'Labour migration', pp. 33, 36.
[3] Kibondo DAR 1951, TNA 202/R/3/A/2/1951.
[4] Johan H. Scherer, 'Marriage and bride-wealth in the highlands of Buha', doctoral thesis, Rijksuniversiteit te Utrecht, 1965, pp. 29–31, 37; James L. Brain, 'The Tutsi and the Ha', *Journal of Asian and African studies*, VIII (1973), 44.
[5] Yonge, Kasulu DAR 1957, TNA library.
[6] Mwapachu to Hinden, 16 August 1950, FCB papers 121, RH; Tanganyika, *A ten-year development and welfare plan for Tanganyika* (Dar es Salaam, 1946), p. 41.
[7] Ruthenberg, *Smallholder*, p. 328 (facing).

per head in Tanga Province was estimated to be nearly six times that of Central Province,[1] which, like Buha, remained chiefly a labour reservoir.

Post-war development swelled the labour force in the late 1940s and early 1950s, but thereafter demand levelled off, not keeping pace with growing population.[2] Money wages barely kept pace with inflation. In 1950 a sisal cutter's average wage for a working month, including bonus, was Shs. 26, plus food conventionally valued at Shs. 12. This was probably less in real terms than at any time for sixty years. In 1951 sisal wages increased by seven shillings a month; by 1954 a further six shillings were added. If another five shillings are included for the rising value of food, cutters' money wages in 1954 were 273 per cent higher than in 1939, while the Dar es Salaam price index was 300 per cent higher. No real increase took place until 1958, when trade union activity transformed the situation.[3]

After the war some long-standing sources of labour were not available. Up to 30,000 men from Northern Rhodesia had worked in Tanganyika each year in the late 1930s, but during the war they were attracted away to the Copperbelt.[4] Southern Africa also drew southern Tanganyika into its orbit. A few Tanganyikans had worked there since German times, but large-scale migration began with the war. In 1942 over fifty men, chiefly Nyakyusa, entered Northern Rhodesia each month, but the main target was the Rand because the Witwatersrand Native Labour Association provided free transport from the Tanganyikan border to Johannesburg. In 1945 it forwarded 2,301 Tanganyikans.[5] Having earned a high reputation as underground miners and the cash needed for bus fares, the Nyakyusa thereafter preferred the Copperbelt's higher wages and less authoritarian conditions. In 1947 some 2,000 men from Rungwe district were working there. In 1954, when southward migration probably reached its peak, there were thought to be 7,400 Tanganyikans working in Northern Rhodesia, 3,150 in Southern Rhodesia, and 10,080 on the Rand. Southern Africa's attraction was simply higher wages. In 1954, when sisal cutters earned Shs. 39 a month plus food, surface workers on the Copperbelt earned Shs. 99–121 and underground miners Shs. 110–133.[6]

---

[1] Hawkins, *Trade*, p. 43. [2] See the annual labour census figures in *Labour reports*.
[3] Above, p. 354; tabulation in TNA 24693/11/193; *Labour report*, 1953, p. 82; Iliffe, 'Dockworkers', p. 123; below, p. 541.
[4] *Annual report of the East African sisal industry, 1946* (Tanga, 1947).
[5] Above, p. 162; CS Lusaka to CS Dar es Salaam, 30 July 1942, and WNLA to CS, 17 October 1947, TNA 10218/11/12 and 94.
[6] *Labour report*, 1947, p. 17; Gulliver, 'Nyakyusa migration', pp. 32, 48.

As certain labour sources fell away, other regions experienced greater pressure. Some began large-scale migration for the first time. Shambaa dreaded malarial sisal plantations, but in the 1950s over-population and economic stagnation compelled up to a third of Shambaa taxpayers to work there each year. Agricultural stagnation amidst inflation and rising expectations made migration from Upogoro common after the war. Similar motives, reinforced by a disastrous resettlement programme, converted a steady Ngindo migration into 'a veritable tidal wave' during the early 1950s.[1] Much labour came from outside Tanganyika. Rwanda and Burundi together supplied 12 per cent of Korogwe's sisal workers in 1956, while 11 per cent were from Mozambique and 7 per cent from Northern Rhodesia and Nyasaland.[2] These 'foreigners' often did the unpopular work of cutting sisal. Yet the chief labour exporters remained remote regions of Tanganyika. The early 1950s were the peak years of Ha and Ngoni migration. Neither coffee, reforming legislation, nor official prohibition affected the exodus from Bugufi. Between 1949 and 1958 the numbers crossing the Kyaka ferry to work in Uganda rose from 6,573 to 24,704.[3]

Tanganyika's post-war development was of a specifically colonial kind. It was export-orientated development. Between 1945 and 1955 domestic exports increased from £8,083,588 to £36,199,000, a doubling of value at constant prices. In 1954 domestic exports formed 46 per cent of monetary gross domestic product. Probably a quarter of all productive activity was devoted to exports.[4] Dependence on Britain increased, for one effect of war and planning was to increase the proportion of trade conducted with the metropolis, although this proportion remained small by colonial standards. Whereas in 1936 27 per cent of Tanganyika's imports were from the United Kingdom, the figure rose in 1948 to 47 per cent, falling again by 1961 to 37 per cent. The proportion of Tanganyika's exports which went to the United Kingdom in those years was 23, 52, and 36 per cent.[5] Much of the

[1] Lushoto DAR 1952, TNA 72/62/6/III/234; Larson, 'History', pp. 364–5; Crosse-Upcott, 'Social structure', pp. 79–89.

[2] P. H. Gulliver, 'Alien Africans in the Tanga region', duplicated, 1956, p. 34, Cory papers, ULD.

[3] *Labour reports*, 1949, p. 23, 1958, p. 18.

[4] Tanganyika, *Blue book*, 1945, p. 186; Tanganyika, *Development plan 1961–4*, p. 6; Henry Bienen, *Tanzania: party transformation and economic development* (Princeton, 1969), p. 269 n. 12; Ehrlich in Low and Smith, *History*, III, 312.

[5] Tanganyika, *Blue books*, 1936, pp. 144 and 177, 1948, p. 213; Great Britain, *Report... on the administration of Tanganyika for the year 1950*, p. 308; Tanganyika, *Budget survey 1962–63* (Dar es Salaam, 1962), pp. 13–14.

increase was due to London's emergence as Europe's main sisal market during the war. After 1945 Tanganyika became somewhat closer to a British colony in an economic sense, following a pattern common throughout British Africa at that time. Yet Tanganyika's wealth increased less quickly than that of other countries. It scarcely felt the post-war industrial development taking place in Kenya and Uganda, Northern Rhodesia and West Africa. In 1925 Cameron had thought Tanganyika more advanced than Nigeria.[1] Thirty years later it was among Britain's poorest territories.

By the late 1950s Tanganyika displayed an extraordinary range of levels of development and technology. 'Walking through Meru country', an observer commented, 'one can see men, women and children cultivating with digging sticks, men, women and children using iron hoes, men ploughing with oxen, and some men ploughing with tractors.'[2] The same juxtaposed diversity was evident in such cultural activities as dance. In 1960 a visitor observed four popular dance styles in Upangwa. One was a long-established mode, two dated from the war, and the fourth – preferred by the young – was a variant of *dansi*, which penetrated the countryside after broadcasting began in 1951. In Ukerewe and elsewhere it replaced the 'era of the dance' by individualised dancing in an international style.[3] This coexistence of diverse technologies and cultural modes was the concrete evidence that postwar Tanganyika was becoming a more complicated country.

These patterns of change intertwined with long-term trends. Maize continued to oust 'old-fashioned' millet and sorghum as the staple food of the savannah, notably in Sukumaland where the area of sorghum fell between 1950 and 1969 from some 200,000 hectares to less than 40,000.[4] Manioc also continued to spread, either as famine reserve and cash crop in Kigoma and the Kilombero valley, or as high-yielding substitute for preferred grains in Ukerewe, Ukara, Unyiha, and Usambara.[5] The quality of the rains and the harvest still chiefly determined economic prosperity. Drought still caused serious food shortages, but relief measures became increasingly efficient as transport improved. Twice in the period, in 1948–50 and 1952–5,

---

[1] Cameron, *Tanganyika service*, p. 16. [2] Puritt, 'Meru', p. 186.
[3] Gerhard Kubik, 'Musikinstrumente und Tänze bei den Wapangwa', *Mitteilungen der anthropologischen Gesellschaft in Wien*, XCI (1961), 145–7; Hartwig, 'Historical and social role', p. 56; Ranger, *Dance*, ch. 5.
[4] L. C. Brown, 'Sorghum in western Tanganyika', duplicated, Ukiriguru, n.d., pp. 17–19 (in ULD).
[5] Kigoma DAR 1954, TNA 180/27/22/140; Ruthenberg, *Smallholder*, pp. 25, 77, 105, 146; Knight, *Ecology and change*, pp. 138–42.

drought caused famines which in the past would have killed enormous numbers, but although several Sandawe died in 1948–50 there is no evidence of deaths in the later famine.[1]

There were still areas where settlement was retreating before the natural ecosystem. They were labour-exporting areas. In Buha sleeping-sickness concentrations disintegrated during the war owing to lack of supervision, soil exhaustion, and probably the continuing drain of labour, so that sleeping-sickness cases in Kibondo district rose to 272 in 1949 and 161 in 1955.[2] In Kondoa, similarly, the disease returned in 1947. Continuing emigration made population growth in Unyamwezi lower than anywhere else in the territory and too low to recolonise the land.[3] Yet these were exceptions, for the post-war decade was generally a time of rapid colonisation, a major advance in man's struggle with nature. Even Kongwa's creaking bulldozers regained small areas for human settlement, but the chief impetus came from change within African societies. One was population growth, now widespread and increasingly rapid, which swelled Tanganyika's African population from 7,410,269 in 1948 to 8,665,336 in 1957.[4] Returning to Unyakyusa in 1955 after twenty years, Professor Wilson noticed the disappearance of pasture. Lakeshore Haya began to colonise the wastelands of Karagwe and Biharamulo. Chagga developed a type of banana which would grow in the dry, wind-swept lowlands. Devoting the volcanic soil of their central plateau to coffee, Nyiha pushed food plots into the surrounding bush, converting it gradually into treeless cultivation steppe and driving back the game until fences could be neglected. High coffee prices enabled some growers in Karagwe to buy cattle from Usukuma and begin to restock the highlands. More commonly, however, the colonist was not a herdsman but a tractor farmer. The acquisitiveness of Meru and Arusha grain farmers powered the land rush which first cultivated the plains below Mount Meru. In 1953 the Chagga Council began to allocate blocks of up to 300 acres in the plains to farmers cultivating maize with tractors.[5] Throughout

[1] Newman, *Sandawe*, pp. 76–9; Brooke, 'Heritage', pp. 17–18; B. J. Dudbridge, 'Report on the 1949/1950 famine in the Maswa district', typescript, n.d., RH. For a severe famine in Ungindo, see Crosse-Upcott, 'Social structure', p. 70.
[2] Kibondo DARs 1951 and 1957, TNA 202/R/3/A/2.
[3] Tanganyika, *African census 1957*, p. 42; Ford, *Trypanosomiases*, p. 215.
[4] Tanganyika, *African census 1957*, p. 18.
[5] Wilson, *Communal rituals*, p. 205; M. A. Hirst, 'A migration survey in Bukoba town', Department of Geography, Makerere University, 1971, p. 61; Maro, 'Population', p. 153; Knight, *Ecology and change*, p. 13; S. M. Kachuchuru, 'A historical survey of

Tanganyika control of the *Grenzwildnisse* became an important political issue.

The most notable advances were in Mbulu and Usukuma, which were two of the five problem areas for which post-war administrators devised special development schemes, the others being Kondoa, Usambara, and Uluguru. The administrators responsible for these plans saw themselves as protectors of the peasants, fearing the human and political consequences if peasant society disintegrated. Rarely realising that their policy of maximising participation in the world economy was the chief solvent of rural society, officials instead identified two enemies. One was the African capitalist farmer. Officials felt deeply, if obscurely, that capitalism was somehow improper for Africans, like gin or politics. 'This is obviously a capitalist community', one wrote of Mbozi, 'and amongst natives...is to be depracated.'[1] Policy therefore aimed to resist rural capitalism, attempting, for example, to preserve communal land tenure. The peasant's second enemy was thought to be himself, for his short time-horizon led him to ruin his land unless prevented. For agriculturalists the post-war priority was to rehabilitate eroded land so that positive development could follow.[2] Erosion was thought to have several causes: overconcentration of men and animals in limited areas, shifting cultivation, the feckless burning of bush and trash, cultivation of slopes, failure to construct anti-erosion barriers, and many others. The remedy was instruction backed by native authority legislation. As a prominent agriculturalist put it, 'the African must be compelled to help himself'.[3]

The Mbulu Development Scheme was an outstanding success, opening 1,700 square kilometres of new pasture through communal bush-clearing and achieving a 17 per cent reduction of the cattle herds in order to relieve the congestion of the Iraqw people, who had been pinned against the rift valley escarpment by the spread of tsetse. Ironically, the scheme was so successful that the Iraqw could partly abandon the intensive agriculture which Europeans admired at Kainam.[4] This indicated the reasons for the scheme's success: it was a *development* scheme which reduced agricultural drudgery while

Banyambo economy in Karagwe district 1860–1960', M.A. thesis, University of Dar es Salaam, 1975, pp. 156–7; above, p. 455; Clemm, 'White mountain', pp. 319–20.
[1] Agricultural Assistant Tukuyu to Mbeya, 3 February 1944, TNA 33/A/3/13/615.
[2] Tanganyika, *Ten-year development plan*, p. 14.
[3] Rounce to Hinden, 2 March 1945, FCB papers 121, RH.
[4] Schultz, *Veränderungen*, pp. 179–85; correspondence in TNA 38504/1.

increasing the land available to cattle-owners and grain-farmers. By contrast, the Sukumaland Development Scheme was only partially successful. A gigantic piece of social engineering costing some £2,000,000, it sought to redistribute Sukuma population from over-populated Mwanza and Kwimba districts by clearing tsetse bush and providing water supplies in the peripheral Geita, Maswa, and Shinyanga districts, while also requiring Sukuma to protect their land by adopting a balanced system of mixed farming. The second part of the scheme failed. Farming was not intensified – cotton yields scarcely changed during the decade – and the enforcement measures aroused bitter hostility until they were abandoned amidst disorder in 1958. But as an aid to continued recolonisation the scheme succeeded. Between 1947 and 1966 an estimated 5,500 square kilometres of Sukumaland was reclaimed from tsetse, mostly in Geita, Maswa, and Shinyanga. In the decade after 1948 Geita's population rose by 93 per cent. In 1956 the district produced a third of Tanganyika's total cotton output. Instead of encouraging balanced peasant husbandry, the Sukumaland Scheme stimulated a capitalist land rush.[1]

Thus the Mbulu and Sukumaland Schemes succeeded in so far as they coincided with African drives towards capitalism and colonisation. This conclusion is supported by the failure of the other three schemes, all in areas of agricultural involution. In Kondoa the object was to remedy erosion on the Kolo Plateau by relocating in the surrounding plains the men and animals driven from them by tsetse. Ill-planned, dependent on compulsion, and enmeshed in local hostility to the chief who enforced the measures, the scheme collapsed in the later 1950s.[2] The Usambara Scheme centred on hillside terracing, at the cost of enormous labour, and also became enmeshed with opposition to the native authority. It was abandoned in 1958, its improvement measures – terraces, manure, irrigation – surviving only on plots producing vegetables for the Tanga market.[3] Drudgery and political conflict also killed the Uluguru Scheme, which again centred on terracing an overpopulated mountain area lacking a profitable cash crop.[4] In such deprived regions government could not offer the

---

[1] Malcolm, *Sukumaland, passim;* de Wilde, *Experiences,* II, 415–50; Maguire, '*Uhuru*', pp. 19–30; Ford, *Trypanosomiases,* pp. 198–201; *Agricultural report,* 1956, p. 36.

[2] Correspondence in TNA 46/D/3/7; John D. Kesby, 'Warangi reaction to agricultural change', EAISR conference paper, 1965.

[3] Correspondence in TNA 33049/I–V; Attems in Ruthenberg, *Smallholder,* pp. 137–74.

[4] Young and Fosbrooke, *Land and politics, passim;* F. H. Page-Jones and J. R. P. Soper, 'A departmental enquiry into the disturbed situation in the Uluguru chiefdom', duplicated, 1955, Cory papers, ULD; Mlahagwa, 'Agricultural change', *passim.*

incentives to make worthwhile the drudgery involved in schemes which attacked only the symptoms and not the causes of deprivation. Successful schemes took place only in regions which were able to develop within the framework of the colonial economy.

Nation-building

After the war the Colonial Office resolved not to retreat from Africa in disarray but to take the initiative in creating viable and friendly successor states. 'In a word', the Colonial Secretary declared in 1947, 'we are nation-building.'[1] So far as East Africa was concerned, Britain's main concern was Kenya, which was a potential base for operations in the Middle East, had a valuable port at Mombasa, and included a European community whose aspirations, unacceptable to the Labour Party and so to any government of the 1940s, were the main obstacle to nation-building. The war had demonstrated the advantages of uniting the three East African administrations, the need for a common representative body, and the dangers of settler predominance. In December 1945, therefore, government proposed to unite the territories' common services with a nominated Central Legislative Assembly containing equal unofficial representation of the three races. European hostility forced the abandonment of racial parity in order to salvage administrative union, but federation remained the long-term objective. For Britain – as for contemporary Africans – the obstacle to rational policies was race. Tanganyika, intrinsically unimportant, was seen as the point of balance between white-dominated Kenya and black-dominated Uganda.[2]

Within each territory devolution meant gradually transforming two institutions: the Executive Council, an inner cabinet of officials established in Tanganyika in 1920; and the Legislative Council, set up in 1926 as a forum where administrators debated legislation and public issues with nominated unofficials. Colonial Office policy was gradually to incorporate unofficials into the Executive Council. Three Europeans and an Asian were nominated in 1939, the first African followed in 1951, and in 1948 Executive Councillors were made responsible for particular government departments. In 1945 the first two Africans were nominated to Legislative Council: Chief Abdiel Shangali of Machame and Chief Kidaha Makwaia of Busiha. They were joined in

[1] Quoted in Haqqi, *Colonial policy*, p. 117.
[2] Correspondence in CO 822/108, 111, 114.

June 1947 by Chief Adam Sapi of Uhehe and in April 1948 by a Tanga-educated Muslim teacher from Dar es Salaam, Juma Mwindadi. This made unofficial representation four Africans, three Asians, and seven Europeans, with fifteen European officials preserving an official majority.[1] Twice between 1945 and 1948 the unofficials declined the offer of a majority in the council.[2] Tanganyika's constitutional progress was meagre, as the first U.N. Visiting Mission complained in 1948.[3] The Colonial Office took this criticism seriously. When Twining left for Tanganyika in 1949 he had instructions to 'reform the old-fashioned Colonial constitution' before the U.N. returned in 1951.[4]

As a career administrator and natural autocrat Twining cared little for constitutions. What Tanganyika needed, he believed, was economic development and good administration, not politics.[5] Yet he had his orders and he toured the country sounding unofficial views. After experience in Mauritius and the Caribbean, he admired Tanganyika's race relations but found that political interest was slight. Legislative Councillors urged him to preserve the status quo. The Asian community impressed him. 'They are the best I have met in the colonies', Twining wrote. 'They are compactly organised and disciplined. Their representatives in Council take a reasonable view...I should like to adopt a more positive policy regarding the Indians.'[6] The Europeans were disappointing. Apart from a few rabid settler politicians in the Northern Province, 'There is a general apathy towards politics amounting to indifference'.[7] This was an underestimate, and so was Twining's assessment of African politics, for having missed the wartime ferment and arrived at a moment of temporary quiescence, he concluded that 'very little interest is taken in anything other than strictly local affairs'.[8] Twining's enquiries stirred only mild interest. In June 1949 a multi-racial group formed a Tanganyika Electoral Association to advocate elections to the Legislative Council, but it aroused more suspicion than support.[9]

In October 1949 Twining offered the Colonial Office his constitu-

[1] Taylor, *Political development*, chs. 3–4.
[2] Cohen to Twining, 1 November 1949, Hall papers, ULD.
[3] UN, *Report of the visiting mission, 1948*, pp. 3–4.
[4] Lord Twining, 'The last nine years in Tanganyika', *African affairs*, LVIII (1959), 16.
[5] Bates, *Gust of plumes*, pp. 224–5.
[6] Twining to Cohen, 11 October 1949, Hall papers, ULD.
[7] Bates, *Gust of plumes*, p. 221.
[8] Twining to Cohen, 11 October 1949, Hall papers, ULD.
[9] *Tanganyika standard* (weekly), 9 and 16 July 1949.

tional proposals. Urban ratepayers should elect township authorities and Tanga should follow Dar es Salaam towards municipal status. Each province should by June 1950 have a multi-racial council like that created in Lake Province in 1949, the African members being elected from native authority councils and the non-Africans directly. 'Within a relatively short time' each municipality and provincial council should elect one African and one non-African to the Legislative Council, which would retain its official majority. Twining proposed to form the council's unofficial members into a committee to consider these suggestions. He regarded them as novel, not knowing that they were almost identical to those which the African Association had accepted in 1946.[1] The Colonial Office welcomed the plan. 'If you can keep up to this programme', Cohen replied, 'it will certainly help us in the U.N.'[2] Offered the proposals in November 1949, the unofficial members formed a Committee on Constitutional Development to hear evidence and formulate an agreed programme. Its proceedings inaugurated Tanganyika's 'time of politics'.

The Europeans were divided into three factions. The largest and most vociferous had as its core the 'red-eyed' settlers, the small coffee and grain farmers of the north. Alarmed by plans for U.N. trusteeship and racial parity in the Central Legislative Assembly, a public meeting at Arusha in February 1946 formed a European Union of Tanganyika. In 1947 this expanded into the Northern Province Council and in October 1949 it was further enlarged into the Tanganyika European Council, which also attracted European 'groundnutters' at Kongwa, many poorer settlers in the Southern Highlands, and other European segregationists.[3] To the Constitutional Committee the Council advocated an elected majority of Europeans in an overall unofficial majority on the Legislative Council, separate voters' rolls, 'a large influx of independent Europeans', and territorial segregation as in Kenya. Its success in winning European support probably surprised Twining and certainly disturbed the general complacency about Tanganyika's race relations.[4] Against the revival of settler traditionalism, however, there stood two smaller factions which realised that overt European domination was anachronistic. One consisted of sisal

[1] Twining to Cohen, 11 October 1949, Hall papers, ULD; above, p. 432.
[2] Cohen to Twining, 1 November 1949, Hall papers, ULD.
[3] *Tanganyika standard*, 2 March 1946; Twining to Cohen, 11 October 1949, Hall papers, ULD; Bates, 'British administration', pp. 325–30; information from Dr Alistair Ross (to whom I owe many insights into European politics).
[4] Tanganyika, 'Committee on constitutional development: evidence', I, 93–107; Bates, 'British administration', p. 333; *The Times*, 23 February 1950.

planters and other capitalists more concerned with economic than racial interests. Its spokesman was Sir Eldred Hitchcock, resident director of Bird and Company. Like Twining, Hitchcock favoured a colour-blind meritocracy, and he urged the Constitutional Committee to recommend equal representation for each race as 'a working compromise'.[1] This aligned him with the third element in the European community, represented by the committee's most influential member, Ivor Bayldon, an ambitious farmer with a genuine belief in multi-racialism who had a personal following in the Southern Highlands and was to become the country's leading European politician of the 1950s.

While Europeans were openly split, Asians concealed their divisions behind a facade of unity. Three issues divided them. One arose from the communal rivalry, culminating in massacre and emigration, which accompanied India's partition in 1947. Tanganyika's Asians had to choose between India and Pakistan. In Kigoma, for example, the Muslim majority boycotted the celebration of India's independence ordered by the Indian Association in July 1947, instead forming a Muslim Association.[2] The second dilemma was that independence for India and Pakistan forced Asians to decide whether to be expatriates or Tanganyikans. This helped to destroy the Indian Association, which was superseded by an Association of the Nationals of India and an Asian Association, the latter formed by young men who looked forward to a secular, multi-racial Tanganyikan state.[3] Yet this raised a third dilemma, for Asians who chose a Tanganyikan future had to decide whether to be a racial group or to belong to the territorial society either as individuals or religious communities. Ismaili Khojas chose the latter course in 1952 when the Aga Khan ordered them to resign from Asian societies and seek their future within Tanganyika as Ismailis, thereby destroying the possibility of a united Asian community.[4] Thus Twining's initiative came at a disastrous moment for Asians, but his admiration of their discipline was justified. The old Indian Association was in decay. It openly confessed that it did not represent Pakistanis. Its last elections had been in 1944. But its committee was composed of community representatives, it had a

[1] Tanganyika, 'Committee on constitutional development: evidence', I, 135.
[2] Savory, 'Public opinion, second quarter 1947', TNA 180/D/2/2/31; M. J. Mulla to Kigoma, 13 October 1949, TNA 180/A/6/3/52; Fleuret, 'Sikhs', p. 198.
[3] J. R. Dharsi to Kigoma, 1 February 1951, TNA 180/A/6/3/57; *The Tanganyikan*, November 1955.
[4] Leslie to PCs, 29 November 1952, TNA 45/988/43.

network of branches headed by businessmen accustomed to obeying headquarters, and it had a simple, appealing programme. Consequently the Asian case to the Constitutional Committee was presented with impressive unity by Indian Association delegates who appeared at every major town to endorse the plan put forward by headquarters. This accepted Twining's idea of parity between African and non-African unofficials, but urged that they should be chosen by provincial councils whose non-African members should be elected by Europeans and Asians voting on a common roll which the more numerous Asians would naturally dominate. Africans might join the common roll in fifty or a hundred years. Because of their divisions, however, Asians were in no hurry for elections. Their chief concern was to resist the Europeans' 'ill-conceived and highly provocative' agitation and to preserve 'the principle of PARAMOUNTCY OF AFRICAN INTERESTS'. Under pressure, Asians, like settlers, reverted to the slogans of the 1920s.[1]

Many Africans, too, met constitutional futurology with old beliefs. The new politics were beyond most political leaders of the mid 1940s. Ali Ponda told the Committee that 'he had little information regarding Legislative Council. He had heard that there were four African Members, but he never heard of what they did.'[2] Among those who did understand were progressive native authorities, and they were deeply suspicious. The Chagga Council urged that the Legislative Council's official majority should remain, with an African majority among the unofficials, but that no elections should take place until Africans could choose their representatives without 'a lot of confusion and tribalism'. Provincial councils should have large African majorities but should on no account supersede native administrations. Bukoba, similarly, revealed a widespread desire to maintain native administrations and a general assumption that a future territorial government would be a vast native authority in which non-Africans would have only advisory functions. Among Africans, as among settlers, Britain's concern with race intensified racialism.[3]

Two African groups responded more positively.[4] One was TAA headquarters, where young men from Makerere had recently gained

[1] Tanganyika, 'Committee on constitutional development: evidence', III, 87–92; Standing committee of the nationals of the Republic of India to AA Dar es Salaam, 6 May 1950, TANU 3.
[2] Tanganyika, 'Committee on constitutional development: evidence', I, 31.
[3] *Ibid.*, I, 52, and II, 212–46.
[4] The Kilosa branch of TAA was a third. See *ibid.*, III, 8–12.

479

leadership. Stimulated and alarmed by the new politics, 'a dozen odd young educated Africans' drafted a memorandum which they persuaded headquarters to adopt and circulate to branches. 'The European Community in this territory', they warned, 'is forcefully clamouring for more seats than the remaining races combined...Our future is at great stake.'[1] 'We as natives are the rightful owners of this country', they told the Committee; '...We wish to reaffirm the correctness of the Tanganyika Government's policy of giving PARA-MOUNTCY to NATIVE INTERESTS.' From this defensive position they advanced to a positive programme. Rejecting 'any policy designed to develop this territory constitutionally on racial lines', they proposed a scheme leading gradually from the immediate election of chiefdom and urban ward councils to the election of a Legislative Council with an unofficial majority chosen on a common roll in the twelfth year, followed a year later by an unofficial majority on the Executive Council, i.e. responsible government. All elections should be on a common roll, and at each stage the structure should be federal and based on 'Tribal Affiliation Units'.[2] The Committee received an even more radical document from TAA's Mwanza branch, drafted by its secretary, a young clerk named Isaac Bhoke Munanka. Condemning 'the Settlers' Supremacy in the ruling of TANGANYIKA, mainly because of their terribly shocking CRUELTY as seen in such neighbouring Dependencies as South Africa, Rhodesia and Kenya', the paper reminded government of 'its PROMISE to the Africans to hand over the rule of the country to them as soon as they are ready for it'. To prepare them for responsible government elected Africans should predominate in all local governments, and an official majority should remain in the Legislative Council until self-government.[3] If Twining was seeking an African voice, it spoke in tones which he can scarcely have expected.

The Constitutional Committee's discussions were dominated by the old conflict between settler leaders, pressing for European equality with all other races combined and immediate communal elections, and Asians insisting on equal representation with Europeans and a common roll for Asians and Europeans if elections must be held. African members took little part but were the main beneficiaries, for deadlock enabled Bayldon to present the multi-racial approach to

[1] Document dated from AA Dar es Salaam, 21 March 1950, TANU 19. The last page or pages are missing. See also below, p. 507.
[2] Tanganyika, 'Committee on constitutional development: evidence', III, 72–86.
[3] *Ibid.*, II, 197–9. See also below, pp. 504–5.

political development. His chief concern was to defer elections until a common roll of all three races was possible, since purely racial elections must return the extremists he opposed. The other Europeans compromised by insisting that Legislative Council elections should be held within three years of the establishment of provincial councils, leaving the method of election undecided. As a tired compromise it was agreed that the Legislative Council should temporarily keep its official majority while the three races should have equal representation under a 'parity' formula.[1] Although parity was less democratic than he desired, Twining endorsed these proposals. They were unacceptable to settler extremists or TAA's Mwanza branch, but moderate opinion – including TAA headquarters – rallied behind parity until the new Conservative government could accept it in June 1952.[2] In accordance with Conservative policy in Kenya and Central Africa, Twining now made parity the basis for a multi-racial state in which each race, as a unit, would have equal political weight.

With Twining's drive behind it, multi-racialism became Tanganyika's official creed. It was a frankly elitist attempt, in Twining's words, 'to build up a community where merit is the criterion, not colour',[3] and he meant merit by European standards – multi-racialism was not multi-culturalism. The programme deprived Africans of many paternalistic protections and established freedom for Europeans to compete, but it also matched the increasing availability of university education and modern technology to a tiny group of privileged Africans and attempted to associate them with government, much as government had interpenetrated with European and Asian leaderships during the 1930s. The African elite was courted, flattered, and strongly attracted by the opportunity to share in a programme which combined self-interest with genuine idealism. A few, notably Kidaha Makwaia, joined the Capricorn Society whose Central African ideas of equal rights for 'civilised' men reached Tanganyika at this time, but Thomas Marealle and Julius Nyerere declined.[4] Several leading Chagga businessmen attended an East African Businessmen's Conference in Nairobi in June 1952 to discuss multi-racial business. Four years later the Tanganyika Farmers' Association separated from its Kenyan parent and invited African members. Many of those at its first meeting were progressive farmers from Arusha. In 1951 Asian

[1] This account is reconstructed from the Hall papers, ULD.
[2] Bates, 'British administration', pp. 318–22.
[3] Quoted in Taylor, *Political development*, p. 221.   [4] Information from Dr Ross.

students were first admitted to Makerere.[1] Post-war development, African capitalism, higher education, immigrant ambitions, and British decolonisation plans all merged to mark out Tanganyika's future as a multi-racial state governed by a colour-blind, capitalist elite, a model for troubled countries to north and south.

For the administration the key issue was local government. A new system to replace indirect rule was doubly acceptable after the war because 'nation-builders' saw it as a means of advancement while conservatives saw it as a counterweight to nationalism. In February 1947 Creech Jones ordered the creation of a system of councils to facilitate 'planned and inter-related change and improvement in all fields'.[2] In 1949 district officers were told to create, gradually, a pyramid of councils from village and sub-chiefdom to chiefdom, district, and provincial levels. The councils were to evolve from existing native authorities by adding commoners, who were eventually to be elected and to share executive power. The main obstacles were diverse political systems – in 1951 Tanganyika contained 435 native administrations – and widespread apathy.[3] In authoritarian Ha chiefdoms the commoners' indifference was such that attempts to form councils were abandoned in 1950. In Uhehe, similarly, 'there is as yet no popular desire to detract from or modify in any way the chief's direct powers'.[4] Other areas, however, showed lively interest in 'democratisation'. The addition of educated commoners to Tanga district's council of headmen in 1945 was generally welcomed. The clan and age-grade systems of Musoma, Tarime, and Arusha lent themselves to conciliar organisation. Perhaps the most successful structure was that established in Unyakyusa, where the balance among chiefs, headmen, and commoners in the indigenous polity fitted neatly into local councils which chose delegates to a Rungwe African District Council.[5] Most commonly the reforms combined success and failure, especially among the small chiefdoms of the western plateau. In Sukumaland local government reform was part of the development scheme. By 1953 a pyramid of 612 parish councils, 55 chiefdom

[1] 'East African inter-territorial business-man's conference', 7–8 June 1952, TANU 3; *Agriculture report*, 1956, p. 5; Goldthorpe, *Elite*, p. 13.

[2] A. Creech Jones, 'The place of African local administration in colonial policy', *JAA*, I (1949), 4.

[3] Twining to Griffiths, 20 September 1950, Cadiz papers, RH.

[4] F. A. Montague and F. H. Page-Jones, 'Some difficulties in the democratisation of native authorities in Tanganyika', *JAA*, III (1951), 22.

[5] See Z. E. Kingdon, 'The initiation of a system of local government by African rural councils in the Rungwe district', *JAA*, III (1951), 186–91.

councils, a Sukumaland Federal Council, and a multi-racial Lake Province Advisory Council existed through enormous administrative effort. Yet the enterprise produced serious tensions. Lower-level councils had few powers and attracted little enthusiasm. 'Only the chiefs and their house-boys sit there', it was alleged, and the same criticism was levelled at the powerful Sukumaland Federal Council through which the chiefs hoped to strengthen their collective authority, for even when commoners were added to it they were often the chiefs' nominees and preserved a discreet silence. As it used the councils to enforce unpopular agricultural rules, government found that it had created not organs of political moderation but targets for political opposition.[1]

In 1952 local government was further complicated by multi-racialism. Officials realised that the crucial problem was the relationship between purely African native administrations, however democratised, and a territorial political system providing for all three races.[2] Cohen and Twining believed that the two should meet at provincial level, where councils could elect Legislative Councillors yet still be sufficiently remote from local affairs to avoid conflict with native administrations. Twining warned the Constitutional Committee that multi-racial *district* councils were neither practicable nor necessary. The committee disagreed, probably because Europeans and Asians wanted a larger share in local government. It recommended new administrative units, to be called counties, which would be either existing districts or groupings of districts with multi-racial councils which would eventually supersede native administrations. This proposal was supported by a constitutional adviser and embodied in the Local Government Ordinance of 1953.[3] This measure introduced elitist, multi-racial capitalism into local politics. Powerful peoples like the Chagga flatly refused county councils, but some less effectively organised groups had multi-racial councils forced upon them during the 1950s, despite angry opposition.[4] As the Constitutional Committee had heard, most Africans were chiefly concerned to defend local

[1] J. V. Shaw, 'The development of African local government in Sukumaland', *JAA*, VI (1954), 171–7; Maguire, '*Uhuru*', pp. 22–6, 40–1, 107.

[2] Surridge to Creech Jones, 9 November 1948, in Bates, 'British administration', p. 352.

[3] 'Future constitutional development in Tanganyika', 18 November 1949, TNA 215/2354/1; Tanganyika, *Report of the committee on constitutional development 1951* (Dar es Salaam, 1951), p. 5; Taylor, *Political development*, pp. 102–3. 1951), p. 5; Taylor, *Political development*, pp. 102–3.

[4] UN, *Report of the visiting mission to trust territories in East Africa, 1954, on Tanganyika* (UNTC T/1142), p. 114; R. C. Pratt, 'Multiracialism and local government in Tanganyika', *Race*, II (1960), 33–49; below, pp. 558–9.

interests. Not only was multi-racial local government, like soil conservation, crop marketing, and education, a point where post-war big government penetrated African societies to impinge on peasant interests, but it was a racial issue on which Africans could unite.

Local government reform was crucial also in another sense. Constant experimentation made it impossible to satisfy the politically ambitious with local government posts and threw both district administration and local politics into disorder, undercutting established authorities without creating stable substitutes. Chiefs were commonly too weak to prevent nominal democratisation but strong enough to stop it becoming much more than nominal. When nationalism penetrated rural areas, therefore, it rarely met effective opposition from local institutions. It was in those areas where local government systems had survived post-war disruption – although not in *all* such areas – that nationalists faced greatest difficulty.[1] Thirty years earlier Cameron had seen his native administrations as 'bulwarks against the agitator'. The bulwarks were breached.

[1] Kilimanjaro was a good example. See below, pp. 515, 525.

CHAPTER 15

The new politics, 1945–55

During 1954 and 1955 a nationalist movement was created in Tanganyika: the Tanganyika African National Union. It sought to usurp central control of the territory by means of popular support and the threat of disorder, with the object of making Tanganyika a nation state similar to those which dominated the twentieth-century world order.[1] This combination of characteristics distinguished TANU from all previous political movements in Tanganyika.

One purpose of this chapter is to explain TANU's emergence. The most penetrating analysis of colonial nationalism refers to India and argues, broadly, that Indian politics took a nationalist form because the expansion of the colonial state and its representative institutions obliged Indians to combine into a territorial organisation in order to advance their interests. Indian nationalism was 'a matching structure of politics' within the framework of British rule.[2] This analysis is based on documentation superior to that available in Tanganyika, where only a few TANU records and private papers are yet accessible, and it probably has much relevance to Tanganyika. As TANU's leader reflected:

Until we were colonised, this 'nation' did not exist, different laws operated among the constituent tribes and there was conflict between them. It was the colonial power which imposed a common law and maintained it by force, until the growth of the independence movement put the flesh of an emotional unity on to the skeleton of legal unity.[3]

Yet the analysis of Indian nationalism requires three qualifications before it can be applied to Tanganyika. First, TANU was formed

---

[1] The definition originates from John Lonsdale, 'The emergence of African nations', in T. O. Ranger (ed.), *Emerging themes of African history* (Nairobi, 1968), p. 201; F. H. Hinsley, *Nationalism and the international system* (London, 1973), *passim.*

[2] Anil Seal, 'Imperialism and nationalism in India', in John Gallagher and others (ed.), *Locality, province, and nation* (Cambridge, 1973), p. 27.

[3] Nyerere, *Freedom and unity,* p. 271.

before the creation of the representative and electoral machinery through which it was to win power, a sequence which was possible because TANU was not a local invention but a deliberate imitation of earlier nationalist movements elsewhere. One difference in a late and imitative nationalism was that the imitators – the educated leaders – played a larger part,[1] especially as expounders of nationalist ideas. The second variation from Indian patterns was therefore the importance of ideas. This does not mean that Tanganyikan nationalism was especially ideological or idealistic, but in nationalism, as in other political actions, men generally followed their interests *as they perceived them*, and it was in altering men's perceptions of their interests that ideology was crucial to Tanganyikan nationalism. Third, it would be misleading to ask why politics took a nationalist form in Tanganyika. The concrete question is why specific people created a specific political movement in specific circumstances, which leads explanation away from short-term responses to colonial government and towards socio-economic change, popular action, and the more distant past. No state – and especially no colonial state – creates a nation. A state creates only subjects. The subjects create the nation, and they bring into the process the whole of their historical experience.[2]

If nationalism was in part a creative response to the imposition of an administrative state on diverse social groups, another response was the politicisation of those groups. Deliberate creation of 'tribal' aggregations and political movements was as much a feature of post-war Tanganyika as was nationalism. Ultimately the two conflicted, but in the post-war decade the situation was more complicated. Nationalism not only grew up alongside other political tendencies; to a considerable extent it grew out of them. The three main elements of Tanganyika's political history which met in TANU came from the capital, the north-east, and the Lake Province. Each in turn predominated, made its contribution to the common store of political experience, and then gave way to the next element, much as each instrument of an orchestra develops a theme before falling silent.

[1] The analogue is Alexander Gerschenkron, *Economic backwardness in historical perspective* (Cambridge, Mass., 1962).

[2] The analogue is E. P. Thompson, *The making of the English working class* (London, 1963).

Tribal aggregation

Post-war circumstances encouraged attempts to reorganise African societies into close-knit tribes. Socio-economic change accentuated regional differentiation and rivalry while strengthening the modernising groups which advocated tribal reconstruction. Local government reform undermined existing structures. Devolution of power to Africans stimulated competition for advantageous positions in the new order. Since government still worked through the units of indirect rule, the most common political organisations of the period were tribal improvement associations. The Sukuma Union is the best example. Three times as numerous as any other 'tribe' in the territory, the Sukuma were increasingly aware of their relative backwardness, while a long-standing cultural conservatism – expressed in indifference to mission work – and government's plans for tribal federation made them increasingly conscious of a common identity. The eighteen schoolteachers and artisans of Mwanza who founded the Sukuma Union in December 1945 had aims ranging from mutual aid and tribal development to 'preserving our language' and maintaining good customs.[1] After a faltering start the union was revitalised in 1950 by a newly-emerged tribal elite. The president, Henry Chagula, was a Makerere-trained teacher, while Paul Bomani, the future cooperative pioneer, was secretary. The union sought representation in the Sukuma Federal Council, tried unsuccessfully to build an independent middle school, and encouraged the use of the Sukuma language. In the past Sukuma had commonly called themselves Sukuma as against Nyamwezi, but Nyamwezi as against anyone else. In 1952, however, even the younger Sukuma of Dar es Salaam broke their ties with the Nyamwezi and formed a Sukuma Union branch.[2] A year later a former policeman, Lameck Bogohe, became the union's full-time secretary and by energetic travelling raised its membership to a peak of 5,814 early in 1954, organised into 32 branches. He also turned the union openly against the Sukumaland Scheme, chiefs, and government. Yet the union achieved little. Government refused it registration and prohibited civil servants from joining. Bogohe was dismissed during a quarrel over funds. Many thought TAA and the cooperative movement more promising lines of action. By 1956 the Sukuma Union

---

[1] F. L. J. Mashaka Ngalaishwa, 'Ilika ipya lya Basukuma' [December 1945] TNA 215/1977/2; Maguire, '*Uhuru*', pp. 75–80.
[2] C. W. Werther, *Zum Victoria Nyanza* (2nd edn, Berlin, n.d.), p. 158; Leslie, *Survey*, p. 44.

487

had almost disappeared, although much of its heightened tribal awareness survived.[1]

Similar tribal associations existed throughout post-war Tanganyika. One other may be described, for besides repeating many features of the Sukuma experience it illustrates other aspects of political tribalism. Moyo wa Uzigua na Nguu, 'The Heart (or Spirit) of Uzigua and Ungulu', came into existence informally in 1938 to collect funds for a Zigua boarding school, but it had deeper origins. One was tension between educated Christian Zigua and hereditary Muslim chiefs. Another was local economic collapse following the penetration of tsetse. The third was the division of Uzigua among several British districts and the loss of the Pangani valley to Shambaa control, which gave Zigua tribalism a strong irredentist element. 'Moyo' became perhaps the country's liveliest tribal improvement society. Backed by the district office, its leaders joined the tribal council and its founder, a teacher named Paul Nkanyemka, became council secretary. Yet like the Sukuma Union it faced the problem of defining the tribe in a region where one group merged almost imperceptibly into another. Not only did Moyo embrace both Zigua and Ngulu – separate 'tribes' on British lists – but both claimed affinity with Shambaa and Bondei, all being supposed descendants of Seuta. In 1951 the provincial commissioner unveiled a clay statue of 'Seuta the Zigua national hero' at native administration headquarters; it was the work of a local student from Makerere.[2] Moyo initially admitted all Seuta's descendants, but it simultaneously advocated the return of the lost Pangani valley – Tambarare, as the area was locally known – from Shambaa to Zigua control. In 1954, on legal advice, the Zigua formed a Tambarare Citizens Union 'to protect the interests of the people of the plains as against those of the hills'. Meanwhile the contradiction in Zigua relations with Shambaa was intensified by Moyo's campaign for the election of a Zigua paramount chief.[3]

Paramountcy movements had existed between the wars among Chagga and Haya,[4] and it is significant that these were the territory's most progressive peoples, for the movements' objects were to unite

---

[1] Maguire, '*Uhuru*', pp. 109, 113, 122–31, 143–6; D. M. Ngalula, 'The life of Lameck Makaranga Bogohe', seminar paper, University College, Dar es Salaam, 1969.

[2] T. R. Sadleir, 'A note on the Handeni museum', *TNR*, XXXIII (1952), 91–2. For Seuta, see Feierman, *Shambaa kingdom*, pp. 52, 66–9. For Moyo, see the correspondence in TNA 6/A/6/1–2.

[3] Morrison to PC Tanga [1954] TNA 304/25/A/1/91; Handeni DAR 1951, TNA 4/962/M/xix.

[4] Rogers, 'Political focus', pp. 564–72; Austen, *Northwest Tanzania*, p. 168.

tribes for collective advancement and to enable educated men to gain power, through election, over hereditary chiefs. Such movements were common after 1945. Paralysed by their divisions, the stateless Bondei suffered Kilindi rule and saw their country – the first to welcome mission education – overtaken by regions able to grow the cash crops which Bonde lacked. In 1948 dissident schoolteachers and traders formed the Bondei Central Union, partly to campaign for a paramount chief. They succeeded a decade later, in alliance with the nationalist movement.[1] Among another classically stateless people with a strong sense of deprivation, the Makonde, educated men also formed a tribal union in the late 1940s to campaign for a paramountcy.[2] Often these movements concealed essentially factional ambitions. This was the case among the Matengo, where in 1956 Chrisostomus Makita was elected paramount chief at the expense of his family's ancient rivals, the Kawanilas, who had British backing.[3] Such was local factionalism that advocates of Nyakyusa and Pare paramountcies could not even agree on candidates. Yet behind these movements there was usually more than personal ambition. The most interesting was that of the Ndendeuli, a stateless people with a strongly egalitarian ideology but little sense of common identity who had been incorporated into the Ngoni chiefdom of Mshope in the 1860s. As the indigenous cultivators of the area, the Ndendeuli benefited most from the introduction of tobacco-growing in the 1930s. They were the keenest members of the cooperative society which demonstrated new methods of collective action and leadership, as also did the Qadiriyya brotherhood which grew in strength as missionaries neglected the Ndendeuli in favour of the Ngoni. When the Chief of Mshope died in 1952 and a succession dispute followed, those Ndendeuli most remote from the chiefdom's capital campaigned successfully for autonomy. Their leaders were prominent Muslims and the separate polity which they created in 1954 was modelled on a cooperative society, with a pyramid of councils and a president elected every three years. The Ndendeuli republic was Tanganyika's best example of a tribal polity created in the colonial period as a result of socio-economic change and the impact of hierarchical institutions on previously stateless people.[4]

Although the tribe was the normal unit of aggregation in the postwar decade, it was not the only one. The Mbeya District Original Tribes Association was a district-wide body designed to resist control

---

[1] 'African clubs and associations, Tanga' [1949?] TNA 45/M/41; below, p. 527.
[2] Liebenow, *Colonial rule*, pp. 196–7. [3] Haule in Iliffe, *Tanzanians*, pp. 166–71.
[4] Newa, 'Ndendeule struggle'; Joseph T. Gallagher, 'The emergence of an African ethnic group: the case of the Ndendeuli', *IJAHS*, VII (1974), 1–26.

by Nyakyusa immigrants. The Kuria Union – a tribal body with members on both sides of the Kenya border – was rivalled by the Mara Union, originally formed in Nairobi by workers from all parts of the East Lake region.[1] Moreover, aggregation could take place in smaller units. While both Haya and Pare had active tribal unions they also formed innumerable clan associations to control land and advance political claims. Tanganyika's pre-colonial units had been so numerous, ill-defined, and situational that colonial aggregation was equally confused. This helped to prevent most tribal improvement societies from achieving anything significant, which in turn made their members more receptive to nationalist politics. Moreover, nationalists were fortunate that Tanganyika had no dominant tribe, that six of its nine largest ethnic groups were situated on its borders, and that the most advanced tribes were relatively small. Yet it would be wrong to think either that local loyalties became stronger after the war – in reality they only became more self-conscious – or that Africans of this period saw an inevitable conflict between tribal and national loyalties. Rather, most Africans assumed that only when their tribal units were strengthened could they be united into a nation. Lameck Bogohe, organiser of the Sukuma Union, was an equally keen member of TAA's Mwanza branch, whose leading activist, Isaac Bhoke Munanka, was also patron of the Mara Union.[2] Like townsmen, political leaders saw their various units and organisations situationally: the tribal union was for local affairs, the wider organisation was for larger problems. Even TANU's founders provided for tribal unions to affiliate to the nationalist party. Only in the late 1950s did the nationalist movement elevate itself above other political organisations and demand exclusive loyalty to the nation. Until that time, parochial and territorial politics interacted to mutual profit.

Popular politics in the north-east

It was in north-eastern Tanganyika – the most developed part of the country, where European pressures were greatest – that the experience of inter-war peasant politics was refined and passed on through a sequence of political actions to contribute to the nationalist

[1] RG to Mbeya, 23 September 1959, TNA 327/A/6/34/I/121; DC Tarime, 'Note of a meeting on 30/10/47 with executive members of the committee of the Kuria Union', TNA 83/3/2/17.
[2] Ngalula, 'Lameck Bogohe'; Idi Marumi to Mwanza, 23 October 1956, TNA 41/A/6/6/300.

movement. It is illuminating to trace this sequence. The initial link with pre-war events took place on Kilimanjaro. Four issues dominated post-war Chagga politics. One was government's desire to break down the particularism of the nineteen chiefs who formed the Chagga Council. A plan for a paramount chief foundered in the 1930s because the other chiefs preferred Petro Itosi Marealle of Marangu to the government's candidate, Abdiel Shangali of Machame. In 1944 the chiefs refused to elect three superior chiefs or *waitori* for the mountain's three main regions, but two years later the provincial commissioner appointed them without further consultation, choosing Petro Itosi, Abdiel, and John Maruma of Rombo. He also provided for the election of commoners to the Chagga Council. It was now clearer than ever that *waitori* were primarily government servants, while other chiefs were naturally offended to be subordinated.[1] Moreover, the cost of administrative reform interacted with the Chagga's second post-war preoccupation, their anxiety to expand educational and other facilities, for between 1946 and 1947 native treasury expenditure on tribal administration rose from £9,039 to £18,210 while educational expenditure increased only from £5,345 to £6,254 and medical expenditure actually fell.[2]

Kilimanjaro's third post-war issue was the African Association's entry into Chagga politics when Joseph Kimalando's branch in Moshi established cells in four mountain chiefdoms by 1947. This coincided with the return to Kilimanjaro after fifteen years absence of Petro Njau and Joseph Merinyo, two gifted peasant politicians of the 1920s who were appalled by the chiefs' growing authority. Moreover, in 1948 government abolished the chiefs' power to prohibit meetings, which had silenced Kilimanjaro's dissidents since 1937. Impatient with TAA's detachment from local issues, Njau and Merinyo took over its mountain branches, confined membership to Chagga, and changed the name to the Kilimanjaro Union, blandly assuring TAA headquarters of continuing cooperation.[3] The Kilimanjaro Union immediately took up the area's fourth political issue: land. Allocation of ex-German land returned to the Chagga by Judge Wilson reopened the conflicts of the 1920s, with Njau and Merinyo accusing the chiefs of favouritism, objecting to the registration of new *vihamba*, and

[1] Rogers, 'Political focus', pp. 790–9.
[2] Hill, 'Memorandum on Chagga native treasury' [July 1947] TNA 12844/II/99A.
[3] Above, p. 427; Rogers, 'Political focus', pp. 816–26; 'Mkutano wa watu wote kufungulia office ya Umoja wa Kilimanjaro tarekh 7 Novemba 1948', TNA 5/583/820; Njau to AA Dar es Salaam, March [?] 1949, TNA 5/584/1.

491

apparently hinting that the land might best be allocated to large-scale progressive farmers like themselves.[1] Perhaps stimulated by growing European political activity, the two politicians also espoused the election of a paramount chief to supersede the *waitori* and unify the tribe.[2]

During the next three years the Kilimanjaro Union pursued this programme in a fascinating *tour de force* of peasant politics which mobilised all the *waitori*'s opponents: dispossessed chiefs, ambitious traders and farmers, old KNPA activists, unprivileged Muslims, clan leaders who resented chiefly power, and young educated men impatient with the old order. The programme was couched in the neo-traditionalist terms of which Njau – once Gutmann's informant – was a master, but the purpose was to put a political party into power. With organisation down to parish level, the Kilimanjaro Union may have had 12,000 subscribing members in 1951.[3] When the Chagga Council condemned the Kilimanjaro Union as 'some how like fascist or communism' and banned public meetings, Njau organised a widely-successful boycott of Chagga Council elections. 'Agitation and division between men and men, household and household' was the result throughout the mountainside during 1950.[4] In the meantime, however, elected members of the Chagga Council had also demanded a paramount chief, and although officials thought this 'politically immature', Twining ordered that the Chagga should choose for themselves.[5] Government and chiefs wanted the paramount to be merely a chairman elected by the Chagga Council from among the *waitori*, but in mid 1951 the people rejected this in favour of the Kilimanjaro Union's plan for a popularly elected chief with maximum independence from the district office.[6]

Meanwhile Njau had found a winning candidate in Thomas Marealle. Grandson of the Germans' collaborator, he not only had the essential chiefly blood, but he was a university-educated moderniser with much administrative experience, he would neutralise his uncle Petro Itosi's popularity, and fifteen years' absence from Kilimanjaro

[1] Njau to PC Northern, 18 June 1949, TNA 5/584/18; Njau, 'Kilimanjaro Chagga Union, amezaliwa Moshi' [July 1949] TNA 5/584/29.
[2] Njau to Hutt, 4 December 1948, TNA 12844/II/205.
[3] Clemm, 'White mountain', p. 222.
[4] Abdiel Shangali to PC Northern, 19 October 1949, TNA 5/584/76; Lewis, Moshi DAR 1949, TNA 69/63/17/2; Abdiel Shangali, 'Report ya nne kwa mwaka ya nchi za Hai Uchagga', 1950, TNA 69/54/MO/113.
[5] Hall to Rogers, 5 September 1951, TNA 12844/III/352; Twining, note on visit to Moshi district, January 1950, TNA 12844/III/277.
[6] Page-Jones to Member for Local Government, 27 July 1951, TNA 12844/III/329.

should make him sufficiently ignorant of Chagga politics to be dependent on his backers. Marealle, however, was quite as shrewd and tough as Njau. Deeply alarmed by the European threat to Tanganyika and the Chagga, he wanted to be paramount but not, as he put it, 'a Paramount Chief *"built on public subscriptions"*'.[1] 'I am most grateful for your support', he told Njau, 'but...convinced as I am of the necessity for unity amongst the Chagga people...I should be anxious not to appear as the candidate of any one particular party.'[2] He won this point, for along with the *waitori* he stood for election in December 1951 as a candidate nominated by the Chagga Council. The Kilimanjaro Union is said to have promised that he 'would abolish the *waitori* system, do away with the coffee cess, and lead the Chagga to greatness as an independent sovereign. He would restore respect to the clans and clan leaders and abolish corruption in the administration. He would speak authoritatively to Government, and they would be forced to listen. Chagga *vihamba* would be safe forever, and more land provided for all.'[3] It was a walkover. Petro Itosi withdrew. Abdiel Shangali won Machame. Everywhere else the voting, although light, was overwhelmingly for Marealle, who won 15,661 of the 24,002 votes.[4] The day of his installation became Chagga Day, a flag was invented, and lively neo-traditionalism accompanied a period of vigorous development and exceptional prosperity, with coffee prices at their peak.

Tanganyika's most prosperous peasant society had produced its most dramatic example of tribal aggregation. Moreover, the Chagga case shows that tribal and supertribal aggregation were not yet seen as incompatible and that local rivalry might itself stimulate men to seek external support. As Njau campaigned against the *waitori* in May 1949 several Meru leaders invited him to extend the Kilimanjaro Union to their district.[5] Their initiative created a Meru affiliate and the Kilimanjaro Union opened its membership to 'the tribes of the whole country of Tanganyika',[6] establishing contact with Arusha, Iraqw, and Masai dissidents, all of them having grievances against government's land utilisation or soil rehabilitation programmes. In October 1952 Chagga, Meru, Arusha, and Masai leaders met to declare their

[1] Marealle to Hinden, 25 May 1949, and to Nicholson, 10 August 1951, FCB papers 121, RH.
[2] Marealle to Njau, 15 September 1951, TNA 12844/III/367.
[3] Rogers, 'Political focus', p. 891 n. 2. A cess is a levy on agricultural produce.
[4] *Ibid.*, p. 900.   [5] Njau to PC Northern, 16 May 1949, TNA 5/584/12.
[6] 'Kanuni na sheria za Kilimanjaro Union', 28 May 1949, TNA 72/44/11/149.

unity.[1] In reality, however, Njau's influence was waning. Once in power, Marealle was distancing himself from the Kilimanjaro Union, as was the successful candidate whom Njau had similarly backed for the Arusha chieftainship, Zephania Sumlei.[2] The Meru Citizens Union severed relations when Njau refused it financial aid.[3] The Masai connection was merely nominal. Yet in May 1953 Njau drafted a plan to convert his organisation into a Tanganyika Citizens Union 'to unite Tanganyika into one body by following the path which united the whole of Kilimanjaro' and 'welcome a general Council of Chiefs as a supreme advisory Body to the Government'.[4] Next month he approached Pare leaders, and he was already in touch with Shambaa politics.[5] Through his actions the political experience of the Chagga was passed on to the other north-eastern peoples.

Chagga politics were essentially domestic. The enemies were local institutions and local chiefs, however supported by government. The initial step towards a politics which openly attacked the colonial regime itself was taken by the Pare. Its origins lay in their consciousness of deprivation relative to their Chagga and Shambaa neighbours. In the 1920s Pare began to grow coffee and joined the KNPA, only to see government uproot their bushes. They responded swiftly to Christian and Muslim teaching, but in 1938 only eleven per cent of Pare children were at school.[6] The basic problem was lack of funds. At the same time, government was anxious to escape from 'the prehistoric system of a flat rate tax' inherited from German times by experimenting with a tax graduated by wealth, but Chagga, Haya, and Ganda all rejected this for fear of partiality by the chiefs who would make the assessments.[7] In 1941 government decided to experiment with the Pare because of their need of funds and eagerness for progress, suggesting that the graduated rate should be modelled on a previous system of tribute to chiefs, known as *mbiru*. The chiefs agreed after some hesitation and the system was introduced in

[1] 'Mkutano wa jumuiya wa Arusha/Meru Federated Citizens Union', 14 October 1952, TNA 472/NA/40/175.
[2] See the correspondence in TNA 472/NA/40 and 472/ASS/35.
[3] Basil P. Mramba, 'Some notes on the political development of the Chagga', B.A. research paper, Makerere University College, 1967, p. 11.
[4] 'Mkutano wa halmashauri na nchama wote wa KCCU, uliokutanika tarehe 2 Mai 1953', and Njau to Twining, 16 July 1953, TNA 5/25/26/163 and 170.
[5] Njau to Minja, 30 June 1953, TNA 4/8/36/191; 'Memorandum', 23 April 1951, TNA 72/44/16/63a.
[6] Above, p. 290; Same DAR 1938, TNA 6/1.
[7] MacMichael on Pim report, 1938, CO 691/158; Hallier diary, 4 April 1935; RH; Griffith, 'Chagga land tenure'; Scott, minute, 19 January 1943, CO 691/181.

1943.[1] Difficulty began a year later. Given wartime conditions, little development resulted from the new tax. The assessing elders proved to be the chiefs' nominees rather than popular representatives, and since they applied varying standards it became necessary to list taxpayers' property. Many Pare chiefs ruled clans who denied their authority. The chiefs had not consulted the people before accepting *mbiru*, which had not been levied for a generation and was not only unknown to younger men but seemed 'reminiscent of the uncivilised and barbarous state of the community' in the past.[2] Clerks and teachers believed they were assessed especially highly. As everywhere in the region, their ambitions were a new and disturbing element in local politics.

Organised opposition began in North Pare in June 1944 when dissidents arranged a joint delegation of protest to the chiefs. Neither this, a petition to the Chief Secretary, nor representations to the provincial commissioner had any effect. Anxious to avoid violence, the dissidents contacted Chagga leaders and offered to pay a flat rate tax which incorporated a two shilling development rate. The crisis came in January 1945 when the Chief of Mamba conscripted 44 men who refused to pay *mbiru* and sent them to Same. Three hundred men followed, after sending messengers to other chiefdoms to implement pre-planned measures. Columns from different chiefdoms converged on Same to form a crowd variously estimated at between 2,000 and 12,000 men. They remained outside the district office for two months, praying, singing hymns, and listening to speeches. Women came daily with food. Leadership fell to Paulo Mashambo, a retired Adventist teacher from Mamba whose oratory helped to maintain discipline. Two delegations to Dar es Salaam had no effect, but a breakthrough came early in March when a lawyer advised the crowd to disperse so that he could petition the government. The authorities agreed only to simplify the *mbiru* system. In July 1945 a small crowd under Mashambo's leadership again assembled briefly at Same. Eight 'ringleaders' were deported, but *mbiru* remained almost impossible to collect and chiefly authority gradually collapsed. In November 1946 – when the leaders were seeking Eliud Mathu's advice on how to win support in Britain – government at last abandoned *mbiru*.

The *mbiru* protest had transcended many divisions in Pare society

[1] The following account is based on Kimambo in Ogot, *War*, pp. 237–58; correspondence in TNA 16516/1–11 and CO 691/186.
[2] M. Hussein to Jackson, 13 March 1945, TNA 30030/1/230A.

and an attempt was made to embody the new-found unity in an organisation. Some say that while demonstrators were assembled at Same a civil servant named Samuel Mshote suggested that the Pare should form a tribal union.[1] At all events, the Pare Union came into being on 4 January 1946, with Mshote as chairman. 'Everyone knows', he explained, 'that no nation or tribe or clan achieves the development of its area or tribe unless it is united.'[2] Yet his scheme met difficulties. It won some support in South Pare, but in the north many young modernisers were simultaneously joining the African Association[3] and the two forms of unity conflicted. Mshote insisted that tribal unity must come first, but the northerners accused him of tribalism. In the south the Pare Union encouraged the celebration of an annual Pare Day, organised such improvement measures as mechanised farming, and later became a nucleus of TANU. In the north the union won little support but encouraged the local African Association branch to degenerate into an embodiment of North Pare particularism.[4] Ironically, the success of the *mbiru* protest – like that of the Kilimanjaro Union – helped to detach its originators from Tanganyika's central political tradition.

Of 23 leaders recommended for deportation during the *mbiru* crisis, six were peasants, eight were traders or craftsmen, and nine were teachers, clerks, or preachers.[5] The latter categories had personal reasons to oppose a graduated rate, but they were able to win much wider support in a social coalition against a 'modernising' measure which threatened the solidarity of rural society. Although some of their techniques – appeals to a supposedly benevolent Chief Secretary or the mobbing of chiefs – were archaic, and although the whole protest was against a specific grievance rather than the whole colonial order, the demonstration at the district office and the attempts to win external support were advances in a logical progress towards open attack on the colonial regime. Yet it is important to distinguish logical process from direct historical connection, for the only evidence of a link forwards from the *mbiru* protest towards nationalist origins was the local administration's view that the protest was the model for political action in Usambara.

In Usambara post-war grievances and aspirations became deeply enmeshed with ancient conflicts. Of the latter, the most important were

[1] 'Manaseh Kaniki of Mbaga-Kindi', duplicated, University of Dar es Salaam, 1970.
[2] S. Mshote, 'Memoranda juu ya sheria', 22 May 1946, in Lukwaro, 'Documents'.
[3] Above, p. 428. [4] See the correspondence in Lukwaro, 'Documents'.
[5] DC Same to CS, 24 February 1945, TNA 16516/1/39.

antagonism between Shambaa commoners and Kilindi rulers, division among the Kilindi between the descendants of Kinyashi and Semboja, and conflict between Vugha's centralising ambitions and the separatism of such sub-chiefdoms as Mlalo. The newer issues were the Usambara Rehabilitation Scheme and the ambitions of Muslim and Lutheran clerks, teachers, and traders. Modern political origins in Usambara are obscure. In April 1945 a native treasury clerk, Samuel Chamshama, planned an Usambara Association to discuss current development proposals. Apparently this stimulated more radical societies, often led by men who bore the name Hoza which signified a commoner married to a Kilindi woman – it is significant of the limitations on political consciousness at this time that opposition to the Kilindi should have been led by commoners who were so close to them.[1] The most extreme dissident was Isaka Hoza, a largely self-educated man who regarded Kilindi rule as illegitimate – he compared it to that of the Stuarts in England – and possessed the wide if sometimes inaccurate knowledge of world events often found among self-educated rural Tanganyikans.[2] The most important of the political societies was known simply as 'the *Chama*', a word originally meaning a secret society or witches' coven but now used to describe a political organisation. The *Chama* was founded in Mlalo, where trade, artisanship, Christianity, and Islam were strong. Mlalo was thrown into disorder in 1942 when its hereditary sub-chief, Hassani Kinyashi, was deposed because he was a worse tax-collector than rain-maker. The paramount chief, Shebuge Magogo, installed his nominee, whose efficient tax-collecting was accompanied by three years of drought. Agitation culminated in the wrecking of the sub-chief's house and a threat to squat outside the district office. Hassani Kinyashi was reinstated, but in October 1946 the government announced its plans to rehabilitate Mlalo – with attendant drudgery and regimentation – and the *Chama* led an opposition which gradually focussed on the ailing paramount chief, who was blamed for Usambara's backwardness and for acquiescing in the rehabilitation scheme.[3] Shebuge Magogo was a grandson of the Semboja who had precipitated Usambara's late nineteenth-century disintegration. In 1929 he had succeeded his

---

[1] Chamshama to Usambara Association, 4 April 1945, and Chamshama, circular, n.d., TNA 72/44/11/4 and 13; J. J. Hozza, 'The Hoza rebellion and after', B.A. thesis, University College, Dar es Salaam, 1969, p. 12; Feierman, 'Concepts', p. 164.

[2] Isaka Hoza to ?, 23 August 1947, TNA 77/44/16/14A.

[3] Hartnoll to CS, 19 June and 28 August 1948, TNA 31207/9 and 14; de Rosemond to Korogwe, 11 October 1946, TNA 4/269/5/1/169; anonymous letter in TNA 72/43/3/83A.

brother, Bila, who had himself replaced Kinyashi, the 'legitimist' candidate. Some men in Usambara thought the rightful king was Bila's son, Abraham Mputa Bila, who claimed the throne in 1946. Others believed that Kinyashi's descendants had the best right, although they did not wish to rule. Yet others, like Isaka Hoza, wanted to restore the clan heads subjected by Mbegha. During 1947 the district officer told the increasingly incapable Shebuge Magogo to appoint a deputy, apparently suggesting Samuel Chamshama, who had support among educated men. Conservatives accused Chamshama of coveting the throne and Magogo instead selected Sem Shemsanga. The activists replied on 4 August 1947 with a demonstration of some 5,000 people at Vugha to demand Magogo's abdication.[1]

The demonstration split Usambara. The court party formed a 'Peace Association' to demand the dissidents' punishment. Shambaa teachers at Minaki school formed 'The Hope of Usambara' to reconcile Shambaa and Kilindi and to advance the country. The dissidents united their societies into a branch of the African Association, presumably desiring its respectability and support, but the association's headquarters disowned them.[2] On 22 November 1947 Shebuge Magogo at last abdicated. Government promptly increased popular representation on the tribal council and instructed the elders of Vugha to choose a new paramount. The *Chama* backed Abraham Mputa Bila, but the elders chose Shebuge Magogo's son, Mputa Magogo. 'The son of a snake is a snake', Isaka Hoza observed, and when *Chama* leaders demonstrated in protest at exclusion from the assembly to ratify Mputa Magogo's succession, several were arrested and the 'African Association, Usambara Branch', was proscribed early in 1949.[3]

Yet it was not dead. During the next decade the British officials responsible for the rehabilitation scheme exploited the paramount and tribal council so ruthlessly that they destroyed much of the Kilindi regime's surviving legitimacy. In Mlalo, Hassani Kinyashi was again deposed in 1948, for indifference to rehabilitation, but had to be reinstated in 1950. By then the two main headmen's areas in Mlalo had

[1] Hozza, 'Hoza rebellion'; Isaka Hoza to ?, 23 August 1947, TNA 77/44/16/14A; 'Mkutano wa mazumbe wa viti', 4–5 June 1947, TNA 72/43/3/70; Lloyd, Korogwe DAR 1947, TNA 72/62/6/III/210.

[2] 'Chama cha Amani: mkutano wa kutafuta njia ya kukomesha uasi', 15–16 August 1947, TNA 72/44/16/12; 'Agenda na maoni ya mkutano mkuu wa kwanza wa chama cha "Tumaini la Usambaa"', 8 January 1948, TNA 72/44/11/46a; Salim Hoza and others to PC Tanga, 24 March 1948, TNA 4/6/2/442; above, p. 429.

[3] Piggott, Lushoto DAR 1948, TNA 72/62/6/III/211; Hozza, 'Hoza rebellion', p. 14.

had twelve headmen in three years. Mtae's native administration followed Vugha's into collapse in 1951. Sem Shemsanga moved into opposition in 1954. Mputa Magogo complained of being treated 'rather as a picture than a human being' but had to enforce rehabilitation measures. His opponents accused his agents of atrocities.[1] Dissidents beat wardrums to summon people to converge on Vugha, broke up council meetings, uprooted permanent crops planted on slopes, cut off the supply of milk to the European community, hired a witch to cast spells on the chief, and employed 'a disaffected Sheikh'.[2] When all these failed they sought outside aid, asking a British parliamentarian to raise their grievances in the House of Commons and then petitioning the United Nations. These measures also proved ineffectual, and instead the Shambaa turned to territorial politics,[3] following a route towards nationalism marked out during a better-known political conflict: the Meru Lands Case.

Meru politics were important because they attracted international attention to Tanganyika and because they contributed the north-eastern region's accumulated political experience to the emerging nationalist movement. Protest originated from Judge Wilson's proposal to remove Meru from two farms at Engare Nanyuki and Leguruki in order to create a homogeneous block of European ranching between Meru and Kilimanjaro.[4] The Meru Chief, Santi, gave his reluctant approval in 1948, but he was not the hereditary chief and had the support of only one Meru faction. The Meru were experiencing the tensions of 'peasantisation' as Christian coffee farmers – less than a third of all Meru – struggled for the leadership of the tribe, having already during the war secured control of the Lutheran church which became the framework for organised resistance to Judge Wilson's proposals.[5] As a final complication, government reorganised Meru native administration in 1948 by creating representative councils dominated by age-set rather than clan leaders, the government anthropologist having apparently based his recommendations chiefly on his knowledge of the neighbouring, but very

[1] Hill to Member for Development and Works, 9 January 1950, TNA 33049/IV/332; Macmillan, Lushoto DAR 1949, TNA 72/62/6/III/221; Thorne, Lushoto DAR 1954, TNA 4/962/1954; Mahanya Kibanga to PC Tanga, 20 August 1952, TNA 72/44/16/123.
[2] Chant, 'Usambara scheme annual report 1951', TNA 33049/IV/411; Macmillan, Lushoto DAR 1949, TNA 72/62/6/III/221.
[3] Usambara Union to Victor Collins M.P., n.d., TNA 4/6/2/503; 'Petition from representatives of the Washambala concerning Tanganyika', UNTC T/PET.2/170 of 31 August 1954; below, p. 526.
[4] Above, p. 451.
[5] Below, p. 546.

499

different, Arusha. The new constitution could not be implemented without first deporting eleven of Chief Santi's critics.[1]

Early in 1949 the Colonial Office at last approved Judge Wilson's proposals and the district officer told the Meru that Santi had agreed. The most articulate protest came from the 28-year-old secretary of TAA's Arusha branch, Kirilo Japhet.[2] Meru insisted that the Engare Nanyuki land – pasture with salt and water supplies and 513 settled taxpayers plus their dependents[3] - was greatly superior to the low, hot, malarial, tsetse-infested, and waterless alternative land offered them at Kingori. Emerging popular leaders contacted Petro Njau and formed the Meru Citizens Union. On 6 July 1951 government announced that the Meru would if necessary be evicted by force from Engare Nanyuki and Leguruki. Funds were collected to hire a lawyer and those threatened with eviction formed a 'Committee of Four' led by the local evangelist and teacher, Raphael Mbise. On 23 August they sent a letter of protest to the Colonial Secretary and to the United Nations.[4] Next day over 2,000 Meru met under the auspices of the Citizens Union and resolved that 'anyone accepting compensation will be ostracised and cursed by the tribe'.[5] The leaders decided to oppose eviction passively. Stiffened perhaps by a Conservative electoral victory, government apparently resolved to act before the detested United Nations could interfere.[6] On 17 October 1951 7 British officers (one wearing his ceremonial sword) reached Engare Nanyuki with 66 armed police and 100 Kikuyu labourers to carry out Operation Exodus. While the Meru watched from a hill, the officers listed each man's property as it was removed from his house, which was then bulldozed. The property was taken by lorry to Kingori, followed by some of the stock until the Meru removed the remainder themselves. Some 25 people were arrested and 2 Meru died, for reasons which were inevitably disputed. Engare Nanyuki was deserted.[7]

[1] Puritt, 'Meru', pp. 113–14; Arusha DAR 1948, TNA 69/63/16/84.
[2] Anton Nelson, *The Freemen of Meru* (Nairobi, 1967), pp. 25–6.
[3] The Colonial Office figure. See the notes of a discussion between Fabian Colonial Bureau and Colonial Office representatives, 5 December 1950, FCB papers 122, RH.
[4] Above, p. 493; Kirilo Japhet and Earle Seaton, *The Meru land case* (Nairobi, 1967), pp. 31–3; 'Statement of No. 7523 Det.-Sgt. Paulo, of Arusha', 13 July 1951, TNA 468; Puritt, 'Meru', p. 4; Munya Lengoroi and others to UN, 23 August 1951, Japhet papers, TNA.
[5] 'Transcription of a report by D/Sergeant Paulo and Constable Boniface', 28 August 1951, TNA 468.
[6] Stubbings to Raia wa Ngare Nanyuki, 31 October 1951, Japhet papers, TNA; Nelson, *Freemen*, pp. 35–7.
[7] Nelson, *Freemen*, ch. 9.

So also was Kingori. Rather than remain there, evicted families took refuge with kinsmen or even squatted on European farms. Young men talked wildly of violence, settlers wore pistols, and crime multiplied, but generally discipline held.[1] Raphael Mbise sent an account of Exodus to Chief Koinange in Kenya, who passed it on to a British parliamentarian and to the United Nations.[2] The next steps are obscure,[3] but on 9 June 1952 Meru leaders asked to be represented when the Trusteeship Council considered their petition. A public meeting chose Japhet and Earle Seaton, a West Indian lawyer practising in Moshi, as representatives. Seaton presented their case on 30 June and Japhet restated it on 21 July, when the Trusteeship Council deprecated the need to use force but rejected a Soviet resolution calling for the restoration of the Meru to their land. Japhet spoke twice again in later debates, but no further action resulted. The British had already stated that they would not restore the two farms.[4] Events at home were also moving against the resistance. Twining allocated increased funds to the Meru area and again reorganised the native administration. Santi was obliged to resign and the Meru Citizens Union took a large part in formulating a new constitution, only to find itself divided between conservatives from West Meru and radicals from the east where the evictions had taken place. In the voting for a new chief during 1953 Raphael Mbise, the eastern candidate, lost to Sylvanus Kaaya from the west, an educated member of the hereditary ruling clan. By the end of 1953 wealthy cattle owners from West Meru were grazing their beasts at Kingori, where 404 Meru taxpayers were already living. Criticisms of expensive and fruitless trips to New York were heard.[5]

In the wider political context, however, the Meru campaign had already done its work of connecting the popular politics of the north-east to TAA's territorial tradition. Japhet was a TAA secretary and TAA headquarters was aware of the gravity of events in Meru by May 1951.[6] At that time the Meru relied chiefly on the Kilimanjaro Union and Kenyan politicians, but the Chagga alliance collapsed when

---

[1] Munya Lengoroi to Congress of Peoples against Imperialism [November 1951?] Japhet papers, TNA; Nelson, *Freemen*, p. 49; Puritt, 'Meru', p. 9; *Tanganyika standard*, 28 June 1952.

[2] Nelson, *Freemen*, p. 43.

[3] For a possible hint, see Bildad Kaggia, *Roots of freedom* (Nairobi, 1975), p. 100.

[4] Japhet and Seaton, *Land case*, pp. 19–61.

[5] Minutes and correspondence in TNA 12844/IV; Puritt, 'Meru', p. 70; Arusha DARs 1954–6, TNA 471/R/3/3/1; Great Britain, *Observations*, p. 23.

[6] TAA Dar es Salaam to Cohen, 21 May 1951, TNA 41736/1.

Njau refused financial aid for the New York trip, while Kenyan contacts became counter-productive after an emergency was declared there in October 1952. Meanwhile Japhet left New York in July 1952 for London, where he met the young student Julius Nyerere. On 26 September 1952 Japhet wrote from London (saying it was his second letter) asking if TAA wished him to include anything in his next statement at the United Nations.[1] Seaton met TAA leaders in Dar es Salaam. In subsequent correspondence the secretary, Abdulwahid Sykes, acknowledged that the Meru protest 'is a matter for all the Africans of Tanganyika' but explained that headquarters had no funds, although it approached its branches.[2] In terms of political action TAA too was a broken reed, but the contacts bore fruit in 1953 when Japhet returned, after a period in California, with a new political awareness. 'The Ngare Nanyuki eviction has made the English word "development" a dirty word for us', he told an American friend.[3] In August 1953 a missionary in Arusha warned government: 'Beware of Kirilo...[who] is talking in terms of self-determination, African District Commissioners, and all the unrealistic cant which...is current coinage in American University circles.'[4] Visiting Dar es Salaam, Japhet renewed contact with Nyerere, now president of TAA. 'Government wants badly to hear the last of our Lands Case', he reported excitedly,

but I have been asked by Mr. Kandoro and Mr. Nyerere of the Tanganyika African Association to go on safari and tell the whole country about the Meru eviction and my adventures in the United Nations. The eviction woke our Meru people up to the indignity of being ruled without our consent by foreigners. Now we nationalists are going to wake up all Tanganyika.[5]

'I am writing this in great heart', he soon added; 'I have just come back after one and a half months turn in the Eastern, Central and Lake Provinces. It is all very promising.'[6] His visit to Sukumaland had aroused keen interest. 'The British Government is much more of a dictatorship than a democracy', a meeting of the Lake Province Growers Association was told in March 1954. 'This we know because UNO...said that the Wameru had been cheated out of their land, but

[1] Above, p. 494; Japhet and Seaton, *Land case*, p. 46; Japhet to Sykes, 26 September 1952, Japhet papers, TNA.
[2] Sablak to TAA Dar es Salaam, 29 November 1952, and Sykes to Sablak, 8 December 1952, TANU 3; S. A. Kandoro, *Mwito wa uhuru* (Dar es Salaam, 1961), p. 21.
[3] Nelson, *Freemen*, p. 68.
[4] Fosbrooke to PC Arusha, 15 August 1953, TNA 468.
[5] Nelson, *Freemen*, pp. 72–3.
[6] Japhet to Nelson, 9 November 1953, Japhet papers, TNA.

the Tanganyika Government ignored the fact that UNO judged against it.'[1]

The grievances of one area were becoming the grievances of all, to be explained by the nature of the colonial regime. And the political strands were also coming together, for the three men who cycled through Sukumaland in September and October 1953 represented the three political elements which fused to form the Tanganyikan nationalist movement. Kirilo Japhet embodied the popular politics of the north-east, Abbas Sykes was secretary of TAA in Dar es Salaam, and ahead of them rode Saadani Kandoro, firebrand and full-time organiser of Sukumaland's political awakening.[2]

The politicisation of the Lake Province

During the 1930s the headquarters of the African Association stimulated the formation of provincial branches which drifted apart, gathered local energies, and then revitalised headquarters when it was in decay. In the 1940s and 1950s the cycle was repeated, and this time revitalisation came from the Lake Province. TAA's decay in the late 1940s was evident. Some branches, notably Moshi and Usangi, were absorbed into tribal politics. Others, such as Ujiji, were concerned solely with township affairs.[3] Long-established branches in Dodoma, Singida, Bagamoyo, and elsewhere survived with their aging and inactive leaders unchanged from year to year. There were exceptions. The Tanga branch was taken over in the early 1950s by disgruntled men from Makerere, notably Godfrey Kayamba and Steven Mhando, who in 1951 presented a U.N. visiting mission with a document denouncing multi-racial parity and demanding 'nothing short but complete Freedom'.[4] But such energy was rare indeed.

The contrast in Lake Province was remarkable. There TAA made three important contributions to Tanganyika's political development in the early 1950s. Its provincial organisation, imitated from TAGSA, penetrated the countryside and drew energy from rural grievances. Its leadership was more professional than anything previously seen in Tanganyika. And it added a frontal attack on the colonial regime and a demand for rapid independence to TAA's programme. There

[1] Maguire, '*Uhuru*', p. 107.
[2] Kandoro, *Mwito*, pp. 25–6; Maguire, '*Uhuru*', pp. 150–1; Listowel, *Making*, pp. 214–15.
[3] Above, pp. 412, 429; McHenry, 'Study', pp. 408–9.
[4] 'Petition from the African Association, Tanga branch', UNTC T/PET.2/130 of 5 October 1951; Mbuli, 'Tanga'.

were probably two reasons for this radicalism. One was that Sukumaland, the core of the region, was at this time experiencing the
tensions of peasantisation which Kilimanjaro and Buhaya had felt in
the 1920s, but whereas the political energy generated in those two areas
had been channelled into local politics, Lake Province was already
within a framework of territorial politics and Sukumaland's political
energies flowed into TAA and TANU. Here, as so often, unevenness
of development was the key to political change. The second reason
for radicalism was the existence in Mwanza of a small group of
activists. The most influential was the cooperative organiser, Paul
Bomani, but he was chiefly concerned with commercial affairs. The
most active politician was Isaac Bhoke Munanka, a Kuria born in 1927
and trained as a clerk at Tabora school. A young man of strong
and simple convictions but little judgment, Munanka was to be a
storm-centre of Tanganyikan politics for a decade. He first intervened
in territorial politics in 1950 when he drafted the memorandum which
TAA's Mwanza branch submitted to the Constitutional Committee
denouncing settler political ambitions and demanding that government should start to prepare Africans for independence.[1] Preparation
for self-government was the Mwanza leaders' theme for the next four
years. It was not new, but it was stated with a new persistence.
Moreover, when the Constitutional Committee made large concessions
to the settlers, Munanka resigned his government post in January 1952
to devote more time to politics.[2] In this he was joined by another
activist, Saadani Kandoro. A Manyema from Ujiji, Kandoro had been
a schoolteacher and clerk before turning to trade. He delighted in the
Swahili language and exchanged verses with a group of Manyema
friends including Amri Abedi, later a leading Muslim. Their poems
reveal increasing political awareness. In one written in 1948 Kandoro
urged that Africans should choose their own representatives and use
Swahili in the Legislative Council. A year later, under a pseudonym,
he stressed the need to 'begin the work of speaking for Africa'. In
1952 Amri Abedi followed with a poem on *uhuru*.[3] Meanwhile
Kandoro had formed a society, 'Rightway', to act as a ginger group
within TAA, and his trading journeys had taken him to Kenya and
Mwanza. There he met Munanka and Bomani, debating late into the
night 'ways of freeing the country from slavery'. When Munanka

[1] Above, p. 480; Maguire, '*Uhuru*', p. 136.
[2] Kandoro, *Mwito*, p. 19.
[3] S. A. Kandoro, *Mashairi ya Saadani* (Dar es Salaam, 1972), pp. 142–3, 136–7; M. M.
Mulokozi, 'Revolution and reaction in Swahili poetry', *Umma*, IV (1974), 132.

resigned, Bomani suggested they invite Kandoro to be TAA's full-time secretary in Lake Province. He took up the post during 1952.[1]

The triumvirate first sought to revitalise TAA. New rules laid down that no officer of the provincial branch might work for government or an alien employer and that district branches must pay all funds above Shs. 200 a year to provincial headquarters. The leaders next turned to the territorial organisation, urging in May 1952 that it should call a territorial conference and choose a more specifically political name – apparently one suggestion was TANU. Concern with both local and territorial issues characterised their programme, which ranged from opposition to cattle culling and crop cesses to demands for elected African representatives and a target date for independence.[2] By championing local grievances they gathered support. Since 1949 one lively TAA branch had existed in Busega, a frontier area east of Mwanza, where the local organiser, a farmer-trader named Stephano Sanja, was at odds with the chief. A similar branch opened in June 1952 among the Sukuma colonists of Geita.[3] When Kirilo Japhet and Abbas Sykes arrived in September 1953, Kandoro began recruiting tours, imitating the successful methods of the cooperatives and Sukuma Union. During January 1954 he held seventeen public meetings in six districts. A month earlier Munanka had attempted unsuccessfully to attend a pan-African meeting in Lusaka.[4]

By mid 1953 the British were seriously alarmed at political developments in Lake Province and took the long-contemplated step of prohibiting civil servants from belonging to TAA, the Asian Association, or the Tanganyika European Council – later adding the Sukuma Union – in order to preserve political impartiality.[5] TAA's headquarters protested that this was 'equivalent to banning the Tanganyika African Association',[6] but the Sukumaland campaign was little affected. It culminated when Twining visited Mwanza in February 1954. Bhoke Munanka submitted a list of local grievances claiming that 'destocking has taught every African that it is Government's purpose to make the Africans beggars' and that the cotton cess was 'intended to impoverish the people from birth to death, and to

[1] Kandoro, *Mwito*, pp. 1–20; Maguire, '*Uhuru*', pp. 136–7.
[2] Maguire, '*Uhuru*', p. 138; Kandoro, *Mwito*, pp. 2–3, 22–5.
[3] Maguire,'*Uhuru*',pp. 113–19,140–1; correspondence in TNA 41/A/6/6 and 251/30/3/1.
[4] Maguire, '*Uhuru*', pp. 150–3; Kandoro, *Mwito*, p. 31.
[5] Vicars-Harris, circular, 1 August 1953, TNA 7/3/2/145.
[6] Nyerere to Twining, 10 August 1953, TANU 49.

make them carriers of loads, hewers of wood and drawers of water
for other races'.[1] Furious, Twining refused to meet a TAA deputation
and instead denounced them to the assembled chiefs as 'a lot of
uneducated, ignorant people' who 'are trying to undermine the policy
of Government' and 'destroy the position of the Chiefs'. 'They
represent nobody except themselves', he claimed. '...I have no
intention of encouraging them. The people whom I am going to
encourage are the people who are members of Councils and...the
Chiefs and the Native Authorities.'[2] This confrontation ensured that
the emerging nationalist movement would face the open hostility of
the British regime. The activists protested fruitlessly to the Secretary
of State,[3] and a campaign of victimisation began in the countryside.
In Maswa the chiefs decided to call first on TAA and Sukuma Union
members for communal labour and sought power to flog their critics.
In May 1954 native authority approval was made a prerequisite for
meetings throughout the Lake Province.[4]

The political movement had meanwhile spread beyond Sukumaland. TAA's branch in Musoma, formed in 1947, was revived in 1952
by traders led by Selemani Kitundu and adopted the full Mwanza
programme, as did the neighbouring Tarime branch.[5] In Bukoba
TAA was revitalised by Ali Migeyo, an illiterate Muslim trader-politician
who had been active in the crisis of 1937. Early in 1952 he attended
the meeting which approved new rules for the provincial branch and
gathered from Munanka – 'an exceptionally bright young man' – his
first vague understanding of independence.[6] In Ali Migeyo's hands
TAA's campaign in Bukoba concentrated on old-fashioned issues:
hostility between commoners and chiefs, often centring on *nyarubanja*,
and opposition to agricultural officials seeking to enforce the destruction of banana plants infested with weevils. It was a popular
campaign, for during 1952–3 Bukoba provided Shs. 6,200 of the Shs.
9,346 reaching TAA's provincial headquarters, but the campaign
reached its almost inevitable climax in December 1953 when Ali Migeyo
held an unauthorised meeting at notoriously dissident Kamachumu
and the police dispersed the crowd with tear-gas – its first use in

[1] Bhoke Munanka to Twining, 1 February 1954, TNA 215/1332/XIII/188.
[2] 'Address by H.E. the Governor to the chiefs of the Mwanza district', 17 February 1954, TNA 215/1332/XIII.
[3] Kandoro, *Mwito*, pp. 46–50.   [4] Maguire, '*Uhuru*', pp. 170–1.
[5] Musoma historical report (answers to a historical questionnaire sent to TANU branches by the party's research section during 1964) TANU 53; TAA Tarime to PC Lake, 23 July 1954, TNA 215/1921/1/74.
[6] Mutahaba, *Portrait*, p. 19.

Tanganyika.[1] The Lake Province leaders protested to the Colonial Office and a sympathetic parliamentarian. They contemplated petitioning the United Nations. But meanwhile the incident had attracted more important attention. On 15 December 1953 Munanka and Kandoro visited Bukoba in the company of TAA's new territorial president, Julius Nyerere.[2] The strands were drawing closer.

Julius Nyerere and the formation of TANU

Although most of the impetus towards nationalism came from Sukumaland and the north-east, it could not have produced an effective nationalist movement without a simultaneous assertion of leadership from Dar es Salaam. Without it the result would have been a dispersal of energy similar to that which had aborted the political awakening of the mid 1940s. Dar es Salaam's revival between 1949 and 1953 took place in two stages. One was a reaction to Twining's 'cock-shy' of 1949, which by stimulating settler demands also alerted two groups of Africans in the capital. One consisted of men who had been student politicians at Makerere in the 1940s: Vedast Kyaruzi, a Haya doctor; Hamza Mwapachu, a British-trained social welfare worker; Steven Mhando, an articulate Bondei teacher; and Luciano Tsere, an Iraqw doctor. The other group contained educated townsmen who had fought in Burma, notably Dossa Aziz, James Mkande, and Abdulwahid and Ally Sykes. Early in 1950 these groups jointly drafted a memorandum to the Constitutional Committee proposing phased constitutional advance to responsible government in thirteen years. A general meeting of TAA adopted this memorandum in March 1950 and elected Kyaruzi president with Abdulwahid Sykes as secretary.[3] The new leaders planned a political campaign, investigated the law governing political meetings and processions, criticised repressive measures proposed after a dock strike, invited the Indian High Commissoner to speak on 'India's own struggle for freedom', and protested to a visiting British minister at the lack of higher education, the slow Africanisation of the civil service, and growing settler influence. During 1951 the leaders met Andrew Cohen of the Colonial Office and sought 'a declaration of a period, after which they will consider giving at least self-government to us'. The U.N. mission of

[1] Kandoro, *Mwito*, p. 32; Mutahaba, *Portrait*, pp. 20–1; Maguire, '*Uhuru*', pp. 152–3.
[2] Kandoro, *Mwito*, pp. 29–30, 51–60.
[3] Listowel, *Making*, pp. 121, 186–91; Sykes to CS, 27 March 1950, TNA 19325/11/171; above, p. 480.

1951 noticed that during the previous three years TAA had made 'a great advance towards political maturity and towards a better organization'.[1] Its interests were also widening. It congratulated Nkrumah when he took power in Ghana and it established contact with the Fabian Colonial Bureau.[2] But by the end of 1951 the momentum was fading. Kyaruzi was posted to Morogoro Prison Hospital and the presidency passed to Thomas Plantan, a former askari with little education. Older, less active leaders took over once more. Parity appeared to satisfy them. Letters went unanswered. No money was available to aid the Meru. To secure a minimal income, one room in the New Street headquarters was let to an Asian laundry. Late in 1952 the association apparently had no president and held no meetings. Activists in Mwanza considered transferring territorial headquarters there. The cycle of decay seemed to have begun again.[3]

Julius Nyerere's election as president in April 1953 checked TAA's decline. He was 31 and the son of a government chief among the backward and previously stateless Zanaki, whose egalitarianism the young Nyerere had inherited. Christianity was another foundation of his character, for he had been one of the first Zanaki to become a Roman Catholic. A first-generation convert of sparkling intelligence, Nyerere had been the archetypal mission boy whose academic success had carried him from local primary school to Tabora, Makerere, and finally Edinburgh University in October 1949.[4] His friends' recollections suggest a slight, diffident, but ambitious and competitive young man gradually emancipating himself from the intellectual constraints of a mission education without abandoning its moral or cultural imperatives. One part of the young Nyerere was student politician. He had been the African Association's first president at Makerere and an active member while teaching at Tabora in 1946. In Britain he had joined the Fabian Colonial Bureau, had sympathised with the Fabian

---

[1] Mkande to Member for Law and Order, 27 April 1950, TNA 19325/11/178; *Tanganyika standard*, 6 May 1950; Sykes to Standing committee of the nationals of India, 4 June 1950, TANU 3; *Tanganyika opinion*, 16 June 1950; TAA Dar es Salaam to Dugdale, 30 August 1950, TNA 19325/11/188; TAA Dar es Salaam to Cohen, 21 May 1951, TNA 41736/1; UN, *Report of the visiting mission to trust territories in East Africa, 1951, on Tanganyika* (UNTC T/946), p. 12.

[2] Marealle to Nicholson, 14 March 1951, and Nicholson to Sykes, 24 April 1951, FCB papers 121, RH; Nicholson to Marealle, 20 March 1951, TANU 3.

[3] Listowel, *Making*, p. 213; TAA Dar es Salaam to Lennox-Boyd, 11 January 1952, TNA 41736/18; Sykes to Nicholson, 24 November 1952, and to Sablak, 8 December 1952, TANU 3; Maguire, '*Uhuru*', p. 142.

[4] There is no adequate biography. See William E. Smith, *Nyerere of Tanzania* (London, 1973); Listowel, *Making*, pp. 170–207.

variety of gradualist socialism, had written for the Fabians an angry but unpublished pamphlet on East Africa's racial problems, had interested himself in Ghana and the Central African Federation, and apparently had sat at the feet of George Padmore, the West Indian pan-Africanist who had been Nkrumah's mentor. Nyerere had been in Britain when the great issues of race and liberation in Africa were first being defined. His political concerns were not the grass-roots material problems on which most politicians build careers but the grand issues of political morality. Nyerere could have been a great teacher, and had he not lived in the Africa of the 1950s he might well have remained one.

When Nyerere returned late in 1952, Tanganyika was not yet ready for mass nationalism. It had only relatively minor grievances over land alienation and settler control. It had no vigorous tradition of elite politics. It had no powerful indigenous polity. It had no electoral system to stimulate political organisation. Local issues were provoking political action in several regions, but only in Meru and Sukumaland was it action against the very existence of colonial rule. A mass nationalist movement therefore had to stress Tanganyika's future dangers and to imitate methods employed in the different circumstances of India and Ghana. This could be Nyerere's contribution, for almost alone among Tanganyikans he had the knowledge of world events and the understanding of political theory to organise a movement which did not grow from local necessities. Nyerere was racially sensitive, hated foreign rule, feared Conservative complicity with settler ambitions, and knew that Africa was moving towards conflict and liberation.[1] But he was no natural politician, no Nkrumah hungry for power. In Britain he apparently contemplated ordination. He wished to prolong his studies, but government refused to extend his grant. He feared to be rushed into commitment and action.[2] A journalist reported him as saying later:

At Edinburgh, I was certain I was coming back to get myself involved full-time in politics... I had been away three years; now I would give myself three years to look at the country before taking up politics fully. And I nearly did my three years. By 1953 it was quite clear to me: it must be the politics of independence.[3]

[1] These points appear in his essay, 'The race problem in East Africa', in Nyerere, *Freedom and unity*, pp. 23–9.
[2] Listowel, *Making*, p. 205; Twining to Lyttleton, 20 December 1951, TNA 23140/III/465; information from Dr Ross.
[3] Smith, *Nyerere*, p. 50.

Events probably forced a final decision on him. He accepted a teaching post a few miles outside Dar es Salaam and settled there with his newly-married wife in February 1953. Having studied and taught at Tabora and Makerere, he knew almost every Tanganyikan secondary school graduate of the 1940s. In Dar es Salaam he met again Joseph Kasella Bantu, once a fellow teacher and now active in TAA. He also met young townsmen like the Sykes brothers who wanted to revitalise TAA. Nyerere shared their impatience but insisted that any political movement must take TAA as its basis or risk dividing the country.[1] In April 1953 his friends engineered his election as TAA's president. With a middle-aged trader, John Rupia, as treasurer, the young men took control of the association. Kasella Bantu was secretary, aided by Dossa Aziz, and the committee included several Kenyans and Nyasas active in urban and labour affairs. In August 1953 Nyerere addressed a meeting publicising the new African Commercial Employees Association.[2]

During 1953 the elements came together. In August civil servants had to quit TAA, which both destroyed the likely opposition to the association's transformation and raised the danger that it might fall into irresponsible hands. In September, with Nyerere's encouragement, Kirilo Japhet and Abbas Sykes toured Lake Province. Nyerere was apparently at an up-country teachers' conference in December 1953 when he heard of the Kamachumu incident. He hastened to investigate and probably first learned the extent of TAA's conflict with government in Lake Province. The next step is obscure, but the logic of the situation is clear. The danger – at the height of Mau Mau – was that the unsophisticated militants of Lake Province might provoke disorder and thereby either break TAA's unity – carrying out a 'green revolution'[3] against established political leaders such as happened in Kenya, Senegal, and Sierra Leone – or embroil TAA in open confrontation with government, thereby enormously complicating the nationalists' task. Writing from Ukerewe in June 1954, Hamza Mwapachu identified the dilemma:

Closer investigation of African opinion reveals growing suspicion of the Government and a more alert political consciousness than one came across

[1] Information from Mr Kasella Bantu.
[2] Listowel, *Making*, p. 221; *Tanganyika standard*, 19 June 1953; A. C. A. Tandau, 'The history of the Tanganyika Federation of Labour from 1955 to 1962', typescript translation by George Kaunda of A. C. A. Tandau, *Historia ya kuundwa kwa T.F.L. (1955–1962) na kuanzishwa kwa NUTA (1964)* (Dar es Salaam, n.d.), p. 2 (all page numbers refer to the translation); below, p. 537.
[3] I owe the phrase to Dr Christopher Clapham.

a decade ago. What is lacking is leadership. All potential leaders are in the civil service and the element of hazard is still great for them to leave their secured positions to offer the people their leadership. In fact a deplorable and serious situation is fast developing whereby this leadership is being snatched by an ill-informed, ill-fitted element of the community in attempts to meet the demand. It is a challenge to all educated Africans in this Territory.[1]

Nyerere had already written to the Mwanza leaders, early in 1954, warning them of their danger and protesting at their action in cabling the Colonial Office about the Kamachumu incident without head-quarters' approval. Munanka replied that these were the ideas of people who were not confronted by the country's problems.[2] At a TAA meeting at Dodoma in April 1954 Nyerere found open tension between older and younger members, the latter including a teacher named Oscar Kambona.[3] Nyerere probably sympathised with the younger radicals, but he must in any case satisfy them or watch TAA fragment.

One of Nyerere's greatest political gifts was to react *creatively* to situations which pressed on him, not merely satisfying demands but by his response transforming a political context to his own advantage.[4] He did this now. Early in 1954 a group of activists – apparently including Japhet, Rupia, Kandoro, and one of the Sykes brothers – began to discuss a new constitution,[5] the draft being Nyerere's and based on the constitutions of Britain's Labour Party and Ghana's Convention People's Party. The new constitution enabled any African to join TAA on payment of a shilling entrance fee and a subscription of fifty cents a month. There were three major differences from TAA's previous constitution. First, trade unions, cooperatives, and tribal unions could affiliate themselves and pay a political levy, and there were to be youth's and women's sections. Second, the supreme organ was to be the annual delegates' conference which would elect a national executive committee (NEC) to formulate policy, while daily business was conducted by elected officers and a central committee appointed by the president – innovations clearly designed to give up-country leaders a share in decision-making, to provide offices for TAA's notables in Dar es Salaam, and to increase central control, which

[1] Mwapachu to Nicholson, 19 June 1954, FCB papers 121, RH.
[2] Kandoro, *Mwito*, p. 71.
[3] 'Minutes za mkutano wa kumkaribisha Bwana Nyerere', 23 April 1954, Suleiman papers, TNA; Chiume, *Kwacha*, pp. 58–9.
[4] Pratt, *Critical phase*, p. 202.
[5] M. J. H. Lugazia to *Tanganyika standard*, 26 December 1957, TANU 34; Japhet and Seaton, *Land case*, p. 62; Listowel, *Making*, pp. 222–3.

was further strengthened by empowering headquarters to appoint and pay all officers (except at branch level) and receive all but thirty per cent of the funds collected by branches. Mwanza was not to rival Dar es Salaam as Dodoma had done in the 1940s. The third and most important innovation was in TAA's aims: 'to prepare the people of Tanganyika for self-Government and Independence, and to fight relentlessly until Tanganyika is self-governing and independent'; to fight tribalism and 'build up a united nationalism'; to secure elected African majorities on public bodies; to advance education, trade unions, and cooperatives; to oppose discrimination, land alienation, immigration, and European-dominated federation; and to cooperate with other national movements for Africa's liberation.[1]

From the old TAA the new association inherited individual membership open only to Africans and the framework of provincial and local branches. The aim of preparing Tanganyika for independence, rather than demanding 'self-government now', probably came from Mwanza. Many of the particular objectives were the common coin of African politics. The innovations were the tightly controlled structure, the pan-Africanism, and the coherence of the programme. They were Nyerere's contribution.

Reorganisation was urgently needed. In April 1954 an ordinance required associations to secure government recognition, submitting their constitutions. Politicians waited to learn whether elections for the new legislature with parity representation would be held, especially in Dar es Salaam, and Nyerere wanted TAA to be ready to organise African voters, although government eventually announced in June 1954 that the first legislature with racial parity would be nominated rather than elected.[2] A U.N. mission was due late in 1954. In preparation for these developments, Nyerere called TAA's first territorial conference for seven years to meet in Dar es Salaam on 7 July 1954.

The photograph taken after that meeting fixed its character.[3] Only seventeen men were present for most of the time. Their very clothes divide them into two groups. Nyerere, slight and youthful, sits in the

[1] 'The Tanganyika African Association: constitution', enclosed in DC Singida to PC Central, 29 June 1954, TNA 68/R/2/3.
[2] Nyerere to CS, 6 March 1954, and Nicholson to Tobias, 14 July 1954, FCB papers 123, RH; Martin Lowenkopf, 'Political parties in Uganda and Tanganyika', M.Sc. (Econ.) thesis, University of London, 1961, p. 134.
[3] Photograph in Kandoro, *Mwito*, facing p. 72. Minutes in *ibid.*, pp. 74–82 (and originals in TANU 49). For other accounts, see Frederick, 'Kimalando', p. 27; Ngalula, 'Lameck Bogohe'.

centre, wearing the mission teacher's white shirt, shorts, and socks. On his right, in white jacket and striped tie, is the heavy, respectable figure of Vice-President Rupia. Behind him, in dapper town clothes, are Abdulwahid Sykes, Dossa Aziz, and a sprinkling of contemporaries from Dar es Salaam: Ally Sykes, Saidi Tewa, Joseph Kasella Bantu, C. O. Millinga, and their friend Patrick Kunambi from Morogoro. One other man wears city clothes: Germano Pacha, the young trader representing Tabora. The other men in the picture are provincials. On Nyerere's left sits Joseph Kimalando from Moshi, the most experienced TAA activist present. Also in the front row, relaxed and travelled, is Kirilo Japhet from Meru. All the others are from Lake Province. Kandoro, squat, belligerent, pushes forward from the back row. Lameck Bogohe stands tall beside him. Selemani Kitwana, Kisung'uta Gabora, and Abubakari Irangi stare doubtfully at the camera in market-day clothes. Tanganyika's two modern political elements, townsmen and peasants, mingle uneasily.

It had been an odd meeting. Opened with prayers, the entire first session was spent restoring relations between headquarters and Lake Province by letting the provincial leaders win. Their cable to the Colonial Office was approved because of Dar es Salaam's lethargy. The headquarters secretary was disowned for not consulting Lake Province leaders before allowing Ali Migeyo to be prosecuted for misappropriating TAA funds. These concessions were necessary to Nyerere's success on the second day, when the new constitution was approved, apparently unchanged. The meeting also altered the association's name to TANU. A variety of issues occupied the third day. Some of those present thought its high point was Nyerere's statement that since Tanganyika was not a colony it owed no allegiance to the Queen. Only in retrospect did the full significance of this 'Saba Saba'[1] meeting appear.

The first phase of nationalist growth (*July 1954 – November 1955*)

As up-country delegates departed and Dar es Salaam leaders continued full-time jobs, their first task was to impose their design on TAA's branches. Letters to secretaries and district officers insisted that branches either affiliate to TANU or hand over their property. Sukuma leaders moved first, instructing their branches, with roughly 5,000 members, to elect new officers and register with government as

[1] Seventh of the seventh, i.e. 7 July.

TANU.[1] Their impetus was swiftly checked. In August 1954 TANU's branch chairman at Malampaka, Stanley Kaseko, held a meeting without the local chief's permission and was gaoled. Government resolved to act before it lost control of Sukumaland. In October it refused to register TANU branches there and banned party activity (although not individual membership). Kandoro was ordered back to Ujiji. Bomani concentrated on cooperatives. Munanka worked with a car-dealer and headed what was virtually an underground movement.[2] Ironically, the ban probably did TANU a crucial service, for it is unlikely that Nyerere could long have controlled the Lake Province branch as it then existed.

Kirilo Japhet had little more success in establishing powerful TANU organisation. The Arusha branch quickly registered itself and affiliated the Arusha and Meru Citizens Unions. Representatives of the latter attended TANU meetings until late in 1957. In May 1955 party leaders resolved to create village branches throughout Arusha district. In reality, however, TANU could as yet offer the Meru little aid. The Meru Citizens Union was decaying. Japhet was becoming a substantial farmer and had little time for TANU work. He was eventually replaced as provincial chairman in February 1958. Meanwhile the Arusha branch stagnated.[3]

Most branches responded to news of the Saba Saba meeting by changing their names to TANU, registering themselves with government, retaining their former officers, and doing little else. Germano Pacha's branch at Tabora was registered in December 1954 but apparently did not hold a meeting outside the town until November 1955.[4] In Dodoma Ali Ponda and Hassan Suleiman changed their branch to TANU and took no further action until December 1955.[5] In Bagamoyo, 60 kilometres from the capital, it took three months for TAA's leaders, Mtumwa Makusudi and Sheikh Muhammad Ramiya,

[1] Juma Athmani to Nansio, 28 September 1954, TNA 158/A/6/7/1/47; Allen to Bukoba, 21 September 1954, TNA 215/2818/1/32; Maguire, '*Uhuru*', p. 180.

[2] Correspondence in TNA 215/1921/1/77–91; RS to TANU Mwanza, 7 October 1954, and Scott to Kandoro, 3 November 1954, FCB papers 121, RH; Maguire, '*Uhuru*', pp. 178–83.

[3] TAA Arusha, application for registration, 30 June 1954, TNA 472/A/6/3/13; 'Mambo yaliyozungumzwa katika mkutano wa halmashauri ya jimbo tarehe 3 Novemba 1957', TANU 35; TANU Arusha to Olkarsis, 21 May 1955, TNA 472/A/6/3/4; 'Mambo ya mkutano wa provincial executive committee ya TANU jimbo la kaskazini', 6 January 1957, and 'Mambo yaliyozungumzwa katika mkutano wa halmashauri ya TANU jimbo la kaskazini', 22–23 February 1958, TANU 35.

[4] Tabora historical report, TANU 53; Pacha to Tabora, 26 November 1955, TNA 47/A/6/11/1.

[5] Hajivayanis and others in Iliffe, *Tanzanians*, pp. 251–2.

to learn of TANU's existence. Then they bought membership cards in Dar es Salaam but took no political action until 1955.[1] Visiting Ujiji, Kandoro gave a distinctly cautious tone to his public speech. TANU's objects, he said, were:

(a) to defend or fight for our rights; (b) to do everything possible with the object in mind for a self-Govt.; (c) to fight for equal pay where the work and skill or experience is the same; (d) to see that Govt. fulfils her duty towards its subjects and vice versa; (e) to further trading spirit among Africans with a view to ousting Indian traders.

I must make it clear to you all that it is more than stupidity to ignore the good work done by the Govt. We must appreciate what good the Govt. has done for us.[2]

TAA's territorial structure was of immense value to TANU, ensuring that it need not work outwards from a single town or tribe and thereby provoke particularistic opposition. Yet not all TAA branches accepted the Saba Saba decisions unquestioningly. The Mafia Island branch did not rename itself TANU until 1956.[3] Some, notably Tanga,[4] were so weakened by the ban on civil servants that they could not provide TANU with a nucleus. At least one, Usangi, had lost contact with territorial politics.[5] More important were those which actively resisted TANU. TAA's president in Lindi reacted to an early TANU statement by publicly doubting whether Tanganyika would be ready for self-government in less than 200 years.[6] But the main difficulty was in Kilimanjaro and Bukoba. After Thomas Marealle's election in 1951 his opponents allied with the rump of the old TAA in Moshi, led by Joseph Kimalando. After the Saba Saba meeting Kimalando publicised TANU's programme and the Kilimanjaro Union denounced it as 'a racial group', declaring support for Twining's multi-racialism. This conflict continued until Kimalando lost TANU's leadership in April 1956, when he promptly reformed a TAA branch in opposition to TANU. The futile dispute helped to prevent TANU making any serious impact on Kilimanjaro at this

[1] Nimtz, 'Sufi order', pp. 485–8; correspondence in TNA 7/3/2/149–71.
[2] Report by Daudi Amri on TANU meeting, 12 August 1954, copy in my possession. I owe this reference to Dr Larson.
[3] TAA Mafia to DC Mafia, 8 November 1955, and R. Makange to DC Mafia, 20 September 1956, TNA 177/S/1/5/5 and 6.
[4] DC Tanga urban to TANU Tanga, 7 November 1955, TNA 304/25/A/1/155; Mbuli, 'Tanga'.
[5] Lukwaro, 'Records', pp. 1–3; DC Same to PC Tanga, 20 January 1956, TNA 304/25/A/1/174.
[6] *Tanganyika standard*, 7 February 1955.

period.[1] Bukoba's problem arose from Ali Migeyo's campaign in 1953 and his subsequent prosecution for misappropriating TAA funds. In his absence TAA and its property were taken over by conservatives led by Elias Lushakuzi. Learning of TANU's formation, they rejected the constitution, especially its financial provisions. Meanwhile a 'centre' group led by Herbert Rugizibwa visited Mwanza and returned resolved to affiliate to TANU. The dispute was not resolved until June 1955. TANU remained unregistered and unable to hold meetings in Bukoba until March 1956.[2]

Thus TAA's branches gave TANU a vital structure but little impetus, once the Sukuma branches were banned. If TANU was to transform Tanganyikan politics, the impetus must come from headquarters. It came slowly. Nyerere and his colleagues did not want TANU to become a mass movement rapidly lest lack of leadership should cause it to run out of control.[3] Instead they concentrated on the capital and on *preparing* Tanganyika for independence. 'At the moment our greatest concern is the educational and economic development of our people', Nyerere explained in September 1954.[4] Moreover, their jobs left little time for politics. Nyerere had to walk in from Pugu twice a week and often type his own letters. The European press dismissed TANU's programme as unrealistic, while few Asian or European leaders paid it any attention. Among Dar es Salaam's Africans the party met much suspicion and incredulity. 'From long ago', a TAA elder told Nyerere at his first public meeting, 'we have believed that we should be ruled until the end of the world!'[5]

Two events offered TANU a political break-through. One was Oscar Kambona's appointment as full-time secretary, on the understanding that he must raise his own salary by enrolling members.[6] He proved a talented and enthusiastic recruiter. The other event was the U.N.

[1] 'Mambo ya mkutano wa Wachagga', 2 January 1954, TNA 471/A/6/22/3; Njau to *Tanganyika standard*, 26 October 1954, TNA 5/25/7/230; 'Mambo ya mkutano wa executive committee ya jimbo la kaskazini', 12 August 1956, TANU 35; 'Minutes of a meeting', 4 January 1957, TNA 5/25/7/289.
[2] DC Bukoba to PC Lake, 22 July and 28 August 1954, TNA 215/2818/1/21 and 30; J. F. Mutafungwa to DC Bukoba, 17 March 1955, E. Lushakuzi to TANU Bukoba, 22 March 1955, and TANU Bukoba to DC Bukoba, 17 April 1956, TNA 71/A/6/16/1, 3, 17; Hydén, *Political development*, p. 119.
[3] Nyerere to Selwyn-Clarke, 4 July 1955, FCB papers 121, RH; Lowenkopf, 'Parties', pp. 134–6.
[4] Nyerere to Nicholson, 15 September 1954, FCB papers 121, RH.
[5] Ulotu Abubaker Ulotu, *Historia ya TANU* (Dar es Salaam, 1971), p. 188. (This book is a slightly amended version of an untitled, duplicated draft in TANU headquarters. I shall refer to the original [in TANU 9] as 'Historia ya TANU'.)
[6] E. B. M. Barongo, *Mkiki mkiki wa siasa Tanganyika* (Dar es Salaam, 1966), pp. 80–2.

visiting mission's arrival in August 1954. TANU's representatives demanded more rapid development, the end of parity after three years, elections in Dar es Salaam, recognition that Tanganyika was 'primarily an African country', and a timetable for constitutional advance. Pressed by the mission, Nyerere suggested that independence might come in 25 years.[1] Recognising the mission's sympathy, TANU's NEC decided in October that Nyerere should visit New York and attend the Trusteeship Council's discussion of the mission's report if it was favourable.[2] The report appeared in January 1955 and exceeded all TANU's hopes, accepting the feasibility of self-government within one generation and describing TANU as 'a national movement'.[3] Nyerere's statement to the Trusteeship Council on 7 March 1955 was a personal triumph and established the predominant tone of TANU's subsequent campaign. TANU, government, and United Nations were all concerned to prepare Tanganyika for non-racial independence, he urged, but he insisted 'that although Tanganyika is multi-racial in population, it is primarily African'.[4]

The real importance of Nyerere's trip was its impact in Tanganyika, especially in Dar es Salaam where part of the money for the fare was raised. In February 1955 many Africans still feared to join TANU lest government should ban it. By contrast, when Nyerere told TANU's first mass meeting on 20 March 1955 that self-government might come in 20–25 years, voices in the crowd protested that it was too long.[5] Both Nyerere and others were struck by the crowd's discipline. TANU then had some 2,000 members in Dar es Salaam. Four months later there were over 5,000.[6] 'The intentions, aims, and entrance procedures (*malango*) of TANU are the talk of the town', Kambona told a meeting.[7] By June 1955 he was enrolling a hundred members a day and Nyerere ordered that ward branches should be formed in order to maintain discipline.[8] 'In spite of our own reluctance to let TANU swell out into a mass movement', he wrote in July, 'TANU is swelling out very rapidly.'[9] The pattern of TANU's support in Dar es Salaam needs study, but financial returns for 1958 show the bulk of support in the old African quarters – Kariakoo, Ilala, Gerezani – which sug-

[1] Taylor, *Political development*, pp. 96–7.
[2] Kambona to Fabian Society, 18 October 1955, FCB papers 121, RH.
[3] UN, *Visiting mission report, 1954*, pp. 185, 213.
[4] Nyerere, *Freedom and unity*, pp. 35–9.
[5] *Tanganyika standard*, 10 February and 21 March 1955.
[6] Nyerere to Selwyn-Clarke, 4 July 1955, FCB papers 121, RH.
[7] Manuscript notes of a public meeting [1955?] TANU 49.   [8] Ulotu, *Historia*, p. 48.
[9] Nyerere to Selwyn-Clarke, 4 July 1955, FCB papers 121, RH.

gests a party based among *fadhahausi* and permanent employees, the town's most stable elements.[1] By September 1955 Dar es Salaam – with some 110,000 people – had taken some 25,000 of the 40,000–45,000 TANU membership cards issued throughout the country.[2] It was the base from which TANU conquered Tanganyika.

Nyerere saw little of this urban excitement. On returning from New York he had to resign his job[3] and spent six months in Musoma, where he installed his family. He had every intention of continuing political activity,[4] and local pressures remained strong. Orphaned by TANU's proscription in Sukumaland, TAA's branches in Musoma and neighbouring districts faced much hostility. 'The very day I entered TANU', an early member in Tarime recalled, 'my brother avoided me...and said that I was Mau Mau.' In November 1955 there were still only 110 members in the district.[5] TANU's organiser in Musoma, Selemani Kitundu, arranged meetings for Nyerere at which there was intense excitement.[6] Late in September 1955 Nyerere returned to Dar es Salaam to take up effective leadership.

He found the situation transformed. The capital was politicised. Some 40,000 attended his first public meeting. A Matumbi townswoman of formidable energy, Bibi Titi Mohamed, had helped Kambona to enrol 5,000 women members.[7] Reports of Nyerere's trip to America passed along the network of correspondence and newspaper-reading to the furthest parts of the country. In sleepy Manyoni, Dominikus Misano sent his subscription to Dar es Salaam and remained TANU's local leader until Independence. The first member in Kahama district heard of TANU from a medical dresser and obtained a card by post. A group of civil servants in Njombe sent four delegates to Dar es Salaam for a supply of cards. TANU's branch in Iramba district was formed by mission teachers who read of the party in the newspapers and hoped to use its support in a feud with the local chief. An observer recalled that TANU's initial up-country audiences were generally dominated by junior civil servants.[8]

TANU's success also activated Tanganyika's other communications

[1] Lists in TANU 67. [2] *Tanganyika standard*, 27 September 1955.
[3] Nyerere to Lynch, 22 March 1955, FCB papers 121, RH.
[4] Nyerere to Selwyn-Clarke, 4 July 1955, FCB papers 121, RH.
[5] 'Historia ya TANU', p. 39; Ulotu, *Historia*, pp. 38–9.
[6] Nyerere to Selwyn-Clarke, 4 July 1955, FCB papers 121, RH; Moronda, 'Makongoro'.
[7] *Tanganyika standard*, 27 September 1955; Kambona to Fabian Society, 18 October 1955, FCB papers 121, RH.
[8] D. J. Misano to SG, 18 August 1955, TANU 56; Kahama historical report, TANU 53; information from Dr J. D. Graham; Iramba historical report, TANU 43; information from W. H. Whiteley.

network: the chains of commercial exchange stretching outwards from export-producing to food-supplying and labour-exporting regions. Here the pioneer district was Rufiji, which supplied the capital with rice and much labour, especially dockworkers. TANU's pioneer there was a local man, Saidi Chamwenye, who had been an active party member in the capital. He and other travellers formed local cells, while others obtained cards by post. In July 1955 Bibi Titi had to go and sort out the different groups. Kambona and Nyerere followed in October, reporting that it was the strongest branch outside the capital, with some 5,000 members. 'Rufiji is *the* TANU district', Nyerere declared.[1]

Such missions from headquarters were TANU's third means of expansion. Kambona began to hold meetings outside the capital in April 1955. The influx of funds bought a Land-Rover, which made long-distance tours possible. Given that in impoverished Tanganyika its funds must come from innumerable tiny entrance fees, TANU now had to grow or die. In this context Nyerere undertook his first major recruiting tour in November 1955, travelling down the southern coast, with an excursion to Nachingwea, and then turning inland to Lake Nyasa before heading back through Iringa and Morogoro to the capital. He found small groups of TANU members in most districts. His aims were to strengthen them, to explain his programme, and simply to show himself in an area he had never visited. He met much suspicion. 'At the beginning', the Mtwara branch recalled, 'people here thought they were just being cheated and robbed.'[2] Moreover, memories of Maji Maji remained vivid:

National freedom – *uhuru* – was an uncomplicated principle, and it needed no justification to the audiences of the first few TANU speakers. All that was required was an explanation of its relevance to their lives, and some reasonable assurance that it could be obtained through the methods proposed by TANU.

The first requirement was not difficult. It is never really difficult for people to acknowledge their own human equality with other men; and it is easy to demonstrate the denial of that equality which is inherent in a colonial situation and the consequent structure of social privilege. In Tanganyika the second requirement was, at the beginning, more difficult. Memories of the Hehe and Maji Maji wars against the German colonialists, and of their ruthless suppression, were deeply ingrained in the minds of our people...The people, particularly the elders, asked, 'How can we win without guns? How can we make sure that there is not going to be a repetition of the Hehe and

[1] Correspondence in TANU 54; *Tanganyika standard*, 22 October 1955 and 25 June 1956.
[2] Mtwara historical report, TANU 43.

Maji Maji wars?' It was therefore necessary for TANU to start by making the people understand that peaceful methods of struggle for independence were possible and could succeed.[1]

'It is another Kinjikitile', men said in Ungindo. 'It is Hongo all over again', elders warned in Uvidunda; 'they are false prophets who will bring disaster to us again; we can never drive out the Europeans with words.'[2] This response was almost universal in the south, especially among the elderly. The difference between the two movements appeared only gradually. 'When TANU came [to Uzungwa] we elders resisted strongly...lest this Nyerere should deceive us like that Mbunga, Hongo...But when we saw that the Europeans were just watching him and when we were told that it was a war of words, then all of us approved.'[3] Elsewhere in Tanganyika Mau Mau often took Maji Maji's place and Nyerere had to convince people that TANU would not commit 'things of the forest'.[4] Uhehe, the scene of Tanganyika's greatest resistance, was relatively apathetic throughout the nationalist campaign, while in Ulanga the predominant memory of resistance was that of the Ndamba against Bena and Mbunga invaders.[5] In Mbulu and Singida, perhaps, memories of revolt may have stimulated positive responses to TANU,[6] but this is uncertain. In Tanganyika the connections between resistance and nationalism were overwhelmingly negative.

Yet Nyerere's tour marked a new stage in TANU's development. For him it was a discovery of Tanganyika. He was already drawing strength from his audiences, and even negative responses stirred by memories of rebellion were responses. Moreover, TANU had started to grow not only by incorporating TAA branches or responding to local initiatives but by deliberate campaigning. Earlier political awakenings, notably in 1943–7, had drained away into the sands of particularism. Deliberate campaigning might prevent that. No longer was TANU merely one of Tanganyika's many post-war political tendencies. It was a true nationalist movement. Kandoro fixed the moment in a memorable poem. 'The ants have come together', he wrote, 'and the snake has grown angry.'[7]

---

[1] Nyerere, *Freedom and unity*, pp. 1–2.
[2] Gwassa and Iliffe, *Records*, p. 29; Akeroyd, 'Bitterness'.
[3] Lupituko Mwamkemwa in MMRP I/IR/2/69.
[4] *Mwangaza*, 7 July 1956.
[5] Membership figures in 'Historia ya TANU', pp. 103–5; Larson, 'History', p. 37; below, p. 534.
[6] Malley, 'Dagharo Gharghara'; Jellicoe, 'Turu resistance', pp. 10–11.
[7] Kandoro, *Mashairi*, p. 138.

CHAPTER 16

The nationalist victory, 1955–61

The United Tanganyika Party

'When Julius Nyerere...set up Tanu', Governor Twining later recalled, 'I read his original Manifesto very carefully. It demanded that Africa should be for the Africans, Tanganyika for the black Tanganyikans. We Europeans were not even allowed to join. This policy of black racialism was contrary to the principles of the Trusteeship Agreement and to the policy of the British Government.'[1] In order to establish multi-racialism in Kenya and Central Africa, Britain was prepared to impose it also on Tanganyika where immigrant races were less important. It was not necessarily intended to be a permanent arrangement – this remains unknown – but it meant neglecting Tanganyika's preparation for independence. In August 1955 Twining met the Colonial Secretary, Alan Lennox-Boyd. No record of their discussion is yet available, but Lennox-Boyd probably approved a campaign against TANU. To lead it Twining chose Ivor Bayldon, leader of the thirty unofficials – ten from each race – appointed to the Legislative Council in March 1955. Most of these unofficials signed the announcement of the United Tanganyika Party's formation in February 1956.[2] The party aimed 'to build up a non-racial Tanganyika nation', self-governing within the Commonwealth, by extending the franchise slowly to wealthier, better educated, and more responsible Africans, taking care that no one race predominated. The party's structure was modelled on the British Conservative Party, with a former Conservative Party official, Brian Willis, as General Director.[3]

Among Europeans UTP did not attract the 'red-eyed settlers', who

[1] Quoted in Listowel, *Making*, p. 163.
[2] *Tanganyika standard*, 17 February 1956; Bates, *Gust of plumes*, p. 267; Listowel, *Making*, pp. 165–6; information from Dr Ross.
[3] Constitution in TNA 5/25/24/403A; statement of beliefs and aims in TNA 18/A/6/4; Lowenkopf, 'Parties', p. 123.

despised multi-racialism and rightly judged that their interests needed stronger protection than it offered. Instead, UTP won two European groups: middle-class amateurs, often women, who ran many branches and shared Bayldon's paternalistic idealism, and businessmen alarmed by TANU's apparent radicalism and its imperviousness to European influence. UTP's founders included Sir Eldred Hitchcock and Sir Charles Phillips, who was an Executive Councillor, resident director of Wigglesworth and Company, and director of several of Tanganyika's largest firms. Large companies probably financed UTP: £4,000 was promised before the party was announced, the Tanganyika Cotton Company donated £500 to bolster 'stable economic and political conditions', and several bank managers joined UTP committees.[1] Like Zanzibari Arabs and Ganda chiefs, progressive Europeans sought to defeat nationalism with its own techniques.

Asians were even more divided. Two leadership groups contested the succession to the defunct Indian Association. One contained such older notables as A. Y. A. Karimjee, Bohra leader and Mayor of Dar es Salaam, and V. M. Nazerali, president of the Ismailia Council – men who disliked 'politics', believed in cooperating with government, and sat in Twining's Legislative Council. As in the 1920s their rivals were young professional men who in 1950 formed the Asian Association, a small organisation – early in 1957 it had about a thousand members – designed to reconcile Indians and Pakistanis through secular nationalism in Nehru's manner. Its leader was an ambitious lawyer, M. N. Rattansey.[2] When Legislative Councillors sent delegates to oppose Nyerere at the U.N. in 1955, the Asian Association declared them unrepresentative. It thereby established an uneasy alliance with TANU, which exchanged its support in the struggle within the Asian community for the Asian backing needed to make its non-racialism appear genuine. By contrast, Asian Legislative Councillors helped to launch UTP and Karimjee later became its treasurer.

Although UTP was conceived and dominated by immigrants, it won some African support. Half the African Legislative Councillors backed it. By 1957 nearly two-thirds of its members were Africans.[3] This support arose chiefly from the divisions which nationalism had opened among Africans.

[1] Tyrrell to Chesham, 4 February 1956, Chesham papers 3, YUL; *Tanganyika standard*, 29 October 1956; D. F. Keeka to Dodoma, 29 April 1957, TNA 435/A/6/8/II/111.
[2] See its journal, *The Tanganyikan*.
[3] *Tanganyika standard*, 17 February 1956; UN, *Visiting mission report, 1957*, p. 35.

The social composition of TANU, 1955–8

As TANU's membership grew the party became increasingly diverse until no one social group predominated, but certain patterns of support recurred. First, there were areas where the commercial economy provided the framework of political organisation. The best example was Sukumaland, where individual membership remained legal after party organisation was proscribed. Behind Sukuma support for TANU lay hostility to the Sukumaland Scheme and the government and chiefs who enforced it, but these grievances were linked to territorial nationalism through lines of communication and leadership based on postwar cotton-growing and trade. Dr Maguire has described TANU's Sukuma activists as

traders, teachers, mission employees or catechists; former government clerks, police officers or medical aides – men who had broken the bonds of rural life through education, experience, travel, study and employment...When the farmers came to the trading centers to get supplies, they fraternized with the traders. When the traders tilled their own fields, they were neighbors of the farmers. While trading centers and mission stations were the initial focal points for leadership, the network of contacts spread easily from there into the countryside...An elder out of sympathy with the local headman or alien chief, an ambitious young committee member of a primary cotton cooperative society, a farmer tired of rules and regulations – any of these men might become the representative, the messenger, the intermediate link from dissident leaders to followers.[1]

The network was perfectly illustrated by TANU's growth in Kisesa, a trading settlement near Mwanza. TANU's first member there was Zacharia Madilla, a cotton farmer and cooperative society chairman. Visiting Mwanza on cooperative business, he heard TANU mentioned in conversation and joined, cautiously paying his subscription through Lameck Bogohe's window. On returning home he hid his membership card and rule book, but they were discovered by James Malashi, the cooperative society's young clerk, who recruited the court clerk and the chief's deputy. Zacharia Madilla then fetched membership cards from Dar es Salaam, and so the movement grew and incidentally enhanced the pioneers' local standing, for James Malashi became TANU's paid district secretary and Zacharia Madilla met national leaders and allowed his house to become a party office.[2] Similar

[1] Maguire, '*Uhuru*', pp. 217–18.
[2] Christina Taabu, 'Historia ya kuzaliwa TANU – Kisessa, Sukuma chiefdom', typescript, n.d., TNA library.

processes operated in other export-producing districts. In Rungwe, for example, TANU's first public meetings were in trading centres, several local leaders belonged to cooperative committees, and party dues were collected at cooperative buying centres. According to Mr Mwaikambo, 'It became difficult to become a member of the [cooperative] society if one was not a member of TANU.'[1] By 1960 some 58 per cent of TANU's members in Rungwe were registered with the four of its fifteen branches situated in Tukuyu town, the main trading and rice-marketing centres at Kyela and Masoko, and the principal coffee-growing area at Mwakaleli.[2]

Yet involvement in the territorial economy did not guarantee nationalist support. Sukumaland was untypical because its local government system was exceptionally weak, it was experiencing the first serious impact of capitalism, and TANU's normal party organisation was proscribed. In more commercialised Bukoba, for example, TANU was still obstructed by diversity of interests and opinions. With the district's leading radical, Ali Migeyo, in gaol and its leading conservative, Elias Lushakuzi, helping to found UTP, the moderate faction led by Herbert Rugizibwa controlled TANU until April 1958. Rugizibwa toured assiduously, aided by a full-time secretary named Edward Barongo, but between August 1955 and January 1957 TANU's local membership scarcely changed.[3] Two disputes split the branch. One pitted coffee traders, led by Rugizibwa, against the cooperative society's monopoly of coffee-buying. The other arose in 1957 when Ali Migeyo was released from prison and elected district chairman. Reopening his lifelong campaign against *nyarubanja*, he was promptly prohibited from speaking in several areas and was suspended by Provincial Chairman Rugizibwa lest TANU be proscribed. This brought Nyerere to Bukoba. 'He found me to be fool on taking such steps and allowed Mr. Ali Migeyo to carry on his job as Bukoba District Chairman', Rugizibwa explained. 'As a consequence I had no alternative but to resign', which in turn angered Bukoba's political elders.[4] Beneath the surface of personality conflicts lay a developed peasant society's divisions of status, interest, and political belief.

[1] J. S. D. Mwaikambo, 'Kagwina coffee growers society', B.A. thesis, University College, Dar es Salaam, 1959.

[2] H. A. M. Mwakangale, 'Taarifa la District Secretary la mwaka 1959/1960', TANU 86.

[3] Rugizibwa to Bukoba, 6 August 1955, TNA 71/A/6/16/5; Rugizibwa to SG, 25 January 1957, TNA 215/1921/1/108.

[4] Rugizibwa to Bukoba, 24 April 1958, and Suedi Kagasheki and others to Bukoba, 7 May 1958, TNA 64/WL/A/6/4/12 and 13.

Whether this aided UTP in Bukoba is uncertain, but it was among the party's earliest and strongest branches.[1]

In Kilimanjaro the UTP branch formed in December 1957 was predominantly the TAA committee which Joseph Kimalando had revived after losing office in TANU. However, UTP leaders regarded this alliance as a defeat, for it was made only after Marealle II and the Chagga Council had rejected a formal appeal to rally the Chagga behind the party.[2] Two considerations had inspired UTP's appeal. One was TANU's continuing weakness on Kilimanjaro. In December 1956 its provincial secretary, M. K. Simon, toured several chiefdoms. In Useri 70 people attended the first TANU meeting ever held. At Mashati Simon was forbidden to hold a meeting. At Mkuu he sold ten rule books. A handful of TANU members attended a meeting at Keni but no new ones joined. Nobody appeared to listen to him in Mwika, while his meeting at Mamba was cancelled because there was a baptism and everyone was drunk. Marangu provided an audience of 50, of whom 7 joined, raising the local membership to 45. In Kirua his initial audience was only 4, while at his last stop, in Kilema, the chief forbade him to speak.[3] The tour illustrated the drudgery of political organisation and the unresponsiveness of Kilimanjaro. Early in 1957 the district branch could not pay its officers' salaries and faced closure. By July the leaders believed that 'the party is now beginning to gather strength', but in February 1958 there were still only 7,710 TANU members among the 365,000 people in Moshi district. Of these, 5,080 were registered in Moshi town (presumably including many from the mountain), 2,000 in Hai division, 450 in Vunjo, and 180 in Rombo.[4] Hai was the stronghold of Chief Abdiel Shangali and the opposition to Marealle II. Marealle was the UTP's second reason for seeking Chagga support. Well acquainted with Bayldon, he was prominent among the progressive chiefs whom Twining favoured and he drew much support from TANU's antagonist, the Kilimanjaro Union. Yet the Chagga Council was unlikely to accept Bayldon's appeal. Of all Tanganyika's peoples the Chagga were most vehemently hostile to European ambitions. Moreover, Marealle was a shrewd man with a

[1] Taylor, *Political development*, p. 145; Hydén, *Political development*, p. 132.

[2] Kimalando to RS, 20 March 1958, TNA 5/25/24/403A; Kathleen M. Stahl, 'The Chagga', in P. H. Gulliver (ed.), *Tradition and transition in East Africa* (London, 1969), p. 216.

[3] M. K. Simon, 'Repoti ya Provincial Secretary', 4–20 December 1956, TANU 35/21.

[4] Simon to branches, 11 February 1957, TANU 35/25; 'Mambo ya mkutano wa halmashauri ya jimbo', 14 July 1957, TANU 35/43; 'Mambo yaliyozungumzwa katika mkutano wa halmashauri ya TANU jimbo la kaskazini', 22–3 February 1958, TANU 25/70.

strong racial consciousness and a determination to discourage party politics on Kilimanjaro. So long as he retained widespread support, neither UTP nor TANU could flourish there.

As centrally-directed recruiting mounted, TANU penetrated beyond the commercially prosperous areas to food-producing and labour-exporting regions. Here its pattern of support often depended on the relationship between the degree of governmental interference with agriculture and the local power balance between official chiefs and educated men. The simplest situation was where educated men excluded from local power allied with TANU against the chiefs and the agricultural regulations they enforced. Usambara was an example. 'The African Association, Usambara Branch' which had attacked the Usambara Scheme and the Kilindi chief had been banned in 1949. Its leaders maintained a clandestine existence, organised passive resistance, and subverted native authorities, but they needed external allies. Abandoned by TAA, they turned to Petro Njau and formed a 'Shambaa Citizens Union under the Kilimanjaro Freemen's Union', but Mputa Magogo's hostility led government to ban it.[1] Shortly afterwards TANU reached Usambara from the lowland trading centres, like the nineteenth-century forces of change whose impact the party often paralleled. Legend now shrouds Nyerere's reception in January 1956. Some say that Mputa Magogo forbade him, as an outsider, to enter Vugha. Certainly Nyerere addressed crowded meetings and recruited a nucleus of members, chiefly among Mputa Magogo's enemies. 'The Shambaa Citizens Union', Mr Hozza writes, 'just changed its name and handed over the offices to TANU.'[2] Three years of vicious conflict followed until the TANU branch was registered in August 1959. Several activists were punished for collecting subscriptions or ignoring conservation rules. Some of the chief's supporters apparently joined UTP. But territorial events and hatred of conservation rules gradually gave TANU victory. The Usambara Scheme was abandoned in 1958. 'Some of the steepest hillsides have been laid bare', the district officer reported, 'and there is hardly a tie ridge to be seen outside the school shambas.'[3] In April 1960 TANU's provincial chairman wrote the epitaph of the Kilindi state:

In this district there are not less than 34 clans. Among all these clans there

[1] Above, pp. 496–9; 'Mapatano baina ya Kilimanjaro Union na raia wa Ushambaa', 15 February 1955, TNA 72/44/11/153A; RG to Lushoto, 16 January 1957, TNA 72/58/24/11/174.
[2] Hozza, 'Hoza rebellion', p. 20.　　　[3] Lushoto DAR 1958, TNA 304/R/3/1.

was only one which claimed to be superior to the other 33. This clan, known as the Kilindi, is the one which held the native government...from village headman and chief to sultan. The other 33 clans were quick to grasp that to be considered inferior people was no good thing...

After a time the rulers even felt themselves to be superior to their brothers of the Kilindi clan...Because of this, those Kilindi who did not rule joined with the 33 clans, and the 34 clans became one thing...

By being misgoverned by their native authorities, all Shambaa know the disgrace of being ruled.[1]

Mobilisation of agricultural grievances by local outgroups was a common pattern of nationalist growth. TANU's pioneers in Uluguru were the Kingalu family of Matombo who were excluded from local government positions and led a campaign against terracing and the chieftainship which culminated in the police shooting a TANU demonstrator in July 1955.[2] In Kondoa, where Muslims predominated in local government, the Roman Catholic schoolteachers of Haubi linked their campaign against the rehabilitation scheme to TANU. As Mr Kesby has written, 'the Haubi people used TANU as a means to their own, Warangi, ends'.[3] Under different circumstances, Christian modernisers of the Bondei Central Union formed TANU's local nucleus and used its legitimacy to secure their candidate's election as the paramount chief whom the Bondei had been unable to agree upon since Kiva.[4] Yet it would oversimplify TANU's diversity to think that its pioneers were always the local elite. In food-producing and labour-exporting regions educated men were rather easily absorbed into government or mission jobs because they paid better than agriculture. Thus domesticated, educated men sometimes opposed TANU. Among the Makonde, for example, government had nominated Muslim traders or Christian teachers as *liwalis*. TANU opposed them under the leadership of Lawi Sijaona, a Christian who had failed to become a *liwali*. In Masasi the Anglican church's long predominance led some Christian teachers and chiefs to oppose TANU, whose supporters came largely from less privileged clans.[5] Local elites often had their own ambitions. Opposed to government and the Chief of Usambara, the Tambarare Citizens Union which embodied Zigua irredentism seemed a natural ally for TANU. In January 1956

[1] S. S. Shemsanga to SG, 20 April 1960, TANU 57/29.
[2] Barongo, *Mkiki mkiki wa siasa*, pp. 88–91; above, p. 474.
[3] John D. Kesby, '"We" and "them" among the Warangi', *Makerere sociological journal*, 1 (1965), 32; correspondence in TNA 256/A/6/1/1.
[4] Tanga rural DAR 1958, TNA 304/R/3/1; Muheza historical report, TANU 43.
[5] Liebenow, *Colonial rule*, chs. 7–11; Newala and Masasi historical reports, TANU 53.

Nyerere spoke at Tambarare's office in Mombo and 300 people joined TANU. But when TANU declined Tambarare's request for affiliation, UTP branches appeared in Mombo and Handeni, led by Michael Kikurwe, a Zigua traditionalist, and Petro Mntambo, a former TAA activist and Legislative Councillor who had signed UTP's manifesto. Tambarare split, but most militants apparently allied with UTP, which may partly explain its unusual strength in Tanga Province.[1]

TANU not only adapted itself to Tanganyika's diverse societies but sometimes changed them. Its radicalism was strongest on the coast. In Bagamoyo, for example, TANU's leaders were predominantly Manyema and mass politics swamped the Shomvi notables, who were regarded as timid and held no party offices after 1955.[2] In Pangani conflict between TANU and UTP was especially bitter because some of the Shomvi *mamwinyi* ('masters') joined UTP in the hope of resisting status reversal. A UTP organiser complained:

If a UTP member goes into a Bar, all the other people in the bar leave.
If a UTP member gets on a bus, everyone else gets off, and then the conductor forces the UTP member to leave...
If relatives of UTP members die (Muslims) no one will go to the funeral.[3]

'Great respect is given to the *mamwinyi* here', a TANU leader wrote after UTP's defeat; 'the difficulty here is of people rather than of clans. Consequently the political problem is to take care that this "mwinyi-ism" does not enter the politics of TANU.'[4] Mafia Island provided another illustration of the complexity of TANU's relations with coastal society. Status distinctions between those of Arab, free, or servile ancestry remained strong in Mafia. During 1957 UTP established itself quite vigorously, but support waned as TANU's objectives and territorial preponderance became clear. In the more prosperous and stratified south of the island Africans of slave descent predominated and provided many TANU leaders, but in the more conservative north men of Arab ancestry or affiliation were the first to align themselves with the party. The situation was illustrated in the northern village which Dr Caplan studied in 1965, where TANU's elected secretary

[1] Korogwe historical report, TANU 53; Tambarare Citizens Union to SG, 8 October 1956, and Kisenge to Tambarare Citizens Union, 16 October 1956, TANU 55/76 and 69; M. L. Kikurwe to Lushoto, 31 August 1957, TNA 72/58/24/III/22; DC Tanga urban to RG, 8 April 1958, TNA 304/A/6/1/IV/5; below, p. 562.
[2] Nimtz, 'Sufi order', pp. 483–507.
[3] Willis to Pangani, 4 November 1957, TNA 31/A/6/13/5.
[4] S. S. Shemsanga to SG, 20 April 1960, TANU 57/29.

came from a family of successful freedmen with many high-status affiliations and was himself a pious *mwalimu* with a wife of free ancestry.[1]

UTP's greatest support was in Tanga. Some resulted from Zigua irredentism and some from UTP's liberal expenditure, but much was probably due to tension between largely unskilled immigrants and the town's elite of Muslim notables and educated Christians, a tension expressed during the dock strike of 1939. Many notables initially regarded TANU as an uncivilised intrusion and its members as 'backward-looking people'.[2] UTP consequently found support among established townsmen. Its local leaders included Sheikh Mohamed Salim Msellem and Mohamed Barwani, from old coastal families, and Khalidi Kirama, a former *akida* prominent in TAA and other elite organisations.[3] Much ostracism, intimidation, and minor disorder followed. During 1958 Dr Wijeyewardene found that few villagers in nearby Mtangata would eat with UTP members. 'The horror people feel towards the UTP', he noted, 'is in many ways similar to a horror of witchcraft.'[4] Even in 1960, after TANU's victory, a dispute over Legislative Council candidates led urban notables to complain that TANU's provincial leaders 'are people originating from outside the town, and it is only right that the town's Legislative Councillor should be chosen by the townspeople themselves'.[5] By contrast, Dar es Salaam experienced little conflict. The influence of TANU's headquarters, the absence of nineteenth-century notables, the preponderance of recent immigrants, and the sheer amorphousness of African society made it 'almost 100 per cent a TANU town' by 1957.[6]

TANU's coastal origins attracted some prestige inland. 'We knew that it came from the coast, so we joined', it was later recalled in Ulanga.[7] But coastal society's most valuable contribution was its language. With strong British support, Swahili had become the universal language of communication with other tribes. In such regions as central Unyamwezi and coastal Uzaramo it was spoken even among neighbours,[8] but the more common situation was described by Dr O'Barr for North Pare, where the Pare language 'continues to be

---

[1] Caplan, *Choice*, ch. 7.   [2] Mbuli, 'Tanga'.
[3] DC Tanga urban to RG, 11 April 1958, TNA 304/A/6/1/IV/6; P. S. E. Mhando to SG, 23 November 1956, TANU 55/118.
[4] G. E. T. Wijeyewardene, 'Administration and politics in two Swahili communities', EAISR conference paper, 1959.
[5] S. B. Nguli and others to SG, 20 May 1960, TANU 57/32.
[6] Leslie, *Survey*, p. 268.   [7] Mzee Ekonga in MMRP 9/68/1/3/22.
[8] Abrahams, *Peoples*, p. 29; Swantz, *Ritual*, p. 81.

used as the language of mother and her children, of the kitchen, of farming, of respect, and of Pare tradition. Swahili is the language of more recently introduced situations like schools, hospital, post office, the national government, and the political party.'[1] There were remote areas where little Swahili was spoken. Few Tatoga or Iraqw knew it, and few women in several regions.[2] But only in Usukuma, Mbulu, and Masailand did Nyerere need an interpreter during the nationalist campaign.[3] Swahili was TANU's sole official language, enabling leaders to speak directly to each other and to the people almost everywhere, permitting a transferable party bureaucracy, and preventing the emergence of an English-speaking elite of political patrons. Some even hold that TANU was chiefly a party of local minorities and especially of the Swahili-speaking communities found in small townships throughout the country,[4] but this is an oversimplification. Many Swahili communities provided TANU with nuclei of support, but in many regions from Bonde to Unyakyusa – especially the more prosperous regions – the party's composition was quite different. On the other hand, Swahili was the focus of TANU's limited cultural nationalism, while the convoluted, Arabised language admired by colonial society and used by Shaaban Robert gave ground to Nyerere's preference for Bantu forms.[5] It was a subtle index of African predominance.

TANU's radicalism appeared also in its appeal to women. Their changing status remains difficult to chart, but since the 1930s their personal freedom and range of choice had probably increased while their security had diminished – a trend which paralleled the growth of capitalism and, given the previous bias against female individuality, probably was a measure of emancipation. Bridewealth was an indicator of change. After increasing rapidly in the early colonial period it continued to rise, but perhaps little more quickly than earnings, except in Usambara. In some advanced areas like Kilimanjaro the overall importance of bridewealth may have declined as some indulgent parents forwent it altogether. More often bridewealth

---

[1] William O'Barr, 'An ethnography of modernization: Pare traditionality and the impact of recent changes', Ph.D. thesis, Northwestern University, 1970, p. 224.

[2] Schultz, *Veränderungen*, pp. 26, 78; G. T. Bell, *Report on the development of Mbulu district* (Dar es Salaam, 1951); Knight, *Ecology and change*, p. 4.

[3] J. Bakempenja to TANU Central Committee, 11 December 1958, TANU 28; *Uganda argus*, 10 April 1962.

[4] Bienen, *Tanzania*, pp. 42–8, 71; above, p. 384.

[5] John Allen, 'A note on Dr Nyerere's translation of *Julius Caesar*', *Makerere journal*, IX (1964), 56–7.

continued to supersede brideservice, but this could make it more difficult for poor young men to marry, as in Bukwaya where Roman Catholic missionaries tried to stabilise marriage by making bridewealth compulsory but succeeded only in encouraging a trend to patriliny and making it harder for young men to form stable unions. Yet the most common change was increased use of cash to replace or purchase cattle, which probably assisted young men to marry; certainly Nyakyusa men began to marry earlier, and whatever else colonialism did in Tanganyika, it did much to emancipate the young. The monetisation of bridewealth may have reduced marital stability, but it probably widened a woman's choice of partners. In Unyakyusa both the divorce rate and the age of women at marriage increased.[1] Monetisation probably reduced polygyny, a trend encouraged by colonial law, urbanisation, land shortage, alternative investment opportunities, and Christianity. The Northern Province had the country's greatest land shortage, the highest proportion of Christians, and the fewest polygynists, while the proportion of married Nyakyusa men who were polygynous fell between 1934 and 1957 from 44 to 38 per cent.[2] Meanwhile female education expanded and towns continued to emancipate. Women owned a quarter of the houses in Mwanza in 1956.[3] Yet the extent of change should not be exaggerated. Illiteracy, exploitation, and drudgery remained most women's lot, especially in remote areas.

Women's status in TANU retained many ambiguities. Nyerere was concerned to raise their position and TANU's first constitution provided for a women's section. It was formed during 1955 by Bibi Titi Mohamed, who first recruited Dar es Salaam's women brewers and then organised house-to-house canvassing until Kambona could report 'a revolution [in] the role of women in African society'.[4] The movement spread. 'We men', Gogo villagers declared, 'do not wish that we alone should be members [of TANU], forgetting the women...Unity is not for men alone.'[5] Most branches had women's sections with 'Lady Chairmen' and officers, much like *beni* societies.

[1] Wilson, 'Zig-zag change', pp. 399–409; Feierman, 'Concepts', pp. 104–14; B. G. M. Sundkler, 'Marriage problems in the church in Tanganyika', *International review of missions*, xxxiv (1945), 260; Hugo Huber, *Marriage and the family in rural Bukwaya* (Fribourg, Switzerland, 1973), *passim*; Beidelman, 'Matrilineal peoples', pp. 44–5.
[2] Tanganyika, *African census 1957*, pp. 61, 78; Wilson, 'Zig-zag change', p. 404.
[3] Mwanza urban DAR 1956, TNA 41/R/3/3/2/20.
[4] Barongo, *Mkiki mkiki wa siasa*, pp. 83, 92–6; Kambona to Fabian Society, 18 October 1955, FCB papers 121, RH.
[5] TANU Dodoma to SG, 4 September 1956, TANU 29.

Outstanding women occasionally gained larger responsibility, especially in the west, where Hima women were often chiefs. Normally, however, TANU attracted innumerable ordinary women who enjoyed its entertainment and social activities. Their participation aroused some male hostility. Several elders initially complained that it was wrong for a woman like Bibi Titi to address men. In one Haya village the men closed down the women's section.[1] Discussion at a party conference revealed the limits of emancipation:

Bibi Titi Mohamed said it was necessary that women should be eligible for employment, but a married woman should not be allowed to work in the party without her husband's consent...Mzee Takadiri said that he agreed with Bibi Titi that they should not accept a married woman to work in TANU without receiving a letter from her husband after seeking his consent...The meeting applauded this elder.[2]

Like every successful movement in Tanganyika's modern history, TANU fed on generational tension. Its Youth League, formed in 1956, provided vigorous support and numerous disciplinary problems. Scanty evidence suggests that it contained a disproportionately large number of young men who had failed to enter middle or secondary school. Like James Malashi, several became TANU secretaries, latter-day catechists. Most were probably of common birth, as was the norm among TANU's leaders.[3] The idea that the 'standard seven leaver' was the key to African nationalism is oversimplified, but government's post-war emphasis on primary education was probably one important reason for TANU's growth. It probably also explained the success of the party's Swahili newspaper, *Mwafrika*, which was launched in 1957 and achieved a circulation of over 20,000. Yet in 1960 Tanganyika still had only four newspapers and three radio sets per thousand people, while TANU's history yields ample evidence that word of mouth remained the most important form of political communication.[4]

TANU harnessed other forms of social radicalism. Where only favoured lineages occupied colonial chieftainships, their rivals were often available for recruitment. Such rivalry was TANU's basis in Singida. In Unyamwezi 'the first party supporters were often local

[1] Barongo, *Mkiki mkiki wa siasa*, p. 94; J. B. Kamugisha, 'Factors contributing to success or failure of self-help schemes', B.A. thesis, University College, Dar es Salaam, 1969.
[2] Hassan Issa, 'Safari ya Tabora', typescript, n.d., copy in my possession. I owe this document to Mr K. M. Kiwanuka.
[3] Maguire, '*Uhuru*', p. 322; Lowenkopf, 'Parties', p. 155.
[4] Lowenkopf, 'Parties', p. 180; Pratt, *Critical phase*, p. 21. Generally, see Judith Molloy, 'Political communication in Lushoto district', Ph.D. thesis, University of Kent, 1971.

dissidents and village rebels'. In the Ihangiro chiefdom of Buhaya the dissident *ab'obumoi* of the 1930s were TANU's nucleus.[1] Tension between village and chiefdom could also be exploited. TANU spread in Kahama during 1959 among groups of neighbours who cooperated to thresh millet, their 'millet chiefs' becoming leaders of a parallel government which fined those refusing to join the party.[2] Affiliation was often a collective decision. The people of a Gogo village told party organisers that 'they were not yet ready to be written down that day; and they promised that when the delegates returned on their second journey, they would undoubtedly be ready to be written down'.[3] A particularly interesting question for future research is whether stateless peoples with participatory political traditions were more responsive to nationalism than hierarchical peoples.[4] Songea district provides one example. Although its Ngoni chiefs showed some initial interest in TANU, owing to temporary discontent with British policy, they soon realised that nationalism threatened their positions. TANU's main strength was therefore in Songea township, around the Peramiho mission, and especially among the formerly stateless Ndendeuli. Those who held office under Undendeuli's republican constitution often resisted TANU, but other Ndendeuli held no positions, had experience of popular organisations, and were impatient for development. When Nyerere visited Nyamtumbo late in 1955 Ndendeuli welcomed him warmly. Led by Hassan Mang'unyuka – organiser of the Ndendeuli secession and TANU chairman for a decade – 'the Ndendeuli joined TANU early and very enthusiastically. The Namtumbo TANU Committee was strong and used to meet every Friday, after prayers.'[5]

Yet chiefs did not necessarily oppose TANU. A particularly diverse group, their reactions were varied and complex. Probably a majority resisted nationalism. One unreliable survey of eighteen districts showed 32 chiefs supporting TANU and 71 opposing it.[6] Opposition was obviously likely where TANU was introduced by the chief's opponents, as in Usambara and Kondoa, or where chiefs lacked hereditary status and depended on government support, as among the *liwalis* of the south-east. Yet many chiefs supported TANU openly or covertly. Some had personal reasons. The elderly and autocratic

[1] Jellicoe, 'Social change', pp. 125, 176, 218; Miller, 'Village leadership', p. 132; Byansheko, 'Hatua', TANU 49; above, p. 416.
[2] Abrahams, *Political organization*, pp. 168–71.
[3] TANU Dodoma to SG, 4 September 1956, TANU 29.
[4] I owe this point to Dr Richard Rathbone.
[5] Newa, 'Ndendeule struggle', pp. 81–4, 105–10.
[6] Ulotu, *Historia*, p. 27 (omitting the figure for Kilimanjaro, which is not in the original).

Makongoro of Ikizu resented the regimentation and backwardness which his chiefdom experienced. An enthusiastic moderniser, TAA sympathiser, and early supporter of Nyerere, he openly encouraged TANU. So did Chrisostomus Makita of Mbinga, who profited from connections with TANU in seeking the Matengo paramountcy.[1] Often local rivalries shaped the chiefs' behaviour. Throughout the south there was remarkable correlation (except in Ungoni) between chiefs' attitudes to TANU and their predecessors' reactions to Maji Maji. While the *liwalis* – the new *akidas* – were predominantly hostile, the more indigenous Ngindo chiefs unanimously favoured nationalism. TANU's opponents in Masasi included successors of Nakaam and Matola. Joseph Mbeyela was regarded as a supporter, Merere as an opponent.[2] Memories of rebellion doubtless coloured these responses, but it was probably more important that TANU polarised local politics as had Maji Maji. In Ulanga, for example, TANU was introduced by Ndamba seeking independence from the Bena Chief Towegale. These pioneers found keen support because 'the citizens ...thought TANU would help them in their tribal struggle'.[3] By contrast, it is said that 'Mtemi Towegare of Ubena (Malinyi) and Sultan Mtohanje of Kiberege saw Tanu as another Maji Maji. They told their people to keep away from it. "We should not accept Tanu cards", they declared, "because either our elders or we ourselves will be hanged. We should prefer British rule only."'[4] In reality the aristocrats were divided. While his son imprisoned the first TANU organisers who appeared, Towegale himself tried to capture the movement as he had previously sought to patronise the African Association. Late in 1956 he made a relative the local TANU secretary and visited party headquarters in Dar es Salaam, whose Organising Secretary blandly told the district officer that he and Towegale had 'reached a gentlemen's agreement'.[5] Yet local antagonisms were beyond gentlemanly control. When TANU was at last registered in Ulanga in 1958 the more extreme Ndamba militants were denied office but the local party remained deeply hostile to chieftainship.

Of all Tanganyikans, the chiefs had the most divided loyalties. Vulnerable and closely supervised, they were the points of maximum

[1] Moronda, 'Makongoro'; Haule in Iliffe, *Tanzanians*, pp. 169–71.
[2] Nachingwea historical report, TANU 43; Masasi historical report, TANU 53; information from Dr J. D. Graham; Mbeya DAR 1960, TNA library.
[3] 'TANU katika Ulanga', typescript, n.d., copy in my possession. I owe this source to Dr Larson. See also Larson, 'History', pp. 372–84.
[4] Petro Moto in MMRP 9/68/1/4/6.
[5] SG to DC Mahenge, 10 October 1956, TANU 29/64.

tension between rulers and subjects, and they often shared popular antipathy to European rule. 'My face is my membership card', one told a hostile crowd.[1] The greatest dilemma faced educated and progressive chiefs who had been the leading Africans of the inter-war period but became the leading casualties of the nationalist movement. One was the sophisticated, vacillating Kidaha Makwaia – 'our Hamlet', in Nyerere's phrase – who alienated nationalists by apparent acquiescence in the East African High Commission and Operation Exodus, became a multi-racial symbol as the first African member of the Executive Council and a founder of UTP, resigned when the party refused to declare Tanganyika primarily an African country, and then unsuccessfully offered himself for selection as a TANU candidate in the 1958 election.[2] More successful was Abdallah Fundikira, Makerere-educated brother of the Chief of Unyanyembe, who contested Western Province in 1958 and won TANU's support when Nyamwezi particularism facilitated his election.[3] Most successful of all was Adam Sapi, Mkwawa's Makerere-educated grandson, who stood aside from party politics but sympathised with TANU and held many public offices after 1961. As TANU's strength increased, the chiefs' dilemma became more perplexing and the fence more crowded. Recognising UTP's weakness, Twining decided, apparently at Marealle's suggestion, to rely more on the chiefs. In May 1957 he inaugurated a Chiefs' Convention, warning them that 'the tribal system and the office of chief' were threatened by those who 'base their appeal on the emotional attractions of extreme nationalism, which in effect is nothing more than racialism'.[4] The tactic failed, for although some chiefs were ready to fight TANU, most realised that their future depended on compromising with it. TANU encouraged them by claiming disingenuously that nationalism sought to supersede only the colonial power.[5]

The chiefs' varied reactions demonstrate that response to TANU was not determined simply by men's interests but by how they perceived their interests. Perception was shaped by ideology, both as prevailing opinion and as ideas propagated by politicians. Records of TANU speeches, even in remote villages, say little of local issues but

[1] Abrahams, *Political organization*, p. 154.
[2] Smith, *Nyerere*, p. 53; Maguire, '*Uhuru*', pp. 52–8; *Tanganyika standard*, 17 February 1956; Makwaia to SG, 8 October 1958, TANU 95/49.
[3] Listowel, *Making*, pp. 317–18; Bienen, *Tanzania*, pp. 59–60.
[4] Tanganyika, *First convention of representative chiefs, 1957* (Dar es Salaam, 1957), p. 1.
[5] *Sauti ya TANU*, 23 June 1958.

much of the large themes of freedom and unity, justice and dignity, while Nyerere himself deliberately eschewed parochial grievances. Although detailed analysis often reveals TANU's absorption into particularistic conflicts and shows its local leaders not as village Hampdens but rural Macbeths,[1] village Hampdens nevertheless existed. Early in 1955 a veteran of the First World War, with only elementary education, wrote in his diary:

We do not want foreigners to rule Tanganyika...What have the Europeans in Europe done for the blacks of Tanganyika? Why were we conscripted and sent to war to die!? What did we have to gain from fighting other Europeans?...The European was poor when he arrived in this country; now he is rich and fat...Every year we suffer a loss on our foodstuffs...We are human beings and Europeans are human beings...No man is superior to another here on earth.[2]

Ideology was especially important in nationalism's early years when politics remained dangerous, when lack of elections prevented TANU from offering its supporters protection or political leverage, and when leaders could only promise what would happen 'when we rule ourselves'. Nationalists had to demonstrate the connection between local or personal interests and their own larger demands, and they had to convince people that nationalism could win. This was done best by showing that it had succeeded elsewhere. 'We cannot overcome these people by conflict', Nyerere explained, '...[but] they have left India, a country they greatly loved because of their large property there – without fighting...Nigeria is hoping to gain its freedom this year.'[3] Celebrating Africa Day or wearing Ghanaian dress demonstrated that TANU was part of a larger, irresistible liberation movement. Like the chief who admitted a *hongo*, the aspiring Macbeth who gave Nyerere a platform unleashed unanticipated passions and ideas.

In public, at least, Nyerere's confidence was growing. In December 1956 he spoke of Independence in ten years, although his first priority was to have Tanganyika declared not a multi-racial territory but a primarily African country to be governed democratically.[4] Success in New York and with the crowds was elevating him above TANU's other leaders. His very lack of a political base in any region or social group

[1] I owe this formulation to Professor Gallagher.
[2] Diary of Ramadhani Willibald Ligonja, quoted in L. E. Larson, 'The African voice: protest and improvement in the Ulanga district, 1945–1954', seminar paper, University of Dar es Salaam, 1972. The classic village Hampden was Isaka Hoza. See above, p. 497.
[3] Typescript for *Mwafrika*, dated 21 December 1957, TANU 47.
[4] Nyerere, *Freedom and unity*, p. 44.

was becoming an asset. His confidence in his supporters grew. 'The trouble with these Government Officials', he gibed, 'is that they are so contemptuous of the masses and yet so frightened of them that... they cannot think of a Public meeting without imagining grim faces who but for the Police Force and the Ordinance, would loot and burn every house.'[1] He saw rather the crowds' discipline, attentiveness, and gaiety, and they emboldened him to liberate emotions which others feared. 'To be ruled is a *disgrace*', he proclaimed repeatedly. Yet he never underestimated the potential for violence which events in Kenya had revealed so brutally. Instead, idealism and caution joined in an appeal to the best in men which gave him moral authority even over his adversaries. 'Good gentlemen of England', he declared, '...You are not being vanquished by arrows, nor by guns or pangas. No indeed, you are being vanquished by the *spirit* of the people whom you rule.'[2] Tanganyikan nationalism was not simply about interests and their organisation. It was also about passions and their liberation.

Labour, trade, religion, and nationalism

The Labour Inspector asked him, why was he not in the queue with others; he replied that a gang leader do not do that, and it has been a rule since long ago. The Inspector then told him that he was proud even his master Nyerere is not as proud as he and he continued to say that he was becoming big headed because of Nyerere.[3]

It was in such everyday relationships that most men experienced nationalism. Workers were one example. The labour movement which they had created from below during the 1940s had collapsed in the riot of 1950. Thereafter government discouraged trade unionism, except among craftsmen, and instead fostered the staff associations and joint negotiating procedures of 'welfare capitalism'.[4] Trade unionism was revived by educated men seeking to create a labour movement from above, on a territorial scale, and with the overt leadership which most earlier labour actions had lacked. The chief pioneers were clerks in the capital's commercial firms who in 1951 founded an African Commercial Employees Association, probably modelled on a parallel Asian organisation. The leading activists – notably M. M. Kamaliza and M. M. Mpangala – were close to TAA

[1] Nyerere to Tanganyika standard, 20 February 1958, TANU 34/92.
[2] *Sauti ya TANU*, 19 June 1959.
[3] E. E. Akena to LC, 15 August 1956, LD 99/66/69, TNA.
[4] Above, p. 404; *Labour report*, 1953, pp. 109–10.

and TANU, whose headquarters they used as their office until 1955. They hoped to form a Tanganyika African Trade Union Congress, but government was hostile and the territory's scattered groups of organised workers proved keen but difficult to coordinate when approached in April 1955.[1]

The breakthrough came three months later when the Kenyan trade unionist, Tom Mboya, visited Dar es Salaam to address leaders of the four main workers' organisations: the ACEA, TAGSA, the Railway African Union (recently reconstituted), and a staff association of African clerks in Dar es Salaam port. Mboya later explained:

The Civil Servants Association...was the only union which was then national in character...[The others] had in almost all cases tried to build from the bottom upwards, and each one was trying to form a little union...

The British concept, that a trade union should develop from the bottom and that experience should be gained by a man as he moves up the ladder, is impossible to adopt in Africa. The whole emphasis has to be given from the top.[2]

On 7 October 1955 the leaders launched a central organisation, the Tanganyika Federation of Labour. Its president was J. B. A. Ohanga, leader of RAU, and its general secretary was Rashidi Kawawa, a Muslim civil servant who was president of TAGSA. The founders apparently planned a general union of which all workers would be individual members, but government refused to register this, presumably judging it too unwieldy to follow 'proper' trade union practice and possibly fearing its potential strength. Instead the organisers had to form industrial unions on the British model and affiliate them to the TFL.[3] Partly from fear of repression and partly because civil servants must eschew politics, the TFL did not affiliate to TANU. 'While preserving the independence of the labour movement from political control', its constitution declared, the federation aimed 'to encourage workers to register and vote, to exercise their full rights and responsibilities of citizenship, and to perform their rightful part in the political life of the nation'.[4]

As table VII shows, the TFL initiated a union growth 'probably unequalled in Africa'. By 1961, 42 per cent of Tanganyika's workers

[1] Tandau, 'History', pp. 1–4.
[2] Tom Mboya, *Freedom and after* (London, 1963), pp. 197–9.
[3] Tandau, 'History', pp. 6–12, 45; William H. Friedland, *Vuta kamba: the development of trade unions in Tanganyika* (Stanford, 1969), pp. 45–52, 140–1.
[4] 'Tanganyika Federation of Labour: constitution', TANU 23/8; Friedland, *Vuta kamba*, pp. 116–20.

Table VII. *Membership of registered trade unions, strikes, and man-days lost, 1951–61*

Date	Unions	Members	Industrial disputes	Man-days lost
1951	0	0	73	12,775
1952	1	381	82	15,923
1953	6	960	61	6,812
1954	7	—	43	7,842
1955	22	2,714	42	12,562
1956	25	13,390	54	58,066
1957	25	35,153	114	165,328
1958	30	46,528	153	296,746
1959	35	80,606	—	—
1960	40	95,393	—	—
1961	35	203,000	—	—

SOURCES: Scott, 'Trade unions', table 1; D. T. Jack, *Report on the state of industrial relations in the sisal industry* (Dar es Salaam, 1959), p. 2.

were unionised, compared with 12 per cent in Uganda and 8 per cent in Kenya.[1] A wave of strikes demonstrated new-found solidarity. When the Domestic and Hotel Workers Union struck in 1956, building workers and commercial employees came out in sympathy and only the law prevented dockworkers following them. Public support for strikers was shown in TANU-backed boycotts of buses and bottled beer. But unions formed rapidly from above had a distinctive character. A survey of their leaders in 1960 showed that only 2 per cent had been manual workers, 15 per cent craftsmen, and 83 per cent white-collar workers. Leaders were young – 61 per cent were under thirty – with between six and ten years of education. Two-thirds were Christians, four-fifths were born in the countryside, and more than three-fifths were first-generation educated.[2] Thus the unions, like TANU, offered advancement to young men from unprivileged families without full secondary schooling. Manual workers took little active part in union organisation, whose authoritarianism they sometimes resented. They often paid entrance fees but seldom monthly dues, assuming that workers were automatically union members. Unions were permanently in financial disorder. Most

[1] Roger Scott, 'Trade unions and the growth of nationalism in East Africa', East African Academy symposium paper, 1965.
[2] Friedland, *Vuta kamba*, pp. 163–77.

receipts – 94 per cent in 1963 – were spent on administration.[1] The strike weapon was used freely and unofficial strikes were common. Of fifteen strikes in Southern Highlands Province between October 1958 and March 1959, only one was official.[2] Given a regime in disarray, these tactics were very effective. In the three years from 1959 to 1961, average wages rose by 65 per cent.[3] But the tactics encouraged violence of thought and language. 'We shall fight tooth to nail for our rights', a union official declared in September 1961,

by throwing out of gear all Ring-leaders' industries, we shall strain every nerve until we over-throw the Khoja Colonialism that attempts to rule us with a high hand. The Employers refusal to accept arbitration is a clear evidence that they are here not to assist Africans achieve a better living standard, but to suck our blood and leave us in poverty. I would request my friends (Khoja) to eat humble pie before time gets too late or else they shall find themselves burning their fingers.[4]

As every Asian shopkeeper knew, this was as authentic an expression of African feeling as Nyerere's generous idealism.

The new unionism's greatest impact was among the dispersed, largely unskilled, and often migrant sisal workers, whose previous experience of industrial organisation was limited to brief, anonymous stoppages and estate councils of headmen. Their first trade union was formed in Eastern Province in March 1956 by Ohanga and local workers.[5] During 1957 other provincial unions followed and strikes multiplied. While many planters opposed the union, prohibiting meetings and allegedly dismissing workers who joined TANU, some larger employers believed that trade unionism must be domesticated through joint consultative machinery. Late in 1957 they established a Central Joint Council for the Sisal Industry with equal representation of workers and employers, the majority on both sides being chosen by councils representing estate committees. The council also included three representatives each of the TSGA and the Tanganyika Sisal Plantation Workers Union, which won recognition in June 1958.[6] Three years of industrial conflict followed. The employers hoped to

---

[1] Correspondence in RTU 14/1 and 14/11, TNA; Friedland, *Vuta kamba*, p. 89; *Labour report*, 1963, p. 7.
[2] 'Report of the Labour Officer, Mbeya and Southern Highlands Province' [April 1959] TNA 18/C/5/6/III/39.
[3] Tanganyika, *Budget survey 1962–3*, p. 9.
[4] G. P. Kanoni, circular [September 1961] TNA 68/A/6/14/176.
[5] Tandau, 'History', p. 24.
[6] This account is largely based on the papers of Sir Barclay Nihill in Rhodes House, Oxford. He was chairman of the joint council.

tame the union by their influence over estate representatives and by manipulating the complexities of conciliation. Union leaders – notably the talented and ambitious general secretary, Victor Mkello – sought to unionise the whole labour force, gain access to estates, and monopolise negotiations. When estate representatives on the Joint Council accepted a fourteen per cent wage offer in November 1958, the union seized the opportunity to call strikes on several plantations. Most ended quickly, but that at Mazinde Estate lasted 68 days and became a major confrontation between the old and new orders until Government appointed a commissioner who recommended greater union representation on estate committees and the Joint Council.[1] TFL leaders anxious to demonstrate African responsibility now urged Mkello to cooperate, and economic circumstances pointed in the same direction, for late in 1958 sisal prices rose in a boom lasting until 1964. Between August 1958 and March 1960 sisal cutters' average wages rose from Shs. 54 to Shs. 111 per working month.[2] But tasks increased also, for union pressure, mechanisation, and the gradual accretion of settled workers were replacing the casual, migrant pattern of sisal labour by a permanent, better-paid workforce, as was happening also in urban industry.[3] When the union demanded that local workers should replace long-distance migrants, employers wholeheartedly agreed. Between 1958 and 1961 Silabu's recruits fell from 32,569 to 3,180. In 1965 the bureau closed.[4] The colonial labour system gave way to a fuller acceptance of capitalism. Mkello sought to capitalise on cooperation by demanding a check-off system, a closed shop, and shop stewards, which, as an observer commented, 'would make him the most powerful Trade Union leader in East Africa'.[5] Yet cooperation carried dangers. In September 1961, apparently without consulting Mkello, impatient workers' representatives abandoned and broke the Joint Council.[6]

Part of Mkello's problem may have been his relatively moderate position in the growing tension between trade unionism and nationalism. TANU had aided the TFL's formation and early party officials

[1] D. T. Jack, *Report on the state of industrial relations in the sisal industry* (Dar es Salaam, 1959), *passim*.
[2] 'Minutes of the second meeting of the Central Joint Council', 14 August 1958, and Leechman, 'New wage rates and increased tasks', 15 March 1960, Nihill papers, RH.
[3] Iliffe, 'Dockworkers', pp. 138–47.
[4] Peter R. Lawrence, 'Plantation sisal', in Cliffe, *Cooperation*, pp. 113–14.
[5] Nihill to Leechman, 15 November 1960, Nihill papers, RH.
[6] 'Minutes of the ninth meeting of the Central Joint Council', 7–9 September 1961, Nihill papers, RH.

often doubled as union organisers. In 1958 a party conference prohibited this, although it granted the TFL two seats on the National Executive. Only nine of the 64 union officials surveyed in 1960 held TANU offices but all were TANU members, for workers commonly belonged to both bodies, regarding them situationally as having separate functions. Yet situationalism became increasingly difficult to maintain as TANU's strength increased, its demands for loyalty became more totalitarian, and its governmental responsibilities grew. The TFL had adopted a non-political stance from fear of British oppression but maintained it from fear of absorption by TANU.[1] This fear, together with much personal ambition, lay behind the split within the TFL from October 1960 to September 1961. Rivalry centred on the presidency, left vacant when Kawawa became a minister. The contestants were the ACEA pioneer, Kamaliza, and the militant young leader of the railway workers, Kasanga Tumbo. Kamaliza advocated close cooperation with TANU, which implied subordinating demands for wage increases and rapid Africanisation to party policy. His support came chiefly from unions in private and semi-private industries. Most unions in the public sector backed Tumbo, who demanded maximum Africanisation, higher wages, the abolition of the East African High Commission, and union independence to avoid 'the take-over of the unions by the political party, as in Ghana'. Kamaliza won the contest in September 1961, but the tension remained.[2]

Nevertheless, between 1955 and 1958 TANU had won the support of most wage-earners, then an exploited and potentially radical group. It was also winning African traders. Some 36,000 strong in 1959,[3] they held many party offices and had pioneered many branches. Successful traders had the money which TANU needed before mass membership supplied it. They also had the experience and entrepreneurial attitudes which made men activists, they had access to information and personal contacts needed for political organisation, and they had a material interest in TANU's success, for they expected it to create conditions in which African commerce could flourish, especially in competition with Asians. Like workers they possessed a sectional organisation allied to TANU, the Tanganyika African Traders Union, formed in 1956 under the chairmanship of Clement Mtamila – also chairman of TANU's Central Committee – to organise a cooperative

[1] Friedland, *Vuta kamba*, pp. 116–24.
[2] Tandau, 'History', pp. 33–55; Friedland, *Vuta kamba*, pp. 126–7.
[3] Hawkins, *Trade*, p. 21.

import-export firm by-passing Asian and European wholesalers. Like post-war traders' cooperatives, however, TATU enjoyed little success. Government prohibited it from trading unless registered as a company. Inexperience and lack of capital damaged some agency operations. There were many accusations of corruption. In March 1959 a new committee was elected containing several TANU leaders. Eighteen months later the organisation had a claimed (but improbable) 20,000 members and large hopes of government aid. 'Our Union members', the president declared, 'represent the growing African middle class in this country.'[1]

Class scarcely threatened TANU's nationalist coalition. Religion was a greater danger. Tanganyika's religions were extraordinarily diverse: numerous indigenous faiths, several schools of Islam, and 36 Christian missionary societies.[2] At the census of 1957, 31 per cent of the population declared themselves Muslims and 25 per cent Christians (17 per cent Roman Catholic and 8 per cent Protestant). The growth of Christianity was striking, for in 1914 only some two per cent had been Christians and in 1938 perhaps ten per cent.[3] This post-war expansion was a continental phenomenon whose causes are little understood. In Tanganyika one reason may have been the country's growing complexity, with greater differentiation and competition between regions and individuals. As the apparent religion of modernity, Christianity could appeal both to the beneficiaries of change and to the deprived who sought equality. This perspective reveals several patterns of church growth. One was the expansion of established mission churches through population growth and social pressure on surviving followers of indigenous religions. In these overwhelmingly Christian regions – Ufipa, Ukerewe, Kilimanjaro, Buhaya – the churches' problem was to minister to swollen followings. In Buhaya, for example, the number of Protestants doubled between 1956 and 1965 while Christian marriages halved, partly because ministers were scarce. A proportional decline in Christian marriages began generally in the late 1950s.[4] To meet such problems Roman Catholics revitalised the catechist's ministry. Lutherans followed the same policy in Usambara, drawing evangelists – like TANU and trade unions – from secondary

---

[1] P. M. Varian to Chief Minister, 31 October 1960, TANU 25/161. This file is the source for this paragraph.

[2] *Central Africa*, August 1953.

[3] Tanganyika, *African census 1957*, p. 61; above, p. 230; Thompson, 'Partnership', p. 43.

[4] Adrian Hastings, *Christian marriage in Africa* (London, 1973), pp. 48–9, 137–40.

school rejects.[1] Another kind of church growth was the evangelisation by the mission churches of hitherto neglected areas. In 1946 Lutherans opened a mission to the Mbugu pastoralists of West Usambara who had long held aloof from church and state. Two years later another, wholly African mission began among the Sonjo. Nearly half the 80,000 Luo in North Mara were baptised as Roman Catholics during the thirty years of mission work which began there in 1933.[2] Even more dramatic were regions where minority churches suddenly won mass support, most notably the Anglican Church of Central Tanganyika. Established in 1876, its following remained almost static around 10,000 from 1913 to 1944 but then grew to some 80,000 by 1967. One reason was probably post-war incorporation into the territorial economy, with resulting social change and awareness of backwardness. Another was lay enthusiasm, for converts were recruited largely by unpaid evangelists 'moved to eloquence by the Holy Ghost'.[3] Many of these evangelists belonged to the expanding Revival movement, which stressed lay responsibility. This was also emphasised by the independent churches, but they remained few. Congregations of Watchtower, the African National Church, and the Last Church of God survived in Rungwe, Mbeya, and Mwanza. Tensions provoked by Revival brought minor secessions from mission churches in Bukoba, Dodoma, and Tabora.[4] Further Luo churches entered North Mara from Kenya, notably Roho, Johera, and the African Israel Church Nineveh. Like Revival or the Shambaa church of the early 1920s they stressed the local community as the basis of church life, especially in newly colonised areas, although some also displayed a colourful symbolism and tolerance of such customs as polygyny which were anathema to Balokole. Yet even in North Mara independent churches were marginal groups and numerically insignificant.[5] More important were the structurally similar pentecostal churches. First established in

[1] Nolan in Shorter and Kataza, *Missionaries*, pp. 27–8; Annual report of the Usambara-Digo Lutheran Church, 1957, in Kaniki, 'Lutheran Church', p. 31.

[2] Annual report of the Usambara-Digo Lutheran Church, 1957, in Kaniki, 'Lutheran Church', p. 29; Smedjebacka, *Church autonomy*, pp. 122–7, 253; Perrin Jassy, *La communauté*, p. 58.

[3] Alfred Stanway, 'Rapid church growth among the Wagogo of Tanzania, 1876–1967', duplicated paper, workshop in religious research, Nairobi, 1968; Edward H. Winter and T. O. Beidelman, 'Tanganyika: a study of an African society at national and local levels', in Julian H. Steward (ed.), *Contemporary change in traditional societies*, I (Urbana, 1967), p. 169.

[4] Above, p. 365; David B. Barrett, 'Two hundred independent church movements in East Africa', UEASSC paper, 1966.

[5] In 1966 the Mara churches were thought to have some 2,550 members. See Perrin Jassy, *La communauté*, pp. 91, 207.

the 1920s in the Southern Highlands, where many small congregations existed, pentecostalism flourished in many regions and especially in central Tanganyika. Miss Jellicoe thought its chief appeal in Singida was to 'the submerged tenth': fatherless young men without inheritance, their mothers, and other deprived women, much as two-thirds of the adherents of the Luo independent churches were women. One observer estimated 30,000 pentecostalists in Tanganyika in 1964.[1]

These growing churches were immensely varied, and so were their ministers. Roman Catholics continued to insist that African priests must receive the same rigorous training as their counterparts throughout the world. Success varied in different dioceses. Kwiro did not ordain an African priest until 1948, whereas only four years later Bukoba consecrated its first African bishop, Laurian Rugambwa (a descendant of Chief Kahigi of Kianja) who in 1960 became modern Africa's first cardinal. The proportion of Roman Catholic priests to laymen in Tanganyika was the highest of any extensively Catholic country in Africa, but in 1959 three-quarters of the priests were Europeans.[2] By contrast, in 1960 six of every seven Lutheran ministers were Africans, but even in 1967 not one African pastor of the Usambara-Digo Lutheran Church was a university graduate. The diocese of Central Tanganyika consecrated the first African as an Anglican Assistant Bishop in 1955, but many Anglican priests had only primary schooling. The first African bishop of the Africa Inland Church had some six years of education.[3]

The first steps towards African control of mission churches – notably Rugambwa's consecration – antedated nationalism, but the process accelerated as self-government approached. Sparse evidence suggests that transfer of power was smoothest for Roman Catholics, partly because their African priests were so well trained, partly because Tanganyika's dioceses were elements in a universal hierarchy. But Protestants also found the transition remarkably smooth, partly because missions often lacked staff and money. Its unsettled history made the diocese of Central Tanganyika the most constitutionally

[1] Jellicoe, 'Social change', ch. 9; Lloyd W. Swantz, *Church, mission, and state relations in pre and post independent Tanzania (1955–1964)*, Maxwell Graduate School, Program of Eastern African Studies, occasional paper no. 19 (New York, 1965), p. 14.

[2] Kwiro mission diary, 29 August 1948, Kwiro archives; Swantz, *Church*, pp. 16, 19; Adrian Hastings, *Church and mission in modern Africa* (London, 1967), p. 209 n. 11.

[3] Swantz, *Church*, p. 16; M. H. Y. Kaniki, 'Politics in the Usambara-Digo Lutheran Church, 1961–63', B.A. thesis, University College, Dar es Salaam, 1968; Stanway, 'Church growth'; D. N. M. Ng'hosha, 'The bishop: Jeremiah Kissula', in Iliffe, *Tanzanians*, pp. 211–12, 216.

advanced of all CMS mission fields, while German missions had again been weakened during the Second World War, when the Moravian church in Rungwe and Lutheran work in Meru passed almost entirely under African control.[1] Yet Protestant diversity posed problems. One was to decide the autonomous churches' patterns of government, a vital matter to Protestants. Almost every mission became a diocese with a synod and elected bishop, president, or superintendent. Lutherans generally adopted episcopacy, although they disagreed over apostolic succession and their attempts to install a European bishop in Usambara led to temporary schism.[2] Another problem for Protestants was ecumenism. Historically divided, Lutherans nevertheless formed an autonomous Federation of Lutheran Churches in 1959. Anglicans included the evangelical CMS, favouring union with Protestants, and the Anglo-Catholic UMCA, sympathising with Roman Catholicism, but they finally joined in the Church of the Province of East Africa in 1960. A loose federation of non-Roman churches known as the Christian Council of Tanganyika was created in 1948 by reshaping the Tanganyika Mission Council which had existed since 1934. Its Roman Catholic counterpart was the Tanganyika Episcopal Conference. Among many reasons for ecumenical advance was certainly the desire to speak with unity in an independent state.[3]

Christian attitudes to nationalism were characteristically diverse. Missions were extensively intertwined with the colonial state, which paid nine-tenths of their teachers' salaries. Where Christians were strongly entrenched in local government – as in Ukaguru, Ugogo, Masasi, Songea – nationalists suspected missionaries of obstructing them.[4] In Dodoma a leading missionary took office in UTP. Yet other missionaries, like the Irish-American Maryknoll Fathers in Musoma, sympathised with nationalism and even helped TANU branches to register, while Roman Catholic bishops refused to forbid their teachers to join TANU lest they rob it of good leaders.[5] Moreover, Christian churches were also intertwined with colonial society's critics and contradictions. Controlling 75 per cent of places in primary schools and 56 per cent in secondary schools in 1961,[6] they had inevitably trained many TANU leaders, Nyerere and Kambona (the son of an Anglican priest) being only the most prominent. Such

[1] Hewitt, *Success*, 1, 425; Ranger in Barrett, *Initiatives*, pp. 141–2; above, p. 499.
[2] Smedjebacka, *Church autonomy*, pp. 158–61, 261–5; Kaniki, 'Politics'.
[3] Swantz, *Church*, pp. 8, 10, 19.
[4] Kilosa, Manyoni, Masasi, and Songea historical reports, TANU 43 and 53.
[5] Listowel, *Making*, p. 246.   [6] Swantz, *Church*, p. 37.

leaders gave the party's ideology a distinctly Christian altruism foreign to indigenous ethics. The African-controlled Lutheran church's role in resistance to Operation Exodus shows how far some churches had returned to religion's pre-colonial ambivalence towards the established order.

Indigenous religions continued to lose vitality and followers, but at different speeds in different regions. During the 1957 census 88 per cent of Iraqw men, 86 per cent of Sukuma, and 82 per cent of Turu declared themselves 'pagans', but the proportion was less than 5 per cent among the Luguru, Makonde, Zaramo, Zigua, and other groups.[1] The notion of divine intervention in human affairs may have continued to take a larger place in indigenous faiths. Men from Dar es Salaam visited Kolelo 'to wash the bad smell' thought to cause persistent unemployment.[2] The High God was probably identified increasingly with the Christian God or with Allah. Tiita's chief priest had a cross on his door.[3] Rain-making survived in many areas – in Usambara it was important in politics – and remedies for immediate misfortunes generally endured better than collective rites. These were dying away in many areas. Kinga priests visited Lwembe's shrine in 1954, but only '"bits and pieces" of ritual' survived among the Nyakyusa. 'Fertiliser has replaced the chief', Sukuma elders told an enquirer.[4] While Fipa diviners ascribed misfortune to ancestral spirits, territorial spirits, or sorcery, commoners tended to blame sorcery alone.[5] This trend had gone even further in Dar es Salaam, where even diviners commonly ascribed misfortune to sorcery, partly because they could treat that in the town, partly because sorcery was easily elided with 'scientific' notions of poisoning. During the 1960s diviners in the rural areas surrounding Dar es Salaam ascribed 58 per cent of misfortunes to spirit action and 27.5 per cent to wizardry, but in the town the proportions were 10 and 63 per cent respectively. No less than 700 diviners practised in Dar es Salaam in 1967, treating 8,000–10,000 clients daily. They often recommended a European hospital.[6] In the most developed areas there may have been an increasing tendency to ascribe misfortune to chance or to adopt western medical remedies, but the possible decline of magical beliefs

[1] Tanganyika, *African census 1957*, p. 63.   [2] Swantz, 'Medicine man', p. 81.
[3] Jellicoe, 'Social change', p. 123.
[4] George Park, 'The accumulation of constitutions in Kingaland', Southwestern Anthropological Association paper, San Diego, 1968; Wilson, *Communal rituals*, p. 211; Hatfield, 'The *nfumu*', p. 103.
[5] R. G. Willis, 'Pollution and paradigms', *Man*, VII (1972), 369–70.
[6] Swantz, 'Medicine man', *passim*.

– potentially the most important intellectual change in twentieth-century Tanganyika – has not yet been studied and was probably confined to an enlightened minority.

Witchcraft eradication remained the most dramatic manifestation of indigenous beliefs. Campaigns followed the three traditions observable in the 1930s,[1] but improved communications encouraged the traditions to merge, while declining European control enabled eradication to revert towards witch-hunting. *Mchape* reappeared in Ufipa and the Rukwa valley in 1954–5, 1960 (when several TANU leaders were suspended for supporting it), and 1963–4 (when younger TANU members often used it against their elders). The campaign of 1963–4 concentrated on finding witches rather than eradicating witchcraft. *Mchape* penetrated as far north as Singida in 1959.[2] In the Pangani valley eradicators operated in Gombero in 1950, Usambara in about 1952, and North Pare in 1955, but in the last case, while using the local name *ikago* for their medicine, the eradicators were Yao and Nyasa and employed many *mchape* techniques.[3] The most vital tradition was that of the south-east, with its roots in the Bokero cult, Maji Maji, and Ngoja's great campaigns. In 1949 a Yao eradicator named Songo (probably the Hongo of the Bokero cult) won such popularity in Ulanga that soldiers with loaded rifles and fixed bayonets were needed to disperse the crowds seeking to prevent his deportation.[4] He was followed in the mid 1950s by the greatest post-war eradicator and witch-finder, Nguvumali, an Ngindo who combined the *ulilo* medicine, originating in the Bokero cult, with the mirror used by *mchape* specialists and many other symbols of modernity. His grave on the outskirts of Dar es Salaam became a place of pilgrimage, and when Nguvumali's nephew was banned from practising in the capital in 1956 Nyerere had to resist demands for TANU's intervention.[5] Meanwhile other contemporary ideas were adopted into the eclectic

[1] Above, p. 367.
[2] Willis, 'Kamcape', pp. 1–15; *Tanganyika standard*, 1 April 1955; McHenry, 'Study', p. 416; J. L. Brain, 'More modern witchfinding', *TNR*, LXII (1964), 44–8.
[3] Sutton to East African Lighterage and Stevedoring Company, 29 November 1950, LD 126/4/32, TNA; Edgar V. Winans, *Shambala* (London, 1962), p. 109; I. M. Omari, 'Witchcraft eradication in Kiruru, Pare', seminar paper, University College, Dar es Salaam, 1967.
[4] Swantz, 'Medicine man', p. 156; L. E. Larson, 'Witchcraft eradication sequences among the peoples of the Ulanga district', seminar paper, University of Dar es Salaam, 1973.
[5] Hassan bin Ismail, *Medicine man*, *passim*; L. E. Larson, 'Problems in the study of witchcraft eradication movements in southern Tanzania', *Ufahamu*, VI (1976), 88–100; Swantz, 'Medicine man', pp. 69–70; *Tanganyika standard*, 12 August 1955 and 10 March 1956.

eradication tradition. The impact of nationalism on anti-witchcraft measures was illustrated by the career of Chikanga, a Nyasa diviner who attracted thousands of patients from the Southern Highlands during the late 1950s, combined the *mchape* tradition with that of the region's oracular shrines, and was believed to possess a divine vocation to liberate the whole of Africa from witchcraft.[1] The merging of traditions and degeneration into witch-hunting came together in the horrifying career of Edom Mwasanguti, a Christian Nyakyusa who in 1954 came to believe himself called by God to destroy the murderous witches of Rungwe and its environs. Mwasanguti was specifically a witch-hunter who, as Moravian authorities complained, 'simply identified "native" medicine as "evil" medicine'. His movement was an assault on indigenous beliefs in an increasingly Christian area. Magical implements were burned outside the Ukukwe Council offices and suspects alleged robbery and torture before the authorities ended the campaign, but witchcraft beliefs remained so strong that despite his methods Mwasanguti's services were eagerly sought by neighbouring peoples.[2]

Little is known of relationships between indigenous religions and nationalism. Probably they contributed chiefly to underlying attitudes: Kolelo's enduring hostility to Europeans; villagers' identification of UTP with witchcraft; their tendency to respond collectively to nationalist organisers as to witchcraft eradicators; and especially, if vaguely, TANU's obsession with unanimity, its concern for collective rather than individual freedom. More concrete connections are rarely evident. TANU allegedly owed much to a *laibon*'s support in Masailand. Some conservatives may have hoped that independence would restore the influence of indigenous faiths, as in Umbugwe, but many practitioners – including Dar es Salaam's diviners – took no part in politics, while others who retained substantial influence may have considered TANU a threat to the indigenous order, notably in predominantly 'pagan' Mbulu where the elderly Nade Bea's influence may have been exerted against the nationalist movement.[3] Yet traditionalists generally lacked the skills for modern

---

[1] Alison Redmayne, 'Chikanga', in Mary Douglas, *Witchcraft confessions and accusations* (London, 1970), pp. 103–28; Mariam K. Slater, *African odyssey* (Garden City, N.Y., 1976), ch. 19.

[2] Moravian mission Utengule to Mbeya, 4 December 1957, TNA 18/A/2/15/69, and other papers in this file.

[3] Masai historical report, TANU 43; Gicha Mbee, 'Letter from Mbugwe', *Africa*, xxxv (1965), 198–208; Swantz, 'Medicine man', p. 335; Mbulu historical report, TANU 43; Malley, 'Dagharo Gharghara'.

politics. TANU's leaders were modernists who, like Nyerere, habitually spoke of indigenous religions with an embarrassed smile.[1]

Islam's political role is easier to chart. Not only was it expanding almost as fast as Christianity, but Muslims probably practised their faith more strictly than before. It is true that much cultural resistance survived. Even the professedly Muslim Ngindo rarely practised Islamic marriage, few Zaramo Muslims attended mosques and their female rituals remained essentially non-Islamic, and urban Islam was sometimes very shallow, especially in Dar es Salaam.[2] Yet the faith was probably deepening. Rituals in coastal villages had a larger Islamic content than in German times. Islam flourished in Ujiji in the 1960s, with sixteen functioning mosques (attended regularly by perhaps a third of the population), twelve Koran schools (which most small boys attended), and an informed interest in religious issues.[3] Greater rigour was doubtless partly due to brotherhoods, especially the Qadiriyya, which had lost some pristine fervour but remained very influential. On the other hand Tanganyikan Islam was very conservative. Many teachers still supported themselves by practising magic or herbalism. The country had scarcely felt the impact of the modernist movement which had profoundly influenced the central Islamic world. External contacts were certainly growing. The Pilgrimage remained too expensive for most Muslims, but greater wealth and better communications made it more popular among merchants and *waalimu*. The first Haya apparently went to Mecca in the 1940s, the first Pare in 1960.[4] Yet wider contacts often brought tension. The Ahmadiyya Muslim Mission, which published the first Swahili translation of the Koran in 1954, aroused much hostility among Sunni Muslims who thought it heterodox.[5] Greater contact with Ganda Muslims during the 1940s caused certain Haya leaders to abandon the full Adhuhuri prayer, thereby signifying that Islam's pioneer days were ended, but this revived the old conflict over drums and led several rural communities

[1] E.g. Barongo, *Mkiki mkiki wa siasa*, p. 208.
[2] Crosse-Upcott, 'Social structure', p. 223; Swantz, *Ritual, passim*, esp. pp. 78–9; Leslie, *Survey*, pp. 210–18.
[3] Wijeyewardene, 'Village solidarity', p. 238 n. 2; Peter Lienhardt, 'A controversy over Islamic custom in Kilwa Kivinje', in I. M. Lewis (ed.), *Islam in tropical Africa* (London, 1966), pp. 374–86; Shunya Hino, 'Neighbourhood groups in African urban society', *KUAS*, VI (1971), 19–22.
[4] Hino, 'Neighbourhood groups', p. 26; Juma Kyakuligi to Bakama, 2 June 1947, TNA 285/155/29; Kimambo, 'Texts', p. 42.
[5] DC Rufiji to PC Eastern, 6 September 1956, TNA 274/A/6/12/38; Kiwanuka, 'Islam in Bukoba', pp. 26, 40.

who resented clerical control to separate and preserve the former custom.[1] These were the tensions of modernisation and deprivation.

For most Muslims the chief deprivation was the relative backwardness in secular affairs, and especially in education, which had reversed their status during the colonial period. After the war the Aga Khan initiated an East African Muslim Welfare Society partly designed to advance African Muslims, but it was unable to coordinate the many local associations and committees formed to build schools and advance Muslim interests. Like stateless peoples, Muslims suffered in the colonial period from their egalitarian tradition. In 1956, probably in response to TANU, a Tanganyika African Muslim Union was formed with plans for a branch in each main town, but Muslims were the most non-racial of all Tanganyika's communities and a month later Asian, African, and Arab leaders in Dar es Salaam created an alternative Central Society of Tanganyika Muslims.[2] Neither had much impact. Muslims devoted great energy to education in the 1950s, but it was uncoordinated. Even Tanganyika's brotherhoods were purely regional in scope.

Muslim reactions to TANU were also uncoordinated but were probably more completely positive than those of Christians. Muslim townsmen had been prominent in TAA, Muslim activists like Kandoro and the Sykes brothers helped to create TANU, Muslim trader-politicians were at first its most characteristic leaders, and use of Swahili gave its ideology many Islamic overtones to balance those which its western-educated leaders derived from Christianity. Brotherhoods could contribute greatly, for their predominantly African membership, regional influence, and hierarchical structures enabled a determined *khalifa* like Muhammad bin Ramiya to throw his whole following behind TANU.[3] But almost every kind of Muslim supported nationalism. Amri Abedi, poet and Ahmadi missionary, became Dar es Salaam's first African mayor. Ali Migeyo belonged to Haya Islam's dissident rural element, but the rival persuasion was also represented in TANU's leadership in Bukoba, where Muslims were a local outgroup and joined the party willingly.[4] Inevitably there were exceptions, chiefly among conservative coastal leaders. The most serious dissent came from the All Muslim National Union of Tanganyika, a body apparently confined to Dar es Salaam and led

[1] Kiwanuka, 'Islam in Bukoba', *passim*.
[2] *Tanganyika standard*, 28 January and 8 February 1956.
[3] Nimtz, 'Sufi order', pp. 495–506; Lienhardt in Lewis, *Islam*, p. 378.
[4] Kiwanuka, 'Islam in Bukoba', pp. 56–7, 61–2; Hydén, *Political development*, p. 152.

chiefly by elderly TAA activists. In August 1959 they proposed that independence should be delayed until Muslims achieved educational equality with Christians, but TANU mobilised a host of sheikhs to disagree.[1] It was an example of the problems raised by TANU's very success.

The breakthrough, 1958–9

TANU's confrontation with colonialism was personified in Nyerere's duel with Twining. Heavy, experienced, and overbearing, Twining cared little for ideas but much for power to ensure law and order, economic development, racial harmony, and gradual constitutional progress. Nyerere, youthful and apparently frail, had an intellectual's impatience with less gifted men. He regarded Twining as a matador eyes a bull. 'Twining provided this foil for us', Nyerere recalled. '...He opposed us, thus giving us a foil; yet he only once barred me for three months from speaking all around the country!'[2] Prevented by British policy and his own principles from dividing or destroying TANU – as would initially have been so easy – Twining responded with infuriated snorts and charges. Publicly he declared Nyerere 'quite a reasonable man' but with an exaggerated idea of his own importance. Privately Twining spoke of him with deep contempt and thought him 'a lonely and unimpressive figure', altogether too soft for a nationalist leader. He regarded Nyerere's demand for a non-racial political system with universal suffrage as racialism disguised in idealistic language, likely to give fleeting power to 'self-appointed leaders' whose authority would collapse in economic chaos and political anarchy at the expense of ordinary people of all races.[3] Later events in many parts of Africa proved that this was no foolish prediction. The mistake was to ignore Tanganyika's particularity, and especially to let European arrogance obscure the fact that Tanganyika's problem was not relations between races but relations between Africans with different views of race. Yet even Twining had to adapt to nationalism. His programme during 1956–7 contained three elements. He reversed earlier policies concerning agriculture, land, and education in order to concentrate on building up an African middle class. He strengthened administrative control over nationalist organ-

[1] Yakubu S. Mtungumwa to Post-Elections Committee, 10 August 1959, TANU 11.
[2] Listowel, *Making*, p. 167.
[3] Twining, 'Nine years', p. 21; Heath to Betts, 15 December 1958, FCB papers 121, RH; Bates, *Gust of plumes*, pp. 253, 266; *Tanganyika standard*, 29 October 1956.

isation. And he pressed forward multi-racialism in local and central government.

Agricultural policy collapsed first. It had aimed to stabilise and improve African agriculture through rehabilitation schemes while discouraging African capitalist farming which might threaten social order. It failed because regimentation and drudgery discredited rehabilitation schemes and fuelled TANU's growth, because the cash-crop boom made many Africans anxious to abandon peasant cultivation for capitalist farming, and because government slowly realised that rural capitalism might be politically advantageous. As an official wrote:

I want to see the emergence from our hitherto undifferentiated African society of a substantial number of rich men...able to afford to send their sons overseas for education, to afford motor cars, good houses and the like, and I believe that the emergence of such relatively wealthy individuals in the community will provide a stabilising factor of immense importance.[1]

After 1954, therefore, agricultural policy shifted to the 'focal-point approach': the concentration of advice on progressive farmers whose example might stimulate their more conservative neighbours. Rehabilitation schemes were abandoned. Ridges and terraces disappeared. The change was accompanied by encouragement of African freehold land tenure, a policy urged by the Royal Commission on Land and Population which reported in 1955 and believed freehold would encourage the colour-blind capitalism which alone, in the commission's view, could genuinely develop East Africa.[2] Education policy also changed. Africans criticised the lack of secondary schooling and the emphasis on primary education which made it difficult to advance from primary to middle school. Government gradually came to agree. Its five-year plan for 1957–61 aimed roughly to treble secondary school places and the first sixth form opened at Tabora in 1959.[3]

Twining's second response to nationalism was to tighten administrative control. His instrument was the Societies Ordinance of 1954, which required associations to seek government registration and obtain police permission before collecting subscriptions or holding public meetings. During 1955 legislation also made intercommunal attacks equivalent to sedition, with the onus of proof on the defence.

[1] Malcolm, minute, 29 July 1952, TNA 41822.
[2] Great Britain, *East Africa Royal Commission 1953–1955 report* (Cmd 9475 of 1955); Tanganyika, *Review of land tenure policy, part 1* (Dar es Salaam, 1958).
[3] Cameron and Dodd, *Society*, ch. 9.

This machinery was very effective, although it also stimulated TANU to improve its organisation. The party was in any case anxious to observe the law, believing that disorder could only delay independence. Headquarters proclaimed its desire to restrain 'our followers' ignorance and failure to grasp the things we are clamouring for'. 'Please jump on those who break the law', the Secretary-General urged.[1] In practice, government's handling of TANU depended largely on the attitudes of individual officers, as provincial administration had done since German times. As Nyerere acutely observed, TANU saw government as institutions while British officers often saw it in the old African manner as personal relations.[2] Some older administrators regarded nationalism as a personal challenge to their concern for peasant welfare and proposed to combat it by vigorous touring. This paternalism was especially common among Sukumaland's 'bush governors', as Nyerere contemptuously described them.[3] Many younger officials, by contrast, probably envied Nyerere, a university man of their own mind and generation with a much more attractive future than theirs. His presence brought reason and gaiety to beleaguered district offices.[4] Early in 1957 government's attitude to TANU hardened. The reasons are obscure but may have included a new chief secretary, UTP's increasingly obvious failure, a sense that TANU's growth threatened Britain's whole eastern African policy, and Nyerere's personal success at the U.N. in 1956 when he insisted that Tanganyika must be declared a primarily African state. In January 1957 he was banned from public speaking for some months after an unusually militant speech which government interpreted as incitement against the authorities and the immigrant races.[5] TANU branches in Korogwe, Handeni, Pangani, and Iringa were proscribed. Yet repression came too late. A U.N. mission was due in August 1957. Twining lifted the ban on Nyerere's speeches in July, appointed him to the Legislative Council, and offered him a junior ministry, which he refused.[6]

[1] Mhando to DC Morogoro, 25 April 1957, and SG to DC Kisarawe, 22 November 1956, TANU 29/153 and 110.
[2] Nyerere, *Freedom and unity*, pp. 105–6.
[3] Maguire, '*Uhuru*', p. 206 n. 1; *Sauti ya TANU*, 27 May 1958.
[4] See especially the correspondence in TNA 46/A/6/3/1/158–9.
[5] 'Report of speech by Julius Nyerere on January 27th at Mnazi Mmoja', Chesham papers 19, YUL; 'Asian Socialist Conference: Anti-Colonial Bureau news letter no. 28: March and April 1957: Freedom of speech in Africa, by Julius Nyerere', FCB papers 121, RH.
[6] Bates, *Gust of plumes*, p. 269; Listowel, *Making*, p. 298.

The new Legislative Council had opened in April 1955 with its official majority and ten nominated unofficials from each race. Twining declared it 'likely to continue to be the best arrangement for a long time to come', but in April 1956 he announced elections in certain constituencies during 1958.[1] Each voter would choose one candidate of each race, presumably to encourage moderation. The key question was who would vote. Government proposed high qualifications, but African councillors rejected them and a Legislative Council committee, dominated by UTP, reduced the qualifications to an annual income of £150, eight years education, or tenure of a designated office. Although TANU denounced 'half-caste government' and the highest electoral qualifications in any British colony, the system ensured in practice that a large majority of voters would be Africans.[2] The vital unanswered question is how far the British realised that this electoral system might enable TANU to win power at a stroke. Meanwhile Twining was again reconstructing local government. In the early 1950s government had moved from democratising native authorities to multi-racial county councils, the first being formed in the Lake and Southern Highlands Provinces in May 1955. They soon proved unsatisfactory, partly because powerful native authorities like the Chagga Council resisted incorporation, partly because 'counties' were artificial and remote units. Rather than abandoning multi-racialism, however, government decided to introduce it at the lower level of multi-racial district councils, despite the known opposition of TANU and most chiefs.[3]

This deeper commitment to multi-racialism inaugurated the decisive confrontation between colonial regime and nationalist movement which occupied 1958 and 1959. It began in January 1958 at TANU's annual conference in Tabora. This made two major decisions. One was to fight for *madaraka*, responsible government, by the end of 1959 or adopt positive action. The other concerned TANU's participation in the elections of 1958–9 under the tripartite voting formula. This seriously divided the party on much the same lines as had endangered TAA in 1953–4. TANU had initially threatened to boycott tripartite elections and Nyerere apparently advocated non-participation in April 1957. At that time most observers believed that Africans would be a minority of the electorate, thus enabling the immigrant races to choose

[1] Listowel, *Making*, p. 258; *Tanganyika standard*, 26 April 1956.
[2] Pratt, *Critical phase*, pp. 39–40; Steven Mhando, *TANU and the vote* (Dar es Salaam, n.d.)
[3] Pratt, *Critical phase*, pp. 31–3.

the African representatives. In June 1957, however, government assured the U.N. that Africans would predominate, and Nyerere replied that TANU wished to participate in elections if they were truly free. In July he dismayed some followers by accepting the 'political risk' of appointment to the Legislative Council.[1] Government replied by easing pressure on TANU branches. During August few Africans registered to vote, perhaps expecting a boycott, but TANU ordered its officers to encourage registration and Nyerere told a public meeting early in September that TANU would fight the elections.[2] Meanwhile both Twining and UTP seem to have realised that tripartite voting might enable Africans – who were eventually some two-thirds of voters – to choose TANU candidates for all seats. When Lennox-Boyd visited East Africa in October 1957 Twining raised the possibility of abandoning tripartite voting, but the Colonial Secretary – concerned to press multi-racialism on Kenya's settlers and nationalists – decided that it was too late, although adding that Tanganyika's constitutional progress was if anything too rapid.[3]

When TANU's conference met in January 1958 Nyerere was committed to fighting the elections. A boycott might give UTP a landslide, divide TANU by encouraging opportunists to stand as independents, and perhaps bring violent confrontation with government. Yet many TANU members opposed participation, especially in Sukumaland where Bomani, who agreed with Nyerere, found the party divided between himself and Bhoke Munanka's militants. Some of these believed that only confrontation could win freedom. Others may have calculated more coolly that tripartite voting and high qualifications would favour moderate candidates. At all events, Mwanza's delegation submitted a resolution that tripartite voting was *haramu*, forbidden, while Nyerere demonstrated his militancy by resigning from the Legislative Council.[4]

No full record of the Tabora Conference survives, but its main lines

---

[1] *Tanganyika standard*, 26 October 1956 and 5 April 1957; M. N. Rattansey, 'Tanganyika', 13 November 1956, FCB papers 123, RH; UNTC record, 12 June 1957 (p. 106) and 18 June 1957 (p. 147); Nyerere to Betts, 2 September 1957, FCB papers 121, RH; Lowenkopf, 'Parties', p. 144.

[2] G. W. Y. Hucks, 'Report on the first elections of members to the Legislative Council of Tanganyika', duplicated, 1959, p. 5 (I owe this reference to Dr Walji); R. O. Philip to Arusha, 3 September 1957, TNA 462/A/6/3/77; Barongo, *Mkiki mkiki wa siasa*, p. 100.

[3] Twining, 'Nine years', p. 20; correspondence in TANU 101; Taylor, *Political development*, pp. 155–6.

[4] Listowel, *Making*, p. 305 n. 1; Bhoke Munanka to Maswanya, 6 January 1958, TANU 18; *Sauti ya TANU*, 16 December 1957.

are clear.[1] Abdallah Rashidi from Tanga urged electoral participation. Bhoke Munanka opposed it and another speaker called the Legislative Council 'a house of danger – an evil trap'. Nyerere spoke, to little effect, and the debate was adjourned without agreement. Next day Bhoke Munanka and Nyerere summed up. Nyerere's speech is clouded by legend but was probably one of his finest. TANU had to win an election, he urged, and it could win this one. Not to contest it might entrench UTP in office and provoke the violence which alone could prevent independence:

Imagine that you have a *shamba* and that in front of it there is a pond, with a lot of mud around it. If you want to harvest your crops and carry them out of the *shamba* you must first step into the mud and dirty your feet. What would you prefer? To lose your crops and keep your feet clean? Or to harvest your crops and dirty your feet?[2]

There were 37 votes for participation and 23 against.[3] Nyerere immediately repaired relations with the militants. His public speech after the conference dwelt on *madaraka* in 1959 rather than the election issue. He toured Lake Province and published an attack on the 'lunatics' administering it which was so libellous that he was sued.[4] In the event the minority loyally accepted the conference decision, although Zuberi Mtemvu, TANU's assistant secretary, resigned and formed the African National Congress.[5]

Nyerere now realised that TANU's organisation must be strengthened. He probably hoped to check the indiscipline which had closed some branches, to remedy the financial crisis at headquarters, to satisfy complaints of inefficiency after Kambona left for further education in Britain in 1956, to comply with the amended Societies Ordinance which required political societies to register all their branches, and perhaps to prevent rivals mobilising support. 'My movement has reached a critical step', he told George Padmore in December 1957:

During the last three years we have been trying to make it a popular mass movement. The success we have achieved has surprised even the most optimistic amongst us. We have virtually the whole country behind us,

[1] For accounts, see the pencilled notes (by Bhoke Munanka?) in TANU 18; Hassan Issa, 'Safari ya Tabora'; 'Taarifa ya mkutano mkuu wa mwaka 1957 uliofanyika toka tarehe 21/1/1958 mpaka tarehe 25/1/1958', TANU 51 (reprinted in Kandoro, *Mwito*, pp. 113–36); Barongo, *Mkiki mkiki wa siasa*, pp. 134–47; Listowel, *Making*, pp. 304–8.
[2] Listowel, *Making*, p. 306, quoting Kisenge.
[3] Hassan Issa, 'Safari ya Tabora'. Lowenkopf, 'Parties', p. 158, gives the voting as 37 to 11.
[4] *Sauti ya TANU*, 27 May 1958.   [5] Below, p. 572.

although our registered membership is roughly between 150,000 and 200,000. We can double that membership in twelve months if we want to. Mass support is no longer our immediate problem. The problem as I see it now is one of minute organization.[1]

For this he chose a new general secretary, Elias Kisenge, a former civil servant who had run TAGSA and the Pare Union before becoming TANU's provincial secretary in Tanga. Kisenge bureaucratised TANU. Branches were formed at chiefdom and sub-chiefdom level. Elders', youths', and women's sections multiplied. Paid, transferable secretaries were appointed at district and sub-district level, until by 1959 TANU had 970 paid staff and another 945 officers receiving expenses or allowances.[2] Such professionals gained much local power and could be controlled from above but were sometimes seen as outsiders by local TANU members.[3] Since Tanganyika had few wealthy Africans, TANU's professional staff could be paid only by subscriptions from a mass membership, much as lack of animal transport had maximised the impact of nineteenth-century trade. Between 1956–7 and 1957–8 funds reaching headquarters each year rose from Shs. 159,699 to Shs. 378,281.[4] 'This year', Nyerere reflected in December 1958, '...TANU has entered nearly every village of Tanganyika, and nearly everyone wants to be a TANU member. In truth our main task is to reach these people.'[5] In most regions 1958 was the year when TANU first became predominant in local affairs. Kahama experienced the impact:

The Annual Conference at Tabora resolved to spread TANU until even the smallest child in the village should know the meaning of TANU and freedom. After this decision a great struggle was made to inform the citizens through meetings, conversations, and their communal groups until TANU had announced itself at every house in every village.[6]

This was the general pattern, but one region was excluded. The militants angrily denounced the proscription which still made Lake Province 'the forbidden land of the Tanganyika Administration'.[7] There, in July 1958, the next crisis occurred. It arose from govern-

[1] Nyerere to Padmore, 14 December 1957, TANU 52.
[2] Kisenge, 'Taarifa ya kazi ya chama kwa kipindi cha pili cha mwaka 1959', 27 July 1959, TANU 28. See also Amos, 'Kisenge'.
[3] Hino, 'Occupational differentiation', p. 103.
[4] 'Income and expenditure account for the year ended 30 September 1957', TANU 18; income and expenditure account, 1 October 1957 – 30 September 1958, TANU 28.
[5] Nyerere to 'Wakuu wote wa TANU', 16 December 1958, TANU 28.
[6] Kahama historical report, TANU 53.
[7] Maswanya to Bhoke Munanka, 31 December 1957, TANU 18; Nyerere to Betts, 26 September 1958, TANU 98.

ment's attempt to create a multi-racial district council in Geita district. Recently colonised by vigorous Sukuma cotton-growers, Geita was a frontier area where native authorities, predominantly Zinza, were especially ineffective and voluntary societies of all kinds – cooperatives, Sukuma Union, TAA, TANU – were especially popular. Early in 1958 the Geita chiefs unhappily acquiesced in a multi-racial council, although many of their subjects feared that Europeans and Asians would thereby control their affairs and their land. Opposition was led by Hezeroni Mpandachalo, a farmer and trader with primary education who spoke for peasant activists. On 11 July 1958 he told an illegal public meeting that the people would cease to pay tax, provide labour, or cull cattle unless government disowned multi-racialism and 'UTP chiefs'. Two days later riot police arrested him, dispersing with teargas the crowd which tried to follow them. Some 2,000 people converged on Geita, where Mpandachalo was held, and then continued to Mwanza, where they camped for four days and unsuccessfully petitioned the Chief Secretary. Mwanza's frightened businessmen pressed the police to act and even Bomani urged the demonstrators to return home. They refused, women and children moved to the front, and the police resorted to truncheons and teargas. On 8 August the Governor was shouted down. Unrest spread throughout Sukumaland as dissidents flouted agricultural rules, sought to release prisoners, and threatened courts.[1] These protest techniques – so similar to those employed by Chagga and Haya in 1937 and by Pare in 1945 – show how TANU in Sukumaland expressed the tensions of a peasant society in formation. Knowing that he must inherit the consequences, Nyerere was appalled. 'Here are people', he protested, 'who are just serving out their few remaining years before they leave for their homes. For people like these it is nothing if Tanganyika is to be a land of disorder. In truth, they would be glad. But *we* want to build a Tanganyika which will benefit our children.'[2] Yet in reality government was equally appalled. 'For both the administrators and the administered', Dr Maguire has written, 'the lesson of civil disobedience in Sukumaland in 1958 was that the colonial system no longer enjoyed the minimal assent of the public.'[3] The Sukumaland Scheme collapsed. Multi-racial local government was broken. One plank of Twining's programme was shattered. The other, meanwhile, was bending under ballot boxes.

[1] Maguire, '*Uhuru*', pp. 199–215, 227, 229, 236–41.
[2] *Sauti ya TANU*, 9 December 1958.   [3] Maguire, '*Uhuru*', p. 242.

The elections of 1958–9 were in two stages, allegedly for administrative reasons. In the first, in September 1958, Northern, Eastern, Western, Tanga, and Southern Highlands Provinces were contested. The others voted in February 1959. TANU initially intended to contest only African seats, but shortly before the election it also decided to support, but not nominate, non-African candidates. Their selection was largely in Nyerere's hands. For Asian candidates he turned to the Asian Association. Lacking any similar European ally, TANU simply supported European candidates who 'could be useful in the struggle'.[1] While Asian community leaders stood aside, TANU's support enabled the Asian Association's young professional men to seize leadership positions. The most important was Amir Jamal, a 38-year-old businessman educated in India who was a bitter critic of British rule and the old Asian leaders.[2] His European counterpart was Derek Bryceson, a farmer who had not established himself within UTP and was free to align himself with nationalism.[3] TANU's African candidates were chosen by the NEC after hearing suggestions from provincial committees and affiliated bodies. The choice inevitably exacerbated the party's divisions. Provincial committees naturally proposed local activists, while the NEC, anticipating *madaraka*, preferred potential ministers. In Western Province TANU supported Chief Abdallah Fundikira, who was almost certain of Nyamwezi votes.[4] In Central Province, by contrast, an eligible local government officer, Job Lusinde, declined to stand and the NEC selected Maalim Kihere of Tanga over the Wagogo Union's protests.[5] Nyerere himself stood in Eastern Province and was opposed by Patrick Kunambi, a local chief and TANU founder. Sijaona was a natural choice in the Southern Province. Kawawa of the TFL was chosen for Dar es Salaam; John Keto, a teacher at Minaki, became the candidate for Tanga; and John Mwakangale, secretary of the Rungwe African District Council and a vehement nationalist, stood for the Southern Highlands. The most serious conflicts were in prosperous Northern and West Lake Provinces where local politics were most competitive. Seventeen candidates sought TANU's nomination in Bukoba, and although Barongo, the provincial chairman, was the local favourite, the NEC

[1] Nyerere to [Jhaveri?], 4 January 1959, TANU 95; Nyerere to Mayanja, 25 September 1958, TANU 98.
[2] Listowel, *Making*, p. 219; *Tanganyika standard*, 22 December 1954.
[3] See the correspondence in Chesham papers, YUL.
[4] Listowel, *Making*, pp. 317–18.
[5] Lusinde to TANU, 8 October 1958, and I. A. Msowoya to TANU, 11 November 1958, TANU 95/34 and 68.

preferred George Kahama, general manager of the contentious local cooperative society.[1] In Northern Province, similarly, the local preference was the provincial secretary, M. K. Simon, but the NEC selected Solomon Eliufoo, who was educational secretary of the Lutheran church, son of a pioneer Chagga pastor, and a man with important political contacts on Kilimanjaro.[2] The picture was completed when Bomani was chosen for the Lake Province rather than Bhoke Munanka, who found no constituency.[3]

Meanwhile UTP's hopes were fading. *Utupu*, 'nothingness', had begun encouragingly, but by mid 1957 it was making no headway and its leaders therefore sharpened their criticisms of government. In June 1957 they demanded a constitutional timetable. In July Willis complained that UTP had not received the 'covert support' expected from the administration. In September the party formulated a new programme including a target date for independence, an end to parity, and an advance towards universal suffrage.[4] TANU's decision to contest the election was a setback, however, and as UTP's policy grew more radical it probably lost appeal to conservative Asians and Europeans and to its capitalist backers, who began to contemplate reconciliation with TANU. In June 1958 UTP's business wing even met TANU to discuss an electoral pact, but Nyerere declared that 'TANU cannot unite with a thing which is utterly dead'.[5] Meanwhile a deficit of over £5,000 at the end of 1957 had forced Willis to resign.[6] As elections approached UTP was demoralised. It sponsored formal candidates in only two constituencies: the Southern Highlands, where Bayldon stood alongside a maverick Nyakyusa teacher, Timothy Sankey Mwanjisi; and Tanga Province, where its candidates included David Lead of Mazinde Estate and Petro Mntambo of the Tambarare Citizens Union.

The election of September 1958 was a devastating victory for TANU. Bayldon lost by 954 votes to the 2,962 polled by his TANU-supported opponent. Nyerere defeated Kunambi by 2,628 to 802. Altogether TANU and its allies won 68 per cent of the votes and 13 of the 15 seats,

[1] S. K. N. Luangisa to SG, 26 September 1958, TANU 95/30; Kisenge to Kandoro, 5 September 1958, TANU 98.
[2] 'Mambo yaliyozungumzwa katika mkutano wa halmashauri ya jimbo la kaskazini', 6 April 1958, TANU 35/100.
[3] A list of nominations and selections (written by J. Kasella Bantu) is in TANU 28.
[4] Taylor, *Political development*, pp. 148, 156; Willis to CS, 29 July 1957, in Lowenkopf, 'Parties', p. 125.
[5] Barongo, *Mkiki mkiki wa siasa*, pp. 167, 204; information from Dr Ross.
[6] Lowenkopf, 'Parties', p. 124.

the others going to unopposed Europeans. The only real contest was in Tanga, where Mntambo polled 1,854 votes against Keto's 3,455. The most remarkable contest was in Western Province, where only the Asian seat was fought but 73 per cent of those registered voted. As the Supervisor of Elections reflected, 'To those who know their Tanganyika, the conception of thousands of Africans trudging miles and miles to vote for a single Asian is something quite extraordinary.'[1] UTP recognised defeat. Its branches disappeared, some selling their office equipment to TANU at knock-down prices. Twining declared it 'a failure, because of apathy and because of lack of leadership'.[2] Only Bayldon, the most committed multi-racialist, tried to keep the party alive in the Southern Highlands. It did not contest the elections of February 1959, when TANU won all fifteen seats against little opposition.

'The atmosphere has been suddenly revolutionized', Nyerere wrote in September 1958. '...There is now more than a chance that we may work our democratic revolution here in a manner that might revolutionize the whole trend of events in East and Central Africa.'[3] In retrospect it is clear that the election was the key to Tanganyika's independence. Deliberately or not, the British had made possible a transfer of power which by-passed the struggle over electoral formulae so common in East and Central Africa, thereby making it impossible to use fancy franchises to contain black power throughout the region. At one stroke TANU had won what might have taken a decade of negotiation and gradual advancement.

The British hesitated. After 1945 the Colonial Office had planned for decolonisation within a generation in order to control the process, but officials had neither settled the form of an independent East Africa nor won support for their programme within the Conservative Party, which regarded itself as guardian of Britain's imperial tradition and held office continuously from 1951 to 1964. In reality Britain did not retain control of decolonisation. Ghana's independence in 1957 showed that to plan decolonisation was to accelerate it as Africans competed to inherit power. Elsewhere, too, the initiative passed to local populations. Economic circumstances also changed, for during the 1950s – the only decade of sustained prosperity she had experienced since 1914 – Britain's trade with industrial states, especially in Europe,

[1] Hucks, 'Report', *passim* (quotation on p. 27).
[2] Twining, 'Nine years', p. 22.
[3] Nyerere to Betts, 26 September 1958, TANU 98 (and in FCB papers 121, RH).

grew much faster than her imperial trade. Unilever's African interests, for example, became markedly less profitable than investments elsewhere,[1] while businessmen realised that their interest lay in accommodation with potential successor regimes. Yet businessmen were not especially important to British colonial policy. What mattered was political opinion. This too was changing, but more slowly. The Labour Party in opposition supported nationalist movements more openly than before, but the Conservative Party was deeply divided by the Suez crisis of 1956 and the apparent impossibility of suppressing violence in Cyprus. Suez probably did not reduce Britain's strategic interest in eastern Africa, but it probably did convince the Prime Minister, Macmillan, that decolonisation must be accelerated lest apparently irresistible nationalists should seek communist support. Temporarily, however, fear of right-wing opposition determined Macmillan to press decolonisation in only one area at a time. During 1958 Cyprus had priority and Lennox-Boyd's policy for East Africa remained multi-racial independence 'eventually rather than soon'.[2]

This constraint dominated policy in Tanganyika when Twining's governorship ended in June 1958, just before his programme disintegrated. His successor, Sir Richard Turnbull, was a simpler man, cool, professional, and disillusioned. An experienced provincial commissioner, he had recently directed the ruthlessly efficient suppression of Mau Mau in Nairobi, which appears to have accentuated his dislike of both violence and politicians. Nyerere publicly welcomed his appointment as a reactionary step. 'If a Colonial Governor is not an Arden-Clarke', he wrote, 'then the more embedded he is in the 19th century the better.'[3] In reality, however, Turnbull's fear of violence made him the Arden-Clarke of Tanganyika. Unlike Twining he was not obsessed by race relations. Instead, he feared that government was losing control of the countryside, that its police force – which had always left rural control to the now discredited native authorities – was incapable of meeting an emergency, and that violence might make the country ungovernable by an African successor regime. On first meeting Nyerere, Turnbull made it clear that he was not committed to multi-racialism and that after the

[1] Charles Wilson, *Unilever 1945–1965* (London, 1968), pp. 16–17, 225.
[2] Phillip Darby, *British defence policy east of Suez 1947–1968* (London, 1973), pp. 119, 125, 204–7; Dan Horowitz, 'Attitudes of British Conservatives towards decolonization in Africa', *African affairs*, LXIX (1970), 13–16; Goldsworthy, *Colonial issues*, pp. 309, 365.
[3] *Sauti ya TANU*, 27 March 1958. Arden-Clarke managed Britain's withdrawal from Ghana.

elections he hoped to include elected members in the new ministry.[1] Nyerere responded by paying his fine for libel rather than choosing 'martyrdom' in prison. He reported a 'fairly good working relationship' with the governor. 'There is a level where our respective roles are incompatible', he wrote. 'But I am convinced that we both want an atmosphere in Tanganyika in which political controversy, however hot, can take place in peace and dignity.'[2] In October Turnbull assured the Legislative Council that 'it is not intended, and never has been intended, that parity should be a permanent feature of the Tanganyika scene', but the general political situation prevented him from going further. At a conference with Lennox-Boyd and the other East African governors in January 1959 Turnbull urged that the weakness of his security forces necessitated rapid concessions, but the conference approved a tentative timetable which would give Tanganyika responsible government in 1963–4 and independence in 1970.[3]

On 17 March 1959 Tanganyika faced the most serious crisis of the nationalist period. The Tabora Conference had threatened positive action unless TANU was assured of responsible government by the end of 1959. Turnbull was to open the new Legislative Council on 17 March. TANU wanted to hear a date for responsible government. Turnbull returned from his conference without authority to give one. As 17 March approached, tension mounted. TANU branches pressed for positive action. Officials made their wills. Turnbull prepared an emergency headquarters in government house. Special constables patrolled the deserted streets of Iringa. And politicians negotiated. Nyerere wanted elected ministers to replace civil servants. Turnbull insisted that real power could be transferred only after African civil servants had been trained. He could not grant an elected majority in the Legislative Council or the Council of Ministers but offered TANU four ministries and a post-elections committee to consider further constitutional advance. TANU leaders threatened positive action. Turnbull said he could give no more. The leaders demanded another ministry so that African ministers could outnumber the obligatory Asian and European. Turnbull agreed.[4]

[1] Turnbull to Chesham, 9 January 1959, Chesham papers 5, YUL; Listowel, *Making*, pp. 334–42, 381.
[2] Nyerere to Betts, 26 September 1958, TANU 98.
[3] Listowel, *Making*, pp. 348, 351; Michael Blundell, *So rough a wind* (London, 1964), p. 261.
[4] Chesham to Turnbull, 27 February 1959, and Turnbull to Chesham, 5 and 31 March 1959, Chesham papers 5, YUL; Listowel, *Making*, pp. 349–53; Chesham to *Sunday Times*, n.d., Chesham papers 9, YUL.

On 17 March Turnbull explained the arrangement to the Legislative Council. Nyerere then had to convince TANU's parliamentary party. While Bryceson and Fundikira urged acceptance, Mwakangale and Kawawa feared it might undermine the confidence of the public in their leaders – particularly if the leader of the opposition himself were to cross to the government front bench. When Nyerere took the hint and declared – to Turnbull's irritation – that he would not accept a ministry, the parliamentary party unanimously accepted the arrangement as a temporary measure.[1] Nyerere and Turnbull chose the ministers – Bryceson, Eliufoo, Fundikira, Jamal, Kahama – from TANU's more moderate and experienced representatives. The Post-Elections Committee proposed that all taxpayers should vote at the next election, together with all women who were literate or owned houses. Each of the fifty districts would return a single (almost certainly African) candidate, while eleven special seats would be reserved for Asians and ten for Europeans. In October 1959 Turnbull announced that such elections would take place in September 1960, but on Lennox-Boyd's instructions he did not say whether they would be followed by responsible government.[2]

Again the focus shifted to London. British policy throughout East and Central Africa was in crisis during 1959. Riots led to an emergency in Nyasaland. Eleven 'hard core' Mau Mau detainees died after being beaten at Hola prison camp. Only at Macmillan's insistence did the savagely criticised Lennox-Boyd agree to remain in office until the election in October, while many younger Conservatives became convinced that Britain's African policy must change to forestall violence which would commit British troops and thereby earn the government much unpopularity within Britain. The election of October 1959 took virtually no account of colonial issues, but it returned a large Conservative majority, brought many liberal younger men into parliament, shifted the balance of power within the party towards the left, and at last enabled Macmillan to tackle eastern Africa. Lennox-Boyd retired and the most radical of the younger Conservative leaders, Iain Macleod, was given the Colonial Office. He had never seen a British colony.[3]

---

[1] 'Tanganyika Elected Members' Organisation: minutes of a special meeting', 17 March 1959, Chesham papers 16, YUL.
[2] Tanganyika, *Report of the post elections committee 1959* (Dar es Salaam, 1959); Chesham to ?, 24 September 1959, Chesham papers 5, YUL.
[3] Goldsworthy, *Colonial issues*, pp. 33–5, 363–72; Nigel Fisher, *Iain Macleod* (London, 1973), pp. 141–3.

Between 1959 and 1961 Macleod carried through measures which liberated East Africa and destroyed the Central African Federation. Gone was the old gradualism, the insistence on training an efficient African bureaucracy, and the concern to protect minorities. Macleod held that European settlers had no future unless they cooperated with nationalism. He calculated that little time was available and that existing nationalist leaders were more amenable than the harder men who might oust them if violence occurred. 'Any other policy would have led to terrible bloodshed', he explained later. '...We could not possibly have held by force to our territories in Africa...Of course there were risks in moving quickly. But the risks of moving slowly were far greater.'[1]

Macleod's policy needed suitable nationalist movements to convert into successor regimes. Because TANU and its much-respected leader offered exactly that, Tanganyika was the first territory to experience Macleod's urgency. When TANU threatened that its ministers would resign unless Britain announced during December 1959 that responsible government would come during 1960, Macleod agreed that it should follow the elections planned for September 1960.[2] Most Tanganyikan leaders still expected independence in five or ten years, but Nyerere met Macleod in London during March 1960 to arrange the steps towards internal self-government, found the whole time-scale changed, and began to demand full independence during 1961.[3] TANU won all seats but one in the election of September 1960. On 3 October Nyerere formed his first cabinet. The final steps were decided at a constitutional conference in Dar es Salaam on 27 March 1961. While TANU agreed that the new state should be headed by a governor-general rather than a president, for fear that British civil servants might leave, Macleod accepted TANU's demand that Tanganyika should become independent in December 1961.[4]

[1] Iain Macleod, 'Trouble in Africa', *The Spectator*, 31 January 1964. See also Fisher, *Macleod*, chs. 8–9.
[2] TANU press release [November 1959?] TANU 34/175; Taylor, *Political development*, p. 186.
[3] Robert Heussler, *British Tanganyika* (Durham, N.C., 1971), p. 66 n. 49; Fisher, *Macleod*, p. 152; Pratt, *Critical phase*, pp. 84–6.
[4] Tanganyika, *Report of the Tanganyika constitutional conference 1961* (Dar es Salaam, 1961); Listowel, *Making*, pp. 384–90.

Between past and future, 1959–61

While politicians scrambled to decolonise, ordinary men prepared for the future. The 76,536 Asians and 20,598 Europeans[1] faced the greatest dilemma. TANU's policy refused them special constitutional safeguards but divorced political citizenship from race. Immigrants could choose to stay in Tanganyika and apply for citizenship, remain provisionally but seek British citizenship, or leave. Some chose Tanganyikan citizenship, either from necessity or from prevailing optimism. In Bryceson and Jamal they had examples of apparently successful accommodation with TANU, although its fear of division prevented the party from admitting non-African members. Identification with Tanganyika was easiest for the educated and mobile but more difficult for uneducated shopkeepers who had little future elsewhere and experienced localised boycott and harrassment. Most Asians chose to wait and see, relying on the British citizenship now available to them. But some immigrants prepared to leave, especially among the European farmers of the north whose hard-line leaders had planned to return 'genuine' representatives for European reserved seats in the 1960 election until TANU smothered this dying gasp of settler power.[2] Yet most Europeans stayed. Large farmers, businessmen, and especially sisal planters generally shared the prevailing optimism. Sisal prices were rising and TANU seemed increasingly willing to respect property. 'Nobody asks him to give up his sisal estate', Nyerere assured the planters.[3] By 1961 he was their favourite African. Officials responded similarly. Encouraged by financial incentives, 85 per cent eventually served the independent regime. Their presence was like a pistol at Nyerere's head.[4]

Africans flocked into TANU. Between July 1958 and January 1960 membership probably increased from some 300,000 to about 1,000,000,[5] until it embraced about one person in ten or one adult in five. Unreliable figures suggest that TANU was strongest in developed regions like the Eastern and Tanga Provinces and weakest in the more remote Western and Southern Highlands Provinces. More remarkable is the fact that Shs. 590,408 of the Shs. 1,575,981 reaching headquarters

[1] Tanganyika, *Report on the census of the non-African population, 1957* (Dar es Salaam, 1958), p. 6.
[2] Minutes of the Northern Province Convention of Associations, 29 March, 27 May, and 14 June 1960, RH.
[3] Quoted in *Venture*, January 1959.
[4] Taylor, *Political development*, p. 219; Pratt, *Critical phase*, p. 101.
[5] Barongo, *Mkiki mkiki wa siasa*, p. 176; TANU, 'Historia ya TANU', pp. 103–5.

between October 1958 and January 1960 came from Sukumaland (with only 14 per cent of the country's population).[1] After TANU's electoral victory the Sukumaland branches were reopened on 12 October 1958, not by local radicals – Bhoke Munanka had been given a party office in Dar es Salaam – but by Kisenge, equipped with elaborate instructions to prevent disorder. Partly at Turnbull's insistence, Nyerere himself visited Mwanza in November. 'TANU of today is quite different to the TANU of yesterday', he told the crowds:

He said there was a misguided conception of the power of the TANU membership card – people thought it meant power to open shops without a licence; to refuse to pay taxes and generally to release citizens from their obligations to the law. This is wrong, said Mr. N. TANU intends its members to obey the laws of the country.[2]

Tight control channelled Sukuma subscriptions to headquarters. 'The only place we can look for money now is Mwanza', Bhoke Munanka told Kisenge, 'for...the National Executive decided that all the money should go through their Provinces and you know what this means.'[3] Although violence was avoided, Sukumaland experienced much ferment. Riot police were needed to enforce rinderpest innoculation – the only conservation measure Turnbull maintained – while party activists captured council seats and demanded the deposition of unsympathetic chiefs.[4]

The most dramatic reversal following TANU's victory – so similar in this respect to German or British conquest – was the fall of Marealle II.[5] Declining coffee prices, accusations of corruption and autocracy, and suspicion of collusion with Twining and the Chiefs' Convention fuelled the campaign against him. Its leaders included Eliufoo, a Machame man who was son-in-law of Abdiel Shangali and had been at Makerere with Nyerere. Marealle's opponents established an alliance with TANU in 1955. Three years later, with Nyerere's approval, they formed the Chagga Democratic Party – 'TANU dressed in a tribal robe'[6] – to oppose both Marealle and the paramountcy itself, instead advocating an elected presidency. A referendum in February 1960 showed a majority of eight to one for a presidency,

[1] TANU, 'Historia ya TANU', pp. 103–5; papers in TANU 91.
[2] Public Relations Officer, Lake Province, to DC Ukerewe, 29 November 1958, TNA 158/A/6/7/1/186.
[3] Bhoke Munanka to Kisenge, 5 November 1958, TANU 98.
[4] Maguire, '*Uhuru*', pp. 283–94.
[5] See Clemm, 'White mountain', pp. 231–69; Mramba, 'Political development', *passim*.
[6] Mramba, 'Political development', p. 13.

Eliufoo becoming the first incumbent. 'TANU had won so much local support as a Territorial body', Marealle complained, 'that it was difficult to discredit these self-same Officers in any other movement, however bogus.'[1] In one sense his fall showed that the Chagga recognised that their future lay in Tanganyika's national arena, but it also enabled young, educated Christians to seize Kilimanjaro's local government from their elders, and only with some reluctance was the CDP disbanded in 1960 after TANU had refused it affiliation. In Sukumaland, similarly, even TANU's local leaders wished to preserve the Sukumaland Federal Council in order 'to catch up with other tribes which have made great progress such as the Chagga', but Nyerere ordered its destruction because 'we can't have another Katanga here'.[2]

TANU's victory in 1958–9 brought many parochial interests and perceptions into the party as even the deprived were politicised. The beneficiaries included many hereditary chiefs. Their convention joined the bandwagon in March 1959.[3] Two months later their spokesman within TANU, Chief Fundikira – whom many considered Nyerere's leading rival – urged TANU's parliamentary party to create an advisory territorial council of chiefs, so that historic institutions could buttress TANU's unity after independence. He found little support, and in July 1960 TANU resolved that after independence even the chiefs' role in local government should pass to divisional executive officers.[4] Some chiefs resisted to the last, notably among the Yao rulers of Tunduru, so progressive in the nineteenth century but now remote and obscurantist. In May 1959 TANU still had only 700 members among Tunduru's 75,000 people.[5] But most chiefs sought places in the new order. Their opportunity was the extension of the electorate from 60,000 registered voters in 1958 to 885,000 in 1960, for in Tanganyika universal suffrage often pointed towards counter-revolution. The trend was clearest in Hima chiefdoms. In 1959 TANU's chairmanship in Kasulu passed to Anna Gwassa, a progressive tractor-farmer and sister of Mwami Theresa Ntare of Heru, the country's most powerful chief who herself became Kasulu's Legislative Councillor in 1960. By 1959 TANU's Youth League in Kibondo was lauding Mwami Nyamaliza II, whose family had worked closely with

[1] Marealle to Vickers-Haviland, 27 February 1960, Marealle papers, RH.
[2] Maguire, '*Uhuru*', pp. 281–2; Barongo, *Mkiki mkiki wa siasa*, pp. 211–15.
[3] Tanganyika, *Fifth convention of representative chiefs of Tanganyika, 5th–7th March 1959* (Dar es Salaam, 1959).
[4] 'Tanganyika Elected Members' Organization: report of a further meeting, held on May 29th, 1959', Chesham papers 16, YUL; Kandoro, *Mwito*, pp. 158–63.
[5] J. A. Nzunda to SG, 15 June 1959, TANU 90.

Europeans since German times. Chief S. R. Kasusura of Rusubi gained nearly all the leading positions in TANU's Biharamulo branch. In Kigoma-Ujiji the party's original nucleus had been among Swahili-speaking townsmen, but Chief G. B. Rusimbi of Nkalinzi challenged their control in 1959 and was elected to parliament in 1965. Three years later a Ha first became TANU's district chairman there. An even older rivalry reappeared in Sumbawanga, where the Nkansi and Lyangalile sections of the Fipa ruling family disputed TANU's leadership until both were ousted by educated commoners.[1]

Yet merely to show that ancient loyalties survived is facile. The problem is to analyse the mingling of continuity and change in divided loyalties and ambiguous behaviour. Theresa Ntare represented Kasulu in Dar es Salaam, but TANU's district councillors elected in Kasulu in 1960 were mainly commoners who promptly reduced bridewealth and banned the use of cattle in bridewealth or as loans to secure services, thus striking at the roots of Tusi social control and bringing the district to 'the fringe of civil tribal fightings'.[2] Bugufi showed even greater complexity. By 1960 everyone of importance there belonged to TANU, the chief having unsuccessfully sought its parliamentary nomination. In that year TANU's branch officers tried to turn local government elections into an anti-Tusi campaign, totally without success. Altogether 54 per cent of successful candidates were from landlord families and 23 of the 24 candidates with tenants were elected, but nearly all of these were Christians and many were educated. 'The Tutsi', an observer concluded, 'control the life of the district through a combination of land holding, social patronage and Hutu ambition, and they show a superior talent for politics.'[3] Ambiguity culminated in 1960 in Mbulu, where the NEC chose a Muslim Mbugwe chief as parliamentary candidate rather than a locally favoured Christian doctor from the heavily preponderant Iraqw. An Iraqw chief then won election as an independent who supported all other aspects of TANU policy and even recruited for the party during his campaign.[4] In many colonies, notably Nigeria,

---

[1] Police permits, 16 June 1959 and 23 February 1960, TNA 202/A/6/13/1/118 and 210; Lionel Cliffe (ed.), *One party democracy* (Nairobi, 1967), pp. 371–3, 381, 406–7; McHenry, 'Study', pp. 412–21; police permit, 16 April 1959, TNA 180/A/6/5/127; TANU District Secretary Sumbawanga, 'Mkutano wa sikukuu ya TANU, 8th July 1960', TANU 74/22.

[2] Kasulu DARs 1960 and 1961, TNA library.

[3] R. E. S. Tanner, 'Local government elections in Ngara', *Journal of local administration overseas*, 1 (1962), 173.

[4] G. B. Michael to SG, 21 April 1960, TANU 21/1; Michael to SG, 10 September 1960, TANU 39/60; Nyerere, *Freedom and socialism*, p. 36.

nationalism fragmented when the franchise was extended in this way to those with overwhelmingly parochial interests and perceptions, and earlier popular movements in Tanganyika, from Maji Maji to *beni* societies and TAA, had experienced such fragmentation. TANU escaped it, partly because no ethnic group was large enough to contemplate a separate future, partly because Swahili bridged ethnic differences, and partly because the party machine was already strong before most people obtained the vote.

The corollary of an all-embracing party was diversity of leadership. Nyerere's cabinet of October 1960 contained representatives of at least six factions. Nyerere himself represented educated men. Rural activists entrenched in the cooperative movement provided Bomani, Kahama, and Nsilo Swai, an Indian-educated Chagga economist who had managed the Meru Cooperative Union. Kawawa represented urban labour, Fundikira the chiefs and conservatives, and Bryceson and Jamal the accommodating immigrants. The sixth component of the coalition were TANU's professionals, represented by its secretary-general, Kambona. Not only had popularity made TANU so diverse that no single group could dominate it, but Tanganyika's poverty ensured 'that there existed no really strong local vested interests supporting the maintenance of colonialism or privilege'.[1] Yet poverty also had negative effects. However much TANU encouraged internal democracy, its members, like trade unionists, remained largely passive. 'The political culture... primarily resembles a *subject* culture', an observer wrote of Buhaya. Kimbu compared TANU to the *uwuxala* society, a mass-membership, authoritarian agency of social control, 'a lion from whose power one cannot escape'.[2] These were the notions of hierarchical societies. Elsewhere TANU might be seen as a parental authority or a neutral arbiter in local conflicts, while to many older people in remote areas the party was as distant, alien, and potentially transient as the many other regimes they had endured.[3] Its individual membership, bureaucracy, aspirations to totalitarian loyalty, and predominant individual leader made TANU a classic mass party which was still close to its peak of vitality at independence, but as a late and imitative party it was particularly dependent on leadership.

The approach of independence both strengthened and weakened Nyerere's standing. By 1961 he was the only survivor from TANU's

[1] Nyerere, *Freedom and unity*, p. 1.
[2] Hydén, *Political development*, p. 241; Shorter, *Chiefship*, pp. 141, 145.
[3] Miller, 'Village leadership', p. 233; Gicha Mbee, 'Letter', p. 199; Lusinde Ng'ingo in MMRP 3/68/1/3/3; Feierman, *Shambaa kingdom*, p. 13.

original central committee of 1954.[1] Apart perhaps from Bibi Titi, he was the only leader known throughout the country, and TANU's very diversity strengthened him against any single faction. His personal austerity and tactical wisdom were widely acknowledged. Humble men fearful of victimisation marvelled at his audacity:

> The people with *Mheshimiwa*,
> Seeing him produce the letter,
> Some ran away, some held their hearts
> Waiting and shivering with fear
> To see what would happen.
> They thought: surely we are going to be put in jail;
> To tease a European, and he who rules us.[2]

The British made it clear, moreover, that Nyerere could win concessions denied to others. Yet opposition existed. Outside the party it came from Mtemvu's overtly racialist African National Congress, which advocated 'Africa for Africans only'.[3] Electorally, ANC failed dismally. In 1958 Mtemvu won only 53 votes in Tanga Province. In 1960 the party's three candidates received only 337 votes between them. Yet it had greater success in local government elections, attracting men who had gained nothing from TANU: embittered chiefs and opponents of the VFCU in Sukumaland; some Christian leaders in Newala; traditionalists and religious dissidents in Bukoba.[4] ANC was a long-term danger. In the short term it probably strengthened TANU's discipline and convinced the British of the party's moderation and non-racialism. Freedom to organise an opposition party was in any case essential to democracy, so Nyerere argued.[5] His main concern was with critics within TANU. Some less sophisticated activists thought him too amenable to the British and his immigrant colleagues, a tension which surfaced briefly during the 1960 election.[6] Others were militant trade unionists who feared TANU's growing hegemony, opposed its enthusiasm for East African Federation, and pressed for more rapid Africanisation. Tension culminated on 18 October 1961 when the National Assembly debated the government's

---

[1] Lowenkopf, 'Parties', p. 170.
[2] This song of 1961 is quoted in William H. Friedland, 'For a sociological concept of charisma', *Social forces*, XLIII (1964–5), 24.
[3] 'Petition from the Tanganyika African Congress concerning Tanganyika' (UNTC T/PET.2/L.10/Add.1 of 7 March 1958). ANC's programme is in TANU 10, its constitution in TNA 435/A/6/8/III/295.
[4] Maguire, '*Uhuru*', pp. 338–52; Newala historical report, TANU 53; Hydén, *Political development*, pp. 131–2; Kiwanuka, 'Islam in Bukoba', p. 63.
[5] 'The future of African nationalism', in *Tribune*, 27 May 1960.
[6] Lowenkopf, 'Parties', pp. 148, 170.

plans for political rather than racial citizenship. In response to criticism, Nyerere made this an issue of confidence and furiously denounced 'a substantial number of potential Verwoerds...[who] stand like Hitlers and begin to glorify the race'.[1] He won easily, but the threat remained.

During the two years before independence Nyerere's chief concern was to move from opposition to authority without unnecessarily alienating supporters or unleashing the disorder which he had feared throughout TANU's growth. A curious diarchy resulted, with TANU and the British struggling on the cliff face with a mutual interest in avoiding a plunge into chaos. Nyerere saw the danger. 'It is always a government affair', he complained of visits to district headquarters. 'I am met by...colonial officers, the very men who TANU fought but a few years ago...Then off to one side I notice a few chaps in torn green shirts wielding banners but looking somewhat forlorn.'[2] To meet the danger he encouraged TANU 'to sing a new song, the song of Freedom and Work'.[3] Party branches were to win every district council seat, support adult literacy campaigns, and aid the police. Speeches emphasised that independence meant sacrifices rather than rewards. Nyerere never lost the educated politician's fear of alienation from his followers.

As TANU's leaders began to formulate policy, their first concern was to Africanise the state machinery which was the most valuable legacy of colonialism, thereby absorbing that innovation into Tanganyikan life. The task was immense. The army, some two thousand strong and equipped with First World War rifles, had only three African officers at independence. Africans had been eligible for officer rank in the police since 1949, but in 1960 they held only 28 of the 245 gazetted posts. The first African political officer was appointed in 1955, but six years later no provincial commissioner and only 2 of the 57 district commissioners were Africans. In the civil service Africans held 1,170 of the 4,452 senior and middle grade posts in 1961. The position in the professions was worse. In 1962 only 16 of 184 physicians, one of 84 civil engineers, and 2 of 57 lawyers were Africans. Nyerere himself wished to preserve standards and avoid discrimination amongst Tanganyikan citizens, but during 1960 political pressure forced him to give Africans priority in civil service recruit-

[1] Nyerere, *Freedom and unity*, pp. 126–9.
[2] Quoted in Pratt, *Critical phase*, p. 108.
[3] *Sauti ya TANU*, 11 November 1959.

ment.[1] The need to Africanise made secondary and higher education the government's first priority. In 1962 only 17 Tanganyikans graduated from Makerere and its sister college at Nairobi. Less than 2 per cent of the age group was then at secondary school; the figures for upper and lower primary schools were 9 and 45 per cent respectively. Sixteen per cent of adult Tanganyikans were thought to be literate in 1961.[2]

A second priority was the liberation and unity of Africa. In 1958 TANU had sponsored a conference which created the Pan-African Freedom Movement of East and Central Africa to counter Britain's multi-racial policy for the region. Administered by Bhoke Munanka from TANU headquarters, it often seemed like TANU's Foreign Ministry.[3] Nyerere held that African unity could be advanced by forming regional federations before individual colonies gained independence. In June 1960 he offered to delay Tanganyika's independence 'for a few months' to facilitate an East African Federation, despite opposition from less sophisticated leaders.[4] During 1961 the East African High Commission was reorganised into a Common Services Organisation acceptable to independent Tanganyika, but federation before independence proved unattainable.

TANU's third priority was economic development. The census of 1957 had shown a population of 8,788,466 – roughly double the estimates for the 1920s – at a density of 10 people per square kilometre but with district variations from 88 per square kilometre in Ukerewe to only one in Mpanda. Only 5 per cent of the land was cultivated, although only 4 per cent of the people lived in gazetted towns. The African population – 97 per cent of the total – was thought to have increased since 1948 at 1.75 per cent per year. Life expectation at birth varied from 45 years in Northern Province to only 35 in the west. Infant mortality rates had changed little since 1948. With a gross domestic product estimated at £21 per head – a quarter of Ghana's – Tanganyika was among the world's poorest countries.[5]

The economic advice reaching TANU's leaders, largely from

[1] Julius K. Nyerere, *Freedom and development* (Dar es Salaam, 1973), p. 328; Listowel, *Making*, p. 431; Walter Rodney, 'Policing the countryside in colonial Tanganyika', UEASSC paper, 1973; Pratt, *Critical phase*, pp. 92–3, 107–8; Bienen, *Tanzania*, p. 124.

[2] Pratt, *Critical phase*, pp. 93–4; Hugh W. Stephens, *The political transformation of Tanganyika, 1920–67* (New York, 1968), p. 108.

[3] Richard Cox, *Pan-Africanism in practice* (London, 1964); correspondence in TANU 14, 20, and 58.

[4] Nyerere, *Freedom and unity*, p. 96; Lowenkopf, 'Parties', p. 148.

[5] Tanganyika, *African census 1957*, pp. 13–15, 17–18, 29, 90–1; Rweyemamu, *Underdevelopment*, p. 2; Ehrlich in Low and Smith, *History*, III, 330.

western sources, was to expand the open, capitalist economy of the 1950s:

The World Bank...pronounced the economy fit and well on the basis of peasant cash crop production (which it expected would continue to expand) while proposing that the main thrust of Government investment should be in settlement schemes where African capitalist farmers could be guided 'under close supervision'. The industrial sector was covered by the Arthur D. Little report of 1961 which proposed an industrial policy of import substitution and agricultural processing, and recommended a long list of incentives in order to attract 'private investors'...The Economist Intelligence Unit report on the wholesale and retail trade observed that 'Tanganyika has a low-cost distribution system' and recommended that no attack be made on the Asian dominance of this sector.[1]

This advice dominated government's development plan for 1961–4, which sought, at a cost of £24,000,000, to lay 'firm foundations' for progress towards sustained growth, giving priority to agriculture and pastoralism, communications, and secondary and technical education, while leaving industrial development to private enterprise.[2] TANU bodies scarcely considered the plan, but they were in any case pressing not for any transformation of the economic structure but for its Africanisation: for the return of alienated land, for higher wages in capitalist industries, and for government aid to African traders. There was little effective demand for Nyerere's brand of gradualist socialism, but there was a model of successful development in the cooperative movement which some saw as essentially anti-Asian and others as a workable form of socialism. In July 1960 TANU's National Executive – in strange contrast to the government's development planners – announced opposition to capitalism and support for 'African democratic socialism' on the cooperative model.[3] Equally ambiguous was TANU's policy towards agriculture, which provided an estimated 52 per cent of gross domestic product in 1961.[4] While the NEC resolved to abolish freehold landownership and discourage capitalism, government and rural activists favoured concentration on progressive farmers, mechanisation, and highly-capitalised settlement schemes.

Nyerere's own priority was different. Christianity and socialism joined to focus his concern on the poverty, ignorance, and disease of

[1] A. C. Coulson, 'A simplified political economy of Tanzania', UEASSC paper, 1973.
[2] Tanganyika, *Development plan 1961–4*, pp. 7–8.
[3] Kandoro, *Mwito*, p. 161.
[4] Tanganyika, *Budget survey 1962–3*, p. 4. This figure includes livestock products.

the backward regions from which he came. To underline the country's poverty the environment again demonstrated its cruelty. Late in 1960 the rains failed throughout central and northern Tanganyika, causing a famine which was the north's worst since the 1890s. Colonial innovations – skilful preparation, generous provision of American grain, and the expenditure of £1,300,000 – ensured that it was not a 'famine that kills', but nearly half a million Tanganyikans were receiving famine relief when their country became independent on 9 December 1961.[1] 'This day has dawned because the people of Tanganyika have worked together in unity', Nyerere declared:

All the time that TANU has been campaigning for *Uhuru* we have based our struggle on our belief in the equality and dignity of all mankind...

Yet we know that on the 9th December we shall not have achieved these objects. Poverty, ignorance, and disease must be overcome before we can really establish in this country the sort of society we have been dreaming of. These obstacles are not small ones, they are more difficult to overcome than any alien government. From now on we are fighting not man but nature.[2]

But it was more complicated than that.

---

[1] E. P. Mwaluko, 'Famine relief in the Central Province of Tanganyika, 1961', *Tropical agriculture*, XXXIX (1962), 163–8; *Agriculture report*, 1961, p. 1; Tanganyika, *Budget survey 1962–3*, p. 12; Nyerere, *Freedom and unity*, p. 254.
[2] Nyerere, 'Independence message to TANU', in his *Freedom and unity*, pp. 138–9.

Bibliography

I. DOCUMENTARY SOURCES
Tanzania: Tanzania National Archives, Dar es Salaam

These holdings are the main sources for this book and divide into seven categories:

1. German records. These are described in Iliffe, *German rule*, pp. 211–12. With one exception, I have again used the reference system outlined there. The exception is that the records have recently been catalogued and renumbered, using a system prefixed with the letter G. See National Archives of Tanzania, *Guide to the German records* (2 vols, Dar es Salaam and Marburg, 1973). Where I have consulted records since their renumbering, I have used the new reference system.

2. British secretariat records. These run from 1916 to roughly 1953, when a new, less centralised filing system came into full operation. Unclassified records were generally accessible, but classified files (with rare exceptions) were not. These files have four- or five-figure numbers (except for one numbered 075).

3. British departmental records. These were not accessible, except for a small number of files from the Labour Department (LD) and the Registry of Trade Unions (RTU), for which special permission was obtained.

4. British provincial and district records. These have been centralised in the National Archives. Unclassified files have been used very extensively in this book. They are cited by the archive accession number, followed by the filing number used by the office from which they came. For accession numbers, see Tanzania, *Fourth annual report of the National Archives of Tanzania, 1967/68* (Dar es Salaam, 1969), pp. 9–15.

5. District books. Copies of these are in the archives, although I used the copies available at area offices, Makerere University Library, or the Tanzania National Museum.

6. Private deposits. I have used the papers of Kirilo Japhet and Hassan Suleiman, and mission diaries from Magila, Mkuzi, and Umba.

7. Library. This contains a number of typescripts, manuscripts, and bound volumes of district annual reports.

Bibliography

Tanzania: Tanganyika African National Union, Dar es Salaam

I was given access to a small number of files at party headquarters. For my references to them, see John Iliffe, 'A list of certain records in TANU headquarters, Dar es Salaam', typescript, 1971, in TANU headquarters and ULD.

Tanzania: University Library, Dar es Salaam

I have used five collections of papers housed in the library: those of Hans Cory, a former government sociologist; the collection of the former East African Swahili Committee, listed in *Swahili*, XXXV (1965), 99–115; a volume of papers on constitutional development, dating from 1950 and apparently belonging to R. de Z. Hall; mission diaries from Masasi; and the papers of the Maji Maji Research Project (MMRP) carried out by the University's history department during 1968–9. The Maji Maji papers consist of essays supported by records of interviews. My references to essays should be taken to embrace the supporting interviews as well. The Library also possesses most of the Swahili and German newspapers cited in this book.

Tanzania: Indian Merchants Chamber, Dar es Salaam

Dr S. R. Walji enabled me to consult the Chamber's minute book from 1942 to 1961.

Tanzania: Kipalapala Pastoral Centre, Tabora

Fr P. van Pelt permitted me to read certain unpublished manuscripts lodged at the Centre.

Tanzania: Kwiro Mission, Mahenge

Dr L. E. Larson enabled me to consult the mission diary for the period 1897–1952.

Tanzania: Peramiho Abbey, Songea

I was permitted to consult the mission diaries from Kigonsera, Peramiho, and St Scholastika, together with a few unpublished papers.

Uganda: Makerere University Library, Kampala

The collection includes a number of typescripts and manuscripts concerning Tanganyika, including certain papers from Milo mission.

German Democratic Republic: Deutsches Zentralarchiv, Potsdam

The archive houses the records of the former Colonial Office, which have been given a simple series numbering. They are open without restriction until at least 1914. I have concentrated on the records of German military operations in the 1890s and on administrative records from the period 1905–14. See Helmut Loetzke and Hans-Stephan Brather, *Uebersicht über die Bestände des Deutschen Zentralarchivs Potsdam* (Berlin, 1957).

German Federal Republic: Bundesarchiv-Militärarchiv, Freiburg i.B.

The archive holds the war-diaries and correspondence of the naval and marine units engaged during the Maji Maji rebellion. For a list, see International Council on Archives, *Quellen zur Geschichte Afrikas südlich der Sahara in den Archiven der Bundesrepublik Deutschland* (Zug, 1970), pp. 41–53.

Great Britain: Public Record Office, London

I have consulted four series of files. FO 84 (slave trade) contains correspondence with the Zanzibar consulate, which I have studied for the period 1856–92. CO 691 is the main series of original correspondence concerning Tanganyika; I have read volumes 1–192, covering the period 1916–46 (after which the records were closed). CO 736 contains two volumes (nos. 13 and 21) of minutes of Tanganyika's Executive Council from 1920 to 1940; they were remarkably uninteresting. CO 822 contains original correspondence concerning East Africa in general; I have read only volumes 102–18, which are valuable for the discussion of East Africa's future between 1939 and 1946. See R. B. Pugh, *The records of the Colonial and Dominions Offices* (London, 1964).

Great Britain: United Society for the Propagation of the Gospel, London

The society holds the records of the former Universities Mission to Central Africa. They were kept in packets listed by diocese and episcopate. I consulted correspondence from the episcopates of Tozer, Steere, Smythies, Hine, and Weston.

Great Britain: Rhodes House Library, Oxford

The library has two collections of papers which were important for this book. Those of the Fabian Colonial Bureau (boxes 121–3) include correspondence with Tanganyikan politicians during the 1940s and 1950s. The Oxford Colonial Records Project has collected the papers of former British colonial officers and their families. See Louis B. Frewer, *Manuscript collections of Africana in Rhodes House Library, Oxford* (Oxford, 1968) and *Supplement* (1971).

Great Britain: J. B. Morrell Library, University of York

The library holds papers of the late Marion Lady Chesham, who was involved in settler and nationalist politics in Tanganyika in the 1950s and 1960s. See Alistair Ross, *A guide to the Tanganyikan papers of Marion Lady Chesham* (York, 1975).

II. NEWSPAPERS AND PERIODICALS

Annual reports of the Agriculture Department (Dar es Salaam)
Annual reports of the Labour Department (Dar es Salaam)
Annual reports of the Provincial Commissioners (Dar es Salaam)
Blue books (Dar es Salaam)
Central Africa: a monthly record of the work of the Universities Mission (London)
Chronique trimestrielle de la Société des Missionnaires d'Afrique (Pères Blancs) (Lille)

Bibliography

Dar es Salaam Times (Dar es Salaam)

Deutsch-Ostafrikanische Rundschau (Dar es Salaam)

Deutsch-Ostafrikanische Zeitung (Dar es Salaam)

Deutsche Kolonialzeitung (Berlin)

Die deutschen Schutzgebiete in Afrika und der Südsee (Berlin)

Deutsches Kolonialblatt (Berlin)

Habari za mwezi (Magila)

Kiongozi (Tanga)

Kwetu (Dar es Salaam)

Mambo leo (Dar es Salaam)

Missions-Blätter: illustrierte Zeitschrift für das katholische Volk: Organ der St Benediktus-Genossenschaft für ausländische Missionen zu St Ottilien (St Ottilien)

Mwanafunzi (Dar es Salaam)

Rafiki yangu (Dar es Salaam)

Sauti ya TANU (Dar es Salaam)

Stenographische Berichte über die Verhandlungen des Reichstages (Berlin)

Stenographische Berichte über die Verhandlungen des Reichstages: Anlagenbände (Berlin)

Tanganyika herald (Dar es Salaam)

Tanganyika opinion (Dar es Salaam)

Tanganyika standard (Dar es Salaam)

Tanganyika Times (Dar es Salaam)

The Tanganyikan (Dar es Salaam)

Usambara-Post (Tanga)

III. OTHER WORKS CITED MORE THAN ONCE

Abdallah, Yohanna B. *The Yaos.* Trans. M. Sanderson, Zomba, 1919.

Abdallah bin Hemedi 'lAjjemy. *The Kilindi.* Trans. J. W. T. Allen, Nairobi, 1963.

Abrahams, R. G. *The peoples of Greater Unyamwezi.* London, 1967.

Abrahams, R. G. *The political organization of Unyamwezi.* Cambridge, 1967.

Adams, Alfons M. *Im Dienste des Kreuzes.* St Ottilien, 1899.

Adams, Alfons M. *Lindi und sein Hinterland.* Berlin [1902?]

Akeroyd, Anne V. 'Bitterness in defeat: memories of the Maji-Maji rising in Uvidunda.' Seminar paper, University College, Dar es Salaam, 1969.

Akinola, G. A. 'Slavery and slave revolts in the Sultanate of Zanzibar in the nineteenth century', *Journal of the Historical Society of Nigeria*, VI (1972), 215–28.

Allan, William. *The African husbandman.* Edinburgh, 1967.

Alpers, Edward A. 'The French slave trade in East Africa (1721–1810)', *Cahiers d'études africaines*, X (1970), 80–124.

Alpers, Edward A. *Ivory and slaves in East Central Africa: changing patterns of international trade to the later nineteenth century.* London, 1975.

Amiji, Hatim. 'The Bohras of East Africa', *Journal of religion in Africa*, VII (1975), 27–61.

Amos, E. B. 'The life of Elias Kisenge.' Seminar paper, University College, Dar es Salaam, 1968.

Anderson-Morshead, A. E. M. *The history of the Universities Mission to Central Africa, 1: 1859–1909.* 6th edn, London, 1955.

Arning, Wilhelm. *Deutsch Ostafrika, gestern und heute.* Berlin, 1936.

Augustiny, Julius. 'Geschichte der Häuptlinge von Madschame', *ZES*, XVII (1926–7), 161–201.

Austen, Ralph A. *Northwest Tanzania under German and British rule, 1889–1939.* New Haven, 1968.

Bachmann, T. 'Ambilishiye: Lebensbild eines eingeborenen Evangelisten aus Ostafrika', *Missions-Blatt der Brüdergemeine*, LXXXI (1917), 4–12, 25–48, 57–73, 92–9, 117–21, 137–47, 160–4.

Bailey, F. G. (ed.) *Debate and compromise: the politics of innovation.* Oxford, 1973. [Rayah Feldman, 'Ismani.']

Bald, Detlef. *Deutsch-Ostafrika 1900–1914: eine Studie über Verwaltung, Interessengruppen und wirtschaftliche Erschliessung.* München, 1970.

Barongo, E. B. M. *Mkiki mkiki wa siasa Tanganyika.* Dar es Salaam, 1966.

Barrett, David B. (ed.) *African initiatives in religion.* Nairobi, 1971. [T. O. Ranger, 'Christian independency in Tanzania.']

Bates, Darrell. *A gust of plumes: a biography of Lord Twining.* London, 1972.

Bates, Margaret L. 'Tanganyika under British administration 1920–1955.' D.Phil. thesis, Oxford University, 1957.

Baumann, Oscar. *In Deutsch-Ostafrika während des Aufstandes.* Wien, 1890.

Baumann, Oscar. *Durch Masailand zur Nilquelle.* Berlin, 1894.

Baumann, Oscar. *Usambara und seine Nachbargebiete.* Berlin, 1891.

Becker, Jérôme. *La Vie en Afrique.* 2nd edn, 2 vols, Paris, 1887.

Behr, H. F. von. *Kriegsbilder aus dem Araberaufstand in Deutsch-Ostafrika.* Leipzig, 1891.

Beidelman, T. O. *The matrilineal peoples of eastern Tanzania.* London, 1967.

Bell, R. M. 'The Maji-Maji rebellion in the Liwale district', *TNR*, XXVIII (1950), 38–57.

Bennett, Norman R. 'The Arab power of Tanganyika in the nineteenth century.' Ph.D. thesis, Boston University, 1961.

Bennett, Norman R. *Mirambo of Tanzania, 1840?–1884.* New York, 1971.

Bennett, Norman R. *Studies in East African history.* Boston, 1963.

Bennett, Norman R. (ed.) *Stanley's despatches to the 'New York herald', 1871–1872, 1874–1877.* Boston, 1970.

Berque, Jacques. *French North Africa: the Maghrib between two world wars.* Trans. J. Stewart, London, 1967.

Bienen, Henry. *Tanzania: party transformation and economic development.* Princeton, 1967.

Blohm, Wilhelm. *Die Nyamwezi.* 2 vols, Hamburg, 1931–3.

Boell, L. *Die Operationen in Ost-Afrika: Weltkrieg 1914–1918.* Hamburg, 1951.

Booth, Mike and Cathy. 'Directory of business names for Dar es Salaam township, 1920–1950.' Typescript, 1970, in my possession.

Bösch, Fridolin. *Les Banyamwezi.* Münster, 1930.

Brett, E. A. *Colonialism and underdevelopment in East Africa: the politics of economic change 1919–1939.* London, 1973.

Brode, Heinrich. *British and German East Africa.* English translation, London, 1911.

Brooke, Clarke. 'The heritage of famine in central Tanzania', *TNR*, LXVII (1967), 15–22.

Brown, Walter T. 'A pre-colonial history of Bagamoyo.' Ph.D. thesis, Boston University, 1971.

Burton, Richard F. *The lake regions of central Africa.* Reprinted, 2 vols, New York, 1961.

Burton, Richard F. 'The lake regions of central equatorial Africa', *Journal of the Royal Geographical Society*, XXIX (1859), 1–464.

Burton, Richard F. *Zanzibar: city, island, and coast.* 2 vols, London, 1872.

Busse, Joseph. 'Aus dem Leben von Asyukile Malango', *ZES*, XXXV (1949–50), 191–227.

Büttner, Kurt. *Die Anfänge der deutschen Kolonialpolitik in Ostafrika.* Berlin, 1959.

Byansheko, R. Gervas. 'Hatua ya kudai uhuru.' Manuscript, 1959, TANU headquarters, Dar es Salaam.

Cameron, Donald C. *My Tanganyika service, and some Nigeria.* London, 1939.

Cameron, J. and W. A. Dodd. *Society, schools and progress in Tanzania.* Oxford, 1970.

Cameron, V. L. *Across Africa.* 4th edn, 2 vols, London, 1877.

Caplan, Ann P. *Choice and constraint in a Swahili community.* London, 1975.

Césard, Edmond. 'Le Muhaya', *Anthropos*, XXX (1935), 75–106; XXXI (1936), 97–114, 489–508, 821–49; XXXII (1937), 15–60.

Charsley, S. R. *The princes of Nyakyusa.* Nairobi, 1969.

Chittick, H. Neville. *Kilwa.* 2 vols, Nairobi, 1974.

Chittick, H. Neville and Robert I. Rotberg (ed.). *East Africa and the Orient: cultural syntheses in pre-colonial times.* New York, 1975.

Chiume, M. W. Kanyama. *Kwacha: an autobiography.* Nairobi, 1975.

Choka, Esmail M. 'A biography of Sheikh Yahya bin Abdallah l'Qadiriyya, known as Sheikh Ramiya.' Seminar paper, University College, Dar es Salaam, 1969.

Clemm, Michael von. 'Agricultural productivity and sentiment on Kilimanjaro', *Economic botany*, XVIII (1964), 99–121.

Clemm, Michael von. 'People of the white mountain: the interdependence of political and economic activity amongst the Chagga in Tanganyika with special reference to recent changes.' D.Phil. thesis, Oxford University, 1962.

Cliffe, Lionel and John S. Saul (ed.). *Socialism in Tanzania.* 2 vols, Nairobi, 1972–3. [J. S. Saul, 'Marketing cooperatives in a developing country: the Tanzanian case'.]

Cliffe, Lionel and others (ed.). *Rural cooperation in Tanzania.* Dar es Salaam, 1975.

Clyde, David F. *History of the medical services of Tanganyika.* Dar es Salaam, 1962.

Cooper, Frederick. *Plantation slavery on the East Coast of Africa.* New Haven, 1977.

Cory, Hans. 'Report on land tenure in Bugufi.' Typescript, 1944, Cory papers, ULD.

Cory [Koritschoner], Hans. 'Some East African native songs', *TNR*, IV (1937), 51–64.

Crosse-Upcott, A. R. W. 'The social structure of the KiNgindo-speaking peoples.' Ph.D. thesis, University of Cape Town, 1956.

Culwick, A. T. and G. M. 'A study of population in Ulanga, Tanganyika Territory', *Sociological review*, XXX (1938), 365–79, and XXXI (1939), 25–43.

Culwick, A. T. and G. M. *Ubena of the rivers*. London, 1935.

Culwick, A. T. and G. M. 'What the Wabena think of indirect rule', *Journal of the Royal African Society*, XXXVI (1937), 176–93.

Dale, Godfrey. 'An account of the principal customs and habits of the natives inhabiting the Bondei country', *Journal of the Anthropological Institute*, XXV (1895), 181–239.

de Froberville, Eugène. 'Notes sur les Va-Ngindo', *Bulletin de la Société de Géographie*, 4th ser., III (1852), 425–43.

de Heusch, Luc. *Le Rwanda et la civilisation interlacustre*. Bruxelles, 1966.

Dempwolff, Otto. *Die Sandawe*. Hamburg, 1916.

de Wilde, John C. and others. *Experiences with agricultural development in tropical Africa*. 2 vols, Baltimore, 1967.

Eggert, Johanna. *Missionsschule und sozialer Wandel in Ostafrika: der Beitrag der deutschen evangelischen Missionsgesellschaften zur Entwicklung des Schulwesens in Tanganyika 1891–1939*. Bielefeld, 1970.

Ekemode, Gabriel O. 'German rule in north-east Tanzania, 1885–1914.' Ph.D. thesis, University of London, 1973.

Farler, J. P. 'The Usambara country in East Africa', *Proceedings of the Royal Geographical Society*, I (1879), 81–97.

Feierman, Steven. 'Concepts of sovereignty among the Shambaa and their relation to political action.' D.Phil. thesis, Oxford University, 1972.

Feierman, Steven. *The Shambaa kingdom: a history*. Madison, 1974.

Fischer, G. A. *Das Massai-Land*. Hamburg, 1885.

Fisher, Nigel. *Iain Macleod*. London, 1973.

Fleuret, Anne K. 'Social organization and adaptation among Sikhs in Tanzania.' Ph.D. thesis, University of California at Santa Barbara, 1975.

Ford, John. *The role of the trypanosomiases in African ecology: a study of the tsetse fly problem*. Oxford, 1971.

Frederick, S. W. 'The life of Joseph Kimalando', *TNR*, LXX (1969), 21–8.

Freeman-Grenville, G. S. P. *The French at Kilwa Island*. Oxford, 1965.

Friedland, William H. *Vuta kamba: the development of trade unions in Tanganyika*. Stanford, 1969.

Fuggles-Couchman, N. R. *Agricultural change in Tanganyika 1945–1960*. Stanford, 1964.

Furse, Ralph. *Aucuparius: recollections of a recruiting officer*. London, 1962.

Gallagher, Joseph T. 'Islam and the emergence of the Ndendeuli.' Ph.D. thesis, Boston University, 1971.

Gann, L. H. and Peter Duignan (ed.). *Colonialism in Africa 1870–1960*. 5 vols, Cambridge, 1969–75.

Bibliography

Gemuseus, Oskar and Joseph Busse. *Ein Gebundener Jesu Christi: das Lebensbild des Fiwombe Malakilindu.* Hamburg, 1950.

Gicha Mbee. 'Letter from Mbugwe', *Africa*, xxxv (1965), 198–208.

Gifford, Prosser and W. Roger Louis (ed.). *Britain and Germany in Africa.* New Haven, 1967. [H. A. Turner, 'Bismarck's imperialist venture'; R. A. Austen, 'The official mind of indirect rule: British policy in Tanganyika, 1916–1939'.]

Giraud, Victor. *Les lacs de l'Afrique équatoriale.* Paris, 1890.

Gleiss, Franz. *An meinen Hirten! Was Negerchristen in Usambara und Tanga an ihren Hirten in der Notzeit 1922–25 zu schreiben hatten.* Bethel bei Bielefeld, 1926.

Goldsworthy, David. *Colonial issues in British politics 1945–1961.* Oxford, 1971.

Goldthorpe, J. E. *An African elite: Makerere College students 1922–1960.* Nairobi, 1965.

Gottlieb, Manuel. 'The extent and character of differentiation in Tanzanian agricultural and rural society 1967–1969', *The African review*, III (1973), 241–61.

Götzen, G. A. von. *Deutsch-Ostafrika im Aufstand 1905–6.* Berlin, 1909.

Graham, James D. 'Changing patterns of wage labor in Tanzania: a history of the relations between African labor and European capitalism in Njombe district, 1931–1961.' Ph.D. thesis, Northwestern University, 1968.

Graham, James D. 'Indirect rule: the establishment of "chiefs" and "tribes" in Cameron's Tanganyika', *TNR*, LXXVII (1976), 1–9.

Gray, Richard (ed.). *The Cambridge History of Africa*, IV. Cambridge, 1975.

Gray, Richard and David Birmingham (ed.). *Pre-colonial African trade.* London, 1970. [Andrew Roberts, 'Nyamwezi trade.']

Gray, Robert F. 'The Mbugwe tribe', *TNR*, xxxVIII (1955), 39–50.

Great Britain. *Joint select committee on closer union in East Africa, II: minutes of evidence.* London, 1931.

Great Britain. *A plan for the mechanised production of groundnuts in east and central Africa* (Cmd 7030 of 1947).

Great Britain. *Report of the United Nations visiting mission to Tanganyika, 1954: observations of the administering authority* (Col. 935 of 1955).

Gregory, Robert G. *India and East Africa: a history of race relations within the British Empire 1890–1939.* Oxford, 1971.

Griffith, A. W. M. 'Chagga land tenure report.' Typescript, 1930, Cory papers, ULD.

Gröschel, P. *Zehn Jahre christlicher Kulturarbeit in Deutsch-Ostafrika.* Berlin, 1911.

Guga, Timilai H. I. 'Research into the history of the Usambara-Digo Church and biographies of some pastors.' Trans. M. H. K. Mbwana, typescript, 1965, MUL.

Guillebaud, C. W. *An economic survey of the sisal industry of Tanganyika.* 2nd edn, Welwyn, 1958; 3rd edn, Welwyn, 1966.

Gulliver, P. H. 'Interim report on land and population in the Arusha chiefdom.' Duplicated, 1957, TNA library.

Gulliver, P. H. *Land tenure and social change among the Nyakyusa.* Kampala, 1958.

Gulliver, P. H. *Neighbours and networks: the idiom of kinship in social action among the Ndendeuli of Tanzania.* Berkeley, 1971.

Gulliver, P. H. 'Nyakyusa labour migration', *Rhodes-Livingstone journal*, XXI (1957), 32–63.

Gupta, P. S. *Imperialism and the British labour movement, 1914–1964.* London, 1975.

Gutmann, Bruno. *Das Dschaggaland und seine Christen.* Leipzig, 1925.

Gutmann, Bruno. *Das Recht der Dschagga.* München, 1926.

Gutmann, Bruno (ed.). *Briefe aus Afrika.* Leipzig, 1925.

Gwassa, G. C. K. 'The outbreak and development of the Maji Maji war 1905–7.' Ph.D. thesis, University of Dar es Salaam, 1973.

Gwassa, G. C. K. and John Iliffe (ed.). *Records of the Maji Maji rising: part one.* Nairobi, 1968.

Haqqi, S. A. H. *The colonial policy of the Labour government (1945–51).* Aligarh, 1960.

Harjula, Raimo. *God and the sun in Meru thought.* Helsinki, 1969.

Harlow, Vincent and E. M. Chilver (ed.). *History of East Africa*, II. Oxford, 1965.

Harries, Lyndon (ed.). *Swahili prose texts.* London, 1965.

Hartwig, Gerald W. *The art of survival in East Africa: the Kerebe and long-distance trade, 1800–1895.* New York, 1976.

Hartwig, Gerald W. 'The historical and social role of Kerebe music', *TNR*, LXX (1969), 41–56.

Hassan bin Ismail. *The medicine man: swifa ya Nguvumali.* Trans. P. Lienhardt, Oxford, 1968.

Hassan Issa. 'Safari ya Tabora.' Typescript, n.d., in my possession.

Hatfield, Colby R. 'The *nfumu* in tradition and change: a study of the position of religious practitioners among the Sukuma of Tanzania.' Ph.D. thesis, Catholic University of America, Washington D.C., 1968.

Hawkins, H. C. G. *Wholesale and retail trade in Tanganyika.* New York, 1965.

Hellberg, Carl-J. *Missions on a colonial frontier west of Lake Victoria.* Trans. E. Sharpe, Lund, 1965.

Hellberg, Carl-J. 'Andrea Kajerero: the man and his church.' Typescript, 1957, MUL.

Hemedi bin Abdallah el Buhriy. *Utenzi wa vita vya Wadachi kutamalaki Mrima 1307 A.H.* Trans. J. W. T. Allen, 2nd edn, Dar es Salaam, 1960.

Hewitt, Gordon. *The problems of success: a history of the Church Missionary Society 1910–1942*, I. London, 1971.

Hill, M. F. *Permanent way.* 2 vols, Nairobi, 1950–7.

Hino, Shunya. 'Neighbourhood groups in African urban society: social relations and consciousness of Swahili people of Ujiji', *KUAS*, VI (1971), 1–30.

Hino, Shunya. 'The occupational differentiation of an African town', *KUAS*, II (1968), 75–107.

Hino, Shunya. 'Social stratification of a Swahili town', *KUAS*, II (1968), 51–74.

Holmes, Charles F. 'A history of the Bakwimba of Usukuma, Tanzania, from earliest times to 1945.' Ph.D. thesis, Boston University, 1969.

Hordern, Charles. *Military operations, East Africa*, I. London, 1941.

Hozza, J. J. 'The Hoza rebellion and after.' B.A. thesis, University College, Dar es Salaam, 1969.

585

Hucks, G. W. Y. 'Report on the first elections of members to the Legislative Council of Tanganyika.' Duplicated, 1959.

Hydén, Göran. *Political development in rural Tanzania.* Reprinted, Nairobi, 1974.

Iliffe, John. 'A history of the dockworkers of Dar es Salaam', *TNR*, LXXI (1970), 119–48.

Iliffe, John. 'The organization of the Maji Maji rebellion', *JAH*, VIII (1967), 495–512.

Iliffe, John. *Tanganyika under German rule 1905–1912.* Cambridge, 1969.

Iliffe, John (ed.). *Modern Tanzanians.* Nairobi, 1973.

Ishumi, A. G. 'Embandwa cult in Buhaya: a socio-historical study.' Typescript, 1970, in Mr Ishumi's possession.

Jack, D. T. *Report on the state of industrial relations in the sisal industry.* Dar es Salaam, 1959.

Jacobs, Alan H. 'The traditional political organization of the pastoral Masai.' D.Phil. thesis, Oxford University, 1965.

Japhet, Kirilo and Earle Seaton. *The Meru land case.* Nairobi, 1967.

Jellicoe, Marguerite. 'Praising the sun', *Transition*, XXXI (1967), 27–31.

Jellicoe, Marguerite. 'The shrine in the desert', *Transition*, XXXIV (1967–8), 43–9.

Jellicoe, Marguerite. 'Social change in Singida: a case study of four settlements in Wahi.' M.A. thesis, Makerere University College, 1967.

Jellicoe, Marguerite. 'The Turu resistance movement', *TNR*, LXX (1969), 1–12.

Johanssen, E. *Führung und Erfahrung in 40 jährigem Missionsdienst.* 3 vols, Bethel bei Bielefeld, n.d.

Johnson, W. P. *Nyasa, the great water.* Reprinted, New York, 1969.

Johnston, P. H. 'Some notes on land tenure on Kilimanjaro', *TNR*, XXI (1946), 1–20.

Kabembo, A. 'African politics in Ujiji.' Duplicated, 1969, in my possession.

Kandoro, S. A. *Mashairi ya Saadani.* Dar es Salaam, 1972.

Kandoro, S. A. *Mwito wa uhuru.* Dar es Salaam, 1961.

Kaniki, M. H. Y. 'Politics in the Usambara-Digo Lutheran Church, 1961–63'. B.A. thesis, University College, Dar es Salaam, 1968.

Kaniki, M. H. Y. (ed.) 'The Lutheran Church in Usambara.' Duplicated, University College, Dar es Salaam, n.d.

Karonda, F. Amani. 'Mazungumzo ya vita vya Ujiji bayna ya taifa mbili hizi Wamanyema na Watanganyika, siku ya 3rd April, 1932.' Typescript, 1933, copy in my possession.

Karp, Mark (ed.). *African dimensions.* Boston, 1975. [Norman R. Bennett, 'Isike, Ntemi of Unyanyembe'.]

Katoke, Israel K. *The Karagwe kingdom: a history of the Abanyambo of north western Tanzania c. 1400–1915.* Nairobi, 1975.

Kaundinya, R. *Erinnerungen aus meinen Pflanzerjahren in Deutsch-Ostafrika.* Leipzig, 1918.

Kayamba, H. M. T. *African problems.* London, 1948.

Kayamba, H. M. T. 'Notes on the Wadigo', *TNR*, XXIII (1947), 80–96.

Kibira, Josiah. *Aus einer afrikanischen Kirche.* Bethel bei Bielefeld, 1963.

Kieran, John A. P. 'The Holy Ghost Fathers in East Africa, 1863 to 1914.' Ph.D. thesis, University of London, 1966.

Kilimanjaro Native Cooperative Union. *Annual report 1960–1*. Moshi, 1961.

Kimambo, Isaria N. *A political history of the Pare of Tanzania c. 1500–1900*. Nairobi, 1969.

Kimambo, Isaria N. (ed.) 'The history of the Pare to 1900: oral texts.' Duplicated, University College, Dar es Salaam, n.d.

Kimambo, Isaria N. and A. J. Temu (ed.). *A history of Tanzania*. Nairobi. 1969.

Kiwanuka, K. Mayanja. 'The politics of Islam in Bukoba district.' B.A. thesis, University of Dar es Salaam, 1973.

Kjekshus, Helge. *Ecology control and economic development in East African history*. London, 1977.

Klamroth, Martin. 'Der literarische Charakter des ostafrikanischen Islams', *Die Welt des Islams*, I (1913), 21–31.

Knappert, Jan. *Swahili Islamic poetry*. Leiden, 1971.

Knappert, Jan. *Traditional Swahili poetry*. Leiden, 1967.

Knight, C. Gregory. *Ecology and change: rural modernization in an African community*. New York, 1974.

Kollmann, Paul. *The Victoria Nyanza*. Trans. H. A. Nesbitt, London, 1899.

Kootz-Kretschmer, Elise. *Die Safwa*. 3 vols, Berlin, 1926–9.

Krapf, J. L. *Travels, researches, and missionary labours during an eighteen years' residence in eastern Africa*. 2nd edn, London, 1968.

Kuczynski, R. R. *Demographic survey of the British colonial empire*, II. London, 1949.

Die Landesgesetzgebung des Deutsch-Ostafrikanischen Schutzgebiets. 2 vols, Dar es Salaam, 1911.

Langheld, Wilhelm. *Zwanzig Jahre in deutschen Kolonien*. Berlin, 1909.

Larson, Lorne E. 'A history of the Mahenge (Ulanga) district, c. 1860–1957.' Ph.D. thesis, University of Dar es Salaam, 1976.

Leslie, J. A. K. *A survey of Dar es Salaam*. London, 1963.

Lettow-Vorbeck, Paul von. *My reminiscences of East Africa*. English translation, 2nd edn, London, n.d.

Lewis, I. M. (ed.) *Islam in tropical Africa*. London, 1966.

Lichtenheld, G. 'Ueber Rinderrassen, Rinderzucht und ihre wirtschaftliche Bedeutung in Deutsch-Ostafrika', *Der Pflanzer*, IX (1913).

Liebenow, J. Gus. *Colonial rule and political development in Tanzania: the case of the Makonde*. Nairobi, 1971.

Listowel, Judith. *The making of Tanganyika*. London, 1965.

Low, D. A. and Alison Smith (ed.). *History of East Africa*, III. Oxford, 1976.

Lowenkopf, Martin. 'Political parties in Uganda and Tanganyika.' M.Sc. (Econ.) thesis, University of London, 1961.

Lukwaro, E. A. (ed.) 'Documents concerning the Wapare Union.' Typescript, 1970, in my possession.

Lukwaro, E. A. (ed.) 'Records of the African Association, Upare.' Duplicated, 1970, in my possession.

Lumley, E. K. *Forgotten Mandate: a British district officer in Tanganyika*. London, 1976.

Bibliography

Maguire, G. A. *Toward 'Uhuru' in Tanzania*. Cambridge, 1969.

Malcolm, D. W. *Sukumaland*. London, 1953.

Malley, A. L. 'Dagharo Gharghara.' Seminar paper, University College, Dar es Salaam, n.d.

Mapunda, O. B. and G. P. Mpangara. *The Maji Maji war in Ungoni*. Nairobi, 1969.

Maro, Paul S. 'Population and land resources in northern Tanzania: the dynamics of change 1920–1970.' Ph.D. thesis, University of Minnesota, 1974.

Martin, B. G. *Muslim brotherhoods in nineteenth-century Africa*. Cambridge, 1976.

Martin, B. G. 'Muslim politics and resistance to colonial rule: Shaykh Uways b. Muhammad al-Barawi and the Qadiriya brotherhood in East Africa', *JAH*, x (1969), 471–86.

Mbuli, J. J. 'The Tanganyika African Association in Tanga.' Seminar paper, University of Dar es Salaam, 1970.

McCleery, H. H. 'Report of an enquiry into landownership in Dar es Salaam.' Typescript, 1939, ULD.

McHenry, Dean E. 'A study of the rise of TANU and the demise of British rule in Kigoma region, western Tanzania', *The African review*, III (1973), 403–21.

Merensky, A. *Deutsche Arbeit am Njassa*. Berlin, 1894.

Methner, Wilhelm. *Unter drei Gouverneuren*. Breslau, 1938.

Middleton, John and E. H. Winter (ed.). *Witchcraft and sorcery in East Africa*. London, 1963.

Miller, Norman N. 'Village leadership and modernization in Tanzania: rural politics among the Nyamwezi people of Tabora region.' Ph.D. thesis, Indiana University, 1966.

Millroth, Berta. *Lyuba: traditional religion of the Sukuma*. Uppsala, 1965.

Mlahagwa, Josiah R. 'Agricultural change in the Uluguru mountains during the colonial period, with particular emphasis from 1945–60.' M.A. thesis, University of Dar es Salaam, 1974.

'Moravian Church, Central Tanzania: extracts from *Periodical accounts*.' Typescript, MUL.

Moronda, E. Brendrire. 'Chief Makongoro: a man and leader of people.' Typescript [1967?] in Mr Moronda's possession.

Morris-Hale, Walter. *British administration in Tanganyika from 1920 to 1945, with special references to the preparation of Africans for administrative positions*. Genève, 1969.

Mosley, Leonard. *Duel for Kilimanjaro*. London, 1963.

Moyse-Bartlett, H. *The King's African Rifles: a study in the military history of East and Central Africa 1890–1945*. Aldershot, 1956.

Mramba, Basil P. 'Some notes on the political development of the Chagga of Kilimanjaro.' B.A. research paper, Makerere University College, 1967.

Mugongo, Nicholas. 'Les mémoires d'un catéchiste noir.' Manuscript, n.d., Kipalapala archives.

Müller, Fritz Ferdinand. *Deutschland – Zanzibar – Ostafrika: Geschichte einer deutschen Kolonialeroberung 1884–1890*. Berlin, 1959.

Mutahaba, G. R. *Portrait of a nationalist: the life of Ali Migeyo*. Nairobi, 1969.

Mwenda, Edward A. 'Historia na maendeleo ya Ubena', *Swahili*, XXXIII (1963), 99–123.

Nchoti, Elias. 'Some aspects of the iron industry of Geita c. 1850–1950 A.D.' M.A. thesis, University of Dar es Salaam, 1975.

Nelson, Anton. *The Freemen of Meru*. Nairobi, 1967.

New, Charles. *Life, wanderings, and labours in eastern Africa*. 2nd edn, London, 1874.

Newa, John B. M. 'The Ndendeule struggle against Ngoni feudalism and British imperialism.' B.A. thesis, University College, Dar es Salaam, 1970.

Newman, James L. *The ecological basis for subsistence change among the Sandawe of Tanzania*. Washington D.C., 1970.

Ngalula, D. M. 'The life of Lameck Makaranga Bogohe.' Seminar paper, University College, Dar es Salaam, 1969.

Nicholls, C. S. *The Swahili coast: politics, diplomacy and trade on the East African littoral 1798–1856*. London, 1971.

Nigmann, Ernst. *Die Wahehe*. Berlin, 1908.

Nimtz, August H. 'The role of the Muslim Sufi order in political change: an overview and micro-analysis from Tanzania.' Ph.D. thesis, Indiana University, 1973.

Njau, Filipo. *Aus meinem Leben*. Trans. B. Gutmann, Erlangen, 1960.

Nyerere, Julius K. *Freedom and socialism*. Dar es Salaam, 1968.

Nyerere, Julius K. *Freedom and unity*. Dar es Salaam, 1966.

Oded, Arye. *Islam in Uganda*. New York, 1974.

Ogot, Bethwell A. (ed.). *Hadith 2*. Nairobi, 1970. [J. A. Kieran, 'Abushiri and the Germans.']

Ogot, Bethwell A. (ed.). *War and society in Africa: ten studies*. London, 1972. [G. C. K. Gwassa, 'African methods of warfare during the Maji Maji war 1905–1907'; Isaria N. Kimambo, 'Mbiru: popular protest in colonial Tanzania 1944–1947.']

Oliver, Roland. *The missionary factor in East Africa*. 2nd edn, London, 1965.

Oliver, Roland (ed.). *The Cambridge history of Africa*, III. Cambridge, 1977.

Perham, Margery (ed.). *Ten Africans*. 2nd edn, London, 1963. ['The story of Martin Kayamba.']

Perrin Jassy, Marie-France. *La communauté de base dans les églises africaines*. Bandundu, 1970.

Pocock, David F. '"Difference" in East Africa: a study of caste and religion in modern Indian society', *Southwestern journal of anthropology*, XIII (1957), 289–300.

Pratt, R. Cranford. *The critical phase in Tanzania 1945–1968: Nyerere and the emergence of a socialist strategy*. Cambridge, 1976.

Prince, Tom von. *Gegen Araber und Wahehe: Erinnerungen aus meiner ostafrikanischen Leutnantszeit 1890–1895*. Berlin, 1914.

Puritt, Paul. 'The Meru of Tanzania: a study of their social and political organization.' Ph.D. thesis, University of Illinois, 1970.

Ranger, T. O. *The African churches of Tanzania*. Nairobi, n.d.

Ranger, T. O. *Dance and society in eastern Africa 1890–1970: the beni 'ngoma'*. London, 1975.

589

Bibliography

Ranger, T. O. 'Witchcraft eradication movements in central and southern Tanzania and their connection with the Maji Maji rising.' Seminar paper, University College, Dar es Salaam, 1966.

Ranger, T. O. and I. N. Kimambo (ed.). *The historical study of African religion.* London, 1972. [M. Wright, 'Nyakyusa cults and politics in the later nineteenth century'; E. A. Alpers, 'Towards a history of the expansion of Islam in East Africa: the matrilineal peoples of the southern interior'; G. C. K. Gwassa, 'Kinjikitile and the ideology of Maji Maji'; T. O. Ranger, 'Missionary adaptation of African religious institutions: the Masasi case.']

Raum, O. F. *Chaga Childhood.* London, 1940.

Redmayne, Alison. 'Mkwawa and the Hehe wars', *JAH*, ix (1968), 409–36.

Redmayne, Alison. 'The Wahehe people of Tanganyika.' D.Phil thesis, Oxford University, 1964.

Redmond, Patrick M. 'A political history of the Songea Ngoni from the mid-nineteenth century to the rise of the Tanganyika African National Union.' Ph.D. thesis, University of London, 1972.

Reichard, Paul. *Deutsch-Ostafrika: das Land und seine Bewohner.* Leipzig, 1892.

Reining, Priscilla C. 'The Haya: the agrarian system of a sedentary people.' Ph.D. thesis, University of Chicago, 1967.

Renault, François. *Lavigerie, l'esclavage Africain, et l'Europe, 1868–1892.* 2 vols, Paris, 1971.

Renner, Frumentius (ed.). *Der fünfarmige Leuchter: Beiträge zum Werden und Wirken der Benediktinerkongregation von St Ottilien.* 2 vols, St Ottilien, 1971.

Richter, Julius. *Geschichte der Berliner Missionsgesellschaft 1824–1924.* Berlin, 1924.

Rigby, Peter. *Cattle and kinship among the Gogo.* Ithaca, 1969.

Roberts, Andrew (ed.). *Tanzania before 1900.* Nairobi, 1968.

Robinson, Ronald E. 'The journal and the transfer of power 1947–51', *Journal of administration overseas,* xiii (1974), 255–8.

Rogers, Susan G. 'The search for political focus on Kilimanjaro: a history of Chagga politics 1916–1952, with special reference to the cooperative movement and indirect rule.' Ph.D. thesis, University of Dar es Salaam, 1972.

Rotberg, R. I. and A. A. Mazrui (ed.). *Protest and power in black Africa.* New York, 1970. [R. D. Jackson, 'Resistance to German invasion of the Tanganyikan coast, 1888–1891'.]

Rounce, N. V. and others. *A record of investigations and observations on the agriculture of the cultivation steppe of Sukuma and Nyamwezi with suggestions as to lines of progress.* Dar es Salaam, 1942.

Ruthenberg, Hans (ed.). *Smallholder farming and smallholder development in Tanzania: ten case studies.* München, 1968.

Rwehumbiza, Philibert. 'Clemens Kiiza: pioneer of Tanzania nationalism.' Seminar paper, University of Dar es Salaam, 1970.

Rweyemamu, Justinian. *Underdevelopment and industrialization in Tanzania.* Nairobi, 1973.

Sago, Laurent. 'A history of labour migration in Kasulu district Tanzania, 1928–1960.' M.A. thesis, University of Dar es Salaam, 1974.

Schanz, Johannes. *Am Fusse der Bergriesen Ostafrikas: Geschichte der Leipziger Mission am Kilimandjaro.* Leipzig, 1912.

Schmidt, Peter R. 'An investigation of Early and Late Iron Age cultures through oral tradition and archaeology: an interdisciplinary case study in Buhaya, Tanzania.' Ph.D. thesis, Northwestern University, 1974.

Schmidt, Peter R. 'A new look at interpretations of the Early Iron Age in East Africa', *History in Africa*, II (1975), 127–36.

Schmidt, Rochus. *Geschichte des Araberaufstandes in Ost-Afrika.* Frankfurt a.O., 1892.

Schnee, Heinrich. *Deutsch-Ostafrika im Weltkriege.* Leipzig, 1919.

Schnee, Heinrich (ed.). *Deutsches Kolonial-Lexicon.* 3 vols, Leipzig, 1920.

Schultz, Jürgen. *Agrarlandwirtschaftliche Veränderungen in Tanzania.* München, 1971.

Schweitzer, Georg. *Emin Pasha, his life and work.* Trans. R. W. Felkin, 2 vols, Westminster, 1898.

Schynse, August. *Mit Stanley und Emin Pascha durch Deutsch Ost-Afrika.* Köln, 1890.

Sheriff, Abdul M. H. 'The rise of a commercial empire: an aspect of the economic history of Zanzibar, 1770–1875.' Ph.D. thesis, University of London, 1971.

Shorter, Aylward. *Chiefship in western Tanzania: a political history of the Kimbu.* Oxford, 1972.

Shorter, Aylward and Eugene Kataza (ed.). *Missionaries to yourselves: African catechists today.* London, 1972. [Francis Nolan, 'History of the catechist in eastern Africa.']

Sicard, S. von. *The Lutheran Church on the coast of Tanzania 1887–1914.* Lund, 1970.

Sick, Eberhard von. 'Die Waniaturu', *Baessler-Archiv*, V (1915), 1–62.

Smedjebacka, Henrik. *Lutheran Church autonomy in northern Tanzania 1940–1963.* Åbo, 1973.

Smith, William E. *Nyerere of Tanzania.* London, 1973.

Stahl, Kathleen M. *History of the Chagga people of Kilimanjaro.* The Hague, 1964.

Stanway, Alfred. 'Rapid church growth among the Wagogo of Tanzania, 1876–1967.' Duplicated, workshop in religious research, Nairobi, 1968.

Stirnimann, Hans. 'Zur Gesellschaftsordnung und Religion der Pangwa', *Anthropos*, LXII (1967), 394–418.

Stuart-Watt, Eva. *Africa's dome of mystery.* London, 1929.

Stuhlmann, Franz. *Handwerk und Industrie in Ostafrika.* Hamburg, 1910.

Stuhlmann, Franz. *Mit Emin Pascha ins Herz von Afrika.* Berlin, 1894.

Sutton, J. E. G. 'Dar es Salaam: a sketch of a hundred years', *TNR*, LXXI (1970), 1–19.

Swann, A. J. *Fighting the slave-hunters in central Africa.* London, 1910.

Swantz, Lloyd W. *Church, mission, and state relations in pre and post independent Tanzania (1955–1964).* Maxwell Graduate School, Program of Eastern African Studies, occasional paper no. 19 (New York, 1965).

Swantz, Lloyd, W. 'The role of the medicine man among the Zaramo of Dar es Salaam.' Ph.D. thesis, University of Dar es Salaam, 1974.

Swantz, Marja-Liisa. *Ritual and symbol in transitional Zaramo society with special reference to women.* Lund, 1970.

Swartz, Marc J. and others (ed.). *Political anthropology.* Chicago, 1966. [G. K. Park, 'Kinga priests.']

Swynnerton, C. F. M. 'An experiment in control of tsetse-flies at Shinyanga, Tanganyika Territory', *Bulletin of entomological research,* XV (1924–5), 313–37.

Swynnerton, R. J. M. and A. L. B. Bennett. *All about 'KNCU' coffee.* Moshi, 1948.

Sykes, D. A. 'The life of Mzee bin Sudi.' Seminar paper, University College, Dar es Salaam, 1969.

Symes, Stewart. *Tour of duty.* London, 1946.

Tambila, Anse. 'A history of the Tanga sisal labour force: 1936–1964.' M.A. thesis, University of Dar es Salaam, 1974.

Tandau, A. C. A. 'The history of the Tanganyika Federation of Labour from 1955 to 1962.' Trans. G. Kaunda, typescript, n.d., copy in my possession.

Tanganyika. *African census report 1957.* Dar es Salaam, 1963.

Tanganyika. *Budget survey 1962–3.* Dar es Salaam, 1962.

Tanganyika. 'Committee on constitutional development: evidence and memoranda submitted to the fact-finding sub-committee 1950.' Duplicated, 3 vols, Dar es Salaam, 1950.

Tanganyika. *Development plan for Tanganyika 1961/62 – 1963/64.* Dar es Salaam, 1962.

Tanganyika. *An outline of post-war development proposals.* Dar es Salaam, 1944.

Tanganyika. *Report of the Central Development Committee.* Dar es Salaam, 1940.

Tanganyika. *Report of the commission appointed to enquire into the disturbances which occurred in the port of Tanga during the month of August 1939.* Dar es Salaam, 1940.

Tanganyika. *Report of the committee appointed to consider and advise on questions relating to the supply and welfare of native labour in the Tanganyika Territory, 22 November 1937.* Dar es Salaam, 1938.

Tanganyika. *A ten-year development and welfare plan for Tanganyika Territory.* Dar es Salaam, 1946.

Tanganyika African National Union. 'Historia ya TANU.' Duplicated, n.d., TANU headquarters.

Tanner, R. E. S. 'The sorcerer in northern Sukumaland', *Southwestern journal of anthropology,* XII (1966), 437–43.

Tanzania. *Guide to the German records.* 2 vols, Dar es Salaam and Marburg, 1973.

Taylor, J. Clagett. *The political development of Tanganyika.* Stanford, 1963.

Taylor, John V. *Processes of growth in an African church.* London, 1958.

ten Raa, Eric. 'Bush foraging and agricultural development: a history of Sandawe famines', *TNR,* LXIX (1968), 33–40.

ten Raa, Eric. 'Sandawe musical and other sound producing instruments', *TNR,* LX (1963), 23–48, and LXII (1964), 91–5.

ten Raa, Eric. 'Sandawe prehistory and the vernacular tradition', *Azania,* IV (1969), 91–103.

Tetzlaff, Rainer. *Koloniale Entwicklung und Ausbeutung: Wirtschafts- und Sozialgeschichte Deutsch-Ostafrikas 1885–1914.* Berlin, 1970.

Thomas, Keith. *Religion and the decline of magic.* Reprinted, Harmondsworth, 1973.

Thompson, A. R. 'Partnership in education in Tanganyika 1919–1961.' M.A. thesis, University of London, 1965.

Thomson, Joseph. *To the central African lakes and back.* 2nd edn, 2 vols, London, 1968.

Twining, Lord. 'The last nine years in Tanganyika', *African affairs,* LVIII (1959), 15–24.

Ulotu, Ulotu Abubaker. *Historia ya TANU.* Dar es Salaam, 1971.

United Nations. *Report of the United Nations visiting mission to East Africa on Tanganyika, 1948* (UNTC T/218).

United Nations. *Report of the United Nations visiting mission to trust territories in East Africa, 1954, on Tanganyika* (UNTC T/1142).

United Nations. *United Nations visiting mission to trust territories in East Africa, 1957: report on the trust territory of Tanganyika* (UNTC T/1345).

Unomah, Alfred C. 'Economic expansion and political change in Unyanyembe (ca. 1840 to 1900).' Ph.D. thesis, University of Ibadan, 1972.

Van der Burgt, J. M. M. 'Zur Entvölkerungsfrage Unjamwesis und Usumbwas', *Koloniale Rundschau,* V (1913), 705–28.

Van Hekken, P. M. and H. U. E. Thoden van Velzen. *Land scarcity and rural inequality in Tanzania: some case studies from Rungwe district.* The Hague, 1972.

Velten, C. *Safari za Wasuaheli.* Göttingen, 1901.

Velten, C. 'Suaheli Gedichte', *MSOS,* XX (1917), 61–182, and XXI (1918), 135–83.

Versteijnen, Frits. *The Catholic mission of Bagamoyo.* Bagamoyo, 1968.

Volkens, Georg. *Der Kilimandscharo.* Berlin, 1897.

Walji, Shirin R. 'Business enterprise and leadership in the Ismaili community, 1914–1968'. Seminar paper, University of Dar es Salaam, 1970.

Walji, Shirin R. 'A history of the Ismaili community in Tanzania'. Ph.D. thesis, University of Wisconsin, 1974.

Walji, Shirin R. 'Ismailis on mainland Tanzania, 1850–1948.' M.A. thesis, University of Wisconsin, 1969.

Waller, Horace (ed.). *The last journals of David Livingstone.* 2 vols, London, 1874.

Washausen, Helmut. *Hamburg und die Kolonialpolitik des Deutschen Reiches 1880 bis 1890.* Hamburg, 1968.

Wehler, Hans-Ulrich. *Bismarck und der Imperialismus.* Köln, 1969.

Wehrmeister, Cyrillus. *Vor dem Sturm: eine Reise durch Deutsch-Ostafrika vor und bei dem Aufstande 1905.* St Ottilien, 1906.

Weidner, Fritz. *Die Haussklaverei in Ostafrika.* Jena, 1915.

Weigt, Ernst. *Europäer in Ostafrika.* Köln, 1955.

Weule, Karl. *Native life in East Africa.* Trans. A. Werner, London, 1909.

Whiteley, W. H. (ed.) 'Maisha ya Hamed bin Muhammed el Murjebi yaani Tippu Tip', *Swahili,* XXVIII–XXIX (1958–9), supplement.

Widenmann, A. *Die Kilimandscharo-Bevölkerung.* Gotha, 1899.

Wijeyewardene, G. E. T. 'Some aspects of village solidarity in Ki-Swahili speaking coastal communities of Kenya and Tanganyika'. Ph.D. thesis, Cambridge University, 1961.

Bibliography

Willis, Roy G. 'Changes in mystical concepts and practices among the Fipa', *Ethnology*, VII (1968), 139–57.

Willis, Roy G. *The Fipa and related peoples of south-west Tanzania and north-east Zambia*. London, 1966.

Willis, Roy G. 'Kamcape: an anti-sorcery movement in south-west Tanzania', *Africa*, XXXVIII (1968), 1–15.

Willis, Roy G. 'Kaswa: oral tradition of a Fipa prophet', *Africa*, XL (1970), 248–56.

Willis, Roy G. *Man and beast*. Reprinted, St Albans, 1975.

Wilson, D. B. *Report of the malaria unit, Tanga, 1933–34*. Dar es Salaam, 1936.

Wilson, Godfrey and Monica. *The analysis of social change*. Reprinted, Cambridge, 1968.

Wilson, Monica. *Communal rituals of the Nyakyusa*. London, 1959.

Wilson, Monica. *Good company: a study of Nyakyusa age-villages*. Reprinted, Boston, 1963.

Wilson, Monica. *Rituals of kinship among the Nyakyusa*. London, 1957.

Wilson, Monica. 'Traditional art among the Nyakyusa', *South African archaeological bulletin*, XIX (1964), 57–63.

Wilson, Monica. 'Zig-zag change', *Africa*, XLVI (1976), 399–409.

Winter, E. H. 'Some aspects of political organization and land tenure among the Iraqw', *KUAS*, II (1968), 1–29.

Wright, Fergus C. *African consumers in Nyasaland and Tanganyika: an enquiry into the distribution and consumption of commodities among Africans carried out in 1952–1953*. London, 1955.

Wright, Marcia. 'Chief Merere and the Germans', *TNR*, LXIX (1968), 41–9.

Wright, Marcia. *German missions in Tanganyika 1891–1941*. Oxford, 1971.

Wright, Marcia. 'Local roots of policy in German East Africa', *JAH*, IX (1968), 621–30.

Yoneyama, Toshinao. 'The life and society of the Iraqw', *KUAS*, IV (1969), 77–114.

Young, Roland and Henry Fosbrooke. *Land and politics among the Luguru of Tanganyika*. London, 1960.

Zimmermann, Alfred. *Geschichte der deutschen Kolonialpolitik*. Berlin, 1914.

Index

595

Index

Makerere College, 340–1, 355–6, 358–60, 420, 422, 426, 428, 430, 445–6, 481–2, 574
Makita, C., 291–2, 489, 534
Makonde tribe
  settlement, 8–9, 74
  matriliny, 16
  politics, 21, 56, 330–1, 489, 527, 572
  employers, 73, 463
  religion, 79
  Maji Maji, 174–5, 194
  Islam, 213
  famine, 269
  labourers, 306, 387, 463
Makongoro, Ikizu chief, 328, 534
Makongoro, Sukuma chief, 190
Makua tribe, 28, 74, 81, 162, 174–5, 194, 222, 257, 306, 527
Makwaia, Chief, 214
Makwaia, D. P. K., 431, 447, 475, 481, 535
Malakilindu, F., 226
Malangali school, 339
Malango, Asyukile, 226, 237
malaria, 12, 35, 244, 250, 386
Malashi, J., 523, 532
Malik, S. B., 374
Maliti, J., 277
Mambo, Akida, 408
Mambwe tribe, 162, 306, 308
Mandate, 246–7, 262, 265–6, 301, 303, 378, 423–4, 430, 432
Mandawa, Chief, 117
Mang'unyuka, Hassan, 533
manioc, 69, 72, 312, 314, 350, 462, 471
Manyema
  long-distance trade, 46, 48–50, 52, 74
  labourers, 161–2
  Islam, 212, 214, 369
  Christianity, 222
  in Bagamoyo, 369, 382, 384, 415, 528
  in Ujiji, 382–4
  in Dar es Salaam, 385, 387, 390, 408
Mara Union, 490
Marealle I, 101–2, 105, 120–1, 144, 154, 291
Marealle, P. I., 280, 491–3
Marealle, T., 412 n. 1, 446–7, 481, 492–4, 515–16, 525–6, 535, 568–9
Marini society, see beni dance
markets, see trade
maroon communities, 73
marriage
  pre-colonial, 16–17
  and Christianity, 219–20, 297, 299–300, 360, 531, 543

colonial change, 297, 299–301, 450, 461, 530–1
  and Islam, 297, 550
  see also bridewealth, polygyny
Maruma, J., 491
Maryknoll Fathers, 546
Mashambo, P., 495
Masai tribe
  early history, 7–8, 23, 42, 51–2, 58–9
  pastoralism, 15,·312–13
  iron-working, 18–19
  and agriculturalists, 20, 23, 59–60, 66, 124, 132, 252, 351, 493–4
  religion, 29, 32, 205, 330, 549
  famine, 70, 124, 576
  politics, 102–3, 124, 143, 145, 252, 330, 493–4, 549
  rinderpest, 124, 143
  labourers, 161–2
  Christianity, 230
  tsetse, 270
Masanja, Chief, 254
Masanja, B., 446 n. 6
Masasi, Chief, 253
Masasi mission
  and Ngoni, 55, 230
  Christianity, 84, 221–2, 225, 227, 229–30, 237, 358–9
  Maji Maji, 175, 181, 233
  First World War, 255, 269–70
  initiation rites, 336
  politics, 527, 534
Mascarene Islands, 39, 41
Mashombo, Chief, 81
Master, K. A., 264
Masudi, N. E. G., 407, 417, 422, 431, 433
Mataka, Chief, 78, 187–8, 198–9, 213
Matengo tribe, 55, 117, 187, 287, 291, 306–7, 489, 534
Mathu, E., 422, 495
Matola dynasty, 74, 175, 194, 221, 534
Matola, C., 266–7, 407–8, 410
Matola, L., 265–6
matriliny, 16, 300
Matumbi tribe, 9, 133, 168–72, 176, 179, 195–6, 199–202, 231, 238, 256, 331
Maulidi, see Islam
Mawalla, S., 154, 277
Mayembe, Chief, 78
Mbararia, Chief, 120
Mbatyan, laibon, 102, 205
Mbegha, Chief, 10–13, 22, 28, 62, 122, 498
Mbeya District Original Tribes Association, 489–90
Mbeyela, Chief, 113, 188–9, 191, 198
Mbeyela, J., 534

606

Sukumaland Development Scheme, 474,
    482–3, 487–8, 505–6, 523, 559, 568
Suleiman, H., 419–22, 425–6, 433, 514
Suleiman bin Nasor, 208, 235
Sumbwa tribe, 41, 67–8, 165–6, 216, 305,
    330, 390, 518, 533, 558
Sumlei, Z., 494
Sunderji, Kassum, 374
Sunderland club, 393
Sururu, Ibrahim, 413
Swahili
    pre-colonial, 37, 79
    German period, 208–10
    British period, 331, 338–9, 529–30, 532
    poetry, 39, 234, 379–80, 407, 504, 520,
        530
    culture, 361, 384, 388, 530
    newspapers, 377, 532
    and nationalism, 529–30, 571
    Koran, 550
Swai, N., 571
Swedi, J., 229
Swetu, Chief, 104, 112
Swynnerton, C. F. M., 270–2
Sykes, Abbas, 503, 505, 510
Sykes, Abdulwahid, 404, 502, 507, 510,
    513
Sykes, Ally, 392, 507, 510, 513
Sykes, Kleist, 408, 410
Symes, Sir S., 339, 356, 374
syphilis, 81

Tabora
    nineteenth century, 41, 46, 48, 68, 80,
        129, 135–6, 141
    colonial period, 103–4, 107, 132, 251,
        381
    Asians, 141
    Maji Maji, 190
    Islam, 211–12, 214, 369
    school, 328, 338, 341, 446, 553
    politics, 403, 421–2, 432, 514
Taibali Essaji Sachak and Co., 304
Taita tribe, 59, 66
Takadiri, Mzee, 532
Tambarare Citizens Union, 488, 527–9,
    561–2
Tanga Indian Association, 140
Tanga town
    trade, 42, 71
    politics, 92, 96, 266–8, 381, 428–9, 503,
        515, 529
    Asians, 139–41
    school, 209
    First World War, 241–3
    Islam, 369
    see also strikes

Tanga Young Comrades Club, 392–3
Tanganyika, named, 247
Tanganyika African Association, *see*
    African Association
Tanganyika African Government
    Servants Association, 396, 420–3,
    434, 503, 538, 558
Tanganyika African Muslim Union, 551
Tanganyika African National Union
    origins, 485–6, 505, 511–13, 521–2
    constitution and structure, 511–13,
        554, 557–8, 571
    membership, 517–18, 558, 567
    finance, 519, 557–8, 567–8
    Tabora conference (1958), 532, 542,
        555–8, 564
    in Provinces: Dar es Salaam, 377,
        516–18, 529, 531, 560; Tanga, 496,
        515, 526–9, 554, 558, 560–2; Lake,
        513–14, 518, 523–4, 534, 558–9, 561,
        567–70; Northern, 514–16, 525–6,
        560–1, 568–70; Western, 514, 518,
        532–3, 535, 558, 560, 562, 569–70;
        Central, 514, 518, 527, 531–3, 560;
        Eastern, 514–15, 519–20, 527–9, 534,
        560; Southern, 515, 520, 527, 533–4,
        560, 569; West Lake, 516, 524, 532–3,
        560–1, 570; Southern Highlands,
        518, 520, 524, 534–5, 554, 560–2
    and tribal unions, 490, 511, 568–9
    and trade unions, 511, 537–42, 572
    Youth League, 511, 531–2, 558
    women, 511, 518, 530–2, 558
    and Mau Mau, 518, 520, 537
    and Maji Maji, 519–20, 534
    and religion, 527, 533, 543–52, 570
    and cultural nationalism, 530
    and chiefs, 533–5, 568–70
    and traders, 542–3
    responsible government, 555, 557, 560,
        564–6
    Independence, 566, 576
    policies, 572–6
    and socialism, 575
Tanganyika African Traders Union,
    542–3
Tanganyika African Welfare and
    Commercial Association, 347, 393–5,
    411
Tanganyika Citizens Union, 494
Tanganyika Cotton Co., 522
Tanganyika Electoral Association, 476
Tanganyika Episcopal Conference, 546
Tanganyika European Council, 505
Tanganyika Farmers Association, 481
Tanganyika Federation of Labour,
    538–42

613